BRITISH RAILWAYS

LOCOMOTIVES & COACHING STOCK

2020

The Complete Guide to all Locomotives & Coaching Stock which operate on the National Rail network and Eurotunnel

Robert Pritchard

PLATFORM 5

Published by Platform 5 Publishing Ltd,
52 Broadfield Road, Sheffield, S8 0XJ, England.

Printed in England by The Lavenham Press, Lavenham, Suffolk.

ISBN 978 1 909431 58 4

CONTENTS

SECTION 1 – LOCOMOTIVES

SECTION 2 – LOCO-HAULED COACHING STOCK

SECTION 3 – DIESEL MULTIPLE UNITS

SECTION 4 – ELECTRIC MULTIPLE UNITS

SECTION 5 – ON-TRACK MACHINES

SECTION 6 – CODES

COVER PHOTOGRAPHS

Front Cover: New Stadler bi-mode unit 755 410, operated by Greater Anglia, leaves Brundall with the 12.36 Norwich–Great Yarmouth on 29/07/19.
Toby Radziszewski

Back Cover: London Northwestern Railway-liveried 230 004, rebuilt by Vivarail from former LU D78 Stock, is seen passing through the Bedford suburbs with the 16.40 Bedford–Bletchley on 14/05/19. **Brian Carter**

BRITAIN'S RAILWAY SYSTEM

INFRASTRUCTURE & OPERATION

Britain's national railway infrastructure is owned by a "not for dividend" company, Network Rail. In 2014 Network Rail was reclassified as a public sector company, being described by the Government as a "public sector arm's-length body of the Department for Transport".

Most stations and maintenance depots are leased to and operated by Train Operating Companies (TOCs), but some larger stations are controlled by Network Rail. The only exception is the infrastructure on the Isle of Wight: The Island Line franchise uniquely included maintenance of the infrastructure as well as the operation of passenger services. As Island Line is now part of the South Western Railway franchise, both the infrastructure and trains are operated by South Western Railway.

Trains are operated by TOCs over Network Rail tracks (the National Network), regulated by access agreements between the parties involved. In general, TOCs are responsible for the provision and maintenance of the locomotives, rolling stock and staff necessary for the direct operation of services, whilst Network Rail is responsible for the provision and maintenance of the infrastructure and also for staff to regulate the operation of services.

The Department for Transport (DfT) is the franchising authority for the national network, with Transport Scotland overseeing the award of the ScotRail franchise and the Welsh Government overseeing the Wales & Borders franchise.

A franchise is the right to run specified services within a specified area for a period of time, in return for the right to charge fares and, where appropriate, to receive financial support from the Government. Subsidy is payable in respect of socially necessary services. Service standards are monitored by the DfT throughout the duration of the franchise. Franchisees earn revenue primarily from fares and from subsidy. They generally lease stations from Network Rail and earn rental income by sub-letting parts of them, for example to retailers.

TOC's and open access operator's main costs are the track access charges they pay to Network Rail, the costs of leasing stations and rolling stock and of employing staff. Franchisees may do light maintenance work on rolling stock or contract it out to other companies. Heavy maintenance is normally carried out by the Rolling Stock Leasing Companies, according to contracts.

TOCs can take commercial risks, although some franchises are "management contracts", where ticket revenues pass directly to the DfT. Concessions (such as London Overground) see the operator paid a fee to run the service, usually within tightly specified guidelines. Operators running a concession would not normally take commercial risks, although there are usually penalties and rewards in the contract.

Note that a railway "reporting period" is four weeks.

DOMESTIC PASSENGER TRAIN OPERATORS

The majority of passenger trains are operated by Train Operating Companies on fixed-term franchises or concessions. Expiry dates are shown in the list below:

Franchise	*Franchisee*	*Trading Name*
Caledonian Sleeper	Serco (until 31 March 2030)	**Caledonian Sleeper**

This franchise started in April 2015 when operation of the ScotRail and ScotRail Sleeper franchises was separated. Abellio won the ScotRail franchise and Serco the Caledonian Sleeper franchise. Caledonian Sleeper operates four trains nightly between London Euston and Scotland using locomotives hired from GBRf. New CAF Mark 5 rolling stock was introduced during 2019.

Chiltern	Arriva (Deutsche Bahn) (until 11 December 2021)	**Chiltern Railways**

There is an option to extend the franchise by 7 months to July 2022.

Chiltern Railways operates a frequent service between London Marylebone, Oxford, Banbury and Birmingham Snow Hill, with some peak trains extending to Kidderminster. There are also regular services from Marylebone to Stratford-upon-Avon and to Aylesbury Vale Parkway via Amersham (along the London Underground Metropolitan Line). The fleet consists of DMUs of Classes 165, 168 and 172 plus a number of locomotive-hauled rakes used on some of the Birmingham and Oxford route trains, worked by Class 68s hired from DRS.

Cross Country	Arriva (Deutsche Bahn) (until 17 October 2020)	**CrossCountry**

In 2018 competition for the next franchise was stopped, pending the publication of the Rail Review by the Government.

CrossCountry operates a network of long distance services between Scotland, the North-East of England and Manchester to the South-West of England, Reading, Southampton, Bournemouth and Guildford, centred on Birmingham New Street. These trains are mainly formed of diesel Class 220/221 Voyagers, supplemented by a small number of HSTs on the NE–SW route. Inter-urban services also link Nottingham, Leicester and Stansted Airport with Birmingham and Cardiff. These trains use Class 170 DMUs.

Crossrail	MTR (until 27 May 2023)	**TfL Rail**

There is an option to extend the concession by 2 years to May 2025.

This is a new concession which started in May 2015. Initially Crossrail took over the Liverpool Street–Shenfield stopping service from Greater Anglia, using a fleet of Class 315 EMUs, with the service branded "TfL Rail". New Class 345 EMUs are being introduced on this route and are also now used between Paddington and Hayes & Harlington and Paddington and Reading (initially in 7-car formation). TfL Rail currently also operates the former Heathrow Connect stopping service that uses Class 360 EMUs. The opening of Crossrail through central London has been delayed and operation through new tunnels beneath central London, from Shenfield and Abbey Wood in the east to Reading and Heathrow Airport in the west is now expected in summer 2021. It will then be branded the "Elizabeth Line".

East Coast **London North Eastern Railway**

Franchise awarded to Stagecoach/Virgin Trains in 2015 but was terminated just over 3 years later in 2018 (having originally been due to operate until 2023) after the franchise failed. Currently operated on an interim basis by the DfT's "Operator of Last Resort". It is due to be relet in the future as part of a new public/private East Coast partnership.

LNER operates frequent long distance trains on the East Coast Main Line between London King's Cross, Leeds, Lincoln, Harrogate, York, Newcastle-upon-Tyne and Edinburgh, with less frequent services to Bradford, Skipton, Hull, Glasgow, Stirling, Aberdeen and Inverness. The former BR HST fleet was phased out at the end of 2019 and the Class 91 + Mark 4 sets are due to be phased out by summer 2020 as a new fleet of 65 Hitachi Class 800 and 801 "Azuma" trains are introduced (these are a mix of bi-mode and electric, 5- and 9-car units).

East Midlands Abellio (until 21 August 2027) **East Midlands Railway**

There is an option to extend the franchise by 2 years to August 2029.

EMR operates a mix of long distance high speed services on the Midland Main Line (MML), from London St Pancras to Sheffield (to Leeds at peak times and with some extensions to York/Scarborough), Nottingham (plus peak-hour trains to Lincoln) and Corby, and local and regional services ranging from the long distance Norwich–Liverpool route to Nottingham–Skegness, Nottingham–Mansfield–Worksop, Newark–Matlock and Derby–Crewe. It also operates local services in Lincolnshire. Trains on the MML are worked by a fleet of Class 222 DMUs and 12 HSTs, whilst the local and regional fleet consists of DMU Classes 153, 156 and 158.

East Anglia Abellio (Netherlands Railways) (60%)/Mitsui Group (40%) (until 11 October 2025) **Greater Anglia**

There is an option to extend the franchise by 1 year to October 2026.

Greater Anglia operates main line trains between London Liverpool Street, Ipswich and Norwich and local trains across Norfolk, Suffolk and parts of Cambridgeshire. It also runs local and commuter services into Liverpool Street from the Great Eastern (including Southend, Braintree and Clacton) and West Anglia (including Ely/Cambridge and Stansted Airport) routes. It operates a varied fleet of Class 90s with locomotive-hauled Mark 3 sets, DMUs of Classes 153, 156 and 170 and EMUs of Classes 317, 321, 360 and 379. The first of a completely new fleet of trains (Class 755 bi-mode units) were introduced in summer 2019, followed by the Class 745 EMUs in early 2020 and new trains (Classes 720, 745 and 755) will be introduced across all routes by spring 2021.

Essex Thameside Trenitalia (until 10 November 2029) **c2c**

There is an option to extend the franchise by 6 months to May 2030.

c2c operates an intensive, principally commuter, service from London Fenchurch Street to Southend and Shoeburyness via both Upminster and Tilbury. The fleet consists of 74 Class 357 EMUs, plus six Class 387s.

Great Western First Group (until 31 March 2020) **Great Western Railway**

Direct Award extension expected to March 2022, with the option of a further 2 year extension to March 2024.

Great Western Railway operates long distance trains from London Paddington to South Wales, the West Country and Worcester and Hereford. In addition there are frequent trains along the Thames Valley corridor to Newbury/Bedwyn and Oxford, plus local and regional trains throughout the South-West including the Cornish, Devon and Thames Valley branches, the Reading–Gatwick North Downs Line and Cardiff–Portsmouth Harbour and Bristol–Weymouth regional routes. Long distance services are now in the hands of a new fleet of Class 800/802 bi-mode InterCity Express Trains. DMUs of Classes 165 and 166 are used on the Thames Valley branches and North Downs routes as well as on local services around Bristol and across to Cardiff. Class 387 EMUs are used between Paddington, Reading, Didcot Parkway and Newbury. Classes 143, 150 and 158 and a fleet of short 4-car HSTs are used on local and regional trains in the South-West. A small fleet of Class 57s is maintained to work the overnight "Cornish Riviera" Sleeper service between London Paddington and Penzance formed of Mark 3 coaches.

London Rail Arriva (Deutsche Bahn) (until 25 May 2024) **London Overground**

This is a concession and is different from other rail franchises, as fares and service levels are set by Transport for London instead of by the DfT. There is an option to extend the concession by 2 years to May 2026.

London Overground operates services on the Richmond–Stratford North London Line and the Willesden Junction–Clapham Junction West London Line, plus the East London Line from Highbury & Islington to New Cross and New Cross Gate, with extensions to Clapham Junction (via Denmark Hill), Crystal Palace and West Croydon. It also runs services from London Euston to Watford Junction. All these use Class 378 EMUs, with new Class 710s recently introduced on the Watford route. Class 710s now operate services on the Gospel Oak–Barking line. London Overground also operates some suburban services from London Liverpool Street – to Chingford, Enfield Town and Cheshunt. These use Class 315 and 317 EMUs, but are to be replaced by AC only Class 710s during 2020.

Merseyrail Electrics Serco (50%)/Abellio (Netherlands Railways) (50%) (until 22 July 2028) **Merseyrail**

Under the control of Merseytravel PTE instead of the DfT. Franchise reviewed every five years to fit in with the Merseyside Local Transport Plan.

Merseyrail operates services between Liverpool and Southport, Ormskirk, Kirkby, Hunts Cross, New Brighton, West Kirby, Chester and Ellesmere Port, using Class 507 and 508 EMUs. A new fleet of Class 777 EMUs will be introduced in 2020–21.

Northern Arriva (Deutsche Bahn) (until 31 March 2025) **Northern**

There is an option to extend the franchise by 1 year to March 2026.

Northern operates a range of inter-urban, commuter and rural services throughout the North of England, including those around the cities of Leeds, Manchester, Sheffield, Liverpool and Newcastle. The network extends from Chathill in the north to Nottingham in the south, and Cleethorpes in the east to St Bees in the west. Long distance services include Leeds–Carlisle, Morpeth–Carlisle and York–Blackpool North. The operator uses a large fleet of DMUs of Classes 142, 144, 150, 153, 155, 156, 158, 170 and 195 plus EMU Classes 319, 321, 322, 323, 331 and 333. The new fleets of DMUs (Class 195) and EMUs (Class 331) are now being introduced on a number of routes, and will be followed by Class 769 bi-mode diesel electric units (converted from Class 319s). Most of the Class 142 Pacers have now been replaced and all Class 142/144 Pacers are due to be replaced by summer 2020.

ScotRail Abellio (Netherlands Railways) (until 31 March 2022) **ScotRail**

ScotRail provides almost all passenger services within Scotland and also trains from Glasgow to Carlisle via Dumfries, some of which extend to Newcastle-upon-Tyne (jointly operated with

Northern). The company operates a large fleet of DMUs of Classes 156, 158 and 170 and EMU Classes 314, 318, 320, 334, 380 and 385. Two locomotive-hauled Mark 2 sets are also used on Fife Circle commuter trains, hauled by Class 68s hired from DRS. In 2018 the first of a fleet of refurbished HSTs entered service on InterCity services and this has been supplemented by a number of unrefurbished HSTs which are used between Edinburgh/Glasgow and Aberdeen and Inverness and also Inverness–Aberdeen. All HSTs should be refurbished by the end of 2020.

South Eastern | Govia (Go-Ahead/Keolis) (until 1 April 2020) | **Southeastern**

The franchise competition was scrapped in 2019. It will either be restarted (in which case another extension to Govia will be required) or the DfT will take over as "Operator of Last Resort".

Southeastern operates all services in the south-east London suburbs, the whole of Kent and part of Sussex, which are primarily commuter services to London. It also operates domestic High Speed trains on HS1 from London St Pancras to Ashford, Ramsgate, Dover and Faversham with additional peak services on other routes. EMUs of Classes 375, 376, 377, 465 and 466 are used, along with Class 395s on the High Speed trains.

South Western | First Group (70%)/MTR (30%) (until 17 August 2024) | **South Western Railway**

There is an option to extend the franchise by 11 months to July 2025.

South Western Railway operates trains from London Waterloo to destinations across the South and South-West including Woking, Basingstoke, Southampton, Portsmouth, Salisbury, Exeter, Reading and Weymouth, as well as suburban services from Waterloo. SWR also runs services between Ryde and Shanklin on the Isle of Wight, using former London Underground 1938 stock (Class 483s). The rest of the fleet consists of DMU Classes 158 and 159 and EMU Classes 442, 444, 450, 455, 456, 458 and 707. A new fleet of Bombardier Class 701s are under construction to replace Classes 455, 456, 458 and 707 in 2020–21 with a fleet of five third rail Vivarail units (converted former LU D78 stock) on order to replace the 1938 Stock on the Isle of Wight.

Thameslink, Southern & Great Northern (TSGN) | Govia (Go-Ahead/Keolis) (until 18 September 2021) | **Govia Thameslink Railway**

There is an option to extend the franchise by 2 years to September 2023.

Govia operates this franchise, the largest in Great Britain, as a management contract. The former Southern franchise was combined with Thameslink/Great Northern in 2015. GTR uses four brands within the franchise: "Thameslink" for trains between Cambridge North, Peterborough, Bedford and Rainham, Sevenoaks, East Grinstead, Brighton, Littlehampton and Horsham via central London and also on the Sutton/Wimbledon loop using new Class 700 EMUs. "Great Northern" comprises services from London King's Cross and Moorgate to Welwyn Garden City, Hertford North, Peterborough, Cambridge and King's Lynn using Class 365, 387 and 717 EMUs. "Southern" operates predominantly commuter services between London, Surrey and Sussex and "metro" services in South London, as well as services along the south Coast between Southampton, Brighton, Hastings and Ashford, plus the cross-London service from South Croydon to Milton Keynes. Class 171 DMUs are used on Ashford–Eastbourne and London Bridge–Uckfield services, whilst all other services are in the hands of Class 313, 377, 455 and 700 EMUs. Finally, the premium "Gatwick Express" operates non-stop trains between London Victoria, Gatwick Airport and Brighton using Class 387/2 EMUs.

Trans-Pennine Express First Group (until 31 March 2023) **TransPennine Express**

There is an option to extend the franchise by 2 years to March 2025.

TransPennine Express operates predominantly long distance inter-urban services linking major cities across the North of England, along with Edinburgh and Glasgow in Scotland. The main services are Manchester Airport/Manchester Piccadilly–Newcastle/Redcar Central/Hull plus Liverpool–Scarborough and Liverpool–Newcastle–Edinburgh along the North Trans-Pennine route via Huddersfield, Leeds and York, and Manchester Airport–Cleethorpes along the South Trans-Pennine route via Sheffield. TPE also operates Manchester Airport–Edinburgh/Glasgow and Liverpool–Glasgow. The fleet consists of Class 185 DMUs, plus three new fleets being introduced: Class 68s+Mark 5A sets on Liverpool–Scarborough and Manchester Airport–Redcar Central, Class 397s on Manchester Airport/Liverpool–Scotland and Class 802 bi-mode units on Liverpool–Edinburgh and Manchester Airport–Newcastle.

Wales & Borders KeolisAmey (until 15 October 2033) **Transport for Wales**

Franchise procured by the Welsh Government.

Transport for Wales Rail operates a mix of long distance, regional and local services throughout Wales, including the Valley Lines network of lines around Cardiff, and also through services to the English border counties and to Manchester and Birmingham. The fleet consists of DMUs of Classes 142, 143, 150, 153, 158, 170 and 175 and two locomotive-hauled Mark 3 sets: one used on a premium Welsh Government sponsored service on the Cardiff–Holyhead route, and one used between Manchester/Crewe and Holyhead (both are hauled by a Class 67). Rebuilt Class 230 D-Trains are to be introduced on a number of routes from late 2019 and new Stadler and CAF fleets introduced on other routes from 2022.

West Coast Partnership First Group (70%)/Trenitalia (30%) (until 31 March 2031) **Avanti West Coast**

There is an option to extend the franchise by 3 years to March 2034.

Avanti West Coast operates long distance services along the West Coast Main Line from London Euston to Birmingham/Wolverhampton, Manchester, Liverpool, Blackpool North and Glasgow using Class 390 Pendolino EMUs. It also operates Class 221 Voyagers on the Euston–Chester–Holyhead route and a small number of trains from Wolverhampton to Shrewsbury, whilst a mix of Class 221s and 390s are used on the Euston–Birmingham–Glasgow/Edinburgh route.

West Midlands Trains Abellio (70%)/JR East (15%)/Mitsui (15%) (until 31 March 2026) **West Midlands Railway/ London Northwestern**

There is an option to extend the franchise by 2 years to March 2028.

West Midlands Trains operates services under two brand names. West Midlands Railway trains are local and regional services around Birmingham, including to Stratford-upon-Avon, Worcester, Hereford, Redditch, Rugeley and Shrewsbury. WMR is managed by a consortium of 16 councils and the Department for Transport. London Northwestern is the brand used for long distance and regional services from London Euston to Northampton and Birmingham/Crewe and also between Birmingham and Liverpool, Bedford–Bletchley and Watford Junction–St Albans Abbey. The fleet consists of DMU Classes 139, 153, 170 and 172 and EMU Classes 319, 323 and 350. Class 230 D-Trains were introduced onto the Bedford–Bletchley route in 2019 and new CAF DMUs and Bombardier EMUs will also be introduced on a number of routes in 2020–21.

NON-FRANCHISED SERVICES

The following operators run non-franchised, or "open access" services (* special seasonal services):

Operator	*Trading Name*	*Route*
Heathrow Airport Holdings	Heathrow Express	London Paddington–Heathrow Airport

Heathrow Express is a frequent express passenger service between London Paddington and Heathrow Airport using Class 332 EMUs, now operated by Great Western Railway as part of its franchise.

Hull Trains (part of First)	Hull Trains	London King's Cross–Hull

Hull Trains operates seven trains a day (weekdays) from Hull to London King's Cross via the East Coast Main Line. New Class 802s are being introduced during late 2019/early 2020, replacing the Class 180 DMUs. One train in each direction starts back from and extends to Beverley.

Grand Central (part of Arriva)	Grand Central	London King's Cross–Sunderland/ Bradford Interchange

Grand Central operates five trains a day from Sunderland and four trains a day from Bradford Interchange to London King's Cross using Class 180 DMUs.

Locomotive Services (TOC)	Locomotive Services	

Locomotive Services operates various excursions across the network.

North Yorkshire Moors Railway Enterprises	North Yorkshire Moors Railway	Pickering–Grosmont–Whitby/ Battersby, Sheringham–Cromer*

The North Yorkshire Moors Railway operates services on the national network between Grosmont and Whitby or Grosmont and Battersby as an extension of its Pickering–Grosmont services and also operates services between Sheringham and Cromer on behalf of the North Norfolk Railway.

South Yorkshire Supertram	Stagecoach Supertram	Meadowhall South–Rotherham Parkgate

South Yorkshire Supertram holds a passenger licence to allow the operation of the pilot tram-train service linking Sheffield city centre with Rotherham Central and Rotherham Parkgate.

Tyne & Wear PTE	Tyne & Wear Metro	Pelaw–Sunderland

Tyne & Wear Passenger Transport Executive holds a passenger license to allow the operation of its Metro service over Network Rail tracks between Pelaw and Sunderland.

Vintage Trains	Vintage Trains	Birmingham Snow Hill–Stratford-upon-Avon*

Vintage Trains operates steam-hauled services on a seasonal basis.

West Coast Railway Company	West Coast Railway Company	Fort William–Mallaig* York–Settle–Carlisle* Carnforth–York–Scarborough*

WCRC operates steam-hauled services on these routes on a seasonal basis and other excursions across the network.

INTERNATIONAL PASSENGER OPERATORS

Eurostar International operates passenger services between London St Pancras and mainland Europe. The company, established in 2010, is jointly owned by SNCF (the national operator of France): 55%, SNCB (the national operator of Belgium): 5% and Patina Rail: 40%. Patina Rail is made up of Canadian-based Caisse de dépôt et placement du Québec (CDPG) and UK-based Hermes Infrastructure (owning 30% and 10% respectively). This 40% was previously owned by the UK Government until it was sold in 2015.

In addition, a service for the conveyance of accompanied road vehicles through the Channel Tunnel is provided by the tunnel operating company, Eurotunnel. All Eurotunnel services are operated in top-and-tail mode by the powerful Class 9 Bo-Bo-Bo locomotives.

FREIGHT TRAIN OPERATORS

The following operators operate freight services or empty passenger stock workings under "Open Access" arrangements:

Colas Rail: Colas Rail operates a number of On-Track Machines and also supplies infrastructure monitoring trains for Network Rail. It also operates a number of different freight flows, including oil and timber. Colas Rail has a small but varied fleet consisting of Class 37s, 56s, 66s, 67s and 70s.

DB Cargo (UK): Still the biggest freight operator in the country, DBC (EWS until bought by Deutsche Bahn, when it was initially called DB Schenker) provides a large number of infrastructure trains to Network Rail and also operates coal, steel, intermodal and aggregate trains nationwide. The core fleet is Class 66s. Of the original 250 ordered, 79 have moved to DB's French and Polish operations, although some of the French locos do return to the UK when major maintenance is required. Around 20 Class 60s are also used on heavier trains, the remainder of the fleet has been stored or sold.

DBC's six Class 59/2s are used alongside the Mendip Rail 59/0s and 59/1s on stone traffic from the Mendip quarries and around the South-East, although Freightliner is due to take over the Mendip stone traffic later in 2019. DBC's fleet of Class 67s are used on passenger or standby duties for Transport for Wales and LNER and also on excursions or special trains. Class 90s see some use on West Coast Main Line freight traffic. The Class 92s are mainly used on a limited number of overnight freights on High Speed 1.

DBC also operates the Class 325 EMUs for Royal Mail and a number of excursion trains.

Devon & Cornwall Railways (part of Cappagh Construction Contractors (London)): DCRail specialises in short-term freight haulage contracts, using

Class 56s or four Class 60s recently acquired from DB Cargo and returned to service.

Direct Rail Services: DRS has built on its original nuclear flask traffic to operate a number of different services. The main flows are intermodal plus the provision of crews and locomotives to Network Rail for autumn RailHead Treatment Trains and also infrastructure trains. DRS has a varied fleet of locomotives, with Class 20s, 37s, 57s and 66s working alongside new Class 68s and diesel-electric Class 88s. Class 68s are hired to Chiltern Railways, TransPennine Express and ScotRail for passenger work. Its Class 68s are also used on some excursion work.

Freightliner: Freightliner (owned by Genesee & Wyoming) operates container trains from the main Ports at Southampton, Felixstowe, Tilbury and Thamesport to major cities including London, Manchester, Leeds and Birmingham. It also operates trains of coal, cement, infrastructure and aggregates. Most services are worked by Class 66s, with Class 70s mainly used on some of the heavier intermodal trains and cement trains from the Peak District. A small fleet of Class 86 and 90 electrics are used on intermodal trains on the Great Eastern and West Coast Main Lines, the Class 86s mainly being used in pairs on the WCML between Crewe and Coatbridge.

GB Railfreight: GBRf (owned by Infracapital) operates a mixture of traffic types, mainly using Class 66s together with a small fleet of Class 73s on infrastructure duties and test trains in the South-East and ten Class 60s acquired from Colas Rail in 2018. The company has also now purchased a number of Class 56s and owns a single Class 59, 59003. Some of the Class 56s are being rebuild as Class 69s with a new GM engine. A fleet of Class 92s is also used on some intermodal flows to and from Dollands Moor or through the Channel Tunnel to Calais. Traffic includes coal, intermodal, biomass, aggregates and gypsum as well as infrastructure services for Network Rail and London Underground. GBRf also supplies Class 92s to Caledonian Sleeper and owns three former Colas Rail Class 47s.

GBRf also operates some excursion trains, including those using the preserved Class 201 "Hastings" DEMU.

Loram (UK): Loram has a freight license and operates a limited number of trains, most hauling On-Track Machines using hired-in locomotives.

Rail Operations Group: This company mainly facilitates rolling stock movements by providing drivers or using locomotives hired from other companies or by using its own fleet of Class 47s or Class 37s hired from Europhoenix or Class 57s hired from DRS.

West Coast Railway Company: WCRC has a freight licence but doesn't operate any freight as such – only empty stock movements. Its fleet of Class 47s, supplemented by a smaller number of Class 33s, 37s and 57s, is used on excursion work nationwide.

In addition, Amey, Balfour Beatty Rail, Harsco Rail, Swietelsky Babcock Rail (SB Rail) and VolkerRail operate trains formed of On-Track Machines.

PROVISION OF INFORMATION

This book has been compiled with care to be as accurate as possible, but some information is not easily available and the publisher cannot be held responsible for any errors or omissions. We would like to thank the companies and individuals who have been helpful in supplying information to us. The authors of this series of books are always pleased to receive notification of any inaccuracies that may be found, to enhance future editions. Please send comments to:

Robert Pritchard, Platform 5 Publishing Ltd, 52 Broadfield Road, Sheffield, S8 0XJ, England. **e-mail:** robert.pritchard@platform5.com. **Tel:** 0114 255 2625.

UPDATES

This book is updated to the start of January 2020. The Platform 5 railway magazine "**Today's Railways UK**" publishes Stock Changes every month to update this book. The magazine also contains news and rolling stock information on the railways of Great Britain and Ireland and is published on the second Monday of every month. For further details of **Today's Railways UK**, please contact Platform 5 Publishing Ltd.

NEW DMUS & EMUS ON ORDER

Where possible all trains for which firm orders have been placed are listed in this book, however, there are several orders for new DMUs and EMUs for which the unit number and/or vehicle number series' have not yet been confirmed. These are summarised in the table below:

Class	*Manufacturer*	*Operator*	*Quantity*	*Delivery dates*
197/0[1]	CAF	Transport for Wales	51 x 2-car	2022–24
197/1[1]	CAF	Transport for Wales	26 x 3-car	2022
231[2]	Stadler	Transport for Wales	11 x 4-car	2022
711[3]	Bombardier	c2c	6 x 10-car	2021
398[4]	Stadler	Transport for Wales	36 x 3-car	2022
756/0[5]	Stadler	Transport for Wales	7 x 3-car	2023
756/1[5]	Stadler	Transport for Wales	17 x 4-car	2023
803[6]	Hitachi	First Group (ECML)	5 x 5-car	2021
804[7]	Hitachi	East Midlands Railway	33 x 5-car	2021–22
tbc[8]	Hitachi	Avanti West Coast	10 x 7-car	2022
tbc[9]	Hitachi	Avanti West Coast	13 x 5-car	2022

[1] Civity DMUs.
[2] FLIRT DMUs.
[3] Aventra EMUs. Funded by Porterbrook.
[4] FLIRT bi-mode electric/battery multiple units.
[5] FLIRT tri-mode diesel/electric/battery multiple units.
[6] EMUs for First Group's planned East Coast open access operation. Funded by Beacon Rail.
[7] Bi-mode units. Funded by Rock Rail.
[8] EMUs. Funded by Rock Rail.
[9] Bi-mode units. Funded by Rock Rail.

1. LOCOMOTIVES

INTRODUCTION

This section contains details of all locomotives which can run on Britain's national railway network, plus those of Eurotunnel.

Locomotives currently approved for use on the national railway network fall into the four broad types: passenger, freight, mixed traffic and shunting.

Passenger

The number of dedicated passenger locomotives has not changed significantly in recent years. However, the number is expected to decline in the future as new multiple unit stock replaces some of the remaining locomotive-hauled or propelled trains. Classes 43 (HST) and 91 and some members of Classes 57, 67, 68, 73/9, 90 and 92 are dedicated to franchised and Open Access passenger operations. Excursion trains have a few dedicated locomotives but mainly use locomotives that are best described as mixed traffic.

Freight

By far the most numerous locomotives are those used solely for bulk commodity and intermodal freight. Since 1998 a large number of new Class 66 locomotives have replaced many former BR designs and in more recent years smaller numbers of Class 70s have also been introduced. There are however a significant number of BR era Class 20, 37, 47, 56, 60, 73/1, 86, 90 and 92 locomotives still in use; their number has increased slightly as some locomotives have been reinstated to cope with demand. In addition there is a small fleet of Class 59s acquired privately in the 1980s and 1990s and a small number of re-engined Class 57s in use.

Mixed Traffic

In addition to their use on passenger and commodity freight workings these locomotives are used for stock movements and specialist infrastructure and test trains. The majority, but not all, are fitted with Electric Train Supply. Locomotives from Classes 20, 33, 37, 47, 57, 67, 68, 73/9, 88 and 90 fall into this category. Also included under this heading are preserved locomotives permitted to operate on the national railway network. Although these have in the past solely operated excursion trains they are increasingly seeing occasional use on other types of trains.

Shunting

Very few shunting locomotives are now permitted to operate freely on the National Railway network. The small number that are have to be fitted with a plethora of safety equipment in order to have engineering acceptance. They are mainly used for local workings such as trips between yards or stock movements between depots and stations. Otherwise, shunting locomotives are not permitted to venture from depots or yards onto the National Railway network other than into defined limits within interface infrastructure. Remotely-controlled driverless shunters are not included in this book. However, all ex-BR shunting locomotives are listed under Section 1.1 "Diesel Shunting Locomotives".

Locomotives which are owned by, for example, DB Cargo or Freightliner, which have been withdrawn from service and are awaiting disposal are listed in the main part of the book. Locomotives which are awaiting disposal at scrapyards are listed in the "Locomotives Awaiting Disposal" section.

Only preserved locomotives which are currently used on the National Railway network are included. Others, which may still be Network Rail registered but not at present certified for use, are not included, but can be found in the Platform 5 book, "Preserved Locomotives of British Railways".

LAYOUT OF INFORMATION

Locomotive classes are listed in numerical order of class. Principal details and dimensions are quoted for each class in metric and/or imperial units as considered appropriate bearing in mind common UK usage.

The heading "Total" indicates how many of that particular class are listed in this book.

Where numbers actually carried are different from those officially allocated, these are noted in class headings where appropriate. Where locomotives have been recently renumbered, the most immediate previous number is shown in parentheses. Each entry is laid out as in the following example:

No.	*Detail*	*Livery*	*Owner*	*Pool*	*Allocn.*	*Name*
60091	+*	**DB**	DB	WCBT	TO	Barry Needham

Detail Differences. Only detail differences which currently affect the areas and types of train which locomotives may work are shown. Where such differences occur within a class or part class, they are shown in the "Detail" column alongside the individual locomotive number.

Codes: Codes are used to denote the livery, owner, pool and depot of each locomotive. Details of these will be found in section 6 of this book.

The owner is the responsible custodian of the locomotive and this may not always be the legal owner. Actual ownership can be very complicated. Some vehicles are owned by finance/leasing companies. Others are owned by subsidiary companies of a holding company or by an associate company of the responsible custodian or operator.

Depot allocation codes for all locomotives are shown in this book (apart from shunting locomotives where the actual location of each is shown). It should be noted that today much locomotive maintenance is undertaken away from these depots. This may be undertaken at fuelling points, berthing sidings or similar, or by mobile maintenance teams. Therefore locomotives in particular may not return to their "home" depots as often as in the past.

(S) denotes that the locomotive is stored (the actual location is shown).

Names: Only names carried with official sanction are listed. Names are shown in UPPER/lower case characters as actually shown on the name carried on the locomotive.

Builders: These are shown in the class headings. More details and a full list of builders can be found in section 6.7.

GENERAL INFORMATION

CLASSIFICATION AND NUMBERING

All locomotives are classified and allocated numbers under the TOPS numbering system, introduced in 1972. This comprises a two-digit class number followed by a three-digit serial number.

For diesel locomotives, class numbers offer an indication of engine horsepower as shown in the table below.

Class No. Range	*Engine hp*
01–14	0–799
15–20	800–1000
21–31	1001–1499
32–39	1500–1999
40–54, 57	2000–2999
55–56, 58–70	3000+

For electric locomotives class numbers are allocated in ascending numerical order under the following scheme:

Class 71–80	Direct current and DC/diesel dual system locomotives.
Class 81 onwards	Alternating current and AC/DC dual system locomotives.

Numbers in the 89101–89999 series are allocated to locomotives which have been deregistered but subsequently re-registered for use on the national railway network and whose original number has already been reused. These numbers are normally only carried inside locomotive cabs and are not carried externally in normal circumstances.

WHEEL ARRANGEMENT

For main line locomotives the number of driven axles on a bogie or frame is denoted by a letter (A = 1, B = 2, C = 3 etc) and the number of non-powered axles is denoted by a number. The use of the letter "o" after a letter indicates each axle is individually powered, whilst the "+" symbol indicates bogies are inter-coupled.

For shunting locomotives, the Whyte notation is used. In this notation the number of leading wheels are given, followed by the number of driving wheels and then the trailing wheels.

UNITS OF MEASUREMENT

All dimensions and weights are quoted for locomotives in an "as new" condition with all necessary supplies (eg oil, water and sand) on board. Dimensions are quoted in the order length x width. Lengths quoted are over buffers or couplers as appropriate. All widths quoted are maxima. Where two different wheel diameter dimensions are shown, the first refers to powered wheels and the second refers to non-powered wheels. All weights are shown as metric tonnes (t = tonnes).

HAULAGE CAPABILITY OF DIESEL LOCOMOTIVES

The haulage capability of a diesel locomotive depends upon three basic factors:

1. Adhesive weight. The greater the weight on the driving wheels, the greater the adhesion and more tractive power can be applied before wheelslip occurs.

2. The characteristics of its transmission. To start a train the locomotive has to exert a pull at standstill. A direct drive diesel engine cannot do this, hence the need for transmission. This may be mechanical, hydraulic or electric. The present British Standard for locomotives is electric transmission. Here the diesel engine drives a generator or alternator and the current produced is fed to the traction motors. The force produced by each driven wheel depends on the current in its traction motor. In other words, the larger the current, the harder it pulls. As the locomotive speed increases, the current in the traction motor falls, hence the *Maximum Tractive Effort* is the maximum force at its wheels the locomotive can exert at a standstill. The electrical equipment cannot take such high currents for long without overheating. Hence the *Continuous Tractive Effort* is quoted which represents the current which the equipment can take continuously.

3. The power of its engine. Not all power reaches the rail, as electrical machines are approximately 90% efficient. As the electrical energy passes through two such machines (the generator or alternator and the traction motors), the *Power at Rail* is approximately 81% (90% of 90%) of the engine power, less a further amount used for auxiliary equipment such as radiator fans, traction motor blowers, air compressors, battery charging, cab heating, Electric Train Supply (ETS) etc. The power of the locomotive is proportional to the tractive effort times the speed. Hence when on full power there is a speed corresponding to the continuous tractive effort.

HAULAGE CAPABILITY OF ELECTRIC LOCOMOTIVES

Unlike a diesel locomotive, an electric locomotive does not develop its power on board and its performance is determined only by two factors, namely its weight and the characteristics of its electrical equipment. Whereas a diesel locomotive tends to be a constant power machine, the power of an electric locomotive varies considerably. Up to a certain speed it can produce virtually a constant tractive effort. Hence power rises with speed according to the formula given in section three above, until a maximum speed is reached at which tractive effort falls, such that the power also falls. Hence the power at the speed corresponding to the maximum tractive effort is lower than the maximum speed.

BRAKE FORCE

Brake Force (also known as brake power) is a measure of the braking power of a locomotive. The Brake Force available is dependant on the adhesion between the rail and the wheels being braked and the normal reaction of the rail on the wheels being braked (and hence on the weight per braked wheel). A locomotive's Brake Force is shown on its data panels so operating staff can ensure sufficient brake power is available for specific trains.

ELECTRIC TRAIN SUPPLY (ETS)

A number of locomotives are equipped to provide a supply of electricity to the train being hauled to power auxiliaries such as heating, cooling fans, air conditioning and kitchen equipment. ETS is provided from the locomotive by means of a separate alternator (except Class 33 locomotives, which have a DC generator). The ETS index of a locomotive is a measure of the electrical power available for train supply. Class 55 locomotives provide an ETS directly from one of their traction generators into the train supply.

Similarly, most locomotive-hauled carriages also have an ETS index, which in this case is a measure of the power required to operate equipment mounted in the carriage. The sum of the ETS indices of all the hauled vehicles in a train must not exceed the ETS index of the locomotive.

ETS is commonly (but incorrectly) known as ETH (Electric Train Heating), which is a throwback to the days before locomotive-hauled carriages were equipped with electrically powered auxiliary equipment other than for train heating.

ROUTE AVAILABILITY (RA)

This is a measure of a railway vehicle's axle load. The higher the axle load of a vehicle, the higher the RA number on a scale from 1 to 10. Each Network Rail route has a RA number and in general no vehicle with a higher RA number may travel on that route without special clearance.

MULTIPLE WORKING

Multiple working between vehicles (ie two or more powered vehicles being driven from one cab) is facilitated by jumper cables connecting the vehicles. However, not all types of locomotive are compatible with each other, and a number of different systems are in use. Some are compatible with others, some are not. BR used "multiple working codes" to designate which locomotives were compatible. The list below shows which classes of locomotives are compatible with each other – the former BR multiple working code being shown in brackets. It should be noted that some locomotives have had the equipment removed or made inoperable.

With other classes:
Classes 20, 25, 31, 33, 37 40 & 73/1*. (Blue Star)
Classes 56 & 58. (Red Diamond)
Classes 59, 66, 67, 68, 70, 73/9 & 88.
* DRS has since adapted the systems so its Classes 20/3, 37 & 57 can work with each other only.

With other members of same class only:
Class 43, Class 47 (Green Circle), Class 50 (Orange Square), Class 60.

PUSH-PULL OPERATION

Some locomotives are modified to operate passenger and service (formed of laboratory, test and inspection carriages) trains in "push-pull" mode – which allows the train to be driven from either end – either with locomotives at each end (both under power) or with a driving brake van at one end and a locomotive at the other. Various different systems are now in use. Electric locomotive Classes 86, 87, 90 & 91 use a time-division multiplex (TDM) system for push-pull working which utilises the existing Railway Clearing House (RCH) jumper cables fitted to carriages. Previously these cables had only been used to control train lighting and public address systems.

More recently locomotives of Classes 67 and 68 have used the Association of American Railroads (AAR) system.

ABBREVIATIONS

Standard abbreviations used in this section of the book are:

a	Train air brake equipment only.
b	Drophead buckeye couplers.
c	Scharfenberg couplers.
d	Fitted with retractable Dellner couplers.
e	European Railway Traffic Management System (ERTMS) signalling equipment fitted.
k	Fitted with Swinghead Automatic "buckeye" combination couplers.
p	Train air, vacuum and electro-pneumatic brakes.
r	Radio Electric Token Block signalling equipment fitted.
s	Slow Speed Control equipment.
v	Train vacuum brake only.
x	Train air and vacuum brakes ("Dual brakes").
+	Additional fuel tank capacity.
§	Sandite laying equipment.

In all cases use of the above abbreviations indicates the equipment in question is normally operable. The definition of non-standard abbreviations and symbols is detailed in individual class headings.

1.1. DIESEL SHUNTING LOCOMOTIVES

All BR design shunting locomotives still in existence, apart from those considered to be preserved, are listed together in this section. Preserved shunting locomotives are listed in the Platform 5 publication "Preserved Locomotives of British Railways" (a small number are listed in both that book and in this publication).

Few shunting locomotives have engineering acceptance and are equipped to operate on Network Rail infrastructure (beyond interface infrastructure), but those that are known to be permitted are indicated here.

For shunting locomotives, instead of the two-letter depot code, actual locations at the time of publication are given. Pool codes for shunting locomotives are not shown.

CLASS 03 BR/GARDNER 0-6-0

Built: 1958–62 by BR at Swindon or Doncaster Works.
Engine: Gardner 8L3 of 152 kW (204 hp) at 1200 rpm.
Transmission: Mechanical. Fluidrive type 23 hydraulic coupling to Wilson-Drewry CA5R7 gearbox with SCG type RF11 final drive.
Maximum Tractive Effort: 68 kN (15300 lbf).
Continuous Tractive Effort: 68 kN (15300 lbf) at 3.75 mph.
Train Brakes: Air & vacuum.
Brake Force: 13 t.
Weight: 31.3 t.
Design Speed: 28.5 mph.
Fuel Capacity: 1364 litres.
Train Supply: Not equipped.
Dimensions: 7.93 x 2.59 m.
Wheel Diameter: 1092 mm.
Maximum Speed: 28.5 mph.
Route Availability: 1.
Total: 3.

Number	*Notes*	*Livery*	*Owner*	*Location*
03084		**G**	WC	West Coast Railway Company, Carnforth Depot
03196		**B**	WC	West Coast Railway Company, Carnforth Depot
D2381	v	**G**	WC	West Coast Railway Company, Carnforth Depot

CLASS 07 BR/RUSTON & HORNSBY 0-6-0

Built: 1962 by Ruston & Hornsby, Lincoln.
Engine: Paxman 6RPHL Mk III of 205 kW (275 hp) at 1360 rpm.
Transmission: Electric. One AEI RTB 6652 traction motor.
Maximum Tractive Effort: 126 kN (28240 lbf).
Continuous Tractive Effort: 71 kN (15950 lbf) at 4.38 mph.
Train Brakes: Vacuum.
Brake Force:
Weight: 43.6 t.
Design Speed: 20 mph.
Fuel Capacity: 1400 litres.
Total: 1.
Dimensions: 8.17 x 2.59 m.
Wheel Diameter: 1067 mm.
Maximum Speed: 20 mph.
Train Supply: Not equipped.

07007	v	**B**	AF	Arlington Fleet Services, Eastleigh Works, Hants

CLASS 08 BR/ENGLISH ELECTRIC 0-6-0

Built: 1955–62 by BR at Crewe, Darlington, Derby Locomotive, Doncaster or Horwich Works.
Engine: English Electric 6KT of 298 kW (400 hp) at 680 rpm.
Main Generator: English Electric 801.
Traction Motors: Two English Electric 506.
Maximum Tractive Effort: 156 kN (35000 lbf).
Continuous Tractive Effort: 49 kN (11100 lbf) at 8.8 mph.
Power at Rail: 194 kW (260 hp).
Brake Force: 19 t.
Weight: 49.6–50.4 t.
Design Speed: 20 mph.
Fuel Capacity: 3037 litres.
Train Supply: Not equipped.
Train Brakes: Air & vacuum.
Dimensions: 8.92 x 2.59 m.
Wheel Diameter: 1372 mm.
Maximum Speed: 15 mph.
Route Availability: 5.
Total: 170.

* Locomotives with engineering acceptance to operate on Network Rail infrastructure. 08850 has acceptance for use between Battersby and Whitby only, for rescue purposes.

† – Fitted with remote control equipment.

Non-standard liveries:

08308 All over ScotRail Caledonian Sleeper purple.
08401 Dark green.
08423 Dark blue.
08442 Dark grey lower bodyside & light grey upper bodyside.
08445 Yellow, blue & green.
08447 Lilac.
08502 Mid blue.
08568 Dark grey lower bodyside & light grey upper bodyside. Red solebar stripe.
08598 Yellow.
08600 Red with a light grey roof.
08630 Black with red cabsides and solebar stripe.
08645 All over black with a white cross.
08682 Multi-coloured.
08774 Red with a light grey roof.
08870 Light grey.
08899 Crimson lake.
08913 Yellow, blue & green.
08956 Serco Railtest green.

Number	*Notes*	*Livery*	*Owner*	*Location*
08220	v	**B**	EE	Nottingham Transport Heritage Centre, Ruddington
08308	a	**0**	RL	Weardale Railway, Wolsingham, County Durham
08331		**K**	20	Midland Railway-Butterley, Derbyshire
08375	a	**RL**	RL	Victoria Group, Port of Boston, Boston
08389	a†	**E**	HN	Celsa Steel UK, Tremorfa Steelworks, Cardiff
08401	a	**0**	HU	Hams Hall Distribution Park, Coleshill, Warwickshire
08405	a†	**E**	RS	East Midlands Railway, Neville Hill Depot, Leeds
08410	* a	**GW**	GW	Great Western Railway, Long Rock Depot, Penzance
08411	a	**B**	RS	RSS, Rye Farm, Wishaw, Sutton Coldfield (S)

08417	* a	**Y**	NR	Loram (UK), RTC Business Park, Derby
08418	a	**E**	WC	West Coast Railway Company, Carnforth Depot
08423	a	**0**	RL	PD Ports, Teesport, Grangetown, Middlesbrough
08428	ak	**E**	HN	Barrow Hill Roundhouse, Chesterfield, Derbys (S)
08441	* a	**RS**	RS	Hitachi, Bounds Green Depot, London
08442	a	**0**	AV	Arriva TrainCare, Eastleigh Depot, Hampshire (S)
08445	a	**0**	HU	Daventry International Railfreight Terminal, Crick
08447	a	**0**	RU	John G Russell (Transport), Hillington, Glasgow (S)
08451	*	**B**	AM	Alstom, Longsight Depot, Manchester
08454	*	**B**	AM	Alstom, Widnes Technology Centre, Merseyside
08460	a	**RS**	RS	GB Railfreight, Eastleigh East Yard
08472	* a	**WA**	WA	Hitachi, Craigentinny Depot, Edinburgh
08480	* a	**RS**	RS	Greater Anglia, Crown Point Depot, Norwich
08483	* a	**K**	GW	Great Western Railway, Laira Depot, Plymouth (S)
08484	a	**RS**	RS	Hitachi Rail Europe, Newton Aycliffe, Co Durham
08485	a	**B**	WC	West Coast Railway Company, Carnforth Depot
08499	a	**B**	CS	Colas Rail, Canton Depot, Cardiff
08500		**E**	HN	Nemesis Rail, Burton-upon-Trent, Staffordshire (S)
08502		**0**	HN	East Kent Light Railway, Shepherdswell, Kent (S)
08507	a	**RB**	RV	Arlington Fleet Services, Eastleigh Works
08511	a	**RS**	RS	GB Railfreight, Eastleigh East Yard
08516	a	**LW**	AV	Arriva TrainCare, Barton Hill Depot, Bristol
08523	*	**B**	RL	Weardale Railway, Wolsingham, County Durham
08525		**ST**	EM	East Midlands Railway, Neville Hill Depot, Leeds (S)
08527		**FA**	HN	Attero Recycling, Rossington, Doncaster
08530	*	**FL**	FL	Freightliner, Trafford Park FLT
08531	* a	**FH**	FL	Freightliner, Felixstowe FLT
08536		**B**	RS	RSS, Rye Farm, Wishaw, Sutton Coldfield (S)
08567		**E**	AF	Arlington Fleet Services, Eastleigh Works, Hants
08568		**0**	RS	RSS, Rye Farm, Wishaw, Sutton Coldfield (S)
08571	* a	**WA**	WA	Daventry International Railfreight Terminal, Crick
08573		**K**	RL	Weardale Railway, Wolsingham, County Durham
08575		**FL**	FL	Nemesis Rail, Burton-upon-Trent, Staffordshire (S)
08578		**E**	HN	Quinton Rail Technology Centre, Long Marston, Warks (S)
08580	*	**RS**	RS	Hitachi, Bounds Green Depot, London
08585	*	**FH**	FL	Freightliner, Southampton Maritime FLT
08588		**RL**	RL	Loram (UK), RTC Business Park, Derby
08593		**E**	RS	RSS, Rye Farm, Wishaw, Sutton Coldfield (S)
08596	* a†	**WA**	WA	Hitachi, Craigentinny Depot, Edinburgh
08598		**0**	AD	RSS, Rye Farm, Wishaw, Sutton Coldfield
08600	a	**0**	AD	AV Dawson, Ayrton Rail Terminal, Middlesbrough
08602		**B**	BT	Bombardier Transportation, Derby Works (S)
08605	†	**DB**	RV	Ecclesbourne Valley Railway, Wirksworth, Derbyshire
08611	*	**B**	AM	Alstom, Wembley Depot, London
08613		**RL**	RL	Weardale Railway, Wolsingham, County Durham
08615	*	**HU**	WA	Tata Steel, Shotton Works, Deeside
08616		**LM**	WM	West Midlands Trains, Tyseley Depot, Birmingham
08617	*	**B**	AM	Alstom, Oxley Depot, Wolverhampton
08622		**K**	RL	Hanson Cement, Ketton Cement Works, nr Stamford
08623		**DB**	HN	Breedon, Hope Cement Works, Derbys (S)
08624	*	**FH**	FL	Freightliner, Felixstowe FLT

08629		**KB**	GE	Gemini Rail Group, Wolverton Works, Milton Keynes
08630	†	**K**	HN	Celsa Steel UK, Tremorfa Steelworks, Cardiff
08631		**B**	LD	Weardale Railway, Wolsingham, County Durham
08632	†	**RS**	RS	GB Railfreight, Bescot Yard
08641	*	**B**	GW	Great Western Railway, Laira Depot, Plymouth
08643		**B**	MR	Aggregate Industries, Merehead Rail Terminal
08644	*	**B**	GW	Great Western Railway, Laira Depot, Plymouth
08645	*	**0**	GW	Great Western Railway, Long Rock Depot, Penzance
08648	*	**K**	RL	ScotRail, Inverness Depot
08649		**KB**	GE	Gemini Rail Group, Wolverton Works, Milton Keynes
08650		**B**	MR	RSS, Rye Farm, Wishaw, Sutton Coldfield
08652		**B**	MR	Aggregate Industries, Merehead Rail Terminal
08653		**E**	HN	Quinton Rail Technology Centre, Long Marston, Warks (S)
08663	* a	**B**	PO	GB Railfreight, Dagenham Car Terminal
08669	* a	**WA**	WA	Wabtec Rail, Doncaster Works
08670	* a	**RS**	RS	GB Railfreight, Bescot Yard
08676		**E**	HN	East Kent Light Railway, Shepherdswell, Kent (S)
08678	a	**WC**	WC	West Coast Railway Company, Carnforth Depot
08682		**0**	BT	Bombardier Transportation, Derby Works (S)
08683	*	**RS**	RS	Greater Anglia, Crown Point Depot, Norwich
08685		**E**	HN	East Kent Light Railway, Shepherdswell, Kent (S)
08690		**ST**	EM	East Midlands Railway, Neville Hill Depot, Leeds (S)
08691	*	**FL**	FL	Freightliner, Crewe Basford Hall Yard, Cheshire
08696	* a	**B**	AM	Alstom, Wembley Depot, London
08700		**B**	RL	Bombardier Transportation, Ilford Works, London
08701	a	**RX**	HN	Quinton Rail Technology Centre, Long Marston, Warks (S)
08703	a	**E**	RS	DB Cargo UK, Springs Branch Depot, Wigan
08704		**RB**	RV	Ecclesbourne Valley Railway, Wirksworth, Derbys
08706	†	**E**	HN	RSS, Rye Farm, Wishaw, Sutton Coldfield (S)
08709		**E**	RS	RSS, Rye Farm, Wishaw, Sutton Coldfield (S)
08711	k	**RX**	HN	Nemesis Rail, Burton-upon-Trent, Staffordshire (S)
08714		**E**	HN	Breedon, Hope Cement Works, Derbys (S)
08721	*	**B**	AM	Alstom, Widnes Technology Centre, Merseyside
08724	*	**WA**	WA	Wabtec Rail, Doncaster Works
08730		**KB**	GE	Gemini Rail Group, Springburn Depot, Glasgow
08735	†	**AW**	AV	Arriva TrainCare, Eastleigh Depot
08737		**G**	LD	L&NWR Heritage Company, Crewe Diesel Depot
08738		**RS**	RS	Arriva TrainCare, Eastleigh Depot
08742	†	**RX**	HN	Barrow HIll Roundhouse, Chesterfield, Derbys (S)
08743		**B**	SU	SembCorp Utilities UK, Wilton, Middlesbrough
08752	†	**RS**	RS	Gemini Rail Group, Wolverton Works, Milton Keynes
08754	*	**B**	RL	ScotRail, Inverness Depot
08756		**DG**	RL	Weardale Railway, Wolsingham, County Durham
08757		**RG**	PO	Telford Steam Railway, Shropshire
08762		**RL**	RL	L&NWR Heritage Company, Crewe Diesel Depot
08764	*	**B**	AM	Alstom, Polmadie Depot, Glasgow
08765		**HN**	HN	Barrow Hill Roundhouse, Chesterfield, Derbys (S)
08774	a	**0**	AD	AV Dawson, Ayrton Rail Terminal, Middlesbrough
08780		**B**	LD	L&NWR Heritage Company, Crewe Diesel Depot
08782	a†	**CU**	HN	Barrow HIll Roundhouse, Chesterfield, Derbys (S)
08783		**E**	EY	European Metal Recycling, Kingsbury, nr Tamworth

08785	* a	**FL**	FL	LH Group, Barton-under-Needwood, Staffordshire
08786	a	**DG**	HN	Barrow Hill Roundhouse, Chesterfield, Derbys (S)
08787		**B**	MR	Hanson Aggregates, Whatley Quarry, near Frome
08788	*	**RL**	RL	PD Ports, Teesport, Grangetown, Middlesbrough
08790	*	**B**	AM	Alstom, Edge Hill Depot, Liverpool
08798		**E**	HN	Barrow Hill Roundhouse, Chesterfield, Derbys (S)
08799	a	**E**	HN	East Kent Light Railway, Shepherdswell, Kent (S)
08802	†	**RX**	HN	RSS, Rye Farm, Wishaw, Sutton Coldfield (S)
08804	†	**E**	HN	East Kent Light Railway, Shepherdswell, Kent (S)
08805		**FO**	WM	West Midlands Trains, Soho Depot, Birmingham
08809		**RL**	RL	Hanson Cement, Ketton Cement Works, nr Stamford
08810	a	**LW**	AV	Arriva TrainCare, Eastleigh Depot, Hampshire
08818		**GB**	HN	GB Railfreight, Garston Car Terminal, Liverpool
08822	*	**IC**	GW	Great Western Railway, St Philip's Marsh Depot, Bristol
08823	a	**HU**	HU	Tata Steel, Shotton Works, Deeside
08824	ak	**K**	HN	Barrow HIll Roundhouse, Chesterfield, Derbys (S)
08834		**HN**	HN	Northern, Allerton Depot, Liverpool
08836	*	**GW**	GW	Great Western Railway, Reading Depot
08846		**B**	RS	East Midlands Railway, Neville Hill Depot, Leeds
08847	*	**CD**	RL	PD Ports, Teesport, Grangetown, Middlesbrough
08850	*	**B**	NY	North Yorkshire Moors Railway, Grosmont Depot
08853	* a	**WA**	WA	Wabtec Rail, Doncaster Works
08865		**E**	HN	Bombardier Transportation, Central Rivers Depot, Barton-under-Needwood
08868		**AW**	HN	Arriva TrainCare, Crewe Depot, Cheshire
08870		**O**	RL	Weardale Railway, Wolsingham, County Durham
08871		**CD**	RL	Bombardier Transportation, Ilford Works, London
08872		**E**	HN	European Metal Recycling, Attercliffe, Sheffield (S)
08873	*	**RX**	HU	LH Group, Barton-under-Needwood, Staffordshire (S)
08874	*	**SL**	RL	Weardale Railway, Wolsingham, County Durham
08877		**DG**	HN	Celsa Steel UK, Tremorfa Steelworks, Cardiff
08879		**E**	HN	Breedon, Hope Cement Works, Derbys (S)
08885		**B**	RL	Weardale Railway, Wolsingham, County Durham (S)
08887	* a	**B**	AM	Alstom, Polmadie Depot, Glasgow
08891	*	**FL**	FL	Nemesis Rail, Burton-upon-Trent, Staffordshire (S)
08892		**DR**	HN	Bombardier Transportation, Old Dalby Test Centre, Asfordby
08899		**O**	EM	East Midlands Railway, Derby Etches Park Depot
08903		**B**	SU	SembCorp Utilities UK, Wilton, Middlesbrough
08904		**E**	HN	HNRC, Worksop Depot, Nottinghamshire
08905		**E**	HN	Breedon, Hope Cement Works, Derbys (S)
08908		**ST**	EM	East Midlands Railway, Neville Hill Depot, Leeds (S)
08912		**B**	AD	AV Dawson, Ayrton Rail Terminal, Middlesbrough (S)
08918		**DG**	HN	Nemesis Rail, Burton-upon-Trent, Staffordshire (S)
08921		**E**	RS	RSS, Rye Farm, Wishaw, Sutton Coldfield (S)
08922		**DG**	PO	EMD, Longport Works, Stoke-on-Trent§
08924	†	**GB**	HN	Celsa Steel UK, Tremorfa Steelworks, Cardiff
08925		**G**	GB	GB Railfreight, Whitemoor Yard, March, Cambs
08927		**G**	RS	RSS, Rye Farm, Wishaw, Sutton Coldfield
08933		**B**	MR	Aggregate Industries, Merehead Rail Terminal
08934	a	**VP**	GB	Barrow Hill Roundhouse, Chesterfield, Derbys (S)
08936		**B**	RL	Weardale Railway, Wolsingham, County Durham

08937		**G**	BD	Dartmoor Railway, Meldon Quarry, nr Okehampton
08939		**RS**	RS	Felixstowe FLT
08943		**HN**	HN	Barrow HIll Roundhouse, Chesterfield, Derbys
08947		**B**	MR	Hanson Aggregates, Whatley Quarry, near Frome
08948	c	**EP**	EU	Eurostar, Temple Mills Depot, London
08950		**ST**	EM	East Midlands Railway, Neville Hill Depot, Leeds (S)
08954	*	**B**	AM	Alstom, Polmadie Depot, Glasgow
08956		**0**	LO	Bombardier Transportation, Old Dalby Test Centre, Asfordby

Class 08/9. Reduced height cab. Converted 1985–87 by BR at Landore.

08994	a	**E**	HN	Nemesis Rail, Burton-upon-Trent, Staffordshire (S)

Other numbers or names carried:

08308	"23"
08423	"H011" / "14"
08451	LONGSIGHT TMD
08460	SPIRIT OF THE OAK
08484	CAPTAIN NATHANIEL DARELL
08499	REDLIGHT
08525	DUNCAN BEDFORD
08568	St. Rollox
08585	Vicky
08588	"H047"
08602	"004"
08605	"WIGAN2"
08613	"H064"
08615	UNCLE DAI
08616	TYSELEY 100 / 3783
08617	Steve Purser
08622	"H028" / "19"
08624	Rambo PAUL RAMSEY
08629	Wolverton
08630	"CELSA 3"
08641	Pride of Laira
08644	Laira Diesel Depot 50 Years 1962–2012
08645	St. Piran
08649	Bradwell
08669	Bob Machin
08678	"555"
08682	Lionheart
08690	DAVID THIRKILL
08691	Terri
08737	D3905
08743	Bryan Turner
08754	"H041"
08757	EAGLE C.U.R.C.
08762	"H067"
08774	ARTHUR VERNON DAWSON
08780	FRED
08787	"08296"
08790	M.A. SMITH
08805	Robin Jones 40 YEARS SERVICE
08809	"24"
08810	RICHARD J. WENHAM EASTLEIGH DEPOT DECEMBER 1989 – JULY 1999
08818	MOLLY / "CELSA 4"
08822	Dave Mills
08823	KEVLA
08824	"IEMD 01"
08846	"003"
08870	"H024"
08871	"H074"
08885	"H042" / "18"
08899	Midland Counties Railway 175 1839–2014
08903	John W Antill
08924	"CELSA 2"
08927	D4157
08937	D4167
08950	DAVID LIGHTFOOT

CLASS 09 BR/ENGLISH ELECTRIC 0-6-0

Built: 1959–62 by BR at Darlington or Horwich Works.
Engine: English Electric 6KT of 298 kW (400 hp) at 680 rpm.
Main Generator: English Electric 801.
Traction Motors: English Electric 506.
Maximum Tractive Effort: 111 kN (25000 lbf).
Continuous Tractive Effort: 39 kN (8800 lbf) at 11.6 mph.
Power at Rail: 201 kW (269 hp).
Brake Force: 19 t.
Weight: 49 t.
Design Speed: 27 mph.
Fuel Capacity: 3037 litres.
Train Supply: Not equipped.
Train Brakes: Air & vacuum.
Dimensions: 8.92 x 2.59 m.
Wheel Diameter: 1372 mm.
Maximum Speed: 27 mph.
Route Availability: 5.
Total: 10.

Class 09/0. Built as Class 09.

09002	**G**	GB	GB Railfreight, Whitemoor Yard, March, Cambs
09006	**E**	HN	Nemesis Rail, Burton-upon-Trent, Staffordshire (S)
09007	**G**	LN	London Overground, Willesden Depot, London
09009	**G**	GB	Miles Platting Stone Terminal, Greater Manchester
09014	**DG**	HN	Nemesis Rail, Burton-upon-Trent, Staffordshire (S)
09022	**B**	VG	Victoria Group, Port of Boston, Boston
09023	**E**	EY	European Metal Recycling, Attercliffe, Sheffield (S)

Class 09/1. Converted from Class 08 1992–93 by RFS Industries, Kilnhurst. 110 V electrical equipment.

09106	**HN**	HN	Celsa Steel UK, Tremorfa Steelworks, Cardiff

Class 09/2. Converted from Class 08 1992 by RFS Industries, Kilnhurst. 90 V electrical equipment.

09201	**DG**	HN	Breedon, Hope Cement Works, Derbys (S)
09204	**AW**	AV	Arriva TrainCare, Crewe Depot, Cheshire

Other numbers or names carried:

09007	D3671
09106	"6"

1.2. MAIN LINE DIESEL LOCOMOTIVES

CLASS 19

Experimental locomotive being rebuilt by Artemis Intelligent Power from a Mark 3B Driving Brake Van. Part of a project funded by the Rail Safety & Standards Board (RSSB) to test the viability of combining hydrostatic transmission to reduce engine emissions. Conversion work is taking place at the Bo'ness & Kinneil Railway. Full details awaited.

Built: 1988 by BR Derby Works.
Engine: 2 x JCB diesel engines.
Main Generator:
Traction Motors:
Maximum Tractive Effort:
Continuous Tractive Effort:
Power at Rail:
Brake Force:
Design Speed:
Fuel Capacity:
Train Supply:
Train Brakes:
Dimensions: 18.83 x 2.71 m.
Weight:
Maximum Speed:
Route Availability:
Total: 1.

19001 (82113) **B** AV BO

CLASS 20 ENGLISH ELECTRIC Bo-Bo

Built: 1957–68 by English Electric at Vulcan Foundry, Newton-le-Willows or by Robert Stephenson & Hawthorns at Darlington.
Engine: English Electric 8SVT Mk II of 746 kW (1000 hp) at 850 rpm.
Main Generator: English Electric 819/3C.
Traction Motors: English Electric 526/5D or 526/8D.
Maximum Tractive Effort: 187 kN (42000 lbf).
Continuous Tractive Effort: 111 kN (25000 lbf) at 11 mph.
Power at Rail: 574 kW (770 hp).
Brake Force: 35 t.
Weight: 73.4–73.5 t.
Design Speed: 75 mph.
Fuel Capacity: 1727 litres.
Train Supply: Not equipped.
Train Brakes: Air & vacuum.
Dimensions: 14.25 x 2.67 m.
Wheel Diameter: 1092 mm.
Maximum Speed: 75 mph.
Route Availability: 5.
Total: 32.

Non-standard liveries/numbering:

20056 Yellow with grey cabsides and red solebar. Carries No. "81".
20066 Dark blue with yellow stripes. Carries No. "82".
20088 RFS grey. Carries No. 2017.
20110 Carries original number D8110.
20142 LUL Maroon.
20168 White with green cabsides and solebar. Carries No. "2".
20227 LUL Maroon.
20906 White. Carries No. "3".

Class 20/0. Standard Design.

20007	**G**	EE	MOLO	SK	
20016	**B**	HN	HNRS	LM (S)	
20056	**0**	HN	HNRL	SC (S)	
20066	**0**	HN	HNRL	HO	
20081	**B**	HN	HNRS	LM (S)	
20088	**0**	HN	HNRS	LM (S)	
20096	**B**	HN	GBEE	BH	Ian Goddard 1938–2016
20107	**B**	HN	GBEE	BH	
20110	**G**	HN	HNRS	BQ (S)	
20118	**FO**	HN	GBEE	BH	Saltburn-by-the-Sea
20121	**HN**	HN	HNRL	BH (S)	
20132	**FO**	HN	GBEE	BH	Barrow Hill Depot
20142	**0**	20	MOLO	SK	SIR JOHN BETJEMAN
20168	**0**	HN	HNRL	HO	SIR GEORGE EARLE
20189	**B**	20	MOLO	SK	
20205	**B**	2L	MOLO	SK	
20227	**0**	2L	MOLO	SK	SHERLOCK HOLMES

Class 20/3. Direct Rail Services refurbished locomotives. Details as Class 20/0 except:

Refurbished: 15 locomotives were refurbished 1995–96 by Brush Traction at Loughborough (20301–305) or 1997–98 by RFS(E) at Doncaster (20306–315). Disc indicators or headcode panels removed.

Train Brakes: Air.
Maximum Speed: 60 mph (+ 75 mph).
Weight: 73 t (+ 76 t).
Fuel Capacity: 2909 (+ 4909) litres.
Brake Force: 35 t (+ 31 t).
RA: 5 (+ 6).

20301	(20047)	r	**DS**	DR	XHSS	BH (S)	
20302	(20084)	r	**DS**	DR	XHCK	KM	
20303	(20127)	r	**DS**	DR	XHCK	KM	Max Joule 1958–1999
20304	(20120)	r	**DS**	DR	XHSS	BH (S)	
20305	(20095)	r	**DS**	DR	XHCK	KM	
20308	(20187)	r+	**DS**	DR	XHSS	BH (S)	
20309	(20075)	r+	**DS**	DR	XHSS	BH (S)	
20311	(20102)	r+	**HN**	HN	XHCK	BH	
20312	(20042)	r+	**DS**	DR	XHSS	BH (S)	
20314	(20117)	r+	**HN**	HN	XHCK	BH	

Class 20/9. Harry Needle Railroad Company (former Hunslet-Barclay/ DRS) locomotives. Details as Class 20/0 except:

Refurbished: 1989 by Hunslet-Barclay at Kilmarnock.
Train Brakes: Air.
Fuel Capacity: 1727 (+ 4727) litres.
RA: 5 (+ 6).

20901	(20101)		**GB**	HN	GBEE	BH	
20903	(20083)	+	**DR**	HN	HNRS	BU (S)	
20904	(20041)		**DR**	HN	HNRS	BU (S)	
20905	(20225)	+	**GB**	HN	GBEE	BH	Dave Darwin
20906	(20219)		**0**	HN	HNRL	HO	

CLASS 25 BR/BEYER PEACOCK/SULZER Bo-Bo

Built: 1965 by Beyer Peacock at Gorton.
Engine: Sulzer 6LDA28-B of 930 kW (1250 hp) at 750 rpm.
Main Generator: AEI RTB15656. **Traction Motors**: AEI 253AY.
Maximum Tractive Effort: 200 kN (45000 lbf).
Continuous Tractive Effort: 93 kN (20800 lbf) at 17.1 mph.
Power at Rail: 708 kW (949 hp). **Train Brakes**: Air & vacuum.
Brake Force: 38 t. **Dimensions**: 15.39 x 2.73 m.
Weight: 71.5 t. **Wheel Diameter**: 1143 mm.
Design Speed: 90 mph. **Maximum Speed**: 60 mph.
Fuel Capacity: 2270 litres. **Route Availability**: 5.
Train Supply: Not equipped. **Total**: 1.

Carries original number D7628.

Only certified for use on Network Rail tracks between Whitby and Battersby, as an extension of North Yorkshire Moors Railway services.

25278	**GG**	NY	MBDL	NY	SYBILLA

CLASS 31 BRUSH/ENGLISH ELECTRIC A1A-A1A

Built: 1958–62 by Brush Traction at Loughborough.
Engine: English Electric 12SVT of 1100 kW (1470 hp) at 850 rpm.
Main Generator: Brush TG160-48. **Traction Motors**: Brush TM73-68.
Maximum Tractive Effort: 160 kN (35900 lbf).
Continuous Tractive Effort: 83 kN (18700 lbf) at 23.5 mph.
Power at Rail: 872 kW (1170 hp). **Train Brakes**: Air & vacuum.
Brake Force: 49 t. **Dimensions**: 17.30 x 2.67 m.
Weight: 106.7–111 t. **Wheel Diameter**: 1092/1003 mm.
Design Speed: 90 mph. **Maximum Speed**: 90 mph.
Fuel Capacity: 2409 litres. **Route Availability**: 5.
Train Supply: Not equipped. **Total**: 1.

31128	**B**	NS	NRLO	BU	CHARYBDIS

CLASS 33 BRCW/SULZER Bo-Bo

Built: 1959–62 by the Birmingham Railway Carriage & Wagon Company at Smethwick.
Engine: Sulzer 8LDA28 of 1160 kW (1550 hp) at 750 rpm.
Main Generator: Crompton Parkinson CG391B1.
Traction Motors: Crompton Parkinson C171C2.
Maximum Tractive Effort: 200 kN (45000 lbf).
Continuous Tractive Effort: 116 kN (26000 lbf) at 17.5 mph.
Power at Rail: 906 kW (1215 hp). **Train Brakes**: Air & vacuum.
Brake Force: 35 t. **Dimensions**: 15.47 x 2.82 (2.64 m 33/2).
Weight: 76-78 t. **Wheel Diameter**: 1092 mm.
Design Speed: 85 mph. **Maximum Speed**: 85 mph.

Fuel Capacity: 3410 litres. **Route Availability**: 6.
Train Supply: Electric, index 48 (750 V DC only).
Total: 5.

Non-standard numbering: 33012 Carries original number D6515.

Class 33/0. Standard Design.

33012	**G**	71	MBDL	SW	Lt Jenny Lewis RN
33025	**WC**	WC	AWCA	CS	
33029	**WC**	WC	AWCA	CS	
33030	**DR**	WC	AWCX	CS (S)	

Class 33/2. Built to former Loading Gauge of Tonbridge–Battle Line.
Equipped with slow speed control.

33207	**WC**	WC	AWCA	CS	Jim Martin

CLASS 37 ENGLISH ELECTRIC Co-Co

Built: 1960–66 by English Electric at Vulcan Foundry, Newton-le-Willows or by Robert Stephenson & Hawthorns at Darlington.
Engine: English Electric 12CSVT of 1300 kW (1750 hp) at 850 rpm.
Main Generator: English Electric 822/10G.
Traction Motors: English Electric 538/A.
Maximum Tractive Effort: 247 kN (55500 lbf).
Continuous Tractive Effort: 156 kN (35000 lbf) at 13.6 mph.
Power at Rail: 932 kW (1250 hp). **Train Brakes**: Air & vacuum.
Brake Force: 50 t. **Dimensions**: 18.75 x 2.74 m.
Weight: 102.8–108.4 t. **Wheel Diameter**: 1092 mm.
Design Speed: 90 mph. **Maximum Speed**: 80 mph.
Fuel Capacity: 4046 (+ 7683) litres. **Route Availability**: 5 (§ 6).
Train Supply: Not equipped. **Total**: 66.

Non-standard numbering:

37057 Also carries original number D6757.
37240 Carries original number 6940.
37424 Also carries the number 37558.
37667 Carries original number D6851.
37703 Carries the number 37067.
37905 Also carries original number D6838.

Class 37/0. Standard Design.

37025		**BL**	37	COTS	NM	Inverness TMD
37038	a	**DI**	DR	XHNC	KM	
37057		**G**	CS	COTS	NM	
37059	ar+	**DI**	DR	XHNC	KM	
37069	ar+	**DI**	DR	XHNC	KM	
37099		**CS**	CS	COTS	NM	MERL EVANS 1947–2016
37116	+	**CS**	CS	COTS	NM	
37146		**CE**	EP	EPUK	LR (S)	
37165	a+	**CE**	WC	AWCX	CS (S)	
37175	a	**CS**	CS	COTS	NM	

37190		**B**	LD	MBDL	CL	
37198	+	**Y**	NR	MBDL	ZA (S)	
37207		**B**	EP	MBDL	LR (S)	
37218	ar+	**DI**	DR	XHNC	KM	
37219		**CS**	CS	COTS	NM	Jonty Jarvis 8-12-1998 to 18-3-2005
37240		**F**	NB	MBDL	NM (S)	
37254		**CS**	CS	COTS	NM	Cardiff Canton
37259	ar	**DS**	DR	XHNC	KM	

Class 37/4. Refurbished with electric train supply equipment. Main generator replaced by alternator. Regeared (CP7) bogies. Details as Class 37/0 except:
Main Alternator: Brush BA1005A. **Power At Rail:** 935 kW (1254 hp).
Traction Motors: English Electric 538/5A.
Maximum Tractive Effort: 256 kN (57440 lbf).
Continuous Tractive Effort: 184 kN (41250 lbf) at 11.4 mph.
Weight: 107 t. **Design Speed:** 80 mph.
Fuel Capacity: 7683 litres.
Train Supply: Electric, index 30.

37401	ar	**BL**	DR	XHAC	KM	Mary Queen of Scots
37402	a	**BL**	DR	XHAC	KM	Stephen Middlemore 23.12.1954–8.6.2013
37403		**BL**	SP	XHAC	KM	Isle of Mull
37405	ar	**DS**	DR	XHAC	KM	
37407		**BL**	DR	XHAC	KM	Blackpool Tower
37409	ar	**BL**	DR	XHAC	KM	Lord Hinton
37418		**BL**	SB	COTS	NM	
37419	ar	**IC**	DR	XHAC	KM	Carl Haviland 1954–2012
37421		**CS**	CS	COTS	NM	
37422	ar	**DR**	DR	XHSS	CR (S)	
37423	ar	**DR**	DR	XHAC	KM	Spirit of the Lakes
37424		**BL**	DR	XHAC	KM	Avro Vulcan XH558
37425	ar	**DS**	DR	XHSS	ZA (S)	Sir Robert McAlpine/Concrete Bob

Class 37/5. Refurbished without train supply equipment. Main generator replaced by alternator. Regeared (CP7) bogies. Details as Class 37/4 except:
Power At Rail: 932 kW (1250 hp).
Maximum Tractive Effort: 248 kN (55590 lbf).
Weight: 106.1–110.0 t.
Train Supply: Not equipped.

37510	a	**EX**	EP	SROG	LR	Orion
37516	s	**WC**	WC	AWCA	CS	Loch Laidon
37517	as	**LH**	WC	AWCX	CS (S)	
37518	ar	**WC**	WC	AWCA	CS	
37521		**CS**	LD	LSLO	CL	

Class 37/6. Originally refurbished for Nightstar services. Main generator replaced by alternator. UIC jumpers. Details as Class 37/5 except:
Maximum Speed: 90 mph. **Train Brake:** Air.
Train Supply: Not equipped, but electric through wired.

37601	ad	**EX**	EP	GROG	LR	Perseus
37602	ar	**DS**	DR	XHSS	ZG (S)	

37603	a	**DS**	DR	XHSS	LW (S)	
37604	a	**DS**	DR	XHSS	LW (S)	
37605	ar	**DS**	DR	XHSS	ZA (S)	
37606	a	**DS**	DR	XHSS	CR (S)	
37607	ar	**DR**	HN	COTS	BH	
37608	ard	**EX**	EP	GROG	LR	Andromeda
37609	a	**DI**	DR	XHSS	LW (S)	
37610	ar	**BL**	HN	COTS	BH	
37611	ad	**EX**	EP	GROG	LR	Pegasus
37612	a	**DR**	HN	COTS	BH	

Class 37/5 continued.

37667	ars	**G**	LD	LSLO	CL	
37668	e	**WC**	WC	AWCA	CS	
37669	e	**WC**	WC	AWCA	CS	
37676	a	**WC**	WC	AWCA	CS (S)	Loch Rannoch
37685	a	**WC**	WC	AWCA	CS	Loch Arkaig

Class 37/7. Refurbished locomotives. Main generator replaced by alternator. Regeared (CP7) bogies. Ballast weights added. Details as Class 37/5 except:
Main Alternator: GEC G564AZ (37800) Brush BA1005A (others).
Maximum Tractive Effort: 276 kN (62000 lbf).
Weight: 120 t. **Route Availability**: 7.

37703		**DR**	DR	XHSS	BO	
37706		**WC**	WC	AWCA	CS	
37710		**LH**	WC	AWCX	CS (S)	
37712	a	**WC**	WC	AWCX	CS (S)	
37716		**DI**	DR	XHNC	KM	
37800	d	**EX**	EP	GROG	LR	Cassiopeia
37884	d	**EX**	EP	GROG	LR	Cerpheus

Class 37/9. Refurbished locomotives. New power unit. Main generator replaced by alternator. Ballast weights added. Details as Class 37/4 except:
Engine: * Mirrlees 6MB275T of 1340 kW (1800 hp) or † Ruston 6RK270T of 1340 kW (1800 hp) at 900 rpm.
Main Alternator: Brush BA15005A.
Maximum Tractive Effort: 279 kN (62680 lbf).
Weight: 120 t. **Route Availability**: 7.
Train Supply: Not equipped.

37901	*	**EX**	EP	EPUK	LR	Mirrlees Pioneer
37905	†	**G**	UR	UKRM	LR (S)	
37906	†	**FO**	UR	UKRM	BL (S)	

Class 97/3. Class 37s refurbished for use on the Cambrian Lines which are signalled by ERTMS. Details as Class 37/0.

97301	(37100)	e	**Y**	NR	QETS	ZA	
97302	(37170)	e	**Y**	NR	QETS	ZA	Ffestiniog & Welsh Highland Railways/Rheilffyrdd Ffestiniog ac Eryri
97303	(37178)	e	**Y**	NR	QETS	ZA	
97304	(37217)	e	**Y**	NR	QETS	ZA	John Tiley

CLASS 40 ENGLISH ELECTRIC 1Co-Co1

Built: 1961 by English Electric at Vulcan Foundry, Newton-le-Willows.
Engine: English Electric 16SVT Mk2 of 1492 kW (2000 hp) at 850 rpm.
Main Generator: English Electric 822/4C.
Traction Motors: English Electric 526/5D or EE526/7D.
Maximum Tractive Effort: 231 kN (52000 lbf).
Continuous Tractive Effort: 137 kN (30900 lbf) at 18.8 mph.
Power at Rail: 1160 kW (1550 hp).
Brake Force: 51 t.
Weight: 132 t.
Design Speed: 90 mph.
Fuel Capacity: 3250 litres.
Train Supply: Steam heating.
Train Brakes: Air & vacuum.
Dimensions: 21.18 x 2.78 m.
Wheel Diameter: 914/1143 mm.
Maximum Speed: 90 mph.
Route Availability: 6.
Total: 2.

40013 Carries original number D213
40145 Carries original number 345.

40013	**G**	ST	LSLO	CL	Andania
40145	**B**	40	CFSL	BQ	

CLASS 43 BREL/PAXMAN Bo-Bo

Built: 1975–82 by BREL at Crewe Works.
Engine: MTU 16V4000R41R of 1680kW (2250 hp) at 1500 rpm.
(* Paxman 12VP185 of 1680 kW (2250 hp) at 1500 rpm.)
Main Alternator: Brush BA1001B.
Traction Motors: Brush TMH68–46 or GEC G417AZ (43124–152); frame mounted.
Maximum Tractive Effort: 80 kN (17980 lbf).
Continuous Tractive Effort: 46 kN (10340 lbf) at 64.5 mph.
Power at Rail: 1320 kW (1770 hp).
Brake Force: 35 t.
Weight: 70.25–75.0 t.
Design Speed: 125 mph.
Fuel Capacity: 4500 litres.
Train Supply: Three-phase electric.
Train Brakes: Air.
Dimensions: 17.79 x 2.74 m.
Wheel Diameter: 1020 mm.
Maximum Speed: 125 mph.
Route Availability: 5.
Total: 193.

† Buffer fitted.
§ Modified Great Western Railway power cars that can operate with power door fitted short sets.

43013, 43014 & 43062 are fitted with measuring apparatus & front-end cameras.

Power cars 43013 and 43321 carry small commemorative plates to celebrate 40 years of the HST, reading "40 YEARS 1976–2016".

Non-standard liveries:

43206 and 43312 Original HST blue & yellow. Carry the numbers 43006 and 43112
43238 and 43274 Red
43172 We Shall Remember Them.

43003		**SI**	A	HAPC	HA	
43004	§	**GW**	A	EFPC	LA	Caerphilly Castle
43005	§	**GW**	A	EFPC	LA	
43009		**FB**	A	EFPC	LA (S)	
43010		**FB**	A	EFPC	LA (S)	
43012		**SI**	A	HAPC	HA	
43013	†	**Y**	P	QCAR	ZA	Mark Carne CBE
43014	†	**Y**	P	QCAR	ZA	The Railway Observer
43015		**SI**	A	HAPC	HA	
43016	§	**GW**	A	EFPC	LA	
43017		**FB**	A	SCEL	EP (S)	
43018		**FB**	A	SCEL	HA (S)	
43020		**FB**	A	EFPC	EP (S)	MTU Power. Passion. Partnership
43021		**SI**	A	HAPC	HA	
43022		**FB**	A	EFPC	LA (S)	The Duke of Edinburgh's Award Diamond Anniversary 1956–2016
43023		**FB**	A	EFPC	PM (S)	SQN LDR HAROLD STARR ONE OF THE FEW
43024		**FB**	A	SCEL	EP (S)	
43025		**FB**	A	SCEL	EP (S)	
43026		**SI**	A	HAPC	HA	
43027		**FB**	A	EFPC	PM (S)	
43028		**SI**	A	HAPC	HA	
43029		**FB**	A	EFPC	LA (S)	
43030		**SI**	A	HAPC	HA	
43031		**SI**	A	HAPC	HA	
43032		**SI**	A	HAPC	HA	
43033		**SI**	A	HAPC	HA	
43034		**SI**	A	HAPC	HA	
43035		**SI**	A	HAPC	HA	
43036		**SI**	A	HAPC	HA	
43037		**SI**	A	HAPC	HA	
43040	§	**GW**	A	EFPC	LA	
43041	§	**GW**	A	EFPC	LA	St Catherine's Castle
43042	§	**GW**	A	EFPC	LA	Tregenna Castle
43043	*	**ST**	P	EMPC	NL	
43044	*	**ST**	P	EMPC	NL	
43045	*	**ST**	P	EMPC	NL	
43046	*	**ST**	P	EMPC	NL	
43047	*	**ST**	P	EMPC	NL	
43048	*	**ST**	P	EMPC	NL	T.C.B. Miller MBE
43049	*	**ST**	P	EMPC	NL	Neville Hill
43050	*	**ST**	P	EMPC	NL	
43052	*	**ST**	P	EMPC	NL	
43053		**FB**	P	SBXL	LM (S)	
43054	*	**ST**	P	EMPC	NL	
43055	*	**ST**	P	EMPC	NL	The Sheffield Star 125 Years
43056		**FB**	P	SBXL	LM (S)	
43058	*	**ST**	P	EMPC	NL	
43059	*	**ST**	P	EMPC	NL	
43060	*	**ST**	P	EMPC	NL	

43061	*	**ST**	P	SBXL	TY (S)	
43062		**Y**	P	QCAR	ZA	John Armitt
43063		**FB**	P	SBXL	LA (S)	
43064	*	**ST**	P	EMPC	NL	
43066	*	**ST**	P	EMPC	NL	
43069		**FB**	P	SBXL	LM (S)	
43070		**FB**	P	SBXL	LM (S)	
43071		**FB**	P	SBXL	LA (S)	
43073	*	**ST**	P	EMPC	NL	
43075	*	**ST**	P	SBXL	TY (S)	
43076	*	**ST**	P	EMPC	NL	IN SUPPORT OF HELP for HEROES
43078		**FB**	P	SBXL	LM (S)	
43079		**FB**	P	SBXL	LM (S)	
43081	*	**ST**	P	EMPC	NL	
43082	*	**ST**	P	EMPC	NL	RAILWAY children – Fighting for street children
43083	*	**ST**	P	EMPC	NL	
43086		**FB**	P	SBXL	LA (S)	
43087		**FB**	P	SBXL	LM (S)	
43088		**FB**	FG	EFPC	LA (S)	
43089	*	**ST**	P	EMPC	NL	
43091		**FB**	P	SBXL	LM (S)	
43092	§	**GW**	FG	EFPC	LA	Cromwell's Castle
43093	§	**GW**	FG	EFPC	LA	Old Oak Common HST Depot 1976–2018
43094	§	**GW**	FG	EFPC	LA	
43097	§	**GW**	FG	EFPC	LA	Environment Agency
43098	§	**GW**	FG	EFPC	LA	
43122	§	**GW**	FG	EFPC	LA	
43124		**SI**	A	HAPC	HA	
43125		**SI**	A	HAPC	HA	
43126		**SI**	A	HAPC	HA	
43127		**SI**	A	HAPC	HA	
43128		**SI**	A	HAPC	HA	
43129		**SI**	A	HAPC	HA	
43130		**SI**	A	HAPC	HA	
43131		**SI**	A	HAPC	HA	
43132		**SI**	A	HAPC	HA	
43133		**SI**	A	HAPC	HA	
43134		**SI**	A	HAPC	HA	
43135		**SI**	A	HAPC	HA	
43136		**SI**	A	HAPC	HA	
43137		**SI**	A	HAPC	HA	
43138		**SI**	A	HAPC	HA	
43139		**SI**	A	HAPC	HA	
43140		**SI**	A	HAPC	HA	
43141		**SI**	A	HAPC	HA	
43142		**SI**	A	HAPC	HA	
43143		**SI**	A	HAPC	HA	
43144		**SI**	A	HAPC	HA	
43145		**SI**	A	HAPC	HA	

43146	**SI**	A	HAPC	HA	
43147	**SI**	A	HAPC	HA	
43148	**SI**	A	HAPC	HA	
43149	**SI**	A	HAPC	HA	
43150	**SI**	A	HAPC	HA	
43151	**SI**	A	HAPC	HA	
43152	**SI**	A	HAPC	HA	
43153 §	**GW**	FG	EFPC	LA	Chûn Castle
43154 §	**GW**	FG	EFPC	LA	Compton Castle
43155 §	**GW**	FG	EFPC	LA	
43156	**FB**	FG	EFPC	LA (S)	Dartington International Summer School
43158 §	**GW**	FG	EFPC	LA	
43159	**FB**	P	SBXL	LM (S)	
43160	**FB**	FG	EFPC	LA (S)	Sir Moir Lockhead OBE
43161	**FB**	P	SBXL	LA (S)	
43162	**FB**	FG	EFPC	LA (S)	Exeter Panel Signalbox 21st Anniversary 2009
43163	**SI**	A	HAPC	HA	
43164	**SI**	A	HAPC	HA	
43165	**FB**	A	SCEL	EP (S)	
43168	**SI**	A	HAPC	HA	
43169	**SI**	A	HAPC	HA	
43170 §	**GW**	A	EFPC	LA	Chepstow Castle
43171	**FB**	A	EFPC	LA (S)	
43172	**AL**	A	EFPC	LA (S)	Harry Patch The last survivor of the trenches
43174	**FB**	A	SCEL	EP (S)	
43175	**SI**	A	HAPC	HA	
43176	**SI**	A	HAPC	HA	
43177	**SI**	A	HAPC	HA	
43179	**SI**	A	HAPC	HA	
43180	**FB**	P	SBXL	LA (S)	
43181	**SI**	A	HAPC	HA	
43182	**SI**	A	HAPC	HA	
43183	**SI**	A	HAPC	HA	
43185	**IC**	A	SCEL	EP (S)	
43186 §	**GW**	A	EFPC	LA	Taunton Castle
43187 §	**GW**	A	EFPC	LA	
43188 §	**GW**	A	EFPC	LA	
43189 §	**GW**	A	EFPC	LA	Launceston Castle
43190	**FB**	A	SCEL	EP (S)	
43191	**FB**	A	EFPC	EP (S)	
43192 §	**GW**	A	EFPC	LA	
43193	**FB**	P	SBXL	LM (S)	
43194 §	**GW**	FG	EFPC	LA	Okehampton Castle
43195	**FB**	FG	EFPC	LA (S)	
43196	**FB**	P	EFPC	LA (S)	
43197	**FB**	P	SBXL	LM (S)	
43198 §	**GW**	FG	EFPC	LA	Driver Stan Martin 25 June 1950 – 6 November 2004/Driver Brian Cooper 15 June 1947 – 5 October 1999

Class 43/2. Rebuilt LNER, CrossCountry and East Midlands Railway (former Grand Central) power cars. Power cars have been renumbered by adding 200 to their original number or 400 to their original number (EMR), except 43123 which became 43423.

43206 (43006)	**0**	A	IECP	EP (S)	
43207 (43007)	**XC**	A	EHPC	LA	
43208 (43008)	**VE**	A	IECP	EH (S)	
43238 (43038)	**0**	A	IECP	NL (S)	
43239 (43039)	**VE**	A	IECP	EH (S)	
43251 (43051)	**VE**	P	EMPC	GA (S)	
43257 (43057)	**VE**	P	EMPC	NL (S)	
43272 (43072)	**VE**	P	EMPC	GA (S)	
43274 (43074)	**0**	P	EMPC	GA (S)	
43277 (43077)	**VE**	P	EMPC	GA (S)	
43285 (43085)	**XC**	P	EHPC	LA	
43290 (43090)	**VE**	P	EMPC	GA (S)	
43295 (43095)	**VE**	A	IECP	GA (S)	
43296 (43096)	**VE**	A	IECP	GA (S)	
43299 (43099)	**VE**	P	EMPC	GA (S)	
43300 (43100)	**VE**	P	IECP	NL (S)	
43301 (43101)	**XC**	P	EHPC	LA	
43302 (43102)	**VE**	P	EMPC	GA (S)	
43303 (43103)	**XC**	P	EHPC	LA	
43304 (43104)	**XC**	A	EHPC	LA	
43305 (43105)	**VE**	A	IECP	GA (S)	
43306 (43106)	**VE**	A	IECP	GA (S)	
43307 (43107)	**VE**	A	IECP	GA (S)	
43308 (43108)	**VE**	A	IECP	GA (S)	
43309 (43109)	**VE**	A	IECP	NL (S)	
43310 (43110)	**VE**	A	IECP	GA (S)	
43311 (43111)	**VE**	A	IECP	EP (S)	
43312 (43112)	**0**	A	IECP	EP (S)	
43313 (43113)	**VE**	A	IECP	BN (S)	
43314 (43114)	**VE**	A	IECP	GA (S)	
43315 (43115)	**VE**	A	IECP	EP (S)	
43316 (43116)	**VE**	A	IECP	NL (S)	
43317 (43117)	**VE**	A	IECP	GA (S)	
43318 (43118)	**VE**	A	IECP	NL (S)	
43319 (43119)	**VE**	A	IECP	GA (S)	
43320 (43120)	**VE**	A	IECP	EP (S)	
43321 (43121)	**XC**	P	EHPC	LA	
43357 (43157)	**XC**	P	EHPC	LA	
43366 (43166)	**XC**	A	EHPC	LA	
43367 (43167)	**VE**	A	IECP	EP (S)	
43378 (43178)	**XC**	A	EHPC	LA	
43384 (43184)	**XC**	A	EHPC	LA	
43423 (43123) †	**EA**	A	EMPC	DY	'VALENTA' 1972–2010
43465 (43065) †	**EA**	A	EMPC	DY	

43467 (43067) †	**EA**	A	EMPC	DY	Nottinghamshire Fire and Rescue Service/ British Transport Police Nottingham
43468 (43068) †	**EA**	A	EMPC	DY	
43480 (43080) †	**EA**	A	EMPC	DY	West Hampstead PSB
43484 (43084) †	**EA**	A	EMPC	DY	

CLASS 47 BR/BRUSH/SULZER Co-Co

Built: 1963–67 by Brush Traction, at Loughborough or by BR at Crewe Works.
Engine: Sulzer 12LDA28C of 1920 kW (2580 hp) at 750 rpm.
Main Generator: Brush TG160-60 Mk4 or TM172-50 Mk1.
Traction Motors: Brush TM64-68 Mk1 or Mk1A.
Maximum Tractive Effort: 267 kN (60000 lbf).
Continuous Tractive Effort: 133 kN (30000 lbf) at 26 mph.
Power at Rail: 1550 kW (2080 hp).
Train Brakes: Air.
Brake Force: 61 t.
Dimensions: 19.38 x 2.79 m.
Weight: 111.5–120.6 t.
Wheel Diameter: 1143 mm.
Design Speed: 95 mph.
Maximum Speed: 95 mph.
Fuel Capacity: 3273 (+ 5887).
Route Availability: 6 or 7.
Train Supply: Not equipped.
Total: 48.

Class 47s exported for use abroad are listed in section 1.6 of this book.

Non-standard liveries/numbering:

47270 Also carries original number 1971.
47501 Carries original number D1944.
47614 Carries original number 1733.
47739 GBRf dark blue.
47773 Also carries original number D1755.
47798 Royal Train claret with Rail Express Systems markings.
47805 Carries original number D1935.
47810 Carries original number D1924.
47830 Also carries original number D1645.

Recent renumbering:

47593 was renumbered from 47790 in 2019.
47614 was renumbered from 47853 in 2019.

Class 47/0. Standard Design. Built with train air and vacuum brakes.

47194 +	**F**	WC	AWCX	CS (S)	
47237 x+	**WC**	WC	AWCA	CS	
47245 x+	**WC**	WC	AWCA	CS	
47270 +	**B**	WC	AWCA	CS	SWIFT

Class 47/3. Built with train air and vacuum brakes. Details as Class 47/0 except: **Weight:** 113.7 t.

47355 a+	**K**	WC	AWCX	CS (S)
47368	**F**	WC	AWCX	CS (S)

Class 47/4. Electric Train Supply equipment.
Details as Class 47/0 except:

Weight: 120.4–125.1 t. **Fuel Capacity**: 3273 (+ 5537) litres.
Train Supply: Electric, index 66. **Route Availability**: 7.

47492 x	**RX**	WC	AWCX	CS (S)	
47501 x+	**GG**	LD	LSLO	CL	CRAFTSMAN
47526 x	**BL**	WC	AWCX	CS (S)	
47580 x	**BL**	47	MBDL	TM	County of Essex
47593	**BL**	LD	LSLO	CL	Galloway Princess
47614 +	**B**	LD	LSLO	CL	

Class 47/7. Previously fitted with an older form of TDM.
Details as Class 47/4 except:

Weight: 118.7 t. **Fuel Capacity**: 5887 litres.
Maximum Speed: 100 mph.

47703	**FR**	HN	HNRL	ZB
47714	**AR**	HN	HNRL	Old Dalby
47715	**N**	HN	HNRL	WS

Class 47/7. Former Railnet dedicated locomotives.
Details as Class 47/0 except:

Fuel Capacity: 5887 litres.

47727	**CA**	GB	GBDF	LR	Edinburgh Castle/ Caisteal Dhùn Èideann
47739	**0**	GB	GBDF	LR	
47746 x	**WC**	WC	AWCA	CS	Chris Fudge 29.7.70 – 22.6.10
47749 d	**B**	GB	GBDF	LR	CITY OF TRURO
47760 x	**WC**	WC	AWCA	CS	
47768	**RX**	WC	AWCX	CS (S)	
47769	**V**	HN	HNRS	BH (S)	Resolve
47772 x	**WC**	WC	AWCA	CS	Carnforth TMD
47773 x	**GG**	70	MBDL	TM	
47776 x	**RX**	WC	AWCX	CS (S)	
47786	**WC**	WC	AWCA	CS	Roy Castle OBE
47787	**WC**	WC	AWCX	CS (S)	

Class 47/4 continued. Route Availability: 6.

47798 x	**0**	NM	MBDL	YK	Prince William
47802 +	**WC**	WC	AWCA	CS	
47804	**WC**	WC	AWCA	CS	
47805 +	**GG**	LD	LSLO	CL	Roger Hosking MA 1925–2013
47810 +	**GG**	LD	LSLO	CL	Crewe Diesel Depot
47811 +	**GL**	LD	DHLT	CL (S)	
47812 +	**RB**	RO	GROG	LR	
47813 +	**RO**	RO	GROG	LR	Jack Frost
47815 +	**RO**	RO	GROG	LR	Lost Boys 68–88
47816 +	**GL**	LD	DHLT	CL (S)	
47818 +	**DS**	AF	MBDL	ZG (S)	
47826 +	**WC**	WC	AWCA	CS	

47828 +	**IC**	D0	AWCA	CS	
47830 +	**GG**	FL	DFLH	CB	BEECHING'S LEGACY
47832 +	**WC**	WC	AWCA	CS	
47841 +	**IC**	LD	LSLS	Margate (S)	The Institution of Mechanical Engineers
47843 +	**RB**	RO	SROG	LR (S)	
47847 +	**BL**	RO	SROG	LR (S)	
47848 +	**RB**	RO	GROG	LR	
47851 +	**WC**	WC	AWCA	CS	
47854 +	**WC**	WC	AWCA	CS	Diamond Jubilee

CLASS 50 ENGLISH ELECTRIC Co-Co

Built: 1967–68 by English Electric at Vulcan Foundry, Newton-le-Willows.
Engine: English Electric 16CVST of 2010 kW (2700 hp) at 850 rpm.
Main Generator: English Electric 840/4B.
Traction Motors: English Electric 538/5A.
Maximum Tractive Effort: 216 kN (48500 lbf).
Continuous Tractive Effort: 147 kN (33000 lbf) at 23.5 mph.
Power at Rail: 1540 kW (2070 hp).
Brake Force: 59 t.
Weight: 116.9 t.
Design Speed: 105 mph.
Fuel Capacity: 4796 litres.
Train Supply: Electric, index 61.
Train Brakes: Air & vacuum.
Dimensions: 20.88 x 2.78 m.
Wheel Diameter: 1092 mm.
Maximum Speed: 90 mph.
Route Availability: 6.
Total: 5.

Non-standard numbering:

50007 Running with the number 50014 on one side.
50050 Also carries original number D400.

50007	**GB**	50	CFOL	KR	Hercules
50008	**B**	HT	HTLX	LR	Thunderer
50044	**B**	50	CFOL	KR	Exeter
50049	**GB**	50	CFOL	KR	Defiance
50050	**B**	NB	MBDL	NM	Fearless

CLASS 52 BR/MAYBACH C-C

Built: 1961–64 by BR at Swindon Works.
Engine: Two Maybach MD655 of 1007 kW (1350 hp) each at 1500 rpm.
Transmission: Hydraulic. Voith L630rV.
Maximum Tractive Effort: 297 kN (66700 lbf).
Continuous Tractive Effort: 201 kN (45200 lbf) at 14.5 mph.
Power at Rail: 1490 kW (2000 hp). **Train Brakes:** Air & vacuum.
Brake Force: 83 t. **Dimensions:** 20.70 m x 2.78 m.
Weight: 110 t. **Wheel Diameter:** 1092 mm.
Design Speed: 90 mph. **Maximum Speed:** 90 mph.
Fuel Capacity: 3900 litres. **Route Availability:** 6.
Train Supply: Steam heating. **Total:** 1.

Never allocated a number in the 1972 number series.

D1015	**B**	DT	MBDL	KR	WESTERN CHAMPION

CLASS 55 ENGLISH ELECTRIC Co-Co

Built: 1961 by English Electric at Vulcan Foundry, Newton-le-Willows.
Engine: Two Napier-Deltic D18-25 of 1230 kW (1650 hp) each at 1500 rpm.
Main Generators: Two English Electric 829/1A.
Traction Motors: English Electric 538/A.
Maximum Tractive Effort: 222 kN (50000 lbf).
Continuous Tractive Effort: 136 kN (30500 lbf) at 32.5 mph.
Power at Rail: 1969 kW (2640 hp). **Train Brakes:** Air & vacuum.
Brake Force: 51 t. **Dimensions:** 21.18 x 2.68 m.
Weight: 100 t. **Wheel Diameter:** 1092 mm.
Design Speed: 105 mph. **Maximum Speed:** 100 mph.
Fuel Capacity: 3755 litres. **Route Availability:** 5.
Train Supply: Electric, index 66. **Total:** 4.

Non-standard numbering:

55002 Carries original number D9002.
55009 Carries original number D9009.
55016 Carries original number D9016.

55002	**GG**	NM	MBDL	YK	THE KING'S OWN YORKSHIRE LIGHT INFANTRY
55009	**B**	DP	MBDL	BH	ALYCIDON
55016	**GG**	LD	MBDL	CL (S)	GORDON HIGHLANDER
55022	**B**	LD	MBDL	CL	ROYAL SCOTS GREY

CLASS 56 BRUSH/BR/RUSTON Co-Co

Built: 1976–84 by Electroputere at Craiova, Romania (as sub-contractors for Brush) or BREL at Doncaster or Crewe Works.
Engine: Ruston Paxman 16RK3CT of 2460 kW (3250 hp) at 900 rpm.
Main Alternator: Brush BA1101A.
Traction Motors: Brush TM73-62.
Maximum Tractive Effort: 275 kN (61800 lbf).
Continuous Tractive Effort: 240 kN (53950 lbf) at 16.8 mph.
Power at Rail: 1790 kW (2400 hp).
Brake Force: 60 t.
Weight: 126 t.
Design Speed: 80 mph.
Fuel Capacity: 5228 litres.
Train Supply: Not equipped.
Train Brakes: Air.
Dimensions: 19.36 x 2.79 m.
Wheel Diameter: 1143 mm.
Maximum Speed: 80 mph.
Route Availability: 7.
Total: 32.

All equipped with Slow Speed Control.

Class 56s exported for use abroad are listed in section 1.6 of this book.

Non-standard liveries:

56009 All over blue.
56303 All over dark green.

56007	**B**	GB	UKRS	LT (S)	
56009	**0**	EO	UKRS	LT (S)	
56018	**FER**	GB	UKRS	LT (S)	
56031	**FER**	GB	GBGS	LT (S)	
56032	**FER**	GB	GBGS	LT (S)	
56037	**E**	GB	GBGS	LT (S)	
56038	**FER**	GB	UKRS	LT (S)	
56049	**CS**	CS	COFS	NM	Robin of Templecombe 1938–2013
56051	**CS**	CS	COFS	NM	Survival
56060	**FER**	GB	UKRS	LT (S)	
56065	**FER**	GB	UKRS	LT (S)	
56069	**FER**	GB	GBGS	LT (S)	
56077	**LH**	GB	UKRS	LT (S)	
56078	**CS**	CS	COFS	NM	
56081	**FO**	GB	GBGD	LR	
56087	**CS**	BN	COFS	NM	
56090	**CS**	BN	COFS	NM	
56091	**DC**	DC	HTLX	LR	Driver Wayne Gaskell The Godfather
56094	**CS**	CS	COFS	NM	
56096	**CS**	BN	COFS	NM	
56098	**FO**	GB	GBGD	LR	
56103	**DC**	DC	HTLX	LR	
56104	**FO**	GB	UKRL	LR (S)	
56105	**CS**	BN	COFS	NM	
56106	**FER**	GB	UKRS	LR (S)	
56113	**CS**	BN	COFS	NM	
56128	**F**	GB		LT (S)	

56301 (56045)	**FA**	56	UKRL	LR	
56302 (56124)	**CS**	CS	COFS	NM	PECO The Railway Modeller 2016 70 Years
56303 (56125)	**0**	GB	HTLX	LR	
56311 (56057)	**DC**	GB	GBGS	LT (S)	
56312 (56003)	**DC**	GB	GBGD	LR	

CLASS 57 BRUSH/GM Co-Co

Built: 1964–65 by Brush Traction at Loughborough or BR at Crewe Works as Class 47. Rebuilt 1997–2004 by Brush Traction at Loughborough.
Engine: General Motors 12 645 E3 of 1860 kW (2500 hp) at 904 rpm.
Main Alternator: Brush BA1101D (recovered from Class 56).
Traction Motors: Brush TM64-68 Mark 1 or Mark 1A.
Maximum Tractive Effort: 244.5 kN (55000 lbf).
Continuous Tractive Effort: 140 kN (31500 lbf) at ?? mph.
Power at Rail: 1507 kW (2025 hp).
Train Brakes: Air.
Brake Force: 80 t.
Dimensions: 19.38 x 2.79 m.
Weight: 120.6 t.
Wheel Diameter: 1143 mm.
Design Speed: 75 mph.
Maximum Speed: 75 mph.
Fuel Capacity: 5550 litres.
Route Availability: 6
Train Supply: Not equipped.
Total: 33.

Non-standard livery: 57604 Original Great Western Railway green.

Class 57/0. No Train Supply Equipment. Rebuilt 1997–2000.

57001 (47356)	**WC**	WC	AWCA	CS (S)	
57002 (47322)	**DI**	DR	XHCK	KM	RAIL EXPRESS
57003 (47317)	**DI**	DR	XHCK	KM	
57004 (47347)	**DS**	DR	XHSS	LW (S)	
57005 (47350)	**AZ**	WC	AWCX	CS (S)	
57006 (47187)	**WC**	WC	AWCX	CS (S)	
57007 (47332)	**DI**	DR	XHSS	KM (S)	John Scott 12.5.45–22.5.12
57008 (47060)	**DS**	DR	XHSS	LW (S)	
57009 (47079)	**DS**	DR	XHSS	LW (S)	
57010 (47231)	**DI**	DR	XHSS	LW (S)	
57011 (47329)	**DS**	DR	XHSS	LW (S)	
57012 (47204)	**DS**	DR	XHSS	LW (S)	

Class 57/3. Electric Train Supply Equipment. Former Virgin Trains locomotives fitted with retractable Dellner couplers. Rebuilt 2002–04. Details as Class 57/0 except:

Engine: General Motors 12645F3B of 2050 kW (2750 hp) at 954 rpm.
Main Alternator: Brush BA1101F (recovered from Class 56) or Brush BA1101G.
Fuel Capacity: 5887 litres.
Train Supply: Electric, index 100.
Design Speed: 95 mph.
Maximum Speed: 95 mph.
Brake Force: 60 t.
Weight: 117 t.

57301 (47845) d	**DI**	P	GROG	LR	Goliath
57302 (47827) d	**DS**	DR	XHSS	ZG (S)	Chad Varah
57303 (47705) d	**DI**	P	XHAC	KM	Pride of Carlisle

57304	(47807) d	**DI**	DR	XHVT	KM	Pride of Cheshire
57305	(47822) d	**VN**	P	GROG	LR	Northern Princess
57306	(47814) d	**DI**	P	XHAC	KM	Her Majesty's Railway Inspectorate 175
57307	(47225) d	**DI**	DR	XHVT	KM	LADY PENELOPE
57308	(47846) d	**DI**	DR	XHVT	KM	Jamie Ferguson
57309	(47806) d	**DI**	DR	XHVT	KM	Pride of Crewe
57310	(47831) d	**DI**	P	XHAC	KM	Pride of Cumbria
57311	(47817) d	**DS**	DR	XHSS	LW (S)	Thunderbird
57312	(47330) d	**RO**	P	GROG	LR	
57313	(47371)	**PC**	WC	AWCA	CS	
57314	(47372)	**WC**	WC	AWCA	CS	
57315	(47234)	**WC**	WC	AWCA	CS	
57316	(47290)	**WC**	WC	AWCA	CS	

Class 57/6. Electric Train Supply Equipment. Prototype ETS loco. Rebuilt 2001. Details as Class 57/0 except:

Main Alternator: Brush BA1101E.
Train Supply: Electric, index 95.
Design Speed: 95 mph.
Brake Force: 60 t.
Fuel Capacity: 3273 litres.
Weight: 113t.
Maximum Speed: 95 mph.

57601	(47825)	**PC**	WC	AWCA	CS	Windsor Castle

Class 57/6. Electric Train Supply Equipment. Great Western Railway locomotives. Rebuilt 2004. Details as Class 57/3.

57602	(47337)	**GW**	P	EFOO	PZ	Restormel Castle
57603	(47349)	**GW**	P	EFOO	PZ	Tintagel Castle
57604	(47209)	**0**	P	EFOO	PZ	PENDENNIS CASTLE
57605	(47206)	**GW**	P	EFOO	PZ	Totnes Castle

CLASS 58 BREL/RUSTON Co-Co

Built: 1983–87 by BREL at Doncaster Works.
Engine: Ruston Paxman 16RK3CT of 2460 kW (3250 hp) at 1000 rpm.
Main Alternator: Brush BA1101B.
Traction Motors: Brush TM73-62.
Maximum Tractive Effort: 275 kN (61800 lbf).
Continuous Tractive Effort: 240 kN (53950 lbf) at 17.4 mph.
Power at Rail: 1780 kW (2387 hp).
Brake Force: 60 t.
Weight: 130 t.
Design Speed: 80 mph.
Fuel Capacity: 4214 litres.
Train Supply: Not equipped.
Train Brakes: Air.
Dimensions: 19.13 x 2.72 m.
Wheel Diameter: 1120 mm.
Maximum Speed: 80 mph.
Route Availability: 7.
Total: 2.

All equipped with Slow Speed Control.

Class 58s exported for use abroad are listed in section 1.6 of this book.

58012	**F**	PO	BL (S)
58023	**ML**	PO	LR (S)

CLASS 59 GENERAL MOTORS Co-Co

Built: 1985 (59001–004) or 1989 (59005) by General Motors, La Grange, Illinois, USA or 1990 (59101–104), 1994 (59201) and 1995 (59202–206) by General Motors, London, Ontario, Canada.
Engine: General Motors 16-645E3C two stroke of 2460 kW (3300 hp) at 904 rpm.
Main Alternator: General Motors AR11 MLD-D14A.
Traction Motors: General Motors D77B.
Maximum Tractive Effort: 506 kN (113550 lbf).
Continuous Tractive Effort: 291 kN (65300 lbf) at 14.3 mph.
Power at Rail: 1889 kW (2533 hp).
Train Brakes: Air.
Brake Force: 69 t.
Dimensions: 21.35 x 2.65 m.
Weight: 121 t.
Wheel Diameter: 1067 mm.
Design Speed: 60 (* 75) mph.
Maximum Speed: 60 (* 75) mph.
Fuel Capacity: 4546 litres.
Route Availability: 7.
Train Supply: Not equipped.
Total: 15.

Class 59/0. Owned by Freightliner and GB Railfreight.

59001		**AI**	FL	DFHG	MD	YEOMAN ENDEAVOUR
59002		**AI**	FL	DFHG	MD	ALAN J DAY
59003		**GB**	GB	GBYH	RR	YEOMAN HIGHLANDER
59004		**AI**	FL	DFHG	MD	PAUL A HAMMOND
59005		**AI**	FL	DFHG	MD	KENNETH J PAINTER

Class 59/1. Owned by Freightliner,

59101		**HA**	FL	DFHG	MD	Village of Whatley
59102		**HA**	FL	DFHG	MD	Village of Chantry
59103		**HA**	FL	DFHG	MD	Village of Mells
59104		**HA**	FL	DFHG	MD	Village of Great Elm

Class 59/2. Owned by DB Cargo.

59201	*	**DB**	FL	DFHG	MD	
59202	*	**DB**	FL	DFHG	MD	Alan Meddows Taylor MD Mendip Rail Limited
59203	*	**DB**	FL	DFHG	MD	
59204	*	**DB**	FL	DFHG	MD	
59205	*b	**DB**	FL	DFHG	MD	
59206	*b	**DB**	FL	DFHG	MD	John F. Yeoman Rail Pioneer

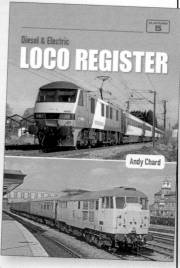

CLASS 60 BRUSH/MIRRLEES Co-Co

Built: 1989–93 by Brush Traction at Loughborough.
Engine: Mirrlees 8MB275T of 2310 kW (3100 hp) at 1000 rpm.
Main Alternator: Brush BA1006A.
Traction Motors: Brush TM2161A.
Maximum Tractive Effort: 500 kN (106500 lbf).
Continuous Tractive Effort: 336 kN (71570 lbf) at 17.4 mph.
Power at Rail: 1800 kW (2415 hp).
Brake Force: 74 t (+ 62 t).
Weight: 129 t (+ 131 t).
Design Speed: 62 mph.
Fuel Capacity: 4546 (+ 5225) litres.
Train Supply: Not equipped.
Train Brakes: Air.
Dimensions: 21.34 x 2.64 m.
Wheel Diameter: 1118 mm.
Maximum Speed: 60 mph.
Route Availability: 8.
Total: 100.

All equipped with Slow Speed Control.

* Refurbished locomotives.

60034, 60064, 60070, 60072, 60073, 60077, 60084 and 60090 carry their names on one side only.

60500 originally carried the number 60016.

Non-standard and Advertising liveries:

60026 Beacon Rail (blue).
60028 Cappagh (blue).
60066 Powering Drax (silver).
60081 Original Great Western Railway green.
60099 Tata Steel (silver).

60001	*	**DB**	DB	WCAT	TO	
60002	+*	**CS**	BN	GBTG	RR	
60003	+	**E**	DB	WQCA	TO (S)	FREIGHT TRANSPORT ASSOCIATION
60004	+	**E**	GB	WQCA	TO (S)	
60005	+	**E**	DB	WQDA	TO (S)	
60006		**CU**	X	WQCA	TO (S)	
60007	+*	**DB**	DB	WCBT	TO	The Spirit of Tom Kendell
60008		**E**	GB	WQCA	TO (S)	Sir William McAlpine
60009	+	**E**	DB	WQCA	TO (S)	
60010	+*	**DB**	DB	WQAA	TO (S)	
60011		**DB**	DB	WCAT	TO	
60012	+	**E**	DB	WQCA	TO (S)	
60013		**EG**	DB	WQCA	TO (S)	Robert Boyle
60014		**EG**	GB	WQCA	TO (S)	
60015	+*	**DB**	DB	WCBT	TO	
60017	+*	**DB**	DB	WCBT	TO	
60018		**E**	GB	WQCA	TO (S)	
60019	*	**DB**	DB	WCAT	TO	Port of Grimsby & Immingham
60020	+*	**DB**	DB	WCBT	TO	The Willows
60021	+*	**GB**	BN	GBTG	RR	PENYGHENT
60022	+	**E**	DB	WQCA	TO (S)	
60023	+	**E**	DB	WQCA	TO (S)	

60024	*	**DB**	DB	WCAT	TO	Clitheroe Castle
60025	+	**E**	DB	WQCA	TO (S)	
60026	+*	**0**	BN	GBTG	RR	HELVELLYN
60027	+	**E**	DB	WQCA	TO (S)	
60028	+	**0**	DC	HTLX	TO	
60029		**E**	DC	HTLX	TO	
60030	+	**E**	DB	WQCA	TO (S)	
60031		**E**	DB	WQCA	TO (S)	
60032		**F**	DB	WQCA	TO (S)	
60033	+	**CU**	DB	WQCA	TO (S)	Tees Steel Express
60034		**EG**	DB	WQCA	TO (S)	Carnedd Llewelyn
60035		**E**	DB	WQBA	TO (S)	
60036		**E**	DB	WQCA	TO (S)	GEFCO
60037	+	**E**	DB	WQCA	TO (S)	
60038	+	**E**	DB	WQCA	TO (S)	
60039	*	**DB**	DB	WCAT	TO	Dove Holes
60040	*	**DB**	DB	WCAT	TO	The Territorial Army Centenary
60041	+	**E**	DB	WQCA	TO (S)	
60042		**E**	DB	WQCA	TO (S)	
60043		**E**	DB	WQCA	TO (S)	
60044	*	**DB**	DB	WCAT	TO	Dowlow
60045		**E**	DB	WQBA	TO (S)	The Permanent Way Institution
60046	+	**DC**	DC	HTLX	TO	William Wilberforce
60047	*	**CS**	BN	GBTG	RR	
60048		**E**	DB	WQCA	TO (S)	
60049		**E**	DB	WQBA	TO (S)	
60050		**E**	X	WQDA	TO (S)	
60051	+	**E**	DB	WQCA	TO (S)	
60052	+	**E**	DB	WQCA	TO (S)	Glofa Twr – The last deep mine in Wales – Tower Colliery
60053		**E**	DB	WQCA	TO (S)	
60054	+*	**DB**	DB	WCBT	TO	
60055	+	**DC**	DC	HTLX	TO	Thomas Barnardo
60056	+*	**CS**	BN	GBTG	RR	
60057		**EG**	DB	WQCA	TO (S)	Adam Smith
60058	+	**E**	DB	WQCA	TO (S)	
60059	+*	**DB**	DB	WCBT	TO	Swinden Dalesman
60060		**EG**	PO	WQDA	TO (S)	
60061		**F**	DB	WQCA	TO (S)	
60062	*	**DB**	DB	WCAT	TO	Stainless Pioneer
60063	*	**DB**	DB	WCAT	TO	
60064	+	**EG**	DB	WQCA	TO (S)	Back Tor
60065		**E**	DB	WCAT	TO	Spirit of JAGUAR
60066	*	**AL**	DB	WCAT	TO	
60067		**EG**	DB	WQCA	TO (S)	
60068		**EG**	DB	WQCA	TO (S)	
60069		**E**	DB	WQCA	TO (S)	Slioch
60070	+	**F**	DB	WQCA	TO (S)	John Loudon McAdam
60071	+	**E**	DB	WQBA	TO (S)	Ribblehead Viaduct
60072		**EG**	DB	WQCA	TO (S)	Cairn Toul
60073		**EG**	DB	WQCA	TO (S)	Cairn Gorm

60074	*	**DB**	DB	WCAT	TO	
60075		**E**	DB	WQCA	TO (S)	
60076	*	**CS**	BN	GBTG	RR	Dunbar
60077	+	**EG**	DB	WQCA	TO (S)	Canisp
60078		**ML**	DB	WQCA	TO (S)	
60079	*	**DB**	DB	WQAB	TO (S)	
60080	+	**E**	DB	WQCA	TO (S)	
60081	+	**O**	LD	WQDA	TO (S)	
60082		**EG**	DB	WQCA	CE (S)	
60083		**E**	DB	WQCA	TO (S)	
60084		**EG**	DB	WQCA	TO (S)	Cross Fell
60085	*	**CS**	BN	GBTG	RR	
60086		**EG**	X	WQCA	TO (S)	
60087	*	**CS**	BN	GBTG	RR	
60088		**F**	DB	WQCA	TO (S)	
60089	+	**E**	DB	WQCA	TO (S)	
60090	+	**EG**	DB	WQCA	TO (S)	Quinag
60091	+*	**DB**	DB	WCBT	TO	Barry Needham
60092	+*	**DB**	DB	WCBT	TO	
60093		**E**	DB	WQCA	TO (S)	
60094		**E**	DB	WQBA	TO (S)	Rugby Flyer
60095	*	**GB**	BN	GBTG	RR	
60096	+*	**CS**	BN	GBTG	RR	
60097	+	**E**	DB	WQCA	TO (S)	
60098	+	**E**	DB	WQCA	TO (S)	
60099		**AL**	DB	WQCA	TO (S)	
60100	*	**DB**	DB	WCAT	TO	Midland Railway - Butterley
60500		**E**	DB	WQCA	TO (S)	

CLASS 66 GENERAL MOTORS/EMD Co-Co

Built: 1998–2008 by General Motors/EMD, London, Ontario, Canada (Model JT42CWR (low emission locomotives Model JT42CWRM)) or 2013–16 by EMD/Progress Rail, Muncie, Indiana (66752–779).
Engine: General Motors 12N-710G3B-EC two stroke of 2385 kW (3200 hp) at 904 rpm. 66752–779 GM 12N-710G3B-T2.
Main Alternator: General Motors AR8/CA6.
Traction Motors: General Motors D43TR.
Maximum Tractive Effort: 409 kN (92000 lbf).
Continuous Tractive Effort: 260 kN (58390 lbf) at 15.9 mph.
Power at Rail: 1850 kW (2480 hp).
Brake Force: 68 t.
Weight: 127 t.
Design Speed: 87.5 mph.
Fuel Capacity: 6550 litres.
Train Supply: Not equipped.
Train Brakes: Air.
Dimensions: 21.35 x 2.64 m.
Wheel Diameter: 1120 mm.
Maximum Speed: 75 mph.
Route Availability: 7.
Total: 388.

All equipped with Slow Speed Control.

Class 66s previously used in the UK but now in use abroad are listed in section 1.6 of this book. Some of the DBC 66s moved to France return to Great Britain from time to time for maintenance or operational requirements.

Class 66 delivery dates. The Class 66 design and delivery evolved over an 18-year period, with more than 400 locomotives delivered. For clarity the delivery dates (by year) for each batch of locomotives is as follows:

66001–250	EWS (now DB Cargo). 1998–2000 (some now in use in France or Poland, ten sold to GB Railfreight and five on long-term hire to DRS).
66301–305	Fastline. 2008. Now used by DRS.
66401–410	DRS. 2003. Now in use with GB Railfreight or Colas Rail and renumbered 66733–737 and 66742–746 (66734 since scrapped).
66411–420	DRS. 2006. Now leased by Freightliner (66411/412/417 exported to Poland).
66421–430	DRS. 2007
66431–434	DRS. 2008
66501–505	Freightliner. 1999
66506–520	Freightliner. 2000
66521–525	Freightliner. 2000 (66521 since scrapped).
66526–531	Freightliner. 2001
66532–537	Freightliner. 2001
66538–543	Freightliner. 2001
66544–553	Freightliner. 2001
66554	Freightliner. 2002†
66555–566	Freightliner. 2002
66567–574	Freightliner. 2003. 66573–574 now used by Colas Rail and renumbered 66846–847.
66575–577	Freightliner. 2004. Now used by Colas Rail and renumbered 66848–850.
66578–581	Freightliner. 2005. Now used by GBRf and renumbered 66738–741.
66582–594	Freightliner. 2007 (66582/583/584/586 exported to Poland).
66595–599	Freightliner. 2008 (66595 exported to Poland).
66601–606	Freightliner. 2000
66607–612	Freightliner. 2002 (66607/609/611/612 exported to Poland)
66613–618	Freightliner. 2003
66619–622	Freightliner. 2005
66623–625	Freightliner. 2007 (66624/625 exported to Poland).
66701–707	GB Railfreight. 2001
66708–712	GB Railfreight. 2002
66713–717	GB Railfreight. 2003
66718–722	GB Railfreight. 2006
66723–727	GB Railfreight. 2006
66728–732	GB Railfreight. 2008
66747–749	Built in 2008 as 20078968-004/006/007 (DE 6313/15/16) for Crossrail AG in the Netherlands but never used. Sold to GB Railfreight in 2012.
66750–751	Built in 2003 as 20038513-01/04 and have worked in the Netherlands, Germany and Poland. GBRf secured these two locomotives on lease in 2013.
66752–772	GB Railfreight. 2014
66773–779	GB Railfreight. 2016
66780–789	GB Railfreight. 1998–2000. Former DBC locomotives acquired in 2017 that have been renumbered in the GBRf number series.

66790–792 Built in 2002 as 20018352-3/4/5 (T66403–405) for CargoNet, Norway. Sold to Beacon Rail and leased to GBRf from 2019 (due to come into service from spring 2020).
66951–952 Freightliner. 2004
66953–957 Freightliner. 2008 (66954 exported to Poland).

Advertising and non-standard liveries:

66109 PD Ports (dark blue).
66587 Ocean Network Express (pink with white stripes).
66709 MSC – blue with images of a container ship.
66718 London Underground 150, (black).
66720 Day and night (various colours, different on each side).
66721 London Underground 150 (white with tube map images). Also carries the numbers 1933 and 2013.
66723 Also carries the number ZA723.
66747 Newell & Wright (blue, white & red).
66775 Also carries the number F231.
66779 BR dark green.
66780 Cemex (grey, blue & red).
66783 Biffa (red & orange).

Class 66/0. DB Cargo-operated locomotives.

All fitted with Swinghead Automatic "Buckeye" Combination Couplers except 66001 and 66002.

66031, 66091, 66108, 66122 and 66126 are on long-term hire to DRS.

† Fitted with additional lights and drawgear for Lickey banking duties.

t Fitted with tripcocks for working over London Underground tracks between Harrow-on-the-Hill and Amersham.

66001 t	**DB**	DB	WBAE	TO	
66002	**E**	DB	WBAE	TO	
66003	**E**	DB	WBAE	TO	
66004	**E**	DB	WBAR	TO	
66005	**MT**	DB	WBAE	TO	Maritime Intermodal One
66006	**E**	DB	WBAR	TO	
66007	**E**	DB	WBAR	TO	
66009	**DB**	DB	WBAE	TO	
66011	**E**	DB	WBAE	TO	
66012	**E**	DB	WBAE	TO	
66013	**E**	DB	WBAE	TO	
66014	**E**	DB	WBAR	TO	
66015	**E**	DB	WBAR	TO	
66017 t	**DB**	DB	WBAR	TO	
66018	**DB**	DB	WBAE	TO	
66019 t	**DB**	DB	WBAR	TO	
66020	**DB**	DB	WBAE	TO	
66021	**DB**	DB	WBAR	TO	
66023	**E**	DB	WBAT	TO	
66024	**E**	DB	WBAE	TO	
66025	**E**	DB	WBAR	TO	

66027	**DB**	DB	WBAE	TO	
66030	**E**	DB	WBAR	TO	
66031	**E**	DB	XHIM	KM	
66034	**DB**	DB	WBAE	TO	
66035	**DB**	DB	WBAE	TO	Resourceful
66037	**E**	DB	WBAR	TO	
66039	**E**	DB	WBAE	TO	
66040	**E**	DB	WBAR	TO	
66041	**DB**	DB	WBAR	TO	
66043	**E**	DB	WQBA	TO (S)	
66044	**DB**	DB	WBAE	TO	
66047	**MT**	DB	WBAE	TO	Maritime Intermodal Two
66050	**E**	DB	WBAE	TO	EWS Energy
66051	**MT**	DB	WBAR	TO	Maritime Intermodal Four
66053	**E**	DB	WBAE	TO	
66054	**E**	DB	WBAR	TO	
66055 †	**DB**	DB	WBAR	TO	Alain Thauvette
66056 †	**E**	DB	WBLE	TO	
66057 †	**E**	DB	WBLE	TO	
66059 †	**E**	DB	WBLE	TO	
66060	**E**	DB	WBAR	TO	
66061	**E**	DB	WBAE	TO	
66063	**E**	DB	WBAE	TO	
66065	**DB**	DB	WBAR	TO	
66066	**DB**	DB	WBAR	TO	Geoff Spencer
66067	**E**	DB	WBAR	TO	
66068	**E**	DB	WBAR	TO	
66069	**E**	DB	WBAR	TO	
66070	**DB**	DB	WBAT	TO	
66074	**DB**	DB	WBAE	TO	
66075	**E**	DB	WBAE	TO	
66076	**E**	DB	WBAE	TO	
66077	**DB**	DB	WBAR	TO	
66078	**DB**	DB	WBAE	TO	
66079	**E**	DB	WBAR	TO	James Nightall G.C.
66080	**E**	DB	WBAE	TO	
66082	**DB**	DB	WBAE	TO	
66083	**E**	DB	WBAR	TO	
66084	**E**	DB	WBAR	TO	
66085	**DB**	DB	WBAR	TO	
66086	**E**	DB	WBAE	TO	
66087	**E**	DB	WBAE	TO	
66088	**E**	DB	WBAE	TO	
66089	**E**	DB	WBAR	TO	
66090	**MT**	DB	WBAE	TO	Maritime Intermodal Six
66091	**E**	DB	XHIM	KM	
66092	**E**	DB	WBAE	TO	
66093	**E**	DB	WBAE	TO	
66094	**DB**	DB	WBAE	TO	
66095	**E**	DB	WBAE	TO	
66096	**E**	DB	WBAR	TO	

66097	**DB**	DB	WBAE	TO	
66098	**E**	DB	WBAE	TO	
66099 r	**E**	DB	WBBE	TO	
66100 r	**DB**	DB	WBBE	TO	Armistice 100 1918–2018
66101 r	**DB**	DB	WBBE	TO	
66102 r	**E**	DB	WBBE	TO	
66103 r	**E**	DB	WBBE	TO	
66104 r	**DB**	DB	WBBT	TO	
66105 r	**DB**	DB	WBAR	TO	
66106 r	**E**	DB	WBBE	TO	
66107 r	**DB**	DB	WBBT	TO	
66108 r	**E**	DB	XHIM	KM	
66109	**AL**	DB	WBAR	TO	Teesport Express
66110 r	**E**	DB	WBBE	TO	
66111 r	**E**	DB	WBAE	TO	
66112 r	**E**	DB	WBBE	TO	
66113 r	**DB**	DB	WBBE	TO	
66114 r	**DB**	DB	WBBT	TO	
66115	**DB**	DB	WBAE	TO	
66116	**E**	DB	WBAE	TO	
66117	**DB**	DB	WBAE	TO	
66118	**DB**	DB	WBAE	TO	
66119	**E**	DB	WBAE	TO	
66120	**E**	DB	WBAE	TO	
66121	**E**	DB	WBAE	TO	
66122	**E**	DB	XHIM	KM	
66124	**DB**	DB	WBAR	TO	
66125	**E**	DB	WBAE	TO	
66126	**E**	DB	XHIM	KM	
66127	**E**	DB	WBAT	TO	
66128	**DB**	DB	WBAE	TO	
66129	**E**	DB	WBAR	TO	
66130	**DB**	DB	WBAR	TO	
66131	**DB**	DB	WBAE	TO	
66133	**E**	DB	WBAE	TO	
66134	**DB**	DB	WBAE	TO	
66135	**DB**	DB	WBAE	TO	
66136	**DB**	DB	WBAE	TO	
66137	**DB**	DB	WBAE	TO	
66138	**E**	DB	WQAB	TO (S)	
66139	**E**	DB	WBAE	TO	
66140	**E**	DB	WBAE	TO	
66142	**MT**	DB	WBAR	TO	Maritime Intermodal Three
66143	**E**	DB	WBAE	TO	
66144	**E**	DB	WBAR	TO	
66145	**E**	DB	WQAB	TO (S)	
66147	**E**	DB	WBAE	TO	
66148	**MT**	DB	WBAE	TO	Maritime Intermodal Seven
66149	**DB**	DB	WBAE	TO	
66150	**DB**	DB	WBAE	TO	
66151	**E**	DB	WBAE	TO	

66152	**DB**	DB	WBAE	TO	Derek Holmes Railway Operator
66154	**E**	DB	WBAE	TO	
66155	**E**	DB	WBAE	TO	
66156	**E**	DB	WBAE	TO	
66158	**E**	DB	WBAE	TO	
66160	**E**	DB	WBAR	TO	
66161	**E**	DB	WBAE	TO	
66162	**MT**	DB	WBAR	TO	Maritime Intermodal Five
66164	**E**	DB	WBAE	TO	
66165	**DB**	DB	WBAR	TO	
66167	**DB**	DB	WBAE	TO	
66168	**E**	DB	WBAR	TO	
66169	**E**	DB	WBAR	TO	
66170	**E**	DB	WBAE	TO	
66171	**E**	DB	WBAR	TO	
66172	**E**	DB	WBAE	TO	PAUL MELLENEY
66174	**E**	DB	WBAE	TO	
66175	**DB**	DB	WBAE	TO	
66176	**E**	DB	WBAR	TO	
66177	**E**	DB	WBAT	TO	
66181	**E**	DB	WBAR	TO	
66182	**DB**	DB	WQAB	TO (S)	
66183	**E**	DB	WBAE	TO	
66185	**DB**	DB	WBAE	TO	DP WORLD London Gateway
66186	**E**	DB	WBAR	TO	
66187	**E**	DB	WBAE	TO	
66188	**E**	DB	WBAR	TO	
66192	**DB**	DB	WBAR	TO	
66194	**E**	DB	WBAR	TO	
66197	**E**	DB	WBAE	TO	
66198	**E**	DB	WBAR	TO	
66199	**E**	DB	WBAE	TO	
66200	**E**	DB	WBAE	TO	
66206	**DB**	DB	WBAR	TO	
66207	**E**	DB	WBAE	TO	
66221	**E**	DB	WBAR	TO	
66230	**DB**	DB	WQAB	TO (S)	

Class 66/3. Former Fastline-operated locomotives now operated by DRS. Low emission. Details as Class 66/0 except:

Engine: EMD 12N-710G3B-T2 two stroke of 2420 kW (3245 hp) at 904 rpm.
Traction Motors: General Motors D43TRC.
Fuel Capacity: 5150 litres.

66301	**DR**	BN	XHIM	KM	Kingmoor TMD
66302	**DR**	BN	XHIM	KM	Endeavour
66303	**DR**	BN	XHIM	KM	
66304	**DR**	BN	XHIM	KM	
66305	**DR**	BN	XHIM	KM	

Class 66/4. Low emission. Macquarie Group-owned. Details as Class 66/3.

66413	**FG**	MQ	DFIN	LD	Lest We Forget
66414	**FH**	MQ	DFIN	LD	
66415	**FG**	MQ	DFIN	LD	You Are Never Alone
66416	**FH**	MQ	DFIN	LD	
66418	**FH**	MQ	DFIN	LD	PATRIOT – IN MEMORY OF FALLEN RAILWAY EMPLOYEES
66419	**FG**	MQ	DFIN	LD	
66420	**FH**	MQ	DFIN	LD	
66421	**DR**	MQ	XHIM	KM	Gresty Bridge TMD
66422	**DR**	MQ	XHIM	KM	
66423	**DR**	MQ	XHIM	KM	
66424	**DR**	MQ	XHIM	KM	
66425	**DR**	MQ	XHIM	KM	
66426	**DR**	MQ	XHIM	KM	
66427	**DR**	MQ	XHIM	KM	
66428	**DR**	MQ	XHIM	KM	Carlisle Eden Mind
66429	**DR**	MQ	XHIM	KM	
66430	**DR**	MQ	XHIM	KM	
66431	**DR**	MQ	XHIM	KM	
66432	**DR**	MQ	XHIM	KM	
66433	**DR**	MQ	XHIM	KM	
66434	**DR**	MQ	XHIM	KM	

Class 66/5. Standard design. Freightliner-operated locomotives. Details as Class 66/0.

66501	**FL**	P	DFIM	LD	Japan 2001
66502	**FL**	P	DFIM	LD	Basford Hall Centenary 2001
66503	**FG**	P	DFIM	LD	The RAILWAY MAGAZINE
66504	**FH**	P	DFIM	LD	
66505	**FL**	P	DFIM	LD	
66506	**FL**	E	DFIM	LD	Crewe Regeneration
66507	**FL**	E	DFIM	LD	
66508	**FL**	E	DFIM	LD	
66509	**FL**	E	DFIM	LD	
66510	**FL**	E	DFIM	LD	
66511	**FL**	E	DFIM	LD	
66512	**FL**	E	DFIM	LD	
66513	**FL**	E	DFIM	LD	
66514	**FL**	E	DFIM	LD	
66515	**FL**	E	DFIM	LD	
66516	**FL**	E	DFIM	LD	
66517	**FL**	E	DFIM	LD	
66518	**FL**	E	DFIM	LD	
66519	**FL**	E	DFIM	LD	
66520	**FL**	E	DFIM	LD	
66522	**FL**	E	DFIM	LD	
66523	**FL**	E	DFIM	LD	
66524	**FL**	E	DFIM	LD	
66525	**FL**	E	DFIM	LD	

66526	**FL**	P	DFIM	LD	Driver Steve Dunn (George)
66528	**FH**	P	DFIM	LD	Madge Elliot MBE Borders Railway Opening 2015
66529	**FL**	P	DFIM	LD	
66531	**FL**	P	DFIM	LD	
66532	**FL**	P	DFIM	LD	P&O Nedlloyd Atlas
66533	**FL**	P	DFIM	LD	Hanjin Express/Senator Express
66534	**FL**	P	DFIM	LD	OOCL Express
66536	**FL**	P	DFIM	LD	
66537	**FL**	P	DFIM	LD	
66538	**FL**	E	DFIM	LD	
66539	**FL**	E	DFIM	LD	
66540	**FL**	E	DFIM	LD	Ruby
66541	**FL**	E	DFIM	LD	
66542	**FL**	E	DFIM	LD	
66543	**FL**	E	DFIM	LD	
66544	**FL**	P	DFIM	LD	
66545	**FL**	P	DFIM	LD	
66546	**FL**	P	DFIM	LD	
66547	**FL**	P	DFIM	LD	
66548	**FL**	P	DFIM	LD	
66549	**FL**	P	DFIM	LD	
66550	**FL**	P	DFIM	LD	
66551	**FL**	P	DFIM	LD	
66552	**FL**	P	DFIM	LD	Maltby Raider
66553	**FL**	P	DFIM	LD	
66554	**FL**	E	DFIM	LD	
66555	**FL**	E	DFIM	LD	
66556	**FL**	E	DFIM	LD	
66557	**FL**	E	DFIM	LD	
66558	**FL**	E	DFIM	LD	
66559	**FL**	E	DFIM	LD	
66560	**FL**	E	DFIM	LD	
66561	**FL**	E	DFIM	LD	
66562	**FL**	E	DFIM	LD	
66563	**FL**	E	DFIM	LD	
66564	**FL**	E	DFIM	LD	
66565	**FL**	E	DFIM	LD	
66566	**FL**	E	DFIM	LD	
66567	**FL**	E	DFIM	LD	
66568	**FL**	E	DFIM	LD	
66569	**FL**	E	DFIM	LD	
66570	**FL**	E	DFIM	LD	
66571	**FL**	E	DFIM	LD	
66572	**FL**	E	DFIM	LD	

Class 66/5. Freightliner-operated low emission locomotives. Details as Class 66/3.

66585	**FL**	MQ	DFIN	LD	
66587	**AL**	MQ	DFIN	LD	AS ONE, WE CAN
66588	**FL**	MQ	DFIN	LD	

66589	**FL**	MQ	DFIN	LD	
66590	**FL**	MQ	DFIN	LD	
66591	**FL**	MQ	DFIN	LD	
66592	**FL**	MQ	DFIN	LD	Johnson Stevens Agencies
66593	**FL**	MQ	DFIN	LD	3MG MERSEY MULTIMODAL GATEWAY
66594	**FL**	MQ	DFIN	LD	NYK Spirit of Kyoto
66596	**FL**	BN	DFIN	LD	
66597	**FL**	BN	DFIN	LD	Viridor
66598	**FL**	BN	DFIN	LD	
66599	**FL**	BN	DFIN	LD	

Class 66/6. Freightliner-operated locomotives with modified gear ratios. Details as Class 66/0 except:

Maximum Tractive Effort: 467 kN (105080 lbf).
Continuous Tractive Effort: 296 kN (66630 lbf) at 14.0 mph.
Design Speed: 65 mph. **Maximum Speed:** 65 mph.

66601	**FL**	P	DFHH	LD	The Hope Valley
66602	**FL**	P	DFHH	LD	
66603	**FL**	P	DFHH	LD	
66604	**FL**	P	DFHH	LD	
66605	**FL**	P	DFHH	LD	
66606	**FL**	P	DFHH	LD	
66607	**FL**	P	DFHH	LD	
66610	**FL**	P	DFHH	LD	
66613	**FL**	E	DFHH	LD	
66614	**FL**	E	DFHH	LD	1916 POPPY 2016
66615	**FL**	E	DFHH	LD	
66616	**FL**	E	DFHH	LD	
66617	**FL**	E	DFHH	LD	
66618	**FL**	E	DFHH	LD	Railways Illustrated Annual Photographic Awards Alan Barnes
66619	**FL**	E	DFHH	LD	Derek W. Johnson MBE
66620	**FL**	E	DFHH	LD	
66621	**FL**	E	DFHH	LD	
66622	**FL**	E	DFHH	LD	

Class 66/6. Freightliner-operated low emission locomotive with modified gear ratios. Details as Class 66/6 except:

Fuel Capacity: 5150 litres.

66623	**FG**	MQ	DFHH	LD

Class 66/7. Standard design. GB Railfreight-operated locomotives. Details as Class 66/0.

66701	**GB**	E	GBBT	RR	
66702	**GB**	E	GBBT	RR	Blue Lightning
66703	**GB**	E	GBBT	RR	Doncaster PSB 1981–2002
66704	**GB**	E	GBBT	RR	Colchester Power Signalbox
66705	**GB**	E	GBBT	RR	Golden Jubilee
66706	**GB**	E	GBBT	RR	Nene Valley
66707	**GB**	E	GBBT	RR	Sir Sam Fay GREAT CENTRAL RAILWAY

66708	**GB**	E	GBBT	RR	Jayne
66709	**AL**	E	GBBT	RR	Sorrento
66710	**GB**	E	GBBT	RR	Phil Packer BRIT
66711	**AI**	E	GBBT	RR	Sence
66712	**GB**	E	GBBT	RR	Peterborough Power Signalbox
66713	**GB**	E	GBBT	RR	Forest City
66714	**GB**	E	GBBT	RR	Cromer Lifeboat
66715	**GB**	E	GBBT	RR	VALOUR – IN MEMORY OF ALL RAILWAY EMPLOYEES WHO GAVE THEIR LIVES FOR THEIR COUNTRY
66716	**GB**	E	GBBT	RR	LOCOMOTIVE & CARRIAGE INSTITUTION CENTENARY 1911–2011
66717	**GB**	E	GBBT	RR	Good Old Boy

66718–751. GB Railfreight locomotives.

Details as Class 66/0 except 66718–732/747–749 as below:

Engine: EMD 12N-710G3B-T2 two stroke of 2420 kW (3245 hp) at 904 rpm.
Traction Motors: General Motors D43TRC.
Fuel Capacity: 5546 litres (66718–722) or 5150 litres (66723–732/747–749).

66747–749 were originally built for Crossrail AG in the Netherlands.

66750/751 were originally built for mainland Europe in 2003.

66718	**AL**	E	GBLT	RR	Sir Peter Hendy CBE
66719	**GB**	E	GBLT	RR	METRO-LAND
66720	**0**	E	GBLT	RR	
66721	**AL**	E	GBLT	RR	Harry Beck
66722	**GB**	E	GBLT	RR	Sir Edward Watkin
66723	**GB**	E	GBLT	RR	Chinook
66724	**GB**	E	GBLT	RR	Drax Power Station
66725	**GB**	E	GBLT	RR	SUNDERLAND
66726	**GB**	E	GBLT	RR	SHEFFIELD WEDNESDAY
66727	**MT**	E	GBLT	RR	Maritime One
66728	**GB**	P	GBLT	RR	Institution of Railway Operators
66729	**GB**	P	GBLT	RR	DERBY COUNTY
66730	**GB**	P	GBLT	RR	Whitemoor
66731	**GB**	P	GBLT	RR	interhub GB
66732	**GB**	P	GBLT	RR	GBRf The First Decade 1999–2009 John Smith – MD

66733	(66401) r	**GB**	P	GBFM	RR	Cambridge PSB
66735	(66403)	**GB**	P	GBBT	RR	PETERBOROUGH UNITED
66736	(66404) r	**GB**	P	GBFM	RR	WOLVERHAMPTON WANDERERS
66737	(66405) r	**GB**	P	GBFM	RR	Lesia
66738	(66578) r	**GB**	BN	GBBT	RR	HUDDERSFIELD TOWN
66739	(66579) r	**GB**	BN	GBFM	RR	Bluebell Railway
66740	(66580) r	**GB**	BN	GBFM	RR	Sarah
66741	(66581)	**GB**	BN	GBBT	RR	Swanage Railway
66742	(66406, 66841)	**GB**	BN	GBBT	RR	ABP Port of Immingham Centenary 1912–2012
66743	(66407, 66842) r	**M**	BN	GBFM	RR	

66744 (66408, 66843)	**GB**	BN	GBBT	RR	Crossrail
66745 (66409, 66844)	**GB**	BN	GBRT	RR	Modern Railways The first 50 years
66746 (66410, 66845) r	**M**	BN	GBFM	RR	
66747 (20078968-007)	**AL**	GB	GBEB	RR	Made in Sheffield
66748 (20078968-004)	**GB**	GB	GBEB	RR	West Burton 50
66749 (20078968-006)	**GB**	GB	GBEB	RR	Christopher Hopcroft MBE 60 Years Railway Service
66750 (20038513-01)	**GB**	BN	GBEB	RR	Bristol Panel Signal Box
66751 (20038513-04) c	**GB**	BN	GBEB	RR	Inspiration Delivered Hitachi Rail Europe

66752–779. Low emission. New build locomotives. Details as Class 66/3.

66752	**GB**	GB	GBEL	RR	The Hoosier State
66753	**GB**	GB	GBEL	RR	EMD Roberts Road
66754	**GB**	GB	GBEL	RR	Northampton Saints
66755	**GB**	GB	GBEL	RR	Tony Berkeley OBE RFG Chairman 1997–2018
66756	**GB**	GB	GBEL	RR	Royal Corps of Signals
66757	**GB**	GB	GBEL	RR	West Somerset Railway
66758	**GB**	GB	GBEL	RR	The Pavior
66759	**GB**	GB	GBEL	RR	Chippy
66760	**GB**	GB	GBEL	RR	David Gordon Harris
66761	**GB**	GB	GBEL	RR	Wensleydale Railway Association 25 Years 1990–2015
66762	**GB**	GB	GBEL	RR	
66763	**GB**	GB	GBEL	RR	Severn Valley Railway
66764	**GB**	GB	GBEL	RR	
66765	**GB**	GB	GBEL	RR	
66766	**GB**	GB	GBEL	RR	
66767	**GB**	GB	GBEL	RR	
66768	**GB**	GB	GBEL	RR	
66769	**GB**	GB	GBEL	RR	
66770	**GB**	GB	GBEL	RR	
66771	**GB**	GB	GBEL	RR	Amanda
66772	**GB**	GB	GBEL	RR	Maria
66773	**GB**	GB	GBNB	RR	Pride of GB Railfreight
66774	**GB**	GB	GBNB	RR	
66775	**GB**	GB	GBNB	RR	HMS Argyll
66776	**GB**	GB	GBNB	RR	Joanne
66777	**GB**	GB	GBNB	RR	Annette
66778	**GB**	GB	GBNB	RR	Cambois Depot 25 Years
66779	**0**	GB	GBEL	RR	EVENING STAR

66780–789. Standard design. Former DB Cargo locomotives acquired by GB Railfreight in 2017. Details as Class 66/0. Fitted with Swinghead Automatic "Buckeye" Combination Couplers.

† Fitted with additional lights and drawgear formerly used for Lickey banking duties.

66780 (66008)	**AL**	GB	GBOB	RR	The Cemex Express
66781 (66016)	**GB**	GB	GBOB	RR	
66782 (66046)	**GB**	GB	GBOB	RR	
66783 (66058) †	**AL**	GB	GBOB	RR	The Flying Dustman
66784 (66081)	**GB**	GB	GBOB	RR	Keighley & Worth Valley Railway 50th Anniversary 1968–2018
66785 (66132)	**GB**	GB	GBOB	RR	
66786 (66141)	**GB**	GB	GBOB	RR	
66787 (66184)	**GB**	GB	GBOB	RR	
66788 (66238)	**GB**	GB	GBOB	RR	LOCOMOTION 15
66789 (66250)	**BL**	GB	GBOB	RR	British Rail 1948–1997
66790 (T66403)		BN			
66791 (T66404)		BN			
66792 (T66405)		BN			

Class 66/8. Standard design. Colas Rail locomotives. Details as Class 66/0.

66846 (66573)	**CS**	BN	COLO	HJ	
66847 (66574)	**CS**	BN	COLO	HJ	Terry Baker
66848 (66575)	**CS**	BN	COLO	HJ	
66849 (66576)	**CS**	BN	COLO	HJ	Wylam Dilly
66850 (66577)	**CS**	BN	COLO	HJ	David Maidment OBE

Class 66/9. Freightliner locomotives. Low emission "demonstrator" locomotives. Details as Class 66/3.

* **Fuel Capacity**: 5905 litres.

66951 *	**FL**	E	DFIN	LD
66952	**FL**	E	DFIN	LD

Class 66/5. Freightliner-operated low emission locomotives. Owing to the 665xx number range being full, subsequent deliveries of 66/5s were numbered from 66953 onwards. Details as Class 66/5 (low emission).

66953	**FL**	BN	DFIN	LD	
66955	**FL**	BN	DFIN	LD	
66956	**FL**	BN	DFIN	LD	
66957	**FL**	BN	DFIN	LD	Stephenson Locomotive Society 1909–2009

CLASS 67 ALSTOM/GENERAL MOTORS Bo-Bo

Built: 1999–2000 by Alstom at Valencia, Spain, as sub-contractors for General Motors (General Motors model JT42 HW-HS).
Engine: GM 12N-710G3B-EC two stroke of 2385 kW (3200 hp) at 904 rpm.
Main Alternator: General Motors AR9A/HEP7/CA6C.
Traction Motors: General Motors D43FM.
Maximum Tractive Effort: 141 kN (31770 lbf).
Continuous Tractive Effort: 90 kN (20200 lbf) at 46.5 mph.
Power at Rail: 1860 kW.
Brake Force: 78 t.
Weight: 90 t.
Train Brakes: Air.
Dimensions: 19.74 x 2.72 m.
Wheel Diameter: 965 mm.

Design Speed: 125 mph.
Fuel Capacity: 4927 litres.
Train Supply: Electric, index 66.
Maximum Speed: 125 mph.
Route Availability: 8.
Total: 30.

All equipped with Slow Speed Control and Swinghead Automatic "Buckeye" Combination Couplers.

Non-standard liveries:

67026 Diamond Jubilee silver.
67029 All over silver with DB logos.

67001	**AB**	DB	WAWC	CE	
67002	**AB**	DB	WAAC	CE	
67003	**AB**	DB	WQAA	TO (S)	
67004 r	**DB**	DB	WABC	CE	
67005	**RZ**	DB	WAAC	CE	Queen's Messenger
67006	**RZ**	DB	WAAC	CE	Royal Sovereign
67007 r	**E**	DB	WQAA	CE (S)	
67008	**E**	DB	WACC	CE	
67009 r	**E**	DB	WQBA	CE (S)	
67010	**DB**	DB	WAAC	CE	
67011 r	**E**	DB	WQBA	CE (S)	
67012	**CM**	DB	WAWC	CE	
67013	**DB**	DB	WAWC	CE	
67014	**CM**	DB	WAWC	CE	
67015	**DB**	DB	WAAC	CE	
67016	**E**	DB	WAAC	CE	
67017	**E**	DB	WQAA	TO (S)	
67018	**DB**	DB	WQAA	CE (S)	Keith Heller
67019	**E**	DB	WQBA	TO (S)	
67020	**E**	DB	WAWC	CE	
67021	**PC**	DB	WAAC	CE	
67022	**E**	DB	WQAA	CE (S)	
67023	**CS**	BN	COTS	RU	Stella
67024	**PC**	DB	WAAC	CE	
67025	**TW**	DB	WACC	TO	
67026	**0**	DB	WQBA	CE (S)	Diamond Jubilee
67027	**CS**	BN	COTS	RU	Charlotte
67028	**DB**	DB	WAAC	CE	
67029	**0**	DB	WACC	CE	Royal Diamond
67030 r	**E**	DB	WQAA	CE (S)	

CLASS 68 VOSSLOH/STADLER Bo-Bo

New Vossloh/Stadler mixed-traffic locomotives operated by DRS.

Built: 2012–16 by Vossloh/Stadler, Valencia, Spain.
Engine: Caterpillar C175-16 of 2800 kW (3750 hp) at 1740 rpm.
Main Alternator: ABB WGX560.
Traction Motors: 4 x AMXL400 AC frame mounted ABB 4FRA6063.
Maximum Tractive Effort: 317 kN (71260 lbf).

Continuous Tractive Effort: 258 kN (58000 lbf) at 20.5 mph.
Power at Rail:
Brake Force: 73 t.
Weight: 85 t.
Design Speed: 100 mph.
Fuel Capacity: 5600 litres.
Train Supply: Electric, index 96.
Train Brakes: Air & rheostatic.
Dimensions: 20.50 x 2.69 m.
Wheel Diameter: 1100 mm.
Maximum Speed: 100 mph.
Route Availability: 7.
Total: 34.

68008–015 have been modified to operate in push-pull mode on the Chiltern Railways locomotive-hauled sets.

68019–034 have been modified to operate with the new TransPennine Express Mark 5A stock.

68001	**DI**	BN	XHVE	CR	Evolution
68002	**DI**	BN	XHVE	CR	Intrepid
68003	**DI**	BN	XHVE	CR	Astute
68004	**DI**	BN	XHVE	CR	Rapid
68005	**DI**	BN	XHVE	CR	Defiant
68006	**SR**	BN	XHVE	CR	Daring
68007	**SR**	BN	XHVE	CR	Valiant
68008	**DI**	BN	XHVE	CR	Avenger
68009	**DI**	BN	XHVE	CR	Titan
68010	**CM**	BN	XHCE	CR	Oxford Flyer
68011	**CM**	BN	XHCE	CR	
68012	**CM**	BN	XHCE	CR	
68013	**CM**	BN	XHCE	CR	
68014	**CM**	BN	XHCE	CR	
68015	**CM**	BN	XHCE	CR	
68016	**DI**	BN	XHVE	CR	Fearless
68017	**DI**	BN	XHVE	CR	Hornet
68018	**DI**	BN	XHVE	CR	Vigilant
68019	**TP**	BN	TPEX	CR	Brutus
68020	**TP**	BN	TPEX	CR	Reliance
68021	**TP**	BN	TPEX	CR	Tireless
68022	**TP**	BN	TPEX	CR	Resolution
68023	**TP**	BN	TPEX	CR	Achilles
68024	**TP**	BN	TPEX	CR	Centaur
68025	**TP**	BN	TPEX	CR	Superb
68026	**TP**	BN	XHTP	CR	Enterprise
68027	**TP**	BN	TPEX	CR	Splendid
68028	**TP**	BN	TPEX	CR	Lord President
68029	**TP**	BN	TPEX	CR	Courageous
68030	**TP**	BN	XHTP	CR	Black Douglas
68031	**TP**	BN	TPEX	CR	Felix
68032	**TP**	BN	TPEX	CR	Destroyer
68033	**DI**	DR	XHVE	CR	
68034	**DI**	DR	XHVE	CR	

CLASS 69 BRUSH/BR/RUSTON/EMD Co-Co

These locomotives are heavy rebuilds of Class 56s for GB Railfreight, with new General Motors engines, the same type as used in the Class 66s. The first rebuild is due to be completed in May 2020 and it is planned that a total of 16 locomotives will be rebuilt. Full details awaited.

Built: 1976–84 by Electroputere at Craiova, Romania (as sub-contractors for Brush) or BREL at Doncaster or Crewe Works. Rebuilt 2019–21 by ElectroMotive Diesel Services, Longport.
Engine: General Motors 12N-710G3B-T2 two stroke of 2385 kW (3200 hp) at 904 rpm.
Main Alternator:
Traction Motors:
Maximum Tractive Effort:
Continuous Tractive Effort:
Power at Rail:
Brake Force:
Weight:
Design Speed:
Fuel Capacity:
Train Supply: Not equipped.
Train Brakes: Air.
Dimensions: 19.36 x 2.79 m.
Wheel Diameter:
Maximum Speed:
Route Availability:

69001	(56311)	GB
69002	(56031)	GB
69003	(56018)	GB
69004		GB
69005		GB
69006		GB
69007		GB
69008		GB
69009		GB
69010		GB
69011		GB
69012		GB
69013		GB
69014		GB
69015		GB
69016		GB

CLASS 70 GENERAL ELECTRIC Co-Co

GE "PowerHaul" locomotives. 70012 was badly damaged whilst being unloaded in 2011 and was returned to Pennsylvania.

70801 (built as 70099) is a Turkish-built demonstrator that arrived in Britain in 2012. Colas Rail leased this locomotive and then in 2013 ordered a further nine locomotives (70802–810) that were delivered in 2014. 70811–817 followed in 2017.

Built: 2009–17 by General Electric, Erie, Pennsylvania, USA or by TÜLOMSAS, Eskişehir, Turkey (70801).

▲ In the colours of the Cornish flag, 08645 is seen at Penzance Long Rock depot on 13/04/19. **Robert Pritchard**

▼ RMS Locotec-liveried 08762 is seen at Crewe LNWR Heritage depot on 08/06/19. **Robert Pritchard**

▲ In white livery and carrying internal No. "3", 20906 is seen at Hope Cement Works on 03/02/19. The Class 20s based here are used to take trains from the cement works to the exchange sidings at Earles. **Robert Pritchard**

▼ BR blue-liveried 31128 passes Roby with the Branch Line Society's "The Sunday Yicker" railtour to Crewe on 09/06/19. **Steven Harrow**

▲ BR green-liveried 33012 (D6515) and West Coast Railway Company maroon-liveried 33029 double-head "The Marching Crompton" railtour away from Weymouth on 23/03/19. **Stephen Ginn**

▼ West Coast Railway Company maroon-liveried 37685 passes Crawford with 5Z38 09.00 Fort William–Carnforth empty stock on 15/06/19. **Robin Ralston**

▲ Colas Rail-liveried 37099 brings up the rear of 1Q86 10.14 March–Derby RTC Network Rail test train at Saxilby on 29/06/19 (led by 37521). **Robert Pritchard**

▲ ScotRail InterCity-liveried 43182 and 43151 pass Bardrill with the 12.35 Stirling–Inverness on 20/09/19. **Ian Lothian**

▲ BR revised blue-liveried 47593 is seen at Carlisle Kingmoor depot on 20/07/19, with 68022 to the right. **Robert Pritchard**

▼ GB Railfreight-liveried 50049 and 50007 (running as 50014 on one side) are seen at Penzance Long Rock open day on 13/04/19. **Robert Pritchard**

▲ Colas Rail-liveried 56087 passes Didcot Parkway with 6L39 Bridgend–Dagenham Dock on 03/06/19. **Steve Stubbs**

▼ Pullman-liveried 57601 arrives at Weymouth with 1Z80, the 10.05 Northern Belle luxury train from London Victoria on 11/08/19. **Stephen Ginn**

▲ Aggregate Industries-liveried 59005 passes Berkley Marsh, near Frome, with 6C78 14.39 Acton–Whatley Quarry on 13/08/19. **Glen Batten**

▼ DB Cargo-liveried 60100 passes Lincoln Central with 6M00 14.30 Humber–Kingsbury loaded bogie tanks on 02/07/18. **Robert Pritchard**

▲ One of six DB Cargo 66s now in the Maritime blue livery, 66047 passes Saxilby with 4L45 10.04 Wakefield Europort–Felixstowe on 03/09/19. **Robert Pritchard**

▲ Royal Scotsman maroon-liveried 66746 leads the 11.10 Boat of Garten–Dundee Royal Scotsman luxury train through Glen Garry, between Dalnaspidal and Dalnacardoch (near Pitlochry), on 27/06/19. **Dave McAlone**

▲ Pullman-liveried 67021 and 67024 arrive at Exeter St David's with 1Z80 17.30 Bath Spa–Penzance Belmond British Pulman on 01/06/19. **Tim Squires**

▼ New DRS-liveried 68034 and 68002 top-and-tail 6M22 15.12 Torness Power Station–Carlisle Kingmoor nuclear flasks at Symington on 02/07/19. **Robin Ralston**

▲ Freightliner-liveried 70015 approaches Rotherham Masborough with 4O31 17.50 Leeds–Southampton Maritime intermodal on 27/06/19. **Robert Pritchard**

▼ Caledonian Sleeper-liveried 73970 passes Coatbridge Central with a 5Z12 08.10 Fort William–Polmadie Mark 5 Sleeper test on 09/03/19. **Ian Lothian**

▲ BR electric blue-liveried 86259 is seen at Lichfield Trent Valley after arriving light engine from Rugby on 20/12/18. **John Stretton**

▼ New DRS-liveried 88004 and 68034 power 6C22 07.27 Carlisle Kingmoor–Sellafield nuclear flask train on 03/07/19. **Dave McAlone**

▲ Freightliner-liveried 90046 and 90041 pass Springfield, near Gretna Junction, with 4M49 14.05 Coatbridge–Crewe intermodal on 14/10/18. **Robin Ralston**

▼ In Virgin Trains East Coast livery with LNER branding, 91126 arrives at York with the 07.00 London King's Cross–Edinburgh on 30/07/19. **Robert Pritchard**

▲ Caledonian Sleeper-liveried 92010 passes Bletchley with a rake of new Mark 5 Sleeper stock as 5Z11 09.30 Polmadie–Wembley on 30/06/19. **Mark Beal**

▲ Eurotunnel Class 9/7 9711 is seen under repair in Coquelles depot on 03/09/19.
David Haydock

▼ Hunslet/Schöma Channel Tunnel maintenance locomotive 0041 is seen in Coquelles yard on 19/09/19.
David Haydock

Engine: General Electric PowerHaul P616LDA1 of 2848 kW (3820 hp) at 1500 rpm.
Main Alternator: General Electric GTA series.
Traction Motors: AC-GE 5GEB30.
Maximum Tractive Effort: 544 kN (122000 lbf).
Continuous Tractive Effort: 427 kN (96000 lbf) at ?? mph.
Power at Rail:
Train Brakes: Air.
Brake Force: 96.7 t.
Dimensions: 21.71 x 2.64 m.
Weight: 129 t.
Wheel Diameter: 1066 mm.
Design Speed: 75 mph.
Maximum Speed: 75 mph.
Fuel Capacity: 6000 litres.
Route Availability: 7.
Train Supply: Not equipped.
Total: 36.

Class 70/0. Freightliner locomotives.

70001	**FH**	MQ	DFGI	LD	PowerHaul
70002	**FH**	MQ	DFGI	LD	
70003	**FH**	MQ	DFGI	LD	
70004	**FH**	MQ	DHLT	LD (S)	The Coal Industry Society
70005	**FH**	MQ	DFGI	LD	
70006	**FH**	MQ	DFGI	LD	
70007	**FH**	MQ	DFGI	LD	
70008	**FH**	MQ	DFGI	LD	
70009	**FH**	MQ	DHLT	LD (S)	
70010	**FH**	MQ	DFGI	LD	
70011	**FH**	MQ	DFGI	LD	
70013	**FH**	MQ	DHLT	LD (S)	
70014	**FH**	MQ	DFGI	LD	
70015	**FH**	MQ	DFGI	LD	
70016	**FH**	MQ	DFGI	LD	
70017	**FH**	MQ	DHLT	LD (S)	
70018	**FH**	MQ	DHLT	LD (S)	
70019	**FH**	MQ	DHLT	LD (S)	
70020	**FH**	MQ	DFGI	LD	

Class 70/8. Colas Rail locomotives.

70801	**CS**	LF	COLO	CF
70802	**CS**	LF	COLO	CF
70803	**CS**	LF	COLO	CF
70804	**CS**	LF	COLO	CF
70805	**CS**	LF	COLO	CF
70806	**CS**	LF	COLO	CF
70807	**CS**	LF	COLO	CF
70808	**CS**	LF	COLO	CF
70809	**CS**	LF	COLO	CF
70810	**CS**	LF	COLO	CF
70811	**CS**	BN	COLO	CF
70812	**CS**	BN	COLO	CF
70813	**CS**	BN	COLO	CF
70814	**CS**	BN	COLO	CF
70815	**CS**	BN	COLO	CF
70816	**CS**	BN	COLO	CF
70817	**CS**	BN	COLO	CF

1.3. ELECTRO-DIESEL & ELECTRIC LOCOMOTIVES

CLASS 73/1 BR/ENGLISH ELECTRIC Bo-Bo

Electro-diesel locomotives which can operate either from a DC supply or using power from a diesel engine.

Built: 1965–67 by English Electric Co. at Vulcan Foundry, Newton-le-Willows.
Engine: English Electric 4SRKT of 447 kW (600 hp) at 850 rpm.
Main Generator: English Electric 824/5D.
Electric Supply System: 750 V DC from third rail.
Traction Motors: English Electric 546/1B.
Maximum Tractive Effort (Electric): 179 kN (40000 lbf).
Maximum Tractive Effort (Diesel): 160 kN (36000 lbf).
Continuous Rating (Electric): 1060 kW (1420 hp) giving a tractive effort of 35 kN (7800 lbf) at 68 mph.
Continuous Tractive Effort (Diesel): 60 kN (13600 lbf) at 11.5 mph.
Maximum Rail Power (Electric): 2350 kW (3150 hp) at 42 mph.
Train Brakes: Air, vacuum & electro-pneumatic († Air & electro-pneumatic).
Brake Force: 31 t.
Dimensions: 16.36 x 2.64 m.
Weight: 77 t.
Wheel Diameter: 1016 mm.
Design Speed: 90 mph.
Maximum Speed: 90 mph.
Fuel Capacity: 1409 litres.
Route Availability: 6.
Train Supply: Electric, index 66 (on electric power only). **Total**: 30.

Formerly numbered E6007–E6020/E6022–E6026/E6028–E6049 (not in order).

Locomotives numbered in the 732xx series are classed as 73/2 and were originally dedicated to Gatwick Express services.

There have been two separate Class 73 rebuild projects. For GBRf 11 locomotives were rebuilt at Brush, Loughborough with a 1600 hp MTU engine (renumbered 73961–971). For Network Rail 73104/211 were rebuilt at RVEL Derby (now Loram) with 2 x QSK19 750 hp engines (now 73951/952).

Non-standard liveries and numbering:

73110 Carries original number E6016.
73128 Two-tone grey.
73139 Light blue & light grey.
73235 Plain dark blue.

73101	**PC**	GB	GBSD	ZG (S)	
73107	**GB**	GB	GBED	SE	Tracy
73109	**GB**	GB	GBED	SE	
73110	**B**	GB	GBBR	ZG (S)	
73119	**GB**	GB	GBED	SE	Borough of Eastleigh
73128	**GB**	GB	GBED	SE	O.V.S. BULLEID C.B.E.
73133	**TT**	TT	MBED	ZG	
73134	**IC**	GB	GBBR	LB (S)	Woking Homes 1885–1985

73136		**GB**	GB	GBED	SE	Mhairi
73138		**Y**	NR	QADD	ZA	
73139		**0**	GB	GBSD	ZG (S)	
73141		**GB**	GB	GBED	SE	Charlotte
73201	†	**B**	GB	GBED	SE	Broadlands
73202	†	**SN**	P	MBED	SL	Graham Stenning
73212	†	**GB**	GB	GBED	SE	Fiona
73213	†	**GB**	GB	GBED	SE	Rhodalyn
73235	†	**0**	P	HYWD	BM	

CLASS 73/9 (RVEL) BR/RVEL Bo-Bo

The 7395x number series is reserved for rebuilt Network Rail locomotives.

Rebuilt: Re-engineered by RVEL Derby 2013–15.
Engine: 2 x QSK19 of 560 kW (750 hp) at 1800 rpm (total 1120 kw (1500 hp)).
Main Alternator: 2 x Marathon Magnaplus.
Electric Supply System: 750 V DC from third rail.
Traction Motors: English Electric 546/1B.
Maximum Tractive Effort (Electric): 179 kN (40000 lbf).
Maximum Tractive Effort (Diesel): 179 kN (40000 lbf).
Continuous Rating (Electric): 1060 kW (1420 hp) giving a tractive effort of 35 kN (7800 lbf) at 68 mph.
Continuous Tractive Effort (Diesel): 990 kW (1328 hp) giving a tractive effort of 33 kN (7420 lbf) at 68 mph.
Maximum Rail Power (Electric): 2350 kW (3150 hp) at 42 mph.
Train Brakes: Air.
Brake Force: 31 t.
Weight: 77 t.
Dimensions: 16.36 x 2.64 m.
Maximum Speed: 90 mph.
Wheel Diameter: 1016 mm.
Fuel Capacity: 2260 litres.
Route Availability: 6.
Train Supply: Not equipped.

73951	(73104)	**Y**	LO	QADD	ZA	Malcolm Brinded
73952	(73211)	**Y**	LO	QADD	ZA	Janis Kong

CLASS 73/9 (GBRf) BR/BRUSH Bo-Bo

GBRf Class 73s rebuilt at Brush Loughborough. 73961–965 are normally used on Network Rail contracts and 73966–971 are used by Caledonian Sleeper.

Rebuilt: Re-engineered by Brush, Loughborough 2014–16.
Engine: MTU 8V4000 R43L of 1195 kW (1600 hp) at 1800 rpm.
Main Alternator: Lechmotoren SDV 87.53-12.
Electric Supply System: 750 V DC from third rail (73961–965 only).
Traction Motors: English Electric 546/1B.
Maximum Tractive Effort (Electric): 179 kN (40000 lbf).
Maximum Tractive Effort (Diesel): 179 kN (40000 lbf).
Continuous Rating (Electric): 1060 kW (1420 hp) giving a tractive effort of 35 kN (7800 lbf) at 68 mph.
Continuous Tractive Effort (Diesel):

Maximum Rail Power (Electric): 2350 kW (3150 hp) at 42 mph.
Train Brakes: Air. **Brake Force**: 31 t.
Weight: 77 t. **Dimensions**: 16.36 x 2.64 m.
Maximum Speed: 90 mph. **Wheel Diameter**: 1016 mm.
Fuel Capacity: 1409 litres. **Route Availability**: 6.
Train Supply: Electric, index 38 (electric & diesel).

73961 (73209)	**GB**	GB	GBNR	SE	Alison
73962 (73204)	**GB**	GB	GBNR	SE	Dick Mabbutt
73963 (73206)	**GB**	GB	GBNR	SE	Janice
73964 (73205)	**GB**	GB	GBNR	SE	Jeanette
73965 (73208)	**GB**	GB	GBNR	SE	

73966–971 have been rebuilt for Caledonian Sleeper but their third rail electric capability has been retained. They have a higher Train Supply index and a slightly higher fuel capacity. Details as 73961–965 except:
Fuel Capacity: 1509 litres. **Train Supply**: Electric, index 96.

73005 and 73006 were originally assembled at Eastleigh Works.

73966 (73005)	d	**CA**	GB	GBCS	EC
73967 (73006)	d	**CA**	GB	GBCS	EC
73968 (73117)	d	**CA**	GB	GBCS	EC
73969 (73105)	d	**CA**	GB	GBCS	EC
73970 (73103)	d	**CA**	GB	GBCS	EC
73971 (73207)	d	**CA**	GB	GBCS	EC

CLASS 86 BR/ENGLISH ELECTRIC Bo-Bo

Built: 1965–66 by English Electric Co at Vulcan Foundry, Newton-le-Willows or by BR at Doncaster Works.
Electric Supply System: 25 kV AC 50 Hz overhead.
Traction Motors: AEI 282BZ axle hung.
Maximum Tractive Effort: 207 kN (46500 lbf).
Continuous Rating: 3010 kW (4040 hp) giving a tractive effort of 85 kN (19200 lbf) at 77.5 mph.
Maximum Rail Power: 4550 kW (6100 hp) at 49.5 mph.
Train Brakes: Air. **Brake Force**: 40 t.
Dimensions: 17.83 x 2.65 m. **Weight**: 83–86.8 t.
Wheel Diameter: 1156 mm. **Train Supply**: Electric, index 74.
Design Speed: 110–125 mph. **Maximum Speed**: 100 mph.
Route Availability: 6. **Total**: 21.

Formerly numbered E3101–E3200 (not in order).

Class 86s exported for use abroad are listed in section 1.6 of this book.

Class 86/1. Class 87-type bogies & motors. Details as above except:

Traction Motors: GEC 412AZ frame mounted.
Maximum Tractive Effort: 258 kN (58000 lbf).
Continuous Rating: 3730 kW (5000 hp) giving a tractive effort of 95 kN (21300 lbf) at 87 mph.
Maximum Rail Power: 5860 kW (7860 hp) at 50.8 mph.

Wheel Diameter: 1150 mm.
Design Speed: 110 mph. **Maximum Speed**: 110 mph.

86101	**CA**	LD	GBCH	ZG (S)	Sir William A Stanier FRS

Class 86/2. Standard design rebuilt with resilient wheels & Flexicoil suspension. Details as in main class heading.

Non-standard livery:

86259 BR "Electric blue". Also carries number E3137.

86251	**V**	FL	EPEX	CB (S)	
86259 x	**0**	PP	MBEL	WN	Les Ross/Peter Pan

Class 86/4. Details as Class 86/2 except:

Traction Motors: AEI 282AZ axle hung.
Maximum Tractive Effort: 258 kN (58000 lbf).
Continuous Rating: 2680 kW (3600 hp) giving a tractive effort of 89kN (20000lbf) at 67 mph.
Maximum Rail Power: 4400 kW (5900 hp) at 38 mph.
Weight: 83–83.9 t.
Design Speed: 100 mph. **Maximum Speed**: 100 mph.

86401	**CA**	EL	GBCH	WN	Mons Meg

Class 86/6. Freightliner-operated locomotives.

Previously numbered in the Class 86/0 and 86/4 series'. 86608 was also regeared and renumbered 86501 between 2000 and 2016.

Details as Class 86/4 except:
Traction Motors: AEI 282AZ axle hung.
Maximum Speed: 75 mph. **Train Supply**: Electric, isolated.

86604	**FL**	FL	DFNC	CB
86605	**FL**	FL	DFNC	CB
86607	**FL**	FL	DFNC	CB
86608	**FL**	FL	DFNC	CB
86609	**FL**	FL	DFNC	CB
86610	**FL**	FL	DFNC	CB
86612	**FL**	FL	DFNC	CB
86613	**FL**	FL	DFNC	CB
86614	**FL**	FL	DFNC	CB
86622	**FH**	FL	DFNC	CB
86627	**FL**	FL	DFNC	CB
86628	**FL**	FL	DFNC	CB
86632	**FL**	FL	DFNC	CB
86637	**FH**	FL	DFNC	CB
86638	**FL**	FL	DFNC	CB
86639	**FL**	FL	DFNC	CB

CLASS 87 BREL/GEC Bo-Bo

Built: 1973–75 by BREL at Crewe Works.
Electric Supply System: 25 kV AC 50 Hz overhead.
Traction Motors: GEC G412AZ frame mounted.
Maximum Tractive Effort: 258 kN (58000 lbf).
Continuous Rating: 3730 kW (5000 hp) giving a tractive effort of 95 kN (21300 lbf) at 87 mph.
Maximum Rail Power: 5860 kW (7860 hp) at 50.8 mph.
Train Brakes: Air.
Brake Force: 40 t.
Dimensions: 17.83 x 2.65 m.
Weight: 83.3 t.
Wheel Diameter: 1150 mm.
Train Supply: Electric, index 95.
Design Speed: 110 mph.
Maximum Speed: 110 mph.
Route Availability: 6.
Total: 1.

Class 87s exported for use abroad are listed in section 1.6 of this book.

87002	**CA**	LD	GBCH	ZG (S)	Royal Sovereign

CLASS 88 VOSSLOH/STADLER Bo-Bo

New Vossloh/Stadler bi-mode DRS locomotives.

Built: 2015–16 by Vossloh/Sladler, Valencia, Spain.
Electric Supply System: 25 kV AC 50 Hz overhead.
Engine: Caterpillar C27 12-cylinder 708 kW (950 hp) at 1750 rpm.
Main Alternator: ABB AMXL400.
Traction Motors: ABB AMXL400.
Maximum Tractive Effort (Electric): 317 kN (71 260 lbf).
Maximum Tractive Effort (Diesel): 317 kN (71 260 lbf).
Continuous Rating: 4000 kW (5360 hp) giving a tractive effort of 258 kN (58000 lbf) at 28 mph (electric).
Maximum Rail Power:
Train Brakes: Air, regenerative & rheostatic.
Brake Force: 73 t.
Dimensions: 20.50 x 2.69 m.
Weight: 85 t.
Wheel Diameter: 1100 mm.
Fuel Capacity: 1800 litres.
Train Supply: Electric, index 96.
Design Speed: 100 mph.
Maximum Speed: 100 mph.
Route Availability: 7.
Total: 10.

88001	**DI**	BN	XHVE	KM	Revolution
88002	**DI**	BN	XHVE	KM	Prometheus
88003	**DI**	BN	XHVE	KM	Genesis
88004	**DI**	BN	XHVE	KM	Pandora
88005	**DI**	BN	XHVE	KM	Minerva
88006	**DI**	BN	XHVE	KM	Juno
88007	**DI**	BN	XHVE	KM	Electra
88008	**DI**	BN	XHVE	KM	Ariadne
88009	**DI**	BN	XHVE	KM	Diana
88010	**DI**	BN	XHVE	KM	Aurora

CLASS 90 GEC Bo-Bo

Built: 1987–90 by BREL at Crewe Works (as sub-contractors for GEC).
Electric Supply System: 25 kV AC 50 Hz overhead.
Traction Motors: GEC G412CY frame mounted.
Maximum Tractive Effort: 258 kN (58000 lbf).
Continuous Rating: 3730 kW (5000 hp) giving a tractive effort of 95kN (21300lbf) at 87 mph.
Maximum Rail Power: 5860 kW (7860 hp) at 68.3 mph.
Train Brakes: Air.
Brake Force: 40 t.
Weight: 84.5 t.
Design Speed: 110 mph.
Train Supply: Electric, index 95.
Dimensions: 18.80 x 2.74 m.
Wheel Diameter: 1150 mm.
Maximum Speed: 110 mph.
Route Availability: 7.
Total: 50.

Advertising livery: 90024 Malcolm Logistics (blue).

90001 b	**GA**	P	IANA	NC	Crown Point
90002 b	**GA**	P	IANA	NC	Eastern Daily Press 1870–2010 SERVING NORFOLK FOR 140 YEARS
90003 b	**GA**	P	IANA	NC	
90004 b	**GA**	P	IANA	NC	City of Chelmsford
90005 b	**GA**	P	IANA	NC	Vice-Admiral Lord Nelson
90006 b	**GA**	P	IANA	NC	Modern Railways Magazine/ Roger Ford
90007 b	**GA**	P	IANA	NC	Sir John Betjeman
90008 b	**GA**	P	IANA	NC	The East Anglian
90009 b	**GA**	P	IANA	NC	
90010 b	**GA**	P	IANA	NC	
90011 b	**GA**	P	IANA	NC	East Anglian Daily Times Suffolk & Proud
90012 b	**GA**	P	IANA	NC	Royal Anglian Regiment
90013 b	**GA**	P	IANA	NC	
90014 b	**GA**	P	IANA	NC	Norfolk and Norwich Festival
90015 b	**GA**	P	IANA	NC	Colchester Castle
90016	**FL**	FL	DFLC	CB	
90017	**E**	DB	WQBA	CE (S)	
90018	**DB**	DB	WQAA	CE (S)	The Pride of Bellshill
90019	**DB**	DB	WEDC	CE	Multimodal
90020	**E**	DB	WEDC	CE	Collingwood
90021	**FS**	DB	WQAB	CE (S)	
90022	**EG**	DB	WQBA	CE (S)	Freightconnection
90023	**E**	DB	WQBA	CE (S)	
90024	**AL**	DB	WQAB	CE (S)	
90025	**F**	DB	WQBA	CE (S)	
90026	**E**	DB	WEDC	CE	
90027	**F**	DB	WQBA	CE (S)	Allerton T&RS Depot
90028	**DB**	DB	WEDC	CE	Sir William McAlpine
90029	**DB**	DB	WEDC	CE	
90030	**E**	DB	WQBA	CE (S)	
90031	**E**	DB	WQBA	CE (S)	The Railway Children Partnership Working For Street Children Worldwide

90032	**E**	DB	WQBA	CE (S)	
90033	**FE**	DB	WQBA	CE (S)	
90034	**DR**	DB	WEDC	CE	
90035	**DB**	DB	WEAC	CE	
90036	**DB**	DB	WEDC	CE	Driver Jack Mills
90037	**E**	DB	WEDC	CE	Spirit of Dagenham
90038	**FE**	DB	WQBA	CE (S)	
90039	**E**	DB	WEDC	CE	
90040	**DB**	DB	WEAC	CE	
90041	**FL**	FL	DFLC	CB	
90042	**FH**	FL	DFLC	CB	
90043	**FH**	FL	DFLC	CB	
90044	**FF**	FL	DFLC	CB	
90045	**FH**	FL	DFLC	CB	
90046	**FL**	FL	DFLC	CB	
90047	**FF**	FL	DFLC	CB	
90048	**FF**	FL	DFLC	CB	
90049	**FH**	FL	DFLC	CB	
90050	**FF**	AV	DHLT	CB (S)	

CLASS 91 GEC Bo-Bo

Built: 1988–91 by BREL at Crewe Works (as sub-contractors for GEC).
Electric Supply System: 25 kV AC 50 Hz overhead.
Traction Motors: GEC G426AZ.
Maximum Tractive Effort: 190 kN (43 000 lbf).
Continuous Rating: 4540 kW (6090 hp) giving a tractive effort of 170kN at 96mph.
Maximum Rail Power: 4700 kW (6300 hp) at ?? mph.
Train Brakes: Air.
Brake Force: 45 t.
Weight: 84 t.
Design Speed: 140 mph.
Train Supply: Electric, index 95.
Dimensions: 19.41 x 2.74 m.
Wheel Diameter: 1000 mm.
Maximum Speed: 125 mph.
Route Availability: 7.
Total: 31.

Locomotives were originally numbered in the 910xx series, but were renumbered upon completion of overhauls at Bombardier, Doncaster by the addition of 100 to their original number. The exception to this rule was 91023 which was renumbered 91132.

91114 has been fitted with a second pantograph for evaluation purposes.

Advertising liveries:

91101 Flying Scotsman (red, white & purple).
91110 Battle of Britain (black and grey).
91111 For the fallen (various with poppy and Union Jack vinyls).

91101	**AL**	E	IECA	BN	FLYING SCOTSMAN
91102	**VE**	E	IECA	BN	City of York
91103	**VE**	E	SAXL	BN (S)	
91104	**VE**	E	IECA	BN	
91105	**VE**	E	IECA	BN	

91106	**VE**	E	IECA	BN	
91107	**VE**	E	IECA	BN	SKYFALL
91108	**VE**	E	SAXL	ZB (S)	
91109	**VE**	E	IECA	BN	Sir Bobby Robson
91110	**AL**	E	IECA	BN	BATTLE OF BRITAIN MEMORIAL FLIGHT
91111	**AL**	E	IECA	BN	For the Fallen
91112	**VE**	E	IECA	BN	
91113	**VE**	E	IECA	BN	
91114	**VE**	E	IECA	BN	Durham Cathedral
91115	**VE**	E	IECA	BN	Blaydon Races
91116	**VE**	E	IECA	BN	
91117	**EX**	EP	EPEX	LR (S)	
91118	**VE**	E	IECA	BN	The Fusiliers
91119	**IC**	E	IECA	BN	Bounds Green INTERCITY Depot 1977–2017
91120	**EX**	EP	EPEX	LR (S)	
91121	**VE**	E	IECA	BN	
91122	**VE**	E	IECA	BN	
91124	**VE**	E	IECA	BN	
91125	**VE**	E	IECA	BN	
91126	**VE**	E	IECA	BN	Darlington Hippodrome
91127	**VE**	E	IECA	BN	
91128	**VE**	E	IECA	BN	INTERCITY 50
91129	**VE**	E	IECA	BN	
91130	**VE**	E	IECA	BN	Lord Mayor of Newcastle
91131	**VE**	E	IECA	BN	
91132	**VE**	E	IECA	BN	

CLASS 92 BRUSH Co-Co

Built: 1993–96 by Brush Traction at Loughborough.
Electric Supply System: 25 kV AC 50 Hz overhead or 750 V DC third rail.
Traction Motors: Asea Brown Boveri design. Model 6FRA 7059B (Asynchronous 3-phase induction motors).
Maximum Tractive Effort: 400 kN (90 000 lbf).
Continuous Rating: 5040 kW (6760 hp) on AC, 4000 kW (5360 hp) on DC.
Maximum Rail Power:
Train Brakes: Air.
Brake Force: 63 t.
Dimensions: 21.34 x 2.67 m.
Weight: 126 t.
Wheel Diameter: 1070 mm.
Design Speed: 140 km/h (87 mph).
Maximum Speed: 140 km/h (87 mph).
Train Supply: Electric, index 180 (AC), 108 (DC).
Route Availability: 7.
Total: 33.

* Fitted with TVM430 signalling equipment to operate on High Speed 1.

Class 92s exported for use abroad are listed in section 1.6 of this book.

Advertising livery: 92017 Stobart Rail (two-tone blue & white).

92004		**EG**	DB	WQBA	CE (S)	Jane Austen
92006	d	**CA**	GB	GBSL	WB	
92007		**EG**	DB	WQBA	CE (S)	Schubert
92008		**EG**	DB	WQBA	CE (S)	Jules Verne
92009	*	**DB**	DB	WQBA	CE (S)	Marco Polo
92010	*d	**CA**	GB	GBST	WB	
92011	*	**EG**	DB	WFBC	CE	Handel
92013		**EG**	DB	WQBA	CE (S)	Puccini
92014	d	**CA**	GB	GBSL	WB	
92015	*	**DB**	DB	WFBC	CE	
92016	*	**DB**	DB	WQBA	CE (S)	
92017		**AL**	DB	WQBA	CE (S)	Bart the Engine
92018	*d	**CA**	GB	GBST	WB	
92019	*	**EG**	DB	WFBC	CE	Wagner
92020	d	**GB**	GB	GBSL	WB	
92021		**EP**	GB	GBSD	LB (S)	Purcell
92023	*d	**CA**	GB	GBSL	WB	
92028	d	**GB**	GB	GBST	WB	
92029		**EG**	DB	WQAB	CE (S)	Dante
92031	*	**DB**	DB	WQBA	CE (S)	
92032	*d	**GB**	GB	GBST	WB	IMechE Railway Division
92033	d	**CA**	GB	GBSL	WB	
92035		**EG**	DB	WQBA	CE (S)	Mendelssohn
92036	*	**EG**	DB	WFBC	CE	Bertolt Brecht
92037		**EG**	DB	WQBA	CE (S)	Sullivan
92038	*d	**CA**	GB	GBST	WB	
92040		**EP**	GB	GBSD	LB (S)	Goethe
92041	*	**EG**	DB	WFBC	CE	Vaughan Williams
92042	*	**DB**	DB	WFBC	CE	
92043	*d	**GB**	GB	GBST	WB	
92044	*	**EP**	GB	GBST	WB	Couperin
92045		**EP**	GB	GBSD	LB (S)	Chaucer
92046		**EP**	GB	GBSD	LB (S)	Sweelinck

1.4. EUROTUNNEL LOCOMOTIVES

DIESEL LOCOMOTIVES

0001–10 are registered on TOPS as 21901–910.

0001–0005 Krupp MaK Bo-Bo

Channel Tunnel maintenance and rescue train locomotives.
Built: 1991–92 by MaK at Kiel, Germany (Model DE 1004).
Engine: MTU 12V396 TC 13 of 950 kW (1275 hp) at 1800 rpm.
Main Alternator: ABB. **Traction Motors:** ABB.
Maximum Tractive Effort: 305 kN (68600 lbf).
Continuous Tractive Effort: 140 kN (31500 lbf) at 20 mph.
Power At Rail: 750 kW (1012 hp). **Dimensions:** 14.40 x ?? m.
Brake Force: 120 kN. **Wheel Diameter:** 1000 mm.
Train Brakes: Air. **Weight:** 90 t.
Maximum Speed: 100 km/h. **Design Speed:** 120 km/h.
Fuel Capacity: 3500 litres. **Multiple Working:** Within class.
Train Supply: Not equipped. **Signalling System:** TVM430 cab signalling.

0001	**GY**	ET	CT
0002	**GY**	ET	CT
0003	**GY**	ET	CT
0004	**GY**	ET	CT
0005	**GY**	ET	CT

0006–0010 Krupp MaK Bo-Bo

Channel Tunnel maintenance and rescue locomotives. Rebuilt from Netherlands Railways/DB Cargo Nederland Class 6400. 0006/07 were added to the ET fleet in 2011, and 0008–10 in 2016. 0010 is used for shunting at Coquelles.

Built: 1990–91 by MaK at Kiel, Germany (Model DE 6400).
Engine: MTU 12V396 TC 13 of 1180 kW (1580 hp) at 1800 rpm.
Main Alternator: ABB. **Traction Motors:** ABB.
Maximum Tractive Effort: 290 kN (65200 lbf).
Continuous Tractive Effort: 140 kN (31500 lbf) at 20 mph.
Power At Rail: 750 kW (1012 hp). **Dimensions:** 14.40 x ?? m.
Brake Force: 120 kN. **Wheel Diameter:** 1000 mm.
Train Brakes: Air. **Weight:** 80 t.
Maximum Speed: 120 km/h. **Design Speed:** 120 km/h.
Fuel Capacity: 2900 litres. **Multiple Working:** Within class.
Train Supply: Not equipped.

Not fitted with TVM 430 cab signalling so have to operate with another locomotive/s when used on HS1.

0006	(6456)	**GY**	ET	CT
0007	(6457)	**GY**	ET	CT
0008	(6450)	**GY**	ET	CT
0009	(6451)	**GY**	ET	CT
0010	(6447)	**EB**	ET	CO

0031–0042 HUNSLET/SCHÖMA 0-4-0

Built: 1989–90 by Hunslet Engine Company at Leeds as 900 mm gauge.
Rebuilt: 1993–94 by Schöma in Germany to 1435 mm gauge as Type CFL 200 DCL-R.
Engine: Deutz F10L 413 FW of 170 kW (230 hp) at 2300 rpm.
Transmission: Mechanical Clark 5421-179 type.
Maximum Tractive Effort: 68 kN (15300 lbf).
Continuous Tractive Effort: 47 kN (10570 lbf) at 5 mph.
Power At Rail: 130.1 kW (175 hp).
Brake Force:
Weight: 25 t. (* 28 t.)
Maximum Speed: 48 km/h (* 75 km/h).
Fuel Capacity: 450 litres.
Train Supply: Not equipped.
Dimensions: 7.87 (* 10.94) x 2.69 m.
Wheel Diameter: 1010 mm.
Train Brakes: Air.
Multiple Working: Not equipped.

* Rebuilt with inspection platforms to check overhead catenary (Type CS 200).

0031		**GY**	ET	CT	FRANCES
0032		**GY**	ET	CT	ELISABETH
0033		**GY**	ET	CT	SILKE
0034		**GY**	ET	CT	AMANDA
0035		**GY**	ET	CT	MARY
0036		**GY**	ET	CT	LAURENCE
0037		**GY**	ET	CT	LYDIE
0038		**GY**	ET	CT	JENNY
0039	*	**GY**	ET	CT	PACITA
0040		**GY**	ET	CT	JILL
0041	*	**GY**	ET	CT	KIM
0042		**GY**	ET	CT	NICOLE

ELECTRIC LOCOMOTIVES

9005–9840 BRUSH/ABB Bo-Bo-Bo

Built: 1993–2002 by Brush Traction, Loughborough.
Electric Supply System: 25 kV AC 50 Hz overhead.
Traction Motors: Asea Brown Boveri design. Asynchronous 3-phase motors. Model 6FHA 7059 (as built). Model 6FHA 7059C (7000 kW rated locos).
Maximum Tractive Effort: 400kN (90 000 lbf).
Continuous Rating: Class 9/0: 5760 kW (7725 hp). Class 9/7 and 9/8: 7000 kW (9387 hp).
Maximum Rail Power:
Brake Force: 50 t.
Weight: 136 t.
Maximum Speed: 140 km/h.
Train Supply: Electric.
Multiple Working: TDM system.
Dimensions: 22.01 x 2.97 x 4.20 m.
Wheel Diameter: 1250 mm.
Design Speed: 140 km/h.
Train Brakes: Air.

Class 9/0 Original build locos. Built 1993–94.

9005	**EB**	ET	CO	JESSYE NORMAN

9007	**EB**	ET	CO	DAME JOAN SUTHERLAND[1]
9011	**EB**	ET	CO	JOSÉ VAN DAM[1]
9013	**EB**	ET	CO	MARIA CALLAS[1]
9015	**EB**	ET	CO	LÖTSCHBERG 1913[1]
9018	**EB**	ET	CO	WILHELMENIA FERNANDEZ
9022	**EB**	ET	CO	DAME JANET BAKER
9024	**EB**	ET	CO	GOTTHARD 1882
9026	**EB**	ET	CO	FURKATUNNEL 1982
9029	**EB**	ET	CO	THOMAS ALLEN
9033	**EB**	ET	CO	MONTSERRAT CABALLE
9036	**EB**	ET	CO	ALAIN FONDARY[1]
9037	**EB**	ET	CO	

Class 9/7. Increased power freight shuttle locos. Built 2001–02 (9711–23 built 1998–2001 as 9101–13 and rebuilt as 9711–23 2010–12).

9701	**EB**	ET	CO
9702	**EB**	ET	CO
9703	**EB**	ET	CO
9704	**EB**	ET	CO
9705	**EB**	ET	CO
9706	**EB**	ET	CO
9707	**EB**	ET	CO

9711	(9101)	**EB**	ET	CO
9712	(9102)	**EB**	ET	CO
9713	(9103)	**EB**	ET	CO
9714	(9104)	**EB**	ET	CO
9715	(9105)	**EB**	ET	CO
9716	(9106)	**EB**	ET	CO
9717	(9107)	**EB**	ET	CO
9718	(9108)	**EB**	ET	CO
9719	(9109)	**EB**	ET	CO
9720	(9110)	**EB**	ET	CO
9721	(9111)	**EB**	ET	CO
9722	(9112)	**EB**	ET	CO
9723	(9113)	**EB**	ET	CO

Class 9/8 Locos rebuilt from Class 9/0 by adding 800 to the loco number. Uprated to 7000 kW.

90xx and 98xx locomotives have a cab in the blunt end for shunting, except 9840 which does not have this feature.

9801	**EB**	ET	CO	LESLEY GARRETT
9802	**EB**	ET	CO	STUART BURROWS
9803	**EB**	ET	CO	BENJAMIN LUXON
9804	**EB**	ET	CO	
9806	**EB**	ET	CO	REGINE CRESPIN
9808	**EB**	ET	CO	ELISABETH SODERSTROM
9809	**EB**	ET	CO	
9810	**EB**	ET	CO	
9812	**EB**	ET	CO	
9814	**EB**	ET	CO	LUCIA POPP

9816	**EB**	ET	CO	
9819	**EB**	ET	CO	MARIA EWING[1]
9820	**EB**	ET	CO	NICOLAI GHIAROV
9821	**EB**	ET	CO	
9823	**EB**	ET	CO	DAME ELISABETH LEGGE-SCHWARZKOPF
9825	**EB**	ET	CO	
9827	**EB**	ET	CO	BARBARA HENDRICKS
9828	**EB**	ET	CO	
9831	**EB**	ET	CO	
9832	**EB**	ET	CO	RENATA TEBALDI
9834	**EB**	ET	CO	MIRELLA FRENI
9835	**EB**	ET	CO	NICOLAI GEDDA
9838	**EB**	ET	CO	HILDEGARD BEHRENS
9840	**EB**	ET	CO	

[1] nameplates carried on one side only.

1.5. LOCOMOTIVES AWAITING DISPOSAL

Locomotives that are still extant but best classed as awaiting disposal are listed here.

66048 EMD, Longport Works

1.6. LOCOMOTIVES EXPORTED FOR USE ABROAD

This section details former British Railways (plus privatisation era) diesel and electric locomotives that have been exported from Great Britain for use in industrial locations or with a main line operator abroad. Not included are locos that are classed as "preserved" abroad. These are included in the Platform 5 "Preserved Locomotives of British Railways" publication.

(S) denotes locomotives that are stored.

Number	*Other no./name*	*Location*
Class 03		
03156		Ferramenta Pugliese, Terlizzi, Bari, Italy
Class 47		
47375	92 70 00 47375-5	Continental Railway Solution, Hungary
Class 56		
56101	92 55 0659 001-5	FLOYD, Hungary
56115	92 55 0659 002-3	FLOYD, Hungary
56117	92 55 0659 003-1	FLOYD, Hungary (S) Budapest Keleti
Class 58		
58001		DB, France, (S) Alizay
58004		DB, France, (S) Alizay
58005		DB, France, (S) Alizay
58006		DB, France, (S) Alizay
58007		DB, France, (S) Alizay
58009		DB, France, (S) Alizay
58010		DB, France, (S) Alizay
58011		DB, France, (S) Alizay
58013		DB, France, (S) Alizay
58015	L54	Transfesa, Spain, Monforte del Cid, Alicante
58018		DB, France, (S) Alizay
58020	L43	Transfesa, Spain, Monforte del Cid, Alicante
58021		DB, France, (S) Alizay
58024	L42	Transfesa, Spain, Monforte del Cid, Alicante
58025		DB, Spain, (S) Albacete
58026		DB, France, (S) Alizay
58027	L52	DB, Spain, (S) Albacete
58029	L44	Transfesa, Spain, (S) Monforte del Cid, Alicante
58030	L46	Transfesa, Spain, Monforte del Cid, Alicante
58031	L45	Transfesa, Spain, Monforte del Cid, Alicante
58032		DB, France, (S) Alizay
58033		DB, France, (S) Alizay
58034		DB, France, (S) Alizay
58035		DB, France, (S) Alizay
58036		DB, France, (S) Alizay

58038		DB, France, (S) Alizay
58039		DB, France, (S) Alizay
58040		DB, France, (S) Alizay
58041	L36	Transfesa, Spain, (S) Albacete
58042		DB, France, (S) Alizay
58043	L37	Transfesa, Spain, Monforte del Cid, Alicante
58044		DB, France, (S) Woippy, Metz
58046		DB, France, (S) Alizay
58047	L51	Transfesa, Spain, Monforte del Cid, Alicante
58049		DB, France, (S) Alizay
58050	L53	DB, Spain, (S) Albacete

Class 66

66010	ECR, France
66022	ECR, France
66026	ECR, France
66028	ECR, France
66029	ECR, France
66032	ECR, France
66033	ECR, France
66036	ECR, France
66038	ECR, France
66042	ECR, France
66045	ECR, France
66049	ECR, France
66052	ECR, France
66062	ECR, France
66064	ECR, France
66071	ECR, France
66072	ECR, France
66073	ECR, France
66123	ECR, France
66146	DBC, Poland
66153	DBC, Poland
66157	DBC, Poland
66159	DBC, Poland
66163	DBC, Poland
66166	DBC, Poland
66173	DBC, Poland
66178	DBC, Poland
66179	ECR, France
66180	DBC, Poland
66189	DBC, Poland
66190	ECR, France
66191	ECR, France
66193	ECR, France
66195	ECR, France
66196	DBC, Poland
66201	ECR, France
66202	ECR, France
66203	ECR, France
66204	ECR, France
66205	ECR, France
66208	ECR, France
66209	ECR, France
66210	ECR, France
66211	ECR, France
66212	ECR, France
66213	ECR, France
66214	ECR, France
66215	ECR, France
66216	ECR, France
66217	ECR, France
66218	ECR, France
66219	ECR, France
66220	DBC, Poland
66222	ECR, France
66223	ECR, France
66224	ECR, France
66225	ECR, France
66226	ECR, France
66227	DBC, Poland
66228	ECR, France
66229	ECR, France
66231	ECR, France
66232	ECR, France
66233	ECR, France
66234	ECR, France

66235		ECR, France
66236		ECR, France
66237		DBC, Poland
66239		ECR, France
66240		ECR, France
66241		ECR, France
66242		ECR, France
66243		ECR, France
66244		ECR, France
66245		ECR, France
66246		ECR, France
66247		ECR, France
66248		DBC, Poland
66249		ECR, France
66411	66013	FL, Poland
66412	66015	FL, Poland
66417	66014	FL, Poland
66527	66016	FL, Poland
66530	66017	FL, Poland
66535	66018	FL, Poland
66582	66009	FL, Poland
66583	66010	FL, Poland
66584	66011	FL, Poland
66586	66008	FL, Poland
66595		FL, Poland
66608	66603	FL, Poland
66609	66605	FL, Poland
66611	66604	FL, Poland
66612	66606	FL, Poland
66624	66602	FL, Poland
66625	66601	FL, Poland
66954		FL, Poland

Class 86

86213	91 52 00 87703-2	Lancashire Witch	Bulmarket, Bulgaria
86215	91 55 0450 005-8		FLOYD, Hungary
86217	91 55 0450 006-6		FLOYD, Hungary

86218	91 55 0450 004-1		FLOYD, Hungary
86228	91 55 0450 007-4		FLOYD, Hungary
86231	91 52 00 85005-4	Lady of the Lake	Bulmarket, Bulgaria
86232	91 55 0450 003-3		FLOYD, Hungary
86233			Bulmarket, Bulgaria (S) Ruse
86234			Bulmarket, Bulgaria
86235	91 52 00 87704-0	Novelty	Bulmarket, Bulgaria
86242	91 55 0450 008-2		FLOYD, Hungary
86248	91 55 0450 001-7		FLOYD, Hungary
86250	91 55 0450 002-5		FLOYD, Hungary
86424	91 55 0450 009-0		FLOYD, Hungary (S) Budapest
86701	91 52 00 87701-6	Orion	Bulmarket, Bulgaria
86702	91 52 00 87702-4	Cassiopeia	Bulmarket, Bulgaria

Class 87

87003	91 52 00 87003-7		BZK, Bulgaria
87004	91 52 00 87004-5	Britannia	BZK, Bulgaria
87006	91 52 00 87006-0		BZK, Bulgaria
87007	91 52 00 87007-8		BZK, Bulgaria
87008	87008-9		BZK, Bulgaria (S) Ruse
87009	91 52 00 87009-4		Bulmarket, Bulgaria
87010	91 52 00 87010-2		BZK, Bulgaria
87012	91 52 00 87012-8		BZK, Bulgaria
87013	91 52 00 87013-6		BZK, Bulgaria
87014	87014-7		BZK, Bulgaria (S) Sofia
87017	91 52 00 87017-7	Iron Duke	Bulmarket, Bulgaria
87019	91 52 00 87019-3		BZK, Bulgaria
87020	91 52 00 87020-1		BZK, Bulgaria
87022	91 52 00 87022-7		BZK, Bulgaria
87023	91 52 00 87023-5	Velocity	Bulmarket, Bulgaria
87025	91 52 00 87025-0		Bulmarket, Bulgaria
87026	91 52 00 87026-8		BZK, Bulgaria
87028	91 52 00 87028-4		BZK, Bulgaria
87029	91 52 00 87029-2		BZK, Bulgaria
87033	91 52 00 87033-4		BZK, Bulgaria
87034	91 52 00 87034-2		BZK, Bulgaria

Class 92

92001	91 53 0 472 002-1	Mircea Eliade	Transagent Rail, Croatia
92002	91 53 0 472 003-9	Lucian Blaga	Transagent Rail, Croatia
92003		Beethoven	DB Cargo, Romania (S)
92005	91 53 0 472-005-4		Transagent Rail, Croatia
92012	91 53 0 472 001-3	Mihai Eminescu	Transagent Rail, Croatia
92022		Charles Dickens	DB Cargo, Bulgaria (S) Aurubis
92024	91 53 0 472 004-7	Marin Preda	Transagent Rail, Croatia
92025	91 52 1 688 025-1	Oscar Wilde	DB Cargo, Bulgaria
92026		Britten	DB Cargo, Romania
92027	91 52 1 688 027-7	George Eliot	DB Cargo, Bulgaria
92030	91 52 1 688 030-1	Ashford	DB Cargo, Bulgaria
92034	91 52 1 688 034-3	Kipling	DB Cargo, Bulgaria
92039	91 53 0 472 006-2	Eugen Ionescu	DB Cargo, Romania

2. LOCO-HAULED COACHING STOCK

INTRODUCTION

This section contains details of all locomotive-hauled or propelled coaching stock, often referred to as carriages, which can run on Britain's national railway network.

The number of locomotive-hauled or propelled carriages in use on the national railway network is much fewer than was once the case. Those that remain fall into two distinct groups.

Firstly, there are those used by franchised and open access operators for regular timetabled services. Most of these are formed in fixed or semi-fixed formations with either locomotives or a locomotive and Driving Brake Carriage at either end which allows for push-pull operation. There are also a small number of mainly overnight and peak-hour trains with variable formations that use conventional locomotive haulage.

Secondly there are those used for what can best be described as excursion trains. These include a wide range of carriage types ranging from luxurious saloons to those more suited to the "bucket and spade" seaside type of excursion. These are formed into sets to suit the requirements of the day. From time to time some see limited use with franchised and open access operators to cover for stock shortages and times of exceptional demand such as major sporting events.

In addition, there remain a small number of carriages referred to as "Service Stock" which are used internally within the railway industry and are not used to convey passengers.

FRANCHISED & OPEN ACCESS OPERATORS

For each operator regularly using locomotive-hauled carriages brief details are given here of the sphere of operation. For details of operators using HSTs see Section 2.2.

Caledonian Sleeper
This franchise, operated by Serco, started in 2015 when the Anglo-Scottish Sleeper operation was split from the ScotRail franchise. Caledonian Sleeper comprises seating and sleeping car services between London Euston and Scotland using sets of new CAF Mark 5 Sleeping Cars and seated carriages.

GBRf is contracted to supply the motive power for the Sleepers. Class 92s are used between London Euston and Edinburgh/Glasgow Central and rebuilt Class 73/9s between Edinburgh and Inverness, Aberdeen and Fort William.

Chiltern Railways
Chiltern operates four sets of Mark 3 carriages hauled by DRS Class 68 locomotives on its Mainline services between London Marylebone and Birmingham Moor Street/Kidderminster (plus one train to Oxford). Another set, that has not been refurbished with sliding doors, is used on a peak-hour commuter service between Marylebone and Bicester North or Banbury. All trains operate as push-pull sets.

Greater Anglia
The Inter-City service between London Liverpool Street and Norwich is operated using 11 sets of Mark 3 carriages with Class 90 locomotives in push-pull formations. These sets are currently being replaced by Class 745 EMUs, with that process due to be complete by April 2020.

Great Western Railway
The "Night Riviera" seating and sleeping car service between London Paddington and Penzance uses sets of Mark 3 carriages hauled by Class 57/6 locomotives.

London North Eastern Railway
At the start of 2020 LNER operates 23 sets of Mark 4 carriages with Class 91 locomotives in push-pull formations on its Inter-City services between London King's Cross and Yorkshire, North-East England and Scotland. These trains are currently being replaced by new Class 800/801 "Azuma" units, with that process due to be complete by summer 2020.

North Yorkshire Moors Railway
In addition to operating the North Yorkshire Moors Railway between Pickering and Grosmont the company operates through services to Whitby and occasionally Battersby. A fleet of Mark 1 passenger carriages and Pullman Cars are used for these services. It also operates the "North Norfolkman" services on behalf of the North Norfolk Railway between Sheringham and Cromer.

ScotRail
ScotRail operates two sets of Mark 2 carriages supplied by DRS on peak-hour services between Edinburgh and Fife using Class 68s.

Transport for Wales
The Monday–Friday Welsh Government sponsored train between Cardiff and Holyhead uses Mark 3 carriages in push-pull mode with a Class 67. A second similarly formed set is used for weekday trains between Crewe or Manchester and Chester/North Wales. These carriages are also used for relief trains, particularly in connection with sports fixtures at Cardiff and busy ferry sailings to and from Holyhead. The Mark 3s are due to be replaced by Mark 4s during the first half of 2020, with further turns introduced between Manchester and Holyhead, and the Manchester train becoming DMU operated.

West Coast Railway Company
WCRC operates two sets of Mark 1/2 carriages on its steam-hauled "Jacobite" trains between Fort William and Mallaig. These trains normally operate between late April and late October.

EXCURSION TRAIN OPERATORS

Usually, three types of companies will be involved in the operation of an excursion train. There will be the promoter, the rolling stock provider and the train operator. In many cases two or more of these roles may be undertaken by the same or associated companies. Only a small number of Train Operating Companies facilitate the operation of excursion trains. This takes various forms ranging from the complete package of providing and operating the train, through offering a "hook up and haul" service, to operating the train for a third party rolling stock custodian.

DB Cargo UK
DBC currently operates its own luxurious train of Mark 3 carriages, called the Company Train. It also offers a hook up and haul service and regularly operates the Royal Train and the Belmond British Pullman as well as trains for Riviera Trains and Locomotives Services and their client promoters.

Direct Rail Services
DRS operates a fleet of Mark 2 carriages originally intended for use on excursion trains. These are currently hired to ScotRail for use on regular timetabled services. The company also offers a hook up and haul service for Riviera Trains and its client promoters.

GB Railfreight
GBRf initially operated excursion trains using the preserved Class 201 "Hastings" DEMU. It now also operates a small number of company excursions using hired carriages. The company also offers a hook up and haul service operating the Royal Scotsman luxury train, as well as trains for Riviera Trains and its client promoters.

Locomotive Services
This vertically integrated company gained a license in 2017. From its base at Crewe excursion trains are operated using its fleet of steam and diesel locomotives and Mark 1/2 carriages.

Rail Operations Group
This company operates a small number of excursion trains using hired in carriages. It also offers a hook up and haul service.

Vintage Trains
This vertically integrated company gained a licence in September 2018. From its base at Tyseley it operates the "Shakespeare Express" steam service between Birmingham and Stratford-upon-Avon. It also operates excursions using its fleet of steam and diesel locomotives and Mark 1/2 carriages and Pullman cars.

West Coast Railway Company
This vertically integrated company has its own fleet of steam and diesel locomotives as well as a full range of different carriage types. It operates its own regular trains, including the luxury Northern Belle, the "Jacobite" steam service between Fort William and Mallaig, the "Dalesman" steam and diesel services over the Settle & Carlisle route and numerous excursion trains for itself and client promoters. In addition, it offers a hook up and haul service operating trains for The Princess Royal Locomotive Trust, Locomotives Services and the Scottish Railway Preservation Society.

LAYOUT OF INFORMATION

Carriages are listed in numerical order of painted number in batches according to type.

Where a carriage has been renumbered, the former number is shown in parentheses. If a carriage has been renumbered more than once, the original number is shown first in parentheses, followed by the most recent previous number.

Each carriage entry is laid out as in the following example (previous number(s) column may be omitted where not applicable):

No.	*Prev. No.*	*Notes*	*Livery*	*Owner*	*Operator*	*Depot/Location*
82301	(82117)	g	**CM**	AV	*CR*	AL

Codes: Codes are used to denote the livery, owner, operator and depot/ location of each carriage. Details of codes used can be found in Section 6 of this book.

The owner is the responsible custodian of the carriage and this may not always be the legal owner. Actual ownership can be very complicated. Some vehicles are owned by finance/leasing companies. Others are owned by subsidiary companies of a holding company or by an associate company of the responsible custodian or operator.

The operator is the organisation which facilitates the use of the carriage and may not be the actual train operating company which runs the train. If no operator is shown the carriage is considered to be not in use.

The depot is the facility primarily responsible for the carriages maintenance. Light maintenance and heavy overhauls may be carried out elsewhere.

The location is where carriages not in use are currently being kept or are stored.

GENERAL INFORMATION

CLASSIFICATION AND NUMBERING

Seven different numbering systems were in use on British Rail. These were the British Rail series, the four pre-nationalisation companies' series', the Pullman Car Company's series and the UIC (International Union of Railways) series. In this book BR number series carriages and former Pullman Car Company series are listed separately. There is also a separate listing of "Saloon" type carriages, that includes pre-nationalisation survivors, which are permitted to run on the national railway system, Locomotive Support Carriages and Service Stock. Please note the Mark 2 Pullman carriages were ordered after the Pullman Car Company had been nationalised and are therefore numbered in the British Rail series. The new CAF Mark 5 carriages have been allocated numbers in the British Rail series.

Also listed separately are the British Rail and Pullman Car Company number series carriages used on North Yorkshire Moors Railway and North Norfolk Railway services on the national railway network. This is due to their very restricted sphere of operation.

The BR number series grouped carriages of a particular type together in chronological order. Major modifications affecting type of accommodation resulted in renumbering into a more appropriate or new number series. Since privatisation such renumbering has not always taken place resulting in renumbering which has been more haphazard and greater variations within numbering groups.

With the introduction of the TOPS numbering system, coaching stock (including multiple unit vehicles) retained their original BR number unless this conflicted with a locomotive number. Carriages can be one–five digits, although no one or two-digit examples remain in use on the national network. BR generally numbered "Service Stock" in a six-digit wagon number series.

UNITS OF MEASUREMENT

All dimensions and weights are quoted for carriages in an "as new" condition or after a major modification, such as fitting with new bogies etc. Dimensions are quoted in the order length x width. Lengths quoted are over buffers or couplers as appropriate. All widths quoted are maxima. All weights are shown as metric tonnes (t = tonnes).

DIMENSIONS

Carriage lengths are summarised as follows:

Mark 1: 19.35 m or 17.37 m.
Mark 2: 19.66 m.
Mark 3: 23.00 m.
Mark 3 HST: 23.00 m.
Mark 4: 23.00 m.
Mark 5: 22.20 m.
Mark 5A: 22.20–22.37 m.

DETAILED INFORMATION & CODES

Under each type heading, the following details are shown:

- "Mark" of carriage (see below).
- Descriptive text.
- Number of First Class seats, Standard Class seats, lavatory compartments and wheelchair spaces shown as F/S nT nW respectively. A number in brackets indicates tip-up seats (in addition to the regular seats).
- Bogie type (see below).
- Additional features.
- ETS Index.
- Weight: All weights are shown as metric tonnes.

BOGIE TYPES

Gresley. LNER design of bogie first used in the "Gresley" era. Used by BR on some Mark 1 catering carriages. Now used for some saloons.

BR Mark 1 (BR1). Double bolster leaf spring bogie. Generally 90 mph, but Mark 1 bogies may be permitted to run at 100 mph with special maintenance. Weight: 6.1 t.

BR Mark 2 (BR2). Single bolster leaf-spring bogie used on certain types of non-passenger stock and suburban stock (all now withdrawn). Weight: 5.3 t.

COMMONWEALTH (C). Heavy, cast steel coil spring bogie. 100 mph. Weight: 6.75t.

B4. Coil spring fabricated bogie. Generally 100 mph, but B4 bogies may be permitted to run at 110 mph with special maintenance. Weight: 5.2 t.

B5. Heavy duty version of B4. 100 mph. Weight: 5.3 t.

B5 (SR). A bogie originally used on Southern Region EMUs, similar in design to B5. Now also used on locomotive-hauled carriages. 100 mph.

BT10. A fabricated bogie designed for 125 mph. Air suspension.

T4. A 125 mph bogie designed by BREL (now Bombardier Transportation).

BT41. Fitted to Mark 4 carriages, designed by SIG in Switzerland. At present limited to 125 mph, but designed for 140 mph.

CAF. Fitted to CAF Mark 5 and Mark 5A carriages.

BRAKES

Air braking is now standard on British main line trains. Carriages with other equipment are denoted:

b Air braked, through vacuum pipe.
v Vacuum braked.
x Dual braked (air and vacuum).

HEATING & VENTILATION

Electric heating and ventilation is now standard on British main-line trains. Certain carriages for use on excursion services may also have steam heating facilities, or be steam heated only. All carriages used on North Yorkshire Moors Railway and North Norfolk Railway trains have steam heating.

NOTES ON ELECTRIC TRAIN SUPPLY

The sum of ETS indices in a train must not be more than the ETS index of the locomotive or generator van. The normal voltage on British trains is 1000 V. Suffix "X" denotes 600 amp wiring instead of 400 amp. Trains whose ETS index is higher than 66 must be formed completely of 600 amp wired stock. Class 33 and 73/1 locomotives cannot provide a suitable electric train supply for Mark 2D, Mark 2E, Mark 2F, Mark 3, Mark 3A, Mark 3B or Mark 4 carriages. Class 55 locomotives provide an ETS directly from one of their traction generators into the train line. Consequently voltage fluctuations can result in motor-alternator flashover. Thus these locomotives are not suitable for use with Mark 2D, Mark 2E, Mark 2F, Mark 3, Mark 3A, Mark 3B or Mark 4 carriages unless modified motor-alternators are fitted. Such motor alternators were fitted to Mark 2D and 2F carriages used on the East Coast Main Line, but few remain fitted.

PUBLIC ADDRESS

It is assumed all carriages are now fitted with public address equipment, although certain stored carriages may not have this feature. In addition, it is assumed all carriages with a conductor's compartment have public address transmission facilities, as have catering carriages.

COOKING EQUIPMENT

It is assumed that Mark 1 catering carriages have gas powered cooking equipment, whilst Mark 2, 3 and 4 catering carriages have electric powered cooking equipment unless stated otherwise.

ADDITIONAL FEATURE CODES

d	Central Door Locking.
dg	Driver–Guard communication equipment.
f	Facelifted or fluorescent lighting.
h	"High density" seating
k	Composition brake blocks (instead of cast iron).
n	Day/night lighting.
pg	Public address transmission and driver-guard communication.
pt	Public address transmission facility.
q	Catering staff to shore telephone.
w	Wheelchair space.

BUILD DETAILS

Lot Numbers

Carriages ordered under the auspices of BR were allocated a lot (batch) number when ordered and these are quoted in class headings and sub-headings.

Builders

These are shown for each lot. More details and a full list of builders can be found in section 6.7.

Information on sub-contracting works which built parts of carriages eg the underframes etc is not shown.

In addition to the above, certain vintage Pullman cars were built or rebuilt at the following works:

Metropolitan Carriage & Wagon Company, Birmingham (later Alstom).
Midland Carriage & Wagon Company, Birmingham.
Pullman Car Company, Preston Park, Brighton.
Conversions have also been carried out at the Railway Technical Centre, Derby, LNWR Crewe and Blakes Fabrications, Edinburgh.

THE DEVELOPMENT OF BR STANDARD COACHES

Mark 1

The standard BR coach built from 1951 to 1963 was the Mark 1. This type features a separate underframe and body. The underframe is normally 64 ft 6 in long, but certain vehicles were built on shorter (57 ft) frames. Tungsten lighting was standard and until 1961, BR Mark 1 bogies were generally provided. In 1959 Lot No. 30525 (Open Standard) appeared with fluorescent lighting and melamine interior panels, and from 1961 onwards Commonwealth bogies were fitted in an attempt to improve the quality of ride which became very poor when the tyre profiles on the wheels of the BR1 bogies became worn. Later batches of Open Standard and Open Brake Standard retained the features of Lot No. 30525, but compartment vehicles – whilst utilising melamine panelling in Standard Class – still retained tungsten lighting. Wooden interior finish was retained in First Class vehicles where the only change was to fluorescent lighting in open vehicles (except Lot No. 30648, which had tungsten lighting). In later years many Mark 1 coaches had BR 1 bogies replaced by B4. More recently a small number of carriages have had BR1 bogies replaced with Commonwealth bogies.

XP64

In 1964, a new prototype train was introduced. Known as "XP64", it featured new seat designs, pressure heating & ventilation, aluminium compartment doors and corridor partitions, foot pedal operated toilets and B4 bogies. The vehicles were built on standard Mark 1 underframes. Folding exterior doors were fitted, but these proved troublesome and were later replaced with hinged doors. All XP64 coaches have been withdrawn, but some have been preserved.

Mark 2

The prototype Mark 2 vehicle (W13252) was produced in 1963. This was a Corridor First of semi-integral construction and had pressure heating & ventilation, tungsten lighting, and was mounted on B4 bogies. This vehicle has now been preserved at the Mid Norfolk Railway. The production build was similar, but wider windows were used. The Open Standard vehicles used a new seat design similar to that in the XP64 and fluorescent lighting was provided. Interior finish reverted to wood. Mark 2 vehicles were built from 1964–66.

Mark 2A–2C

The Mark 2A design, built 1967–68, incorporated the remainder of the features first used in the XP64 coaches, ie foot pedal operated toilets (except Open Brake Standard), new First Class seat design, aluminium compartment doors and partitions together with fluorescent lighting in first class compartments. Folding gangway doors (lime green coloured) were used instead of the traditional one-piece variety.

Mark 2B coaches had wide wrap around doors at vehicle ends, no centre doors and a slightly longer body. In Standard Class there was one toilet at each end instead of two at one end as previously. The folding gangway doors were red.

Mark 2C coaches had a lowered ceiling with twin strips of fluorescent lighting and ducting for air conditioning, but air conditioning was never fitted.

Mark 2D–2F

These vehicles were fitted with air conditioning. They had no opening top-lights in saloon windows, which were shallower than previous ones.

Mark 2E vehicles had smaller toilets with luggage racks opposite. The folding gangway doors were fawn coloured.

Mark 2F vehicles had a modified air conditioning system, plastic interior panels and InterCity 70 type seats.

Mark 3

The Mark 3 design has BT10 bogies, is 75 ft (23 m) long and is of fully integral construction with InterCity 70 type seats. Gangway doors were yellow (red in Kitchen Buffet First) when new, although these were changed on refurbishment. Locomotive-hauled coaches are classified Mark 3A, Mark 3 being reserved for HST trailers. A new batch of Open First and Open Brake First, classified Mark 3B, was built in 1985 with Advanced Passenger Train-style seating and revised lighting. The last vehicles in the Mark 3 series were the driving brake vans ("Driving Van Trailers") built for West Coast Main Line services but now used elsewhere.

A number of Mark 3 vehicles have been converted for use as HST trailers with CrossCountry, Grand Central and Great Western Railway.

Mark 4

The Mark 4 design was built by Metro-Cammell for use on the East Coast Main Line after electrification and featured a body profile suitable for tilting trains, although tilt is not fitted, and is not intended to be. This design is suitable for 140 mph running, although is restricted to 125 mph because the signalling system on the route is not suitable for the higher speed. The bogies for these coaches were built by SIG in Switzerland and are designated BT41. Power operated sliding plug exterior doors are standard. All Mark 4s were rebuilt with completely new interiors in 2003–05 for GNER and referred to as "Mallard" stock. These rakes generally run in fixed formations and are now mostly still operated by London North Eastern Railway.

New CAF carriages have recently been introduced by Caledonian Sleeper and TransPennine Express. CAF has designated them "Mark 5" and "Mark 5A" but it should be emphasised that these are not a development of the BR standard coach.

2.1. BRITISH RAILWAYS NUMBER SERIES COACHING STOCK

KITCHEN FIRST

Mark 1. Spent most of its life as a Royal Train vehicle and was numbered 2907 for a time. 24/–. B5 bogies. ETS 2.

Lot No. 30633 Swindon 1961. 41 t.

325	**VN**	WC	*WC*	CS	DUART

PULLMAN KITCHEN

Mark 2. Pressure Ventilated. Built with First Class seating but this has been replaced with a servery area. Gas cooking. 2T. B5 bogies. ETS 6.

Lot No. 30755 Derby 1966. 40 t.

504	**PC**	WC	*WC*	CS	ULLSWATER
506	**PC**	WC	*WC*	CS	WINDERMERE

PULLMAN OPEN FIRST

Mark 2. Pressure Ventilated. 36/– 2T. B4 bogies. ETS 5.

Lot No. 30754 Derby 1966. 35 t.

Non-standard livery: 546 Maroon & beige.

546	**0**	WC		CS	CITY OF MANCHESTER
548	**PC**	WC	*WC*	CS	GRASMERE
549	**PC**	WC	*WC*	CS	BASSENTHWAITE
550	**PC**	WC	*WC*	CS	RYDAL WATER
551	**PC**	WC	*WC*	CS	BUTTERMERE
552	**PC**	WC	*WC*	CS	ENNERDALE WATER
553	**PC**	WC	*WC*	CS	CRUMMOCK WATER

PULLMAN OPEN BRAKE FIRST

Mark 2. Pressure Ventilated. 30/– 2T. B4 bogies. ETS 4.

Lot No. 30753 Derby 1966. 35 t.

586	**PC**	WC	*WC*	CS	DERWENTWATER

BUFFET FIRST

Mark 2F. Air conditioned. Converted 1988–89/91 at BREL, Derby from Mark 2F Open Firsts. 1200/03/11/20/21 have Stones equipment, others have Temperature Ltd. 25/– 1T 1W. B4 bogies. d. ETS 6X.

1200/03/11/20. Lot No. 30845 Derby 1973. 33 t.
1207/10/12/21. Lot No. 30859 Derby 1973–74. 33 t.

1200	(3287, 6459)	**BG**	RV	*RV*	BU	
1203	(3291)	**CC**	LS	*LS*	CL	
1207	(3328, 6422)	**V**	WC		CS	
1210	(3405, 6462)	**FS**	ER		WO	
1211	(3305)	**PC**	LS	*LS*	CL	SNAEFELL
1212	(3427, 6453)	**BG**	RV	*RV*	BU	
1220	(3315, 6432)	**FS**	ER		WO	
1221	(3371)	**IC**	WC		CS	

KITCHEN WITH BAR

Mark 1. Built with no seats but three Pullman-style seats now fitted in bar area. B5 bogies. ETS 1.

Lot No. 30624 Cravens 1960–61. 41 t.

1566	**VN**	WC	*WC*	CS	CAERDYDD

KITCHEN BUFFET UNCLASSIFIED

Mark 1. Built with 23 loose chairs. All remaining vehicles were refurbished with 23 fixed polypropylene chairs and fluorescent lighting. 1683/91 were further refurbished with 21 chairs, wheelchair space and carpets. ETS 2 (* 2X).

Now used on excursion trains with the seating area adapted to various uses including servery and food preparation areas, with some or all seating removed.

1651–91. Lot No. 30628 Pressed Steel 1960–61. Commonwealth bogies. 39 t.
1730. Lot No. 30512 BRCW 1960–61. B5 bogies. 37 t.

1651		**CC**	RV	*RV*	ZG
1657		**BG**	RV	*RV*	BU
1666	x	**M**	RP	*WC*	CS
1671	x*	**CH**	RV	*RV*	ZG
1683		**RB**	RV		BU
1691		**BG**	RV	*RV*	BU
1730	x	**M**	SP	*SP*	BO

BUFFET STANDARD

Mark 1. These carriages are basically an open standard with two full window spaces removed to accommodate a buffet counter, and four seats removed to allow for a stock cupboard. All remaining vehicles now have fluorescent lighting. –/44 2T. Commonwealth bogies. ETS 3.

1861 has had its toilets replaced with store cupboards.

1813–32. Lot No. 30520 Wolverton 1960. 38 t.
1840. Lot No. 30507 Wolverton 1960. 37 t.
1859–63. Lot No. 30670 Wolverton 1961–62. 38 t.
1882. Lot No. 30702 Wolverton 1962. 38 t.

1813	x	**CH**	RV	*RV*	ZG	1860	x	**M**	WC	*WC*	CS
1832	x	**CH**	RV	*RV*	ZG	1861	x	**M**	WC	*WC*	CS
1840	v	**M**	WC	*WC*	CS	1863	x	**CH**	LS		CL
1859	x	**M**	SP	*SP*	BO	1882	x	**M**	WC	*WC*	CS

KITCHEN UNCLASSIFIED

Mark 1. These carriages were built as Unclassified Restaurants. They were rebuilt with buffet counters and 23 fixed polypropylene chairs, then further refurbished by fitting fluorescent lighting. Further modified for use as servery vehicle with seating removed and kitchen extended. ETS 2X.

1953. Lot No. 30575 Swindon 1960. B4/B5 bogies. 36.5 t.
1961. Lot No. 30632 Swindon 1961. Commonwealth bogies. 39 t.

1953		**VN**	WC	*WC*	CS	1961	x	**M**	WC	*WC*	CS

HM THE QUEEN'S SALOON

Mark 3. Converted from an Open First built 1972. Consists of a lounge, bedroom and bathroom for HM The Queen, and a combined bedroom and bathroom for the Queen's dresser. One entrance vestibule has double doors. Air conditioned. BT10 bogies. ETS 9X.

Lot No. 30886 Wolverton 1977. 36 t.

2903 (11001) **RP** NR *RT* ZN

HRH THE DUKE OF EDINBURGH'S SALOON

Mark 3. Converted from an Open Standard built 1972. Consists of a combined lounge/dining room, a bedroom and a shower room for the Duke, a kitchen and a valet's bedroom and bathroom. Air conditioned. BT10 bogies. ETS 15X.

Lot No. 30887 Wolverton 1977. 36 t.

2904 (12001) **RP** NR *RT* ZN

ROYAL HOUSEHOLD SLEEPING CAR

Mark 3A. Built to similar specification as Sleeping Cars 10647–729. 12 sleeping compartments for use of Royal Household with a fixed lower berth and a hinged upper berth. 2T plus shower room. Air conditioned. BT10 bogies. ETS 11X.

Lot No. 31002 Derby/Wolverton 1985. 44 t.

2915		**RP**	NR	*RT*	ZN

HRH THE PRINCE OF WALES'S DINING CAR

Mark 3. Converted from HST TRUK (kitchen car) built 1976. Large kitchen retained, but dining area modified for Royal use seating up to 14 at central table(s). Air conditioned. BT10 bogies. ETS 13X.

Lot No. 31059 Wolverton 1988. 43 t.

2916	(40512)	**RP**	NR	*RT*	ZN

ROYAL KITCHEN/HOUSEHOLD DINING CAR

Mark 3. Converted from HST TRUK built 1977. Large kitchen retained and dining area slightly modified with seating for 22 Royal Household members. Air conditioned. BT10 bogies. ETS 13X.

Lot No. 31084 Wolverton 1990. 43 t.

2917	(40514)	**RP**	NR	*RT*	ZN

ROYAL HOUSEHOLD CARS

Mark 3. Converted from HST TRUKs built 1976/77. Air conditioned. BT10 bogies. ETS 10X.

Lot Nos. 31083 (* 31085) Wolverton 1989. 41.05 t.

2918	(40515)	**RP**	NR		ZN
2919	(40518) *	**RP**	NR		ZN

ROYAL HOUSEHOLD COUCHETTES

Mark 2B. Converted from Corridor Brake First built 1969. Consists of luggage accommodation, guard's compartment, workshop area, 350 kW diesel generator and staff sleeping accommodation. B5 bogies. ETS 2X (when generator not in use). ETS index ?? (when generator in use).

Lot No. 31044 Wolverton 1986. 48 t.

2920	(14109, 17109)	**RP**	NR	*RT*	ZN

Mark 2B. Converted from Corridor Brake First built 1969. Consists of luggage accommodation, kitchen, brake control equipment and staff accommodation. B5 bogies. ETS 7X.

Lot No. 31086 Wolverton 1990. 41.5 t.

2921 (14107, 17107) **RP** NR *RT* ZN

HRH THE PRINCE OF WALES'S SLEEPING CAR

Mark 3B. Air conditioned. BT10 bogies. ETS 7X.

Lot No. 31035 Derby/Wolverton 1987.

2922 **RP** NR *RT* ZN

ROYAL SALOON

Mark 3B. Air conditioned. BT10 bogies. ETS 6X.

Lot No. 31036 Derby/Wolverton 1987.

2923 **RP** NR *RT* ZN

OPEN FIRST

Mark 1. 42/– 2T. ETS 3. Many now fitted with table lamps.

3058 was numbered DB 975313, 3068 was numbered DB 975606 and 3093 was numbered DB 977594 for a time when in departmental service for BR.

3058–68. Lot No. 30169 Doncaster 1955. B4 bogies. 33 t (* Commonwealth bogies 35 t).
3093. Lot No. 30472 BRCW 1959. B4 bogies. 33 t.
3096–3100. Lot No. 30576 BRCW 1959. B4 bogies. 33 t.

3058	*x **M**	WC	*WC*	CS	FLORENCE
3066	**CC**	RV	*RV*	ZG	
3068	**CC**	RV	*RV*	ZG	
3093	x **M**	WC	*WC*	CS	FLORENCE
3096	x **M**	SP	*SP*	BO	
3097	**CH**	RV	*RV*	ZG	
3098	x **CH**	RV	*RV*	ZG	
3100	x **CC**	LS	*LS*	CL	

Later design with fluorescent lighting, aluminium window frames and Commonwealth bogies.

3128/36/41/43/46/47/48 were renumbered 1058/60/63/65/68/69/70 when reclassified Restaurant Open First, then 3600/05/08/09/06/04/10 when declassified to Open Standard, but have since regained their original numbers. 3136 was numbered DB 977970 for a time when in use with Serco Railtest as a Brake Force Runner.

3105 has had its luggage racks removed and has tungsten lighting.

3105–28. Lot No. 30697 Swindon 1962–63. 36 t.
3130–50. Lot No. 30717 Swindon 1963. 36 t.

3105	x	**M**	WC	*WC*	CS
3106	x	**M**	WC	*WC*	CS
3110	x	**CH**	RV	*RV*	ZG
3112	x	**CH**	RV		ZG
3113	x	**M**	WC	*WC*	CS
3115	x	**M**	SP	*SP*	BO
3117	x	**M**	WC	*WC*	CS
3119	x	**CH**	RV	*RV*	ZG
3120		**CH**	RV	*RV*	ZG
3121		**CH**	RV	*RV*	ZG
3122	x	**CC**	LS	*LS*	CL
3123		**CH**	RV	*RV*	ZG
3125	x	**CC**	LS	*LS*	CL
3128	x	**M**	WC	*WC*	CS
3130	x	**M**	WC	*WC*	CS
3136	x	**M**	WC	*WC*	CS
3141		**CH**	RV	*RV*	ZG
3143	x	**M**	WC	*WC*	CS
3146		**CH**	RV	*RV*	ZG
3147		**CH**	RV	*RV*	ZG
3148		**CC**	LS	*LS*	CL
3149		**CH**	RV	*RV*	ZG
3150		**M**	SP	*SP*	BO

Names:

3105	JULIA
3106	ALEXANDRA
3113	JESSICA
3117	CHRISTINA
3128	VICTORIA
3130	PAMELA
3136	DIANA
3143	PATRICIA

OPEN FIRST

Mark 2D. Air conditioned. Stones equipment. 42/– 2T. B4 bogies. ETS 5.

† Interior modified to Pullman Car standards with new seating, new panelling, tungsten lighting and table lights.

Lot No. 30821 Derby 1971–72. 34 t.

3174	†	**VN**	WC	*WC*	CS	GLAMIS
3182	†	**VN**	WC	*WC*	CS	WARWICK
3188		**PC**	LS		CL	CADAIR IDRIS

OPEN FIRST

Mark 2E. Air conditioned. Stones equipment. 42/– 2T (* 36/– 2T). B4 bogies. ETS 5.

r Refurbished with new seats.
† Interior modified to Pullman Car standards with new seating, new panelling, tungsten lighting and table lights.

Lot No. 30843 Derby 1972–73. 32.5 t. († 35.8 t).

3223		**RV**	LS		CL	DIAMOND
3229		**PC**	LS	*LS*	CL	SNOWDON
3231	*	**PC**	LS	*LS*	CL	BEN CRUACHAN
3232	dr	**BG**	WC		CS	
3240		**RV**	LS		CL	SAPPHIRE
3247	†	**VN**	WC	*WC*	CS	CHATSWORTH
3267	†	**VN**	WC	*WC*	CS	BELVOIR
3273	†	**VN**	WC	*WC*	CS	ALNWICK
3275	†	**VN**	WC	*WC*	CS	HARLECH

OPEN FIRST

Mark 2F. Air conditioned. 3278–3314/3359–79 have Stones equipment, others have Temperature Ltd. All refurbished in the 1980s with power-operated vestibule doors, new panels and new seat trim. 42/– 2T. B4 bogies. d. ETS 5X.

r Further refurbished with table lamps and modified seats with burgundy seat trim.
u Fitted with power supply for Mark 1 Kitchen Buffet Unclassified.

3278–3314. Lot No. 30845 Derby 1973. 33.5 t.
3325–3426. Lot No. 30859 Derby 1973–74. 33.5 t.
3431–3438. Lot No. 30873 Derby 1974–75. 33.5 t.

3278	r	**BG**	RV	*RV*	BU
3304	r	**BG**	RV	*RV*	BU
3312		**PC**	LS	*LS*	CL
3313	r	**M**	WC	*WC*	CS
3314	r	**BG**	RV	*RV*	BU
3325	r	**V**	RV		ZG
3326	r	**M**	WC	*WC*	CS
3330	r	**CC**	LS	*LS*	CL
3333	r	**BG**	RV	*RV*	BU
3340	r	**BG**	RV	*RV*	BU
3344	r	**PC**	LS	*LS*	CL
3345	r	**BG**	RV	*RV*	BU
3348	r	**PC**	LS	*LS*	CL
3350	r	**M**	WC	*WC*	CS
3352	r	**M**	WC	*WC*	CS
3356	r	**BG**	RV	*RV*	BU
3359	r	**M**	WC	*WC*	CS
3360	r	**PC**	WC	*WC*	CS
3362	r	**PC**	WC	*WC*	CS
3364	r	**BG**	RV	*RV*	BU
3384	r	**PC**	LS	*LS*	CL
3386	r	**BG**	RV	*RV*	BU
3390	r	**BG**	RV	*RV*	BU
3392	r	**M**	WC	*WC*	CS
3395	r	**M**	WC	*WC*	CS
3397	r	**BG**	RV	*RV*	BU
3426	r	**PC**	LS	*LS*	CL
3431	r	**M**	WC	*WC*	CS
3438	r	**PC**	LS	*LS*	CL

Names:

3312	HELVELLYN
3344	SCAFELL
3348	INGLEBOROUGH
3384	PEN-Y-GHENT
3426	BEN NEVIS
3438	BEN LOMOND

OPEN STANDARD

Mark 1. –/64 2T. ETS 4.

4831–36. Lot No. 30506 Wolverton 1959. Commonwealth bogies. 37 t.
4854/56. Lot No. 30525 Wolverton 1959–60. B4 bogies. 33 t.

4831	x	**M**	SP	*SP*	BO
4832	x	**M**	SP	*SP*	BO
4836	x	**M**	SP	*SP*	BO
4854	x	**M**	WC	*WC*	CS
4856	x	**M**	SP	*SP*	BO

OPEN STANDARD

Mark 1. Commonwealth bogies. –/64 2T. ETS 4.

4905. Lot No. 30646 Wolverton 1961. 36 t.
4927–5044. Lot No. 30690 Wolverton 1961–62. 37 t.

4905	x	**M**	WC	*WC*	CS
4927	x	**CC**	RV	*RV*	ZG
4931	v	**M**	WC	*WC*	CS
4940	x	**M**	WC	*WC*	CS
4946	x	**CH**	RV	*RV*	ZG
4949	x	**CH**	RV	*RV*	ZG
4951	x	**M**	WC	*WC*	CS
4954	v	**M**	WC	*WC*	CS
4959		**CH**	RV	*RV*	ZG
4960	x	**M**	WC	*WC*	CS
4973	x	**M**	WC	*WC*	CS
4984	x	**M**	WC	*WC*	CS
4991		**CH**	RV	*RV*	ZG
4994	x	**M**	WC	*WC*	CS
4998		**CH**	RV	*RV*	ZG
5009	x	**CH**	RV		BU
5028	x	**M**	SP	*SP*	BO
5032	x	**M**	WC	*WC*	CS
5033	x	**M**	WC	*WC*	CS
5035	x	**M**	WC	*WC*	CS
5044	x	**M**	WC	*WC*	CS

OPEN STANDARD

Mark 2. Pressure ventilated. –/64 2T. B4 bogies. ETS 4.

Lot No. 30751 Derby 1965–67. 32 t.

5157	v	**CH**	VT	*VT*	TM
5171	v	**M**	WC	*WC*	CS
5177	v	**CH**	VT	*VT*	TM
5191	v	**CH**	VT	*VT*	TM
5198	v	**CH**	VT	*VT*	TM
5200	v	**M**	WC	*WC*	CS
5212	v	**CH**	VT	*VT*	TM
5216	v	**M**	WC	*WC*	CS
5222	v	**M**	WC	*WC*	CS

OPEN STANDARD

Mark 2. Pressure ventilated. –/48 2T. B4 bogies. ETS 4.

Lot No. 30752 Derby 1966. 32 t.

5229		**M**	WC	*WC*	CS
5236	v	**M**	WC	*WC*	CS
5237	v	**M**	WC	*WC*	CS
5239		**M**	WC	*WC*	CS
5249	v	**M**	WC	*WC*	CS

OPEN STANDARD

Mark 2A. Pressure ventilated. –/64 2T (w –/62 2T). B4 bogies. ETS 4.

f Facelifted vehicles.

5278–92. Lot No. 30776 Derby 1967–68. 32 t.
5366–5419. Lot No. 30787 Derby 1968. 32 t.

5278		**M**	WC	*WC*	CS
5292	f	**CC**	RV		BU
5366	f	**CC**	LS	*LS*	CL
5419	w	**M**	WC	*WC*	CS

OPEN STANDARD

Mark 2B. Pressure ventilated. –/62. B4 bogies. ETS 4.

Lot No. 30791 Derby 1969. 32 t.

5487 **M** WC *WC* CS

OPEN STANDARD

Mark 2E. Air conditioned. Stones equipment. Refurbished with new interior panelling. –/64 2T. B4 bogies. d. ETS 5.

s Modified design of seat headrest and centre luggage stack. –/60 2T.

5787. Lot No. 30837 Derby 1972. 33.5 t.
5810. Lot No. 30844 Derby 1972–73. 33.5 t.

5787	s	**DS** DR	*SR*	ML	5810		**DS** DR	*SR*	ML

OPEN STANDARD

Mark 2F. Air conditioned. Temperature Ltd equipment. InterCity 70 seats. All were refurbished in the 1980s with power-operated vestibule doors, new panels and seat trim. They have subsequently undergone a second refurbishment with carpets and new seat trim. –/64 2T. B4 bogies. d. ETS 5X.

q Fitted with two wheelchair spaces. –/60 2T 2W.
s Fitted with centre luggage stack. –/60 2T.
t Fitted with centre luggage stack and wheelchair space. –/58 2T 1W.
† Retention toilets.

5910–55. Lot No. 30846 Derby 1973. 33 t.
5961–6158. Lot No. 30860 Derby 1973–74. 33 t.
6173–83. Lot No. 30874 Derby 1974–75. 33 t.

5910	q	**BG**	RV		BU	5991		**CC**	LS	*LS*	CL
5912		**PC**	LS	*LS*	CL	5995	†	**DS**	DR	*SR*	ML
5919	† pt	**DS**	DR	*SR*	ML	5998		**BG**	RV	*TW*	CF
5921		**AR**	RV	*RV*	BU	6000	t	**M**	WC	*WC*	CS
5929		**BG**	RV	*RV*	BU	6001	†	**DS**	DR	*SR*	ML
5937		**DS**	DR	*SR*	ML	6006		**AR**	RV		BU
5945		**SR**	RV	*SR*	ML	6008	† s	**DS**	DR	*SR*	ML
5950		**AR**	RV	*RV*	BU	6012		**M**	WC	*WC*	CS
5952		**SR**	RV		ZG	6021		**PC**	WC	*WC*	CS
5955		**SR**	RV	*SR*	ML	6022	s	**M**	WC	*WC*	CS
5961	pt	**BG**	RV	*TW*	CF	6024		**BG**	RV	*TW*	CF
5964		**AR**	RV	*RV*	BU	6027	q	**SR**	RV	*SR*	ML
5965	t	**SR**	RV		BU	6042		**AR**	RV	*TW*	CF
5971	†	**DS**	DR	*SR*	ML	6046	†	**DS**	DR	*SR*	ML
5976	t	**SR**	RV		BU	6051		**BG**	RV	*RV*	BU
5985		**AR**	RV	*RV*	BU	6054		**BG**	RV	*TW*	CF
5987		**SR**	RV		BU	6064	†	**DS**	DR	*SR*	ML

6067	pt	**BG**	RV	*TW*	CF	6141	q	**V**	RV		BU
6103		**M**	WC	*WC*	CS	6158		**BG**	RV	*TW*	CF
6115	s	**M**	WC	*WC*	CS	6173	†	**DS**	DR	*SR*	ML
6117	†	**DS**	DR	*SR*	ML	6176	t	**SR**	RV		ZG
6122	†	**DS**	DR	*SR*	ML	6177	s	**SR**	RV		BU
6137	s pt	**SR**	RV		BU	6183	s	**SR**	RV		BU

BRAKE GENERATOR VAN

Mark 1. Renumbered 1989 from BR departmental series. Converted from Gangwayed Brake Van in 1973 to three-phase supply brake generator van for use with HST trailers. Modified 1999 for use with locomotive-hauled stock. B5 bogies. ETS index ??.

Lot No. 30400 Pressed Steel 1958.

6310	(81448, 975325)	**CH**	RV	*RV*	ZG

GENERATOR VAN

Mark 1. Converted from Gangwayed Brake Vans in 1992. B4 (* B5) bogies. ETS index 75.

6311. Lot No. 30162 Pressed Steel 1958. 37.25 t.
6312. Lot No. 30224 Cravens 1956. 37.25 t.
6313. Lot No. 30484 Pressed Steel 1958. 37.25 t.

6311	(80903, 92911)		**CC**	LS	*LS*	CL
6312	(81023, 92925)		**M**	WC	*WC*	CS
6313	(81553, 92167)	*	**PC**	BE	*BP*	SL

BUFFET STANDARD

Mark 2C. Converted from Open Standard by removal of one seating bay and replacing this with a counter with a space for a trolley, now replaced with a more substantial buffet. Adjacent toilet removed and converted to steward's washing area/store. Pressure ventilated. –/55 1T. B4 bogies. ETS 4.

Lot No. 30795 Derby 1969–70. 32.5 t.

6528	(5592)	**M**	WC	*WC*	CS

SLEEPER RECEPTION CAR

Mark 2F. Converted from Open First. These vehicles consist of pantry, microwave cooking facilities, seating area for passengers (with loose chairs, staff toilet plus two bars). Now refurbished again with new "sofa" seating as well as the loose chairs. Converted at RTC, Derby (6700), Ilford (6701–05) and Derby (6706–08). Air conditioned. 6700/01/03/05–08 have Stones equipment and 6702/04 have Temperature Ltd equipment. The number of seats per coach can vary but typically is 25/– 1T (12 seats as "sofa" seating and 13 loose chairs). B4 bogies. d. ETS 5X.

6700–02/04/08. Lot No. 30859 Derby 1973–74. 33.5 t.
6703/05–07. Lot No. 30845 Derby 1973. 33.5 t.

6700	(3347)	**CA**	ER		WO	
6701	(3346)	**CA**	BR		ZM	
6702	(3421)	**FS**	ER		WB	
6703	(3308)	**CA**	ER		WO	
6704	(3341)	**FS**	ER		WO	
6705	(3310, 6430)	**FS**	ER		WO	
6706	(3283, 6421)	**FS**	ER		WO	
6707	(3276, 6418)	**FS**	ER		WO	
6708	(3370)	**PC**	LS	*LS*	CL	MOUNT HELICON

BUFFET FIRST

Mark 2D. Converted from Buffet Standard by the removal of another seating bay and fitting a more substantial buffet counter with boiler and microwave oven. Now converted to First Class with new seating and end luggage stacks. Air conditioned. Stones equipment. 30/– 1T. B4 bogies. d. ETS 5.
Lot No. 30822 Derby 1971. 33 t.

6723	(5641, 6662)	**M**	WC		CS
6724	(5721, 6665)	**M**	WC	*WC*	CS

OPEN BRAKE STANDARD WITH TROLLEY SPACE

Mark 2. This vehicle uses the same bodyshell as Mark 2 Corridor Brake Firsts and has First Class seat spacing and wider tables. Converted from Open Brake Standard by removal of one seating bay and replacing this with a counter with a space for a trolley. Adjacent toilet removed and converted to a steward's washing area/store. –/23. B4 bogies. ETS 4.

Lot No. 30757 Derby 1966. 31 t.

9101	(9398)	v	**CH**	VT	*VT*	TM

OPEN BRAKE STANDARD

Mark 2. These vehicles use the same bodyshell as Mark 2 Corridor Brake Firsts and have First Class seat spacing and wider tables. Pressure ventilated. –/31 1T. B4 bogies. ETS 4.

9104 was originally numbered 9401. It was renumbered when converted to Open Brake Standard with trolley space. Now returned to original layout.

Lot No. 30757 Derby 1966. 31.5 t.

9104	v	**M**	WC	*WC*	CS	9392	v	**M**	WC	*WC*	CS
9391		**M**	WC	*WC*	CS						

OPEN BRAKE STANDARD

Mark 2D. Air conditioned. Stones Equipment. B4 bogies. d. pg. ETS 5.

r Refurbished with new interior panelling –/31 1T.
s Refurbished with new seating –/22 1TD.

Lot No. 30824 Derby 1971. 33 t.

9479	r	**PC**	LS	*LS*	CL	9493	s	**M**	WC	*WC*	CS
9488	s	**SR**	DR	*SR*	ML						

OPEN BRAKE STANDARD

Mark 2E. Air conditioned. Stones Equipment. Refurbished with new interior panelling. –/32 1T (* –/30 1T 1W). B4 bogies. d. pg. ETS 5.

Lot No. 30838 Derby 1972. 33 t.

Non-standard livery: 9502 Pullman umber & cream.

s Modified design of seat headrest.

9497		**CA**	ER		WO	9507	s	**BG**	RV	*TW*	CF
9502	s	**0**	BE	*BP*	SL	9509	s	**AV**	RV		BU
9504	s*	**BG**	RV	*RV*	BU						

OPEN BRAKE STANDARD

Mark 2F. Air conditioned. Temperature Ltd equipment. All were refurbished in the 1980s with power-operated vestibule doors, new panels and seat trim. All now further refurbished with carpets. –/32 1T (w –/30 1T 1W). B4 bogies. d. pg. ETS 5X.

9537 has had all its seats removed for the purpose of carrying luggage.

Lot No. 30861 Derby 1974. 34 t.

9513		**IC**	ER		WO	9526	n	**BG**	RV	*TW*	CF
9520	nw	**AR**	RV	*TW*	CF	9527	n	**SR**	RV	*SR*	ML
9521		**DS**	RV	*DR*	KM	9537	n	**V**	RV		BU
9525		**DS**	DR	*SR*	ML	9539		**SR**	RV	*SR*	ML

DRIVING OPEN BRAKE STANDARD

Mark 2F. Air conditioned. Temperature Ltd equipment. Push & pull (tdm system). Converted from Open Brake Standard, these vehicles originally had half cabs at the brake end. They have since been refurbished and have had their cabs widened and the cab-end gangways removed. Five vehicles (9701–03/08/14) have been converted for use in Network Rail test trains and can be found in the Service Stock section of this book. –/30(+1) 1W. B4 bogies. d. pg. Cowcatchers. ETS 5X.

Lot No. 30861 Derby 1974. Converted Glasgow 1979. Disc brakes. 34 t.

9704	(9512)	**DS**	DR	LW
9705	(9519)	**DS**	DR	LW
9707	(9511)	**DS**	DR	LW
9709	(9515)	**DS**	DR	LW
9710	(9518)	**DS**	DR	LW

OPEN BRAKE UNCLASSIFIED

Mark 2E. Converted from Open Standard with new seating by Railcare, Wolverton. Air conditioned. Stones equipment. Five vehicles (9801/03/06/08/10) are currently used in Network Rail test trains and can be found in the Service Stock section of this book.–/31 2T. B4 bogies. d. ETS 4X.

9800/02. Lot No. 30837 Derby 1972. 33.5 t.
9804–09. Lot No. 30844 Derby 1972–73. 33.5 t.

9800	(5751)	**CA**	ER	PO
9802	(5772)	**CA**	ER	PO
9804	(5826)	**FS**	ER	PO
9805	(5833)	**FS**	ER	PO
9807	(5851)	**FS**	ER	WO
9809	(5890)	**FS**	ER	PO

KITCHEN BUFFET FIRST

Mark 3A. Air conditioned. Converted from HST catering vehicles and Mark 3 Open Firsts. 18/– plus two seats for staff use (* 24/–, † 35 1T, t 23/– 1T 1W). BT10 bogies. d. ETS 14X.

† Refurbished Great Western Railway Sleeper coaches fitted with new Transcal seating.

Non-standard liveries:

10211 EWS dark maroon.
10241 Livery trials.

10211. Lot No. 30884 Derby 1977. 39.8 t.
10212–229. Lot No. 30878 Derby 1975–76. 39.8 t.
10241–259. Lot No. 30890 Derby 1979. 39.8 t.

10211	(40510)		**0**	DB	*DB*	TO
10212	(11049)		**VT**	ER		CP
10217	(11051)	†	**GW**	P	*GW*	PZ
10219	(11047)	†	**GW**	P	*GW*	PZ
10225	(11014)	†	**GW**	P	*GW*	PZ
10229	(11059)	*	**GA**	ER		CP
10241	(10009)	*	**0**	P		IL
10249	(10012)	t	**AW**	AV	*TW*	CF
10259	(10025)	t	**AW**	AV	*TW*	CF

KITCHEN BUFFET FIRST

Mark 3A. Air conditioned. Rebuilt 2011–12 and fitted with sliding plug doors. Interiors originally refurbished for Wrexham & Shropshire with Primarius seating, a new kitchen area and universal-access toilet. Retention toilets. 30/– 1TD 1W. BT10 bogies. ETS 14X.

10271/273/274. Lot No. 30890 Derby 1979. 41.3 t.
10272. Lot No. 30884 Derby 1977. 41.3 t.

10271 (10018, 10236)	**CM**	AV	*CR*	AL
10272 (40517, 10208)	**CM**	AV	*CR*	AL
10273 (10021, 10230)	**CM**	AV	*CR*	AL
10274 (10010, 10255)	**CM**	AV	*CR*	AL

KITCHEN BUFFET STANDARD

Mark 4. Air conditioned. Rebuilt from First to Standard Class with bar adjacent to seating area instead of adjacent to end of coach. Retention toilets. –/30 1T. BT41 bogies. ETS 6X.

Lot No. 31045 Metro-Cammell 1989–92. 43.2 t.

10300	**VE**	E	*LN*	BN
10301	**VE**	E	*LN*	BN
10302	**VE**	E	*LN*	BN
10303	**VE**	E	*LN*	BN
10304	**VE**	E	*LN*	BN
10305	**VE**	E	*LN*	BN
10306	**VE**	E	*LN*	BN
10307	**VE**	E	*LN*	BN
10308	**VE**	E	*LN*	BN
10309	**VE**	E	*LN*	BN
10310	**VE**	E	*LN*	BN
10311	**VE**	E	*LN*	BN
10312	**VE**	E		EH
10313	**VE**	E	*LN*	BN
10315	**VE**	E	*LN*	BN
10317	**VE**	E		ZB
10318	**VE**	E	*LN*	BN
10319	**VE**	E		WB
10320	**VE**	E	*LN*	BN
10321	**VE**	E	*LN*	BN
10323	**VE**	E	*LN*	BN
10324	**VE**	E	*LN*	BN
10325	**VE**	E		EH
10326	**VE**	E	*LN*	BN
10328	**VE**	E		EH
10329	**VE**	E		WS
10330	**VE**	E	*LN*	BN
10331	**VE**	E	*LN*	BN
10332	**VE**	E	*LN*	BN
10333	**VE**	E	*LN*	BN

BUFFET STANDARD

Mark 3A. Air conditioned. Converted from Mark 3 Open Standard at Derby 2006. –/54. d. ETS 13X.

Lot No. 30877 Derby 1975–77. 37.8 t.

10401 (12168)	**GA**	P	*GA*	NC
10402 (12010)	**GA**	P	*GA*	NC
10403 (12135)	**GA**	P	*GA*	NC
10404 (12068)	**GA**	P	*GA*	NC
10405 (12157)	**GA**	P	*GA*	NC
10406 (12020)	**GA**	P	*GA*	NC

BUFFET STANDARD

Mark 3A. Air conditioned. Converted from Mark 3 Kitchen Buffet First 2015–16. –/54. BT10 bogies. d. ETS 13X.

10411–412. Lot No. 30884 Derby 1977. 37.8 t.
10413–416. Lot No. 30878 Derby 1975–76. 37.8 t.
10417. Lot No. 30890 Derby 1979. 37.8 t.

10411	(40519, 10200)	**GA**	P	*GA*	NC
10412	(40506, 10203)	**GA**	P	*GA*	NC
10413	(11034, 10214)	**GA**	P	*GA*	NC
10414	(11041, 10216)	**GA**	P	*GA*	NC
10415	(11043, 10223)	**GA**	P	*GA*	NC
10416	(11035, 10228)	**GA**	P	*GA*	NC
10417	(10011, 10247)	**GA**	P	*GA*	NC

SLEEPING CAR WITH PANTRY

Mark 3A. Air conditioned. Retention toilets. 12 compartments with a fixed lower berth and a hinged upper berth, plus an attendant's compartment (* 11 compartments with a fixed lower berth and a hinged upper berth + one compartment for a disabled person. 1TD). 2T. BT10 bogies. d. ETS 7X.

Non-standard livery: 10546 EWS dark maroon.

Lot No. 30960 Derby 1981–83. 41 t.

10501		**FS**	ER		WO
10502		**FS**	ER		WO
10504		**FS**	LS		KR
10513		**FS**	LS		KR
10519		**FS**	LS		KR
10520		**FS**	LS		KR
10522		**FS**	P		LM
10526		**FS**	P		LM
10527		**FS**	P		LM
10531		**FS**	P		WB
10532		**GW**	P	*GW*	PZ
10534		**GW**	P	*GW*	PZ
10542		**FS**	P		LM
10544		**FS**	P		WB
10546		**0**	DB	*DB*	TO
10551		**FS**	P		WB
10553		**FS**	P		WB
10561		**FS**	P		LM
10563		**GW**	P	*GW*	PZ
10584		**GW**	P	*GW*	PZ
10589		**GW**	P	*GW*	PZ
10590		**GW**	P	*GW*	PZ
10594		**GW**	P	*GW*	PZ
10596		**GW**	P	*GW*	PZ
10598		**FS**	WC		CS
10600		**FS**	ER		WO
10601	*	**GW**	P	*GW*	PZ
10605		**FS**	P		LM
10610		**FS**	WC		CS
10612	*	**GW**	P	*GW*	PZ
10614		**FS**	WC		CS
10616	*	**GW**	P	*GW*	PZ

SLEEPING CAR

Mark 3A. Air conditioned. Retention toilets. 13 compartments with a fixed lower berth and a hinged upper berth (* 11 compartments with a fixed lower berth and a hinged upper berth + one compartment for a disabled person. 1TD). 2T. BT10 bogies. ETS 6X.

10734 was originally 2914 and used as a Royal Train staff sleeping car. It has 12 berths and a shower room and is ETS 11X.

10648–729. Lot No. 30961 Derby 1980–84. 43.5 t.
10734. Lot No. 31002 Derby/Wolverton 1985. 42.5 t.

10648 d*	**FS**	LS		KR	10703 d	**FS**	WC		CS
10650 d*	**FS**	LS		KR	10706 d*	**FS**	P		WB
10675 d	**FS**	LS		KR	10714 d*	**FS**	PO		CS
10680 d*	**FS**	P		LM	10718 d*	**FS**	WC		CS
10683 d	**FS**	LS		KR	10719 d*	**FS**	PO		CS
10688 d	**FS**	LS		CL	10722 d*	**FS**	P		LM
10689 d*	**FS**	P		WB	10729	**VN**	WC	*WC*	CS
10699 d*	**FS**	ER		WB	10734	**VN**	WC	*WC*	CS

Names:

10729	CREWE	10734	BALMORAL

OPEN FIRST

Mark 3A. Air conditioned. All refurbished with table lamps and new seat cushions and trim. 48/– 2T. BT10 bogies. d. ETS 6X.

† Reseated with Standard Class seats: –/68 2T 2W.

Non-standard livery: 11039 EWS dark maroon.

Lot No. 30878 Derby 1975–76. 34.3 t.

11018	**VT**	P		LR	11039	**0**	DB	*DB*	TO
11029 †	**CM**	AV	*CR*	AL	11048	**VT**	P		LR
11031 †	**CM**	AV	*CR*	AL					

OPEN FIRST

Mark 3B. Air conditioned. InterCity 80 seats. All refurbished with table lamps and new seat cushions and trim. Retention toilets. 48/– 1T. BT10 bogies. d. ETS 6X.

† Fitted with disabled toilet and reduced seating, including three Compin Pegasus seats. 37/– 1TD 2W.

Non-standard livery: 11074 Original HST prototype grey & BR blue.

Lot No. 30982 Derby 1985. 36.5 t.

11066	**GA**	P	*GA*	NC	11080	**GA**	P		KP
11067	**GA**	P	*GA*	NC	11081	**GA**	P	*GA*	NC
11068	**GA**	P	*GA*	NC	11082	**GA**	P	*GA*	NC
11069	**GA**	P	*GA*	NC	11085 †	**GA**	P	*GA*	NC
11070	**GA**	P	*GA*	NC	11087 †	**GA**	P	*GA*	NC
11072	**GA**	P	*GA*	NC	11088 †	**GA**	P	*GA*	NC
11073	**GA**	P	*GA*	NC	11090 †	**GA**	P	*GA*	NC
11074	**0**	DA	*DB*	LR	11091	**GA**	P	*GA*	NC
11075	**GA**	P	*GA*	NC	11092 †	**GA**	P	*GA*	NC
11076	**GA**	P	*GA*	NC	11093 †	**GA**	P		KP
11077	**GA**	P	*GA*	NC	11094 †	**GA**	P	*GA*	NC
11078 †	**GA**	P	*GA*	NC	11095 †	**GA**	P	*GA*	NC

11096 †	**GA**	P	*GA*	NC
11098 †	**GA**	P	*GA*	NC
11099 †	**GA**	P	*GA*	NC
11100 †	**GA**	P	*GA*	NC
11101 †	**GA**	P	*GA*	NC

OPEN FIRST

Mark 4. Air conditioned. Rebuilt with new interior by Bombardier Wakefield 2003–05 (some converted from Standard Class vehicles). Retention toilets. 41/– 1T (plus 2 seats for staff use). BT41 bogies. ETS 6X.

11201–11244. Lot No. 31046 Metro-Cammell 1989–92. 41.3 t.
11277–11299. Lot No. 31049 Metro-Cammell 1989–92. 41.3 t.

11201		**VE**	E	*LN*	BN
11219		**VE**	E	*LN*	BN
11229		**VE**	E	*LN*	BN
11241		**VE**	E	*LN*	BN
11244		**VE**	E	*LN*	BN
11277	(12408)	**VE**	E	*LN*	BN
11278	(12479)	**VE**	E	*LN*	BN
11279	(12521)	**VE**	E	*LN*	BN
11280	(12523)	**VE**	E	*LN*	BN
11281	(12418)	**VE**	E	*LN*	BN
11282	(12524)	**VE**	E	*LN*	BN
11283	(12435)	**VE**	E	*LN*	BN
11284	(12487)	**VE**	E	*LN*	BN
11285	(12537)	**VE**	E	*LN*	BN
11286	(12482)	**VE**	E	*LN*	BN
11287	(12527)	**VE**	E	*LN*	BN
11288	(12517)	**VE**	E	*LN*	BN
11289	(12528)	**VE**	E	*LN*	BN
11290	(12530)	**VE**	E	*LN*	BN
11291	(12535)	**VE**	E	*LN*	BN
11295	(12475)	**VE**	E	*LN*	BN
11298	(12416)	**VE**	E	*LN*	BN
11299	(12532)	**VE**	E	*LN*	BN

OPEN FIRST (DISABLED)

Mark 4. Air conditioned. Rebuilt from Open First by Bombardier Wakefield 2003–05. Retention toilets. 42/– 1TD 1W. BT41 bogies. ETS 6X.

Lot No. 31046 Metro-Cammell 1989–92. 40.7 t.

11301	(11215)	**VE**	E	*LN*	BN
11302	(11203)	**VE**	E	*LN*	BN
11303	(11211)	**VE**	E	*LN*	BN
11304	(11257)	**VE**	E	*LN*	BN
11305	(11261)	**VE**	E	*LN*	BN
11306	(11276)	**VE**	E	*LN*	BN
11307	(11217)	**VE**	E	*LN*	BN
11308	(11263)	**VE**	E	*LN*	BN
11309	(11259)	**VE**	E	*LN*	BN
11310	(11272)	**VE**	E	*LN*	BN
11311	(11221)	**VE**	E	*LN*	BN
11312	(11225)	**VE**	E	*LN*	BN
11313	(11210)	**VE**	E	*LN*	BN
11314	(11207)	**VE**	E	*LN*	BN
11315	(11238)	**VE**	E	*LN*	BN
11316	(11227)	**VE**	E	*LN*	BN
11317	(11223)	**VE**	E	*LN*	BN
11318	(11251)	**VE**	E	*LN*	BN
11319	(11247)	**VE**	E	*LN*	BN
11320	(11255)	**VE**	E	*LN*	BN
11321	(11245)	**VE**	E	*LN*	BN
11322	(11228)	**VE**	E	*LN*	BN
11323	(11235)	**VE**	E		EH
11324	(11253)	**VE**	E		EH
11325	(11231)	**VE**	E		EH
11326	(11206)	**VE**	E	*LN*	BN
11327	(11236)	**VE**	E		WB
11328	(11274)	**VE**	E	*LN*	BN
11329	(11243)	**VE**	E		WS
11330	(11249)	**VE**	E		WS

OPEN FIRST

Mark 4. Air conditioned. Rebuilt from Open First by Bombardier Wakefield 2003–05. Separate area for 7 smokers, although smoking is no longer allowed. Retention toilets. 46/– 1TD 1W. BT41 bogies. ETS 6X.

Lot No. 31046 Metro-Cammell 1989–92. 42.1 t.

11401	(11214)	**VE**	E	*LN*	BN
11402	(11216)	**VE**	E	*LN*	BN
11403	(11258)	**VE**	E	*LN*	BN
11404	(11202)	**VE**	E	*LN*	BN
11405	(11204)	**VE**	E	*LN*	BN
11406	(11205)	**VE**	E	*LN*	BN
11407	(11256)	**VE**	E	*LN*	BN
11408	(11218)	**VE**	E	*LN*	BN
11409	(11262)	**VE**	E	*LN*	BN
11410	(11260)	**VE**	E	*LN*	BN
11411	(11240)	**VE**	E	*LN*	BN
11412	(11209)	**VE**	E	*LN*	BN
11413	(11212)	**VE**	E	*LN*	BN
11414	(11246)	**VE**	E	*LN*	BN
11415	(11208)	**VE**	E	*LN*	BN
11416	(11254)	**VE**	E	*LN*	BN
11417	(11226)	**VE**	E	*LN*	BN
11418	(11222)	**VE**	E	*LN*	BN
11419	(11250)	**VE**	E	*LN*	BN
11420	(11242)	**VE**	E	*LN*	BN
11421	(11220)	**VE**	E	*LN*	BN
11422	(11232)	**VE**	E	*LN*	BN
11426	(11252)	**VE**	E	*LN*	BN
11430	(11248)	**VE**	E		ZB

OPEN FIRST

CAF Mark 5A. Air conditioned. Currently entering service with TransPennine Express. Retention toilets. 30/– 1TD 2W. CAF bogies. ETS XX.

CAF Beasain 2017–18. 32.7 t.

11501	**TP**	BN		MA
11502	**TP**	BN		LW
11503	**TP**	BN		MA
11504	**TP**	BN	*TP*	MA
11505	**TP**	BN		MA
11506	**TP**	BN	*TP*	MA
11507	**TP**	BN	*TP*	MA
11508	**TP**	BN	*TP*	MA
11509	**TP**	BN	*TP*	MA
11510	**TP**	BN		MA
11511	**TP**	BN	*TP*	MA
11512	**TP**	BN	*TP*	MA
11513	**TP**	BN	*TP*	MA

OPEN FIRST

Mark 4. Air conditioned. Converted from Kitchen Buffet Standard with new interior by Bombardier Wakefield 2005. Retention toilets. 46/– 1T. BT41 bogies. ETS 6X.

Lot No. 31046 Metro-Cammell 1989–92. 41.3 t.

11998	(10314)	**VE**	E		WS
11999	(10316)	**VE**	E		WS

OPEN STANDARD

Mark 3A. Air conditioned. All refurbished with modified seat backs and new layout and further refurbished with new seat trim. –/76 2T († –/70 2T 1W, t –/72 2T, z –/70 1TD 1T 2W). BT10 bogies. d. ETS 6X.

* Further refurbished with more unidirectional seating and one toilet removed. Retention toilets. –/80 1T.

s Refurbished Sleeper day coaches fitted with new Transcal seating to a 2+2 layout and a universal access toilet. Retention toilets. –/65 1TD 1W.

12170/171 were converted from Open Composites 11909/910, formerly Open Firsts 11009/010.

Non-standard livery: 12092 Original HST prototype grey & BR blue.

12005–167. Lot No. 30877 Derby 1975–77. 34.3 t.
12170/171. Lot No. 30878 Derby 1975–76. 34.3 t.

12005	*	**GA**	P		KP
12009	*	**GA**	P	*GA*	NC
12012	*	**GA**	P	*GA*	NC
12013	*	**GA**	P	*GA*	NC
12015	*	**GA**	P		KP
12016	*	**GA**	P	*GA*	NC
12017	t	**CM**	AV	*CR*	AL
12019	*	**GA**	P	*GA*	NC
12021	*	**GA**	P		KP
12024	*	**GA**	P	*GA*	NC
12026	*	**GA**	P	*GA*	NC
12027	*	**GA**	P	*GA*	NC
12030	*	**GA**	P	*GA*	NC
12031	*	**GA**	P	*GA*	NC
12032	*	**GA**	P	*GA*	NC
12034	*	**GA**	P	*GA*	NC
12035	*	**GA**	P	*GA*	NC
12036	†	**CM**	AV	*CR*	AL
12037	*	**GA**	P		KP
12040	*	**GA**	P	*GA*	NC
12041	*	**GA**	P		KP
12042	*	**GA**	P		KP
12043	†	**CM**	AV	*CR*	AL
12046	*	**GA**	P	*GA*	NC
12049	*	**GA**	P	*GA*	NC
12051	*	**GA**	P	*GA*	NC
12054	†	**CM**	AV	*CR*	AL
12056	*	**GA**	P	*GA*	NC
12057	*	**GA**	P	*GA*	NC
12060	*	**GA**	P	*GA*	NC
12061	*	**GA**	P	*GA*	NC
12062	*	**GA**	P	*GA*	NC
12064	*	**GA**	P	*GA*	NC
12066	*	**GA**	P	*GA*	NC
12067	*	**GA**	P	*GA*	NC
12073	*	**GA**	P	*GA*	NC
12078		**VT**	X		LR
12079	*	**GA**	P	*GA*	NC
12081	*	**GA**	P	*GA*	NC
12082	*	**GA**	P		KP
12084	*	**GA**	P		KP
12089	*	**GA**	P		KP
12090	*	**GA**	P	*GA*	NC
12091	*	**GA**	P	*GA*	NC
12092		**0**	DA		LR
12093	*	**GA**	P	*GA*	NC
12094		**CM**	AV	*CR*	AL
12097	*	**GA**	P	*GA*	NC
12098	*	**GA**	P	*GA*	NC
12099	*	**GA**	P	*GA*	NC
12100	s	**GW**	P	*GW*	PZ
12103	*	**GA**	P	*GA*	NC
12105	*	**GA**	P	*GA*	NC
12107	*	**GA**	P		KP
12108	*	**GA**	P	*GA*	NC
12109	*	**GA**	P	*GA*	NC
12110	*	**GA**	P	*GA*	NC
12111	*	**GA**	P	*GA*	NC
12114	*	**GA**	P	*GA*	NC
12115	*	**GA**	P	*GA*	NC
12116	*	**GA**	P	*GA*	NC
12118	*	**GA**	P	*GA*	NC
12119	t	**CM**	AV	*CR*	AL
12120	*	**GA**	P	*GA*	NC
12122	z	**VT**	P		LR
12125	*	**GA**	P	*GA*	NC
12126	*	**GA**	P	*GA*	NC
12129	*	**GA**	P		KP
12130	*	**GA**	P	*GA*	NC
12132	*	**GA**	P	*GA*	NC
12133		**VT**	P		LR
12137	*	**GA**	P	*GA*	NC
12138		**VT**	P		LR
12139	*	**GA**	P	*GA*	NC
12141	*	**GA**	P	*GA*	NC
12142	s	**GW**	P	*GW*	PZ
12143	*	**GA**	P		LR
12146	*	**GA**	P	*GA*	NC
12147	*	**GA**	P	*GA*	NC
12148	*	**GA**	P	*GA*	NC
12150	*	**GA**	P	*GA*	NC
12151	*	**GA**	P	*GA*	NC
12153	*	**GA**	P	*GA*	NC
12154	*	**GA**	P	*GA*	NC

12159 *	**GA**	P	*GA*	NC
12161 s	**GW**	P	*GW*	PZ
12164 *	**GA**	P	*GA*	NC
12166 *	**GA**	P	*GA*	NC
12167 *	**GA**	P	*GA*	NC
12170 *	**GA**	P		KP
12171 *	**GA**	P	*GA*	NC

OPEN STANDARD

Mark 3A (†) or Mark 3B. Air conditioned. Converted from Mark 3A or 3B Open First. Fitted with new Grammer seating. –/70 2T 1W. BT10 bogies. d. ETS 6X.

12176–181/185. Mark 3B. Lot No. 30982 Derby 1985. 38.5 t.
12182–184. Mark 3A. Lot No. 30878 Derby 1975–76. 38.5 t.

12176 (11064)		**AW**	AV	*TW*	CF
12177 (11065)		**AW**	AV	*TW*	CF
12178 (11071)		**AW**	AV	*TW*	CF
12179 (11083)		**AW**	AV	*TW*	CF
12180 (11084)		**AW**	AV	*TW*	CF
12181 (11086)		**AW**	AV	*TW*	CF
12182 (11013)	†	**AW**	AV	*TW*	CF
12183 (11027)	†	**AW**	AV	*TW*	CF
12184 (11044)	†	**AW**	AV	*TW*	CF
12185 (11089)		**AW**	AV	*TW*	CF

OPEN STANDARD (END)

Mark 4. Air conditioned. Rebuilt with new interior by Bombardier Wakefield 2003–05. Separate area for 26 smokers, although smoking is no longer allowed. Retention toilets. –/76 1T. BT41 bogies. ETS 6X.

12232 was converted from the original 12405.

12200–231. Lot No. 31047 Metro-Cammell 1989–91. 39.5 t.
12232. Lot No. 31049 Metro-Cammell 1989–92. 39.5 t.

12200	**VE**	E	*LN*	BN
12201	**VE**	E	*LN*	BN
12202	**VE**	E	*LN*	BN
12203	**VE**	E	*LN*	BN
12204	**VE**	E		ZB
12205	**VE**	E	*LN*	BN
12207	**VE**	E	*LN*	BN
12208	**VE**	E	*LN*	BN
12209	**VE**	E	*LN*	BN
12210	**VE**	E	*LN*	BN
12211	**VE**	E	*LN*	BN
12212	**VE**	E	*LN*	BN
12213	**VE**	E	*LN*	BN
12214	**VE**	E	*LN*	BN
12215	**VE**	E	*LN*	BN
12216	**VE**	E		WS
12217	**VE**	E		EH
12218	**VE**	E	*LN*	BN
12219	**VE**	E		EH
12220	**VE**	E	*LN*	BN
12222	**VE**	E	*LN*	BN
12223	**VE**	E	*LN*	BN
12224	**VE**	E	*LN*	BN
12225	**VE**	E		EH
12226	**VE**	E	*LN*	BN
12227	**VE**	E		WB
12228	**VE**	E	*LN*	BN
12229	**VE**	E	*LN*	BN
12230	**VE**	E	*LN*	BN
12231	**VE**	E	*LN*	BN
12232	**VE**	E	*LN*	BN

OPEN STANDARD (DISABLED)

Mark 4. Air conditioned. Rebuilt with new interior by Bombardier Wakefield 2003–05. Retention toilets. –/68 2W 1TD. BT41 bogies. ETS 6X.

12331 was converted from Open Standard 12531.

12300–330. Lot No. 31048 Metro-Cammell 1989–91. 39.4 t.
12331. Lot No. 31049 Metro-Cammell 1989–92. 39.4 t.

12300	**VE**	E	*LN*	BN	12317	**VE**	E		ZB
12301	**VE**	E	*LN*	BN	12318	**VE**	E		WS
12302	**VE**	E	*LN*	BN	12319	**VE**	E		ZB
12303	**VE**	E	*LN*	BN	12320	**VE**	E	*LN*	BN
12304	**VE**	E	*LN*	BN	12321	**VE**	E		WB
12305	**VE**	E	*LN*	BN	12322	**VE**	E		ZB
12307	**VE**	E	*LN*	BN	12323	**VE**	E	*LN*	BN
12308	**VE**	E	*LN*	BN	12324	**VE**	E	*LN*	BN
12309	**VE**	E	*LN*	BN	12325	**VE**	E	*LN*	BN
12310	**VE**	E	*LN*	BN	12326	**VE**	E	*LN*	BN
12311	**VE**	E	*LN*	BN	12327	**VE**	E	*LN*	BN
12312	**VE**	E	*LN*	BN	12328	**VE**	E	*LN*	BN
12313	**VE**	E	*LN*	BN	12329	**VE**	E	*LN*	BN
12315	**VE**	E	*LN*	BN	12330	**VE**	E	*LN*	BN
12316	**VE**	E	*LN*	BN	12331	**VE**	E		WS

OPEN STANDARD

Mark 4. Air conditioned. Rebuilt with new interior by Bombardier Wakefield 2003–05. Retention toilets. –/76 1T. BT41 bogies. ETS 6X.

12405 is the second coach to carry that number. It was built from the bodyshell originally intended for 12221. The original 12405 is now 12232.

Lot No. 31049 Metro-Cammell 1989–92. 40.8 t.

12400	**VE**	E	*LN*	BN	12422	**VE**	E	*LN*	BN
12401	**VE**	E	*LN*	BN	12423	**VE**	E	*LN*	BN
12402	**VE**	E	*LN*	BN	12424	**VE**	E	*LN*	BN
12404	**VE**	E	*LN*	BN	12426	**VE**	E	*LN*	BN
12405	**VE**	E	*LN*	BN	12427	**VE**	E	*LN*	BN
12406	**VE**	E	*LN*	BN	12428	**VE**	E	*LN*	BN
12407	**VE**	E	*LN*	BN	12429	**VE**	E	*LN*	BN
12409	**VE**	E	*LN*	BN	12430	**VE**	E	*LN*	BN
12410	**VE**	E	*LN*	BN	12431	**VE**	E	*LN*	BN
12411	**VE**	E	*LN*	BN	12432	**VE**	E	*LN*	BN
12414	**VE**	E	*LN*	BN	12433	**VE**	E	*LN*	BN
12415	**VE**	E	*LN*	BN	12434	**VE**	E	*LN*	BN
12417	**VE**	E	*LN*	BN	12436	**VE**	E	*LN*	BN
12419	**VE**	E	*LN*	BN	12437	**VE**	E	*LN*	BN
12420	**VE**	E	*LN*	BN	12438	**VE**	E		WS
12421	**VE**	E	*LN*	BN	12439	**VE**	E	*LN*	BN

12440	**VE**	E	*LN*	BN
12441	**VE**	E	*LN*	BN
12442	**VE**	E	*LN*	BN
12443	**VE**	E	*LN*	BN
12444	**VE**	E	*LN*	BN
12445	**VE**	E	*LN*	BN
12446	**VE**	E		EH
12447	**VE**	E		EH
12448	**VE**	E	*LN*	BN
12449	**VE**	E		WS
12450	**VE**	E	*LN*	BN
12452	**VE**	E	*LN*	BN
12453	**VE**	E	*LN*	BN
12454	**VE**	E		EH
12458	**VE**	E		WS
12459	**VE**	E	*LN*	BN
12460	**VE**	E	*LN*	BN
12461	**VE**	E	*LN*	BN
12462	**VE**	E		ZB
12463	**VE**	E		WS
12465	**VE**	E	*LN*	BN
12467	**VE**	E	*LN*	BN
12468	**VE**	E	*LN*	BN
12469	**VE**	E	*LN*	BN
12470	**VE**	E	*LN*	BN
12471	**VE**	E		WB
12472	**VE**	E		WS
12473	**VE**	E	*LN*	BN
12474	**VE**	E	*LN*	BN
12476	**VE**	E	*LN*	BN
12477	**VE**	E	*LN*	BN
12478	**VE**	E	*LN*	BN
12480	**VE**	E	*LN*	BN
12481	**VE**	E	*LN*	BN
12483	**VE**	E	*LN*	BN
12484	**VE**	E	*LN*	BN
12485	**VE**	E	*LN*	BN
12486	**VE**	E	*LN*	BN
12488	**VE**	E	*LN*	BN
12489	**VE**	E	*LN*	BN
12513	**VE**	E	*LN*	BN
12514	**VE**	E	*LN*	BN
12515	**VE**	E	*LN*	BN
12518	**VE**	E	*LN*	BN
12520	**VE**	E	*LN*	BN
12522	**VE**	E	*LN*	BN
12526	**VE**	E	*LN*	BN
12533	**VE**	E		ZB
12534	**VE**	E		WS

OPEN STANDARD

Mark 3A. Air conditioned. Rebuilt 2011–13 and fitted with sliding plug doors. Original InterCity 70 seating retained but mainly arranged around tables. Retention toilets. –/72(+6) or * –/69(+4) 1T. BT10 bogies. ETS 6X.

12602–609/614–616/618/620. Lot No. 30877 Derby 1975–77. 36.2 t (* 37.1 t).
12601/613/617–619/621/623/625/627. Lot No. 30878 Derby 1975–76. 36.2 t (* 37.1 t).

12602 (12072)		**CM**	AV	*CR*	AL
12603 (12053)	*	**CM**	AV	*CR*	AL
12604 (12131)		**CM**	AV	*CR*	AL
12605 (11040)	*	**CM**	AV	*CR*	AL
12606 (12048)		**CM**	AV	*CR*	AL
12607 (12038)	*	**CM**	AV	*CR*	AL
12608 (12069)		**CM**	AV	*CR*	AL
12609 (12014)	*	**CM**	AV	*CR*	AL
12610 (12117)		**CM**	AV	*CR*	AL
12613 (11042, 12173)	*	**CM**	AV	*CR*	AL
12614 (12145)		**CM**	AV	*CR*	AL
12615 (12059)	*	**CM**	AV	*CR*	AL
12616 (12127)		**CM**	AV	*CR*	AL
12617 (11052, 12174)	*	**CM**	AV	*CR*	AL
12618 (11008, 12169)		**CM**	AV	*CR*	AL

12619	(11058, 12175)	*	**CM**	AV	*CR*	AL
12620	(12124)		**CM**	AV	*CR*	AL
12621	(11046)	*	**CM**	AV	*CR*	AL
12623	(11019)	*	**CM**	AV	*CR*	AL
12625	(11030)	*	**CM**	AV	*CR*	AL
12627	(11054)	*	**CM**	AV	*CR*	AL

OPEN STANDARD

CAF Mark 5A. Air conditioned. Currently entering service with TransPennine Express. Retention toilets. –/69 1T (* –/59(+6) 1T + bike spaces). CAF bogies. ETS XX.

CAF Beasain 2017–18. 31.8 t (* 31.6 t).

12701		**TP**	BN		MA
12702		**TP**	BN		MA
12703	*	**TP**	BN		MA
12704		**TP**	BN		LW
12705		**TP**	BN		LW
12706	*	**TP**	BN		LW
12707		**TP**	BN		MA
12708		**TP**	BN		MA
12709	*	**TP**	BN		MA
12710		**TP**	BN	*TP*	MA
12711		**TP**	BN	*TP*	MA
12712	*	**TP**	BN	*TP*	MA
12713		**TP**	BN		MA
12714		**TP**	BN		MA
12715	*	**TP**	BN		MA
12716		**TP**	BN	*TP*	MA
12717		**TP**	BN	*TP*	MA
12718	*	**TP**	BN	*TP*	MA
12719		**TP**	BN	*TP*	MA
12720		**TP**	BN	*TP*	MA
12721	*	**TP**	BN	*TP*	MA
12722		**TP**	BN	*TP*	MA
12723		**TP**	BN	*TP*	MA
12724	*	**TP**	BN	*TP*	MA
12725		**TP**	BN	*TP*	MA
12726		**TP**	BN	*TP*	MA
12727	*	**TP**	BN	*TP*	MA
12728		**TP**	BN		MA
12729		**TP**	BN		MA
12730	*	**TP**	BN		MA
12731		**TP**	BN	*TP*	MA
12732		**TP**	BN	*TP*	MA
12733	*	**TP**	BN	*TP*	MA
12734		**TP**	BN	*TP*	MA
12735		**TP**	BN	*TP*	MA
12736	*	**TP**	BN	*TP*	MA
12737		**TP**	BN	*TP*	MA
12738		**TP**	BN	*TP*	MA
12739	*	**TP**	BN	*TP*	MA

DRIVING OPEN BRAKE STANDARD

CAF Mark 5A. Air conditioned. Currently entering service with TransPennine Express. –/64. CAF bogies. ETS XX.

CAF Irun 2017–18. 32.9 t.

12801	**TP**	BN		MA
12802	**TP**	BN		LW
12803	**TP**	BN		MA
12804	**TP**	BN	*TP*	MA
12805	**TP**	BN		MA
12806	**TP**	BN	*TP*	MA
12807	**TP**	BN	*TP*	MA
12808	**TP**	BN	*TP*	MA
12809	**TP**	BN	*TP*	MA
12810	**TP**	BN		MA
12811	**TP**	BN	*TP*	MA
12812	**TP**	BN	*TP*	MA
12813	**TP**	BN	*TP*	MA
12814	**TP**	BN		MA

CORRIDOR FIRST

Mark 1. Seven compartments. 42/– 2T. B4 bogies. ETS 3.

Lot No. 30381 Swindon 1959. 33 t.
Lot No. 30667 Swindon 1962. Commonwealth bogies. 36 t.

13227 x	**CC**	LS	*LS*	CL	13230 xk	**M**	SP	*SP*	BO
13229 xk	**M**	SP	*SP*	BO	13306 x	**M**	WC	*WC*	CS

Name: 13306 JOANNA

OPEN FIRST

Mark 1 converted from Corridor First in 2013–14. 42/– 2T. Commonwealth bogies. ETS 3.

Lot No. 30667 Swindon 1962. 35 t.

13320 x	**M**	WC	*WC*	CS	ANNA

CORRIDOR FIRST

Mark 2A. Seven compartments. Pressure ventilated. 42/– 2T. B4 bogies. ETS 4.

Lot No. 30774 Derby 1968. 33 t.

13440 v	**M**	WC	*WC*	CS

SLEEPER SEATED CARRIAGE WITH BRAKE

CAF Mark 5. Air conditioned. Retention toilets. –/31 1TD 1W. CAF bogies. ETS XX.

CAF Irun 2016–18. 32.5 t.

15001	**CA**	LF	*CA*	PO	15007	**CA**	LF	*CA*	PO
15002	**CA**	LF	*CA*	PO	15008	**CA**	LF	*CA*	PO
15003	**CA**	LF	*CA*	PO	15009	**CA**	LF	*CA*	PO
15004	**CA**	LF	*CA*	PO	15010	**CA**	LF	*CA*	PO
15005	**CA**	LF	*CA*	PO	15011	**CA**	LF	*CA*	PO
15006	**CA**	LF	*CA*	PO					

SLEEPER LOUNGE CAR

CAF Mark 5. Air conditioned. –/30 or –/28 1W. CAF bogies. ETS XX.

CAF Beasain 2016–18. 35.5 t.

15101	**CA**	LF	*CA*	PO	15106	**CA**	LF	*CA*	PO
15102	**CA**	LF	*CA*	PO	15107	**CA**	LF	*CA*	PO
15103	**CA**	LF	*CA*	PO	15108	**CA**	LF	*CA*	PO
15104	**CA**	LF	*CA*	PO	15109	**CA**	LF	*CA*	PO
15105	**CA**	LF	*CA*	PO	15110	**CA**	LF	*CA*	PO

SLEEPING CAR (FULLY ACCESSIBLE)

CAF Mark 5. Air conditioned. Retention toilets. Two fully accessible berths (one with double bed, one with foldable upper bed), two berths with double beds and en-suite toilets and showers, two berths with foldable upper beds. 2TD 2T, plus two showers. CAF bogies. ETS XX.

CAF Castejon/Irun 2016–18. 35.5 t.

15201	**CA**	LF	*CA*	PO
15202	**CA**	LF	*CA*	PO
15203	**CA**	LF	*CA*	PO
15204	**CA**	LF	*CA*	PO
15205	**CA**	LF	*CA*	PO
15206	**CA**	LF	*CA*	PO
15207	**CA**	LF	*CA*	PO
15208	**CA**	LF	*CA*	PO
15209	**CA**	LF	*CA*	PO
15210	**CA**	LF	*CA*	PO
15211	**CA**	LF	*CA*	PO
15212	**CA**	LF	*CA*	PO
15213	**CA**	LF	*CA*	PO
15214	**CA**	LF	*CA*	PO

SLEEPING CAR

CAF Mark 5. Air conditioned. Retention toilets. 6 en-suite toilet/shower and 4 non en-suite compartments with a fixed lower berth and hinged upper berth. 7T. CAF bogies. ETS XX.

CAF Beasain 2016–18. 38.0 t.

15301	**CA**	LF	*CA*	PO
15302	**CA**	LF	*CA*	PO
15303	**CA**	LF	*CA*	PO
15304	**CA**	LF	*CA*	PO
15305	**CA**	LF	*CA*	PO
15306	**CA**	LF	*CA*	PO
15307	**CA**	LF	*CA*	PO
15308	**CA**	LF	*CA*	PO
15309	**CA**	LF	*CA*	PO
15310	**CA**	LF	*CA*	PO
15311	**CA**	LF	*CA*	PO
15312	**CA**	LF	*CA*	PO
15313	**CA**	LF	*CA*	PO
15314	**CA**	LF	*CA*	PO
15315	**CA**	LF	*CA*	PO
15316	**CA**	LF	*CA*	PO
15317	**CA**	LF	*CA*	PO
15318	**CA**	LF	*CA*	PO
15319	**CA**	LF	*CA*	PO
15320	**CA**	LF	*CA*	PO
15321	**CA**	LF	*CA*	PO
15322	**CA**	LF	*CA*	PO
15323	**CA**	LF	*CA*	PO
15324	**CA**	LF	*CA*	PO
15325	**CA**	LF	*CA*	PO
15326	**CA**	LF	*CA*	PO
15327	**CA**	LF	*CA*	PO
15328	**CA**	LF	*CA*	PO
15329	**CA**	LF	*CA*	PO
15330	**CA**	LF	*CA*	PO
15331	**CA**	LF	*CA*	PO
15332	**CA**	LF	*CA*	PO
15333	**CA**	LF	*CA*	PO
15334	**CA**	LF	*CA*	PO
15335	**CA**	LF	*CA*	PO
15336	**CA**	LF	*CA*	PO
15337	**CA**	LF	*CA*	PO
15338	**CA**	LF	*CA*	PO
15339	**CA**	LF	*CA*	PO
15340	**CA**	LF	*CA*	PO

CORRIDOR BRAKE FIRST

Mark 1. Four compartments. 24/– 1T. Commonwealth bogies. ETS 2.

Lot No. 30668 Swindon 1961. 36 t.

17018 (14018)	v	**CH**	VT		TM	BOTAURUS

CORRIDOR BRAKE FIRST

Mark 2A. Four compartments. Pressure ventilated. 24/– 1T. B4 bogies. ETS 4.

17080/090 were numbered 35516/503 for a time when declassified.

17056. Lot No. 30775 Derby 1967–68. 32 t.
17080–102. Lot No. 30786 Derby 1968. 32 t.

17056 (14056)		**CC**	LS		ZG
17080 (14080)		**PC**	LS		ZG
17090 (14090)	v	**CH**	VT		TM
17102 (14102)		**M**	WC	*WC*	CS

COUCHETTE/GENERATOR COACH

Mark 2B. Formerly part of Royal Train. Converted from Corridor Brake First built 1969. Consists of luggage accommodation, guard's compartment, 350 kW diesel generator and staff sleeping accommodation. Pressure ventilated. B5 bogies. ETS 5X (when generator not in use). ETS index ?? (when generator in use).

Lot No. 30888 Wolverton 1977. 46 t.

17105 (14105, 2905)	**BG**	RV	*RV*	BU

CORRIDOR BRAKE FIRST

Mark 2D. Four compartments. Air conditioned. Stones equipment. 24/– 1T. B4 Bogies. ETS 5.

Lot No. 30823 Derby 1971–72. 33.5 t.

17159 (14159)	d	**CC**	LS	*LS*	CL	
17167 (14167)		**VN**	WC	*WC*	CS	MOW COP

OPEN BRAKE UNCLASSIFIED

Mark 3B. Air conditioned. Fitted with hydraulic handbrake. Used as Sleeper day coaches. Refurbished with new Transcal seating 2018. 55/– 1T. BT10 bogies. pg. d. ETS 6X.

Lot No. 30990 Derby 1986. 35.8 t.

17173	**GW**	P	*GW*	PZ
17174	**GW**	P	*GW*	PZ
17175	**GW**	P	*GW*	PZ

CORRIDOR STANDARD

Mark 1. –/48 2T. Eight Compartments. Commonwealth bogies. ETS 4.

Currently in use as part of the Harry Potter World exhibition at Leavesden, near Watford.

Lot No. 30685 Derby 1961–62. 36 t.

18756 (25756)	x	**M**	WC	SH

CORRIDOR BRAKE COMPOSITE

Mark 1. There are two variants depending upon whether the Standard Class compartments have armrests. Each vehicle has two First Class and three Standard Class compartments. 12/18 2T (* 12/24 2T). Commonwealth bogies. ETS 2.

21241–245. Lot No. 30669 Swindon 1961–62. 36 t.
21256. Lot No. 30731 Derby 1963. 37 t.
21266–272. Lot No. 30732 Derby 1964. 37 t.

21241	x	**M**	SP	*SP*	BO
21245	x	**M**	RV		ZG
21256	x	**M**	WC	*WC*	CS
21266	x*	**M**	WC	*WC*	CS
21269	*	**CC**	RV	*RV*	ZG
21272	x*	**CH**	RV	*RV*	ZG

CORRIDOR BRAKE STANDARD

Mark 1. Four compartments. –/24 1T. ETS 2.

35185. Lot No. 30427 Wolverton 1959. B4 bogies. 33 t.
35459/465. Lot No. 30721 Wolverton 1963. Commonwealth bogies. 37 t.

35185	x	**M**	SP	*SP*	BO
35459	x	**M**	WC	*WC*	CS
35465	x	**CC**	LS	*LS*	CL

CORRIDOR BRAKE GENERATOR STANDARD

Mark 1. Four compartments. –/24 1T. Fitted with an ETS generator in the former luggage compartment. ETS 2 (when generator not in use). ETS index ?? (when generator in use).

Lot No. 30721 Wolverton 1963. Commonwealth bogies. 37 t.

35469	x	**CH**	RV	*RV*	ZG

BRAKE/POWER KITCHEN

Mark 2C. Pressure ventilated. Converted from Corridor Brake First (declassified to Corridor Brake Standard) built 1970. Converted by West Coast Railway Company 2000–01. Consists of 60 kVA generator, guard's compartment and electric kitchen. B5 bogies. ETS ? (when generator not in use). ETS index ?? (when generator in use).

Non-standard livery: Brown.

Lot No. 30796 Derby 1969–70. 32.5 t.

35511 (14130, 17130)		**0**	LS	CL

KITCHEN CAR

Mark 1. Converted 1989/2006/2017–19 from Kitchen Buffet Unclassified. 80041/020 had buffet and seating area replaced with additional kitchen and food preparation area. 80043 had a full length kitchen fitted. Fluorescent lighting. Commonwealth or (†) B5 bogies. ETS 2X.

Lot No. 30628 Pressed Steel 1960–61. 39 t (* 36.4 t).

80041 (1690)	x	**M**	RV		ZG
80042 (1646)		**CH**	RV	*RV*	ZG
80043 (1680)	*	**PC**	LS	*LS*	CL
80044 (1659)	†	**CC**	LS	*LS*	CL

DRIVING BRAKE VAN (110 mph)

Mark 3B. Air conditioned. T4 bogies. dg. ETS 5X. Driving Brake Vans converted for use by Network Rail can be found in the Service Stock section of this book.

Non-standard livery: 82146 All over silver with DB logos.

Lot No. 31042 Derby 1988. 45.2 t.

82102	**GA**	P	*GA*	NC
82103	**GA**	P	*GA*	NC
82105	**GA**	P	*GA*	NC
82107	**GA**	P	*GA*	NC
82112	**GA**	P	*GA*	NC
82114	**GA**	P	*GA*	NC
82115	**B**	DA	*DB*	LR
82118	**GA**	P	*GA*	NC
82121	**GA**	P	*GA*	NC
82127	**GA**	P	*GA*	NC
82132	**GA**	P	*GA*	NC
82133	**GA**	P	*GA*	NC
82136	**GA**	P	*GA*	NC
82139	**GA**	P	*GA*	NC
82143	**GA**	P	*GA*	NC
82146	**0**	DB	*DB*	TO
82152	**GA**	P	*GA*	NC

DRIVING BRAKE VAN (140 mph)

Mark 4. Air conditioned. Swiss-built (SIG) bogies. dg. ETS 6X.

Advertising livery: 82205 Flying Scotsman (red, white & purple).

Lot No. 31043 Metro-Cammell 1988. 43.5 t.

82200	**VE**	E	*LN*	BN
82201	**VE**	E	*LN*	BN
82202	**VE**	E	*LN*	BN
82203	**VE**	E		WS
82204	**VE**	E	*LN*	BN
82205	**AL**	E	*LN*	BN
82206	**VE**	E	*LN*	BN
82207	**VE**	E	*LN*	BN
82208	**VE**	E	*LN*	BN
82209	**VE**	E	*LN*	BN
82210	**VE**	E	*LN*	BN
82211	**VE**	E	*LN*	BN
82212	**VE**	E	*LN*	BN
82213	**VE**	E	*LN*	BN
82214	**VE**	E	*LN*	BN
82215	**VE**	E	*LN*	BN
82216	**VE**	E		EH
82217	**VE**	E	*LN*	BN
82218	**VE**	E	*LN*	BN
82219	**VE**	E	*LN*	BN
82220	**VE**	E	*LN*	BN
82222	**VE**	E	*LN*	BN
82223	**VE**	E	*LN*	BN
82224	**VE**	E	*LN*	BN
82225	**VE**	E	*LN*	BN
82226	**TW**	E		EH
82227	**VE**	E	*LN*	BN
82228	**VE**	E		WB
82229	**VE**	E		EH
82230	**VE**	E	*LN*	BN
82231	**VE**	E		ZB

DRIVING BRAKE VAN (110 mph)

Mark 3B. Air conditioned. T4 bogies. dg. ETS 6X.

82301–305 originally converted 2008. 82306–308 converted 2011–12. 82309 converted 2013.

g Fitted with a diesel generator for use while stabled in terminal stations or at depots. 48.5 t.

Lot No. 31042 Derby 1988. 45.2 t.

82301	(82117)	g	**CM**	AV	*CR*	AL
82302	(82151)	g	**CM**	AV	*CR*	AL
82303	(82135)	g	**CM**	AV	*CR*	AL
82304	(82130)	g	**CM**	AV	*CR*	AL
82305	(82134)	g	**CM**	AV	*CR*	AL
82306	(82144)		**AW**	AV	*TW*	CF
82307	(82131)		**AW**	AV	*TW*	CF
82308	(82108)		**AW**	AV	*TW*	CF
82309	(82104)	g	**CM**	AV	*CR*	AL

GANGWAYED BRAKE VAN (100 mph)

Mark 1. Short frame (57 ft). Load 10 t. Adapted 199? for use as Brake Luggage Van. Guard's compartment retained and former baggage area adapted for secure stowage of passengers' luggage. B4 bogies. 100 mph. ETS 1X.

Lot No. 30162 Pressed Steel 1956–57. 30.5 t.

92904 (80867, 99554)		**VN**	WC	*WC*	CS

HIGH SECURITY GENERAL UTILITY VAN

Mark 1. Short frame (57 ft). Load 14 t. Modified with new floors, three roller shutter doors per side and the end doors removed. Commonwealth bogies. ETS 0X.

Lot No. 30616 Pressed Steel 1959–60. 32 t.

94225 (86849, 93849)		**M**	WC	*WC*	CS

GENERAL UTILITY VAN (100 mph)

Mark 1. Short frame (57 ft). Load 14 t. Screw couplers. Adapted 2013/2010 for use as a water carrier with 3000 gallon capacity. ETS 0.

Non-standard livery: 96100 GWR Brown.

96100. Lot No. 30565 Pressed Steel 1959. 30 t. B5 bogies.
96175. Lot No. 30403 York/Glasgow 1958–60. 32 t. Commonwealth bogies.

96100 (86734, 93734)	x	**0**	VT	*VT*	TM
96175 (86628, 93628)	x	**M**	WC	*WC*	CS

KITCHEN CAR

Mark 1 converted from Corridor First in 2008 with staff accommodation. Commonwealth bogies. ETS 3.

Lot No. 30667 Swindon 1961. 35 t.

99316 (13321)	x	**M**	WC	*WC*	CS

BUFFET STANDARD

Mark 1 converted from Open Standard in 2013 by the removal of two seating bays and fitting of a buffet. –/48 2T. Commonwealth bogies. ETS 4.

Lot No. 30646 Wolverton 1961. 36 t.

99318 (4912)	x	**M**	WC	*WC*	CS

KITCHEN CAR

Mark 1 converted from Corridor Standard in 2011 with staff accommodation. Commonwealth bogies. ETS 3.

Lot No. 30685 Derby 1961–62. 34 t.

99712 (18893)	x	**M**	WC	*WC*	CS

OPEN STANDARD

Mark 1 Corridor Standard rebuilt in 1997 as Open Standard using components from 4936. –/64 2T. Commonwealth bogies. ETS 4.

Lot No. 30685 Derby 1961–62. 36 t.

99722 (25806, 18806)	x	**M**	WC	*WC*	CS

LUL 4 TC USED AS HAULED STOCK

The Class 438 4 TC sets were unpowered units designed to work in push-pull mode with Class 430 (4 Rep) tractor units and Class 33/1, 73 and 74 locomotives. They were converted from locomotive-hauled coaching stock built 1952–57.

The vehicles listed are owned by London Underground and used on both special services on the LU Metropolitan Line and on occasional specials on the National Rail network, top-and-tailed by locomotives.

Mark 1. Trailer Brake Second side corridor with Lavatory (TBSK). Lot No. 30229. Metro-Cammell 1957. 35.5 t.

70823	(34970)	**M**	LU	*WC*	RS

Mark 1. Trailer First side corridor with Lavatory (TFK). Lot No. 30019. Swindon 1954. 33.5 t.

71163	(13097)	**M**	LU	*WC*	RS

Mark 1. Driving Trailer Second Open (DTSO).

76297. Lot No. 30086. Eastleigh 1955. 32.0 t.
76324. Lot No. 30149. Swindon 1956. 32.0 t.

76297	(3938)	**M**	LU	*WC*	RS
76324	(4009)	**M**	LU	*WC*	RS

NNR REGISTERED CARRIAGES

These carriages are permitted to operate on the national railway network only between Sheringham and Cromer as an extension of North Norfolk Railway (NNR) "North Norfolkman" services. Only NNR coaches currently registered for use on the national railway network are listed.

KITCHEN BUFFET STANDARD

Mark 1. Built as Unclassified Restaurant. Rebuilt with Buffet Counter and seating reduced. –/23. Commonwealth bogies. Lot No. 30632 Swindon 1960–61. 39 t.

1969 v **CC** NN *NY* NO

OPEN FIRST

Mark 1. 42/–. Commonwealth bogies. Lot No. 30697 Swindon 1962–63. 36 t.

3116 v **CC** NN *NY* NO

OPEN STANDARD

Mark 1. –/48 2T. BR Mark 1 bogies. Lot No. 30121 Eastleigh 1953–55. 32 t.

4372 v **CC** NN *NY* NO

GANGWAYED BRAKE VAN

Mark 1. Short frame (57 ft). Now fitted with a kitchen. BR Mark 1 bogies. Lot No. 30224 Cravens 1955–56. 31.5 t.

81033 v **CC** NN *NY* NO

NYMR REGISTERED CARRIAGES

These carriages are permitted to operate on the national railway network but may only be used to convey fare-paying passengers between Middlesbrough and Whitby on the Esk Valley branch as an extension of North Yorkshire Moors Railway services between Pickering and Grosmont. Only NYMR coaches currently registered for use on the national railway network are listed.

RESTAURANT FIRST

Mark 1. 24/–. Commonwealth bogies. Lot No. 30633 Swindon 1961. 42.5 t.

324	x	**PC**	NY	*NY*	NY	JOS de CRAU

BUFFET STANDARD

Mark 1. –/44 2T. Commonwealth bogies.

Lot No. 30520 Wolverton 1960. 38 t.

1823	v	**M**	NY	*NY*	NY

OPEN STANDARD

Mark 1. –/64 2T (* –/60 2W 2T, † –/60 3W 1T). BR Mark 1 bogies.

3798/3801. Lot No. 30079 York 1953. 33 t.
3860/72. Lot No. 30080 York 1954. 33 t.
3948. Lot No. 30086 Eastleigh 1954–55. 33 t.
4198/4252. Lot No. 30172 York 1956. 33 t.
4286/90. Lot No. 30207 BRCW 1956. 33 t.
4455. Lot No. 30226 BRCW 1957. 33 t.

3798	v	**M**	NY	*NY*	NY
3801	v	**CC**	NY	*NY*	NY
3860	v*	**M**	NY	*NY*	NY
3872	v†	**BG**	NY	*NY*	NY
3948	v	**CC**	NY	*NY*	NY
4198	v	**CC**	NY	*NY*	NY
4252	v*	**CC**	NY	*NY*	NY
4286	v	**CC**	NY	*NY*	NY
4290	v	**M**	NY	*NY*	NY
4455	v	**CC**	NY	*NY*	NY

OPEN STANDARD

Mark 1. –/48 2T. BR Mark 1 bogies.

4786. Lot No. 30376 York 1957. 33 t.
4817. Lot No. 30473 BRCW 1959. 33 t.

4786	v	**CH**	NY	*NY*	NY
4817	v	**M**	NY	*NY*	NY

OPEN STANDARD

Mark 1. Later vehicles built with Commonwealth bogies. –/64 2T.

Lot No. 30690 Wolverton 1961–62. Aluminium window frames. 37 t.

4990	v	**M**	NY	*NY*	NY
5000	v	**M**	NY	*NY*	NY
5029	v	**CH**	NY	*NY*	NY

OPEN BRAKE STANDARD

Mark 1. –/39 1T. BR Mark 1 bogies.

Lot No. 30170 Doncaster 1956. 34 t.

9225 v **M** NY *NY* NY | 9274 v **M** NY *NY* NY

CORRIDOR COMPOSITE

Mark 1. 24/18 1T. BR Mark 1 bogies.

15745. Lot No. 30179 Metro Cammell 1956. 36 t.
16156. Lot No. 30665 Derby 1961. 36 t.

15745 v **M** NY *NY* NY | 16156 v **CC** NY *NY* NY

CORRIDOR BRAKE COMPOSITE

Mark 1. Two First Class and three Standard Class compartments. 12/18 2T. BR Mark 1 bogies.

Lot No. 30185 Metro Cammell 1956. 36 t.

21100 v **CC** NY *NY* NY

CORRIDOR BRAKE STANDARD

Mark 1. –/24 1T. BR Mark 1 bogies.

Lot No. 30233 Gloucester 1957. 35 t.

35089 v **CC** NY *NY* NY

PULLMAN BRAKE THIRD

Built 1928 by Metropolitan Carriage & Wagon Company. –/30. Gresley bogies. 37.5 t.

232 v **PC** NY *NY* NY CAR No. 79

PULLMAN KITCHEN FIRST

Built by Metro-Cammell 1960–61 for East Coast Main Line services. 20/– 2T. Commonwealth bogies. 41.2 t.

318 x **PC** NY *NY* NY ROBIN

PULLMAN PARLOUR FIRST

Built by Metro-Cammell 1960–61 for East Coast Main Line services. 29/– 2T. Commonwealth bogies. 38.5 t.

328 x **PC** NY *NY* NY OPAL

2.2. HIGH SPEED TRAIN TRAILER CARS

HSTs consist of a number of trailer cars (usually between four and nine) with a power car at each end. All trailers are classified Mark 3 and have BT10 bogies with disc brakes and central door locking. Heating is by a 415 V three-phase supply and vehicles have air conditioning. Maximum speed is 125 mph.

The trailer cars have one standard 23m bodyshell for both First and Standard Class, thus facilitating easy conversion from one class to the other. As built all cars had facing seating around tables with Standard Class carriages having nine bays of seats per side which did not line up with the eight windows per side.

All vehicles underwent a mid-life refurbishment in the 1980s with Standard Class seating layouts revised to incorporate unidirectional seating in addition to facing. A further refurbishment programme was completed in November 2000, with each company having a different scheme as follows:

Great Western Trains (later First Great Western). Green seat covers and extra partitions between seat bays.

Great North Eastern Railway. New lighting panels and brown seat covers.

Virgin CrossCountry. Green seat covers. Standard Class vehicles had four seats in the centre of each carriage replaced with a luggage stack. All have now passed to other operators.

Midland Mainline. Grey seat covers, redesigned seat squabs, side carpeting and two seats in the centre of each Standard Class carriage and one in First Class carriages replaced with a luggage stack.

Since then there have been many separate, and very different, refurbishment projects:

Midland Mainline was first to refurbish its vehicles a second time during 2003–04. This involved fitting new fluorescent and halogen ceiling lighting, although the original seats were retained in First and Standard Class, but with blue upholstery.

London St Pancras–Sheffield/Leeds and Nottingham services are now operated by **East Midlands Railway.** Previous operator East Midlands Trains embarked on another, less radical, refurbishment in 2009–10 which included retention of the original seats but with red upholstery in Standard Class and blue in First Class. EMR will be replacing its sets with former LNER sets during the first part of 2020.

First Great Western (now **Great Western Railway**) started a major rebuild of its HST sets in late 2006, with the programme completed in 2008. The new interiors featured new lighting and seating throughout. First Class seats had leather upholstery, and were made by Primarius UK. Standard Class seats were of high-back design by Grammer. A number of sets operated without a full buffet or kitchen car, instead using one of 19 TS vehicles converted to include a "mini buffet" counter for use on shorter distance services. During 2012 15 402xx or 407xx buffet vehicles were converted to Trailer Standards to make the rakes formed as 7-cars up to 8-cars.

Great Western Railway is retaining 11 short 4-car sets for local and regional services. Trailers for these sets are being fitted with power doors and renumbered in the 48xxx and 49xxx series'.

Having increased its sets to 9-car sets in 2004, at the end of 2006 **GNER** embarked on a major rebuild of its HSTs. All vehicles have similar interiors to the Mark 4 "Mallard" fleet, with new Primarius seating. The refurbishment of the 13 sets was completed by **National Express East Coast** in late 2009, these trains were later operated by **Virgin Trains East Coast** and then **London North Eastern Railway**. VTEC refurbished its sets in 2015–16, with the same seats retained but with new upholstery, and leather in First Class. Nine of these sets will transfer to East Midlands Railway in early 2020.

Open access operator **Grand Central** started operation in December 2007 with a new service from Sunderland to London King's Cross. This operator had three sets mostly using stock converted from loco-hauled Mark 3s. The seats in Standard Class have First Class spacing and in most vehicles are all facing. These sets were withdrawn in December 2017 and transferred to East Midlands Trains (now EMR). They were refurbished in 2018–19, with ex-GWR buffet cars used instead of the original Grand Central buffet cars.

CrossCountry reintroduced HSTs to the Cross-Country network from 2008. Five sets were refurbished at Wabtec, Doncaster principally for use on the Plymouth–Edinburgh route. Three of these sets use stock mostly converted from loco-hauled Mark 3s and two are sets ex-Midland Mainline. The interiors are similar to refurbished East Coast sets, although the seating layout is different and one toilet per carriage has been removed in favour of a luggage stack. These sets are currently being fitted with sliding power doors, with all due to be completed by early 2020.

ScotRail started operating HSTs from October 2018. The operator will have a fleet of 17 5-car and nine 4-car former GWR sets (fitted with sliding power doors) for use between Glasgow/Edinburgh and Aberdeen/Inverness, as well as on the Aberdeen–Inverness route. Initially some unrefurbished sets are being used as cover whilst the heavily delayed programme to fit the 26 sets with sliding power doors is completed.

Operator Codes

Operator codes are shown in the heading before each set of vehicles. The first letter is always "T" for HST carriages, denoting a Trailer vehicle. The second letter denotes the passenger accommodation in that vehicle, for example "F" for First. "GS" denotes Guards accommodation and Standard Class seating. This is followed by catering provision, with "B" for buffet, and "K" for a kitchen and buffet:

TC	Trailer Composite
TCK	Trailer Composite Kitchen
TF	Trailer First
TFB	Trailer Buffet First
TFKB	Trailer Kitchen Buffet First
TGFB	Trailer Guard's Buffet First
TSB	Trailer Buffet Standard
TS	Trailer Standard
TGS	Trailer Guard's Standard

Power doors: All HSTs now operated by CrossCountry and Great Western Railway and most operated by ScotRail have been fitted with power sliding doors and retention toilets. Those vehicles completed so far are shown with a "p" in the Notes column.

TRAILER BUFFET STANDARD TSB

19 vehicles converted at Laira 2009–10 from HST TSs for First Great Western. Refurbished with Grammer seating.

40101–119. For Lot No. details see TS. –/70 1T. 35.5 t.

40101	(42170)	**FD**	P	LM
40102	(42223)	**FD**	P	LM
40103	(42316)	**GW**	P	LM
40104	(42254)	**FD**	P	LM
40105	(42084)	**FD**	P	LM
40106	(42162)	**FD**	P	LM
40107	(42334)	**FD**	P	LM
40108	(42314)	**GW**	P	LM
40109	(42262)	**FD**	P	LM
40110	(42187)	**FD**	P	LM
40111	(42248)	**FD**	P	LM
40112	(42336)	**FD**	P	LM
40113	(42309)	**GW**	P	LM
40114	(42086)	**FD**	P	LM
40115	(42320)	**FD**	P	LM
40116	(42147)	**FD**	P	LM
40117	(42249)	**GW**	P	LM
40118	(42338)	**FD**	P	LM
40119	(42090)	**FD**	P	LM

TRAILER BUFFET FIRST TFB

Converted from TSB by fitting First Class seats. Renumbered from 404xx series by subtracting 200. All refurbished by First Great Western and fitted with Primarius leather seating. 23/–.

40204–221. Lot No. 30883 Derby 1976–77. 36.12 t.
40231. Lot No. 30899 Derby 1978–79. 36.12 t.

40204	**EA**	A	*EM*	DY
40205	**EA**	A	*EM*	DY
40207	**FD**	A		EP
40210	**FD**	A		EP
40221	**EA**	A	*EM*	DY
40231	**FD**	A		EP

TRAILER BUFFET STANDARD TSB

Renumbered from 400xx series by adding 400. –/33 1W.

40433 was numbered 40233 for a time when fitted with 23 First Class seats.

40402–426. Lot No. 30883 Derby 1976–77. 36.12 t.
40433. Lot No. 30899 Derby 1978–79. 36.12 t.

40402	**V**	AV	ZR
40424	**GC**	A	DY
40426	**GC**	A	EP
40433	**GC**	A	EP

▲ BR blue & grey-liveried Mark 2F Buffet First 1200 is seen near Penzance on 13/04/19. **Robert Pritchard**

▼ BR carmine & cream-liveried Mark 1 Open First 3068 is seen at Bletchley on 07/07/19. **Mark Beal**

▲ BR chocolate & cream-liveried Mark 1 Open First 3119 is seen near Craigenhill Summit on 23/09/18. **Robin Ralston**

▼ Royal Train-liveried Royal Kitchen/Household Dining Car 2917 is seen near Symington on 28/06/19. **Robin Ralston**

▲ WCRC maroon-liveried Mark 1 Open First 99125 (3113) is seen at Carlisle on 20/07/19. **Robert Pritchard**

▼ Northern Belle-liveried Open First 3182 "Warwick" is seen at Hanslope Junction on 07/07/19. **Mark Beal**

▲ BR chocolate & cream-liveried Mark 1 Open Standard 4959 is seen at Carlisle on 27/04/19. **Ian Beardsley**

▼ BR blue & grey liveried Mark 2F Open Standard 5961 is seen at Penzance on 13/04/19. **Ian Beardsley**

▲ Revised Direct Rail Services-liveried Mark 2F Open Brake Standard 9525 is seen at Great Yarmouth on 06/08/19. **Robert Pritchard**

▼ Great Western Railway-liveried Mark 3A Sleeping Car with Pantry 10601 is seen at London Paddington on 01/06/19. **Robert Pritchard**

▲ Greater Anglia-liveried Mark 3B Open First 11082 is seen at Norwich on 04/09/19. **Robert Pritchard**

▼ TransPennine Express Mark 5A Open First 11501 is seen Earlestown on 11/09/18. **Alan Hart**

▲ Virgin Trains East Coast-liveried Mark 4 Open First 11426 is seen at Doncaster on 17/06/19. **Robert Pritchard**

▼ Arriva Trains Wales-liveried Mark 3A Open Standard 12184 is seen at Llandudno Junction on 09/08/18. **Robert Pritchard**

▲ Chiltern Railways Mainline-liveried Mark 3A Open Standard 12625 is seen at Dorridge on 20/06/19. **Robert Pritchard**

▼ Caledonian Sleeper Mark 5 Sleeping Car 15333 is seen at Bletchley on 30/06/19. **Mark Beal**

▲ Mark 2B Couchette/Generator Coach 17105 is seen at Cottam Power Station on 28/09/19. **Robert Pritchard**

▼ In Virgin Trains East Coast livery with LNER logos, Mark 4 Driving Brake Van 82223 passes Doncaster leading the 14.30 Edinburgh–London King's Cross on 17/06/19. **Robert Pritchard**

▲ WCRC maroon-liveried Mark 1 Kitchen Car 99316 (converted from Corridor First) is seen at London Euston on 14/07/18. **Tony Christie**

▼ BR carmine & cream-liveried Mark 1 Open Standard 3948, one of the North Yorkshire Moors Railway fleet, is seen at Whitby on 19/04/19. **Ian Beardsley**

▲ In Stagecoach long distance livery with new EMR InterCity logos, HST TKBF is seen at Leicester on 19/08/19. **Robert Pritchard**

▼ CrossCountry-liveried HST TS 42097, fitted with sliding doors, is seen near Rotherham Masborough on 06/06/19. **Robert Pritchard**

▲ ScotRail InterCity-liveried HST Trailer Standard 42292 is seen at Jamestown on 14/07/19. **Robin Ralston**

▼ Great Western Railway-liveried HST Trailer Guard's Standard 49104 is seen at Liskeard on 21/07/19. **Tony Christie**

▲ Royal Scotsman Saloon 99961 "State Car No. 1" is seen near Drem on 05/09/18. **Robin Ralston**

▼ Pullman-liveried Pullman Parlour Second 348 "TOPAZ" is seen at Totnes on 22/07/18. **Tony Christie**

▲ BR carmine & cream-liveried Mark 1 Corridor Brake Standard Locomotive Support Coach 35451 is seen at Craigenhill on 18/02/19. **Robin Ralston**

▼ All over dark blue-liveried HST Barrier Vehicle 6340 passes Durham on 04/04/19. **Robert Pritchard**

▲ Arlington Fleet Services-liveried EMU Translator Vehicle 64664 is seen at Great Wymondley, near Hitchin, on 29/06/19. **Mark Beal**

▼ Network Rail yellow Brake Force Runner 96604 is seen at Norwich on 15/03/19. **Robert Pritchard**

▲ Network Rail yellow Ultrasonic Test Coach 62287 is seen at Norwich on 15/03/19. **Robert Pritchard**

▼ Network Rail yellow New Measurement Train Lecture Coach 975984 is seen on the approaches to Sheffield on 22/06/19. **Robert Pritchard**

TRAILER GUARD'S MINIATURE BUFFET FIRST TGFB

Refurbished 2018–20 for ScotRail. Former Great Western Railway vehicles. Primarius leather seating. Fitted with a new corner buffet counter and kitchen. 32/– 1T.

40601–626. For Lot No. details see TF. 39.1 t.

40601	(41032)	p	**SI**	A	*SR*	IS
40602	(41038)	p	**SI**	A	*SR*	IS
40603	(41052)		**SI**			
40604	(41024)	p	**SI**	A	*SR*	IS
40605	(41094)	p	**SI**	A	*SR*	IS
40606	(41104)		**SI**			
40607	(41136)		**SI**			
40608	(41122)	p	**SI**	A	*SR*	IS
40609	(41020)		**SI**			
40610	(41103)	p	**SI**	A	*SR*	IS
40611	(41130)		**SI**			
40612	(41134)	p	**SI**	A	*SR*	IS
40613	(41135)		**SI**			
40614	(41010)		**SI**			
40615	(41022)		**SI**			
40616	(41142)	p	**SI**	A	*SR*	IS
40617	(41144)		**SI**			
40618	(41016)		**SI**			
40619	(41124)		**SI**			
40620	(41158)		**SI**			
40621	(41146)		**SI**			
40622	(41006)		**SI**			
40623	(41180)		**SI**			
40624	(41116)	p	**SI**	A	*SR*	IS
40625	(41137)	p	**SI**	A	*SR*	IS
40626	(41012)		**SI**			

TRAILER KITCHEN BUFFET FIRST TFKB

These vehicles have larger kitchens than the 402xx and 404xx series vehicles, and are used in trains where a full meal service is required. They were renumbered from the 403xx series (in which the seats were unclassified) by adding 400 to the previous number. 17/–.

* Refurbished former GWR vehicles. Primarius leather seating.
m Refurbished former LNER vehicles with Primarius leather seating.

40700–721. Lot No. 30921 Derby 1978–79. 38.16 t.
40722–735. Lot No. 30940 Derby 1979–80. 38.16 t.
40737–753. Lot No. 30948 Derby 1980–81. 38.16 t.
40754–757. Lot No. 30966 Derby 1982. 38.16 t.

40700		**ST**	P	*EM*	NL
40701	m	**VE**	P		GA
40702	m	**VE**	P		GA
40703	*	**FD**	A		ZB
40704	m	**VE**	A		EP
40705	m	**VE**	A		EC
40706	m	**VE**	A		EP
40707	*	**FD**	A		EP
40708	m	**VE**	P		GA
40710	*	**FD**	A		EP
40711	m	**VE**	A		NL
40713	*	**FD**	A		EP
40715	*	**GW**	A		EP
40716	*	**FD**	A		EP
40718	*	**FD**	A		EP
40720	m	**BG**	A		EP
40721	*	**FD**	A		EP
40722	*	**FD**	A		EP
40727	*	**FD**	A		EP
40728		**ST**	P	*EM*	NL
40730		**ST**	P	*EM*	NL
40732		**VE**	P		TY
40733	*	**FD**	A		EP
40734	*	**FD**	A		EP
40735	m	**VE**	A		GA
40737	m	**VE**	A		GA
40739	*	**FD**	A		EP
40740	m	**VE**	A		GA
40741		**ST**	P	*EM*	NL
40742	m	**VE**	A		EP
40743	*	**GW**	A		EP
40746		**ST**	P	*EM*	NL

40748	m	**VE**	A		NL
40749		**ST**	P	*EM*	NL
40750	m	**VE**	A		GA
40751		**VE**	P	*EM*	NL
40752	*	**FD**	A		EP
40753		**ST**	P	*EM*	NL
40754		**ST**	P	*EM*	NL
40755	*	**GW**	A		EP
40756		**ST**	P	*EM*	NL
40757	*	**FD**	A		EP

TRAILER KITCHEN BUFFET FIRST TFKB

These vehicles have been converted from TSBs in the 404xx series to be similar to the 407xx series vehicles. 17/–.

40802/804/811 were numbered 40212/232/211 for a time when fitted with 23 First Class seats.

* Refurbished former GWR vehicles. Primarius leather seating.
m Refurbished former LNER vehicle with Primarius leather seating.

40801–803/805/808/809/811. Lot No. 30883 Derby 1976–77. 38.16 t.
40804/806/807/810. Lot No. 30899 Derby 1978–79. 38.16 t.

40801	(40027, 40427)	*	**GW**	P	LM
40802	(40012, 40412)	*	**FD**	P	LM
40803	(40018, 40418)	*	**GW**	P	LM
40804	(40032, 40432)	*	**FD**	P	LM
40805	(40020, 40420)	m	**VE**	P	TY
40806	(40029, 40429)	*	**FD**	P	LM
40807	(40035, 40435)	*	**FD**	P	LM
40808	(40015, 40415)	*	**FD**	P	LM
40809	(40014, 40414)	*	**FD**	P	LM
40810	(40030, 40430)	*	**FD**	P	LM
40811	(40011, 40411)	*	**FD**	P	LM

TRAILER BUFFET FIRST TFB

Converted from TSB by First Great Western. Refurbished with Primarius leather seating. 23/–.

40900/902/904. Lot No. 30883 Derby 1976–77. 36.12 t.
40901/903. Lot No. 30899 Derby 1978–79. 36.12 t.

40900	(40022, 40422)	**FD**	FG	PM
40901	(40036, 40436)	**GW**	P	LM
40902	(40023, 40423)	**FD**	FG	PM
40903	(40037, 40437)	**GW**	P	LM
40904	(40001, 40401)	**GW**	FG	PM

TRAILER FIRST TF

As built and m 48/– 2T (m† 48/– 1T – one toilet removed for trolley space).
* Refurbished former GWR vehicles. Primarius leather seating.
c Refurbished CrossCountry vehicles with Primarius seating and 2 tip-up seats. One toilet removed. 40/– 1TD 1W.
m Refurbished former LNER vehicles with Primarius leather seating.
px Refurbished CrossCountry vehicles with power doors, Primarius seating

and one toilet removed. 39/– 1TD 1W.
s Fitted with centre luggage stack, disabled toilet and wheelchair space. 46/– 1T 1TD 1W.
w Wheelchair space. 47/– 2T 1W. (41154 47/– 1TD 1T 1W).
x Toilet removed for trolley space (FGW). 48/– 1T.

41004–056. Lot No. 30881 Derby 1976–77. 33.66 t.
41057–120. Lot No. 30896 Derby 1977–78. 33.66 t.
41122–146. Lot No. 30938 Derby 1979–80. 33.66 t.
41149–166. Lot No. 30947 Derby 1980. 33.66 t.
41167/169. Lot No. 30963 Derby 1982. 33.66 t.
41170. Lot No. 30967 Derby 1982. Former prototype vehicle. 33.66 t.
41176. Lot No. 30897 Derby 1977. 33.66 t.
41180. Lot No. 30884 Derby 1976–77. 33.66 t.
41182/183/189. Lot No. 30939 Derby 1979–80. 33.66 t.
41185–187. Lot No. 30969 Derby 1982. 33.66 t.
41190. Lot No. 30882 Derby 1976–77. 33.60 t.
41192. Lot No. 30897 Derby 1977–79. 33.60 t.

41004	*x	**FD**	A		EP
41006	*w	**GW**	A		ZB
41008	*w	**FD**	A		EP
41010	*w	**FD**	A		EP
41012	*w	**GW**	A		ZB
41016	*w	**FD**	A		ZB
41018	*w	**FD**	A		EP
41020	*w	**FD**	A		ZB
41022	*w	**FD**	A	*SR*	IS
41026	px	**XC**	A	*XC*	LA
41028	*w	**FD**	A		EP
41030	*w	**FD**	A		EP
41034	*w	**FD**	A		EP
41035	c	**XC**	A	*XC*	LA
41039	m†	**VE**	A		GA
41040	mw	**VE**	A		GA
41041	s	**ST**	P	*EM*	NL
41044	mw	**VE**	A		GA
41046	s	**ST**	P	*EM*	NL
41052	*w	**FD**	A		EP
41056	*w	**FD**	A		EP
41057		**ST**	P	*EM*	NL
41059	*w	**GW**	FG		LM
41061	w	**ST**	P	*EM*	NL
41062		**VE**	P		TY
41063		**ST**	P	*EM*	NL
41064	s	**ST**	P	*EM*	NL
41066	m†	**VE**	A		NL
41067	s	**ST**	P	*EM*	NL
41068	w	**VE**	P		TY
41069	s	**ST**	P	*EM*	NL
41070	s	**ST**	P	*EM*	NL
41071		**ST**	P	*EM*	NL

41072	s	**ST**	P	*EM*	NL
41075		**ST**	P	*EM*	NL
41076	s	**ST**	P	*EM*	NL
41077		**ST**	P	*EM*	NL
41079		**ST**	P	*EM*	NL
41083	mw	**VE**	P		GA
41084	s	**ST**	P	*EM*	NL
41087	m†	**VE**	A		EP
41088	mw	**VE**	A		EP
41089	*w	**FD**	A		EP
41090	m†	**VE**	A		GA
41091	m†	**VE**	A		EP
41092	mw	**VE**	A		EP
41095	mw	**VE**	P		GA
41097	m†	**VE**	A		GA
41098	mw	**VE**	A		GA
41099	m†	**VE**	A		NL
41100	mw	**VE**	A		NL
41102	*w	**FD**	A		EP
41103	*x	**FD**	A		ZB
41104	*w	**FD**	A	*SR*	IS
41106	*w	**FD**	A		EP
41108	*w	**GW**	P		LM
41110	*w	**FD**	A		EP
41111		**ST**	P	*EM*	NL
41112		**VE**	P		TY
41113	s	**ST**	P	*EM*	NL
41115	m†	**VE**	P		GA
41117		**ST**	P	*EM*	NL
41118	mw	**BG**	A		EP
41120	m†	**VE**	A		NL
41124	*w	**FD**	A	*SR*	IS
41126	*w	**FD**	A	*SR*	IS

41128	*w	**FD**	A		EP
41130	*w	**FD**	A	*SR*	IS
41132	*w	**FD**	A		EP
41135	*w	**FD**	A		EP
41136	*w	**FD**	A		ZB
41138	*w	**FD**	A		EP
41140	*w	**FD**	A	*SR*	IS
41144	*w	**FD**	A	*SR*	IS
41146	*w	**GW**	A		ZB
41149	*w	**GW**	P		LM
41150	mw	**VE**	A		NL
41151	m†	**VE**	A		GA
41152	mw	**VE**	A		GA
41154	w	**VE**	P		TY
41156		**ST**	P	*EM*	NL
41158	*w	**GW**	A	*SR*	IS
41159	m†	**VE**	P		GA
41160	*w	**GW**	FG		PM
41161	*w	**GW**	P		LM
41162	*w	**GW**	P		LM
41164	mw	**VE**	A		EP
41165	mw	**VE**	P		GA
41166	*w	**GW**	FG		PM
41167	*w	**FD**	FG		PM
41169	*w	**FD**	P		LM

41193–195/201–206. Lot No. 30878 Derby 1975–76. 34.3 t. Converted from Mark 3A Open First.
41207–209. Lot No. 30877 Derby 1975–77. Converted from Mark 3A Open Standard.

41170	(41001)	m†	**BG**	A		EP
41176	(42142, 42352)	*w	**GW**	P		LM
41180	(40511)	*w	**FD**	A		ZB
41182	(42278)	*w	**GW**	P		LM
41183	(42274)	*w	**GW**	P		LM
41185	(42313)	m†	**VE**	P		GA
41186	(42312)	*w	**FD**	P		LM
41187	(42311)	*w	**FD**	P		LM
41189	(42298)	*w	**GW**	P		LM
41190	(42088)	m†	**VE**	P		NL
41192	(42246)	*w	**GW**	P		LM

The following carriages have been converted from loco-hauled Mark 3 vehicles.

41193	(11060)	px	**XC**	P	*XC*	LA
41194	(11016)	px	**XC**	P	*XC*	LA
41195	(11020)	px	**XC**	P	*XC*	LA
41204	(11023)		**EA**	A	*EM*	DY
41205	(11036)	w	**EA**	A	*EM*	DY
41206	(11055)		**EA**	A	*EM*	DY
41207	(12033, 42403)		**EA**	A	*EM*	DY
41208	(12112, 42406)	w	**EA**	A	*EM*	DY
41209	(12088, 42409)		**EA**	A	*EM*	DY

TRAILER STANDARD TS

42158 was numbered 41177 for a time when fitted with First Class seats.
42310 was numbered 41188 for a time when fitted with First Class seats.

Standard seating and m –/76 2T.
* Refurbished former Great Western Railway vehicles. Grammer seating. –/80 2T (unless h – high density).
c Refurbished CrossCountry vehicles with Primarius seating. –/82 1T.
§c Refurbished CrossCountry vehicles with Primarius seating and 2 tip-up

seats. –/66 1TD 2W. 42379/380 are –/71 1TD 1T 2W.
d Former Great Western Railway vehicles with universal access toilet and 5, 6 or 7 tip-up seats. –/68 1T 1TD 2W.
h "High density" former Great Western Railway vehicles. –/84 2T.
k "High density" former Great Western Railway refurbished vehicle with disabled persons toilet and 5, 6 or 7 tip-up seats. –/72 1T 1TD 2W.
m Refurbished former LNER vehicles with Primarius seating.
pr Refurbished ScotRail vehicles with power doors and Grammer seating. –/74.
ps Refurbished ScotRail vehicles with power doors and Grammer seating. –/74 1T.
p* Refurbished ScotRail vehicles with power doors, Grammer seating and universal access toilet. –/58 1TD 2W.
px Refurbished CrossCountry vehicles with power doors and Primarius seating. –/80 1T.
pt Refurbished CrossCountry vehicles with power doors, Primarius seating and universal access toilet. –/64 1TD 2W.
u Centre luggage stack (EMR) –/74 2T.
w Centre luggage stack and wheelchair space (EMR) –72 2T 1W.
† Disabled persons toilet (LNER) –/62 1T 1TD 1W.

42003–089/362. Lot No. 30882 Derby 1976–77. 33.6 t.
42091–250. Lot No. 30897 Derby 1977–79. 33.6 t.
42251–305. Lot No. 30939 Derby 1979–80. 33.6 t.
42306–322. Lot No. 30969 Derby 1982. 33.6 t.
42323–341. Lot No. 30983 Derby 1984–85. 33.6 t.
42342/360. Lot No. 30949 Derby 1982. 33.47 t. Converted from TGS.
42343/345. Lot No. 30970 Derby 1982. 33.47 t. Converted from TGS.
42344/361. Lot No. 30964 Derby 1982. 33.47 t. Converted from TGS.
42346/347/350/351/379/380/551–564. Lot No. 30881 Derby 1976–77. 33.66 t. Converted from TF.
42348/349/363/364/381/565–570. Lot No. 30896 Derby 1977–78. 33.66 t. Converted from TF.
42354. Lot No. 30897 Derby 1977. Was TF from 1983 to 1992. 33.66 t.
42353/355–357. Lot No. 30967 Derby 1982. Ex-prototype vehicles. 33.66 t.
42366–378/382/383/401–409. Lot No. 30877 Derby 1975–77. 34.3 t. Converted from Mark 3A Open Standard.
42384. Lot No. 30896 Derby 1977–78. 33.66 t. Converted from TF.
42501/509/513/515/517. Lot No. 30948 Derby 1980–81. 34.8 t. Converted from TFKB.
42502/506/508/514/516. Lot No. 30940 Derby 1979–80. 34.8 t. Converted from TFKB.
42503/504/510/511. Lot No. 30921 Derby 1978–79. 34.8 t. Converted from TFKB.
42505/507/512/518/519. Lot No. 30883 Derby 1976–77. 34.8 t. Converted from TSB.
42520. Lot No. 30899 Derby 1978–79. 34.8 t. Converted from TSB.
42571–579. Lot No. 30938 Derby 1979–80. 33.66 t. Converted from TF.
42580–583. Lot No. 30947 Derby 1980. 33.66 t. Converted from TF.
42584–586. Lot No. 30878 Derby 1975–76. Converted from Mark 3A Open First.

42003	*h	**FD**	A		ZB
42004	p*	**SI**	A	*SR*	IS
42005	*h	**GW**	A		LA
42006	*h	**FD**	A		EP
42007	*d	**FD**	A		ZB
42009	*h	**FD**	A		EP
42010	*h	**FD**	A	*SR*	IS
42012	*k	**FD**	A	*SR*	IS

42013	*h	**FD**	A		EP
42014	*h	**FD**	A		ZB
42015	*k	**GW**	A		LA
42016	*h	**GW**	A		LA
42019	ps	**SI**	A	*SR*	IS
42021	*k	**FD**	A		ZB
42023	*h	**FD**	A		EP
42024	*k	**FD**	A		EP
42025	*h	**FD**	A		EP
42026	*h	**FD**	A		EP
42028	*h	**FD**	A		EP
42029	*h	**FD**	A		EP
42030	*k	**FD**	A	*SR*	IS
42031	*h	**FD**	A		EP
42032	*h	**FD**	A	*SR*	IS
42033	*	**FD**	A		ZB
42034	pr	**SI**	A	*SR*	IS
42035	*	**FD**	A		ZB
42036	px	**XC**	A	*XC*	LA
42037	px	**XC**	A	*XC*	LA
42038	c	**XC**	A	*XC*	LA
42039	*h	**FD**	A		EP
42040	*h	**FD**	A		EP
42041	*h	**FD**	A		EP
42042	*h	**FD**	A		ZB
42043	*h	**FD**	A		EP
42044	*h	**FD**	A		ZB
42045	ps	**SI**	A	*SR*	IS
42046	ps	**SI**	A	*SR*	IS
42047	*	**FD**	A		EP
42048	*h	**FD**	A		EP
42049	*h	**FD**	A		EP
42050	*h	**FD**	A		EP
42051	px	**XC**	A	*XC*	LA
42052	c	**XC**	A	*XC*	LA
42053	c	**XC**	A	*XC*	LA
42054	*	**FD**	A		EP
42055	p*	**SI**	A	*SR*	IS
42056	*	**FD**	A		EP
42057	m	**VE**	A		EP
42058	m	**VE**	A		EP
42059	m	**VE**	A		EP
42060	*h	**FD**	A		EP
42061	*h	**FD**	A		EP
42062	*k	**FD**	A		EP
42063	m	**VE**	A		GA
42064	m	**VE**	A		GA
42065	m	**VE**	A		GA
42066	*k	**FD**	A		EP
42067	*h	**FD**	A		EP
42068	*h	**FD**	A		EP
42069	*k	**FD**	A	*SR*	IS
42070	*h	**FD**	A		EP
42071	*h	**FD**	A		EP
42072	*	**FD**	A		ZB
42074	*h	**FD**	A		EP
42075	ps	**SI**	A	*SR*	IS
42076	*	**FD**	A	*SR*	IS
42077	*	**FD**	A		EP
42078	*	**FD**	A		EP
42079	*h	**FD**	A		EP
42080	*h	**FD**	A		EP
42081	*k	**FD**	A		EP
42083	*h	**FD**	A		EP
42087	*h	**GW**	P		LA
42089	*h	**FD**	A		EP
42091	m†	**VE**	A		NL
42092	*k	**FD**	P		LM
42094	*h	**FD**	FG		LA
42095	*	**FD**	FG		LA
42096	*h	**FD**	A		EP
42097	px	**XC**	A	*XC*	LA
42098	*h	**FD**	A		EP
42099	*h	**FD**	A		EP
42100	u	**ST**	P	*EM*	NL
42103	*k	**FD**	P		LA
42104	m	**VE**	A		EP
42105	*k	**FD**	P		LM
42106	m	**VE**	A		EP
42107	*	**FD**	A		ZB
42108	*h	**FD**	P		LM
42109	m	**VE**	P		GA
42110	m	**VE**	P		GA
42111	u	**ST**	P	*EM*	NL
42112	u	**ST**	P	*EM*	NL
42113	u	**ST**	P	*EM*	NL
42115	*h	**FD**	P		LM
42116	m†	**VE**	A		NL
42117	m	**VE**	P		GA
42118	*h	**FD**	A	*SR*	IS
42119	u	**ST**	P	*EM*	NL
42120	u	**ST**	P	*EM*	NL
42121	u	**ST**	P	*EM*	NL
42122	m	**VE**	A		EP
42123		**VE**	P		TY
42124	u	**ST**	P	*EM*	NL
42125		**VE**	P		TY
42126	*h	**FD**	A		EP
42127	m†	**VE**	A		GA
42128	m†	**VE**	A		GA
42129	*	**GW**	A	*SR*	IS
42130	m	**VE**	P		GA

42131	u	**ST**	P	*EM*	NL
42132	w	**ST**	P	*EM*	NL
42133	u	**ST**	P	*EM*	NL
42134	m	**VE**	A		EP
42135	u	**ST**	P	*EM*	NL
42136	u	**ST**	P	*EM*	NL
42137	u	**ST**	P	*EM*	NL
42139	u	**ST**	P	*EM*	NL
42140	u	**ST**	P	*EM*	NL
42141	u	**ST**	P	*EM*	NL
42143	*	**FD**	A		ZK
42144	*	**FD**	A		EP
42145	*	**FD**	A		ZK
42146	m	**VE**	A		NL
42148	u	**ST**	P	*EM*	NL
42149	u	**ST**	P	*EM*	NL
42150	m	**VE**	A		NL
42151	w	**ST**	P	*EM*	NL
42152	u	**ST**	P	*EM*	NL
42153	u	**ST**	P	*EM*	NL
42154	m	**VE**	A		NL
42155	w	**ST**	P	*EM*	NL
42156	u	**ST**	P	*EM*	NL
42157	u	**ST**	P	*EM*	NL
42158	m	**VE**	A		GA
42159	m†	**VE**	P		GA
42160	m	**VE**	P		GA
42161	m†	**VE**	A		EP
42163	m	**VE**	P		GA
42164		**ST**	P	*EM*	NL
42165		**ST**	P	*EM*	NL
42166	*h	**FD**	P		LM
42167	*h	**FD**	FG		LA
42169	*h	**FD**	P		LM
42171	m	**VE**	A		EP
42172	m	**VE**	A		EP
42173	*k	**FD**	P		LM
42175	*h	**FD**	FG		LA
42176	*h	**GW**	P		LA
42178	*h	**FD**	P		LM
42179	m	**VE**	A		EP
42180	m	**VE**	A		EP
42181	m	**VE**	A		EP
42182	m	**VE**	A		GA
42183	p*	**SI**	A	*SR*	IS
42184	ps	**SI**	A	*SR*	IS
42185	*	**FD**	A		EP
42186	m	**VE**	A		GA
42188	m†	**VE**	A		EP
42189	m†	**VE**	A		GA
42190	m	**VE**	A		GA
42191	m	**VE**	A		GA
42192	m	**VE**	A		GA
42193	m	**VE**	A		GA
42194	u	**VE**	P		TY
42195	*k	**FD**	P		LM
42196	*h	**FD**	A		EP
42197	*h	**FD**	A		EP
42198	m	**VE**	A		NL
42199	m	**VE**	A		NL
42200	*d	**GW**	A	*SR*	IS
42202	*k	**FD**	A		ZB
42205		**VE**	P		EC
42206	*d	**FD**	A	*SR*	IS
42207	*d	**FD**	A		ZB
42208	*	**FD**	A	*SR*	IS
42209	*	**FD**	A	*SR*	IS
42210		**VE**	P		EC
42211	*k	**FD**	A		ZB
42213	*h	**FD**	A		EP
42215	m	**VE**	A		EP
42216	*h	**FD**	A		EP
42217	*k	**FD**	P		LM
42219	m	**VE**	A		EP
42220	w	**ST**	P	*EM*	NL
42221	*h	**FD**	A		EP
42225		**VE**	P		TY
42226	m	**VE**	A		GA
42227		**VE**	P		TY
42228	m	**VE**	P		GA
42229		**VE**	P		TY
42230	u	**ST**	P	*EM*	NL
42231	*h	**FD**	FG		LA
42232	*h	**GW**	P		LM
42233	*h	**FD**	P		LM
42234	px	**XC**	P	*XC*	LA
42235	m	**VE**	A		EP
42236	*h	**FD**	A		EP
42237	m	**VE**	P		GA
42238	m†	**VE**	A		GA
42239	m†	**VE**	A		NL
42240	m	**VE**	A		NL
42241	m	**VE**	A		EP
42242	m	**BG**	A		EP
42243	m	**BG**	A		EP
42244	m	**VE**	A		EP
42245	*	**GW**	A		EP
42247	*h	**FD**	P		LM
42250	*	**GW**	A		ZB
42252	pr	**SI**	A	*SR*	IS
42253	*	**FD**	A		ZB
42255	*d	**FD**	A	*SR*	IS

42256	*	**FD**	A	*SR*	IS
42257	*	**FD**	A		ZB
42259	p*	**SI**	A	*SR*	IS
42260	*h	**FD**	A		EP
42261	*h	**FD**	A	*SR*	IS
42263	*	**FD**	A		ZK
42264	*k	**FD**	A		ZB
42265	p*	**SI**	A	*SR*	IS
42267	*d	**FD**	A	*SR*	IS
42268	*d	**FD**	A		ZB
42269	*	**FD**	A	*SR*	IS
42272	*h	**FD**	A		EP
42275	p*	**SI**	A	*SR*	IS
42276	ps	**SI**	A	*SR*	IS
42277	*	**FD**	A		ZB
42279	*d	**FD**	A		EP
42280	*	**FD**	A		EP
42281	*	**FD**	A		ZB
42283	*h	**FD**	A		EP
42284	*h	**FD**	A		EP
42286	m†	**VE**	P		GA
42287	*k	**FD**	A	*SR*	IS
42288	*h	**FD**	A		ZK
42289	*h	**FD**	A	*SR*	IS
42290	c	**XC**	P	*XC*	LA
42291	p*	**SI**	A	*SR*	IS
42292	p*	**SI**	A	*SR*	IS
42293	ps	**SI**	A	*SR*	IS
42294	*	**FD**	P		LM
42295	*d	**FD**	A	*SR*	IS
42296	*	**FD**	A		EP
42297	*	**FD**	A		ZB
42299	*d	**GW**	A		ZB
42300	*	**GW**	A		ZB
42301	*	**GW**	A	*SR*	IS
42302	*k	**FD**	P		LA
42303	*h	**FD**	P		LM
42304	*h	**FD**	FG		LA
42305	*h	**GW**	P		LM
42306	m	**VE**	P		GA
42307	m	**VE**	P		GA
42308	*h	**FD**	P		LM
42310	*k	**FD**	P		LA
42319	*h	**GW**	P		LM
42321	*h	**FD**	P		LM
42322	m	**VE**	P		GA
42323	m	**VE**	A		GA
42325	*	**FD**	A	*SR*	IS
42326	m	**VE**	P		GA
42327	w	**ST**	P	*EM*	NL
42328	w	**ST**	P	*EM*	NL
42329	w	**ST**	P	*EM*	NL
42330	m	**VE**	P		GA
42331	u	**ST**	P	*EM*	NL
42332	*	**FD**	A		EP
42333	ps	**SI**	A	*SR*	IS
42335	w	**VE**	P		TY
42337	w	**ST**	P	*EM*	NL
42339	w	**ST**	P	*EM*	NL
42340	m	**VE**	A		GA
42341	u	**ST**	P	*EM*	NL

42342	(44082)	px	**XC**	A	*XC*	LA
42343	(44095)	ps	**SI**	A	*SR*	IS
42344	(44092)	*k	**FD**	A	*SR*	IS
42345	(44096)	p*	**SI**	A	*SR*	IS
42346	(41053)	*h	**FD**	A		EP
42347	(41054)	*k	**FD**	A		EP
42348	(41073)	*k	**FD**	A		EP
42350	(41047)	*	**FD**	A		ZB
42351	(41048)	*	**GW**	A		EP
42353	(42001, 41171)	*k	**FD**	P		LM
42354	(42114, 41175)	m	**VE**	A		NL
42355	(42000, 41172)	m	**VE**	A		EP
42356	(42002, 41173)	*k	**GW**	A		EP
42357	(41002, 41174)	m	**VE**	A		EP
42360	(44084, 45084)	p*	**SI**	A	*SR*	IS
42361	(44099, 42000)	*h	**GW**	A		EP
42362	(42011, 41178)	*h	**FD**	A		EP
42363	(41082)	m†	**BG**	A		EP
42364	(41080)	*k	**GW**	P		LM

42366–378 were converted from loco-hauled Mark 3 vehicles for CrossCountry and 42382/383 for First Great Western.

42366	(12007)	pt	**XC**	P	*XC*	LA
42367	(12025)	px	**XC**	P	*XC*	LA
42368	(12028)	c	**XC**	P	*XC*	LA
42369	(12050)	px	**XC**	P	*XC*	LA
42370	(12086)	px	**XC**	P	*XC*	LA
42371	(12052)	pt	**XC**	P	*XC*	LA
42372	(12055)	c	**XC**	P	*XC*	LA
42373	(12071)	c	**XC**	P	*XC*	LA
42374	(12075)	pt	**XC**	P	*XC*	LA
42375	(12113)	px	**XC**	P	*XC*	LA
42376	(12085)	pt	**XC**	P	*XC*	LA
42377	(12102)	px	**XC**	P	*XC*	LA
42378	(12123)	px	**XC**	P	*XC*	LA
42379	(41036)	§c	**XC**	A	*XC*	LA
42380	(41025)	§c	**XC**	A	*XC*	LA
42381	(41058)	*k	**FD**	P		LM
42382	(12128)	*h	**GW**	P		LM
42383	(12172)	*h	**GW**	P		LM
42384	(41078)	w	**ST**	P	*EM*	NL

These carriages were converted from loco-hauled Mark 3 vehicles for Grand Central, now operated by East Midlands Railway. They have a lower density seating layout (most seats arranged around tables). –/62 2T.

42401	(12149)	**EA**	A	*EM*	DY
42402	(12155)	**EA**	A	*EM*	DY
42404	(12152)	**EA**	A	*EM*	DY
42405	(12136)	**EA**	A	*EM*	DY
42407	(12044)	**EA**	A	*EM*	DY
42408	(12121)	**EA**	A	*EM*	DY

These carriages have been converted from TFKB or TSB buffet cars to TS vehicles in 2011–12 (42501–515) and 2013–14 (42516–520) at Wabtec Kilmarnock for FGW. Refurbished with Grammer seating. –/84 1T. 34.8 t.

42501	(40344, 40744)	**FD**	A	EP
42502	(40331, 40731)	**FD**	A	ZB
42503	(40312, 40712)	**FD**	A	EP
42504	(40314, 40714)	**FD**	A	EP
42505	(40428, 40228)	**FD**	A	EP
42506	(40324, 40724)	**FD**	A	EP
42507	(40409, 40209)	**FD**	A	EP
42508	(40325, 40725)	**FD**	A	EP
42509	(40336, 40736)	**GW**	A	EP
42510	(40317, 40717)	**FD**	A	EP
42511	(40309, 40709)	**FD**	A	EP
42512	(40408, 40208)	**GW**	A	EP
42513	(40338, 40738)	**FD**	A	EP
42514	(40326, 40726)	**FD**	A	EP
42515	(40347, 40747)	**FD**	A	EP

42516	(40323, 40723)		**FD**	A		EP
42517	(40345, 40745)		**FD**	A		EP
42518	(40003, 40403)		**FD**	P		LM
42519	(40016, 40416)		**FD**	P		LM
42520	(40234, 40434)		**FD**	P		LM

These carriages have been converted from TF to TS vehicles in 2014 at Wabtec Kilmarnock for FGW. Refurbished with Grammer seating. –/80 1T (pr –/74). 35.5 t.

42551	(41003)	pr	**SI**	A	*SR*	IS
42552	(41007)		**FD**	A		EP
42553	(41009)	pr	**SI**	A	*SR*	IS
42554	(41011)		**GW**	A		LA
42555	(41015)		**FD**	A		ZB
42556	(41017)		**FD**	A		EP
42557	(41019)		**FD**	A		ZB
42558	(41021)		**FD**	A		ZB
42559	(41023)	pr	**SI**	A	*SR*	IS
42560	(41027)		**FD**	A		EP
42561	(41031)	pr	**SI**	A	*SR*	IS
42562	(41037)	pr	**SI**	A	*SR*	IS
42563	(41045)		**FD**	FG		LA
42564	(41051)		**FD**	A		EP
42565	(41085)		**FD**	FG		LA
42566	(41086)		**FD**	FG		LA
42567	(41093)		**FD**	A		ZB
42568	(41101)		**FD**	A		EP
42569	(41105)		**FD**	A		EP
42570	(41114)		**FD**	FG		LA
42571	(41121)	pr	**SI**	A	*SR*	IS
42572	(41123)		**FD**	A	*SR*	IS
42573	(41127)		**FD**	A		EP
42574	(41129)		**FD**	A		ZB
42575	(41131)		**FD**	A		EP
42576	(41133)	pr	**SI**	A	*SR*	IS
42577	(41141)	pr	**SI**	A	*SR*	IS
42578	(41143)	pr	**SI**	A	*SR*	IS
42579	(41145)		**GW**	A	*SR*	IS
42580	(41155)		**FD**	P		LA
42581	(41157)		**GW**	A		EP
42582	(41163)		**FD**	FG		LA
42583	(41153, 42385)		**GW**	P		LM

These carriages were converted from loco-hauled carriages for Grand Central, but have now been converted to TS for East Midlands Railway. –/62 2T.

42584	(11045, 41201)	**EA**	A	*EM*	DY
42585	(11017, 41202)	**EA**	A	*EM*	DY
42586	(11038, 41203)	**EA**	A	*EM*	DY

TRAILER GUARD'S STANDARD TGS

As built and m –/65 1T.
- * Refurbished Great Western Railway vehicles. Grammer seating and toilet removed for trolley store. –/67 (unless h).
- c Refurbished CrossCountry vehicles with Primarius seating. –/67 1T.
- p Refurbished CrossCountry vehicles with power doors and Primarius seating. –/67.
- h "High density" Great Western Railway vehicles. –/71.
- m Refurbished LNER vehicles with Primarius seating.
- s Fitted with centre luggage stack (EMR) –/63 1T. 44027 is –/64 1T.
- t Fitted with centre luggage stack –/61 1T.

44001–090. Lot No. 30949 Derby 1980–82. 33.47 t.
44091–094. Lot No. 30964 Derby 1982. 33.47 t.
44098–100. Lot No. 30970 Derby 1982. 33.47 t.

44001	*	**FD**	A		EP
44002	*h	**FD**	A		EP
44004	*h	**FD**	A		EP
44005	*h	**GW**	A		LA
44007	*h	**FD**	A		EP
44008	*h	**FD**	A		ZB
44009	*h	**FD**	A		EP
44010	*h	**FD**	A	*SR*	IS
44011	*	**FD**	A		EP
44012	p	**XC**	A	*XC*	LA
44013	*h	**FD**	A		EP
44014	*h	**FD**	A		ZB
44015	*	**FD**	A		EP
44016	*h	**FD**	A		EP
44017	c	**XC**	A	*XC*	LA
44018	*	**FD**	A		EP
44019	m	**VE**	A		GA
44020	*h	**FD**	A		EP
44021	p	**XC**	P	*XC*	LA
44022	*h	**FD**	A		EP
44023	*h	**FD**	A	*SR*	IS
44024	*h	**FD**	A		EP
44025	*	**FD**	A		EP
44026	*h	**FD**	A		EP
44027	s	**VE**	P		TY
44028	*	**FD**	A		EP
44029	*	**FD**	A	*SR*	IS
44030	*h	**FD**	A	*SR*	IS
44031	m	**VE**	A		EP
44032	*	**FD**	A	*SR*	IS
44034	*	**FD**	A		EP
44035	*	**FD**	A		EP
44036	*h	**FD**	A		ZB
44037	*h	**FD**	A	*SR*	IS
44038	*	**FD**	A		EP
44039	*	**FD**	A	*SR*	IS
44040	*	**GW**	A		ZB
44041	s	**ST**	P	*EM*	NL
44042	*h	**FD**	P		LA
44043	*h	**FD**	A		EP
44044	s	**ST**	P	*EM*	NL
44045	m	**VE**	A		GA
44046	s	**ST**	P	*EM*	NL
44047	s	**ST**	P	*EM*	NL
44048	s	**ST**	P	*EM*	NL
44049	*	**FD**	A		EP
44050	m	**VE**	P		GA
44051	s	**ST**	P	*EM*	NL
44052	p	**XC**	P	*XC*	LA
44054	s	**ST**	P	*EM*	NL
44056	m	**VE**	A		EP
44057	m	**VE**	P		GA
44058	m	**VE**	A		EP
44059	*	**FD**	A		EP
44060	*h	**FD**	P		LM
44061	m	**VE**	A		GA
44063	m	**VE**	A		NL
44066	*	**FD**	A	*SR*	IS
44068	*h	**FD**	P		LA
44069	*h	**FD**	P		LA
44070	s	**ST**	P	*EM*	NL
44071	s	**ST**	P	*EM*	NL
44072	p	**XC**	P	*XC*	LA
44073	t	**VE**	P		TY
44074	*h	**FD**	P		LM
44075	m	**VE**	P		GA
44076	*h	**FD**	P		LM
44077	m	**VE**	A		NL
44078	*h	**FD**	P		LM
44080	m	**VE**	A		GA

44081	*h	**FD**	P		LM
44085	s	**ST**	P	*EM*	NL
44086	*	**GW**	A	*SR*	IS
44089	t	**V**	AV		ZR
44091	*h	**FD**	P		LM
44093	*h	**FD**	A		EP
44094	m	**VE**	A		NL
44098	m	**BG**	A		EP
44100	*h	**FD**	P		LA

TRAILER COMPOSITE KITCHEN TCK

Converted from Mark 3A Open Standard. Refurbished CrossCountry vehicles with Primarius seating. Small kitchen for the preparation of hot food and stowage space for two trolleys between First and Standard Class. One toilet removed. 30/10 1T.

p Fitted with power doors. 30/8 1T.

45001–005. Lot No. 30877 Derby 1975–77. 34.3 t.

45001	(12004)	p	**XC**	P	*XC*	LA
45002	(12106)	p	**XC**	P	*XC*	LA
45003	(12076)	p	**XC**	P	*XC*	LA
45004	(12077)	p	**XC**	P	*XC*	LA
45005	(12080)		**XC**	P	*XC*	LA

TRAILER COMPOSITE TC

Converted from TF for First Great Western 2014–15. Refurbished with Grammer seating. 24/39 1T.

46001–004. Lot No. 30881 Derby 1976–77. 35.6 t. Converted from TF.
46005–009. Lot No. 30896 Derby 1977–78. 35.6 t. Converted from TF.
46010–013. Lot No. 30938 Derby 1979–80. 35.6 t. Converted from TF.
46014. Lot No. 30963 Derby 1982. 35.6 t. Converted from TF.
46015. Lot No. 30884 Derby 1976–77. 35.6 t. Converted from TF.
46016/017. Lot No. 30939 Derby 1979–80. 35.6 t. Converted from TF.
46018. Lot No. 30969 Derby 1982. 35.6 t. Converted from TF.

46001	(41005)	**FD**	A		EP
46002	(41029)	**FD**	A		EP
46003	(41033)	**FD**	A		EP
46004	(41055)	**FD**	A		EP
46005	(41065)	**FD**	A		EP
46006	(41081)	**FD**	P		LM
46007	(41096)	**FD**	P		LM
46008	(41109)	**FD**	P		LM
46009	(41119)	**FD**	P		LM
46010	(41125)	**FD**	A	*SR*	IS
46011	(41139)	**FD**	A		EP
46012	(41147)	**FD**	P		LM
46013	(41148)	**FD**	P		LM
46014	(41168)	**FD**	P		LM
46015	(40505, 41179)	**FD**	A		EP
46016	(42282, 41181)	**FD**	P		LM
46017	(42270, 41184)	**FD**	P		LM
46018	(42318, 41191)	**FD**	P		LM

TRAILER STANDARD TS

Refurbished for Great Western Railway 2017–20 and fitted with power doors and retention toilets. For use in 4-car sets on local and regional services across the South-West. –/84 1T († –/62 and 5 tip-ups 1TD 2W).

48101–135. For Lot No. details see TS. 36.3 t.

48101	(42093, 48111)	p	**GW**	FG	*GW*	LA
48102	(42218)	p†	**GW**	FG	*GW*	LA
48103	(42168, 48101)	p	**GW**	FG	*GW*	LA
48104	(41107, 42365)	p	**GW**	FG	*GW*	LA
48105	(42266)	p†	**GW**	FG	*GW*	LA
48106	(42258)	p	**GW**	FG	*GW*	LA
48107	(42101)	p	**GW**	FG	*GW*	LA
48108	(42174)	p†	**GW**	FG	*GW*	LA
48109	(42085)	p	**GW**	FG	*GW*	LA
48110	(42315)	p	**GW**	FG	*GW*	LA
48111	(42224)	p†	**GW**	FG	*GW*	LA
48112	(42222)	p	**GW**	FG	*GW*	LA
48113	(42177, 48102)	p	**GW**	FG	*GW*	LA
48114	(42317)	p†	**GW**	FG	*GW*	LA
48115	(42285)	p	**GW**	A	*GW*	LA
48116	(42273)	p	**GW**	A	*GW*	LA
48117	(42271)	p†	**GW**	A	*GW*	LA
48118	(42073)	p	**GW**	A	*GW*	LA
48119	(42204)	p	**GW**	A	*GW*	LA
48120	(42201)	p†	**GW**	A	*GW*	LA
48121	(42027)	p	**GW**	A	*GW*	LA
48122	(42214)	p	**GW**	A	*GW*	LA
48123						
48124	(42212)	p	**GW**	A	*GW*	LA
48125	(42203)	p	**GW**	A	*GW*	LA
48126	(42138)	p†	**GW**	A	*GW*	LA
48127	(42349)	p	**GW**	A	*GW*	LA
48128						
48129	(42008)	p†	**GW**	A	*GW*	LA
48130						
48131	(42102)	p	**GW**	FG	*GW*	LA
48132						
48133						
48134						
48135	(42251)	p†	**GW**	A	*GW*	LA

TRAILER GUARD'S STANDARD TGS

Refurbished for Great Western Railway 2017–20 and fitted with power doors. –/71.

49101–113. For Lot No. details see TGS. 35.7 t.

49101	(44055)	p **GW**	FG	*GW*	LA
49102	(44083)	p **GW**	FG	*GW*	LA
49103	(44097)	p **GW**	FG	*GW*	LA
49104	(44101)	p **GW**	FG	*GW*	LA
49105	(44090)	p **GW**	FG	*GW*	LA
49106	(44033)	p **GW**	A	*GW*	LA
49107	(44064)	p **GW**	A	*GW*	LA
49108	(44067)	p **GW**	A	*GW*	LA
49109	(44003)	p **GW**	A	*GW*	LA
49110	( )	**GW**			
49111	( )	**GW**			
49112	(44079)	p **GW**	FG	*GW*	LA
49113	( )	**GW**			

2.3. HST SET FORMATIONS

GREAT WESTERN RAILWAY

Great Western Railway withdrew its last full length HST sets in spring 2019. The company is retaining and refurbishing 11 4-car sets for use on regional and local services in the South-West. It withdrew a number of other sets used in short formations but still with slam doors at the end of 2019. The position shown here is how the fleet will look once all sets are refurbished by spring 2020.

Number of sets: 11.
Maximum number of daily diagrams: 9.
Formations: 4-cars.
Allocation: Laira (Plymouth).
Other maintenance and servicing depots: Long Rock (Penzance), St Philip's Marsh (Bristol).
Operation: Principally Bristol–Exeter–Plymouth–Penzance and Cardiff–Bristol–Taunton.

Set	*D*	*C*	*B*	*A*
GW01	48103	48102	48101	49101
GW02	48106	48105	48104	49102
GW03	48109	48108	48107	49103
GW04	48112	48111	48110	49104
GW05	48115	48114	48113	49105
GW06	48118	48117	48116	49106
GW07	48121	48120	48119	49107
GW08	48124	48123	48122	49108
GW09	48127	48126	48125	49109
GW10	48130	48129	48128	49110
GW11	48133	48132	48131	49111

Spares:

LA: 48134 48135 49112 49113

EAST MIDLANDS RAILWAY

East Midlands Railway HSTs are concentrated on the St Pancras–Nottingham corridor during the day, with early morning and evening services to Leeds for servicing at Neville Hill.

The fleet NL01–NL12 (nine sets) shown here is to be phased out in early 2020 in favour of former LNER sets, which are in better condition.

The three 6-car sets were transferred from Grand Central at the end of 2017, entering traffic in spring 2018.

Number of sets: 12. **Maximum number of daily diagrams:** 10.
Formations: 8-cars or 6-cars.
Allocation: Neville Hill (Leeds) or Derby Etches Park.
Operation: London St Pancras–Nottingham, Sheffield/Leeds.

Set	*J*	*G*	*F*	*E*	*D*	*C*	*B*	*A*
NL01	41057	41084	40730	42327	42111	42112	42113	44041
NL03	41061	41067	40741	42337	42119	42120	42121	44054
NL04	41077	41064	40749	42151	42164	42165	42153	44047
NL06	41156	41041	40746	42132	42131	42331	42133	44046
NL07	41111	41070	40754	42339	42135	42136	42137	44044
NL08	41071	41072	40753	42329	42139	42140	42141	44048
NL10	41075	41076	40756	42328	42341	42148	42149	44051
NL11	41117	41046	40728	42220	42100	42230	42124	44085
NL12	41079	41069	40700	42155	42156	42157	42152	44070
DY21	41207	40205	41206	42408	42584	42585		
DY22	41208	40221	41205	42401	42405	42404		
DY23	41209	40204	41204	42402	42586	42407		

Spares:

NL: 40751 41063 41113 42384 44071

East Midlands Railway: Former LNER sets to be phased in during early 2020 (former LNER set numbers are shown):

EC51	41120	41150	40748	42091	42146	42150	42154	44094
EC52	41039	41040	40735	42189	42057	42058	42059	44019
EC53	41090	41044	40737	42127	42063	42064	42065	44045
EC57	41151	41152	40740	42128	42182	42186	42190	44080
EC58	41097	41098	40750	42238	42191	42192	42193	44061
EC59	41099	41100	40711	42239	42240	42198	42199	44063
EC61	41115	41165	40702	42159	42160	42109	42110	44057
EC62	41185	41095	40701	42326	42330	42237	42307	44075
EC63	41159	41083	40708	42286	42228	42130	42322	44050

Spares:
NL: 40705 41066 41190 42116 42354 44077

CROSSCOUNTRY

CrossCountry HSTs run in 7-car formation. Sets are currently being fitted with sliding doors, with XC05 the last being completed.

Number of sets: 5. **Maximum number of daily diagrams:** 4.
Formations: 7-cars. **Allocation:** Laira (Plymouth).
Other maintenance depots: Neville Hill (Leeds) or Edinburgh (Craigentinny).
Operation: Edinburgh–Leeds–Plymouth is the core route with some services extending to Dundee or Penzance.

Set	A	B	C	D	E	F	G	
XC01	41193	45001	42342	42097	42377	42374	44021	Refurbished
XC02	41194	45002	42234	42037	42367	42371	44072	Refurbished
XC03	41195	45003	42370	42378	42036	42376	44052	Refurbished
XC04	41026	45004	42375	42369	42051	42366	44012	Refurbished
XC05	41035	45005	42052	42038	42053	42379	44017	

Spares:

LA:	42290	42368	42372	42373	42380

SCOTRAIL

ScotRail is introducing refurbished HSTs onto its Edinburgh/Glasgow–Aberdeen/Inverness services – branded INTER-7-CITY as they will serve Scotland's seven cities. There will ultimately be 17 5-car and nine 4-car sets but the refurbishment programme has been running behind schedule. As a result ScotRail introduced some unrefurbished sets into service. These will steadily be withdrawn as more sets are refurbished and fitted with sliding doors. At the time of writing all sets are running as 4-cars, 5-car sets are to be introduced in 2020.

Number of sets: 26 (by late 2020).
Number of diagrams at start of 2020: 11.
Formations: 4-cars or 5-cars.
Allocation: Power cars: Haymarket (Edinburgh), Trailers: Inverness.
Operation: Edinburgh/Glasgow–Aberdeen, Edinburgh/Glasgow–Inverness, Aberdeen–Inverness.

Set	A	B	C	D	
HA01	41124	42256	42255	44029	
HA02	41144	42295	42032	44039	
HA03	41104	42208	42206	44066	
HA05	41022	42030	42010	44010	
HA06	41158	42200	42129	44086	
HA17	40610	42360	42551	42252	Refurbished
HA18	40624	42265	42553	42293	Refurbished
HA19	40625	42259	42578	42333	Refurbished
HA20	40616	42291	42577	42075	Refurbished
HA21	40612	42055	42576	42276	Refurbished
HA22	40608	42275	42571	42019	Refurbished
HA23	40605	42345	42034	42184	Refurbished
HA24	40604	42183	42559	42343	Refurbished
HA25	40602	42292	42562	42045	Refurbished
HA26	40601	42004	42561	42046	Refurbished
HA31	41126	42344	42261	44030	
HA32	46010	42069	42118	44023	
HA33	41140	42287	42289	44037	

Spares:

IS:	42076	42269	42301	42572	42579

2.4. SALOONS

Several specialist passenger carrying carriages, normally referred to as saloons are permitted to run on the national railway system. Many of these are to pre-nationalisation designs.

WCJS FIRST CLASS SALOON

Built 1892 by LNWR, Wolverton. Originally dining saloon mounted on six-wheel bogies. Rebuilt with new underframe with four-wheel bogies in 1927. Rebuilt 1960 as observation saloon with DMU end. Gangwayed at other end. The interior has a saloon, kitchen, guards vestibule and observation lounge. 19/– 1T. Gresley bogies. 28.5 t. 75 mph. ETS x.

41 (484, 45018) x **M** WC *WC* CS

LNWR DINING SALOON

Built 1890 by LNWR, Wolverton. Mounted on the underframe of LMS General Utility Van 37908 in the 1980s. Contains kitchen and dining area seating 12 at tables for two. 12/–. Gresley bogies. 75 mph. 25.4 t. ETS x.

159 (5159) x **M** WC *WC* CS

GNR FIRST CLASS SALOON

Built 1912 by GNR, Doncaster. Contains entrance vestibule, lavatory, two separate saloons, library and luggage space. 19/– 1T. Gresley bogies. 75 mph. 29.4 t. ETS x.

Non-standard livery: Teak.

807 (4807) x **0** WC *WC* CS

LNER GENERAL MANAGERS SALOON

Built 1945 by LNER, York. Gangwayed at one end with a veranda at the other. The interior has a dining saloon seating 12, kitchen, toilet, office and nine seat lounge. 21/– 1T. B4 bogies. 75 mph. 35.7 t. ETS 3.

1999 (902260) **M** WC CS DINING CAR No. 2

GENERAL MANAGER'S SALOON

Renumbered 1989 from London Midland Region departmental series. Formerly the LMR General Manager's saloon. Rebuilt from LMS period 1 Corridor Brake First M5033M to dia 1654 and mounted on the underframe of BR suburban Brake Standard M43232. Screw couplings have been removed. B4 bogies. 100 mph. ETS 2X.

LMS Lot No. 326 Derby 1927. 27.5 t.

6320 (5033, DM 395707) x **M** PR *PR* SK

SUPPORT CAR

Converted 199? from Courier vehicle converted from Mark 1 Corridor Brake Standard 1986–87. Toilet retained and former compartment area replaced with train manager's office, crew locker room, linen store and dry goods store. The former luggage area has been adapted for use as an engineers' compartment and workshop. B5 bogies. 100 mph. ETS 2.

Lot No. 30721 Wolverton 1963. 35.5 t.

99545 (35466, 80207) **PC** BE *BP* SL BAGGAGE CAR No. 11

SERVICE CAR

Converted from BR Mark 1 Corridor Brake Standard. Commonwealth bogies. 100 mph. ETS 2.

Lot No. 30721 Wolverton 1963.

99886 (35407) x **M** WC *WC* CS 86 SERVICE CAR No. 1

ROYAL SCOTSMAN SALOONS

Built 1960 by Metro-Cammell as Pullman Kitchen Second for East Coast Main Line Services. Rebuilt 2016 as a Spa Car with two large bedrooms with bathroom/spa areas. Commonwealth bogies. xx t. ETS ?.

99337 (CAR No. 337) **M** BE *RS* ZG STATE SPA CAR

Built 1960 by Metro-Cammell as Pullman Kitchen First for East Coast Main Line services. Rebuilt 2013 as dining car. Commonwealth bogies. 38.5 t. ETS ?.

99960 (321 SWIFT) **M** BE *RS* ZG DINING CAR No. 2

Built 1960 by Metro-Cammell as Pullman Parlour First (§ Pullman Kitchen First) for East Coast Main Line services. Rebuilt 1990 as sleeping cars with four twin sleeping rooms (*§ three twin sleeping rooms and two single sleeping rooms at each end). Commonwealth bogies. 38.5 t. ETS ?.

99961 (324 AMBER)	*	**M**	BE	*RS*	ZG	STATE CAR No. 1
99962 (329 PEARL)		**M**	BE	*RS*	ZG	STATE CAR No. 2
99963 (331 TOPAZ)		**M**	BE	*RS*	ZG	STATE CAR No. 3
99964 (313 FINCH)	§	**M**	BE	*RS*	ZG	STATE CAR No. 4

Built 1960 by Metro-Cammell as Pullman Kitchen First for East Coast Main Line services. Rebuilt 1990 as observation car with open verandah seating 32. B4 bogies. 36.95 t. ETS ?.

99965 (319 SNIPE)		**M**	BE	*RS*	ZG	OBSERVATION CAR

Built 1960 by Metro-Cammell as Pullman Kitchen First for East Coast Main Line services. Rebuilt 1993 as dining car. Commonwealth bogies. 38.5 t. ETS ?.

99967 (317 RAVEN)		**M**	BE	*RS*	ZG	DINING CAR No. 1

Mark 3A. Converted 1997 from a Sleeping Car at Carnforth Railway Restoration & Engineering Services. BT10 bogies. Attendant's and adjacent two sleeping compartments converted to generator room containing a 160 kW Volvo unit. In 99968 four sleeping compartments remain for staff use with another converted for use as a staff shower and toilet. The remaining five sleeping compartments have been replaced by two passenger cabins. In 99969 seven sleeping compartments remain for staff use. A further sleeping compartment, along with one toilet, have been converted to store rooms. The other two sleeping compartments have been combined to form a crew mess. 41.5 t. 99968 ETS index ?. 99969 ETS 7X (when generator not in use). ETS index ?? (when generator in use).

Lot No. 30960 Derby 1981–83.

99968 (10541)		**M**	BE	*RS*	ZG	STATE CAR No. 5
99969 (10556)		**M**	BE	*RS*	ZG	SERVICE CAR

"CLUB CAR"

Converted from BR Mark 1 Open Standard at Carnforth Railway Restoration & Engineering Services in 1994. Contains kitchen, pantry and two dining saloons. 20/– 1T. Commonwealth bogies. 100 mph. ETS 4.

Lot No. 30724 York 1963. 37 t.

99993 (5067)	x	**CC**	LS	*LS*	CL	CLUB CAR

BR INSPECTION SALOON

Mark 1. Short frames. Non-gangwayed. Observation windows at each end. The interior layout consists of two saloons interspersed by a central lavatory/kitchen/guards/luggage section. 90 mph. ETS x.

BR Wagon Lot No. 3095 Swindon 1957. B4 bogies. 30.5 t.

999506	**M**	WC	*WC*	CS	

2.5. PULLMAN CAR COMPANY SERIES

Pullman cars have never generally been numbered as such, although many have carried numbers, instead they have carried titles. However, a scheme of schedule numbers exists which generally lists cars in chronological order. In this section those numbers are shown followed by the car's title. Cars described as "kitchen" contain a kitchen in addition to passenger accommodation and have gas cooking unless otherwise stated. Cars described as "parlour" consist entirely of passenger accommodation. Cars described as "brake" contain a compartment for the use of the guard and a luggage compartment in addition to passenger accommodation.

PULLMAN PARLOUR FIRST

Built 1927 by Midland Carriage & Wagon Company. 26/– 2T. Gresley bogies. 41 t. ETS 2.

213	MINERVA	**PC**	BE	*BP*	SL

PULLMAN KITCHEN FIRST

Built 1928 by Metropolitan Carriage & Wagon Company. 20/– 1T. Gresley bogies. 42 t. ETS 4.

238	PHYLISS	**PC**	BE		SL

PULLMAN PARLOUR FIRST

Built 1928 by Metropolitan Carriage & Wagon Company. 24/– 2T. Gresley bogies. 40 t. ETS 4.

239	AGATHA	**PC**	BE		SL
243	LUCILLE	**PC**	BE	*BP*	SL

PULLMAN KITCHEN FIRST

Built 1925 by BRCW. Rebuilt by Midland Carriage & Wagon Company in 1928. 20/– 1T. Gresley bogies. 41 t. ETS 4.

245	IBIS	**PC**	BE	*BP*	SL

PULLMAN PARLOUR FIRST

Built 1928 by Metropolitan Carriage & Wagon Company. 24/– 2T. Gresley bogies. ETS 4.

254	ZENA	**PC**	BE	*BP*	SL

PULLMAN KITCHEN FIRST

Built 1928 by Metropolitan Carriage & Wagon Company. 20/– 1T. Gresley bogies. 42 t. ETS 4.

255	IONE		**PC**	BE	*BP*	SL

PULLMAN KITCHEN COMPOSITE

Built 1932 by Metropolitan Carriage & Wagon Company. Originally included in 6-Pul EMU. Electric cooking. 12/16 1T. EMU bogies. ETS x.

264	RUTH		**PC**	BE		SL

PULLMAN KITCHEN FIRST

Built 1932 by Metropolitan Carriage & Wagon Company. Originally included in "Brighton Belle" EMUs but now used as hauled stock. Electric cooking. 20/– 1T. B5 (SR) bogies (§ EMU bogies). 44 t. ETS 2.

280	AUDREY		**PC**	BE	*BP*	SL
281	GWEN		**PC**	BE	*BP*	SL
283	MONA	§	**PC**	BE		SL
284	VERA		**PC**	BE	*BP*	SL

PULLMAN PARLOUR THIRD

Built 1932 by Metropolitan Carriage & Wagon Company. Originally included in "Brighton Belle" EMUs. –/56 2T. EMU bogies. ETS x.

Non-standard livery: BR Revised Pullman (blue & white lined out in white).

286	CAR No. 86		**0**	BE		SL

PULLMAN BRAKE THIRD

Built 1932 by Metropolitan Carriage & Wagon Company. Originally driving motor cars in "Brighton Belle" EMUs. Traction and control equipment removed for use as hauled stock. –/48 1T. EMU bogies. ETS x.

292	CAR No. 92		**PC**	BE		SL
293	CAR No. 93		**PC**	BE		SL

PULLMAN PARLOUR FIRST

Built 1951 by Birmingham Railway Carriage & Wagon Company. 32/– 2T. Gresley bogies. 39 t. ETS 3.

301	PERSEUS		**PC**	BE	*BP*	SL

Built 1952 by Pullman Car Company, Preston Park using underframe and bogies from 176 RAINBOW, the body of which had been destroyed by fire. 26/– 2T. Gresley bogies. 38 t. ETS 4.

302	PHOENIX		**PC**	BE	*BP*	SL

PULLMAN PARLOUR FIRST

Built 1951 by Birmingham Railway Carriage & Wagon Company. 32/– 2T. Gresley bogies. 39 t. ETS 3.

308	CYGNUS		**PC**	BE	*BP*	SL

PULLMAN BAR FIRST

Built 1951 by Birmingham Railway Carriage & Wagon Company. Rebuilt 1999 by Blake Fabrications, Edinburgh with original timber-framed body replaced by a new fabricated steel body. Contains kitchen, bar, dining saloon and coupé. Electric cooking. 14/– 1T. Gresley bogies. ETS 3.

310	PEGASUS	x	**PC**	LS	*LS*	CL

Also carries "THE TRIANON BAR" branding.

PULLMAN PARLOUR FIRST

Built 1960–61 by Metro-Cammell for East Coast Main Line services. –/36 2T. Commonwealth bogies. 38.5 t. ETS x.

325	AMBER	x	**PC**	WC	*WC*	CS
326	EMERALD	x	**PC**	WC	*WC*	CS

PULLMAN KITCHEN SECOND

Built 1960–61 by Metro-Cammell for East Coast Main Line services. Commonwealth bogies. –/30 1T. 40 t. ETS x.

335	CAR No. 335	x	**PC**	VT	*VT*	TM

PULLMAN PARLOUR SECOND

Built 1960–61 by Metro-Cammell for East Coast Main Line services. 347 is used as an Open First. –/42 2T. Commonwealth bogies. 38.5 t. ETS x.

347	CAR No. 347	x	**M**	WC	*WC*	CS
348	TOPAZ	x	**PC**	WC	*WC*	CS
349	CAR No. 349	x	**PC**	VT	*VT*	TM
350	TANZANITE	x	**PC**	WC	*WC*	CS
351	SAPPHIRE	x	**PC**	WC	*WC*	CS
352	AMETHYST	x	**PC**	WC	*WC*	CS
353	CAR No. 353	x	**PC**	VT		TM

PULLMAN SECOND BAR

Built 1960–61 by Metro-Cammell for East Coast Main Line services. –/24+17 bar seats. Commonwealth bogies. 38.5 t. ETS x.

354	THE HADRIAN BAR	x	**PC**	WC	*WC*	CS

2.6. LOCOMOTIVE SUPPORT CARRIAGES

These carriages have been adapted from Mark 1s and Mark 2s for use as support carriages for heritage steam and diesel locomotives. Some seating is retained for the use of personnel supporting the locomotives operation with the remainder of the carriage adapted for storage, workshop, dormitory and catering purposes. These carriages can spend considerable periods of time off the national railway system when the locomotives they support are not being used on that system. No owner or operator details are included in this section. After the depot code, the locomotive(s) each carriage is usually used to support is given.

CORRIDOR BRAKE FIRST

Mark 1. Commonwealth bogies. ETS 2.

14007. Lot No. 30382 Swindon 1959. 35 t.
17025. Lot No. 30718 Swindon 1963. Metal window frames. 36 t.

14007	(14007, 17007)	x	**M**	NY	LNER 61264
17025	(14025)	v	**M**	CS	LMS 45690

CORRIDOR BRAKE FIRST

Mark 2A. Pressure ventilated. B4 bogies. ETS 4.

14060. Lot No. 30775 Derby 1967–68. 32 t.
17096. Lot No. 30786 Derby 1968. 32 t.

14060	(14060, 17060)	v	**M**	TM	LMS 45596	
17096	(14096)		**PC**	SL	SR 35028	MERCATOR

CORRIDOR BRAKE COMPOSITE

Mark 1. ETS 2.

21096. Lot No. 30185 Metro-Cammell 1956. BR Mark 1 bogies. 32.5 t.
21232. Lot No. 30574 GRCW 1960. B4 bogies. 34 t.
21249. Lot No. 30669 Swindon 1961–62. Commonwealth bogies. 36 t.

21096	x	**M**	NY	LNER 60007
21232	x	**M**	SK	LMS 46201
21249	x	**CC**	SL	New Build 60163

CORRIDOR BRAKE STANDARD

Mark 1. Metal window frames and melamine interior panelling. ETS 2.

35317/322. Lot No. 30699 Wolverton 1962–63. Commonwealth bogies. 37 t.
35451–486. Lot No. 30721 Wolverton 1963. Commonwealth bogies. 37 t.

35317	x	**CC**	CL	Locomotives Services Crewe-based locomotives
35322	x	**M**	CS	WCRC Carnforth-based locomotives
35451	x	**CC**	CL	Locomotives Services Crewe-based locomotives
35461	x	**CH**	CL	GWR 5029
35463	v	**M**	CS	WCRC Carnforth-based locomotives
35468	x	**M**	YK	National Railway Museum locomotives
35470	v	**CH**	TM	Tyseley Locomotive Works-based locos
35476	x	**M**	SK	LMS 46233
35479	v	**M**	SH	LNER 61306
35486	x	**M**	TN	LNER 60009

CORRIDOR BRAKE FIRST

Mark 2C. Pressure ventilated. Renumbered when declassified. B4 bogies. ETS 4.

Lot No. 30796 Derby 1969–70. 32.5 t.

35508 (14128, 17128)		**M**	BQ	LMS 44871/45212/45407

CORRIDOR BRAKE FIRST

Mark 2A. Pressure ventilated. Renumbered when declassified. B4 bogies. ETS 4.

Lot No. 30786 Derby 1968. 32 t.

35517 (14088, 17088)	b	**M**	BQ	LMS 44871/45212/45407
35518 (14097, 17097)	b	**G**	CS	SR 34067

COURIER VEHICLE

Mark 1. Converted 1986–87 from Corridor Brake Standards. ETS 2.

80204/217. Lot No. 30699 Wolverton 1962. Commonwealth bogies. 37 t.
80220. Lot No. 30573 Gloucester 1960. B4 bogies. 33 t.

80204 (35297)	**M**	CS	WCRC Carnforth-based locomotives
80217 (35299)	**M**	CS	WCRC Carnforth-based locomotives
80220 (35276)	**M**	NY	LNER 62005

2.7. 95xxx & 99xxx RANGE NUMBER CONVERSION TABLE

The following table is presented to help readers identify carriages which may still carry numbers in the 95xxx and 99xxx number ranges of the former private owner number series, which is no longer in general use.

9xxxx	*BR No.*	*9xxxx*	*BR No.*	*9xxxx*	*BR No.*
95402	Pullman 326	99350	Pullman 350	99673	550
99025	Pullman 325	99351	Pullman 351	99674	551
99035	35322	99352	Pullman 352	99675	552
99040	21232	99353	Pullman 353	99676	553
99041	35476	99354	Pullman 354	99677	586
99052	Saloon 41	99361	Pullman 335	99678	504
99121	3105	99371	3128	99679	506
99122	3106	99405	35486	99680	17102
99125	3113	99530	Pullman 301	99710	18767
99127	3117	99531	Pullman 302	99716 *	18808
99128	3130	99532	Pullman 308	99718	18862
99131	Saloon 1999	99534	Pullman 245	99721	18756
99241	35449	99535	Pullman 213	99723	35459
99302	13323	99536	Pullman 254	99880	Saloon 159
99304	21256	99537	Pullman 280	99881	Saloon 807
99311	1882	99539	Pullman 255	99883	2108
99312	35463	99541	Pullman 243	99885	2110
99319	17168	99543	Pullman 284	99887	2127
99326	4954	99546	Pullman 281	99953	35468
99327	5044	99547	Pullman 292	99966	34525
99328	5033	99548	Pullman 293	99970	Pullman 232
99329	4931	99670	546	99972	Pullman 318
99347	Pullman 347	99671	548	99973	324
99348	Pullman 348	99672	549	99974	Pullman 328
99349	Pullman 349				

* The number 99716 has also been applied to 3416 for filming purposes.

2.8. SET FORMATIONS

LNER MARK 4 SET FORMATIONS

The LNER Mark 4 sets generally run in fixed formations. Class 91 locomotives are positioned next to Coach B. Sets BN23–BN25/BN27–BN30 were withdrawn in 2019 and the whole fleet is due to be withdrawn by LNER by June 2020. Some coaches will be taken on by Transport for Wales.

Set	B	C	D	E	F	H	K	L	M	DVT
BN01	12207	12417	12415	12414	12307	10307	11298	11301	11401	82207
BN02	12232	12402	12450	12448	12302	10302	11299	11302	11402	82202
BN03	12201	12401	12459	12478	12301	10320	11277	11303	11403	82219
BN04	12202	12480	12421	12518	12327	10303	11278	11304	11404	82209
BN05	12209	12486	12520	12522	12300	10326	11219	11305	11405	82210
BN06	12208	12406	12420	12422	12313	10309	11279	11306	11406	82208
BN07	12231	12411	12405	12489	12329	10323	11280	11307	11407	82204
BN08	12205	12481	12485	12407	12328	10300	11229	11308	11408	82211
BN09	12230	12513	12483	12514	12308	10304	11281	11309	11409	82215
BN10	12214	12419	12488	12443	12305	10331	11282	11310	11410	82205
BN11	12203	12437	12436	12484	12315	10308	11283	11311	11411	82218
BN12	12212	12431	12404	12426	12330	10333	11284	11312	11412	82212
BN13	12228	12469	12430	12424	12311	10313	11285	11313	11413	82213
BN14	12229	12410	12526	12423	12312	10332	11201	11314	11414	82206
BN15	12226	12442	12409	12515	12309	10306	11286	11315	11415	82214
BN16	12213	12428	12445	12433	12304	10315	11287	11316	11416	82222
BN17	12223	12444	12427	12432	12303	10324	11288	11317	11417	82225
BN18	12215	12453	12468	12467	12324	10305	11289	11318	11418	82220
BN19	12211	12434	12400	12470	12310	10318	11290	11319	11419	82201
BN20	12224	12477	12439	12440	12326	10321	11241	11320	11420	82200
BN21	12222	12461	12441	12476	12323	10330	11244	11321	11421	82227
BN22	12210	12452	12460	12473	12316	10301	11291	11322	11422	82230
BN26	12220	12474	12465	12429	12325	10311	11295	11326	11426	82223
Spare	12200				12320	10310		11328		82217
Spare	12218									82224

TRANSPENNINE EXPRESS MARK 5A SET FORMATIONS

These new coaches are used in fixed formations hauled by a Class 68 locomotive in push-pull mode, initially between Liverpool and Scarborough and will be introduced onto the Manchester Airport–Redcar route during 2020.

Set	E	D	C	B	A
TP01	11501	12701	12702	12703	12801
TP02	11502	12704	12705	12706	12802
TP03	11503	12707	12708	12709	12803
TP04	11504	12710	12711	12712	12804
TP05	11505	12713	12714	12715	12805
TP06	11506	12716	12717	12718	12806
TP07	11507	12719	12720	12721	12807
TP08	11508	12722	12723	12724	12808
TP09	11509	12725	12726	12727	12809
TP10	11510	12728	12729	12730	12810
TP11	11511	12731	12732	12733	12811
TP12	11512	12734	12735	12736	12812
TP13	11513	12737	12738	12739	12813
Spare					12814

2.9. SERVICE STOCK

Carriages in this section are used for internal purposes within the railway industry, ie they do not generate revenue from outside the industry. Most are numbered in the former BR departmental number series.

BARRIER, ESCORT & TRANSLATOR VEHICLES

These vehicles are used to move multiple unit, HST and other vehicles around the national railway system.

HST Barrier Vehicles. Mark 1/2A. Renumbered from BR departmental series, or converted from various types. B4 bogies (* Commonwealth bogies).

Non-standard livery: 6340, 6344, 6346 All over dark blue.

6330. Mark 2A. Lot No. 30786 Derby 1968.
6336/38/44. Mark 1. Lot No. 30715 Gloucester 1962.
6340. Mark 1. Lot No. 30669 Swindon 1962.
6346. Mark 2A. Lot No. 30777 Derby 1967.
6348. Mark 1. Lot No. 30163 Pressed Steel 1957.

6330	(14084, 975629)		**FB**	A	*RO*	LR
6336	(81591, 92185)		**FB**	A	*GW*	LA
6338	(81581, 92180)		**FB**	A	*RO*	LR
6340	(21251, 975678)	*	**0**	A	*RO*	LR
6344	(81263, 92080)		**0**	A	*RO*	LR
6346	(9422)		**0**	A	*LN*	EC
6348	(81233, 92963)		**FB**	A	*GW*	LA

Mark 4 Barrier Vehicles. Mark 2A. Converted from Corridor First. B4 bogies. Lot No. 30774 Derby 1968.

6352	(13465, 19465)	**HB**	E	*LN*	BN
6353	(13478, 19478)	**HB**	E	*LN*	BN

EMU Translator Vehicles. Mark 1. Converted 1980 from Restaurant Unclassified Opens. 6376/77 have Tightlock couplers and 6378/79 Dellner couplers. Commonwealth bogies.

Lot No. 30647 Wolverton 1959–61.

6376	(1021, 975973)	**PB**	P	*DB*	TO *(works with 6377)*
6377	(1042, 975975)	**PB**	P	*DB*	TO *(works with 6376)*
6378	(1054, 975971)	**RO**	P	*DB*	TO *(works with 6379)*
6379	(1059, 975972)	**RO**	P	*DB*	TO *(works with 6378)*

Brake Force Runners. Mark 1. Previously used as HST Barrier Vehicles. Converted from Gangwayed Brake Vans in 1994–95. B4 bogies.

6392. Lot No. 30715 Gloucester 1962.
6397. Lot No. 30716 Gloucester 1962.

6392	(81588, 92183)	**PB**	CS	*CS*	ZA
6397	(81600, 92190)	**PB**	CS	*CS*	ZA

HST Barrier Vehicles. Mark 1. Converted from Gangwayed Brake Vans in 1994–95. B4 bogies.

6393. Lot No. 30716 Gloucester 1962.
6394. Lot No. 30162 Pressed Steel 1956–57.
6398/99. Lot No. 30400 Pressed Steel 1957–58.

6393	(81609, 92196)	**PB**	P	*LN*	EC
6394	(80878, 92906)	**PB**	P	*LN*	EC
6398	(81471, 92126)	**PB**	EM	*EM*	NL
6399	(81367, 92994)	**PB**	EM	*EM*	NL

Escort Coaches. Converted from Mark 2A (* Mark 2E) Open Brake Standards. 9419/28 use the same bodyshell as the Mark 2A Corridor Brake First. B4 bogies.

9419. Lot No.30777 Derby 1970.
9428. Lot No.30820 Derby 1970.
9506/08. Lot No.30838 Derby 1972.

9419		**DS**	DR	*DR*	KM
9428		**DS**	DR	*DR*	KM
9506	*	**DS**	DR	*DR*	KM
9508	*	**DS**	DR	*DR*	KM

EMU Translator Vehicles. Converted from Class 508 driving cars.

64664. Lot No. 30979 York 1979–80.
64707. Lot No. 30981 York 1979–80.

64664	**AG**	A	*GB*	ZG	Liwet	*(works with 64707)*
64707	**AG**	A	*GB*	ZG	Labezerin	*(works with 64664)*

EMU Translator Vehicles. Converted from Class 489 DMLVs that had originally been Class 414/3 DMBSOs. Previously used as de-icing coaches.

Lot No. 30452 Ashford/Eastleigh 1959. Mk 4 bogies.

68501	(61281)	**AG**	AF	*RO*	LR
68504	(61286)	**AG**	AF	*RO*	LR

Eurostar Barrier Vehicles. Mark 1. Converted from General Utility Vans with bodies removed. Fitted with B4 bogies for use as Eurostar barrier vehicles.

96380/381. Lot No. 30417 Pressed Steel 1958–59.
96383. Lot No. 30565 Pressed Steel 1959.
96384. Lot No. 30616 Pressed Steel 1959–60.

96380	(86386, 6380)	**B**	EU	*EU*	TI
96381	(86187, 6381)	**B**	EU	*EU*	TI
96383	(86664, 6383)	**B**	EU	*EU*	TI
96384	(86955, 6384)	**B**	EU	*EU*	TI

Brake Force Runners. Converted from Motorail vans built 1998–99 by Marcroft Engineering using underframe and running gear from Motorail General Utility Vans. B5 bogies.

Lot No. 30417 Pressed Steel 1958–59.

96604	(86337, 96156)	**Y**	CS	*CS*	ZA

96606	(86324, 96213)	**Y**	CS	*CS*	ZA
96608	(86385, 96216)	**Y**	CS	*CS*	ZA
96609	(86327, 96217)	**Y**	CS	*CS*	ZA

EMU Translator Vehicles. Converted from various Mark 1s.

Non-standard livery: All over blue.

975864. Lot No. 30054 Eastleigh 1951–54. Commonwealth bogies.
975867. Lot No. 30014 York 1950–51. Commonwealth bogies.
975875. Lot No. 30143 Charles Roberts 1954–55. Commonwealth bogies.
975974/978. Lot No. 30647 Wolverton 1959–61. B4 bogies.
977087. Lot No. 30229 Metro–Cammell 1955–57. Commonwealth bogies.

975864	(3849)	**HB**	E		BU		*(works with 975867)*
975867	(1006)	**HB**	E		BU		*(works with 975864)*
975875	(34643)	**0**	E	*RO*	LR		*(works with 977087)*
975974	(1030)	**AG**	A	*GB*	ZG	Paschar	*(works with 975978)*
975978	(1025)	**AG**	A	*GB*	ZG	Perpetiel	*(works with 975974)*
977087	(34971)	**0**	E	*RO*	LR		*(works with 975875)*

LABORATORY, TESTING & INSPECTION COACHES

These coaches are used for research, testing and inspection on the national railway system. Many are fitted with sophisticated technical equipment.

Plain Line Pattern Recognition Coaches. Converted from BR Mark 2F Buffet First (*) or Open Standard. B4 bogies.

1256. Lot No. 30845 Derby 1973.
5981. Lot No. 30860 Derby 1973–74.

1256	(3296)	*	**Y**	NR	*CS*	ZA
5981			**Y**	NR	*CS*	ZA

Generator Vans. Mark 1. Converted from BR Mark 1 Gangwayed Brake Vans. B5 bogies.

6260. Lot No. 30400 Pressed Steel 1957–58.
6261. Lot No. 30323 Pressed Steel 1957.
6262. Lot No. 30228 Metro-Cammell 1957–58.
6263. Lot No. 30163 Pressed Steel 1957.
6264. Lot No. 30173 York 1956.

6260	(81450, 92116)	**Y**	NR	*CS*	ZA
6261	(81284, 92988)	**Y**	NR	*CS*	ZA
6262	(81064, 92928)	**Y**	NR	*CS*	ZA
6263	(81231, 92961)	**Y**	NR	*CS*	ZA
6264	(80971, 92923)	**Y**	NR	*CS*	ZA

Staff Coach. Mark 2D. Converted from BR Mark 2D Open Brake Standard. Lot No. 30824 Derby 1971. B4 bogies.

9481	**Y**	NR	*CS*	ZA

Test Train Brake Force Runners. Mark 2F. Converted from BR Mark 2F Open Brake Standard. Lot No. 30861 Derby 1974. B4 bogies.

9516	**Y**	NR	*CS*	ZA
9523	**Y**	NR	*CS*	ZA

Driving Trailer Coaches. Converted 2008 at Serco, Derby from Mark 2F Driving Open Brake Standards. Fitted with generator. Disc brakes. B4 bogies.

9701–08. Lot No. 30861 Derby 1974. Converted to Driving Open Brake Standard Glasgow 1974.
9714. Lot No. 30861 Derby 1974. Converted to Driving Open Brake Standard Glasgow 1986.

9701	(9528)	**Y**	NR	*CS*	ZA
9702	(9510)	**Y**	NR	*CS*	ZA
9703	(9517)	**Y**	NR	*CS*	ZA
9708	(9530)	**Y**	NR	*CS*	ZA
9714	(9536)	**Y**	NR	*CS*	ZA

Test Train Brake Coaches. Former Caledonian Sleeper coaches now used for staff accommodation in test trains. Fitted with toilets with retention tanks. Converted from Mark 2E Open Standard with new seating by Railcare Wolverton. B4 bogies.

9801/03. Lot No. 30837 Derby 1972.
9806–10. Lot No. 30844 Derby 1972–73.

9801	(5760)	**FS**	ER	*CS*	ZA
9803	(5799)	**FS**	ER	*CS*	ZA
9806	(5840)	**FS**	ER	*CS*	ZA
9808	(5871)	**FS**	ER	*CS*	ZA
9810	(5892)	**FS**	ER	*CS*	ZA

Ultrasonic Test Coach. Converted from Class 421 EMU MBSO.

62287. Lot No. 30808. York 1970. SR Mark 6 bogies.
62384. Lot No. 30816. York 1970. SR Mark 6 bogies.

62287	**Y**	NR	*CS*	ZA
62384	**Y**	NR	*CS*	ZA

Test Train Brake Force Runners. Converted from Mark 2F Open Standard converted to Class 488/3 EMU TSOLH. These vehicles are included in test trains to provide brake force and are not used for any other purposes. Lot No. 30860 Derby 1973–74. B4 bogies.

72612	(6156)	**Y**	NR	*CS*	ZA
72616	(6007)	**Y**	NR	*CS*	ZA

Structure Gauging Train Coach. Converted from Mark 2F Open Standard converted to Class 488/3 EMU TSOLH. Lot No. 30860 Derby 1973–74. B4 bogies.

72630	(6094)	**Y**	NR	*CS*	ZA *(works with 99666)*

Plain Line Pattern Recognition Coaches. Converted from BR Mark 2F Open Standard converted to Class 488/3 EMU TSOLH. Lot No. 30860 Derby 1973–74. B4 bogies.

72631 (6096)	**Y**	NR	*CS*	ZA
72639 (6070)	**Y**	NR	*CS*	ZA

Driving Trailer Coaches. Converted from Mark 3B 110 mph Driving Brake Vans. Fitted with diesel generator. Lot No. 31042 Derby 1988. T4 bogies.

82111	**Y**	NR		ZA
82124	**Y**	NR		ZA
82129	**Y**	NR		ZA
82145	**Y**	NR		ZA

Structure Gauging Train Coach. Converted from BR Mark 2E Open First then converted to exhibition van. Lot No. 30843 Derby 1972–73. B4 bogies.

99666 (3250)	**Y**	NR	*CS*	ZA	*(works with 72630)*

Inspection Saloon. Converted from Class 202 DEMU TRB at Stewarts Lane for use as a BR Southern Region General Manager's Saloon. Overhauled at FM Rail, Derby 2004–05 for use as a New Trains Project Saloon. Can be used in push-pull mode with suitably equipped locomotives. Eastleigh 1958. SR Mark 4 bogies.

975025 (60755)	**G**	NR	*CS*	ZA	CAROLINE

Overhead Line Equipment Test Coach ("MENTOR"). Converted from BR Mark 1 Corridor Brake Standard. Lot No. 30142 Gloucester 1954–55. Fitted with pantograph. B4 bogies.

975091 (34615)	**Y**	NR	*CS*	ZA

New Measurement Train Conference Coach. Converted from prototype HST TF Lot No. 30848 Derby 1972. BT10 bogies.

975814 (11000, 41000)	**Y**	NR	*CS*	ZA

New Measurement Train Lecture Coach. Converted from prototype HST catering vehicle. Lot No. 30849 Derby 1972–73. BT10 bogies.

975984 (10000, 40000)	**Y**	NR	*CS*	ZA

Radio Survey Coach. Converted from BR Mark 2E Open Standard. Lot No. 30844 Derby 1972–73. B4 bogies.

977868 (5846)	**Y**	NR	*CS*	ZA

Staff Coach. Converted from Royal Household couchette Lot No. 30889, which in turn had been converted from BR Mark 2B Corridor Brake First. Lot No. 30790 Derby 1969. B5 bogies.

977969 (14112, 2906)	**Y**	NR	*CS*	ZA

Track Inspection Train Coach. Converted from BR Mark 2E Open Standard. Lot No. 30844 Derby 1972–73. B4 bogies.

977974 (5854)	**Y**	NR	*CS*	ZA

Electrification Measurement Coach. Converted from BR Mark 2F Open First converted to Class 488/2 EMU TFOH. Lot No. 30859 Derby 1973–74. B4 bogies.

977983 (3407, 72503) **Y** NR *CS* ZA

New Measurement Train Staff Coach. Converted from HST catering vehicle. Lot No. 30884 Derby 1976–77. BT10 bogies.

977984 (40501) **Y** P *CS* ZA

Structure Gauging Train Coaches. Converted from Mark 2F Open Standard converted to Class 488/3 EMU TSOLH or from BR Mark 2D Open First subsequently declassified to Open Standard and then converted to exhibition van. B4 bogies.

977985. Lot No. 30860 Derby 1973–74.
977986. Lot No. 30821 Derby 1971.

977985 (6019, 72715) **Y** NR *CS* ZA *(works with 977986)*
977986 (3189, 99664) **Y** NR *CS* ZA *(works with 977985)*

New Measurement Train Overhead Line Equipment Test Coach. Converted from HST TGS. Lot No. 30949 Derby 1982. BT10 bogies.

977993 (44053) **Y** P *CS* ZA

New Measurement Train Track Recording Coach. Converted from HST TGS. Lot No. 30949 Derby 1982. BT10 bogies.

977994 (44087) **Y** P *CS* ZA

New Measurement Train Coach. Converted from HST catering vehicle. Lot No. 30921 Derby 1978–79. Fitted with generator. BT10 bogies.

977995 (40719, 40619) **Y** P *CS* ZA

Radio Survey Coach. Converted from Mark 2F Open Standard converted to Class 488/3 EMU TSOLH. Lot No. 30860 Derby 1973–74. B4 bogies.

977997 (72613, 6126) **Y** NR *CS* ZA

Track Recording Coach. Purpose built Mark 2. BR Wagon Lot No. 3830 Derby 1976. B4 bogies.

999550 **Y** NR *CS* ZA

Ultrasonic Test Coaches. Converted from Class 421 EMU MBSO and Class 432 EMU MSO.

999602/605. Lot No. 30862 York 1974. SR Mk 6 bogies.
999606. Lot No. 30816. York 1970. SR Mk 6 bogies.

999602 (62483) **Y** NR *CS* ZA
999605 (62482) **Y** NR *CS* ZA
999606 (62356) **Y** NR *CS* ZA

BREAKDOWN TRAIN COACHES

These coaches are formed in trains used for the recovery of derailed railway vehicles and were converted from BR Mark 1 Corridor Brake Standard and General Utility Van. The current use of each vehicle is given.

971001/003/004. Lot No. 30403 York/Glasgow 1958–60. Commonwealth bogies.
971002. Lot No. 30417 Pressed Steel 1958–59. Commonwealth bogies.
975087. Lot No. 30032 Wolverton 1951–52. BR Mark 1 bogies.
975464. Lot No. 30386 Charles Roberts 1956–58. Commonwealth bogies.
975471. Lot No. 30095 Wolverton 1953–55. Commonwealth bogies.
975477. Lot No. 30233 GRCW 1955–57. BR Mark 1 bogies.
975486. Lot No. 30025 Wolverton 1950–52. Commonwealth bogies.

971001	(86560, 94150)	**Y**	NR	*DB*	SP	Tool & Generator Van
971002	(86624, 94190)	**Y**	NR	*DB*	SP	Tool Van
971003	(86596, 94191)	**Y**	NR	*DB*	SP	Tool Van
971004	(86194, 94168)	**Y**	NR	*DB*	SP	Tool Van
975087	(34289)	**Y**	NR	*DB*	SP	Tool & Generator Van
975464	(35171)	**Y**	NR	*DB*	SP	Staff Coach
975471	(34543)	**Y**	NR	*DB*	SP	Staff Coach
975477	(35108)	**Y**	NR	*DB*	SP	Staff Coach
975486	(34100)	**Y**	NR	*DB*	SP	Tool & Generator Van

INFRASTRUCTURE MAINTENANCE COACH

Winterisation Train Coach. Converted from BR Mark 2E Open Standard. Lot No. 30844 Derby 1972–73. B4 bogies.

977869 (5858)	**Y**	NR	*DR*	Perth CS

INTERNAL USER VEHICLES

These vehicles are confined to yards and depots or do not normally move. Details are given of the internal user number (if allocated), type, former identity, current use and location. Many no longer see regular use.

* = Grounded body.

975403 carries its original number 4598.

041474*	BR SPV 975418	Stores Van	Worksop Up Yard
041989*	BR SPV 975423	Stores Van	Toton Depot
042154	BR GUV 93975	Stores van	Ipswich Upper Yard
061202*	BR GUV 93498	Stores Van	Laira Depot, Plymouth
–	BR NA 94322*	Stores Van	WCRC, Carnforth Depot
083602	BR CCT 94494	Stores van	Three Bridges Station
–	BR NB 94548*	Stores Van	WCRC, Carnforth Depot
083637	BR NW 99203	Stores van	Stewarts Lane Depot
083644	BR Ferry Van 889201	Stores van	Eastleigh Depot
083664	BR Ferry Van 889203	Stores van	Eastleigh Depot
–	BR Open Standard 5636	Instruction Coach	St Philip's Marsh Depot
–	BR BV 6360	Barrier vehicle	Neville Hill Depot, Leeds
–	BR BV 6396	Stores van	Longsight Depot (Manchester)
–	BR RFKB 10256	Instruction Coach	Yoker Depot
–	BR RFKB 10260	Instruction Coach	Yoker Depot
–	BR SPV 88045*	Stores Van	Thames Haven Yard
–	BR NL 94003	Stores van	Burton-upon-Trent Depot
–	BR NK 94121	Stores van	Toton Depot
–	BR NB 94438	Stores van	Toton Depot
–	BR CCT 94663*	Stores Van	Mossend Up Yard
–	BR GUV 96139	Stores van	Longsight Depot, Manchester
–	BR Ferry Van 889200	Stores van	Stewarts Lane Depot
–	BR Ferry Van 889202	Stores van	Stewarts Lane Depot
–	SR PMV 977045*	Stores Van	EMD, Longport Works
–	SR CCT 2516*	Stores Van	Eastleigh Depot

Abbreviations:

BV = Barrier Vehicle
CCT = Covered Carriage Truck (a 4-wheeled van similar to a GUV)
GUV = General Utility Van (bogied van with side and end doors)
NAA = Propelling Control Vehicle
NB = High Security Brake Van (converted from Gangwayed Brake Van, gangways removed)
NK= High Security General Utility Van (end doors removed)
NL = Newspaper Van (converted from a GUV)
NW = Bullion Van (converted from a Corridor Brake Standard)
PMV = Parcels & Miscellaneous Van (a 4-wheeled van similar to a CCT but without end doors)
RFKB = Kitchen Buffet First
SPV = Special Parcels Van (a 4-wheeled van converted from a Fish Van)

2.10. COACHING STOCK AWAITING DISPOSAL

This list shows the locations of carriages awaiting disposal. The definition of which vehicles are awaiting disposal is somewhat vague, but often these are vehicles of types not now in normal service, those not expected to see further use or that have originated from preservationists as a source of spares or possible future use or carriages which have been damaged by fire, vandalism or collision.

1201	TM
1252	SH
1253	SH
1258	CS
1644	CS
1650	CS
1652	CS
1655	CS
1658	CL
1663	CS
1670	CS
1679	RO
1696	CL
1800	SH
1883	CL
1954	CL
2108	CS
2110	CS
2127	CS
2131	CS
2833	CS
2909	CS
3045	CL
3051	CL
3060	CL
3091	RO
3107	RO
3140	RO
3241	CS
3255	FA
3277	RO
3279	BU
3292	BU
3295	RO
3303	TO
3309	TM
3318	BU
3331	BU
3334	DE
3336	DE
3351	TM
3358	BU
3368	FA
3379	DE
3388	FA
3399	FA
3400	BU
3408	CS
3416	TM
3417	DE
3424	BU
4362	BU
4796	BU
4799	BU
4849	CS
4860	CS
4932	CS
4997	CS
5027	BU
5054	RO
5179	TM
5183	TM
5186	TM
5194	TM
5331	FA
5386	FA
5420	TM
5453	CS
5463	CS
5478	CS
5491	CS
5569	CS
5631	ME
5657	BU
5710	ZM
5737	CS
5740	CS
5756	CS
5777	BU
5797	RO
5815	SH
5876	SH
5888	SH
5922	DR
5924	DR
5925	SH
5928	TM
5943	CS
5954	ME
5958	SH
5959	DR
5978	SH
6009	SH
6029	SH
6036	DR
6041	CS
6045	SH
6050	CS
6073	SH
6110	ME
6134	SH
6139	ME
6151	SH
6152	DR
6154	SH
6175	CS
6179	CS
6324	CP
6351	BU
6361	NL
6364	CF
6365	CF
6412	CL
6720	FA
6722	LM
7204	CL
7931	BU
9440	SH
9489	CS
9490	BU
9496	DE
9529	DR
9531	DR
10224	CL
10237	LM
10242	LM
10245	CS
10530	ZN
10578	ZN
10588	ZN
10656	ZN
11006	BU
11021	LM
11028	ZB
11033	LM
11079	LM
11097	LM
12096	ZN
12104	LM
12165	LM
13306	CS
13323	CS
13508	RO
17013	CL
17168	CS
18767	SH
18808	SH
18862	CS
21268	RO
34525	CS
35333	ZG
35467	CL
68505	ZG
80212	CS
80374	BU
80403	CS

80404	CS
80414	SL
82101	LW
82126	LW
82138	LM
82150	LM
92114	ZA
92159	CS
92908	CS
93723	BY
94058	BU
94101	CS
94104	TO
94106	BU
94116	BU
94153	WE
94166	BU
94170	CL
94176	BU
94177	TO
94195	BU
94196	CS
94197	BU
94207	TO
94208	TO
94214	CS
94222	CS
94227	HM
94229	CL
94302	Hellifield
94303	Hellifield
94304	MH
94306	Hellifield
94308	CS
94310	WE
94311	WE
94313	WE
94316	TO
94317	TO
94323	Hellifield
94326	Hellifield
94332	CS
94333	Hellifield
94335	CL
94336	CL
94337	WE
94338	WE
94344	TO
94401	CS
94406	CS
94408	CS
94410	WE
94420	CS
94422	TO
94423	BU
94427	WE
94428	CS
94429	HM
94431	CS
94434	CL
94435	TO
94445	WE
94450	WE
94451	WE
94470	TO
94479	TO
94482	CS
94488	BU
94490	BU
94492	WE
94495	Hellifield
94498	CS
94501	TO
94504	Hellifield
94512	CS
94515	ZG
94517	BU
94520	BU
94522	CL
94525	CS
94526	CS
94527	Hellifield
94530	CS
94531	BU
94538	CL
94539	CS
94540	TJ
94542	CS
94545	HM
94546	Hellifield
94547	CS
95300	CS
95410	CS
95727	WE
95754	CS
95761	WE
95763	BU
96110	CS
96132	CS
96135	CS
96164	CS
96165	CS
96170	CS
96178	CS
96182	CS
96191	CS
96192	CS
96371	LR
96372	LM
96373	LM
96374	ZB
96375	LM
96602	Barry
96603	CF
96605	Barry
96607	Barry
99019	CS
99884	CL
975081	BU
975280	BU
975454	TO
975484	CS
975490	BU
975639	CS
975681	Portobello
975682	Portobello
975685	Portobello
975686	Portobello
975687	Portobello
975688	Portobello
975920	Portobello
977085	BU
977095	CS
977169	BU
977241	BU
977450	BU
977618	BY
999509	CL
083439	BU

DS70220 Western Trading Estate Siding, North Acton

Pullman 315 CS
Pullman 316 HN

3. DIESEL MULTIPLE UNITS

INTRODUCTION

This section contains details of all Diesel Multiple Units, usually referred to as DMUs, which can run on Britain's national railway network.

Since the 1980s DMUs have replaced more traditional locomotive-hauled trains on many routes. DMUs today work a wide variety of services, from long distance Intercity to inter-urban and suburban duties.

LAYOUT OF INFORMATION

DMUs are listed in numerical order of set – using current numbers as allocated by the Rolling Stock Library. Individual "loose" vehicles are listed in numerical order after vehicles formed into fixed formations. Where sets or vehicles have been renumbered in recent years, former numbering detail is shown in parentheses. Each entry is laid out as in the following example:

RSL Set No.	*Detail*	*Livery*	*Owner*	*Operator*	*Depot*	*Formation*	
170 518	*	**XC**	P	*XC*	TS	50518	79518

Codes: Codes are used to denote the livery, owner, operator and depot allocation of each Diesel Multiple Unit. Details of these can be found in section 6 of this book. Where a unit or spare car is off-lease, the operator column is left blank.

Detail Differences: Detail differences which currently affect the areas and types of train which vehicles may work are shown, plus differences in interior layout. Where such differences occur within a class, these are shown either in the heading information or alongside the individual set or vehicle number. The following standard abbreviations are used:

- e European Railway Traffic Management System (ERTMS) signalling equipment fitted.
- r Radio Electric Token Block signalling equipment fitted.

Use of the above abbreviations indicates the equipment fitted is normally operable. Meaning of non-standard abbreviations is detailed in individual class headings.

Set Formations: Regular set formations are shown where these are normally maintained. Readers should note set formations might be temporarily varied from time to time to suit maintenance and/or operational requirements. Vehicles shown as "Spare" are not formed in any regular set formation.

Names: Only names carried with official sanction are listed. Names are shown in UPPER/lower case characters as actually shown on the name carried on the vehicle(s). Unless otherwise shown, complete units are regarded as named rather than just the individual car(s) which carry the name.

GENERAL INFORMATION

CLASSIFICATION AND NUMBERING

DMU Classes are listed in class number order.

First generation ("Heritage") DMUs were classified in the series 100–139.
Parry People Movers (not technically DMUs) are classified in the series 139.
Second generation DMUs are classified in the series 140–199.
Diesel Electric Multiple Units are classified in the series 200–249.
Service units are classified in the series 930–999.

First and second generation individual cars are numbered in the series 50000–59999 and 79000–79999.

Parry People Mover cars are numbered in the 39000 series.

DEMU individual cars are numbered in the series 60000–60999, except for a few former EMU vehicles which retain their EMU numbers.

For all new vehicles allocated by the Rolling Stock Library since 2014 6-digit vehicle numbers are being used. The Class 230 D-Train DEMU individual cars are numbered in the 300xxx series.

WHEEL ARRANGEMENT

A system whereby the number of powered axles on a bogie or frame is denoted by a letter (A = 1, B = 2, C= 3 etc) and the number of unpowered axles is denoted by a number is used in this publication. The letter "o" after a letter indicates that each axle is individually powered.

UNITS OF MEASUREMENT

Principal details and dimensions are quoted for each class in metric and/or imperial units as considered appropriate bearing in mind common UK usage.

All dimensions and weights are quoted for vehicles in an "as new" condition with all necessary supplies (eg oil, water, sand) on board. Dimensions are quoted in the order Length – Width. All lengths quoted are over buffers or couplers as appropriate. Where two lengths are quoted, the first refers to outer vehicles in a set and the second to inner vehicles. All width dimensions quoted are maxima. All weights are shown as metric tonnes (t = tonnes).

OPERATING CODES

These codes are used by train operating company staff to describe the various different types of vehicles and normally appear on data panels on the inner (ie non driving) ends of vehicles.

The first part of the code describes whether the car has a motor or a driving cab as follows:

DM Driving motor   DT Driving trailer   M Motor   T Trailer

The next letter is a "B" for cars with a brake compartment.
This is followed by the saloon details:

F First
S Standard
C Composite

L denotes a vehicle with a toilet.
W denotes a Wheelchair space.

Finally vehicles with a buffet or kitchen area are suffixed RB or RMB for a miniature buffet counter.

Where two vehicles of the same type are formed within the same unit, the above codes may be suffixed by (A) and (B) to differentiate between the vehicles.

A composite is a vehicle containing both First and Standard Class accommodation, whilst a brake vehicle is a vehicle containing separate specific accommodation for the conductor.

Where vehicles have been declassified, the correct operating code which describes the actual vehicle layout is quoted in this publication.

BUILD DETAILS

Lot Numbers

Vehicles ordered under the auspices of BR were allocated a Lot (batch) number when ordered and these are quoted in class headings and sub-headings. Vehicles ordered since 1995 have no Lot Numbers, but the manufacturer and location that they were built is given.

Builders

These are shown for each lot. More details and a full list of builders can be found in section 6.7.

Information on sub-contracting works which built parts of carriages eg the underframes etc is not shown.

ACCOMMODATION

The information given in class headings and sub-headings is in the form F/S nT (or TD) nW. For example 12/54 1T 1W denotes 12 First Class and 54 Standard Class seats, one toilet and one space for a wheelchair. A number in brackets (ie (+2)) denotes tip-up seats (in addition to the fixed seats). Tip-up seats in vestibules do not count. The seating layout of open saloons is shown as 2+1, 2+2 or 3+2 as the case may be. Where units have First Class accommodation as well as Standard Class and the layout is different for each class then these are shown separately prefixed by "1:" and "2:".

TD denotes a universal access toilet suitable for use by people with disabilities. By law all trains should be fitted with such facilities by the start of 2020, but a number of trains were not made compliant in time and have been given time-limited dispensations for continued operation.

3.1. DIESEL MECHANICAL & DIESEL HYDRAULIC UNITS

3.1.1. FIRST GENERATION UNIT

CLASS 121 PRESSED STEEL SUBURBAN

First generation unit. Used by Chiltern Railways until 2017, and then sold to Locomotives Services for use as a route learning vehicle.
Construction: Steel.
Engines: Two Leyland 1595 of 112 kW (150 hp) at 1800 rpm.
Transmission: Mechanical. Cardan shaft and freewheel to a four-speed epicyclic gearbox and final drive.
Bogies: DD10.
Brakes: Vacuum.
Couplers: Screw.
Dimensions: 20.45 x 2.82 m.
Gangways: Non gangwayed single cars with cabs at each end.
Wheel arrangement: 1-A + A-1.
Doors: Manually-operated slam.
Maximum Speed: 70 mph.
Seating Layout: 3+2 facing.
Multiple Working: "Blue Square" coupling code. First Generation vehicles cannot be coupled to Second Generation units.

Fitted with central door locking.

Formerly in departmental use as 977828.

DMBS. Lot No. 30518 1960. –/65. 38.0 t.

121 034	**G**	LS	*LS*	CL	55034

3.1.2. PARRY PEOPLE MOVERS

CLASS 139 PPM-60

Gas/flywheel hybrid drive Railcars used on the Stourbridge Junction–Stourbridge Town branch.
Body construction: Stainless steel framework.
Chassis construction: Welded mild steel box section.
Primary Drive: Ford MVH420 2.3 litre 64 kW (86 hp) LPG fuel engine driving through Newage marine gearbox, Tandler bevel box and 4 "V" belt driver to flywheel.
Flywheel Energy Store: 500 kg, 1 m diameter, normal operational speed range 1000–1500 rpm.
Final transmission: 4 "V" belt driver from flywheel to Tandler bevel box, Linde hydrostatic transmission and spiral bevel gearbox at No. 2 end axle.
Braking: Normal service braking by regeneration to flywheel (1 m/s/s); emergency/parking braking by sprung-on, air-off disc brakes (3 m/s/s).
Maximum Speed: 45 mph.
Dimensions: 8.7 x 2.4 m.
Doors: Deans powered doors, double-leaf folding (one per side).
Seating Layout: 1+1 unidirectional/facing.
Multiple Working: Not applicable.

39001–002. DMS. Main Road Sheet Metal, Leyland 2007–08. –/17(+4) 1W. 12.5 t.

139 001	**WM**	P	*WM*	SJ	39001
139 002	**WM**	P	*WM*	SJ	39002

3.1.3. SECOND GENERATION UNITS

All units in this section have air brakes and are equipped with public address, with transmission equipment on driving vehicles and flexible diaphragm gangways. Except where otherwise stated, transmission is Voith 211r hydraulic with a cardan shaft to a Gmeinder GM190 final drive.

CLASS 142 PACER BREL DERBY/LEYLAND

DMS–DMSL. The remaining Class 142s are due to be withdrawn from service by summer 2020.

Construction: Steel underframe, rivetted steel body and roof. Built from Leyland National bus parts on Leyland Bus four-wheeled underframes.
Engines: One Cummins LT10-R of 165 kW (225 hp) at 1950 rpm.
Couplers: BSI at outer ends, bar within unit.
Dimensions: 15.55 x 2.80 m.
Gangways: Within unit only.
Wheel Arrangement: 1-A + A-1.
Doors: Twin-leaf inward pivoting.
Maximum Speed: 75 mph.
Seating Layout: 3+2 mainly unidirectional bus/bench style unless stated.

Multiple Working: Within class and with Classes 143, 144, 150, 153, 155, 156, 158 and 159.

c Units refurbished for Arriva Trains Wales. Fitted with 2+2 individual Chapman seating.
s Fitted with 2+2 individual high-back seating.
t Former First North Western facelifted units – DMS fitted with a luggage/bicycle rack and wheelchair space.
u Merseytravel units – Fitted with 3+2 individual low-back seating.

55543–590. DMS. Lot No. 31003 1985–86. –/62 (c –/46(+6) 2W, s –/56, t –/53 or 55 1W, u –/52 or 54 1W). 24.5 t.
55593–640. DMSL. Lot No. 31004 1985–86. –/59 1T (c –/44(+6) 1T 2W, s –/50 1T, u –/60 1T). 25.0 t.
55701–745. DMS. Lot No. 31013 1986–87. –/62 (c –/46(+6) 2W, s –/56, t –/53 or 55 1W, u –/52 or 54 1W). 24.5 t.
55747–791. DMSL. Lot No. 31014 1986–87. –/59 1T (c –/44(+6) 1T 2W, s –/50 1T, u –/60 1T). 25.0 t.

142 002	c	**AV**	A	*TW*	CF	55543	55593
142 003		**NO**	A		GA	55544	55594
142 004	t	**NO**	A	*NO*	NH	55545	55595
142 006	c	**AV**	A	*TW*	CF	55547	55597
142 007	t	**NO**	A		GA	55548	55598
142 009	t	**NO**	A		GA	55550	55600
142 010	c	**AV**	A	*TW*	CF	55551	55601
142 011	t	**NO**	A	*NO*	NH	55552	55602
142 012	t	**NO**	A		LE	55553	55603
142 013		**NO**	A	*NO*	HT	55554	55604
142 014	t	**NO**	A		GA	55555	55605
142 017	s	**NO**	A		WS	55558	55608
142 018	s	**NO**	A	*NO*	HT	55559	55609
142 019	s	**NO**	A		WS	55560	55610
142 020	s	**NO**	A		WS	55561	55611
142 023	t	**NO**	A	*NO*	HT	55564	55614
142 024	s	**NO**	A		GA	55565	55615
142 027	t	**NO**	A		WS	55568	55618
142 028	t	**NO**	A		GA	55569	55619
142 032	t	**NO**	A		GA	55573	55623
142 034	t	**NO**	A		GA	55575	55625
142 035	t	**NO**	A	*NO*	NH	55576	55626
142 036	t	**NO**	A	*NO*	NH	55577	55627
142 038	t	**NO**	A		GA	55579	55629
142 041	u	**NO**	A	*NO*	NH	55582	55632
142 043	u	**NO**	A	*NO*	NH	55584	55634
142 045	u	**NO**	A	*NO*	NH	55586	55636
142 046	u	**NO**	A		GA	55587	55637
142 047	u	**NO**	A	*NO*	NH	55588	55638
142 049	u	**NO**	A		GA	55590	55640
142 051	u	**NO**	A	*NO*	NH	55701	55747
142 054	u	**NO**	A		GA	55704	55750
142 055	u	**NO**	A	*NO*	NH	55705	55751

142 056	u	**NO**	A		GA	55706	55752
142 058	u	**NO**	A	*NO*	NH	55708	55754
142 060	t	**NO**	A		GA	55710	55756
142 061	t	**NO**	A	*NO*	NH	55711	55757
142 062	t	**NO**	A		GA	55712	55758
142 065	s	**NO**	A	*NO*	HT	55715	55761
142 068	t	**NO**	A	*NO*	HT	55718	55764
142 069	c	**AV**	A	*TW*	CF	55719	55765
142 070	t	**NO**	A	*NO*	HT	55720	55766
142 071	s	**NO**	A	*NO*	HT	55721	55767
142 072	c	**AV**	A	*TW*	CF	55722	55768
142 073	c	**AV**	A	*TW*	CF	55723	55769
142 074	c	**AV**	A	*TW*	CF	55724	55770
142 075	c	**AV**	A	*TW*	CF	55725	55771
142 076	c	**AV**	A	*TW*	CF	55726	55772
142 077	c	**AV**	A	*TW*	CF	55727	55773
142 078	s	**NO**	A	*NO*	NH	55728	55774
142 079	s	**NO**	A		LE	55729	55775
142 080	c	**AV**	A	*TW*	CF	55730	55776
142 081	c	**AV**	A	*TW*	CF	55731	55777
142 082	c	**AV**	A	*TW*	CF	55732	55778
142 083	c	**AV**	A	*TW*	CF	55733	55779
142 084	s	**NO**	A		WS	55734	55780
142 085	c	**AV**	A	*TW*	CF	55735	55781
142 086	s	**NO**	A		CF	55736	55782
142 087	s	**NO**	A	*NO*	HT	55737	55783
142 089	s	**NO**	A		GA	55739	55785
142 090	s	**NO**	A	*NO*	NH	55740	55786
142 091	s	**NO**	A		WS	55741	55787
142 094	s	**NO**	A	*NO*	HT	55744	55790
142 095	s	**NO**	A	*NO*	HT	55745	55791

CLASS 143 PACER ALEXANDER/BARCLAY

DMS–DMSL. Similar design to Class 142, but bodies built by W Alexander with Barclay underframes. The Class 143s are due to be withdrawn from service during 2020.

Construction: Steel underframe, aluminium alloy body and roof. Alexander bus bodywork on four-wheeled underframes.
Engines: One Cummins LT10-R of 165 kW (225 hp) at 1950 rpm.
Couplers: BSI at outer ends, bar within unit.
Dimensions: 15.45 x 2.80 m.
Gangways: Within unit only.
Wheel Arrangement: 1-A + A-1.
Doors: Twin-leaf inward pivoting.
Maximum Speed: 75 mph.
Seating Layout: 2+2 high-back Chapman seating, mainly unidirectional.
Multiple Working: Within class and with Classes 142, 144, 150, 153, 155, 156, 158 and 159.

DMS. Lot No. 31005 Andrew Barclay 1985–86. –/48(+6) 2W. 24.0 t.
DMSL. Lot No. 31006 Andrew Barclay 1985–86. –/44(+6) 1T 2W. 24.5 t.

143 601	**AV**	MG	*TW*	CF	55642	55667
143 602	**AW**	P	*TW*	CF	55651	55668
143 603	**GW**	P	*GW*	EX	55658	55669
143 604	**AW**	P	*TW*	CF	55645	55670
143 605	**AW**	P	*TW*	CF	55646	55671
143 606	**AW**	P	*TW*	CF	55647	55672
143 607	**AW**	P	*TW*	CF	55648	55673
143 608	**AW**	P	*TW*	CF	55649	55674
143 609	**AV**	SG	*TW*	CF	55650	55675
143 610	**AV**	MG	*TW*	CF	55643	55676
143 611	**GW**	P	*GW*	EX	55652	55677
143 612	**GW**	P	*GW*	EX	55653	55678
143 614	**AV**	MG	*TW*	CF	55655	55680
143 616	**AW**	P	*TW*	CF	55657	55682
143 617	**GW**	GW	*GW*	EX	55644	55683
143 618	**GW**	GW	*GW*	EX	55659	55684
143 619	**GW**	GW	*GW*	EX	55660	55685
143 620	**GW**	P	*GW*	EX	55661	55686
143 621	**GW**	P	*GW*	EX	55662	55687
143 622	**AW**	P	*TW*	CF	55663	55688
143 623	**AW**	P	*TW*	CF	55664	55689
143 624	**AW**	P	*TW*	CF	55665	55690
143 625	**AW**	P	*TW*	CF	55666	55691

CLASS 144 PACER ALEXANDER/BREL DERBY

DMS–DMSL or DMS–MS–DMSL. As Class 143, but underframes built by BREL. The Class 144s are due to be withdrawn from service by summer 2020.

Construction: Steel underframe, aluminium alloy body and roof. Alexander bus bodywork on four-wheeled underframes.
Engines: One Cummins LT10-R of 165 kW (225 hp) at 1950 rpm.
Couplers: BSI at outer ends, bar within unit.
Dimensions: 15.45/15.43 x 2.80 m.
Gangways: Within unit only.
Wheel Arrangement: 1-A + A-1.
Doors: Twin-leaf inward pivoting.
Maximum Speed: 75 mph.
Seating Layout: 2+2 high-back Richmond seating, mainly unidirectional.
Multiple Working: Within class and with Classes 142, 143, 150, 153, 155, 156, 158 and 159.

Non-standard livery: 144 012 144evolution (blue & purple).

DMS. Lot No. 31015 BREL Derby 1986–87. –/45(+3) 1W 24.0 t.
MS. Lot No. 31037 BREL Derby 1987. –/58. 23.5 t.
DMSL. Lot No. 31016 BREL Derby 1986–87. –/41(+3) 1T. 24.5 t.

† Prototype demonstrator unit, refurbished as a trial, with new Fainsa seating and a universal access toilet. Details are as follows:
DMS 55812: Lot No. 31015 BREL Derby 1986–87. –/43(+3). 27.2 t
DMSL 55835: Lot No. 31016 BREL Derby 1986–87. –/35 1TD 2W. 28.0 t.

144 001		**NO**	P	*NO*	HT	55801		55824
144 002		**NO**	P	*NO*	HT	55802		55825
144 003		**NO**	P	*NO*	HT	55803		55826
144 004		**NO**	P	*NO*	HT	55804		55827
144 005		**NO**	P	*NO*	HT	55805		55828
144 006		**NO**	P	*NO*	HT	55806		55829
144 007		**NO**	P	*NO*	HT	55807		55830
144 008		**NO**	P	*NO*	HT	55808		55831
144 009		**NO**	P	*NO*	HT	55809		55832
144 010		**NO**	P	*NO*	HT	55810		55833
144 011		**NO**	P	*NO*	HT	55811		55834
144 012	†	**0**	P	*NO*	HT	55812		55835
144 013		**NO**	P	*NO*	HT	55813		55836
144 014		**NO**	P	*NO*	HT	55814	55850	55837
144 015		**NO**	P	*NO*	HT	55815	55851	55838
144 016		**NO**	P	*NO*	HT	55816	55852	55839
144 017		**NO**	P	*NO*	HT	55817	55853	55840
144 018		**NO**	P	*NO*	HT	55818	55854	55841
144 019		**NO**	P	*NO*	HT	55819	55855	55842
144 020		**NO**	P	*NO*	HT	55820	55856	55843
144 021		**NO**	P	*NO*	HT	55821	55857	55844
144 022		**NO**	P	*NO*	HT	55822	55858	55845
144 023		**NO**	P	*NO*	HT	55823	55859	55846

Name: 144 001 THE PENISTONE LINE PARTNERSHIP

CLASS 150/0 SPRINTER BREL YORK

DMSL–MS–DMS. Prototype Sprinter.

Construction: Steel.
Engines: One Cummins NT855R5 of 213 kW (285 hp) at 2100 rpm.
Bogies: BX8P (powered), BX8T (non-powered).
Couplers: BSI at outer end of driving vehicles, bar non-driving ends.
Dimensions: 19.93/19.92 x 2.73 m.
Gangways: Within unit only.
Wheel Arrangement: 2-B + 2-B + B-2.
Doors: Twin-leaf sliding.
Maximum Speed: 75 mph.
Seating Layout: 3+2 (mainly unidirectional).
Multiple Working: Within class and with Classes 142, 143, 144, 153, 155, 156, 158, 159, 170 and 172.

Fitted with a new universal access toilet to meet the 2020 accessibility regulations. Full details awaited.

DMSL. Lot No. 30984 1984. –/72 1T. 35.4 t.
MS. Lot No. 30986 1984. –/92. 35.0 t.
DMS. Lot No. 30985 1984. –/69(+6). 34.7 t.

150 001	**GW**	A	*GW*	EX	55200	55400	55300
150 002	**GW**	A	*GW*	EX	55201	55401	55301

CLASS 150/1 SPRINTER BREL YORK

DMSL–DMS.

Construction: Steel.
Engines: One Cummins NT855R5 of 213 kW (285 hp) at 2100 rpm.
Bogies: BP38 (powered), BT38 (non-powered).
Couplers: BSI.
Dimensions: 19.74 x 2.82 m.
Gangways: Within unit only.
Wheel Arrangement: 2-B + B-2.
Doors: Twin-leaf sliding.
Maximum Speed: 75 mph.
Seating Layout: 3+2 facing as built but units operated by Centro were reseated with mainly unidirectional seating.
Multiple Working: Within class and with Classes 142, 143, 144, 153, 155, 156, 158, 159, 170 and 172.

* Northern units fitted with a new universal access toilet to meet the 2020 accessibility regulations. Chapman seating.
† Northern units fitted with a new universal access toilet to meet the 2020 accessibility regulations. Original Ashbourne seating.

DMSL. Lot No. 31011 1985–86. u –/71 1T, * –/55(+3) 1TD 2W, † –/56(+3) or –/57(+3) 1TD 2W. 38.3 t.
DMS. Lot No. 31012 1985–86. u –/70(+6), * –/65, † –/70(+6) or –/71(+6)). 38.1 t.

150 101	†	**NR**	A	*NO*	NH	52101	57101
150 102	†	**NR**	A	*NO*	NH	52102	57102
150 103	†	**NR**	A	*NO*	NH	52103	57103
150 104	†	**NR**	A	*NO*	NH	52104	57104
150 105	†	**LM**	A	*NO*	NH	52105	57105
150 106	†	**NR**	A	*NO*	NH	52106	57106
150 107	†	**LM**	A	*NO*	NH	52107	57107
150 108	†	**NR**	A	*NO*	NH	52108	57108
150 109	†	**LM**	A	*NO*	NH	52109	57109
150 110	†	**NO**	A	*NO*	NH	52110	57110
150 111	u	**NO**	A	*NO*	NH	52111	57111
150 112	†	**NR**	A	*NO*	NH	52112	57112
150 113	†	**NR**	A	*NO*	NH	52113	57113
150 114	†	**NO**	A	*NO*	NH	52114	57114
150 115	†	**NO**	A	*NO*	NH	52115	57115
150 116	†	**NR**	A	*NO*	NH	52116	57116
150 117	†	**NO**	A	*NO*	NH	52117	57117
150 118	†	**NO**	A	*NO*	NH	52118	57118
150 119	†	**NR**	A	*NO*	NH	52119	57119
150 120	†	**NR**	A	*NO*	NH	52120	57120
150 121	†	**NR**	A	*NO*	NH	52121	57121
150 122	u	**FB**	A	*NO*	NH	52122	57122
150 123	†	**NR**	A	*NO*	NH	52123	57123
150 124	†	**NR**	A	*NO*	NH	52124	57124
150 125	†	**NR**	A	*NO*	NH	52125	57125
150 126	†	**NR**	A	*NO*	NH	52126	57126
150 127	†	**NR**	A	*NO*	NH	52127	57127

150 128	†	**NR**	A	*NO*	NH	52128	57128
150 129	†	**NR**	A	*NO*	NH	52129	57129
150 130	†	**NR**	A	*NO*	NH	52130	57130
150 131	†	**NR**	A	*NO*	NH	52131	57131
150 132	†	**NR**	A	*NO*	NH	52132	57132
150 133	*	**NR**	A	*NO*	NH	52133	57133
150 134	*	**NR**	A	*NO*	NH	52134	57134
150 135	*	**NO**	A	*NO*	NH	52135	57135
150 136	*	**NR**	A	*NO*	NH	52136	57136
150 137	*	**NR**	A	*NO*	NH	52137	57137
150 138	*	**NR**	A	*NO*	NH	52138	57138
150 139	*	**NR**	A	*NO*	NH	52139	57139
150 140	*	**NR**	A	*NO*	NH	52140	57140
150 141	*	**NR**	A	*NO*	NH	52141	57141
150 142	*	**NR**	A	*NO*	NH	52142	57142
150 143	*	**NR**	A	*NO*	NH	52143	57143
150 144	*	**NR**	A	*NO*	NH	52144	57144
150 145	*	**NR**	A	*NO*	NH	52145	57145
150 146	*	**NR**	A	*NO*	NH	52146	57146
150 147	*	**NR**	A	*NO*	NH	52147	57147
150 148	*	**NR**	A	*NO*	NH	52148	57148
150 149	*	**NR**	A	*NO*	NH	52149	57149
150 150	*	**NR**	A	*NO*	NH	52150	57150

CLASS 150/2 SPRINTER BREL YORK

DMSL–DMS.

Construction: Steel.
Engines: One Cummins NT855R5 of 213 kW (285 hp) at 2100 rpm.
Bogies: BP38 (powered), BT38 (non-powered).
Couplers: BSI.
Dimensions: 19.74 x 2.82 m.
Gangways: Throughout.
Wheel Arrangement: 2-B + B-2.
Doors: Twin-leaf sliding.
Maximum Speed: 75 mph.
Seating Layout: 3+2 mainly unidirectional seating as built, but most units have now been refurbished with new 2+2 seating.
Multiple Working: Within class and with Classes 142, 143, 144, 153, 155, 156, 158, 159, 170 and 172.

c Former First North Western units with 3+2 Chapman seating.
p Units refurbished for Arriva Trains Wales with 2+2 Primarius seating.
q Refurbished units for Great Western Railway with new universal access toilet to meet the 2020 accessibility regulations. Original Ashbourne seating. Full details awaited.
t Refurbished units for Transport for Wales with 2+2 Chapman seating and a new universal access toilet to meet the 2020 accessibility regulations.
v Units refurbished for Valley Lines with 2+2 Chapman seating.
w Units refurbished for First Great Western with 2+2 Chapman seating.
* Refurbished units for Great Western Railway with 2+2 Chapman seating and a new universal access toilet to meet the 2020 accessibility regulations.

† Refurbished units for Northern with a new universal access toilet to meet the 2020 accessibility regulations. 3+2 Chapman seating.
§ Refurbished units for Northern with new universal access toilet to meet the 2020 accessibility regulations. Original Ashbourne seating.

150 209 is formed DMS–DMS (two toiletless vehicles).

DMSL. Lot No. 31017 1986–87. * –/50(+4) 1TD 2W, † –/58(+3) 1TD 2W, § –/58 1TD 2W, c –/62 1TD, p –/60(+4) 1T, t –/50 1TD 2W, u –/71 1T), v –/60(+8) 1T, w –/60(+8) 1T. 37.5 t (* 35.8 t, † and § 38.1 t).
DMS. Lot No. 31018 1986–87. * –/58(+10), † –/70(+6), § –/72(+3), c –/70, p –/56(+10) 1W, t –/58(+6), † u –/70(+6), v –/56(+15) 2W, w –/56(+17) 2W. 36.5 t.

150 201	c	**NO**	A	*NO*	NH	52201	57201
150 202	q	**GW**	A	*GW*	EX	52202	57202
150 203	†	**NR**	A	*NO*	NL	52203	57203
150 204	†	**NR**	A	*NO*	NH	52204	57204
150 205	†	**NR**	A	*NO*	NL	52205	57205
150 206	†	**NR**	A	*NO*	NL	52206	57206
150 207	c	**GW**	A	*GW*	EX	52207	57207
150 208	t	**AW**	P	*TW*	CF	52208	57208
150 209		**FB**	A	*NO*	NH	57209	57212
150 210	u	**NO**	A	*NO*	NH	52210	57210
150 211	†	**NR**	A	*NO*	NL	52211	57211
150 213	t	**AW**	P	*TW*	CF	52213	57213
150 214	§	**NR**	A	*NO*	NL	52214	57214
150 215	†	**NR**	A	*NO*	NH	52215	57215
150 216	q	**GW**	A	*GW*	EX	52216	57216
150 217	t	**AW**	P	*TW*	CF	52217	57217
150 218	†	**NR**	A	*NO*	NH	52218	57218
150 219	*	**FB**	P	*GW*	EX	52219	57219
150 220	†	**NR**	A	*NO*	NL	52220	57220
150 221	*	**GW**	P	*GW*	EX	52221	57221
150 222	†	**NR**	A	*NO*	NH	52222	57222
150 223	†	**NR**	A	*NO*	NL	52223	57223
150 224	†	**NR**	A	*NO*	NH	52224	57224
150 225	†	**NR**	A	*NO*	NH	52225	57225
150 226	u	**NO**	A	*NO*	NH	52226	57226
150 227	p	**AW**	P	*TW*	CF	52227	57227
150 228	§	**NR**	P	*NO*	NL	52228	57228
150 229	t	**AW**	P	*TW*	CF	52229	57229
150 230	w	**AW**	P	*TW*	CF	52230	57230
150 231	p	**AW**	P	*TW*	CF	52231	57231
150 232	*	**GW**	P	*GW*	EX	52232	57232
150 233	*	**GW**	P	*GW*	EX	52233	57233
150 234	*	**GW**	P	*GW*	EX	52234	57234
150 235	p	**AW**	P	*TW*	CF	52235	57235
150 236	t	**AW**	P	*TW*	CF	52236	57236
150 237	p	**AW**	P	*TW*	CF	52237	57237
150 238	*	**FB**	P	*GW*	EX	52238	57238
150 239	*	**GW**	P	*GW*	EX	52239	57239

150 240	t	**AW**	P	*TW*	CF	52240	57240
150 241	t	**AW**	P	*TW*	CF	52241	57241
150 242	t	**AW**	P	*TW*	CF	52242	57242
150 243	*	**GW**	P	*GW*	EX	52243	57243
150 244	*	**GW**	P	*GW*	EX	52244	57244
150 245	p	**AW**	P	*TW*	CF	52245	57245
150 246	*	**GW**	P	*GW*	EX	52246	57246
150 247	*	**GW**	P	*GW*	EX	52247	57247
150 248	*	**GW**	P	*GW*	EX	52248	57248
150 249	*	**GW**	P	*GW*	EX	52249	57249
150 250	t	**AW**	P	*TW*	CF	52250	57250
150 251	w	**AW**	P	*TW*	CF	52251	57251
150 252	t	**AW**	P	*TW*	CF	52252	57252
150 253	t	**AW**	P	*TW*	CF	52253	57253
150 254	t	**AW**	P	*TW*	CF	52254	57254
150 255	p	**AW**	P	*TW*	CF	52255	57255
150 256	t	**AW**	P	*TW*	CF	52256	57256
150 257	t	**AW**	P	*TW*	CF	52257	57257
150 258	t	**AW**	P	*TW*	CF	52258	57258
150 259	t	**AW**	P	*TW*	CF	52259	57259
150 260	t	**AW**	P	*TW*	CF	52260	57260
150 261	*	**GW**	P	*GW*	EX	52261	57261
150 262	t	**AW**	P	*TW*	CF	52262	57262
150 263	*	**GW**	P	*GW*	EX	52263	57263
150 264	t	**AW**	P	*TW*	CF	52264	57264
150 265	*	**GW**	P	*GW*	EX	52265	57265
150 266	*	**GW**	P	*GW*	EX	52266	57266
150 267	t	**AW**	P	*TW*	CF	52267	57267
150 268	§	**NR**	P	*NO*	NL	52268	57268
150 269	§	**NR**	P	*NO*	NL	52269	57269
150 270	§	**NR**	P	*NO*	NL	52270	57270
150 271	§	**NR**	P	*NO*	NL	52271	57271
150 272	§	**NR**	P	*NO*	NL	52272	57272
150 273	§	**NR**	P	*NO*	NL	52273	57273
150 274	§	**NR**	P	*NO*	NL	52274	57274
150 275	§	**NR**	P	*NO*	NL	52275	57275
150 276	§	**NR**	P	*NO*	NL	52276	57276
150 277	§	**NR**	P	*NO*	NL	52277	57277
150 278	v	**AW**	P	*TW*	CF	52278	57278
150 279	v	**AW**	P	*TW*	CF	52279	57279
150 280	v	**AW**	P	*TW*	CF	52280	57280
150 281	v	**AW**	P	*TW*	CF	52281	57281
150 282	t	**AW**	P	*TW*	CF	52282	57282
150 283	t	**AW**	P	*TW*	CF	52283	57283
150 284	t	**AW**	P	*TW*	CF	52284	57284
150 285	t	**AW**	P	*TW*	CF	52285	57285

Names:

150 214 The Bentham Line A Dementia-Friendly Railway
150 275 The Yorkshire Regiment Yorkshire Warrior

CLASS 153 SUPER SPRINTER LEYLAND BUS

DMSL. Converted by Hunslet-Barclay, Kilmarnock from Class 155 2-car units.

Construction: Steel underframe, rivetted steel body and roof. Built from Leyland National bus parts on Leyland Bus bogied underframes.
Engine: One Cummins NT855R5 of 213 kW (285 hp) at 2100 rpm.
Bogies: One P3-10 (powered) and one BT38 (non-powered).
Couplers: BSI.
Dimensions: 23.21 x 2.70 m.
Gangways: Throughout.
Wheel Arrangement: 2-B.
Doors: Single-leaf sliding plug.
Maximum Speed: 75 mph.
Seating Layout: 2+2 facing/unidirectional.
Multiple Working: Within class and with Classes 142, 143, 144, 150, 155, 156, 158, 159, 170 and 172.

Cars numbered in the 573xx series were renumbered by adding 50 to their original number so that the last two digits correspond with the set number.

c Chapman seating.
d Richmond seating.
† Refurbished units for Transport for Wales with a new universal access toilet to meet the 2020 accessibility regulations.

153 305/370/373/377/380 are to be converted to bicycle carrying vehicles for use with ScotRail. 153 373/380 are currently on sub-lease to Northern.

52301–52335. DMSL. Lot No. 31026 1987–88. Converted under Lot No. 31115 1991–92. –/72(+3) 1T 1W. (s –/72 1T 1W, t –/72(+2) 1T 1W), † –/59 1TD 2W). 41.2 t.
57301–57335. DMSL. Lot No. 31027 1987–88. Converted under Lot No. 31115 1991–92. –/72(+3) 1T 1W (s –/72 1T 1W, † –/59 1TD 2W). 41.2 t.

153 301	d	**NO**	A	*NO*	NL	52301	
153 302	c	**EM**	A	*EM*	NM	52302	
153 303	c	**AW**	A	*TW*	CF	52303	
153 304	ds	**NO**	A	*NO*	NL	52304	
153 305	d	**U**	A		ZM	52305	
153 306	c	**GA**	P	*TW*	CF	52306	
153 307	d	**NO**	A	*NO*	NL	52307	
153 308	c	**EM**	A	*EM*	NM	52308	
153 309	c	**GA**	P	*TW*	CF	52309	
153 310	c	**EM**	P	*TW*	CF	52310	
153 311	c	**EM**	P	*EM*	NM	52311	
153 312	s	**AW**	A	*TW*	CF	52312	
153 313	cs	**EM**	P	*TW*	CF	52313	
153 314	c	**GA**	P	*TW*	CF	52314	
153 315	ds	**NO**	A	*NO*	NL	52315	
153 316	c	**NO**	P	*NO*	NL	52316	John "Longitude" Harrison Inventor of the Marine Chronometer
153 317	ds	**NO**	A	*NO*	NL	52317	
153 318	d	**EM**	A	*EM*	NM	52318	
153 319	c	**EM**	A	*EM*	NM	52319	
153 320	†c	**TW**	P	*TW*	CF	52320	

153 321	ct	**EM**	P	*TW*	CF	52321	
153 322	c	**GA**	P	*TW*	CF	52322	
153 323	†c	**TW**	P	*TW*	CF	52323	
153 324	c	**NO**	P	*NO*	NL	52324	
153 325	†c	**TW**	P	*TW*	CF	52325	
153 326	c	**EM**	P	*TW*	CF	52326	
153 327	c	**AW**	A	*TW*	CF	52327	
153 328	ds	**NO**	A	*NO*	NL	52328	
153 329	c	**FB**	P	*TW*	CF	52329	
153 330	cs	**NO**	P	*NO*	NL	52330	
153 331	d	**NO**	A	*NO*	NL	52331	
153 332	c	**NO**	P	*NO*	NL	52332	
153 333	†c	**TW**	P	*TW*	CF	52333	
153 334	ct	**LM**	P	*WM*	TS	52334	
153 335	c	**GA**	P	*TW*	CF	52335	
153 351	d	**NO**	A	*NO*	NL	57351	
153 352	ds	**NO**	A	*NO*	NL	57352	
153 353	c	**AW**	A	*TW*	CF	57353	
153 354	c	**LM**	P	*WM*	TS	57354	
153 355	c	**EM**	A	*EM*	NM	57355	
153 356	c	**LM**	P	*WM*	TS	57356	
153 357	c	**EM**	A	*EM*	NM	57357	
153 358	c	**NO**	P	*NO*	NL	57358	
153 359	c	**NO**	P	*NO*	NL	57359	
153 360	c	**NO**	P	*NO*	NL	57360	
153 361	cs	**FB**	P	*TW*	CF	57361	
153 362	cs	**AW**	A	*TW*	CF	57362	
153 363	cs	**NO**	P	*NO*	NL	57363	
153 364	c	**LM**	P	*WM*	TS	57364	
153 365	c	**LM**	P	*WM*	TS	57365	
153 366	c	**LM**	P	*WM*	TS	57366	
153 367	†c	**TW**	P	*TW*	CF	57367	
153 368	d	**EM**	A	*EM*	NM	57368	
153 369	c	**FB**	P	*TW*	CF	57369	
153 370	d	**GW**	A		ZM	57370	
153 371	c	**LM**	P	*WM*	TS	57371	
153 372	d	**EM**	A	*EM*	NM	57372	
153 373	d	**GW**	A	*NO*	NL	57373	
153 374	c	**EM**	A	*EM*	NM	57374	
153 375	c	**LM**	P	*WM*	TS	57375	
153 376	c	**EM**	P	*EM*	NM	57376	X24-EXPEDITIOUS
153 377	d	**GW**	A		ZM	57377	
153 378	d	**NO**	A	*NO*	NL	57378	
153 379	c	**EM**	P	*EM*	NM	57379	
153 380	d	**GW**	A	*NO*	NL	57380	
153 381	c	**EM**	P	*EM*	NM	57381	
153 382	d	**EM**	A	*EM*	NM	57382	
153 383	c	**EM**	P	*EM*	NM	57383	Ecclesbourne Valley Railway 150 Years
153 384	c	**EM**	P	*EM*	NM	57384	
153 385	c	**EM**	P	*EM*	NM	57385	

CLASS 155 SUPER SPRINTER LEYLAND BUS

DMSL–DMS.

Construction: Steel underframe, rivetted steel body and roof. Built from Leyland National bus parts on Leyland Bus bogied underframes.
Engines: One Cummins NT855R5 of 213 kW (285 hp) at 2100 rpm.
Bogies: One P3-10 (powered) and one BT38 (non-powered).
Couplers: BSI.
Dimensions: 23.21 x 2.70 m.
Gangways: Throughout. **Wheel Arrangement:** 2-B + B-2.
Doors: Single-leaf sliding plug. **Maximum Speed:** 75 mph.
Seating Layout: 2+2 facing/unidirectional Chapman seating.
Multiple Working: Within class and with Classes 142, 143, 144, 150, 153, 156, 158, 159, 170 and 172.

DMSL. Lot No. 31057 1988. –/64 1TD 2W. 39.0 t.
DMS. Lot No. 31058 1988. –/76. 40.4 t.

155 341	**NR**	P	*NO*	NL	52341	57341
155 342	**NR**	P	*NO*	NL	52342	57342
155 343	**NR**	P	*NO*	NL	52343	57343
155 344	**NR**	P	*NO*	NL	52344	57344
155 345	**NR**	P	*NO*	NL	52345	57345
155 346	**NR**	P	*NO*	NL	52346	57346
155 347	**NR**	P	*NO*	NL	52347	57347

CLASS 156 SUPER SPRINTER METRO-CAMMELL

DMSL–DMS.

Construction: Steel.
Engines: One Cummins NT855R5 of 213 kW (285 hp) at 2100 rpm.
Bogies: One P3-10 (powered) and one BT38 (non-powered).
Couplers: BSI.
Dimensions: 23.03 x 2.73 m.
Gangways: Throughout. **Wheel Arrangement:** 2-B + B-2.
Doors: Single-leaf sliding. **Maximum Speed:** 75 mph.
Seating Layout: 2+2 facing/unidirectional.
Multiple Working: Within class and with Classes 142, 143, 144, 150, 153, 155, 158, 159, 170 and 172.

† Greater Anglia or East Midlands Railway units fitted with a new universal access toilet to meet the 2020 accessibility regulations. Chapman seating.
* Angel-owned Northern units fitted with a new universal access toilet to meet the 2020 accessibility regulations. Richmond seating.
§ Porterbrook-owned Northern units fitted with a new universal access toilet to meet the 2020 accessibility regulations. Chapman seating.
b Refurbished as a demonstrator unit by Brodies, Kilmarnock with a new universal access toilet to meet the 2020 accessibility regulations. Full details awaited.
c Chapman seating.

m East Midlands Railway units fitted with a new universal access toilet to meet the 2020 accessibility regulations. Chapman seating.
w ScotRail units with new Fainsa seating and universal access toilet to meet the 2020 accessibility regulations.

Non-standard livery: 156406 White with purple doors

Northern promotional vinyls:

156461 Ravenglass & Eskdale Railway
156464 Lancashire DalesRail
156480 Royal Air Force (light blue & white)

DMSL. Lot No. 31028 1988–89. –/74 1TD 1W († –/62 1TD 2W, * –/64(+2) 1TD 2W, § –/62(+2) 1TD 2W), c –/70, m –/62 (+2) 1TD 2W, t –/68 1W, u –/68, w –/66(+3) 1TD 2W). 38.6 t.
DMS. Lot No. 31029 1987–89. –/76 († –/74, *–/72(+4), t & u –/72, w –/76). 36.1 t.

156 401	m	**EM**	P	*EM*	DY	52401	57401
156 402	†cr	**GA**	P	*GA*	NC	52402	57402
156 403	m	**EM**	P	*EM*	DY	52403	57403
156 404	m	**EM**	P	*EM*	DY	52404	57404
156 405	m	**EM**	P	*EM*	DY	52405	57405
156 406	m	**0**	P	*EM*	DY	52406	57406
156 407	†cr	**GA**	P	*GA*	NC	52407	57407
156 408	m	**EM**	P	*EM*	DY	52408	57408
156 410	m	**EM**	P	*EM*	DY	52410	57410
156 411	m	**EM**	P	*EM*	DY	52411	57411
156 413	m	**EM**	P	*EM*	DY	52413	57413
156 414	m	**EM**	P	*EM*	DY	52414	57414
156 415	m	**EM**	P	*EM*	DY	52415	57415
156 416	†cr	**GA**	P	*GA*	NC	52416	57416
156 417	†cr	**GA**	P	*GA*	NC	52417	57417
156 418	†cr	**GA**	P	*GA*	NC	52418	57418
156 419	†cr	**GA**	P	*GA*	NC	52419	57419
156 420	§	**NR**	P	*NO*	NH	52420	57420
156 421	§	**NR**	P	*NO*	HT	52421	57421
156 423	§	**NR**	P	*NO*	NH	52423	57423
156 424	§	**NR**	P	*NO*	NH	52424	57424
156 425	c	**NO**	P	*NO*	NH	52425	57425
156 426	c	**NO**	P	*NO*	NH	52426	57426
156 427	§	**NR**	P	*NO*	NH	52427	57427
156 428	§	**NR**	P	*NO*	NH	52428	57428
156 429	c	**NO**	P	*NO*	NH	52429	57429
156 430	w	**SR**	A	*SR*	CK	52430	57430
156 431	w	**SR**	A	*SR*	CK	52431	57431
156 432	w	**SR**	A	*SR*	CK	52432	57432
156 433	w	**SR**	A	*SR*	CK	52433	57433
156 434	w	**SR**	A	*SR*	CK	52434	57434
156 435	w	**SR**	A	*SR*	CK	52435	57435
156 436	w	**SR**	A	*SR*	CK	52436	57436
156 437	w	**SR**	A	*SR*	CK	52437	57437

156 438	*	**NR**	A	*NO*	HT	52438	57438
156 439	w	**SR**	A	*SR*	CK	52439	57439
156 440	§	**NR**	P	*NO*	NH	52440	57440
156 441	§	**NR**	P	*NO*	HT	52441	57441
156 442	w	**SR**	A	*SR*	CK	52442	57442
156 443	*	**NR**	A	*NO*	HT	52443	57443
156 444	*	**NR**	A	*NO*	HT	52444	57444
156 445	rw	**SR**	A	*SR*	CK	52445	57445
156 446	rw	**SR**	A	*SR*	CK	52446	57446
156 447	u	**FS**	A	*NO*	HT	52447	57447
156 448	*	**NR**	A	*NO*	HT	52448	57448
156 449	u	**FS**	A	*NO*	HT	52449	57449
156 450	rw	**SR**	A	*SR*	CK	52450	57450
156 451	*	**NR**	A	*NO*	HT	52451	57451
156 452	§	**NR**	P	*NO*	NH	52452	57452
156 453	rw	**SR**	A	*SR*	CK	52453	57453
156 454	*	**NR**	A	*NO*	HT	52454	57454
156 455	§	**NR**	P	*NO*	NH	52455	57455
156 456	rw	**SR**	A	*SR*	CK	52456	57456
156 457	rw	**SR**	A	*SR*	CK	52457	57457
156 458	rw	**SR**	A	*SR*	CK	52458	57458
156 459	§	**NR**	P	*NO*	NH	52459	57459
156 460	c	**NO**	P	*NO*	NH	52460	57460
156 461	c	**NO**	P	*NO*	NH	52461	57461
156 462	w	**SR**	A	*SR*	CK	52462	57462
156 463	*	**NR**	A	*NO*	HT	52463	57463
156 464	c	**NO**	P	*NO*	NH	52464	57464
156 465	u	**FS**	A	*NO*	HT	52465	57465
156 466	§	**NR**	P	*NO*	NH	52466	57466
156 467	w	**SR**	A	*SR*	CK	52467	57467
156 468	*	**NR**	A	*NO*	HT	52468	57468
156 469	*	**NR**	A	*NO*	HT	52469	57469
156 470	m	**EM**	A	*EM*	DY	52470	57470
156 471	*	**NR**	A	*NO*	HT	52471	57471
156 472	*	**NR**	A	*NO*	HT	52472	57472
156 473	m	**EM**	A	*EM*	DY	52473	57473
156 474	rw	**SR**	A	*SR*	CK	52474	57474
156 475	*	**NR**	A	*NO*	HT	52475	57475
156 476	rw	**SR**	A	*SR*	CK	52476	57476
156 477	rw	**SR**	A	*SR*	CK	52477	57477
156 478	rb	**SR**	BR	*SR*	CK	52478	57478
156 479	*	**NR**	A	*NO*	HT	52479	57479
156 480	*	**NR**	A	*NO*	HT	52480	57480
156 481	*	**NR**	A	*NO*	HT	52481	57481
156 482	*	**NR**	A	*NO*	HT	52482	57482
156 483	*	**NR**	A	*NO*	HT	52483	57483
156 484	*	**NR**	A	*NO*	HT	52484	57484
156 485	u	**FS**	A	*NO*	HT	52485	57485
156 486	*	**NR**	A	*NO*	HT	52486	57486
156 487	*	**NR**	A	*NO*	HT	52487	57487
156 488	*	**NR**	A	*NO*	HT	52488	57488

156 489	*	**NR**	A	*NO*	HT	52489	57489
156 490	*	**NR**	A	*NO*	HT	52490	57490
156 491	*	**NR**	A	*NO*	HT	52491	57491
156 492	rw	**SR**	A	*SR*	CK	52492	57492
156 493	rw	**SR**	A	*SR*	CK	52493	57493
156 494	w	**SR**	A	*SR*	CK	52494	57494
156 495	w	**SR**	A	*SR*	CK	52495	57495
156 496	u	**FS**	A	*NO*	HT	52496	57496
156 497	m	**EM**	A	*EM*	DY	52497	57497
156 498	m	**EM**	A	*EM*	DY	52498	57498
156 499	rt	**SR**	A	*SR*	CK	52499	57499
156 500	rw	**SR**	A	*SR*	CK	52500	57500
156 501	w	**SR**	A	*SR*	CK	52501	57501
156 502	w	**SR**	A	*SR*	CK	52502	57502
156 503	w	**SR**	A	*SR*	CK	52503	57503
156 504	w	**SR**	A	*SR*	CK	52504	57504
156 505	w	**SR**	A	*SR*	CK	52505	57505
156 506	w	**SR**	A	*SR*	CK	52506	57506
156 507	w	**SR**	A	*SR*	CK	52507	57507
156 508	w	**SR**	A	*SR*	CK	52508	57508
156 509	w	**SR**	A	*SR*	CK	52509	57509
156 510	w	**SR**	A	*SR*	CK	52510	57510
156 511	w	**SR**	A	*SR*	CK	52511	57511
156 512	w	**SR**	A	*SR*	CK	52512	57512
156 513	w	**SR**	A	*SR*	CK	52513	57513
156 514	w	**SR**	A	*SR*	CK	52514	57514

Names:

156 460	Driver John Axon G.C.
156 464	Lancashire DalesRail
156 469	The Royal Northumberland Fusiliers (The Fighting Fifth)
156 480	Spirit of The Royal Air Force
156 483	William George 'Billy' Hardy 14/01/1903 – 10/03/1950

Class 156/9. Former Greater Anglia units transferring to East Midlands Railway. All nine of these units are due to transfer to East Midlands Railway in late 2019/early 2020.

156 902	(156 402)							
156 907	(156 407)							
156 909	(156 409)	†	**EI**	P	*EM*	DY	52409	57409
156 912	(156 412)	†	**GA**	P	*EM*	DY	52412	57412
156 916	(156 416)							
156 917	(156 417)							
156 918	(156 418)							
156 919	(156 419)							
156 922	(156 422)	†	**GA**	P	*EM*	DY	52422	57422

CLASS 158/0 BREL

DMSL(B)–DMSL(A) or DMCL–DMSL or DMSL–MSL–DMSL.

Construction: Welded aluminium.
Engines: 158 701–813/158 880–890/158 950–959: One Cummins NTA855R1 of 260 kW (350 hp) at 2100 rpm.
158 815–862: One Perkins 2006-TWH of 260 kW (350 hp) at 2100 rpm.
158 863–872: One Cummins NTA855R3 of 300 kW (400 hp) at 1900 rpm.
Bogies: One BREL P4 (powered) and one BREL T4 (non-powered) per car.
Couplers: BSI.
Gangways: Throughout.
Doors: Twin-leaf swing plug.
Dimensions: 22.57 x 2.70 m.
Wheel Arrangement: 2-B + B-2.
Maximum Speed: 90 mph.
Seating Layout: 2+2 facing/unidirectional.
Multiple Working: Within class and with Classes 142, 143, 144, 150, 153, 155, 156, 159, 170 and 172.

ScotRail 158s 158 701–736/738–741 are "fitted" for RETB. When a unit arrives at Inverness the cab display unit is clipped on and plugged in.

Transport for Wales units have ERTMS plugged in at Shrewsbury for working the Cambrian Lines.

* Refurbished ScotRail units fitted with Grammer seating, additional luggage racks and cycle stowage areas.
  ScotRail units 158 726–736/738–741 are fitted with Richmond seating.
† Refurbished East Midlands Railway units with Grammer seating.
§ Northern refurbished 3-car units (original seating).
c Chapman seating.
n Fully refurbished Northern units with new Fainsa seating.
p Refurbished ScotRail units with Richmond seating.
s Refurbished Transport for Wales units with Grammer seating.
v Northern units with modifications for operation beyond 2020.
z Refurbished Great Western Railway units. Units 158 745–749/751/762/767 (some formed into 3-car sets) have Richmond seating.

Non-standard livery: 158 773 and 158 774 White with orange doors.

Northern promotional vinyls:

158 784 PTEG: 40 years.
158 787, 158 792–796: Sheffield–Leeds fast service.
158 790/842/843/844/850/853: We Are Northern.
158 860: Keighley & Brontë Country.

DMSL(B). Lot No. 31051 BREL Derby 1989–92. –/68 1TD 1W. († 68(+3) 1TD 2W, § –/64(+3) 1TD 2W, cv –/62 1TD 2W, n –/66 1TD 2W, p –/60(+4) 1TD 2W, s –/64(+4) 1TD 2W, v –/64 1TD 2W, w –/66 1TD 2W, z –/62 1TD 2W). 38.5 t.
MSL. Lot No. 31050 BREL Derby 1991. –/68 1T. 38.5 t.
DMSL(A). Lot No. 31052 BREL Derby 1989–92. –/70 1T († –/74, cv & w –/68 1T, n –/72 1T, * & p –/64(+2) 1T, z –/68) plus cycle stowage area. 38.5 t.

The above details refer to the "as built" condition. The following DMSL(B) have now been converted to DMCL as follows:
52701–736/738–741 (ScotRail). 15/53 1TD 1W (* refurbished sets –/60(+6) 1TD 1W plus cycle stowage area).

158 701	*	**SR**	P	*SR*	IS	52701	57701	
158 702	*	**SR**	P	*SR*	IS	52702	57702	
158 703	*	**SR**	P	*SR*	IS	52703	57703	
158 704	*	**SR**	P	*SR*	IS	52704	57704	
158 705	*	**SR**	P	*SR*	IS	52705	57705	
158 706	*	**SR**	P	*SR*	IS	52706	57706	
158 707	*	**SR**	P	*SR*	IS	52707	57707	
158 708	*	**SR**	P	*SR*	IS	52708	57708	
158 709	*	**SR**	P	*SR*	IS	52709	57709	
158 710	*	**SR**	P	*SR*	IS	52710	57710	
158 711	*	**SR**	P	*SR*	IS	52711	57711	
158 712	*	**SR**	P	*SR*	IS	52712	57712	
158 713	*	**SR**	P	*SR*	IS	52713	57713	
158 714	*	**SR**	P	*SR*	IS	52714	57714	
158 715	*	**SR**	P	*SR*	IS	52715	57715	
158 716	*	**SR**	P	*SR*	IS	52716	57716	
158 717	*	**SR**	P	*SR*	IS	52717	57717	
158 718	*	**SR**	P	*SR*	IS	52718	57718	
158 719	*	**SR**	P	*SR*	IS	52719	57719	
158 720	*	**SR**	P	*SR*	IS	52720	57720	
158 721	*	**SR**	P	*SR*	IS	52721	57721	
158 722	*	**SR**	P	*SR*	IS	52722	57722	
158 723	*	**SR**	P	*SR*	IS	52723	57723	
158 724	*	**SR**	P	*SR*	IS	52724	57724	
158 725	*	**SR**	P	*SR*	IS	52725	57725	
158 726	p	**SR**	P	*SR*	CK	52726	57726	
158 727	p	**SR**	P	*SR*	CK	52727	57727	
158 728	p	**SR**	P	*SR*	CK	52728	57728	
158 729	p	**SR**	P	*SR*	CK	52729	57729	
158 730	p	**SR**	P	*SR*	CK	52730	57730	
158 731	p	**SR**	P	*SR*	CK	52731	57731	
158 732	p	**SR**	P	*SR*	CK	52732	57732	
158 733	p	**SR**	P	*SR*	CK	52733	57733	
158 734	p	**SR**	P	*SR*	CK	52734	57734	
158 735	p	**SR**	P	*SR*	CK	52735	57735	
158 736	p	**SR**	P	*SR*	CK	52736	57736	
158 738	p	**SR**	P	*SR*	CK	52738	57738	
158 739	p	**SR**	P	*SR*	CK	52739	57739	
158 740	p	**SR**	P	*SR*	CK	52740	57740	
158 741	p	**SR**	P	*SR*	CK	52741	57741	
158 745	z	**GW**	P	*GW*	EX	52745	57745	
158 747	z	**GW**	P	*GW*	EX	52747	57747	
158 749	z	**GW**	P	*GW*	EX	52749	57749	
158 750	z	**GW**	P	*GW*	EX	52750	57750	
158 752	§	**NR**	P	*NO*	NL	52752	58716	57752
158 753	§	**NR**	P	*NO*	NL	52753	58710	57753
158 754	§	**NR**	P	*NO*	NL	52754	58708	57754
158 755	§	**NR**	P	*NO*	NL	52755	58702	57755
158 756	§	**NR**	P	*NO*	NL	52756	58712	57756
158 757	§	**NR**	P	*NO*	NL	52757	58706	57757
158 758	§	**NR**	P	*NO*	NL	52758	58714	57758

158 759	§	**NR**	P	*NO*	NL	52759	58713	57759
158 760	z	**GW**	P	*GW*	EX	52760	57760	
158 762	z	**GW**	P	*GW*	EX	52762	57762	
158 763	z	**GW**	P	*GW*	EX	52763	57763	
158 765	z	**GW**	P	*GW*	EX	52765	57765	
158 766	z	**GW**	P	*GW*	EX	52766	57766	
158 767	z	**GW**	P	*GW*	EX	52767	57767	
158 769	z	**GW**	P	*GW*	EX	52769	57769	
158 770	†	**ST**	P	*EM*	NM	52770	57770	
158 773	†	**O**	P	*EM*	NM	52773	57773	
158 774	†	**O**	P	*EM*	NM	52774	57774	
158 777	†	**ST**	P	*EM*	NM	52777	57777	
158 780	†	**ST**	A	*EM*	NM	52780	57780	
158 782	n	**NR**	A	*NO*	NL	52782	57782	
158 783	†	**ST**	A	*EM*	NM	52783	57783	
158 784	v	**NO**	A	*NO*	NL	52784	57784	
158 785	†	**ST**	A	*EM*	NM	52785	57785	
158 786	n	**NR**	A	*NO*	NL	52786	57786	
158 787	v	**NO**	A	*NO*	NL	52787	57787	
158 788	†	**ST**	A	*EM*	NM	52788	57788	
158 789	n	**NR**	A	*NO*	NL	52789	57789	
158 790	v	**NO**	A	*NO*	NL	52790	57790	
158 791	v	**NO**	A	*NO*	NL	52791	57791	
158 792	v	**NO**	A	*NO*	NL	52792	57792	
158 793	v	**NO**	A	*NO*	NL	52793	57793	
158 794	v	**NO**	A	*NO*	NL	52794	57794	
158 795	v	**NO**	A	*NO*	NL	52795	57795	
158 796	v	**NO**	A	*NO*	NL	52796	57796	
158 797	v	**NO**	A	*NO*	NL	52797	57797	
158 798	z	**GW**	P	*GW*	PM	52798	58715	57798
158 799	†	**ST**	P	*EM*	NM	52799	57799	
158 806	†	**ST**	P	*EM*	NM	52806	57806	
158 810	†	**ST**	P	*EM*	NM	52810	57810	
158 812	†	**ST**	P	*EM*	NM	52812	57812	
158 813	†	**ST**	P	*EM*	NM	52813	57813	
158 815	cv	**NO**	A	*NO*	HT	52815	57815	
158 816	cv	**NO**	A	*NO*	HT	52816	57816	
158 817	cv	**NO**	A	*NO*	HT	52817	57817	
158 818	es	**TW**	A	*TW*	MN	52818	57818	
158 819	es	**AW**	A	*TW*	MN	52819	57819	
158 820	es	**TW**	A	*TW*	MN	52820	57820	
158 821	es	**TW**	A	*TW*	MN	52821	57821	
158 822	es	**TW**	A	*TW*	MN	52822	57822	
158 823	es	**TW**	A	*TW*	MN	52823	57823	
158 824	es	**TW**	A	*TW*	MN	52824	57824	
158 825	es	**TW**	A	*TW*	MN	52825	57825	
158 826	es	**TW**	A	*TW*	MN	52826	57826	
158 827	es	**TW**	A	*TW*	MN	52827	57827	
158 828	es	**TW**	A	*TW*	MN	52828	57828	
158 829	es	**TW**	A	*TW*	MN	52829	57829	
158 830	es	**TW**	A	*TW*	MN	52830	57830	

158 831	es	**AW**	A	*TW*	MN	52831	57831
158 832	es	**TW**	A	*TW*	MN	52832	57832
158 833	es	**AW**	A	*TW*	MN	52833	57833
158 834	es	**TW**	A	*TW*	MN	52834	57834
158 835	es	**TW**	A	*TW*	MN	52835	57835
158 836	es	**TW**	A	*TW*	MN	52836	57836
158 837	es	**TW**	A	*TW*	MN	52837	57837
158 838	es	**TW**	A	*TW*	MN	52838	57838
158 839	es	**TW**	A	*TW*	MN	52839	57839
158 840	es	**TW**	A	*TW*	MN	52840	57840
158 841	es	**TW**	A	*TW*	MN	52841	57841
158 842	cv	**NO**	A	*NO*	HT	52842	57842
158 843	cv	**NO**	A	*NO*	HT	52843	57843
158 844	v	**NO**	A	*NO*	HT	52844	57844
158 845	n	**NR**	A	*NO*	HT	52845	57845
158 846	†	**ST**	A	*EM*	NM	52846	57846
158 847	†	**ST**	A	*EM*	NM	52847	57847
158 848	v	**NO**	A	*NO*	HT	52848	57848
158 849	n	**NR**	A	*NO*	HT	52849	57849
158 850	v	**NO**	A	*NO*	HT	52850	57850
158 851	v	**NO**	A	*NO*	HT	52851	57851
158 852	†	**ST**	A	*EM*	NM	52852	57852
158 853	v	**NO**	A	*NO*	HT	52853	57853
158 854	†	**ST**	A	*EM*	NM	52854	57854
158 855	v	**NO**	A	*NO*	HT	52855	57855
158 856	†	**ST**	A	*EM*	NM	52856	57856
158 857	†	**ST**	A	*EM*	NM	52857	57857
158 858	†	**ST**	A	*EM*	NM	52858	57858
158 859	v	**NO**	A	*NO*	HT	52859	57859
158 860	v	**NO**	A	*NO*	HT	52860	57860
158 861	v	**NO**	A	*NO*	HT	52861	57861
158 862	†	**ST**	A	*EM*	NM	52862	57862
158 863	†	**ST**	A	*EM*	NM	52863	57863
158 864	†	**ST**	A	*EM*	NM	52864	57864
158 865	†	**ST**	A	*EM*	NM	52865	57865
158 866	†	**ST**	A	*EM*	NM	52866	57866
158 867	n	**NR**	A	*NO*	NL	52867	57867
158 868	n	**NR**	A	*NO*	NL	52868	57868
158 869	n	**NR**	A	*NO*	NL	52869	57869
158 870	n	**NR**	A	*NO*	NL	52870	57870
158 871	n	**NR**	A	*NO*	NL	52871	57871
158 872	cv	**NO**	A	*NO*	NL	52872	57872

Names:

158 784	Barbara Castle
158 791	County of Nottinghamshire
158 796	Fred Trueman Cricketing Legend
158 797	Jane Tomlinson
158 847	Lincoln Castle Explorer
158 854	The Station Volunteer
158 860	Ian Dewhirst
158 861	Magna Carta 800 Lincoln 2015

Class 158/8. Refurbished South Western Railway and East Midlands Railway units. Converted from former TransPennine Express units at Wabtec, Doncaster in 2007. 2+1 seating in First Class. Refurbished with modifications for operation beyond 2020.

158 885 has been fitted with new ZF transmission as a trial.

Details as Class 158/0 except:

DMCL. Lot No. 31051 BREL Derby 1989–92. 13/40(+2) 1TD 1W. 38.5 t.
DMSL. Lot No. 31052 BREL Derby 1989–92. –/70 1T. 38.5 t.

158 880	(158 737)	**ST**	P	*SW*	SA	52737	57737
158 881	(158 742)	**ST**	P	*SW*	SA	52742	57742
158 882	(158 743)	**ST**	P	*SW*	SA	52743	57743
158 883	(158 744)	**ST**	P	*SW*	SA	52744	57744
158 884	(158 772)	**ST**	P	*SW*	SA	52772	57772
158 885	(158 775)	**ST**	P	*SW*	SA	52775	57775
158 886	(158 779)	**ST**	P	*SW*	SA	52779	57779
158 887	(158 781)	**SW**	P	*SW*	SA	52781	57781
158 888	(158 802)	**SW**	P	*SW*	SA	52802	57802
158 889	(158 808)	**ST**	P	*EM*	NM	52808	57808
158 890	(158 814)	**SW**	P	*SW*	SA	52814	57814

CLASS 158/9 BREL

DMSL–DMS. Units leased by West Yorkshire PTE but managed by Eversholt Rail. Refurbished with new Fainsa seating. Details as Class 158/0 except for seating and toilets.

DMSL. Lot No. 31051 BREL Derby 1990–92. –/66 1TD 2W. 38.5 t.
DMS. Lot No. 31052 BREL Derby 1990–92. –/72 and parcels area. 38.5 t.

158 901	**NR**	E	*NO*	NL	52901	57901
158 902	**NR**	E	*NO*	NL	52902	57902
158 903	**NR**	E	*NO*	NL	52903	57903
158 904	**NR**	E	*NO*	NL	52904	57904
158 905	**NR**	E	*NO*	NL	52905	57905
158 906	**NR**	E	*NO*	NL	52906	57906
158 907	**NR**	E	*NO*	NL	52907	57907
158 908	**NR**	E	*NO*	NL	52908	57908
158 909	**NR**	E	*NO*	NL	52909	57909
158 910	**NR**	E	*NO*	NL	52910	57910

CLASS 158/0 BREL

DMSL(A)–DMSL(B)–DMSL(A). Units reformed as 3-car hybrid sets for Great Western Railway, mainly used between Cardiff and Portsmouth. For vehicle details see above. Formations can be flexible depending on when unit exams become due.

158 950	**GW**	P	*GW*	PM	57751	52761	57761
158 951	**GW**	P	*GW*	PM	52751	52764	57764

158 956	**GW**	P	*GW*	PM	52748	52768	57768
158 957	**GW**	P	*GW*	PM	57748	52771	57771
158 958	**GW**	P	*GW*	PM	57746	52776	57776
158 959	**GW**	P	*GW*	PM	52746	52778	57778

CLASS 159/0 BREL

DMCL–MSL–DMSL. Built as Class 158. Converted before entering passenger service to Class 159 by Rosyth Dockyard.

Construction: Welded aluminium.
Engines: One Cummins NTA855R3 of 300 kW (400 hp) at 1900 rpm.
Bogies: One BREL P4 (powered) and one BREL T4 (non-powered) per car.
Couplers: BSI.
Dimensions: 22.16 x 2.70 m.
Gangways: Throughout.
Wheel Arrangement: 2-B + B-2 + B-2.
Doors: Twin-leaf swing plug.
Maximum Speed: 90 mph.
Seating Layout: 1: 2+1 facing, 2: 2+2 facing/unidirectional.
Multiple Working: Within class and with Classes 142, 143, 144, 150, 153, 155, 156, 158 and 170.

DMCL. Lot No. 31051 BREL Derby 1992–93. 23/28 1TD 1W. 38.5 t.
MSL. Lot No. 31050 BREL Derby 1992–93. –/70(+6) 1T. 38.5 t.
DMSL. Lot No. 31052 BREL Derby 1992–93. –/72 1T. 38.5 t.

159 001	**SW**	P	*SW*	SA	52873	58718	57873
159 002	**SW**	P	*SW*	SA	52874	58719	57874
159 003	**SW**	P	*SW*	SA	52875	58720	57875
159 004	**SW**	P	*SW*	SA	52876	58721	57876
159 005	**SW**	P	*SW*	SA	52877	58722	57877
159 006	**SW**	P	*SW*	SA	52878	58723	57878
159 007	**SW**	P	*SW*	SA	52879	58724	57879
159 008	**SW**	P	*SW*	SA	52880	58725	57880
159 009	**SW**	P	*SW*	SA	52881	58726	57881
159 010	**SW**	P	*SW*	SA	52882	58727	57882
159 011	**SW**	P	*SW*	SA	52883	58728	57883
159 012	**SW**	P	*SW*	SA	52884	58729	57884
159 013	**SW**	P	*SW*	SA	52885	58730	57885
159 014	**SW**	P	*SW*	SA	52886	58731	57886
159 015	**SW**	P	*SW*	SA	52887	58732	57887
159 016	**SW**	P	*SW*	SA	52888	58733	57888
159 017	**SW**	P	*SW*	SA	52889	58734	57889
159 018	**SW**	P	*SW*	SA	52890	58735	57890
159 019	**SW**	P	*SW*	SA	52891	58736	57891
159 020	**SW**	P	*SW*	SA	52892	58737	57892
159 021	**SW**	P	*SW*	SA	52893	58738	57893
159 022	**SW**	P	*SW*	SA	52894	58739	57894

CLASS 159/1 BREL

DMCL–MSL–DMSL. Units converted from Class 158s at Wabtec, Doncaster in 2006–07 for South West Trains.

Details as Class 158/0 except:
Seating Layout: 1: 2+1 facing, 2: 2+2 facing/unidirectional.

DMCL. Lot No. 31051 BREL Derby 1989–92. 24/24(+2) 1TD 2W. 38.5 t.
MSL. Lot No. 31050 BREL Derby 1989–92. –/70 1T. 38.5 t.
DMSL. Lot No. 31052 BREL Derby 1989–92. –/72 1T. 38.5 t.

159 101	(158 800)	**ST**	P	*SW*	SA	52800	58717	57800
159 102	(158 803)	**ST**	P	*SW*	SA	52803	58703	57803
159 103	(158 804)	**ST**	P	*SW*	SA	52804	58704	57804
159 104	(158 805)	**ST**	P	*SW*	SA	52805	58705	57805
159 105	(158 807)	**ST**	P	*SW*	SA	52807	58707	57807
159 106	(158 809)	**ST**	P	*SW*	SA	52809	58709	57809
159 107	(158 811)	**ST**	P	*SW*	SA	52811	58711	57811
159 108	(158 801)	**ST**	P	*SW*	SA	52801	58701	57801

CLASS 165/0 NETWORK TURBO BREL

DMSL–DMS and DMSL–MS–DMS. Chiltern Railways units. Refurbished 2003–05 with First Class seats removed and air conditioning fitted.

Construction: Welded aluminium.
Engines: One Perkins 2006-TWH of 260 kW (350 hp) at 2100 rpm.
Bogies: BREL P3-17 (powered), BREL T3-17 (non-powered).
Couplers: BSI.
Dimensions: 23.50/23.25 x 2.81 m.
Gangways: Within unit only.
Wheel Arrangement: 2-B (+ B-2) + B-2.
Doors: Twin-leaf swing plug.
Maximum Speed: 75 mph.
Seating Layout: 2+2/3+2 facing/unidirectional.
Multiple Working: Within class and with Classes 166, 168, 170 and 172.

Fitted with tripcocks for working over London Underground tracks between Harrow-on-the-Hill and Amersham.

58801–822/58873–878. DMSL. Lot No. 31087 BREL York 1990. –/77(+7) 1TD 2W. 42.1 t.
58823–833. DMSL. Lot No. 31089 BREL York 1991–92. –/77(+7) 1TD 2W. 40.1 t.
MS. Lot No. 31090 BREL York 1991–92. –/106. 37.0 t.
DMS. Lot No. 31088 BREL York 1991–92. –/94. 41.5 t.

165 001	**CR**	A	*CR*	AL	58801		58834
165 002	**CR**	A	*CR*	AL	58802		58835
165 003	**CR**	A	*CR*	AL	58803		58836
165 004	**CR**	A	*CR*	AL	58804		58837
165 005	**CR**	A	*CR*	AL	58805		58838
165 006	**CR**	A	*CR*	AL	58806		58839
165 007	**CR**	A	*CR*	AL	58807		58840
165 008	**CR**	A	*CR*	AL	58808		58841

165 009	**CR**	A	*CR*	AL	58809		58842
165 010	**CR**	A	*CR*	AL	58810		58843
165 011	**CR**	A	*CR*	AL	58811		58844
165 012	**CR**	A	*CR*	AL	58812		58845
165 013	**CR**	A	*CR*	AL	58813		58846
165 014	**CR**	A	*CR*	AL	58814		58847
165 015	**CR**	A	*CR*	AL	58815		58848
165 016	**CR**	A	*CR*	AL	58816		58849
165 017	**CR**	A	*CR*	AL	58817		58850
165 018	**CR**	A	*CR*	AL	58818		58851
165 019	**CR**	A	*CR*	AL	58819		58852
165 020	**CR**	A	*CR*	AL	58820		58853
165 021	**CR**	A	*CR*	AL	58821		58854
165 022	**CR**	A	*CR*	AL	58822		58855
165 023	**CR**	A	*CR*	AL	58873		58867
165 024	**CR**	A	*CR*	AL	58874		58868
165 025	**CR**	A	*CR*	AL	58875		58869
165 026	**CR**	A	*CR*	AL	58876		58870
165 027	**CR**	A	*CR*	AL	58877		58871
165 028	**CR**	A	*CR*	AL	58878		58872
165 029	**CR**	A	*CR*	AL	58823	55404	58856
165 030	**CR**	A	*CR*	AL	58824	55405	58857
165 031	**CR**	A	*CR*	AL	58825	55406	58858
165 032	**CR**	A	*CR*	AL	58826	55407	58859
165 033	**CR**	A	*CR*	AL	58827	55408	58860
165 034	**CR**	A	*CR*	AL	58828	55409	58861
165 035	**CR**	A	*CR*	AL	58829	55410	58862
165 036	**CR**	A	*CR*	AL	58830	55411	58863
165 037	**CR**	A	*CR*	AL	58831	55412	58864
165 038	**CR**	A	*CR*	AL	58832	55413	58865
165 039	**CR**	A	*CR*	AL	58833	55414	58866

CLASS 165/1 NETWORK TURBO BREL

Great Western Railway units. DMSL–MS–DMS or DMSL–DMS. In 2015 GWR removed First Class from all its Class 165s, it was later reinstated on the 3-car units. Air cooling equipment fitted.

Construction: Welded aluminium.
Engines: One Perkins 2006-TWH of 260 kW (350 hp) at 2100 rpm.
Bogies: BREL P3-17 (powered), BREL T3-17 (non-powered).
Couplers: BSI.
Dimensions: 23.50/23.25 x 2.81 m.
Gangways: Within unit only.
Doors: Twin-leaf swing plug.
Wheel Arrangement: 2-B (+ B-2) + B-2.
Maximum Speed: 90 mph.
Seating Layout: 3+2/2+2 facing/unidirectional.
Multiple Working: Within class and with Classes 166, 168, 170 and 172.

58953–969. DMSL. Lot No. 31098 BREL York 1992. 16/51 1TD 2W. 40.8 t.
58879–898. DMSL. Lot No. 31096 BREL York 1992. –/73 1TD 2W. 40.8 t.
MS. Lot No. 31099 BREL 1992. –/106. 38.1 t.
DMS. Lot No. 31097 BREL 1992. –/84. 37.0 t.

▲ West Midlands Railway-liveried Parry People Mover 139 001 arrives at Stourbridge Junction with the 13.50 shuttle from Stourbridge Town on 03/06/19. **Steve Burdett**

▼ Arriva Trains-liveried 142 077 is seen at Bargoed with the 16.32 to Penarth on 04/07/19. **Dave Gommersall**

▲ Great Western Railway-liveried 143 619 and 158 766 leave Torquay with the 09.12 Paignton–Exmouth on 07/08/19. **Tony Christie**

▼ Northern-liveried 144 009 leaves Sheffield with the 11.30 to Hull on 29/06/19. **Robert Pritchard**

▲ New Northern-liveried 150 223 arrives at Hope with the 10.45 Manchester Piccadilly–Sheffield on 03/02/19. **Robert Pritchard**

▼ Transport for Wales-liveried 153 333 and First Group blue-liveried 153 361 stand at Cardiff Central with the 14.35 to Ebbw Vale Town on 07/09/19. **Robert Pritchard**

▲ With EMR Regional branding, East Midlands Trains-liveried 156 404 leaves Norwich with the 16.56 to Manchester Piccadilly on 04/09/19. **Robert Pritchard**

▼ Great Western Railway-liveried 158 769 stands at Cardiff Central with the 14.30 to Portsmouth Harbour on 07/09/19. **Robert Pritchard**

▲ New Northern-liveried 158 845 is seen near Corbridge in the Tyne Valley with the 13.54 Carlisle–Morpeth on 21/09/19. **Robert Pritchard**

▼ South Western Railway-liveried 159 019 passes Eckington working back from Brush Loughborough to Salisbury following refurbishment on 13/09/19. **Dave Gommersall**

▲ Chiltern Railways-liveried 165 028 is seen near Hatton Locks with the 09.34 Birmingham Moor Street–Leamington Spa on 13/09/19. **Paul Biggs**

▼ Great Western Railway green-liveried 166 212 is seen at Bincombe, at the end of the climb from Upwey, with the 15.08 Weymouth–Gloucester on 22/05/19. **Stephen Ginn**

▲ Chiltern Railways Mainline-liveried 168 005 approaches Dorridge with the 16.21 London Marylebone–Birmingham Snow Hill on 20/06/19. **Robert Pritchard**

▼ ScotRail-liveried 170 414 and 170 406 cross Jamestown Viaduct with the 15.16 Perth–Haymarket depot empty stock on 14/07/19. **Robin Ralston**

▲ Southern-liveried 171 804+171 401+171 723 pass Honor Oak Park with the 17.37 London Bridge–Uckfield on 11/07/18. **Robert Pritchard**

▼ West Midlands Railway-liveried 172 006 leaves Coventry Arena with the 16.16 Nuneaton–Leamington Spa on 15/06/19. **Robert Pritchard**

▲ Transport for Wales-liveried 175 006 passes Coedkernew, between Newport and Cardiff, with the 11.31 Manchester Piccadilly–Carmarthen on 16/09/19.
Stewart Armstrong

▼ Grand Central-liveried 180 102 passes Saxilby with the diverted 12.31 Sunderland–London King's Cross on 26/08/19. **Robert Pritchard**

▲ TransPennine Express-liveried 185 130 approaches Sheffield with the 08.53 Manchester Airport–Cleethorpes on 22/06/19. **Robert Pritchard**

▼ New Northern-liveried 195 107 arrives at Sheffield empty stock from Newton Heath on 12/08/19 for crew training. **Robert Pritchard**

▲ Preserved "Hastings" DEMU 1001 passes Little Langford in the Wylye Valley with the "Ludgershall Legionnaire" tour from Hastings to Ludgershall on 14/09/19.
Alan Holding

▼ CrossCountry-liveried 220 011 passes Rotherham Masborough with the 07.30 Birmingham New Street–Newcastle on 20/09/19. **Robert Pritchard**

▲ New Virgin Trains-liveried 221 101 and 221 143 pass Rugeley Trent Valley with the 17.10 London Euston–Holyhead on 15/06/19. **Robert Pritchard**

▼ New East Midlands Railway-liveried 222 104 and 222 015 pass Beeston with the 11.21 Derby–Nottingham empty stock on the launch day of the EMR franchise – 19/08/19. **Tony Christie**

▲ London Northwestern Railway-liveried 230 005 arrives at Bedford St Johns with the 12.01 Bletchley–St Johns on 15/06/19. **Robert Pritchard**

▼ Balfour Beatty Dynamic Track Stabiliser DR 72213 is seen at Long Marston on 20/06/19. **Robert Pritchard**

▲ Network Rail Plasser & Theurer 09-3X Dynamic Tamper DR 73120 is seen at Long Marston on 20/06/19. **Robert Pritchard**

▼ Network Rail Pandrol Jackson Plain Line Stoneblower DR 80210 passes Crewe on 02/07/19. **Cliff Beeton**

▲ Swietelsky Babcock Rail Kirow KRC 250S 25 tonne Diesel Hydraulic Crane DRK 81626 is hauled through Saxilby on 26/08/19. **Robert Pritchard**

▼ Network Rail Windhoff MPVs with Overhead Line Renewal Equipment DR 98004 and DR 98003 pass Lichfield Trent Valley on 29/07/19. **Dave Gommersall**

▲ Network Rail Ballast System Propulsion Machine DR 92331 is seen at Long Marston on 20/06/19. **Robert Pritchard**

▼ Network Rail Independent Drift Snowploughs ADB 965236 and ADB 965234 are powered through Belper by 37259 and 37218 whilst on test after overhaul on 20/08/19. **Tony Christie**

165 101	**GW**	A	*GW*	RG	58953	55415	58916
165 102	**GW**	A	*GW*	RG	58954	55416	58917
165 103	**GW**	A	*GW*	RG	58955	55417	58918
165 104	**GW**	A	*GW*	RG	58956	55418	58919
165 105	**GW**	A	*GW*	RG	58957	55419	58920
165 106	**GW**	A	*GW*	RG	58958	55420	58921
165 107	**GW**	A	*GW*	RG	58959	55421	58922
165 108	**GW**	A	*GW*	RG	58960	55422	58923
165 109	**GW**	A	*GW*	RG	58961	55423	58924
165 110	**GW**	A	*GW*	RG	58962	55424	58925
165 111	**GW**	A	*GW*	RG	58963	55425	58926
165 112	**GW**	A	*GW*	RG	58964	55426	58927
165 113	**GW**	A	*GW*	RG	58965	55427	58928
165 114	**GW**	A	*GW*	RG	58966	55428	58929
165 116	**GW**	A	*GW*	PM	58968	55430	58931
165 117	**GW**	A	*GW*	RG	58969	55431	58932
165 118	**GW**	A	*GW*	PM	58879		58933
165 119	**GW**	A	*GW*	PM	58880		58934
165 120	**GW**	A	*GW*	PM	58881		58935
165 121	**GW**	A	*GW*	RG	58882		58936
165 122	**GW**	A	*GW*	PM	58883		58937
165 123	**GW**	A	*GW*	RG	58884		58938
165 124	**GW**	A	*GW*	RG	58885		58939
165 125	**GW**	A	*GW*	RG	58886		58940
165 126	**GW**	A	*GW*	RG	58887		58941
165 127	**GW**	A	*GW*	PM	58888		58942
165 128	**GW**	A	*GW*	RG	58889		58943
165 129	**GW**	A	*GW*	PM	58890		58944
165 130	**GW**	A	*GW*	RG	58891		58945
165 131	**GW**	A	*GW*	PM	58892		58946
165 132	**GW**	A	*GW*	PM	58893		58947
165 133	**GW**	A	*GW*	RG	58894		58948
165 134	**GW**	A	*GW*	PM	58895		58949
165 135	**GW**	A	*GW*	RG	58896		58950
165 136	**GW**	A	*GW*	RG	58897		58951
165 137	**GW**	A	*GW*	PM	58898		58952

CLASS 166 NETWORK EXPRESS TURBO ABB

DMCL–MS–DMSL. Great Western Railway units, built for Paddington–Oxford/Newbury services. Air conditioned and with additional luggage space compared to the Class 165s. The DMSL vehicles have had their 16 First Class seats declassified.

Construction: Welded aluminium.
Engines: One Perkins 2006-TWH of 260 kW (350 hp) at 2100 rpm.
Bogies: BREL P3-17 (powered), BREL T3-17 (non-powered).
Couplers: BSI.
Dimensions: 23.50 x 2.81 m.
Gangways: Within unit only.
Doors: Twin-leaf swing plug.
Wheel Arrangement: 2-B + B-2 + B-2.
Maximum Speed: 90 mph.

Seating Layout: 1: 2+2 facing, 2: 2+2/3+2 facing/unidirectional.
Multiple Working: Within class and with Classes 165, 168, 170 and 172.

DMCL. Lot No. 31116 ABB York 1992–93. 16/53 1TD 2W. 41.2 t.
MS. Lot No. 31117 ABB York 1992–93. –/91. 39.9 t.
DMSL. Lot No. 31116 ABB York 1992–93. –/84 1T. 39.6 t.

166 201	**FB**	A	*GW*	PM	58101	58601	58122
166 202	**FB**	A	*GW*	PM	58102	58602	58123
166 203	**FB**	A	*GW*	PM	58103	58603	58124
166 204	**GW**	A	*GW*	PM	58104	58604	58125
166 205	**GW**	A	*GW*	PM	58105	58605	58126
166 206	**GW**	A	*GW*	PM	58106	58606	58127
166 207	**FB**	A	*GW*	PM	58107	58607	58128
166 208	**GW**	A	*GW*	PM	58108	58608	58129
166 209	**FB**	A	*GW*	PM	58109	58609	58130
166 210	**GW**	A	*GW*	PM	58110	58610	58131
166 211	**FB**	A	*GW*	PM	58111	58611	58132
166 212	**GW**	A	*GW*	PM	58112	58612	58133
166 213	**GW**	A	*GW*	PM	58113	58613	58134
166 214	**GW**	A	*GW*	PM	58114	58614	58135
166 215	**FB**	A	*GW*	PM	58115	58615	58136
166 216	**GW**	A	*GW*	PM	58116	58616	58137
166 217	**GW**	A	*GW*	PM	58117	58617	58138
166 218	**GW**	A	*GW*	PM	58118	58618	58139
166 219	**GW**	A	*GW*	PM	58119	58619	58140
166 220	**GW**	A	*GW*	PM	58120	58620	58141
166 221	**FB**	A	*GW*	PM	58121	58621	58142

Names:

166 204 Norman Topsom MBE
166 220 Roger Watkins THE GWR MASTER TRAIN PLANNER
166 221 Reading Train Care Depot/READING TRAIN CARE DEPOT *(alt sides)*

CLASS 168 CLUBMAN ADTRANZ/BOMBARDIER

Air conditioned.

Construction: Welded aluminium bodies with bolt-on steel ends.
Engines: One MTU 6R183TD13H of 315 kW (422 hp) at 1900 rpm.
Transmission: Hydraulic. Voith T211rzze to ZF final drive.
Bogies: One Adtranz P3–23 and one BREL T3–23 per car.
Couplers: BSI at outer ends, bar within unit.
Dimensions: Class 168/0: 24.10/23.61 x 2.69 m. Others: 23.62/23.61 x 2.69 m.
Gangways: Within unit only. **Wheel Arrangement:** 2-B (+ B-2 + B-2) + B-2.
Doors: Twin-leaf swing plug. **Maximum Speed:** 100 mph.
Seating Layout: 2+2 facing/unidirectional.
Multiple Working: Within class and with Classes 165 and 166.

Fitted with tripcocks for working over London Underground tracks between Harrow-on-the-Hill and Amersham.

Class 168/0. Original Design. DMSL(A)–MS–MSL–DMSL(B) or DMSL(A)–MSL–MS–DMSL(B).

58451–455 were numbered 58656–660 for a time when used in 168 106–110.

58151–155. DMSL(A). Adtranz Derby 1997–98. –/57 1TD 1W. 44.0 t.
58651–655. MSL. Adtranz Derby 1998. –/73 1T. 41.0 t.
58451–455. MS. Adtranz Derby 1998. –/77. 41.0 t.
58251–255. DMSL(B). Adtranz Derby 1998. –/68 1T. 43.6 t.

168 001	**CL**	P	*CR*	AL	58151	58651	58451	58251
168 002	**CL**	P	*CR*	AL	58152	58652	58452	58252
168 003	**CL**	P	*CR*	AL	58153	58453	58653	58253
168 004	**CL**	P	*CR*	AL	58154	58654	58454	58254
168 005	**CL**	P	*CR*	AL	58155	58655	58455	58255

Class 168/1. These units are effectively Class 170s. DMSL(A)–MSL–MS–DMSL(B) or DMSL(A)–MS–DMSL(B).

58461–463 have been renumbered from 58661–663.

58156–163. DMSL(A). Adtranz Derby 2000. –/57 1TD 2W. 45.2 t.
58456–460. MS. Bombardier Derby 2002. –/76. 41.8 t.
58756–757. MSL. Bombardier Derby 2002. –/73 1T. 42.9 t.
58461–463. MS. Adtranz Derby 2000. –/76. 42.4 t.
58256–263. DMSL(B). Adtranz Derby 2000. –/69 1T. 45.2 t.

168 106	**CL**	P	*CR*	AL	58156	58756	58456	58256
168 107	**CL**	P	*CR*	AL	58157	58757	58457	58257
168 108	**CL**	P	*CR*	AL	58158		58458	58258
168 109	**CL**	P	*CR*	AL	58159		58459	58259
168 110	**CL**	P	*CR*	AL	58160		58460	58260
168 111	**CL**	E	*CR*	AL	58161		58461	58261
168 112	**CL**	E	*CR*	AL	58162		58462	58262
168 113	**CL**	E	*CR*	AL	58163		58463	58263

Class 168/2. These units are effectively Class 170s. DMSL(A)–(MS)–MS–DMSL(B).

58164–169. DMSL(A). Bombardier Derby 2003–04. –/57 1TD 2W. 45.4 t.
58365–367. MS. Bombardier Derby 2006. –/76. 43.3 t.
58464/468/469. MS. Bombardier Derby 2003–04. –/76. 44.0 t.
58465–467. MS. Bombardier Derby 2006. –/76. 43.3 t.
58264–269. DMSL(B). Bombardier Derby 2003–04. –/69 1T. 45.5 t.

168 214	**CL**	P	*CR*	AL	58164		58464	58264
168 215	**CL**	P	*CR*	AL	58165	58365	58465	58265
168 216	**CL**	P	*CR*	AL	58166	58366	58466	58266
168 217	**CL**	P	*CR*	AL	58167	58367	58467	58267
168 218	**CL**	P	*CR*	AL	58168		58468	58268
168 219	**CL**	P	*CR*	AL	58169		58469	58269

Class 168/3. Former South West Trains/TransPennine Express Class 170s taken on by Chiltern Railways in 2015–16 and renumbered in the 168 3xx series. 170 309 was originally numbered 170 399. DMSL(A)–DMSL(B).

50301–308/399. DMCL. Adtranz Derby 2000–01. –/59 1TD 2W. 45.8 t.
79301–308/399. DMSL. Adtranz Derby 2000–01. –/69 1T. 45.8 t.

168 321	(170 301)	**CL**	P	*CR*	AL	50301	79301
168 322	(170 302)	**CL**	P	*CR*	AL	50302	79302
168 323	(170 303)	**CL**	P	*CR*	AL	50303	79303
168 324	(170 304)	**CL**	P	*CR*	AL	50304	79304
168 325	(170 305)	**CL**	P	*CR*	AL	50305	79305
168 326	(170 306)	**CL**	P	*CR*	AL	50306	79306
168 327	(170 307)	**CL**	P	*CR*	AL	50307	79307
168 328	(170 308)	**CL**	P	*CR*	AL	50308	79308
168 329	(170 309)	**CL**	P	*CR*	AL	50399	79399

CLASS 170 TURBOSTAR ADTRANZ/BOMBARDIER

Various formations. Air conditioned.

Construction: Welded aluminium bodies with bolt-on steel ends.
Engines: One MTU 6R183TD13H of 315 kW (422 hp) at 1900 rpm.
Transmission: Hydraulic. Voith T211rzze to ZF final drive.
Bogies: One Adtranz P3–23 and one BREL T3–23 per car.
Couplers: BSI at outer ends, bar within later build units.
Dimensions: 23.62/23.61 x 2.69 m.
Gangways: Within unit only. **Wheel Arrangement**: 2-B (+ B-2) + B-2.
Doors: Twin-leaf sliding plug. **Maximum Speed**: 100 mph.
Seating Layout: 1: 2+1 facing/unidirectional. 2: 2+2 unidirectional/facing.
Multiple Working: Within class and with Classes 150, 153, 155, 156, 158, 159 and 172.

Class 170/1. CrossCountry (former Midland Mainline) units. Lazareni seating. DMSL–MS–DMCL/DMSL–DMCL.

DMSL. Adtranz Derby 1998–99. –/59 1TD 2W. 45.0 t.
MS. Adtranz Derby 2001. –/80. 43.0 t.
DMCL. Adtranz Derby 1998–99. 9/52 1T. 44.8 t

170 101	**XC**	P	*XC*	TS	50101	55101	79101
170 102	**XC**	P	*XC*	TS	50102	55102	79102
170 103	**XC**	P	*XC*	TS	50103	55103	79103
170 104	**XC**	P	*XC*	TS	50104	55104	79104
170 105	**XC**	P	*XC*	TS	50105	55105	79105
170 106	**XC**	P	*XC*	TS	50106	55106	79106
170 107	**XC**	P	*XC*	TS	50107	55107	79107
170 108	**XC**	P	*XC*	TS	50108	55108	79108
170 109	**XC**	P	*XC*	TS	50109	55109	79109
170 110	**XC**	P	*XC*	TS	50110	55110	79110
170 111	**XC**	P	*XC*	TS	50111		79111
170 112	**XC**	P	*XC*	TS	50112		79112
170 113	**XC**	P	*XC*	TS	50113		79113
170 114	**XC**	P	*XC*	TS	50114		79114
170 115	**XC**	P	*XC*	TS	50115		79115
170 116	**XC**	P	*XC*	TS	50116		79116
170 117	**XC**	P	*XC*	TS	50117		79117

Class 170/2. Transport for Wales 3-car units. Previously operated by Greater Anglia. Chapman seating. DMCL–MSL–DMSL.

DMCL. Adtranz Derby 1999. 7/39 1TD 2W. 44.3 t.
MSL. Adtranz Derby 1999. –/74 1T. 42.8 t.
DMSL. Adtranz Derby 1999. –/66 1T. 44.8 t.

170 201		**GA**	P	*TW*	CF	50201	56201	79201
170 202		**GA**	P	*TW*	CF	50202	56202	79202
170 203		**GA**	P	*TW*	CF	50203	56203	79203
170 204		**GA**	P	*TW*	CF	50204	56204	79204
170 205		**GA**	P	*TW*	CF	50205	56205	79205
170 206		**GA**	P	*TW*	CF	50206	56206	79206
170 207		**GA**	P	*TW*	CF	50207	56207	79207
170 208		**GA**	P	*TW*	CF	50208	56208	79208

Class 170/2. Transport for Wales and Greater Anglia 2-car units. Chapman seating. DMSL–DMCL.

DMSL. Bombardier Derby 2002. –/57 1TD 2W. 45.7 t.
DMCL. Bombardier Derby 2002. 9/53 1T. 45.7 t.

170 270		**GA**	P	*TW*	CF	50270	79270
170 271	r	**GA**	P	*GA*	NC	50271	79271
170 272		**GA**	P	*TW*	CF	50272	79272
170 273		**GA**	P	*TW*	CF	50273	79273

Class 170/3. Units built for Hull Trains, now in use with ScotRail. Chapman seating. DMSL–MSL–DMSL.

DMSL(A). Bombardier Derby 2004. –/55 1TD 2W. 46.5 t.
MSL. Bombardier Derby 2004. –/71 1T. 44.7 t.
DMSL(B). Bombardier Derby 2004. –/67 1T. 47.0 t.

170 393	**SR**	P	*SR*	HA	50393	56393	79393
170 394	**SR**	P	*SR*	HA	50394	56394	79394
170 395	**SR**	P	*SR*	HA	50395	56395	79395
170 396	**SR**	P	*SR*	HA	50396	56396	79396

Class 170/3. CrossCountry units. Lazareni seating. DMSL–MS–DMCL.

DMSL. Bombardier Derby 2002. –/59 1TD 2W. 45.4 t.
MS. Bombardier Derby 2002. –/80. 43.0 t.
DMCL. Bombardier Derby 2002. 9/52 1T. 45.8 t.

170 397	**XC**	P	*XC*	TS	50397	56397	79397
170 398	**XC**	P	*XC*	TS	50398	56398	79398

Class 170/4. ScotRail "express" units. Chapman seating. DMCL–MS–DMCL.

Non-standard/Advertising liveries:

170 407 BTP text number 61016 (blue).
170 416, 170 417, 170 419, 170 420 Unbranded Saltire blue with grey doors.

DMCL(A). Adtranz Derby 1999–2001. 9/43 1TD 2W. 45.2 t.
MS. Adtranz Derby 1999–2001. –/76. 42.5 t.
DMCL(B). Adtranz Derby 1999–2001. 9/49 1T. 45.2 t.

170 401	**SR**	P	*SR*	HA	50401	56401	79401
170 402	**SR**	P	*SR*	HA	50402	56402	79402
170 403	**SR**	P	*SR*	HA	50403	56403	79403
170 404	**SR**	P	*SR*	HA	50404	56404	79404
170 405	**SR**	P	*SR*	HA	50405	56405	79405
170 406	**SR**	P	*SR*	HA	50406	56406	79406
170 407	**AL**	P	*SR*	HA	50407	56407	79407
170 408	**SR**	P	*SR*	HA	50408	56408	79408
170 409	**SR**	P	*SR*	HA	50409	56409	79409
170 410	**SR**	P	*SR*	HA	50410	56410	79410
170 411	**SR**	P	*SR*	HA	50411	56411	79411
170 412	**SR**	P	*SR*	HA	50412	56412	79412
170 413	**SR**	P	*SR*	HA	50413	56413	79413
170 414	**SR**	P	*SR*	HA	50414	56414	79414
170 415	**SR**	P	*SR*	HA	50415	56415	79415
170 416	**0**	E	*SR*	HA	50416	56416	79416
170 417	**0**	E	*SR*	HA	50417	56417	79417
170 418	**SR**	E	*SR*	HA	50418	56418	79418
170 419	**0**	E	*SR*	HA	50419	56419	79419
170 420	**0**	E	*SR*	HA	50420	56420	79420

Class 170/4. ScotRail "express" units. Chapman seating. DMCL–MS–DMCL.

DMCL. Bombardier Derby 2003–05. 9/43 1TD 2W. 46.8 t.
MS. Bombardier Derby 2003–05. –/76. 43.7 t.
DMCL. Bombardier Derby 2003–05. 9/49 1T. 46.5 t.

170 425	**SR**	P	*SR*	HA	50425	56425	79425
170 426	**SR**	P	*SR*	HA	50426	56426	79426
170 427	**SR**	P	*SR*	HA	50427	56427	79427
170 428	**SR**	P	*SR*	HA	50428	56428	79428
170 429	**SR**	P	*SR*	HA	50429	56429	79429
170 430	**SR**	P	*SR*	HA	50430	56430	79430
170 431	**SR**	P	*SR*	HA	50431	56431	79431
170 432	**SR**	P	*SR*	HA	50432	56432	79432
170 433	**SR**	P	*SR*	HA	50433	56433	79433
170 434	**SR**	P	*SR*	HA	50434	56434	79434

Class 170/4. ScotRail and Northern units. Originally built as Standard Class only. 170 450–457 were retro-fitted with First Class but those used by Northern are now Standard Class only. Chapman seating. DMSL–MS–DMSL or † DMCL–MS–DMCL.

DMSL/DMCL. Bombardier Derby 2004–05. –/55 1TD 2W († 9/47 1TD 2W). 46.3 t.
MS. Bombardier Derby 2004–05. –/76. 43.4 t.
DMSL/DMCL. Bombardier Derby 2004–05. –/67 1T († 9/49 1T 1W). 46.4 t.

170 450	†	**SR**	P	*SR*	HA	50450	56450	79450
170 451	†	**SR**	P	*SR*	HA	50451	56451	79451
170 452	†	**SR**	P	*SR*	HA	50452	56452	79452
170 453	†	**NR**	P	*NO*	NL	50453	56453	79453
170 454	†	**NR**	P	*NO*	NL	50454	56454	79454
170 455	†	**NR**	P	*NO*	NL	50455	56455	79455
170 456	†	**NR**	P	*NO*	NL	50456	56456	79456

170 457	†	**NR**	P	*NO*	NL	50457	56457	79457
170 458		**NR**	P	*NO*	NL	50458	56458	79458
170 459		**NR**	P	*NO*	NL	50459	56459	79459
170 460		**NR**	P	*NO*	NL	50460	56460	79460
170 461		**NR**	P	*NO*	NL	50461	56461	79461

Class 170/4. ScotRail and Northern units. Standard Class only units. Chapman seating. DMSL–MS–DMSL.

50470–471. DMSL(A). Adtranz Derby 2001. –/55 1TD 2W. 45.1 t.
50472–478. DMSL(A). Bombardier Derby 2004–05. –/57 1TD 2W. 45.8 t.
56470–471. MS. Adtranz Derby 2001. –/76. 42.4 t.
56472–478. MS. Bombardier Derby 2004–05. –/76. 43.0 t.
79470–471. DMSL(B). Adtranz Derby 2001. –/67 1T. 45.1 t.
79472–478. DMSL(B). Bombardier Derby 2004–05. –/67 1T. 45.8 t.

170 470		**SR**	P	*SR*	HA	50470	56470	79470
170 471		**SR**	P	*SR*	HA	50471	56471	79471
170 472		**NR**	P	*NO*	NL	50472	56472	79472
170 473		**NR**	P	*NO*	NL	50473	56473	79473
170 474		**NR**	P	*NO*	NL	50474	56474	79474
170 475		**NR**	P	*NO*	NL	50475	56475	79475
170 476		**NR**	P	*NO*	NL	50476	56476	79476
170 477		**NR**	P	*NO*	NL	50477	56477	79477
170 478		**NR**	P	*NO*	NL	50478	56478	79478

Class 170/5. West Midlands Trains and CrossCountry 2-car units. Lazareni seating. DMSL–DMSL or * DMSL–DMCL (CrossCountry).

DMSL(A). Adtranz Derby 1999–2000. –/55 1TD 2W (* –/59 1TD 2W). 45.8 t.
DMSL(B). Adtranz Derby 1999–2000. –/67 1T (* DMCL 9/52 1T). 45.9 t.

170 501		**WI**	P	*WM*	TS	50501	79501
170 502		**WI**	P	*WM*	TS	50502	79502
170 503		**WI**	P	*WM*	TS	50503	79503
170 504		**WI**	P	*WM*	TS	50504	79504
170 505		**WI**	P	*WM*	TS	50505	79505
170 506		**WI**	P	*WM*	TS	50506	79506
170 507		**WI**	P	*WM*	TS	50507	79507
170 508		**WI**	P	*WM*	TS	50508	79508
170 509		**WI**	P	*WM*	TS	50509	79509
170 510		**WI**	P	*WM*	TS	50510	79510
170 511		**WI**	P	*WM*	TS	50511	79511
170 512		**WI**	P	*WM*	TS	50512	79512
170 513		**WI**	P	*WM*	TS	50513	79513
170 514		**WI**	P	*WM*	TS	50514	79514
170 515		**WI**	P	*WM*	TS	50515	79515
170 516		**WI**	P	*WM*	TS	50516	79516
170 517		**WI**	P	*WM*	TS	50517	79517
170 518	*	**XC**	P	*XC*	TS	50518	79518
170 519	*	**XC**	P	*XC*	TS	50519	79519
170 520	*	**XC**	P	*XC*	TS	50520	79520
170 521	*	**XC**	P	*XC*	TS	50521	79521
170 522	*	**XC**	P	*XC*	TS	50522	79522
170 523	*	**XC**	P	*XC*	TS	50523	79523

Class 170/6. West Midlands Trains and CrossCountry 3-car units. Lazareni seating. DMSL–MS–DMSL or * DMSL–MS–DMCL (CrossCountry).

DMSL(A). Adtranz Derby 2000. –/55 1TD 2W (* –/59 1TD 2W). 45.8 t.
MS. Adtranz Derby 2000. –/74 (* –/80). 42.4 t.
DMSL(B). Adtranz Derby 2000. –/67 1T (* DMCL 9/52 1T). 45.9 t.

170 630		**WI**	P	*WM*	TS	50630	56630	79630
170 631		**WI**	P	*WM*	TS	50631	56631	79631
170 632		**WI**	P	*WM*	TS	50632	56632	79632
170 633		**WI**	P	*WM*	TS	50633	56633	79633
170 634		**WI**	P	*WM*	TS	50634	56634	79634
170 635		**WI**	P	*WM*	TS	50635	56635	79635
170 636	*	**XC**	P	*XC*	TS	50636	56636	79636
170 637	*	**XC**	P	*XC*	TS	50637	56637	79637
170 638	*	**XC**	P	*XC*	TS	50638	56638	79638
170 639	*	**XC**	P	*XC*	TS	50639	56639	79639

CLASS 171 TURBOSTAR BOMBARDIER

DMCL–DMSL or DMCL–MS–MS–DMCL. Southern units. Air conditioned. Chapman seating.

Construction: Welded aluminium bodies with bolt-on steel ends.
Engines: One MTU 6R183TD13H of 315 kW (422 hp) at 1900 rpm.
Transmission: Hydraulic. Voith T211rzze to ZF final drive.
Bogies: One Adtranz P3–23 and one BREL T3–23 per car.
Couplers: Dellner 12 at outer ends, bar within unit (Class 171/8).
Dimensions: 23.62/23.61 x 2.69 m.
Gangways: Within unit only. **Wheel Arrangement:** 2-B (+ B-2 + B-2) + B-2.
Doors: Twin-leaf swing plug. **Maximum Speed:** 100 mph.
Seating Layout: 1: 2+1 facing/unidirectional. 2: 2+2 facing/unidirectional.
Multiple Working: Within class and with EMU Classes 375 and 377 in an emergency.

Class 171/2. 2-car units rebuilt from ScotRail Class 170s. Full details awaited. DMCL–DMSL.

Originally built as 3-car units 170 421/423, but renumbered as Class 171 when fitted with Dellner couplers.

DMCL. Adtranz Derby 1999–2001.
DMSL. Adtranz Derby 1999–2001.

171 201	**SN**	E	*SN*	SU	50421	79421
171 202	**SN**	E	*SN*	SU	50423	79423

Class 171/4. 4-car units rebuilt from ScotRail Class 170s. Full details awaited. DMCL(A)–MS–MS–DMCL(B).

Reformed and renumbered Class 171s in 2016 using vehicles from ScotRail 3-car Class 170s 170 421–424.

DMCL(A). Adtranz Derby 1999–2001.
MS. Adtranz Derby 1999–2001.
DMCL(B). Adtranz Derby 1999–2001.

171 401	**SN**	E	*SN*	SU	50422	56421	56422	79422
171 402	**SN**	E	*SN*	SU	50424	56423	56424	79424

Class 171/7. 2-car units. DMCL–DMSL.

171 721–726 were built as Class 170s (170 721–726), but renumbered as Class 171 when fitted with Dellner couplers.

171 730 was formerly South West Trains unit 170 392, before transferring to Southern in 2007.

50721–726. DMCL. Bombardier Derby 2003. 9/43 1TD 2W. 47.6 t.
50727–729. DMCL. Bombardier Derby 2005. 9/43 1TD 2W. 46.3 t.
50392. DMCL. Bombardier Derby 2003. 9/43 1TD 2W. 46.6 t.
79721–726. DMSL. Bombardier Derby 2003. –/64 1T. 47.8 t.
79727–729. DMSL. Bombardier Derby 2005. –/64 1T. 46.2 t.
79392. DMSL. Bombardier Derby 2003. –/64 1T. 46.5 t.

171 721	**SN**	P	*SN*	SU	50721	79721
171 722	**SN**	P	*SN*	SU	50722	79722
171 723	**SN**	P	*SN*	SU	50723	79723
171 724	**SN**	P	*SN*	SU	50724	79724
171 725	**SN**	P	*SN*	SU	50725	79725
171 726	**SN**	P	*SN*	SU	50726	79726
171 727	**SN**	P	*SN*	SU	50727	79727
171 728	**SN**	P	*SN*	SU	50728	79728
171 729	**SN**	P	*SN*	SU	50729	79729
171 730	**SN**	P	*SN*	SU	50392	79392

Class 171/8. 4-car units. DMCL(A)–MS–MS–DMCL(B).

DMCL(A). Bombardier Derby 2004. 9/43 1TD 2W. 46.5 t.
MS. Bombardier Derby 2004. –/74. 43.7 t.
DMCL(B). Bombardier Derby 2004. 9/50 1T. 46.5 t.

171 801	**SN**	P	*SN*	SU	50801	54801	56801	79801
171 802	**SN**	P	*SN*	SU	50802	54802	56802	79802
171 803	**SN**	P	*SN*	SU	50803	54803	56803	79803
171 804	**SN**	P	*SN*	SU	50804	54804	56804	79804
171 805	**SN**	P	*SN*	SU	50805	54805	56805	79805
171 806	**SN**	P	*SN*	SU	50806	54806	56806	79806

CLASS 172 TURBOSTAR BOMBARDIER

New generation Chiltern Railways and West Midlands Trains Turbostars. Air conditioned.

Construction: Welded aluminium bodies with bolt-on steel ends.
Engines: One MTU 6H1800R83 of 360 kW (483 hp) at 1800 rpm.
Transmission: Mechanical. Supplied by ZF, Germany.
Bogies: B5006 type "lightweight" bogies.
Couplers: BSI at outer ends, bar within unit.
Dimensions: 23.62/23.00 x 2.69 m.
Gangways: 172/0 & 172/1: Within unit only. 172/2: Throughout.
Wheel Arrangement: 2-B (+ B-2) + B-2.

Doors: Twin-leaf sliding plug.
Maximum Speed: 100 mph.
Seating Layout: 2+2 facing/unidirectional.
Multiple Working: Within class and with Classes 150, 153, 155, 156, 158, 159, 165, 166 and 170.

Class 172/0. West Midlands Trains units. Formerly operated by London Overground. DMSL–DMS.

59311–318. DMSL. Bombardier Derby 2009–10. –/57(+4) 1TD 2W. 41.6 t.
59411–418. DMS. Bombardier Derby 2009–10. –/64(+12). 41.5 t.

172 001	**WM**	A	*WM*	TS	59311	59411
172 002	**WM**	A	*WM*	TS	59312	59412
172 003	**WM**	A	*WM*	TS	59313	59413
172 004	**WM**	A	*WM*	TS	59314	59414
172 005	**WM**	A	*WM*	TS	59315	59415
172 006	**WM**	A	*WM*	TS	59316	59416
172 007	**WM**	A	*WM*	TS	59317	59417
172 008	**WM**	A	*WM*	TS	59318	59418

Class 172/1. Chiltern Railways units. DMSL–DMS.

59111–114. DMSL. Bombardier Derby 2009–10. –/60(+5) 1TD 2W. 42.4 t.
59211–214. DMS. Bombardier Derby 2009–10. –/80. 41.8 t.

172 101	**CR**	A	*CR*	AL	59111	59211
172 102	**CR**	A	*CR*	AL	59112	59212
172 103	**CR**	A	*CR*	AL	59113	59213
172 104	**CR**	A	*CR*	AL	59114	59214

Class 172/2. West Midlands Trains 2-car units. DMSL–DMS. Used on local services via Birmingham Snow Hill.

50211–222. DMSL. Bombardier Derby 2010–11. –/52(+11) 1TD 2W. 42.5 t.
79211–222. DMS. Bombardier Derby 2010–11. –/68(+8). 41.9 t.

172 211	**WM**	P	*WM*	TS	50211	79211
172 212	**WM**	P	*WM*	TS	50212	79212
172 213	**WM**	P	*WM*	TS	50213	79213
172 214	**WM**	P	*WM*	TS	50214	79214
172 215	**WM**	P	*WM*	TS	50215	79215
172 216	**WM**	P	*WM*	TS	50216	79216
172 217	**WM**	P	*WM*	TS	50217	79217
172 218	**WM**	P	*WM*	TS	50218	79218
172 219	**WM**	P	*WM*	TS	50219	79219
172 220	**WM**	P	*WM*	TS	50220	79220
172 221	**WM**	P	*WM*	TS	50221	79221
172 222	**WM**	P	*WM*	TS	50222	79222

Class 172/3. West Midlands Trains 3-car units. DMSL–MS–DMS. Used on local services via Birmingham Snow Hill. 172 333/338 are running with misformed formations, as shown.

50331–345. DMSL. Bombardier Derby 2010–11. –/52(+11) 1TD 2W. 42.5 t.
56331–345. MS. Bombardier Derby 2010–11. –/72(+8). 38.8 t.
79331–345. DMS. Bombardier Derby 2010–11. –/68(+8). 41.9 t.

172 331	**WM**	P	*WM*	TS	50331	56331	79331
172 332	**WM**	P	*WM*	TS	50332	56332	79332
172 333	**WM**	P	*WM*	TS	50338	56333	79333
172 334	**WM**	P	*WM*	TS	50334	56334	79334
172 335	**WM**	P	*WM*	TS	50335	56335	79335
172 336	**WM**	P	*WM*	TS	50336	56336	79336
172 337	**WM**	P	*WM*	TS	50337	56337	79337
172 338	**WM**	P	*WM*	TS	50333	56338	79338
172 339	**WM**	P	*WM*	TS	50339	56339	79339
172 340	**WM**	P	*WM*	TS	50340	56340	79340
172 341	**WM**	P	*WM*	TS	50341	56341	79341
172 342	**WM**	P	*WM*	TS	50342	56342	79342
172 343	**WM**	P	*WM*	TS	50343	56343	79343
172 344	**WM**	P	*WM*	TS	50344	56344	79344
172 345	**WM**	P	*WM*	TS	50345	56345	79345

CLASS 175 CORADIA 1000 ALSTOM

Air conditioned.

Construction: Steel.
Engines: One Cummins N14 of 335 kW (450 hp).
Transmission: Hydraulic. Voith T211rzze to ZF Voith final drive.
Bogies: ACR (Alstom FBO) – LTB-MBS1, TB-MB1, MBS1-LTB.
Couplers: Scharfenberg outer ends and bar within unit (Class 175/1).
Dimensions: 23.70 x 2.73 m.
Gangways: Within unit only. **Wheel Arrangement**: 2-B (+ B-2) + B-2.
Doors: Single-leaf swing plug. **Maximum Speed**: 100 mph.
Seating Layout: 2+2 facing/unidirectional.
Multiple Working: Within class and with Class 180.

At the time of writing sets 175 004/005/006/101/109/115 are running with misformed formations, as shown.

Class 175/0. DMSL–DMSL. 2-car units.

DMSL(A). Alstom Birmingham 1999–2000. –/54 1TD 2W. 48.8 t.
DMSL(B). Alstom Birmingham 1999–2000. –/64 1T. 50.7 t.

175 001	**TW**	A	*TW*	CH	50701	79701
175 002	**TW**	A	*TW*	CH	50702	79702
175 003	**TW**	A	*TW*	CH	50703	79703
175 004	**AV**	A	*TW*	CH	50759	79759
175 005	**AV**	A	*TW*	CH	50705	79751
175 006	**TW**	A	*TW*	CH	50706	79765
175 007	**AV**	A	*TW*	CH	50707	79707
175 008	**AV**	A	*TW*	CH	50708	79708
175 009	**TW**	A	*TW*	CH	50709	79709
175 010	**AV**	A	*TW*	CH	50710	79710
175 011	**TW**	A	*TW*	CH	50711	79711

Class 175/1. DMSL–MSL–DMSL. 3-car units.

DMSL(A). Alstom Birmingham 1999–2001. –/54 1TD 2W. 50.7 t.
MSL. Alstom Birmingham 1999–2001. –/68 1T. 47.5 t.
DMSL(B). Alstom Birmingham 1999–2001. –/64 1T. 49.5 t.

175 101	**AV**	A	*TW*	CH	50751	56751	79704
175 102	**AV**	A	*TW*	CH	50702	56752	79752
175 103	**AV**	A	*TW*	CH	50753	56753	79753
175 104	**AV**	A	*TW*	CH	50754	56754	79754
175 105	**AV**	A	*TW*	CH	50755	56755	79755
175 106	**AV**	A	*TW*	CH	50756	56756	79756
175 107	**TW**	A	*TW*	CH	50757	56757	79757
175 108	**AV**	A	*TW*	CH	50758	56758	79758
175 109	**AV**	A	*TW*	CH	50704	56759	79705
175 110	**AV**	A	*TW*	CH	50760	56760	79760
175 111	**AV**	A	*TW*	CH	50761	56761	79761
175 112	**AV**	A	*TW*	CH	50762	56762	79762
175 113	**AV**	A	*TW*	CH	50763	56763	79763
175 114	**AV**	A	*TW*	CH	50764	56764	79764
175 115	**AV**	A	*TW*	CH	50765	56765	79706
175 116	**AV**	A	*TW*	CH	50766	56766	79766

CLASS 180 CORADIA 1000 ALSTOM

Air conditioned.

Construction: Steel.
Engines: One Cummins QSK19 of 560 kW (750 hp) at 2100 rpm.
Transmission: Hydraulic. Voith T312br to Voith final drive.
Bogies: ACR (Alstom FBO): LTB1-MBS2, TB1-MB2, TB1-MB2, TB2-MB2, MBS2-LTB1.
Couplers: Scharfenberg outer ends, bar within unit.
Dimensions: 23.71/23.03 x 2.73 m.
Gangways: Within unit only.
Wheel Arrangement: 2-B + B-2 + B-2 + B-2 + B-2.
Doors: Single-leaf swing plug. **Maximum Speed:** 125 mph.
Seating Layout: 1: 2+1 facing/unidirectional, 2: 2+2 facing/unidirectional.
Multiple Working: Within class and with Class 175.

At the time of writing sets 180 109/113 are running with misformed formations, as shown.

The Hull Trains units are due to transfer to East Midlands Railway in early 2020.

DMSL(A). Alstom Birmingham 2000–01. –/46 2W 1TD. 51.7 t.
MFL. Alstom Birmingham 2000–01. 42/– 1T 1W + catering point. 49.6 t.
MSL. Alstom Birmingham 2000–01. –/68 1T. 49.5 t.
MSLRB. Alstom Birmingham 2000–01. –/56 1T. 50.3 t.
DMSL(B). Alstom Birmingham 2000–01. –/56 1T. 51.4 t.

180 101	**GC**	A	*GC*	HT	50901	54901	55901	56901	59901
180 102	**GC**	A	*GC*	HT	50902	54902	55902	56902	59902
180 103	**GC**	A	*GC*	HT	50903	54903	55903	56903	59903

180 104	**GC**	A	*GC*	HT	50904	54904	55904	56904	59904
180 105	**GC**	A	*GC*	HT	50905	54905	55905	56905	59905
180 106	**GC**	A	*GC*	HT	50906	54906	55906	56906	59906
180 107	**GC**	A	*GC*	HT	50907	54907	55907	56907	59907
180 108	**GC**	A	*GC*	HT	50908	54908	55908	56908	59908
180 109	**FD**	A	*HT*	XW	50909	54909	55913	56909	59909
180 110	**FD**	A		DY	50910	54910	55910	56910	59910
180 111	**FD**	A		DY	50911	54911	55911	56911	59911
180 112	**GC**	A	*GC*	HT	50912	54912	55912	56912	59912
180 113	**FD**	A	*HT*	XW	50913	54913	55909	56913	59913
180 114	**GC**	A	*GC*	HT	50914	54914	55914	56914	59914

Names (carried on DMSL(A):

180 105 THE YORKSHIRE ARTIST ASHLEY JACKSON
180 107 HART OF THE NORTH
180 108 WILLIAM SHAKESPEARE
180 112 JAMES HERRIOT CELEBRATING 100 YEARS 1916–2016
180 114 KIRKGATE CALLING

CLASS 185 DESIRO UK SIEMENS

Air conditioned. Grammer seating in Standard Class and Fainsa in First Class.

Construction: Aluminium.
Engines: One Cummins QSK19 of 560 kW (750 hp) at 2100 rpm.
Transmission: Voith.
Bogies: Siemens.
Couplers: Dellner 12.
Dimensions: 23.76/23.75 x 2.66 m.
Gangways: Within unit only.
Wheel Arrangement: 2-B + 2-B + B-2.
Doors: Double-leaf sliding plug.
Maximum Speed: 100 mph.
Seating Layout: 1: 2+1 facing/unidirectional, 2: 2+2 facing/unidirectional.
Multiple Working: Within class only.

DMCL. Siemens Krefeld 2005–06. 15/18(+8) 2W 1TD + catering point. 55.4 t.
MSL. Siemens Krefeld 2005–06. –/72 1T. 52.7 t.
DMS. Siemens Krefeld 2005–06. –/64(+4). 54.9 t.

185 101	**TP**	E	*TP*	AK	51101	53101	54101
185 102	**TP**	E	*TP*	AK	51102	53102	54102
185 103	**TP**	E	*TP*	AK	51103	53103	54103
185 104	**TP**	E	*TP*	AK	51104	53104	54104
185 105	**TP**	E	*TP*	AK	51105	53105	54105
185 106	**TP**	E	*TP*	AK	51106	53106	54106
185 107	**TP**	E	*TP*	AK	51107	53107	54107
185 108	**TP**	E	*TP*	AK	51108	53108	54108
185 109	**TP**	E	*TP*	AK	51109	53109	54109
185 110	**TP**	E	*TP*	AK	51110	53110	54110
185 111	**TP**	E	*TP*	AK	51111	53111	54111
185 112	**TP**	E	*TP*	AK	51112	53112	54112
185 113	**TP**	E	*TP*	AK	51113	53113	54113
185 114	**TP**	E	*TP*	AK	51114	53114	54114
185 115	**TP**	E	*TP*	AK	51115	53115	54115
185 116	**TP**	E	*TP*	AK	51116	53116	54116

185 117	**TP**	E	*TP*	AK	51117	53117	54117
185 118	**TP**	E	*TP*	AK	51118	53118	54118
185 119	**TP**	E	*TP*	AK	51119	53119	54119
185 120	**TP**	E	*TP*	AK	51120	53120	54120
185 121	**TP**	E	*TP*	AK	51121	53121	54121
185 122	**TP**	E	*TP*	AK	51122	53122	54122
185 123	**TP**	E	*TP*	AK	51123	53123	54123
185 124	**TP**	E	*TP*	AK	51124	53124	54124
185 125	**TP**	E	*TP*	AK	51125	53125	54125
185 126	**TP**	E	*TP*	AK	51126	53126	54126
185 127	**TP**	E	*TP*	AK	51127	53127	54127
185 128	**TP**	E	*TP*	AK	51128	53128	54128
185 129	**TP**	E	*TP*	AK	51129	53129	54129
185 130	**TP**	E	*TP*	AK	51130	53130	54130
185 131	**TP**	E	*TP*	AK	51131	53131	54131
185 132	**TP**	E	*TP*	AK	51132	53132	54132
185 133	**TP**	E	*TP*	AK	51133	53133	54133
185 134	**TP**	E	*TP*	AK	51134	53134	54134
185 135	**TP**	E	*TP*	AK	51135	53135	54135
185 136	**TP**	E	*TP*	AK	51136	53136	54136
185 137	**TP**	E	*TP*	AK	51137	53137	54137
185 138	**TP**	E	*TP*	AK	51138	53138	54138
185 139	**TP**	E	*TP*	AK	51139	53139	54139
185 140	**TP**	E	*TP*	AK	51140	53140	54140
185 141	**TP**	E	*TP*	AK	51141	53141	54141
185 142	**TP**	E	*TP*	AK	51142	53142	54142
185 143	**TP**	E	*TP*	AK	51143	53143	54143
185 144	**TP**	E	*TP*	AK	51144	53144	54144
185 145	**TP**	E	*TP*	AK	51145	53145	54145
185 146	**TP**	E	*TP*	AK	51146	53146	54146
185 147	**TP**	E	*TP*	AK	51147	53147	54147
185 148	**TP**	E	*TP*	AK	51148	53148	54148
185 149	**TP**	E	*TP*	AK	51149	53149	54149
185 150	**TP**	E	*TP*	AK	51150	53150	54150
185 151	**TP**	E	*TP*	AK	51151	53151	54151

CLASS 195 CIVITY CAF

DMS–DMS or DMS–MS–DMS. New units currently being delivered to Northern. Air conditioned.

Construction: Aluminium.
Engines: One Rolls-Royce MTU 6H 1800 R85L of 390 kW (523 hp) per car.
Transmission: Mechanical, supplied by ZF, Germany.
Bogies: CAF.
Couplers: Dellner.
Gangways: Within unit only.
Doors: Sliding plug.
Dimensions: 24.03/23.35 x 2.71 m.
Wheel Arrangement:
Maximum Speed: 100 mph.
Seating Layout: 2+2 facing/unidirectional.
Multiple Working: Within class only.

Class 195/0. DMS–DMS. 2-car units.

DMS(A). CAF Zaragoza/Irun/Newport 2017–20. –/45(+8) 1TD 2W. 43.9 t.
DMS(B). CAF Zaragoza/Irun/Newport 2017–20. –/63(+7). 43.2 t.

195 001	**NR**	E	*NO*	NH	101001	103001
195 002	**NR**	E	*NO*	NH	101002	103002
195 003	**NR**	E	*NO*	NH	101003	103003
195 004	**NR**	E	*NO*	NH	101004	103004
195 005	**NR**	E	*NO*	NH	101005	103005
195 006	**NR**	E	*NO*	NH	101006	103006
195 007	**NR**	E	*NO*	NH	101007	103007
195 008	**NR**	E	*NO*	NH	101008	103008
195 009	**NR**	E	*NO*	NH	101009	103009
195 010	**NR**	E	*NO*	NH	101010	103010
195 011	**NR**	E	*NO*	NH	101011	103011
195 012	**NR**	E	*NO*	NH	101012	103012
195 013	**NR**	E	*NO*	NH	101013	103013
195 014	**NR**	E	*NO*	NH	101014	103014
195 015	**NR**	E	*NO*	NH	101015	103015
195 016	**NR**	E			101016	103016
195 017	**NR**	E			101017	103017
195 018	**NR**	E			101018	103018
195 019	**NR**	E			101019	103019
195 020	**NR**	E			101020	103020
195 021	**NR**	E			101021	103021
195 022	**NR**	E			101022	103022
195 023	**NR**	E			101023	103023
195 024	**NR**	E			101024	103024
195 025	**NR**	E			101025	103025

Class 195/1. DMS–MS–DMS. 3-car units.

DMS(A). CAF Zaragoza/Irun/Newport 2017–20. –/45(+8) 1TD 2W. 43.9 t.
MS. CAF Zaragoza/Irun/Newport 2017–20. –/76(+4).
DMS(B). CAF Zaragoza/Irun/Newport 2017–20. –/63(+7). 43.2 t.

195 101	**NR**	E	*NO*	NH	101101	102101	103101	
195 102	**NR**	E	*NO*	NH	101102	102102	103102	
195 103	**NR**	E	*NO*	NH	101103	102103	103103	
195 104	**NR**	E	*NO*	NH	101104	102104	103104	Deva Victrix
195 105	**NR**	E	*NO*	NH	101105	102105	103105	
195 106	**NR**	E	*NO*	NH	101106	102106	103106	
195 107	**NR**	E	*NO*	NH	101107	102107	103107	
195 108	**NR**	E	*NO*	NH	101108	102108	103108	
195 109	**NR**	E	*NO*	NH	101109	102109	103109	
195 110	**NR**	E	*NO*	NH	101110	102110	103110	
195 111	**NR**	E	*NO*	NH	101111	102111	103111	
195 112	**NR**	E	*NO*	NH	101112	102112	103112	
195 113	**NR**	E	*NO*	NH	101113	102113	103113	
195 114	**NR**	E	*NO*	NH	101114	102114	103114	
195 115	**NR**	E	*NO*	NH	101115	102115	103115	
195 116	**NR**	E	*NO*	NH	101116	102116	103116	Proud to be Northern

195 117	**NR**	E	*NO*	NH	101117	102117	103117	
195 118	**NR**	E	*NO*	NH	101118	102118	103118	
195 119	**NR**	E	*NO*	NH	101119	102119	103119	
195 120	**NR**	E	*NO*	NH	101120	102120	103120	
195 121	**NR**	E	*NO*	NH	101121	102121	103121	
195 122	**NR**	E	*NO*	NH	101122	102122	103122	
195 123	**NR**	E	*NO*	NH	101123	102123	103123	
195 124	**NR**	E	*NO*	NH	101124	102124	103124	
195 125	**NR**	E	*NO*	NH	101125	102125	103125	
195 126	**NR**	E	*NO*	NH	101126	102126	103126	
195 127	**NR**	E	*NO*	NH	101127	102127	103127	
195 128	**NR**	E	*NO*	NH	101128	102128	103128	Calder Champion
195 129	**NR**	E	*NO*	NH	101129	102129	103129	
195 130	**NR**	E	*NO*	NH	101130	102130	103130	
195 131	**NR**	E			101131	102131	103131	
195 132	**NR**	E			101132	102132	103132	
195 133	**NR**	E			101133	102133	103133	

CLASS 196 CIVITY CAF

DMS–DMS or DMS–MS–MS–DMS. New units currently under construction for West Midlands Trains for local services around Birmingham. Air conditioned. Full details awaited. Due to enter service 2020–21.

Construction: Aluminium.
Engines: One Rolls-Royce MTU 6H 1800 R85L of 390 kW (523 hp) per car.
Transmission: Mechanical, supplied by ZF, Germany.
Bogies: CAF.
Couplers: Dellner.
Gangways: Throughout.
Doors: Sliding plug.
Seating Layout: 2+2 facing/unidirectional.
Multiple Working: Within class only.
Dimensions:
Wheel Arrangement:
Maximum Speed:

Class 196/0. DMS–DMS. 2-car units.

DMS(A). CAF Zaragoza/Irun/Newport 2019–20.
DMS(B). CAF Zaragoza/Irun/Newport 2019–20.

196 001	**WM**	CO	121001	124001
196 002	**WM**	CO	121002	124002
196 003	**WM**	CO	121003	124003
196 004	**WM**	CO	121004	124004
196 005	**WM**	CO	121005	124005
196 006	**WM**	CO	121006	124006
196 007	**WM**	CO	121007	124007
196 008	**WM**	CO	121008	124008
196 009	**WM**	CO	121009	124009
196 010	**WM**	CO	121010	124010
196 011	**WM**	CO	121011	124011
196 012	**WM**	CO	121012	124012

Class 196/1. DMS–MS–MS–DMS. 4-car units.

DMS(A). CAF Zaragoza/Irun/Newport 2019–20.
MS(A). CAF Zaragoza/Irun/Newport 2019–20.
MS(B). CAF Zaragoza/Irun/Newport 2019–20.
DMS(B). CAF Zaragoza/Irun/Newport 2019–20.

196 101	**WM**	CO	121101	122101	123101	124101
196 102	**WM**	CO	121102	122102	123102	124102
196 103	**WM**	CO	121103	122103	123103	124103
196 104	**WM**	CO	121104	122104	123104	124104
196 105	**WM**	CO	121105	122105	123105	124105
196 106	**WM**	CO	121106	122106	123106	124106
196 107	**WM**	CO	121107	122107	123107	124107
196 108	**WM**	CO	121108	122108	123108	124108
196 109	**WM**	CO	121109	122109	123109	124109
196 110	**WM**	CO	121110	122110	123110	124110
196 111	**WM**	CO	121111	122111	123111	124111
196 112	**WM**	CO	121112	122112	123112	124112
196 113	**WM**	CO	121113	122113	123113	124113
196 114	**WM**	CO	121114	122114	123114	124114

3.2. DIESEL ELECTRIC UNITS

CLASS 201/202 PRESERVED "HASTINGS" UNIT BR

DMBS–TSL–TSL–TSRB–TSL–DMBS.

Preserved unit made up from two Class 201 short-frame cars and three Class 202 long-frame cars. The "Hastings" units were made with narrow body-profiles for use on the section between Tonbridge and Battle which had tunnels of restricted loading gauge. These tunnels were converted to single track operation in the 1980s thus allowing standard loading gauge stock to be used. The set also contains a Class 411 EMU trailer (not Hastings line gauge) and a Class 422 EMU buffet car.

Construction: Steel.
Engine: One English Electric 4SRKT Mk. 2 of 450 kW (600 hp) at 850 rpm.
Main Generator: English Electric EE824.
Traction Motors: Two English Electric EE507 mounted on the inner bogie.
Bogies: SR Mk 4. (Former EMU TSL vehicles have Commonwealth bogies).
Couplers: Drophead buckeye.
Dimensions: 18.40 x 2.50 m (60000), 20.35 x 2.50 m (60116/118/529), 18.36 x 2.50 m (60501), 20.35 x 2.82 (69337), 20.30 x 2.82 (70262).
Gangways: Within unit only. **Doors:** Manually operated slam.
Wheel arrangement: 2-Bo + 2-2 + 2-2 + 2-2- + 2-2- + Bo-2.
Brakes: Electro-pneumatic and automatic air.
Maximum Speed: 75 mph. **Seating Layout:** 2+2 facing.
Multiple Working: Other ex-BR Southern Region DEMU vehicles.

60000. DMBS. Lot No. 30329 Eastleigh 1957. –/22. 55.0 t.
60116. DMBS. Lot No. 30395 Eastleigh 1957. –/31. 56.0 t.
60118. DMBS. Lot No. 30395 Eastleigh 1957. –/30. 56.0 t.
60501. TSL. Lot No. 30331 Eastleigh 1957. –/52 2T. 29.5 t.
60529. TSL. Lot No. 30397 Eastleigh 1957. –/60 2T. 30.5 t.
69337. TSRB (ex-Class 422 EMU). Lot No. 30805 York 1970. –/40. 35.0 t.
70262. TSL (ex-Class 411/5 EMU). Lot No. 30455 Eastleigh 1958. –/64 2T. 31.5 t.

201 001	**G**	HD	*HD*	SE	60116	60529	70262	69337	60501	60118
Spare	**G**	HD	*HD*	SE	60000					

Names:

60000	Hastings	60118	Tunbridge Wells
60116	Mountfield		

CLASS 220 VOYAGER BOMBARDIER

DMS–MS–MS–DMF. All engines have been derated from 750 hp to 700 hp.

Construction: Steel.
Engine: Cummins QSK19 of 520 kW (700 hp) at 1800 rpm.
Transmission: Two Alstom Onix 800 three-phase traction motors of 275 kW.
Braking: Rheostatic and electro-pneumatic.
Bogies: Bombardier B5005.
Couplers: Dellner 12 at outer ends, bar within unit.
Dimensions: 23.85/23.00 (602xx) x 2.73 m.
Gangways: Within unit only.
Wheel Arrangement: 1A-A1 + 1A-A1 + 1A-A1 + 1A-A1.
Doors: Single-leaf swing plug.
Maximum Speed: 125 m.p.h.
Seating Layout: 1: 2+1 facing/unidirectional, 2: 2+2 mainly unidirectional.
Multiple Working: Within class and with Classes 221 and 222 (in an emergency). Also can be controlled from Class 57/3 locomotives.

DMS. Bombardier Bruges/Wakefield 2000–01. –/42 1TD 1W. 51.1 t.
MS(A). Bombardier Bruges/Wakefield 2000–01. –/66. 45.9 t.
MS(B). Bombardier Bruges/Wakefield 2000–01. –/66 1TD. 46.7 t.
DMF. Bombardier Bruges/Wakefield 2000–01. 26/– 1TD 1W. 50.9 t.

220 001	**XC**	BN	*XC*	CZ	60301	60701	60201	60401
220 002	**XC**	BN	*XC*	CZ	60302	60702	60202	60402
220 003	**XC**	BN	*XC*	CZ	60303	60703	60203	60403
220 004	**XC**	BN	*XC*	CZ	60304	60704	60204	60404
220 005	**XC**	BN	*XC*	CZ	60305	60705	60205	60405
220 006	**XC**	BN	*XC*	CZ	60306	60706	60206	60406
220 007	**XC**	BN	*XC*	CZ	60307	60707	60207	60407
220 008	**XC**	BN	*XC*	CZ	60308	60708	60208	60408
220 009	**XC**	BN	*XC*	CZ	60309	60709	60209	60409
220 010	**XC**	BN	*XC*	CZ	60310	60710	60210	60410
220 011	**XC**	BN	*XC*	CZ	60311	60711	60211	60411
220 012	**XC**	BN	*XC*	CZ	60312	60712	60212	60412

220 013	**XC**	BN	*XC*	CZ	60313	60713	60213	60413
220 014	**XC**	BN	*XC*	CZ	60314	60714	60214	60414
220 015	**XC**	BN	*XC*	CZ	60315	60715	60215	60415
220 016	**XC**	BN	*XC*	CZ	60316	60716	60216	60416
220 017	**XC**	BN	*XC*	CZ	60317	60717	60217	60417
220 018	**XC**	BN	*XC*	CZ	60318	60718	60218	60418
220 019	**XC**	BN	*XC*	CZ	60319	60719	60219	60419
220 020	**XC**	BN	*XC*	CZ	60320	60720	60220	60420
220 021	**XC**	BN	*XC*	CZ	60321	60721	60221	60421
220 022	**XC**	BN	*XC*	CZ	60322	60722	60222	60422
220 023	**XC**	BN	*XC*	CZ	60323	60723	60223	60423
220 024	**XC**	BN	*XC*	CZ	60324	60724	60224	60424
220 025	**XC**	BN	*XC*	CZ	60325	60725	60225	60425
220 026	**XC**	BN	*XC*	CZ	60326	60726	60226	60426
220 027	**XC**	BN	*XC*	CZ	60327	60727	60227	60427
220 028	**XC**	BN	*XC*	CZ	60328	60728	60228	60428
220 029	**XC**	BN	*XC*	CZ	60329	60729	60229	60429
220 030	**XC**	BN	*XC*	CZ	60330	60730	60230	60430
220 031	**XC**	BN	*XC*	CZ	60331	60731	60231	60431
220 032	**XC**	BN	*XC*	CZ	60332	60732	60232	60432
220 033	**XC**	BN	*XC*	CZ	60333	60733	60233	60433
220 034	**XC**	BN	*XC*	CZ	60334	60734	60234	60434

CLASS 221 SUPER VOYAGER BOMBARDIER

* DMS–MS–MS–MSRMB–DMF (Avanti West Coast units) or DMS–MS–(MS)–MS–DMF (CrossCountry units). Built as tilting units but tilt now isolated on CrossCountry sets. All engines have been derated from 750 hp to 700 hp.

Construction: Steel.
Engine: Cummins QSK19 of 520 kW (700 hp) at 1800 rpm.
Transmission: Two Alstom Onix 800 three-phase traction motors of 275 kW.
Braking: Rheostatic and electro-pneumatic.
Bogies: Bombardier HVP.
Couplers: Dellner 12 at outer ends, bar within unit.
Dimensions: 23.67 x 2.73 m.
Gangways: Within unit only.
Wheel Arrangement: 1A-A1 + 1A-A1 + 1A-A1 (+ 1A-A1) + 1A-A1.
Doors: Single-leaf swing plug.
Maximum Speed: 125 mph.
Seating Layout: 1: 2+1 facing/unidirectional, 2: 2+2 mainly unidirectional.
Multiple Working: Within class and with Classes 220 and 222 (in an emergency). Also can be controlled from Class 57/3 locomotives.

* Avanti West Coast units. MSRMB moved adjacent to the DMF. The seating in this vehicle (2+2 facing) can be used by First or Standard Class passengers depending on demand.

Advertising livery: 221 115 Dark grey Bombardier branding on end vehicles.

DMS. Bombardier Bruges/Wakefield 2001–02. –/42 1TD 1W. 58.5 t (* 58.9 t.)
60751–794 MS (* MSRMB). Bombardier Bruges/Wakefield 2001–02. –/66 (* –/52). 54.1 t (* 55.9 t.)
60951–994. MS. Bombardier Bruges/Wakefield 2001–02. –/66 1TD (* –/68 1TD). 54.8 t (* 54.3 t.)
60851–890. MS. Bombardier Bruges/Wakefield 2001–02. –/62 1TD (* –/68 1TD). 54.4 t (* 55.0 t.)
DMF. Bombardier Bruges/Wakefield 2001–02. 26/– 1TD 1W. 58.9 t (* 59.1 t.)

221 101	*	**VW**	BN	*AW*	CZ	60351	60951	60851	60751	60451
221 102	*	**VT**	BN	*AW*	CZ	60352	60952	60852	60752	60452
221 103	*	**VT**	BN	*AW*	CZ	60353	60953	60853	60753	60453
221 104	*	**VT**	BN	*AW*	CZ	60354	60954	60854	60754	60454
221 105	*	**VT**	BN	*AW*	CZ	60355	60955	60855	60755	60455
221 106	*	**VT**	BN	*AW*	CZ	60356	60956	60856	60756	60456
221 107	*	**VT**	BN	*AW*	CZ	60357	60957	60857	60757	60457
221 108	*	**VT**	BN	*AW*	CZ	60358	60958	60858	60758	60458
221 109	*	**VT**	BN	*AW*	CZ	60359	60959	60859	60759	60459
221 110	*	**VT**	BN	*AW*	CZ	60360	60960	60860	60760	60460
221 111	*	**VT**	BN	*AW*	CZ	60361	60961	60861	60761	60461
221 112	*	**VT**	BN	*AW*	CZ	60362	60962	60862	60762	60462
221 113	*	**VT**	BN	*AW*	CZ	60363	60963	60863	60763	60463
221 114	*	**VT**	BN	*AW*	CZ	60364	60964	60864	60764	60464
221 115	*	**AL**	BN	*AW*	CZ	60365	60965	60865	60765	60465
221 116	*	**VT**	BN	*AW*	CZ	60366	60966	60866	60766	60466
221 117	*	**VT**	BN	*AW*	CZ	60367	60967	60867	60767	60467
221 118	*	**VT**	BN	*AW*	CZ	60368	60968	60868	60768	60468
221 119		**XC**	BN	*XC*	CZ	60369	60769	60969	60869	60469
221 120		**XC**	BN	*XC*	CZ	60370	60770	60970	60870	60470
221 121		**XC**	BN	*XC*	CZ	60371	60771	60971	60871	60471
221 122		**XC**	BN	*XC*	CZ	60372	60772	60972	60872	60472
221 123		**XC**	BN	*XC*	CZ	60373	60773	60973	60873	60473
221 124		**XC**	BN	*XC*	CZ	60374	60774	60974	60874	60474
221 125		**XC**	BN	*XC*	CZ	60375	60775	60975	60875	60475
221 126		**XC**	BN	*XC*	CZ	60376	60776	60976	60876	60476
221 127		**XC**	BN	*XC*	CZ	60377	60777	60977	60877	60477
221 128		**XC**	BN	*XC*	CZ	60378	60778	60978	60878	60478
221 129		**XC**	BN	*XC*	CZ	60379	60779	60979	60879	60479
221 130		**XC**	BN	*XC*	CZ	60380	60780	60980	60880	60480
221 131		**XC**	BN	*XC*	CZ	60381	60781	60981	60881	60481
221 132		**XC**	BN	*XC*	CZ	60382	60782	60982	60882	60482
221 133		**XC**	BN	*XC*	CZ	60383	60783	60983	60883	60483
221 134		**XC**	BN	*XC*	CZ	60384	60784	60984	60884	60484
221 135		**XC**	BN	*XC*	CZ	60385	60785	60985	60885	60485
221 136		**XC**	BN	*XC*	CZ	60386	60786		60886	60486
221 137		**XC**	BN	*XC*	CZ	60387	60787	60987	60887	60487
221 138		**XC**	BN	*XC*	CZ	60388	60788	60988	60888	60488
221 139		**XC**	BN	*XC*	CZ	60389	60789	60989	60889	60489
221 140		**XC**	BN	*XC*	CZ	60390	60790		60890	60490
221 141		**XC**	BN	*XC*	CZ	60391	60791	60991		60491
221 142	*	**VT**	BN	*VW*	CZ	60392	60992	60986	60792	60492

221 143 *	**VT**	BN	*VW*	CZ	60393 60993 60994 60793 60493
221 144	**XC**	BN	*XC*	CZ	60394 60794 60990 60494

Names (carried on MS No. 609xx):

221 101 101 SQUADRON
221 114 ROYAL AIR FORCE CENTENARY 1918–2018
221 116 City of Bangor/Dinas Bangor
221 117 The Wrekin Giant
221 142 BOMBARDIER Voyager

CLASS 222 MERIDIAN BOMBARDIER

Construction: Steel.
Engine: Cummins QSK19 of 560 kW (750 hp) at 1800 rpm.
Transmission: Two Alstom Onix 800 three-phase traction motors of 275 kW.
Braking: Rheostatic and electro-pneumatic.
Bogies: Bombardier B5005. **Dimensions:** 23.85/23.00 x 2.73 m.
Couplers: Dellner at outer ends, bar within unit.
Gangways: Within unit only. **Wheel Arrangement:** All cars 1A-A1.
Doors: Single-leaf swing plug. **Maximum Speed:** 125 mph.
Seating Layout: 1: 2+1, 2: 2+2 facing/unidirectional.
Multiple Working: Within class and with Classes 220 and 221 (in an emergency).

222 001–006. 7-car units. DMF–MF–MF–MSRMB–MS–MS–DMS.

The 7-car units were built as 9-car units, before being reduced to 8-car sets and then later to 7-car sets to strengthen all 4-car units to 5-cars. 222 007 was built as a 9-car unit but later reduced to a 5-car unit.

DMRF. Bombardier Bruges 2004–05. 22/– 1TD 1W. 52.8 t.
MF. Bombardier Bruges 2004–05. 42/– 1T. 46.8 t.
MSRMB. Bombardier Bruges 2004–05. –/62. 48.0 t.
MS. Bombardier Bruges 2004–05. –/68 1T. 47.0 t.
DMS. Bombardier Bruges 2004–05. –/38 1TD 1W. 49.4 t.

222 001	**ST**	E	*EM*	DY	60241 60445 60341 60621 60561 60551 60161
222 002	**ST**	E	*EM*	DY	60242 60346 60342 60622 60562 60544 60162
222 003	**ST**	E	*EM*	DY	60243 60446 60343 60623 60563 60553 60163
222 004	**ST**	E	*EM*	DY	60244 60345 60344 60624 60564 60554 60164
222 005	**ST**	E	*EM*	DY	60245 60347 60443 60625 60555 60565 60165
222 006	**ST**	E	*EM*	DY	60246 60447 60441 60626 60566 60556 60166

Names (carried on MSRMB or DMS (222 003)):

222 001 THE ENTREPRENEUR EXPRESS
222 002 THE CUTLERS' COMPANY
222 003 TORNADO
222 004 CHILDREN'S HOSPITAL SHEFFIELD
222 006 THE CARBON CUTTER

222 007–023. 5-car units. DMF–MC–MSRMB–MS–DMS.

DMRF. Bombardier Bruges 2003–04. 22/– 1TD 1W. 52.8 t.
MC. Bombardier Bruges 2003–04. 28/22 1T. 48.6 t.
MSRMB. Bombardier Bruges 2003–04. –/62. 49.6 t.
MS. Bombardier Bruges 2004–05. –/68 1T. 47.0 t.
DMS. Bombardier Bruges 2003–04. –/40 1TD 1W. 51.0 t.

222 007	**ST**	E	*EM*	DY	60247	60442	60627	60567	60167
222 008	**ST**	E	*EM*	DY	60248	60918	60628	60545	60168
222 009	**ST**	E	*EM*	DY	60249	60919	60629	60557	60169
222 010	**ST**	E	*EM*	DY	60250	60920	60630	60546	60170
222 011	**ST**	E	*EM*	DY	60251	60921	60631	60531	60171
222 012	**ST**	E	*EM*	DY	60252	60922	60632	60532	60172
222 013	**ST**	E	*EM*	DY	60253	60923	60633	60533	60173
222 014	**ST**	E	*EM*	DY	60254	60924	60634	60534	60174
222 015	**ST**	E	*EM*	DY	60255	60925	60635	60535	60175
222 016	**ST**	E	*EM*	DY	60256	60926	60636	60536	60176
222 017	**ST**	E	*EM*	DY	60257	60927	60637	60537	60177
222 018	**ST**	E	*EM*	DY	60258	60928	60638	60444	60178
222 019	**ST**	E	*EM*	DY	60259	60929	60639	60547	60179
222 020	**ST**	E	*EM*	DY	60260	60930	60640	60543	60180
222 021	**ST**	E	*EM*	DY	60261	60931	60641	60552	60181
222 022	**ST**	E	*EM*	DY	60262	60932	60642	60542	60182
222 023	**ST**	E	*EM*	DY	60263	60933	60643	60541	60183

Names (carried on MSRMB or DMS):

222 008 Derby Etches Park
222 011 Sheffield City Battalion 1914–1918
222 015 175 YEARS OF DERBY'S RAILWAYS 1839–2014
222 017 LIONS CLUB INTERNATIONAL CENTENARY 1917–2017
222 022 INVEST IN NOTTINGHAM

222 101–104. 4-car former Hull Trains units. DMF–MC–MSRMB–DMS.

DMRF. Bombardier Bruges 2005. 22/– 1TD 1W. 52.8 t.
MC. Bombardier Bruges 2005. 11/46 1T. 47.1 t.
MSRMB. Bombardier Bruges 2005. –/62. 48.0 t.
DMS. Bombardier Bruges 2005. –/40 1TD 1W. 49.4 t.

222 101	**ST**	E	*EM*	DY	60271	60571	60681	60191
222 102	**ST**	E	*EM*	DY	60272	60572	60682	60192
222 103	**ST**	E	*EM*	DY	60273	60573	60683	60193
222 104	**ER**	E	*EM*	DY	60274	60574	60684	60194

CLASS 230 D-TRAIN METRO-CAMMELL/VIVARAIL

The Class 230 D-Train is a DEMU or diesel-battery unit rebuilt from former London Underground D78 Stock by Vivarail at Long Marston. The D-Train uses the bodyshells, bogies and electric traction motors of D78 Stock. Instead of being powered by electricity the motors are instead powered by new underfloor-mounted diesel engines: two per driving car. Modern IGBT electronic controls replace the previous mechanical camshaft controllers, incorporating automotive stop-start technology and dynamic braking.

230 001 was a prototype unit and was followed by 230 002, a prototype diesel-battery hybrid. West Midlands Trains ordered three diesel sets (numbered 230 003–005) for use on the Bedford–Bletchley Marston Vale Line from spring 2019. This was followed by an order by Transport for Wales for five 3-car diesel-battery hybrid sets (numbered 230 006–010) for delivery in 2020.

Vivarail acquired more than 200 redundant D78 Stock vehicles that are stored at Long Marston and it is hoped that orders for further conversions will be forthcoming. South Western Railway has ordered five straight electric sets for the Isle of Wight (to be Class 484).

Construction: Aluminium.
Engine: 2 x Ford Duratorq 3.2 litre engines of 150 kW (200 hp). 230 002 and 230 006–010 have 60 x 24V batteries.
Traction motors: LT118.
Control System: IGBT Inverter. **Braking:** Rheostatic & Dynamic.
Bogies: Bombardier FLEXX1000 flexible-frame.
Dimensions: 18.37/18.12 x 2.85 m.
Couplers: LUL automatic wedgelock. **Gangways:** Within unit only.
Wheel Arrangement: Bo-Bo + 2-2 + Bo-Bo.
Doors: Sliding. **Maximum Speed:** 60 mph.
Seating Layout: Longitudinal or 2+2 facing.
Multiple Working: Within class.

Rebuilt from former London Underground D78 Stock 2016–20. Original D78 numbers are shown alongside the new running numbers.

Class 230/0. Prototype diesel or diesel-battery units.
230 001 is to be exported to the USA.

DMS(A). Metro-Cammell Birmingham 1979–83. 28.0 t (* 27.0 t).
TS. Metro-Cammell Birmingham 1979–83. 20.0 t.
DMS(B). Metro-Cammell Birmingham 1979–83. 28.0 t (* 23.0 t).

230 001	**VI**	VI		LM	300001 (7058)	300201 (17058)	300101 (7511)
230 002 *	**VI**	VI		LM	300002 (7122)	300202 (17091)	300102 (7067)

Class 230/0. West Midlands Trains diesel units.

DMS(A). Metro-Cammell Birmingham 1979–83. –/58(+2). 33.3 t.
DMS(B). Metro-Cammell Birmingham 1979–83. –/40(+7) 1TD 2W. 32.3 t.

230 003	**LN**	VI	*WM*	BY	300003 (7069)	300103 (7127)
230 004	**LN**	VI	*WM*	BY	300004 (7100)	300104 (7500)
230 005	**LN**	VI	*WM*	BY	300005 (7066)	300105 (7128)

Class 230/0. Transport for Wales diesel-battery units. Full details awaited.

DMS(A). Metro-Cammell Birmingham 1979–83.
TS. Metro-Cammell Birmingham 1979–83.
DMS(B). Metro-Cammell Birmingham 1979–83.

230 006	300006 (7098)	300206 (17066)	300106 (7510)
230 007	300007 (7103)	300207 (17063)	300107 (7529)
230 008	300008 (7120)	300208 (17050)	300108 (7065)
230 009	300009 (7055)	300209 (17084)	300109 (7523)
230 010	300010 (7090)	300210 (17071)	300110 (7017)

3.3. DMU VEHICLES IN INDUSTRIAL SERVICE

This list comprises DMU vehicles that have been withdrawn from active service but continue to be used in industrial service (for use in emergency training).

Cl. 142	55574	55624	South Wales Police RFC Ground, Waterton Cross, Bridgend (ex-unit 142 033)

4. ELECTRIC MULTIPLE UNITS

INTRODUCTION

This section contains details of all Electric Multiple Units, usually referred to as EMUs, which can run on Britain's national railway network.

The number of EMUs in operation has been steadily increasing in recent years as both more lines have been opened or have been electrified and as the number of passengers travelling on the network has increased. EMUs work a wide variety of services, from long distance Intercity (such as the Class 390 Pendolinos) to inter-urban and suburban duties.

LAYOUT OF INFORMATION

25 kV AC 50 Hz overhead EMUs and dual voltage EMUs are listed in numerical order of set numbers. Individual "loose" vehicles are listed in numerical order after vehicles formed into fixed formations.

750 V DC third rail EMUs are listed in numerical order of class number, then in numerical order of set number. Some of these use the former Southern Region four-digit set numbers. These are derived from theoretical six digit set numbers which are the four-digit set number prefixed by the first two numbers of the class.

Where sets or vehicles have been renumbered in recent years, former numbering detail is shown alongside current detail. Each entry is laid out as in the following example:

Set No.	*Detail*	*Livery*	*Owner*	*Operator*	*Allocation*	*Formation*
5912	*	**SS**	P	*SW*	WD	77835 62837 67400 77836

Codes: Codes are used to denote the livery, owner, operator and depot allocation of each Electric Multiple Unit. Details of these can be found in section 6 of this book. Where a unit or spare car is off-lease, the operator column is left blank.

Detail Differences: Detail differences which currently affect the areas and types of train which vehicles may work are shown, plus differences in interior layout. Where such differences occur within a class, these are shown either in the heading information or alongside the individual set or vehicle number.

Set Formations: Regular set formations are shown where these are normally maintained. Readers should note set formations might be temporarily varied from time to time to suit maintenance and/or operational requirements. Vehicles shown as "Spare" are not formed in any regular set formation.

Names: Only names carried with official sanction are listed. Names are shown in UPPER/lower case characters as actually shown on the name carried on the vehicle(s). Unless otherwise shown, complete units are regarded as named rather than just the individual car(s) which carry the name.

GENERAL INFORMATION

CLASSIFICATION AND NUMBERING

25 kV AC 50 Hz overhead and "Versatile" EMUs are classified in the series 300–399. 750 V DC third rail EMUs are classified in the series 400–599. More recently dual-voltage units have been numbered in the 700+ series and Hitachi IEP units in the 800+ series. Classes 800 and 802 are bi-mode units which can operate under both diesel or electric power.

Until 2014 EMU individual cars were numbered in the series 61000–78999, except for vehicles used on the Isle of Wight – which are numbered in a separate series, and the Class 378s, 380s and 395s, which took up the 38xxx and 39xxx series'.

For all new vehicles allocated by the Rolling Stock Library since 2014 6-digit vehicle numbers are being used.

Any vehicle constructed or converted to replace another vehicle following accident damage and carrying the same number as the original vehicle is denoted by the suffix" in this publication

WHEEL ARRANGEMENT

A system whereby the number of powered axles on a bogie or frame is denoted by a letter (A = 1, B = 2, C= 3 etc) and the number of unpowered axles is denoted by a number is used in this publication. The letter "o" after a letter indicates that each axle is individually powered.

UNITS OF MEASUREMENT

Principal details and dimensions are quoted for each class in metric and/or imperial units as considered appropriate bearing in mind common UK usage.

All dimensions and weights are quoted for vehicles in an "as new" condition with all necessary supplies (eg oil, water, sand) on board. Dimensions are quoted in the order Length – Width. All lengths quoted are over buffers or couplers as appropriate. Where two lengths are quoted, the first refers to outer vehicles in a set and the second to inner vehicles. All width dimensions quoted are maxima. All weights are shown as metric tonnes (t = tonnes).

Bogie Types are quoted in the format motored/non-motored (eg BP20/BT13 denotes BP20 motored bogies and BT non-motored bogies).

Unless noted to the contrary, all vehicles listed have bar couplers at non-driving ends.

Unless stated, traction motors power details refer to each motored car per unit.

Vehicles ordered under the auspices of BR were allocated a Lot (batch) number when ordered and these are quoted in class headings and sub-headings. Vehicles ordered since 1995 have no Lot Numbers, but the manufacturer and location that they were built is given.

OPERATING CODES

These codes are used by train operating company staff to describe the various different types of vehicles and normally appear on data panels on the inner (ie non driving) ends of vehicles.

A "B" prefix indicates a battery vehicle.
A "P" prefix indicates a trailer vehicle on which is mounted the pantograph, instead of the default case where the pantograph is mounted on a motor vehicle.

The first part of the code describes whether or not the car has a motor or a driving cab as follows:

DM Driving motor   DT Driving trailer   M Motor   T Trailer

The next letter is a "B" for cars with a brake compartment.
This is followed by the saloon details:

F First   S Standard   C Composite

The next letter denotes the style of accommodation, which is "O" for Open for all EMU vehicles still in service.

Finally vehicles with a buffet or kitchen area are suffixed RB or RMB for a miniature buffet counter.

Where two vehicles of the same type are formed within the same unit, the above codes may be suffixed by (A) and (B) to differentiate between vehicles.

A composite is a vehicle containing both First and Standard Class accommodation, whilst a brake vehicle is a vehicle containing separate specific accommodation for the conductor.

ACCOMMODATION

The information given in class headings and sub-headings is in the form F/S nT (or TD) nW. For example 12/54 1T 1W denotes 12 First Class and 54 Standard Class seats, one toilet and one space for a wheelchair. A number in brackets (ie (+2)) denotes tip-up seats (in addition to the fixed seats). Tip-up seats in vestibules do not count. The seating layout of open saloons is shown as 2+1, 2+2 or 3+2 as the case may be. Where units have First Class accommodation as well as Standard Class and the layout is different for each class then these are shown separately prefixed by "1:" and "2:".

TD denotes a universal access toilet suitable for use by people with disabilities. By law all trains should be fitted with such facilities by the start of 2020, but a number of trains were not made compliant in time and have been given time-limited dispensations for continued operation.

4.1. 25 kV AC 50 Hz OVERHEAD & DUAL VOLTAGE UNITS

Except where otherwise stated, all units in this section operate on 25 kV AC 50 Hz overhead only.

CLASS 313 BREL YORK

Inner suburban units.

Formation: DMS–TS–BDMS.
Systems: 25 kV AC overhead/750 V DC third rail (but pantographs removed).
Construction: Steel underframe, aluminium alloy body and roof.
Traction Motors: Four GEC G310AZ of 82.125 kW.
Wheel Arrangement: Bo-Bo + 2-2 + Bo-Bo.
Braking: Disc & rheostatic.
Dimensions: 20.33/20.18 x 2.82 m.
Bogies: BX1.
Couplers: Tightlock.
Gangways: Within unit + end doors.
Control System: Camshaft.
Doors: Sliding.
Maximum Speed: 75 mph.
Seating Layout: 2+2 high back facing.
Multiple Working: Within class.

Class 313/2. Southern units. Refurbished for Brighton Coastway services. 750 V DC only (pantographs removed).

DMS. Lot No. 30879 1976–77. –/64. 37.0 t.
TS. Lot No. 30880 1976–77. –/64(+2). 31.0 t.
BDMS. Lot No. 30885 1976–77. –/64. 37.0 t.

313201	(313101)	**BG**	BN	*SN*	BI	62529	71213	62593
313202	(313102)	**SN**	BN	*SN*	BI	62530	71214	62594
313203	(313103)	**SN**	BN	*SN*	BI	62531	71215	62595
313204	(313104)	**SN**	BN	*SN*	BI	62532	71216	62596
313205	(313105)	**SN**	BN	*SN*	BI	62533	71217	62597
313206	(313106)	**SN**	BN	*SN*	BI	62534	71218	62598
313207	(313107)	**SN**	BN	*SN*	BI	62535	71219	62599
313208	(313108)	**SN**	BN	*SN*	BI	62536	71220	62600
313209	(313109)	**SN**	BN	*SN*	BI	62537	71221	62601
313210	(313110)	**SN**	BN	*SN*	BI	62538	71222	62602
313211	(313111)	**SN**	BN	*SN*	BI	62539	71223	62603
313212	(313112)	**SN**	BN	*SN*	BI	62540	71224	62604
313213	(313113)	**SN**	BN	*SN*	BI	62541	71225	62605
313214	(313114)	**SN**	BN	*SN*	BI	62542	71226	62606
313215	(313115)	**SN**	BN	*SN*	BI	62543	71227	62607
313216	(313116)	**SN**	BN	*SN*	BI	62544	71228	62608
313217	(313117)	**SN**	BN	*SN*	BI	62545	71229	62609
313219	(313119)	**SN**	BN	*SN*	BI	62547	71231	62611
313220	(313120)	**SN**	BN	*SN*	BI	62548	71232	62612

CLASS 314 BREL YORK

Inner suburban units. All units removed from service by the end of 2019.

Formation: DMS–PTS–DMS.
Construction: Steel underframe, aluminium alloy body and roof.
Traction Motors: Four GEC G310AZ (* Brush TM61-53) of 82.125 kW.
Wheel Arrangement: Bo-Bo + 2-2 + Bo-Bo.
Braking: Disc & rheostatic.
Dimensions: 20.33/20.18 x 2.82 m.
Bogies: BX1.
Couplers: Tightlock.
Gangways: Within unit + end doors.
Control System: Thyristor.
Doors: Sliding.
Maximum Speed: 70 mph.
Seating Layout: 3+2 low-back facing.
Multiple Working: Within class and with Class 315.

DMS. Lot No. 30912 1979. –/68. 34.5 t.
PTS. Lot No. 30913 1979. –/76. 33.0 t.
DMS. Lot No. 30912 1979. –/68. 34.5 t.

314202	*	**SC**	SR	GW	64585	71451	64586
314204	*	**SR**	X	ZG	64589	71453	64590
314205	*	**SC**	SR	GW	64591	71454	64592
314209		**SR**	SR	YO	64599	71458	64600
314210		**SC**	SR	YO	64601	71459	64602
314214		**SR**	SR	GW	64609	71463	64610
314215		**SC**	SR	ZH	64611	71464	64612
314216		**SC**	SR	YO	64613	71465	64614

CLASS 315 BREL YORK

Inner suburban units.

Formation: DMS–TS–PTS–DMS.
Construction: Steel underframe, aluminium alloy body and roof.
Traction Motors: Four Brush TM61-53 (* GEC G310AZ) of 82.125 kW.
Wheel Arrangement: Bo-Bo + 2-2 + 2-2 + Bo-Bo.
Braking: Disc & rheostatic.
Dimensions: 20.18 x 2.82 m.
Bogies: BX1.
Couplers: Tightlock.
Gangways: Within unit + end doors.
Control System: Thyristor.
Doors: Sliding.
Maximum Speed: 75 mph.
Seating Layout: 3+2 low-back facing.
Multiple Working: Within class and with Class 314 and 317.

DMS. Lot No. 30902 1980–81. –/74. 38.2 t.
TS. Lot No. 30904 1980–81. –/86. 27.4 t.
PTS. Lot No. 30903 1980–81. –/75(+7) 2W. 33.8 t.
DMS. Lot No. 30902 1980–81. –/74. 38.2 t.

315801	**LO**	E	*LO*	IL	64461	71281	71389	64462
315802	**LO**	E	*LO*	IL	64463	71282	71390	64464
315803	**LO**	E	*LO*	IL	64465	71283	71391	64466
315805	**LO**	E	*LO*	IL	64469	71285	71393	64470
315806	**LO**	E	*LO*	IL	64471	71286	71394	64472

315807		**LO**	E	*LO*	IL	64473	71287	71395	64474
315808		**LO**	E	*LO*	IL	64475	71288	71396	64476
315809		**LO**	E	*LO*	IL	64477	71289	71397	64478
315810		**LO**	E	*LO*	IL	64479	71290	71398	64480
315811		**LO**	E	*LO*	IL	64481	71291	71399	64482
315812		**LO**	E	*LO*	IL	64483	71292	71400	64484
315815		**LO**	E	*LO*	IL	64489	71295	71403	64490
315816		**LO**	E	*LO*	IL	64491	71296	71404	64492
315817		**LO**	E	*LO*	IL	64493	71297	71405	64494
315818		**TF**	E	*XR*	IL	64495	71298	71406	64496
315819		**TF**	E	*XR*	IL	64497	71299	71407	64498
315820		**TF**	E	*XR*	IL	64499	71300	71408	64500
315822		**TF**	E	*LO*	IL	64503	71302	71410	64504
315824		**TF**	E	*XR*	IL	64507	71304	71412	64508
315825		**TF**	E	*LO*	IL	64509	71305	71413	64510
315826		**TF**	E	*XR*	IL	64511	71306	71414	64512
315827		**TF**	E	*LO*	IL	64513	71307	71415	64514
315829		**TF**	E	*XR*	IL	64517	71309	71417	64518
315830		**TF**	E	*XR*	IL	64519	71310	71418	64520
315831		**TF**	E	*LO*	IL	64521	71311	71419	64522
315833		**TF**	E		NN	64525	71313	71421	64526
315834		**TF**	E	*XR*	IL	64527	71314	71422	64528
315836		**TF**	E	*LO*	IL	64531	71316	71424	64532
315837		**TF**	E	*XR*	IL	64533	71317	71425	64534
315838		**TF**	E	*XR*	IL	64535	71318	71426	64536
315839		**TF**	E	*XR*	IL	64537	71319	71427	64538
315843	*	**TF**	E	*XR*	IL	64545	71323	71431	64546
315844	*	**TF**	E	*XR*	IL	64547	71324	71432	64548
315847	*	**TF**	E	*XR*	IL	64553	71327	71435	64554
315848	*	**TF**	E	*XR*	IL	64540	71328	71436	64556
315849	*	**TF**	E	*XR*	IL	64557	71329	71437	64558
315851	*	**TF**	E	*XR*	IL	64561	71331	71439	64562
315852	*	**TF**	E	*XR*	IL	64563	71332	71440	64564
315853	*	**TF**	E	*XR*	IL	64565	71333	71441	64566
315854	*	**TF**	E	*XR*	IL	64567	71334	71442	64568
315856	*	**TF**	E	*XR*	IL	64571	71336	71444	64572
315857	*	**TF**	E	*XR*	IL	64573	71337	71445	64574
315859	*	**TF**	E		NN	64577	71339	71447	64578

Names (carried on DMS):

315817 Transport for London
315829 London Borough of Havering Celebrating 40 years

CLASS 317 BREL YORK/DERBY

Outer suburban units.

Formation: Various, see sub-class headings.
Construction: Steel.
Traction Motors: Four GEC G315BZ of 247.5 kW (except 317 722, see below).
Wheel Arrangement: 2-2 + Bo-Bo + 2-2 + 2-2.

Braking: Disc.
Bogies: BP20 (MS), BT13 (others).
Gangways: Throughout
Doors: Sliding.
Dimensions: 19.83/20.18 x 2.82 m.
Couplers: Tightlock.
Control System: Thyristor.
Maximum Speed: 100 mph.
Seating Layout: Various, see sub-class headings.
Multiple Working: Within class & with Classes 315, 318, 319, 320, 321, 322 and 323.

Class 317/1. Pressure ventilated.

Formation: DTS–MS–TC–DTS.
Seating Layout: 1: 2+2 facing, 2: 3+2 facing.

* Fitted with a universal access toilet to comply with the 2020 accessibility regulations. Full details awaited.

DTS(A). Lot No. 30955 York 1981–82. –/74. 29.5 t.
MS. Lot No. 30958 York 1981–82. –/79. 49.0 t.
TC. Lot No. 30957 Derby 1981–82. 22/46 2T. 29.0 t.
DTS(B). Lot No. 30956 York 1981–82. –/71. 29.5 t.

317 337	*	**TL**	A	*GA*	IL	77036	62671	71613	77084
317 338	*	**TL**	A	*GA*	IL	77037	62698	71614	77085
317 339		**TL**	A	*GA*	IL	77038	62699	71615	77086
317 340		**TL**	A	*GA*	IL	77039	62700	71616	77087
317 341	*	**TL**	A	*GA*	IL	77040	62701	71617	77088
317 342		**TL**	A	*GA*	IL	77041	62702	71618	77089
317 343		**TL**	A	*GA*	IL	77042	62703	71619	77090
317 344		**GA**	A	*GA*	IL	77029	62690	71620	77091
317 345		**GA**	A	*GA*	IL	77044	62705	71621	77092
317 346		**GA**	A	*GA*	IL	77045	62706	71622	77093
317 347		**GA**	A	*GA*	IL	77046	62707	71623	77094
317 348		**TL**	A	*GA*	IL	77047	62708	71624	77095

Names (carried on TC):

317 345 Driver John Webb | 317 348 Richard A Jenner

Class 317/5. Pressure ventilated. Units renumbered from Class 317/1 in 2005 for West Anglia Metro services. Refurbished with new upholstery and Passenger Information Systems. Details as Class 317/1.

The original DTS 77048 was written off after the Cricklewood accident of 1983. A replacement vehicle was built at Wolverton in 1987 and given the same number.

317 501	*	**GA**	A	*GA*	IL	77024	62661	71577	77048^{II}
317 502		**GA**	A	*GA*	IL	77001	62662	71578	77049
317 503		**GA**	A	*GA*	IL	77002	62663	71579	77050
317 504	*	**GA**	A	*GA*	IL	77003	62664	71580	77051
317 505		**GA**	A	*GA*	IL	77004	62665	71581	77052
317 506	*	**GA**	A	*GA*	IL	77005	62666	71582	77053
317 507		**GA**	A	*GA*	IL	77006	62667	71583	77054
317 508		**GA**	A	*GA*	IL	77010	62697	71587	77058
317 509		**GA**	A	*GA*	IL	77011	62672	71588	77059
317 510		**GA**	A	*GA*	IL	77012	62673	71589	77060

317511	**GA**	A	*GA*	IL	77014	62675	71591	77062
317512	**GA**	A	*GA*	IL	77015	62676	71592	77063
317513	**GA**	A	*GA*	IL	77016	62677	71593	77064
317514	**GA**	A	*GA*	IL	77017	62678	71594	77065
317515	**GA**	A	*GA*	IL	77019	62680	71596	77067

Name (carried on TC): 317507 University of Cambridge 800 Years 1209–2009

Class 317/6. Convection heating. Units converted from Class 317/2 by Railcare, Wolverton 1998–99 with Chapman seating.

Formation: DTS–MS–TS–DTC.
Seating Layout: 2+2 facing.

77200–219. DTS. Lot No. 30994 York 1985–86. –/64. 29.5 t.
77280–283. DTS. Lot No. 31007 York 1987. –/64. 29.5 t.
62846–865. MS. Lot No. 30996 York 1985–86. –/71. 49.0 t.
62886–889. MS. Lot No. 31009 York 1987. –/71. 49.0 t.
71734–753. TS. Lot No. 30997 York 1985–86. –/60(+3) 2T. 29.0 t.
71762–765. TS. Lot No. 31010 York 1987. –/60(+3) 2T. 29.0 t.
77220–239. DTC. Lot No. 30995 York 1985–86. 24/36. 29.5 t.
77284–287. DTC. Lot No. 31008 York 1987. 24/36. 29.5 t.

317649	**GA**	A	*GA*	IL	77200	62846	71734	77220
317650	**GA**	A	*GA*	IL	77201	62847	71735	77221
317651	**GA**	A	*GA*	IL	77202	62848	71736	77222
317652	**GA**	A	*GA*	IL	77203	62849	71739	77223
317653	**GA**	A	*GA*	IL	77204	62850	71738	77224
317654	**GA**	A	*GA*	IL	77205	62851	71737	77225
317655	**GA**	A	*GA*	IL	77206	62852	71740	77226
317656	**NC**	A	*GA*	IL	77207	62853	71742	77227
317657	**NC**	A	*GA*	IL	77208	62854	71741	77228
317658	**GA**	A	*GA*	IL	77209	62855	71743	77229
317659	**GA**	A	*GA*	IL	77210	62856	71744	77230
317660	**GA**	A	*GA*	IL	77211	62857	71745	77231
317661	**GA**	A	*GA*	IL	77212	62858	71746	77232
317662	**GA**	A	*GA*	IL	77213	62859	71747	77233
317663	**GA**	A		EP	77214	62860	71748	77234
317664	**GA**	A	*GA*	IL	77215	62861	71749	77235
317665	**GA**	A	*GA*	IL	77216	62862	71750	77236
317666	**NC**	A	*GA*	IL	77217	62863	71752	77237
317667	**GA**	A	*GA*	IL	77218	62864	71751	77238
317668	**GA**	A	*GA*	IL	77219	62865	71753	77239
317669	**NC**	A		EP	77280	62886	71762	77284
317670	**GA**	A	*GA*	IL	77281	62887	71763	77285
317671	**NC**	A	*GA*	IL	77282	62888	71764	77286
317672	**GA**	A	*GA*	IL	77283	62889	71765	77287

Name (carried on DTC): 317654 Richard Wells

Class 317/7. Units converted from Class 317/1 by Railcare, Wolverton 2000 for Stansted Express services between London Liverpool Street and Stansted. Air conditioning. Fitted with luggage stacks. Displaced from Stansted services in 2011 by Class 379s – most units are now operated by London Overground. Toilets have been locked out of use.

* 317722 received new Bombardier MJA 280-8 AC traction motors as part of an Angel trial. Two vehicles (77021 and 62682, now in **GA** livery) also received an interior refurbishment with new Fainsa seating whilst the other two vehicles were left in their Stansted Express condition (still in **NX** livery).

Formation: DTS–MS–TS–DTC.
Seating Layout: 1: 2+1 facing, 2: 2+2 facing.

DTS. Lot No. 30955 York 1981–82. –/52 + catering point. 31.4 t.
MS. Lot No. 30958 York 1981–82. –/62 (* –/64). 51.3 t.
TS. Lot No. 30957 Derby 1981–82. –/42(+5) 1TD 1T 1W. 30.2 t.
DTC. Lot No. 30956 York 1981–82. 22/16 + catering point. 31.6 t.

317708		**LO**	A	*LO*	IL	77007	62668	71584	77055
317709		**LO**	A	*LO*	IL	77008	62669	71585	77056
317710		**LO**	A	*LO*	IL	77009	62670	71586	77057
317714		**LO**	A	*LO*	IL	77013	62674	71590	77061
317719		**LO**	A	*LO*	IL	77018	62679	71595	77066
317722	*	**GA/NX**	A		EP	77021	62682	71598	77069
317723		**LO**	A	*LO*	IL	77022	62683	71599	77070
317729		**LO**	A	*LO*	IL	77028	62689	71605	77076
317732		**LO**	A	*LO*	IL	77031	62692	71608	77079

Class 317/8. Pressure Ventilated. Units refurbished and renumbered from Class 317/1 in 2005–06 at Wabtec, Doncaster for use on Stansted Express services. Displaced from Stansted services in 2011. Toilets have been locked out of use on London Overground units.

Formation: DTS–MS–TC–DTS.
Seating Layout: 1: 2+2 facing, 2: 3+2 facing.

DTS(A). Lot No. 30955 York 1981–82. –/66. 29.5 t.
MS. Lot No. 30958 York 1981–82. –/71. 49.0 t.
TC. Lot No. 30957 Derby 1981–82. 20/42 2T († –/62 2T). 29.0 t.
DTS(B). Lot No. 30956 York 1981–82. –/66. 29.5 t.

317881		**GA**	A	*GA*	IL	77020	62681	71597	77068	
317882		**GA**	A	*GA*	IL	77023	62684	71600	77071	
317883		**GA**	A	*GA*	IL	77000	62685	71601	77072	
317884		**GA**	A	*GA*	IL	77025	62686	71602	77073	
317885		**GA**	A	*GA*	IL	77026	62687	71603	77074	
317886		**GA**	A	*GA*	IL	77027	62688	71604	77075	
317887	†	**LO**	A	*LO*	IL	77043	62704	71606	77077	
317888	†	**LO**	A	*LO*	IL	77030	62691	71607	77078	
317889	†	**LO**	A	*LO*	IL	77032	62693	71609	77080	
317890	†	**LO**	A	*LO*	IL	77033	62694	71610	77081	
317891	†	**LO**	A	*LO*	IL	77034	62695	71611	77082	
317892	†	**LO**	A	*LO*	IL	77035	62696	71612	77083	Ilford Depot

CLASS 318 BREL YORK

Outer suburban units.

Formation: DTS–MS–DTS.
Construction: Steel.
Traction Motors: Four Brush TM 2141 of 268 kW.
Wheel Arrangement: 2-2 + Bo-Bo + 2-2.
Braking: Disc.
Bogies: BP20 (MS), BT13 (others).
Gangways: Within unit.
Doors: Sliding.
Seating Layout: 3+2 facing.
Dimensions: 19.83/19.92 x 2.82 m.
Couplers: Tightlock.
Control System: Thyristor.
Maximum Speed: 90 mph.
Multiple Working: Within class & with Classes 317, 319, 320, 321, 322 and 323.

77240–259. DTS. Lot No. 30999 1985–86. –/55 1TD 2W. 32.0 t.
77288. DTS. Lot No. 31020 1987. –/55 1TD 2W. 32.0 t.
62866–885. MS. Lot No. 30998 1985–86. –/79. 53.0 t.
62890. MS. Lot No. 31019 1987. –/79. 53.0 t.
77260–279. DTS. Lot No. 31000 1985–86. –/69(+2). 31.6 t.
77289. DTS. Lot No. 31021 1987. –/69(+2). 31.6 t.

318 250	**SR**	E	*SR*	GW	77240	62866	77260
318 251	**SR**	E	*SR*	GW	77241	62867	77261
318 252	**SR**	E	*SR*	GW	77242	62868	77262
318 253	**SR**	E	*SR*	GW	77243	62869	77263
318 254	**SR**	E	*SR*	GW	77244	62870	77264
318 255	**SR**	E	*SR*	GW	77245	62871	77265
318 256	**SR**	E	*SR*	GW	77246	62872	77266
318 257	**SR**	E	*SR*	GW	77247	62873	77267
318 258	**SR**	E	*SR*	GW	77248	62874	77268
318 259	**SR**	E	*SR*	GW	77249	62875	77269
318 260	**SR**	E	*SR*	GW	77250	62876	77270
318 261	**SR**	E	*SR*	GW	77251	62877	77271
318 262	**SR**	E	*SR*	GW	77252	62878	77272
318 263	**SR**	E	*SR*	GW	77253	62879	77273
318 264	**SR**	E	*SR*	GW	77254	62880	77274
318 265	**SR**	E	*SR*	GW	77255	62881	77275
318 266	**SR**	E	*SR*	GW	77256	62882	77276
318 267	**SR**	E	*SR*	GW	77257	62883	77277
318 268	**SR**	E	*SR*	GW	77258	62884	77278
318 269	**SR**	E	*SR*	GW	77259	62885	77279
318 270	**SR**	E	*SR*	GW	77288	62890	77289

CLASS 319 BREL YORK

Express and outer suburban units. Units shown * or † have a universal access toilet to comply with the 2020 accessibility regulations. Some units are being rebuilt as bi-modes and are now numbered in the Class 769 or Class 799 series.

Formation: Various, see sub-class headings.
Systems: 25 kV AC overhead/750 V DC third rail.
Construction: Steel.
Traction Motors: Four GEC G315BZ of 268 kW.
Wheel Arrangement: 2-2 + Bo-Bo + 2-2 + 2-2.
Braking: Disc. **Dimensions:** 20.17/20.16 x 2.82 m.
Bogies: P7-4 (MS), T3-7 (others). **Couplers:** Tightlock.
Gangways: Within unit + end doors. **Control System:** GTO chopper.
Doors: Sliding. **Maximum Speed:** 100 mph.
Seating Layout: Various, see sub-class headings.
Multiple Working: Within class & with Classes 317, 318, 320, 321, 322 and 323.

Class 319/0. DTS–MS–TS–DTS. 319002/003/006/007/008 (plus four other units to be identified) are being/are to be converted to Class 769 bi-mode units for Transport for Wales.

Seating Layout: 3+2 facing.

DTS(A). Lot No. 31022 (odd nos.) 1987–88. –/82 (* –/79). 28.2 t (* 30.7 t).
MS. Lot No. 31023 1987–88. –/82 (* –/81). 49.2 t (* 50.9 t).
TS. Lot No. 31024 1987–88. –/77 2T (* –/63 1TD 2W, † –/64 1TD 2W). 31.0 t (*† 32.5 t).
DTS(B). Lot No. 31025 (even nos.) 1987–88. –/78 (* –/79). 28.1 t (* 30.0 t).

319003	*	**TL**	P		LB	77295	62893	71774	77294
319005	*	**TL**	P	*WM*	NN	77299	62895	71776	77298
319007	*	**TL**	P		LB	77303	62897	71778	77302
319009		**TL**	P		LM	77307	62899	71780	77306
319010		**TL**	P		LM	77309	62900	71781	77308
319011		**TL**	P		LM	77311	62901	71782	77310
319012	*	**TL**	P	*WM*	NN	77313	62902	71783	77312
319013	†	**LM**	P	*WM*	NN	77315	62903	71784	77314

Names (carried on TS):

319009 Coquelles | 319011 John Ruskin College

Class 319/2. DTS–MS–TS–DTC. Units converted from Class 319/0.

Seating Layout: 1: 2+1 facing, 2: 2+2/3+2 facing.

DTS. Lot No. 31022 (odd nos.) 1987–88. –/64. 30.0 t.
MS. Lot No. 31023 1987–88. –/73. 51.0 t.
TS. Lot No. 31024 1987–88. –/52 1TD 1T. 31.0 t.
DTC. Lot No. 31025 (even nos.) 1987–88. 18/36. 30.0 t.

319214	*	**TL**	P	*WM*	NN	77317	62904	71785	77316
319215	*	**TL**	P	*WM*	NN	77319	62905	71786	77318
319216	*	**LM**	P	*WM*	NN	77321	62906	71787	77320
319217	*	**TL**	P	*WM*	NN	77323	62907	71788	77322
319218	*	**TL**	P	*WM*	NN	77325	62908	71789	77324
319219	*	**TL**	P	*WM*	NN	77327	62909	71790	77326
319220	*	**TL**	P	*WM*	NN	77329	62910	71791	77328

Class 319/3. DTS–MS–TS–DTS. Converted from Class 319/1 by replacing First Class seats with Standard Class seats.

Refurbished with a new universal access toilet to comply with the 2020 accessibility regulations, except 319 373.

Seating Layout: 3+2 facing.

DTS(A). Lot No. 31063 1990. –/79. 29.0 t.
MS. Lot No. 31064 1990. –/81. 50.6 t.
TS. Lot No. 31065 1990. –/64 1TD 2W. 31.0 t.
DTS(B). Lot No. 31066 1990. –/79. 29.7 t.

319 361	*	**NR**	P	*NO*	AN	77459	63043	71929	77458
319 362	*	**NR**	P		LM	77461	63044	71930	77460
319 363	*	**NR**	P		LM	77463	63045	71931	77462
319 364	*	**NR**	P		LM	77465	63046	71932	77464
319 365	*	**NR**	P		LM	77467	63047	71933	77466
319 366	*	**NR**	P	*NO*	AN	77469	63048	71934	77468
319 367	*	**NR**	P	*NO*	AN	77471	63049	71935	77470
319 368	*	**NR**	P	*NO*	AN	77473	63050	71936	77472
319 369	*	**NR**	P	*NO*	AN	77475	63051	71937	77474
319 370	*	**NR**	P	*NO*	AN	77477	63052	71938	77476
319 371	*	**NR**	P		LM	77479	63053	71939	77478
319 372	*	**TL**	P	*NO*	AN	77481	63054	71940	77480
319 373		**TL**	P		LM	77483	63055	71941	77482
319 374	*	**NR**	P		LM	77485	63056	71942	77484
319 375	*	**NR**	P	*NO*	AN	77487	63057	71943	77486
319 376	*	**NR**	P		LM	77489	63058	71944	77488
319 377	*	**NR**	P		LM	77491	63059	71945	77490
319 378	*	**NR**	P	*NO*	AN	77493	63060	71946	77492
319 379	*	**NR**	P	*NO*	AN	77495	63061	71947	77494
319 380	*	**NR**	P		LM	77497	63062	71948	77496
319 381	*	**NR**	P	*NO*	AN	77973	63093	71979	77974
319 382	*	**NR**	P		LM	77975	63094	71980	77976
319 383	*	**NR**	P	*NO*	AN	77977	63095	71981	77978
319 384	*	**NR**	P	*NO*	AN	77979	63096	71982	77980
319 385	*	**NR**	P	*NO*	AN	77981	63097	71983	77982
319 386	*	**NR**	P	*NO*	AN	77983	63098	71984	77984

Class 319/4. DTC–MS–TS–DTS. Converted from Class 319/0. Refurbished with carpets. DTS(A) converted to composite.

Eight units (319 424/431/434/442/448/450/456/458) have been or are being converted to Class 769 bi-mode units for Northern (see Class 769).

319 422/423/425/427/428/430/432/435–440/443/445/447/449/452/459 are to be converted to Class 769 tri-mode units for Great Western Railway.

Non-standard livery: 319 454 Porterbrook Innovation Hub (blue).

Seating Layout: 1: 2+1 facing 2: 2+2/3+2 facing.

77331–381. DTC. Lot No. 31022 (odd nos.) 1987–88. 12/51 (* 12/50). 30.0t (* 31.0 t).
77431–457. DTC. Lot No. 31038 (odd nos.) 1988. 12/51 (* 12/50). 30.0t (* 31.0 t).
62911–936. MS. Lot No. 31023 1987–88. –/74 (* –/75). 49.2t (* 52.4 t).

62961–974. MS. Lot No. 31039 1988. –/74 (* –/75). 49.2t (* 52.4 t).
71792–817. TS. Lot No. 31024 1987–88. –/67 2T (* –/58 1TD 2W). 31.0t (* 33.7 t).
71866–879. TS. Lot No. 31040 1988. –67 2T (* –/58 1TD 2W). 31.0t (* 33.7 t).
77330–380. DTS. Lot No. 31025 (even nos.) 1987–88. –/71 1W (* –/73). 28.1t (* 30.7 t).
77430–456. DTS. Lot No. 31041 (even nos.) 1988. –/71 1W (* –/73). 28.1t (* 30.7 t).

319421	*	**TL**	P		LM	77331	62911	71792	77330
319422	*	**TL**	P		LB	77333	62912	71793	77332
319423	*	**TL**	P		ZN	77335	62913	71794	77334
319425	*	**TL**	P		LM	77339	62915	71796	77338
319426	*	**NR**	P		LB	77341	62916	71797	77340
319427	*	**TL**	P		ZN	77343	62917	71798	77342
319428	*	**TL**	P		LM	77345	62918	71799	77344
319429	*	**LM**	P	*WM*	NN	77347	62919	71800	77346
319430	*	**TL**	P		LM	77349	62920	71801	77348
319432	*	**TL**	P		LM	77353	62922	71803	77352
319433	*	**LM**	P	*WM*	NN	77355	62923	71804	77354
319435	*	**TL**	P		ZN	77359	62925	71806	77358
319436	*	**TL**	P		LM	77361	62926	71807	77360
319437	*	**TL**	P		LB	77363	62927	71808	77362
319438	*	**TL**	P		LM	77365	62928	71809	77364
319439	*	**TL**	P		ZN	77367	62929	71810	77366
319440	*	**TL**	P		RG	77369	62930	71811	77368
319441	*	**LM**	P	*WM*	NN	77371	62931	71812	77370
319443	*	**TL**	P		LB	77375	62933	71814	77374
319444	*	**TL**	P		ZA	77377	62934	71815	77376
319445	*	**TL**	P		LB	77379	62935	71816	77378
319446	*	**TL**	P		ZN	77381	62936	71817	77380
319447	*	**TL**	P		ZN	77431	62961	71866	77430
319449	*	**TL**	P		ZN	77435	62963	71868	77434
319451		**FU**	P		LM	77439	62965	71870	77438
319452	*	**TL**	P		LB	77441	62966	71871	77440
319453		**FU**	P		LM	77443	62967	71872	77442
319454		**0**	P		LM	77445	62968	71873	77444
319455		**FU**	P		LM	77447	62969	71874	77446
319457	*	**LM**	P	*WM*	NN	77451	62971	71876	77450
319459	*	**TL**	P		ZN	77455	62973	71878	77454
319460	*	**LM**	P	*WM*	NN	77457	62974	71879	77456

Name (carried on TS): 319444 City of St Albans

CLASS 320 BREL YORK

Suburban units. In 2016–19 ScotRail received 320401/403/404/411–418/420 (ex-Class 321s) which were refurbished and reformed as 3-cars.

Formation: DTS–MS–DTS.
Construction: Steel
Traction Motors: Four Brush TM2141B of 268 kW.
Wheel Arrangement: 2-2 + Bo-Bo + 2-2.
Braking: Disc. **Dimensions:** 19.95 x 2.82 m.
Bogies: P7-4 (MS), T3-7 (others). **Couplers:** Tightlock.

Gangways: Within unit.
Doors: Sliding.
Seating Layout: 3+2 facing.
Multiple Working: Within class & with Classes 317, 318, 319, 321, 322 and 323.
Control System: Thyristor.
Maximum Speed: 90 mph.

Class 320/3. Original build.

DTS(A). Lot No. 31060 1990. –/51(+4) 1TD 2W. 31.7 t.
MS. Lot No. 31062 1990. –/78. 52.6 t.
DTS(B). Lot No. 31061 1990. –/73(+2). 31.6 t.

320 301	**SR**	E	*SR*	GW	77899	63021	77921
320 302	**SR**	E	*SR*	GW	77900	63022	77922
320 303	**SR**	E	*SR*	GW	77901	63023	77923
320 304	**SR**	E	*SR*	GW	77902	63024	77924
320 305	**SR**	E	*SR*	GW	77903	63025	77925
320 306	**SR**	E	*SR*	GW	77904	63026	77926
320 307	**SR**	E	*SR*	GW	77905	63027	77927
320 308	**SR**	E	*SR*	GW	77906	63028	77928
320 309	**SR**	E	*SR*	GW	77907	63029	77929
320 310	**SR**	E	*SR*	GW	77908	63030	77930
320 311	**SR**	E	*SR*	GW	77909	63031	77931
320 312	**SR**	E	*SR*	GW	77910	63032	77932
320 313	**SR**	E	*SR*	GW	77911	63033	77933
320 314	**SR**	E	*SR*	GW	77912	63034	77934
320 315	**SR**	E	*SR*	GW	77913	63035	77935
320 316	**SR**	E	*SR*	GW	77914	63036	77936
320 317	**SR**	E	*SR*	GW	77915	63037	77937
320 318	**SR**	E	*SR*	GW	77916	63038	77938
320 319	**SR**	E	*SR*	GW	77917	63039	77939
320 320	**SR**	E	*SR*	GW	77918	63040	77940
320 321	**SR**	E	*SR*	GW	77919	63041	77941
320 322	**SR**	E	*SR*	GW	77920	63042	77942

Class 320/4. Former London Midland Class 321s reduced to 3-car formation and refurbished as Class 320/4s by Wabtec Doncaster or Wabtec Kilmarnock 2015–19.

The original vehicles 71966 and 77960 from 321 418 (now 320 418) and 78114 and 63082 from 321 420 (now 320 420) were written off after the Watford Junction accident in 1996. The undamaged vehicles were formed together as 321 418 whilst four new vehicles were built in 1997, taking the same numbers as the scrapped vehicles, and these became the second 321 420.

DTS(A). Lot No. 31060 1990. –/54(+4) 1TD 2W. 32.0 t.
MS. Lot No. 31062 1990. –/79. 52.2 t.
DTS(B). Lot No. 31061 1990. –/74(+2). 32.0 t.

320 401	(321 401)	**SR**	E	*SR*	GW	78095	63063	77943
320 403	(321 403)	**SR**	E	*SR*	GW	78097	63065	77945
320 404	(321 404)	**SR**	E	*SR*	GW	78098	63066	77946
320 411	(321 411)	**SR**	E	*SR*	GW	78105	63073	77953
320 412	(321 412)	**SR**	E	*SR*	GW	78106	63074	77954
320 413	(321 413)	**SR**	E	*SR*	GW	78107	63075	77955

320414	(321414)	**SR**	E	*SR*	GW	78108	63076	77956
320415	(321415)	**SR**	E	*SR*	GW	78109	63077	77957
320416	(321416)	**SR**	E	*SR*	GW	78110	63078	77958
320417	(321417)	**SR**	E	*SR*	GW	78111	63079	77959
320418	(321418)	**SR**	E	*SR*	GW	78112	63080	77962
320420	(321420)	**SR**	E	*SR*	GW	78114ᴵᴵ	63082ᴵᴵ	77960ᴵᴵ

CLASS 321 BREL YORK

Outer suburban units.

Formation: DTC (DTS on Class 321/9)–MS–TS–DTS.
Construction: Steel.
Traction Motors: Four Brush TM2141C of 268 kW (* Four TSA010163 AC motors of 300 kW).
Wheel Arrangement: 2-2 + Bo-Bo + 2-2 + 2-2.
Braking: Disc (* and regenerative). **Dimensions**: 19.95 x 2.82 m.
Bogies: P7-4 (MS), T3-7 (others). **Couplers**: Tightlock.
Gangways: Within unit.
Control System: Thyristor (* IGBT Inverter).
Doors: Sliding. **Maximum Speed**: 100 mph.
Seating Layout: 1: 2+2 facing, 2: 3+2 facing.
Multiple Working: Within class & with Classes 317, 318, 319, 320, 322 and 323.

Class 321/3.

* "Renatus" rebuilt units with completely new interiors, air conditioning and Quantum seating, still arranged to a 3+2 layout in Standard Class. Fitted with new TSA AC traction motors.

DTC. Lot No. 31053 1988–90. 16/57 (321 347–366 16/56) (* 16/31(+4) 1TD 2W. 29.7 t (* 34.1 t).
MS. Lot No. 31054 1988–90. –/82 (* –/80). 51.5 t (* 53.8 t).
TS. Lot No. 31055 1988–90. –/75 2T (* –/78 1T). 29.1 t (* 31.7 t).
DTS. Lot No. 31056 1988–90. –/78 (* –/76). 29.7 t (* 32.8 t.)

321301	*	**GR**	E	*GA*	IL	78049	62975	71880	77853
321302	*	**GR**	E	*GA*	IL	78050	62976	71881	77854
321303	*	**GR**	E	*GA*	IL	78051	62977	71882	77855
321304	*	**GR**	E	*GA*	IL	78052	62978	71883	77856
321305	*	**GR**	E	*GA*	IL	78053	62979	71884	77857
321306	*	**GR**	E	*GA*	IL	78054	62980	71885	77858
321307	*	**GR**	E	*GA*	IL	78055	62981	71886	77859
321308	*	**GR**	E	*GA*	IL	78056	62982	71887	77860
321309	*	**GR**	E	*GA*	IL	78057	62983	71888	77861
321310	*	**GR**	E	*GA*	IL	78058	62984	71889	77862
321311	*	**GR**	E	*GA*	IL	78059	62985	71890	77863
321312	*	**GR**	E	*GA*	IL	78060	62986	71891	77864
321313	*	**GR**	E	*GA*	IL	78061	62987	71892	77865
321314	*	**GR**	E	*GA*	IL	78062	62988	71893	77866
321315	*	**GR**	E	*GA*	IL	78063	62989	71894	77867
321316	*	**GR**	E	*GA*	IL	78064	62990	71895	77868

321 317	*	**GR**	E	*GA*	IL	78065	62991	71896	77869
321 318	*	**GR**	E	*GA*	IL	78066	62992	71897	77870
321 319	*	**GR**	E	*GA*	IL	78067	62993	71898	77871
321 320	*	**GR**	E	*GA*	IL	78068	62994	71899	77872
321 321	*	**GR**	E	*GA*	IL	78069	62995	71900	77873
321 322	*	**GR**	E	*GA*	IL	78070	62996	71901	77874
321 323	*	**GR**	E	*GA*	IL	78071	62997	71902	77875
321 324	*	**GR**	E	*GA*	IL	78072	62998	71903	77876
321 325	*	**GR**	E	*GA*	IL	78073	62999	71904	77877
321 326	*	**GR**	E	*GA*	IL	78074	63000	71905	77878
321 327	*	**GR**	E	*GA*	IL	78075	63001	71906	77879
321 328	*	**GR**	E	*GA*	IL	78076	63002	71907	77880
321 329	*	**GR**	E	*GA*	IL	78077	63003	71908	77881
321 330	*	**GR**	E	*GA*	IL	78078	63004	71909	77882
321 331		**NC**	E	*GA*	IL	78079	63005	71910	77883
321 332		**NC**	E	*GA*	IL	78080	63006	71911	77884
321 333		**NC**	E	*GA*	IL	78081	63007	71912	77885
321 334		**NC**	E	*GA*	IL	78082	63008	71913	77886
321 335		**NC**	E	*GA*	IL	78083	63009	71914	77887
321 336		**NC**	E	*GA*	IL	78084	63010	71915	77888
321 337		**NC**	E	*GA*	IL	78085	63011	71916	77889
321 338		**NC**	E	*GA*	IL	78086	63012	71917	77890
321 339		**NC**	E	*GA*	IL	78087	63013	71918	77891
321 340		**NC**	E	*GA*	IL	78088	63014	71919	77892
321 341		**NC**	E	*GA*	IL	78089	63015	71920	77893
321 342		**NC**	E	*GA*	IL	78090	63016	71921	77894
321 343		**NC**	E	*GA*	IL	78091	63017	71922	77895
321 344		**NC**	E	*GA*	IL	78092	63018	71923	77896
321 345		**NC**	E	*GA*	IL	78093	63019	71924	77897
321 346		**NC**	E	*GA*	IL	78094	63020	71925	77898
321 347		**NC**	E	*GA*	IL	78131	63105	71991	78280
321 348		**NC**	E	*GA*	IL	78132	63106	71992	78281
321 349		**NC**	E	*GA*	IL	78133	63107	71993	78282
321 350		**NC**	E	*GA*	IL	78134	63108	71994	78283
321 351		**NC**	E	*GA*	IL	78135	63109	71995	78284
321 352		**NC**	E	*GA*	IL	78136	63110	71996	78285
321 353		**NC**	E	*GA*	IL	78137	63111	71997	78286
321 354		**NC**	E	*GA*	IL	78138	63112	71998	78287
321 355		**NC**	E	*GA*	IL	78139	63113	71999	78288
321 356		**NC**	E	*GA*	IL	78140	63114	72000	78289
321 357		**NC**	E	*GA*	IL	78141	63115	72001	78290
321 358		**NC**	E	*GA*	IL	78142	63116	72002	78291
321 359		**GA**	E	*GA*	IL	78143	63117	72003	78292
321 360		**NC**	E	*GA*	IL	78144	63118	72004	78293
321 361		**GA**	E	*GA*	IL	78145	63119	72005	78294
321 362		**GA**	E	*GA*	IL	78146	63120	72006	78295
321 363		**GA**	E	*GA*	IL	78147	63121	72007	78296
321 364		**GA**	E	*GA*	IL	78148	63122	72008	78297
321 365		**GA**	E	*GA*	IL	78149	63123	72009	78298
321 366		**GA**	E	*GA*	IL	78150	63124	72010	78299

Names (carried on TS):

321 334 Amsterdam
321 336 GEOFFREY FREEMAN ALLEN
321 342 R. Barnes
321 343 RSA RAILWAY STUDY ASSOCIATION
321 351 London Southend Airport
321 361 Phoenix

Class 321/4.

The DTCs of 321 421–437 have had 12 First Class seats declassified.

Units 321 401/403/404/411–418/420 have been refurbished as Class 320/4 3-car units for ScotRail (their TS vehicles are stored or have been scrapped).

† 321 448 received an interior refurbishment as an Eversholt demonstrator unit. Fitted with two different types of interior using seats supplied by Quantum it acted as the pilot unit for the "Renatus" work being carried out on the Class 321/3s. 78130 and 63104 have a "suburban" interior with a 3+2 seating layout and 78279 and 71990 have a "metro" interior with 2+2 seating. It is also fitted with the new TSA AC traction motors.

Non-standard livery: 321 448 Eversholt demonstrator (silver with blue doors and multi-coloured stripes).

DTC. Lot No. 31067 1989–90. 28/40 (321 421–437 16/52, 321 438–447 16/56). 29.8 t. († 16/30(+4) 1TD 2W 33.9 t).
MS. Lot No. 31068 1989–90. –/79 (321 438–447 –/82). 51.6 t († –/82. 54.0 t).
TS. Lot No. 31069 1989–90. –/74 2T (321 438–447 –/75 2T). 29.2 t († –/62 1T. 31.7 t).
DTS. Lot No. 31070 1989–90. –/78. 29.8 t. († –/58. 33.2 t).

321402	**FB**	E	*GA*	IL	78096	63064	71950	77944
321405	**FB**	E	*GA*	IL	78099	63067	71953	77947
321406	**FB**	E	*GA*	IL	78100	63068	71954	77948
321407	**FB**	E	*GA*	IL	78101	63069	71955	77949
321408	**FB**	E	*GA*	IL	78102	63070	71956	77950
321409	**FB**	E	*GA*	IL	78103	63071	71957	77951
321410	**FB**	E	*GA*	IL	78104	63072	71958	77952
321419	**FB**	E	*GA*	IL	78113	63081	71967	77961
321421	**NC**	E	*GA*	IL	78115	63083	71969	77963
321422	**NC**	E	*GA*	IL	78116	63084	71970	77964
321423	**NC**	E	*GA*	IL	78117	63085	71971	77965
321424	**NX**	E	*GA*	IL	78118	63086	71972	77966
321425	**NC**	E	*GA*	IL	78119	63087	71973	77967
321426	**NX**	E	*GA*	IL	78120	63088	71974	77968
321427	**NX**	E	*GA*	IL	78121	63089	71975	77969
321428	**NX**	E	*GA*	IL	78122	63090	71976	77970
321429	**NX**	E	*GA*	IL	78123	63091	71977	77971
321430	**NX**	E	*GA*	IL	78124	63092	71978	77972
321431	**NX**	E	*GA*	IL	78151	63125	72011	78300
321432	**NC**	E	*GA*	IL	78152	63126	72012	78301
321433	**NC**	E	*GA*	IL	78153	63127	72013	78302
321434	**NC**	E	*GA*	IL	78154	63128	72014	78303
321435	**NC**	E	*GA*	IL	78155	63129	72015	78304

321436		**NC**	E	*GA*	IL	78156	63130	72016	78305
321437		**NC**	E	*GA*	IL	78157	63131	72017	78306
321438		**GA**	E	*GA*	IL	78158	63132	72018	78307
321439		**GA**	E	*GA*	IL	78159	63133	72019	78308
321440		**GA**	E	*GA*	IL	78160	63134	72020	78309
321441		**GA**	E	*GA*	IL	78161	63135	72021	78310
321442		**GA**	E	*GA*	IL	78162	63136	72022	78311
321443		**GA**	E	*GA*	IL	78125	63099	71985	78274
321444		**NC**	E	*GA*	IL	78126	63100	71986	78275
321445		**NC**	E	*GA*	IL	78127	63101	71987	78276
321446		**NC**	E	*GA*	IL	78128	63102	71988	78277
321447		**GA**	E	*GA*	IL	78129	63103	71989	78278
321448	†	**0**	E	*GA*	IL	78130	63104	71990	78279
Spare		**FB**	E		ZK (S)	71951	71968		
Spare		**LM**	E		ZB (S)	71959			
Spare		**LM**	E		LM (S)	71963			

Names (carried on TS):

321409 Dame Alice Owen's School 400 Years of Learning
321428 The Essex Commuter
321442 Crouch Valley 1889–2014
321444 Essex Lifeboats
321446 George Mullings

Class 321/9. DTS(A)–MS–TS–DTS(B).

DTS(A). Lot No. 31108 1991. –/45(+6) 1TD 2W. 31.7 t.
MS. Lot No. 31109 1991. –/79. 52.1 t.
TS. Lot No. 31110 1991. –/78. 30.6 t.
DTS(B). Lot No. 31111 1991. –/79. 30.6 t.

321901	**NB**	E		CY	77990	63153	72128	77993
321902	**NB**	E		CY	77991	63154	72129	77994
321903	**NB**	E	*NO*	NL	77992	63155	72130	77995

CLASS 322 BREL YORK

Units built for use on Stansted Airport services, used for a number of years with ScotRail before transfer to Northern.

Formation: DTS–MS–TS–DTS.
Construction: Steel.
Traction Motors: Four Brush TM2141C of 268 kW.
Wheel Arrangement: 2-2 + Bo-Bo + 2-2 + 2-2.
Braking: Disc.
Bogies: P7-4 (MS), T3-7 (others).
Gangways: Within unit.
Doors: Sliding.
Dimensions: 19.95/19.92 x 2.82 m.
Couplers: Tightlock.
Control System: Thyristor.
Maximum Speed: 100 mph.
Seating Layout: 3+2 facing.
Multiple Working: Within class & with Classes 317, 318, 319, 320, 321 and 323.

DTS(A). Lot No. 31094 1990. –/54(+4) 1TD 2W. 31.7 t.
MS. Lot No. 31092 1990. –/83. 52.1 t.

TS. Lot No. 31093 1990. –/80 1T. 30.6 t.
DTS(B). Lot No. 31091 1990. –/79. 30.6 t.

322481	**NB**	E	*NO*	NL	78163	63137	72023	77985
322482	**NB**	E	*NO*	NL	78164	63138	72024	77986
322483	**NB**	E	*NO*	NL	78165	63139	72025	77987
322484	**NB**	E	*NO*	NL	78166	63140	72026	77988
322485	**NB**	E	*NO*	NL	78167	63141	72027	77989

CLASS 323 HUNSLET TRANSPORTATION PROJECTS

Suburban units.

Formation: DMS–PTS–DMS.
Construction: Welded aluminium alloy.
Traction Motors: Four Holec DMKT 52/24 asynchronous of 146 kW.
Wheel Arrangement: Bo-Bo + 2-2 + Bo-Bo.
Braking: Disc & regenerative.
Bogies: SRP BP62 (DMS), BT52 (PTS).
Gangways: Within unit.
Doors: Sliding plug.
Dimensions: 23.37/23.44 x 2.80 m.
Couplers: Tightlock.
Control System: IGBT Inverter.
Maximum Speed: 90 mph.
Seating Layout: 3+2 facing/unidirectional.
Multiple Working: Within class & with Classes 317, 318, 319, 320, 321 and 322.

DMS(B) vehicles 65003 and 65005 in 323203/205 and 65019 and 65021 in 323219/221 switched between units following accident damage and were not returned to their original sets, instead swapping numbers.

* Fitted with a universal access toilet to comply with the 2020 accessibility regulations.

DMS(A). Lot No. 31112 Hunslet 1992–93. –/98 († –/82, * –/97). 41.0 t.
TS. Lot No. 31113 Hunslet 1992–93. –/88(+5) 1T 2W. († –/80(+5) 1T 2W, * –/81(+3) 1TD 2W). 39.4t.
DMS(B). Lot No. 31114 Hunslet 1992–93. –/98 († –/82, * –/97). 41.0 t.

323201	*	**WI**	P	*WM*	SO	64001	72201	65001
323202	*	**WI**	P	*WM*	SO	64002	72202	65002
323203	*	**WI**	P	*WM*	SO	64003	72203	65003
323204	*	**WI**	P	*WM*	SO	64004	72204	65004
323205		**WI**	P	*WM*	SO	64005	72205	65005
323206		**WI**	P	*WM*	SO	64006	72206	65006
323207		**WI**	P	*WM*	SO	64007	72207	65007
323208		**WI**	P	*WM*	SO	64008	72208	65008
323209	*	**WI**	P	*WM*	SO	64009	72209	65009
323210		**WI**	P	*WM*	SO	64010	72210	65010
323211		**WI**	P	*WM*	SO	64011	72211	65011
323212		**WI**	P	*WM*	SO	64012	72212	65012
323213		**WI**	P	*WM*	SO	64013	72213	65013
323214	*	**WI**	P	*WM*	SO	64014	72214	65014
323215		**WI**	P	*WM*	SO	64015	72215	65015
323216	*	**WI**	P	*WM*	SO	64016	72216	65016
323217	*	**WI**	P	*WM*	SO	64017	72217	65017
323218	*	**WI**	P	*WM*	SO	64018	72218	65018

323 219	*	**WI**	P	*WM*	SO	64019	72219	65019
323 220		**WI**	P	*WM*	SO	64020	72220	65020
323 221	*	**WI**	P	*WM*	SO	64021	72221	65021
323 222	*	**WI**	P	*WM*	SO	64022	72222	65022
323 223	†	**NO**	P	*NO*	AN	64023	72223	65023
323 224	†	**NO**	P	*NO*	AN	64024	72224	65024
323 225	†	**NO**	P	*NO*	AN	64025	72225	65025
323 226	*	**NR**	P	*NO*	AN	64026	72226	65026
323 227		**NO**	P	*NO*	AN	64027	72227	65027
323 228		**NO**	P	*NO*	AN	64028	72228	65028
323 229	*	**NR**	P	*NO*	AN	64029	72229	65029
323 230		**NO**	P	*NO*	AN	64030	72230	65030
323 231		**NO**	P	*NO*	AN	64031	72231	65031
323 232		**NO**	P	*NO*	AN	64032	72232	65032
323 233		**NO**	P	*NO*	AN	64033	72233	65033
323 234	*	**NR**	P	*NO*	AN	64034	72234	65034
323 235		**NO**	P	*NO*	AN	64035	72235	65035
323 236	*	**NR**	P	*NO*	AN	64036	72236	65036
323 237		**NO**	P	*NO*	AN	64037	72237	65037
323 238	*	**NR**	P	*NO*	AN	64038	72238	65038
323 239	*	**NR**	P	*NO*	AN	64039	72239	65039
323 240	*	**WI**	P	*WM*	SO	64040	72340	65040
323 241		**WI**	P	*WM*	SO	64041	72341	65041
323 242		**WI**	P	*WM*	SO	64042	72342	65042
323 243		**WI**	P	*WM*	SO	64043	72343	65043

CLASS 325 ABB DERBY

Postal units based on Class 319s. Compatible with diesel or electric locomotive haulage. Built for dual voltage use, but 750 V DC third rail shoe gear has been removed as it is not required on current duties.

Formation: DTPMV–MPMV–TPMV–DTPMV.
System: 25 kV AC overhead.
Construction: Steel.
Traction Motors: Four GEC G315BZ of 268 kW.
Wheel Arrangement: 2-2 + Bo-Bo + 2-2 + 2-2.
Braking: Disc.
Bogies: P7-4 (MPMV), T3-7 (others).
Gangways: None.
Doors: Roller shutter.
Multiple Working: Within class.
Dimensions: 19.33 x 2.82 m.
Couplers: Drop-head buckeye.
Control System: GTO Chopper.
Maximum Speed: 100 mph.

DTPMV. Lot No. 31144 1995. 29.1 t.
MPMV. Lot No. 31145 1995. 49.5 t.
TPMV. Lot No. 31146 1995. 30.7 t.

325 001	**RM**	RM	*DB*	CE	68300	68340	68360	68301
325 002	**RM**	RM	*DB*	CE	68302	68341	68361	68303
325 003	**RM**	RM	*DB*	CE	68304	68342	68362	68305
325 004	**RM**	RM	*DB*	CE	68306	68343	68363	68307
325 005	**RM**	RM	*DB*	CE	68308	68344	68364	68309

325006	**RM**	RM	*DB*	CE	68310	68345	68365	68311
325007	**RM**	RM	*DB*	CE	68312	68346	68366	68313
325008	**RM**	RM	*DB*	CE	68314	68347	68367	68315
325009	**RM**	RM	*DB*	CE	68316	68349	68368	68317
325011	**RM**	RM	*DB*	CE	68320	68350	68370	68321
325012	**RM**	RM	*DB*	CE	68322	68351	68371	68323
325013	**RM**	RM	*DB*	CE	68324	68352	68372	68325
325014	**RM**	RM	*DB*	CE	68326	68353	68373	68327
325015	**RM**	RM	*DB*	CE	68328	68354	68374	68329
325016	**RM**	RM	*DB*	CE	68330	68355	68375	68331

Name (carried on one side of each DTPMV):

325008 Peter Howarth CBE

CLASS 331 CIVITY CAF

New units currently entering service with Northern.

Formation: DMS–PTS–DMS or DMS–PTS–TS–DMS.
Construction: Aluminium.
Traction Motors: Four TSA asynchronous of 220 kW.
Wheel Arrangement: Bo-Bo + 2-2 + Bo-Bo or Bo-Bo + 2-2 + 2-2 + Bo-Bo.
Braking: Disc & regenerative.
Bogies: CAF.
Gangways: Within unit.
Doors: Sliding plug.
Heating & ventilation: Air conditioning.
Seating: 2+2 facing/unidirectional.
Dimensions: 24.03/23.35 x 2.55 m.
Couplers: Dellner.
Control System: IGBT Inverter.
Maximum Speed: 100 mph.
Multiple Working: Within class.

Class 331/0. DMS–PTS–DMS. 3-car units.

DMS. CAF Zaragoza/Newport 2017–20. –/45(+8) 1TD 2W. 40.8 t.
PTS. CAF Zaragoza/Newport 2017–20. –/76(+4). 34.9 t.
DMS. CAF Zaragoza/Newport 2017–20. –/63(+7). 39.8 t.

331001	**NR**	E	*NO*	AN	463001	464001	466001
331002	**NR**	E	*NO*	AN	463002	464002	466002
331003	**NR**	E	*NO*	AN	463003	464003	466003
331004	**NR**	E	*NO*	AN	463004	464004	466004
331005	**NR**	E	*NO*	AN	463005	464005	466005
331006	**NR**	E	*NO*	AN	463006	464006	466006
331007	**NR**	E	*NO*	AN	463007	464007	466007
331008	**NR**	E	*NO*	AN	463008	464008	466008
331009	**NR**	E	*NO*	AN	463009	464009	466009
331010	**NR**	E	*NO*	AN	463010	464010	466010
331011	**NR**	E	*NO*	AN	463011	464011	466011
331012	**NR**	E	*NO*	AN	463012	464012	466012
331013	**NR**	E	*NO*	AN	463013	464013	466013
331014	**NR**	E	*NO*	AN	463014	464014	466014
331015	**NR**	E	*NO*	AN	463015	464015	466015
331016	**NR**	E	*NO*	AN	463016	464016	466016
331017	**NR**	E	*NO*	AN	463017	464017	466017

331 018	**NR**	E	*NO*	AN	463018	464018	466018	
331 019	**NR**	E	*NO*	AN	463019	464019	466019	
331 020	**NR**	E	*NO*	AN	463020	464020	466020	
331 021	**NR**	E			463021	464021	466021	
331 022	**NR**	E			463022	464022	466022	
331 023	**NR**	E			463023	464023	466023	
331 024	**NR**	E			463024	464024	466024	
331 025	**NR**	E			463025	464025	466025	
331 026	**NR**	E			463026	464026	466026	
331 027	**NR**	E			463027	464027	466027	
331 028	**NR**	E			463028	464028	466028	
331 029	**NR**	E			463029	464029	466029	
331 030	**NR**	E			463030	464030	466030	
331 031	**NR**	E			463031	464031	466031	

Class 331/1. DMS–PTS–TS–DMS. 4-car units.

DMS. CAF Zaragoza/Newport 2017–19. –/45(+8) 1TD 2W. 40.8 t.
PTS. CAF Zaragoza/Newport 2017–19. –/76(+4). 34.9 t.
TS. CAF Zaragoza/Newport 2017–19. –/76(+4). 30.1 t.
DMS. CAF Zaragoza/Newport 2017–19. –/63(+7). 39.8 t.

331 101	**NR**	E	*NO*	NL	463101	464101	465101	466101
331 102	**NR**	E	*NO*	AN	463102	464102	465102	466102
331 103	**NR**	E	*NO*	AN	463103	464103	465103	466103
331 104	**NR**	E	*NO*	NL	463104	464104	465104	466104
331 105	**NR**	E	*NO*	AN	463105	464105	465105	466105
331 106	**NR**	E	*NO*	NL	463106	464106	465106	466106
331 107	**NR**	E	*NO*	AN	463107	464107	465107	466107
331 108	**NR**	E	*NO*	NL	463108	464108	465108	466108
331 109	**NR**	E	*NO*	NL	463109	464109	465109	466109
331 110	**NR**	E	*NO*	NL	463110	464110	465110	466110
331 111	**NR**	E	*NO*	AN	463111	464111	465111	466111
331 112	**NR**	E	*NO*	AN	463112	464112	465112	466112

Names (carried on driving cars):

331 106 Proud to be Northern | 331 110 Proud to be Northern

CLASS 332 HEATHROW EXPRESS CAF/SIEMENS

Dedicated Heathrow Express units. Five units were increased from 4-car to 5-car in 2002. Operate in coupled pairs at peak times. This class is unique in not being fitted with TPWS equipment (as the route operated is ATP only).

Formation: DMS–TS–PTS–(TS)–DMF.
Construction: Steel.
Traction Motors: Two Siemens monomotors asynchronous of 350 kW.
Wheel Arrangement: B-B + 2-2 + 2-2 (+ 2-2) + B-B.
Braking: Disc.
Bogies: CAF.
Gangways: Within unit.
Doors: Sliding plug.
Dimensions: 23.74/23.35/23.14 x 2.75 m.
Couplers: Scharfenberg 10L.
Control System: IGBT Inverter.
Maximum Speed: 100 mph.

Heating & ventilation: Air conditioning.
Seating: 1: 1+1 facing/unidirectional, 2: 2+2 mainly unidirectional.
Multiple Working: Within class.

Advertising livery: Tata Communications (various colours).

DMS. CAF 1997–98. –/43(+8). 49.9 t.
72400–413. TS. CAF 1997–98. –/64(+11). 38.4 t.
PTS. CAF 1997–98. –/39(+11) 1TD 2W. 47.6 t.
72414–418. TS. CAF 2002. –/56 35.8 t.
DMF. CAF 1997–98. 20/–. 49.5 t.

332001	**AL**	HE	*HE*	OH	78400	72412	63400		78401
332002	**AL**	HE	*HE*	OH	78402	72409	63406		78403
332003	**AL**	HE	*HE*	OH	78404	72407	63402		78405
332004	**AL**	HE	*HE*	OH	78406	72405	63403		78407
332005	**AL**	HE	*HE*	OH	78408	72411	63404	72417	78409
332006	**AL**	HE	*HE*	OH	78410	72410	63405	72415	78411
332007	**AL**	HE	*HE*	OH	78412	72401	63401	72414	78413
332008	**AL**	HE	*HE*	OH	78414	72413	63407	72418	78415
332009	**AL**	HE	*HE*	OH	78416	72400	63408	72416	78417
332010	**AL**	HE	*HE*	OH	78418	72402	63409		78419
332011	**AL**	HE	*HE*	OH	78420	72403	63410		78421
332012	**AL**	HE	*HE*	OH	78422	72404	63411		78423
332013	**AL**	HE	*HE*	OH	78424	72408	63412		78425
332014	**AL**	HE		OH	78426	72406	63413		78427

CLASS 333 CAF/SIEMENS

West Yorkshire area suburban units.

Formation: DMS–PTS–TS–DMS.
Construction: Steel.
Traction Motors: Two Siemens monomotors asynchronous of 350 kW.
Wheel Arrangement: B-B + 2-2 + 2-2 + B-B.
Braking: Disc.
Bogies: CAF.
Gangways: Within unit.
Doors: Sliding plug.
Heating & ventilation: Air conditioning.
Dimensions: 23.74/23.35 x 2.75 m.
Couplers: Dellner 10L.
Control System: IGBT Inverter.
Maximum Speed: 100 mph.
Multiple Working: Within class.
Seating Layout: 3+2 facing/unidirectional.

333001–008 were made up to 4-car units from 3-car units in 2002.

333009–016 were made up to 4-car units from 3-car units in 2003.

DMS(A). (odd Nos.) CAF Zaragoza 2001. –/90. 50.0 t.
PTS. CAF Zaragoza 2001. –/73(+7) 1TD 2W. 46.0 t.
TS. CAF Zaragoza 2002–03. –/100. 38.5 t.
DMS(B). (even Nos.) CAF Zaragoza 2001. –/90. 50.0 t.

333001	**NR**	A	*NO*	NL	78451	74461	74477	78452
333002	**NR**	A	*NO*	NL	78453	74462	74478	78454
333003	**NR**	A	*NO*	NL	78455	74463	74479	78456
333004	**NR**	A	*NO*	NL	78457	74464	74480	78458

333005	**YR**	A	*NO*	NL	78459	74465	74481	78460
333006	**YR**	A	*NO*	NL	78461	74466	74482	78462
333007	**NR**	A	*NO*	NL	78463	74467	74483	78464
333008	**NR**	A	*NO*	NL	78465	74468	74484	78466
333009	**NR**	A	*NO*	NL	78467	74469	74485	78468
333010	**NR**	A	*NO*	NL	78469	74470	74486	78470
333011	**NR**	A	*NO*	NL	78471	74471	74487	78472
333012	**NR**	A	*NO*	NL	78473	74472	74488	78474
333013	**NR**	A	*NO*	NL	78475	74473	74489	78476
333014	**NR**	A	*NO*	NL	78477	74474	74490	78478
333015	**NR**	A	*NO*	NL	78479	74475	74491	78480
333016	**YR**	A	*NO*	NL	78481	74476	74492	78482

CLASS 334 JUNIPER ALSTOM BIRMINGHAM

Outer suburban units.

Formation: DMS–PTS–DMS.
Construction: Steel.
Traction Motors: Two Alstom ONIX 800 asynchronous of 270 kW.
Wheel Arrangement: 2-Bo + 2-2 + Bo-2.
Braking: Disc.
Dimensions: 21.01/19.94 x 2.80 m.
Bogies: Alstom LTB3/TBP3.
Couplers: Dellner.
Gangways: Within unit.
Control System: IGBT Inverter.
Doors: Sliding plug.
Maximum Speed: 90 mph.
Heating & ventilation: Air conditioning.
Seating Layout: 2+2 facing/unidirectional (3+2 in PTS).
Multiple Working: Within class.

DMS(A). Alstom Birmingham 1999–2001. –/64. 42.6 t.
PTS. Alstom Birmingham 1999–2001. –/55 1TD 1W. 39.4 t.
DMS(B). Alstom Birmingham 1999–2001. –/59(+3). 42.6 t.

334001	**SR**	E	*SR*	GW	64101	74301	65101
334002	**SR**	E	*SR*	GW	64102	74302	65102
334003	**SR**	E	*SR*	GW	64103	74303	65103
334004	**SR**	E	*SR*	GW	64104	74304	65104
334005	**SR**	E	*SR*	GW	64105	74305	65105
334006	**SR**	E	*SR*	GW	64106	74306	65106
334007	**SR**	E	*SR*	GW	64107	74307	65107
334008	**SR**	E	*SR*	GW	64108	74308	65108
334009	**SR**	E	*SR*	GW	64109	74309	65109
334010	**SR**	E	*SR*	GW	64110	74310	65110
334011	**SR**	E	*SR*	GW	64111	74311	65111
334012	**SR**	E	*SR*	GW	64112	74312	65112
334013	**SR**	E	*SR*	GW	64113	74313	65113
334014	**SR**	E	*SR*	GW	64114	74314	65114
334015	**SR**	E	*SR*	GW	64115	74315	65115
334016	**SR**	E	*SR*	GW	64116	74316	65116
334017	**SR**	E	*SR*	GW	64117	74317	65117
334018	**SR**	E	*SR*	GW	64118	74318	65118
334019	**SR**	E	*SR*	GW	64119	74319	65119

334020	**SR**	E	*SR*	GW	64120	74320	65120
334021	**SR**	E	*SR*	GW	64121	74321	65121
334022	**SR**	E	*SR*	GW	64122	74322	65122
334023	**SR**	E	*SR*	GW	64123	74323	65123
334024	**SR**	E	*SR*	GW	64124	74324	65124
334025	**SR**	E	*SR*	GW	64125	74325	65125
334026	**SR**	E	*SR*	GW	64126	74326	65126
334027	**SR**	E	*SR*	GW	64127	74327	65127
334028	**SR**	E	*SR*	GW	64128	74328	65128
334029	**SR**	E	*SR*	GW	64129	74329	65129
334030	**SR**	E	*SR*	GW	64130	74330	65130
334031	**SR**	E	*SR*	GW	64131	74331	65131
334032	**SR**	E	*SR*	GW	64132	74332	65132
334033	**SR**	E	*SR*	GW	64133	74333	65133
334034	**SR**	E	*SR*	GW	64134	74334	65134
334035	**SR**	E	*SR*	GW	64135	74335	65135
334036	**SR**	E	*SR*	GW	64136	74336	65136
334037	**SR**	E	*SR*	GW	64137	74337	65137
334038	**SR**	E	*SR*	GW	64138	74338	65138
334039	**SR**	E	*SR*	GW	64139	74339	65139
334040	**SR**	E	*SR*	GW	64140	74340	65140

CLASS 345 AVENTRA BOMBARDIER DERBY

These 9-car units are being delivered for London's Crossrail/Elizabeth Line. Some units are in service as 7-car units, both on services between Liverpool Street and Shenfield and from Paddington to Hayes & Harlington and Reading ahead of the heavily delayed opening of the full Elizabeth Line, now not expected until summer 2021. By late 2019 the whole fleet had been built, but with many units stored at Old Oak Common, Old Dalby, Worksop or Derby.

The design is marketed as "Aventra" by Bombardier and is a development on the successful Electrostar design. There is an option for a further 14 9-car units.

Formation: DMS–PMS–MS–MS*–TS–MS*–MS–PMS–DMS.
* Initially these MS vehicles are missing from some units. For units in traffic that are missing these vehicles, the missing vehicles are shown in *italics*.
System: 25 kV AC overhead.
Construction: Aluminium.
Traction Motors: Two Bombardier asynchronous of 265 kW.
Wheel Arrangement: 2-Bo + Bo-2 + Bo-Bo (+ Bo-2) + 2-2 (+ 2-Bo) + Bo-Bo + 2-Bo + Bo-2.
Braking: Disc & regenerative.
Bogies: FLEXX B5000 inside-frame.
Gangways: Within unit.
Doors: Sliding plug (three per vehicle).
Dimensions: 23.62/22.50 m x 2.78 m.
Couplers: Dellner.
Control System: IGBT Inverter.
Maximum Speed: 90 mph.
Heating & ventilation: Air conditioning.
Seating Layout: Mostly longitudinal, with some 2+2 facing.
Multiple Working: Within class.

DMS(A). Bombardier Derby 2015–19. –/46. 39.0 t.
PMS(A). Bombardier Derby 2015–19. –/46(+6). 37.1 t.
MS(A). Bombardier Derby 2015–19. –/46(+6). 36.5 t.
MS(B). Bombardier Derby 2015–19. –/49(+3). 31.4 t.
TS. Bombardier Derby 2015–19. –/38(+12). 29.7 t.
MS(C). Bombardier Derby 2015–19. –/49(+3). 31.4 t.
MS(D). Bombardier Derby 2015–19. –/46(+6). 37.2 t.
PMS(B). Bombardier Derby 2015–19. –/46(+6). 37.1 t.
DMS(B). Bombardier Derby 2015–19. –/46. 39.0 t.

345001	**XR**	XR			340101	340201	340301	340401	340501	340601	340701	340801	340901
345002	**XR**	XR			340102	340202	340302	340402	340502	340602	340702	340802	340902
345003	**XR**	XR	*XR*	OC	340103	340203	340303	*340403*	340503	*340603*	340703	340803	340903
345004	**XR**	XR			340104	340204	340304	340404	340504	340604	340704	340804	340904
345005	**XR**	XR	*XR*	OC	340105	340205	340305	*340405*	340505	*340605*	340705	340805	340905
345006	**XR**	XR	*XR*	OC	340106	340206	340306	*340406*	340506	*340606*	340706	340806	340906
345007	**XR**	XR	*XR*	OC	340107	340207	340307	*340407*	340507	*340607*	340707	340807	340907
345008	**XR**	XR	*XR*	OC	340108	340208	340308	*340408*	340508	*340608*	340708	340808	340908
345009	**XR**	XR	*XR*	OC	340109	340209	340309	*340409*	340509	*340609*	340709	340809	340909
345010	**XR**	XR	*XR*	OC	340110	340210	340310	*340410*	340510	*340610*	340710	340810	340910
345011	**XR**	XR	*XR*	OC	340111	340211	340311	*340411*	340511	*340611*	340711	340811	340911
345012	**XR**	XR	*XR*	OC	340112	340212	340312	*340412*	340512	*340612*	340712	340812	340912
345013	**XR**	XR	*XR*	OC	340113	340213	340313	*340413*	340513	*340613*	340713	340813	340913
345014	**XR**	XR	*XR*	OC	340114	340214	340314	*340414*	340514	*340614*	340714	340814	340914
345015	**XR**	XR	*XR*	OC	340115	340215	340315	*340415*	340515	*340615*	340715	340815	340915
345016	**XR**	XR	*XR*	OC	340116	340216	340316	*340416*	340516	*340616*	340716	340816	340916
345017	**XR**	XR	*XR*	OC	340117	340217	340317	*340417*	340517	*340617*	340717	340817	340917
345018	**XR**	XR			340118	340218	340318	340418	340518	340618	340718	340818	340918
345019	**XR**	XR			340119	340219	340319	340419	340519	340619	340719	340819	340919
345020	**XR**	XR	*XR*	OC	340120	340220	340320	*340420*	340520	*340620*	340720	340820	340920

345021	**XR**	XR			340121	340221	340321	340421	340521
					340621	340721	340821	340921	
345022	**XR**	XR	*XR*	OC	340122	340222	340322	*340422*	340522
					340622	340722	340822	340922	
345023	**XR**	XR		WS(S)	340123	340223	340323	340423	340523
					340623	340723	340823	340923	
345024	**XR**	XR			340124	340224	340324	340424	340524
					340624	340724	340824	340924	
345025	**XR**	XR			340125	340225	340325	340425	340525
					340625	340725	340825	340925	
345026	**XR**	XR		WS(S)	340126	340226	340326	340426	340526
					340626	340726	340826	340926	
345027	**XR**	XR	*XR*	OC	340127	340227	340327	340427	340527
					340627	340727	340827	340927	
345028	**XR**	XR	*XR*	OC	340128	340228	340328	340428	340528
					340628	340728	340828	340928	
345029	**XR**	XR	*XR*	OC	340129	340229	340329	*340429*	340529
					340629	340729	340829	340929	
345030	**XR**	XR	*XR*	OC	340130	340230	340330	340430	340530
					340630	340730	340830	340930	
345031	**XR**	XR			340131	340231	340331	340431	340531
					340631	340731	340831	340931	
345032	**XR**	XR			340132	340232	340332	340432	340532
					340632	340732	340832	340932	
345033	**XR**	XR			340133	340233	340333	340433	340533
					340633	340733	340833	340933	
345034	**XR**	XR	*XR*	OC	340134	340234	340334	340434	340534
					340634	340734	340834	340934	
345035	**XR**	XR	*XR*	OC	340135	340235	340335	340435	340535
					340635	340735	340835	340935	
345036	**XR**	XR			340136	340236	340336	340436	340536
					340636	340736	340836	340936	
345037	**XR**	XR	*XR*	OC	340137	340237	340337	340437	340537
					340637	340737	340837	340937	
345038	**XR**	XR	*XR*	OC	340138	340238	340338	*340438*	340538
					340638	340738	340838	340938	
345039	**XR**	XR	*XR*	OC	340139	340239	340339	*340439*	340539
					340639	340739	340839	340939	
345040	**XR**	XR	*XR*	OC	340140	340240	340340	*340440*	340540
					340640	340740	340840	340940	
345041	**XR**	XR			340141	340241	340341	340441	340541
					340641	340741	340841	340941	
345042	**XR**	XR	*XR*	OC	340142	340242	340342	*340442*	340542
					340642	340742	340842	340942	
345043	**XR**	XR			340143	340243	340343	340443	340543
					340643	340743	340843	340943	
345044	**XR**	XR	*XR*	OC	340144	340244	340344	*340444*	340544
					340644	340744	340844	340944	
345045	**XR**	XR		WS(S)	340145	340245	340345	340445	340545
					340645	340745	340845	340945	

345 046	**XR**	XR		WS(S)	340146	340246	340346	340446	340546
					340646	340746	340846	340946	
345 047	**XR**	XR	*XR*	OC	340147	340247	340347	*340447*	340547
					340647	340747	340847	340947	
345 048	**XR**	XR		WS(S)	340148	340248	340348	340448	340548
					340648	340748	340848	340948	
345 049	**XR**	XR	*XR*	OC	340149	340249	340349	*340449*	340549
					340649	340749	340849	340949	
345 050	**XR**	XR			340150	340250	340350	340450	340550
					340650	340750	340850	340950	
345 051	**XR**	XR	*XR*	OC	340151	340251	340351	*340451*	340551
					340651	340751	340851	340951	
345 052	**XR**	XR	*XR*	OC	340152	340252	340352	*340452*	340552
					340652	340752	340852	340952	
345 053	**XR**	XR			340153	340253	340353	340453	340553
					340653	340753	340853	340953	
345 054	**XR**	XR			340154	340254	340354	340454	340554
					340654	340754	340854	340954	
345 055	**XR**	XR	*XR*	OC	340155	340255	340355	*340455*	340555
					340655	340755	340855	340955	
345 056	**XR**	XR	*XR*	OC	340156	340256	340356	*340456*	340556
					340656	340756	340856	340956	
345 057	**XR**	XR	*XR*	OC	340157	340257	340357	*340457*	340557
					340657	340757	340857	340957	
345 058	**XR**	XR			340158	340258	340358	340458	340558
					340658	340758	340858	340958	
345 059	**XR**	XR	*XR*	OC	340159	340259	340359	*340459*	340559
					340659	340759	340859	340959	
345 060	**XR**	XR		WS(S)	340160	340260	340360	340460	340560
					340660	340760	340860	340960	
345 061	**XR**	XR		WS(S)	340161	340261	340361	340461	340561
					340661	340761	340861	340961	
345 062	**XR**	XR	*XR*	OC	340162	340262	340362	*340462*	340562
					340662	340762	340862	340962	
345 063	**XR**	XR	*XR*	OC	340163	340263	340363	*340463*	340563
					340663	340763	340863	340963	
345 064	**XR**	XR	*XR*	OC	340164	340264	340364	*340464*	340564
					340664	340764	340864	340964	
345 065	**XR**	XR	*XR*	OC	340165	340265	340365	*340465*	340565
					340665	340765	340865	340965	
345 066	**XR**	XR	*XR*	OC	340166	340266	340366	*340466*	340566
					340666	340766	340866	340966	
345 067	**XR**	XR			340167	340267	340367	340467	340567
					340667	340767	340867	340967	
345 068	**XR**	XR			340168	340268	340368	340468	340568
					340668	340768	340868	340968	
345 069	**XR**	XR			340169	340269	340369	340469	340569
					340669	340769	340869	340969	
345 070	**XR**	XR			340170	340270	340370	340470	340570
					340670	340770	340870	340970	

CLASS 350 DESIRO UK SIEMENS

Outer suburban and long distance units.

Formation: DMC–TC–PTS–DMC.
Systems: 25 kV AC overhead (350/1s built with 750 V DC, but equipment currently decommissioned).
Construction: Welded aluminium.
Traction Motors: 4 Siemens 1TB2016-0GB02 asynchronous of 250 kW.
Wheel Arrangement: Bo-Bo + 2-2 + 2-2 + Bo-Bo.
Braking: Disc & regenerative.
Bogies: SGP SF5000.
Gangways: Throughout.
Doors: Sliding plug.
Dimensions: 20.34 x 2.79 m.
Couplers: Dellner 12.
Control System: IGBT Inverter.
Maximum Speed: 110 mph.
Heating & ventilation: Air conditioning.
Seating Layout: Various, see sub-class headings.
Multiple Working: Within class.

Class 350/1. Original-build units owned by Angel Trains. Formerly part of an aborted South West Trains 5-car Class 450/2 order. 2+2 seating.

Seating Layout: 1: 2+2 facing, 2: 2+2 facing/unidirectional.

Non-standard and advertising liveries:

350 101/102/104/106/115/116/123/129/130 Grey with green doors.
350 110 Project 110 (silver centre cars).

* Refurbished. Guard's office removed in TC vehicle with extra luggage racks in its place.

DMS(A). Siemens Krefeld 2004–05. –/60. 48.7 t.
TC. Siemens Krefeld/Prague 2004–05. 24/32 1T. 36.2 t.
PTS. Siemens Krefeld/Prague 2004–05. –/50(+9) 1TD 2W. 45.2 t.
DMS(B). Siemens Krefeld 2004–05. –/60. 49.2 t.

350 101	*	**0**	A	*WM*	NN	63761	66811	66861	63711
350 102		**0**	A	*WM*	NN	63762	66812	66862	63712
350 103		**LM**	A	*WM*	NN	63765	66813	66863	63713
350 104		**0**	A	*WM*	NN	63764	66814	66864	63714
350 105		**LM**	A	*WM*	NN	63763	66815	66868	63715
350 106	*	**0**	A	*WM*	NN	63766	66816	66866	63716
350 107		**LM**	A	*WM*	NN	63767	66817	66867	63717
350 108		**LM**	A	*WM*	NN	63768	66818	66865	63718
350 109		**LM**	A	*WM*	NN	63769	66819	66869	63719
350 110	*	**AL**	A	*WM*	NN	63770	66820	66870	63720
350 111		**LM**	A	*WM*	NN	63771	66821	66871	63721
350 112		**LM**	A	*WM*	NN	63772	66822	66872	63722
350 113	*	**LM**	A	*WM*	NN	63773	66823	66873	63723
350 114		**LM**	A	*WM*	NN	63774	66824	66874	63724
350 115	*	**0**	A	*WM*	NN	63775	66825	66875	63725
350 116	*	**0**	A	*WM*	NN	63776	66826	66876	63726
350 117		**LM**	A	*WM*	NN	63777	66827	66877	63727
350 118		**LM**	A	*WM*	NN	63778	66828	66878	63728

350 119		**LM**	A	*WM*	NN	63779	66829	66879	63729
350 120		**LM**	A	*WM*	NN	63780	66830	66880	63730
350 121		**LM**	A	*WM*	NN	63781	66831	66881	63731
350 122		**LM**	A	*WM*	NN	63782	66832	66882	63732
350 123	*	**0**	A	*WM*	NN	63783	66833	66883	63733
350 124		**LM**	A	*WM*	NN	63784	66834	66884	63734
350 125		**LM**	A	*WM*	NN	63785	66835	66885	63735
350 126		**LM**	A	*WM*	NN	63786	66836	66886	63736
350 127		**LM**	A	*WM*	NN	63787	66837	66887	63737
350 128		**LM**	A	*WM*	NN	63788	66838	66888	63738
350 129	*	**0**	A	*WM*	NN	63789	66839	66889	63739
350 130	*	**0**	A	*WM*	NN	63790	66840	66890	63740

Class 350/2. Owned by Porterbrook Leasing.

Seating Layout: 1: 2+2 facing, 2: 3+2 facing/unidirectional.

At the time of writing sets 350 233/246/264 are running with misformed formations, as shown.

DMS(A). Siemens Krefeld 2008–09. –/70. 43.7 t.
TC. Siemens Prague 2008–09. 24/42 1T. 35.3 t.
PTS. Siemens Prague 2008–09. –/61(+9) 1TD 2W. 42.9 t.
DMS(B). Siemens Krefeld 2008–09. –/70. 44.2 t.

350 231	**LI**	P	*WM*	NN	61431	65231	67531	61531
350 232	**LI**	P	*WM*	NN	61432	65232	67532	61532
350 233	**LM**	P	*WM*	NN	61433	65233	67533	61546
350 234	**LI**	P	*WM*	NN	61434	65234	67534	61534
350 235	**LM**	P	*WM*	NN	61435	65235	67535	61535
350 236	**LM**	P	*WM*	NN	61436	65236	67536	61536
350 237	**LM**	P	*WM*	NN	61437	65237	67537	61537
350 238	**LM**	P	*WM*	NN	61438	65238	67538	61538
350 239	**LI**	P	*WM*	NN	61439	65239	67539	61539
350 240	**LI**	P	*WM*	NN	61440	65240	67540	61540
350 241	**LM**	P	*WM*	NN	61441	65241	67541	61541
350 242	**LM**	P	*WM*	NN	61442	65242	67542	61542
350 243	**LM**	P	*WM*	NN	61443	65243	67543	61543
350 244	**LI**	P	*WM*	NN	61444	65244	67544	61544
350 245	**LI**	P	*WM*	NN	61445	65245	67545	61545
350 246	**LM**	P	*WM*	NN	61446	65246	67546	61564
350 247	**LM**	P	*WM*	NN	61447	65247	67547	61547
350 248	**LM**	P	*WM*	NN	61448	65248	67548	61548
350 249	**LM**	P	*WM*	NN	61449	65249	67549	61549
350 250	**LM**	P	*WM*	NN	61450	65250	67550	61550
350 251	**LM**	P	*WM*	NN	61451	65251	67551	61551
350 252	**LI**	P	*WM*	NN	61452	65252	67552	61552
350 253	**LI**	P	*WM*	NN	61453	65253	67553	61553
350 254	**LI**	P	*WM*	NN	61454	65254	67554	61554
350 255	**LM**	P	*WM*	NN	61455	65255	67555	61555
350 256	**LM**	P	*WM*	NN	61456	65256	67556	61556
350 257	**LI**	P	*WM*	NN	61457	65257	67557	61557
350 258	**LI**	P	*WM*	NN	61458	65258	67558	61558

350 259	**LI**	P	*WM*	NN	61459	65259	67559	61559
350 260	**LM**	P	*WM*	NN	61460	65260	67560	61560
350 261	**LM**	P	*WM*	NN	61461	65261	67561	61561
350 262	**LI**	P	*WM*	NN	61462	65262	67562	61562
350 263	**LI**	P	*WM*	NN	61463	65263	67563	61563
350 264	**LM**	P	*WM*	NN	61464	65264	67564	61533
350 265	**LM**	P	*WM*	NN	61465	65265	67565	61565
350 266	**LM**	P	*WM*	NN	61466	65266	67566	61566
350 267	**LI**	P	*WM*	NN	61467	65267	67567	61567

Class 350/3. Owned by Angel Trains.

Seating Layout: 1: 2+2 facing, 2: 2+2 facing/unidirectional.

DMS(A). Siemens Krefeld 2014. –/60. 44.2 t.
TC. Siemens Krefeld 2014. 24/36 1T. 36.3 t.
PTS. Siemens Krefeld 2014. –/50(+9) 1TD 2W. 44.0 t.
DMS(B). Siemens Krefeld 2014. –/60. 45.0 t.

350 368	**LN**	A	*WM*	NN	60141	60511	60651	60151
350 369	**LN**	A	*WM*	NN	60142	60512	60652	60152
350 370	**LN**	A	*WM*	NN	60143	60513	60653	60153
350 371	**LN**	A	*WM*	NN	60144	60514	60654	60154
350 372	**LN**	A	*WM*	NN	60145	60515	60655	60155
350 373	**LN**	A	*WM*	NN	60146	60516	60656	60156
350 374	**LN**	A	*WM*	NN	60147	60517	60657	60157
350 375	**LN**	A	*WM*	NN	60148	60518	60658	60158
350 376	**LN**	A	*WM*	NN	60149	60519	60659	60159
350 377	**LN**	A	*WM*	NN	60150	60520	60660	60160

Names (carried on one side of PTS):

350 375 Vic Hall
350 377 Graham Taylor OBE

Class 350/4. Owned by Angel Trains. Units still operated by TransPennine Express will transfer to West Midlands Trains in early 2020.

Seating Layout: 1: 2+1 facing, 2: 2+2 facing/unidirectional.

DMS(A). Siemens Krefeld 2013–14. –/56. 44.2 t.
TC. Siemens Krefeld 2013–14. 19/24 1T. 36.2 t.
PTS. Siemens Krefeld 2013–14. –/42 1TD 1T. 44.6 t.
DMS(B). Siemens Krefeld 2013–14. –/56. 45.0 t.

350 401	**LN**	A	*WM*	NN	60691	60901	60941	60671
350 402	**TP**	A	*TP*	AK	60692	60902	60942	60672
350 403	**LN**	A	*TP*	AK	60693	60903	60943	60673
350 404	**LN**	A	*WM*	NN	60694	60904	60944	60674
350 405	**LN**	A	*WM*	NN	60695	60905	60945	60675
350 406	**LN**	A	*TP*	AK	60696	60906	60946	60676
350 407	**LN**	A	*TP*	AK	60697	60907	60947	60677
350 408	**TP**	A	*TP*	AK	60698	60908	60948	60678
350 409	**TP**	A	*TP*	AK	60699	60909	60949	60679
350 410	**LN**	A	*WM*	NN	60700	60910	60950	60680

CLASS 357 ELECTROSTAR
ADTRANZ/BOMBARDIER DERBY

Provision for 750 V DC supply if required.

Formation: DMS–MS–PTS–DMS.
Construction: Welded aluminium alloy underframe, sides and roof with steel ends. All sections bolted together.
Traction Motors: Two Adtranz asynchronous of 250 kW.
Wheel Arrangement: 2-Bo + 2-Bo + 2-2 + Bo-2.
Braking: Disc & regenerative.
Bogies: Adtranz P3-25/T3-25.
Gangways: Within unit.
Doors: Sliding plug.
Dimensions: 20.40/19.99 x 2.80 m.
Couplers: Tightlock.
Control System: IGBT Inverter.
Maximum Speed: 100 mph.
Heating & ventilation: Air conditioning.
Seating Layout: 3+2 facing/unidirectional.
Multiple Working: Within class.

Class 357/0. Owned by Porterbrook Leasing.

DMS(A). Adtranz Derby 1999–2001. –/71. 40.7 t.
MS. Adtranz Derby 1999–2001. –/78. 36.7 t.
PTS. Adtranz Derby 1999–2001. –/58(+4) 1TD 2W. 39.5 t.
DMS(B). Adtranz Derby 1999–2001. –/71. 40.7 t.

357 001	**C2**	P	*C2*	EM	67651	74151	74051	67751
357 002	**C2**	P	*C2*	EM	67652	74152	74052	67752
357 003	**C2**	P	*C2*	EM	67653	74153	74053	67753
357 004	**C2**	P	*C2*	EM	67654	74154	74054	67754
357 005	**C2**	P	*C2*	EM	67655	74155	74055	67755
357 006	**C2**	P	*C2*	EM	67656	74156	74056	67756
357 007	**C2**	P	*C2*	EM	67657	74157	74057	67757
357 008	**C2**	P	*C2*	EM	67658	74158	74058	67758
357 009	**C2**	P	*C2*	EM	67659	74159	74059	67759
357 010	**C2**	P	*C2*	EM	67660	74160	74060	67760
357 011	**C2**	P	*C2*	EM	67661	74161	74061	67761
357 012	**C2**	P	*C2*	EM	67662	74162	74062	67762
357 013	**C2**	P	*C2*	EM	67663	74163	74063	67763
357 014	**C2**	P	*C2*	EM	67664	74164	74064	67764
357 015	**C2**	P	*C2*	EM	67665	74165	74065	67765
357 016	**C2**	P	*C2*	EM	67666	74166	74066	67766
357 017	**C2**	P	*C2*	EM	67667	74167	74067	67767
357 018	**C2**	P	*C2*	EM	67668	74168	74068	67768
357 019	**C2**	P	*C2*	EM	67669	74169	74069	67769
357 020	**C2**	P	*C2*	EM	67670	74170	74070	67770
357 021	**C2**	P	*C2*	EM	67671	74171	74071	67771
357 022	**C2**	P	*C2*	EM	67672	74172	74072	67772
357 023	**C2**	P	*C2*	EM	67673	74173	74073	67773
357 024	**C2**	P	*C2*	EM	67674	74174	74074	67774
357 025	**C2**	P	*C2*	EM	67675	74175	74075	67775
357 026	**C2**	P	*C2*	EM	67676	74176	74076	67776
357 027	**C2**	P	*C2*	EM	67677	74177	74077	67777

357 028	**C2**	P	*C2*	EM	67678	74178	74078	67778
357 029	**C2**	P	*C2*	EM	67679	74179	74079	67779
357 030	**C2**	P	*C2*	EM	67680	74180	74080	67780
357 031	**C2**	P	*C2*	EM	67681	74181	74081	67781
357 032	**C2**	P	*C2*	EM	67682	74182	74082	67782
357 033	**C2**	P	*C2*	EM	67683	74183	74083	67783
357 034	**C2**	P	*C2*	EM	67684	74184	74084	67784
357 035	**C2**	P	*C2*	EM	67685	74185	74085	67785
357 036	**C2**	P	*C2*	EM	67686	74186	74086	67786
357 037	**C2**	P	*C2*	EM	67687	74187	74087	67787
357 038	**C2**	P	*C2*	EM	67688	74188	74088	67788
357 039	**C2**	P	*C2*	EM	67689	74189	74089	67789
357 040	**C2**	P	*C2*	EM	67690	74190	74090	67790
357 041	**C2**	P	*C2*	EM	67691	74191	74091	67791
357 042	**C2**	P	*C2*	EM	67692	74192	74092	67792
357 043	**C2**	P	*C2*	EM	67693	74193	74093	67793
357 044	**C2**	P	*C2*	EM	67694	74194	74094	67794
357 045	**C2**	P	*C2*	EM	67695	74195	74095	67795
357 046	**C2**	P	*C2*	EM	67696	74196	74096	67796

Names (carried on DMS(A) and DMS(B) (one plate on each)):

357 001 BARRY FLAXMAN
357 002 ARTHUR LEWIS STRIDE 1841–1922
357 003 SOUTHEND city.on.sea
357 004 TONY AMOS
357 005 SOUTHEND: 2017 Alternative City of Culture
357 006 DIAMOND JUBILEE 1952–2012
357 007 Sir Andrew Foster
357 011 JOHN LOWING
357 018 Remembering our Fallen 88 1914–1918
357 028 London, Tilbury & Southend Railway 1854–2004
357 029 THOMAS WHITELEGG 1840–1922
357 030 ROBERT HARBEN WHITELEGG 1871–1957

Class 357/2. Owned by Angel Trains.

DMS(A). Bombardier Derby 2001–02. –/71. 40.7 t.
MS. Bombardier Derby 2001–02. –/78. 36.7 t.
PTS. Bombardier Derby 2001–02. –/58(+4) 1TD 2W. 39.5 t.
DMS(B). Bombardier Derby 2001–02. –/71. 40.7 t.

357 201	**C2**	A	*C2*	EM	68601	74701	74601	68701
357 202	**C2**	A	*C2*	EM	68602	74702	74602	68702
357 203	**C2**	A	*C2*	EM	68603	74703	74603	68703
357 204	**C2**	A	*C2*	EM	68604	74704	74604	68704
357 205	**C2**	A	*C2*	EM	68605	74705	74605	68705
357 206	**C2**	A	*C2*	EM	68606	74706	74606	68706
357 207	**C2**	A	*C2*	EM	68607	74707	74607	68707
357 208	**C2**	A	*C2*	EM	68608	74708	74608	68708
357 209	**C2**	A	*C2*	EM	68609	74709	74609	68709
357 210	**C2**	A	*C2*	EM	68610	74710	74610	68710
357 211	**C2**	A	*C2*	EM	68611	74711	74611	68711

Names (carried on DMS(A) and DMS(B) (one plate on each)):

357 201 KEN BIRD
357 202 KENNY MITCHELL
357 203 HENRY PUMFRETT
357 204 DEREK FOWERS
357 205 JOHN D'SILVA
357 206 MARTIN AUNGIER
357 207 JOHN PAGE
357 208 DAVE DAVIS
357 209 JAMES SNELLING

Class 357/3. Owned by Angel Trains. In 2015–16 17 Class 357/2s (357 212–228) were reconfigured as "high density" units 357 312–328 with fewer seats and more standing room for shorter distance workings.

Seating Layout: 2+2 facing/unidirectional.

DMS(A). Bombardier Derby 2001–02. –/56. 40.7 t.
MS. Bombardier Derby 2001–02. –/60. 36.7 t.
PTS. Bombardier Derby 2001–02. –/50 1TD 2W. 39.5 t.
DMS(B). Bombardier Derby 2001–02. –/56. 40.7 t.

357 312	(357 212)	**C2**	A	*C2*	EM	68612	74712	74612	68712
357 313	(357 213)	**C2**	A	*C2*	EM	68613	74713	74613	68713
357 314	(357 214)	**C2**	A	*C2*	EM	68614	74714	74614	68714
357 315	(357 215)	**C2**	A	*C2*	EM	68615	74715	74615	68715
357 316	(357 216)	**C2**	A	*C2*	EM	68616	74716	74616	68716
357 317	(357 217)	**C2**	A	*C2*	EM	68617	74717	74617	68717
357 318	(357 218)	**C2**	A	*C2*	EM	68618	74718	74618	68718
357 319	(357 219)	**C2**	A	*C2*	EM	68619	74719	74619	68719
357 320	(357 220)	**C2**	A	*C2*	EM	68620	74720	74620	68720
357 321	(357 221)	**C2**	A	*C2*	EM	68621	74721	74621	68721
357 322	(357 222)	**C2**	A	*C2*	EM	68622	74722	74622	68722
357 323	(357 223)	**C2**	A	*C2*	EM	68623	74723	74623	68723
357 324	(357 224)	**C2**	A	*C2*	EM	68624	74724	74624	68724
357 325	(357 225)	**C2**	A	*C2*	EM	68625	74725	74625	68725
357 326	(357 226)	**C2**	A	*C2*	EM	68626	74726	74626	68726
357 327	(357 227)	**C2**	A	*C2*	EM	68627	74727	74627	68727
357 328	(357 228)	**C2**	A	*C2*	EM	68628	74728	74628	68728

Names (carried on DMS(A) and DMS(B) (one plate on each)):

357 313 UPMINSTER I.E.C.C.
357 317 ALLAN BURNELL
357 327 SOUTHEND UNITED

CLASS 360/0 DESIRO UK SIEMENS

Outer suburban/express units.

Formation: DMC–PTS–TS–DMC.
Construction: Welded aluminium.
Traction Motors: Four Siemens 1TB2016-0GB02 asynchronous of 250 kW.
Wheel Arrangement: Bo-Bo + 2-2 + 2-2 + Bo-Bo.
Braking: Disc & regenerative.
Bogies: SGP SF5000.
Gangways: Within unit.
Dimensions: 20.34 x 2.80 m.
Couplers: Dellner 12.
Control System: IGBT Inverter.

Doors: Sliding plug. **Maximum Speed:** 100 mph.
Heating & ventilation: Air conditioning.
Seating Layout: 1: 2+2 facing, 2: 3+2 facing/unidirectional.
Multiple Working: Within class.

DMC(A). Siemens Krefeld 2002–03. 8/59. 45.0 t.
PTS. Siemens Vienna 2002–03. –/60(+9) 1TD 2W. 43.6 t.
TS. Siemens Vienna 2002–03. –/78. 34.3 t.
DMC(B). Siemens Krefeld 2002–03. 8/59. 44.1 t.

360 101	**FB**	A	*GA*	IL	65551	72551	74551	68551
360 102	**FB**	A	*GA*	IL	65552	72552	74552	68552
360 103	**FB**	A	*GA*	IL	65553	72553	74553	68553
360 104	**FB**	A	*GA*	IL	65554	72554	74554	68554
360 105	**FB**	A	*GA*	IL	65555	72555	74555	68555
360 106	**FB**	A	*GA*	IL	65556	72556	74556	68556
360 107	**FB**	A	*GA*	IL	65557	72557	74557	68557
360 108	**FB**	A	*GA*	IL	65558	72558	74558	68558
360 109	**FB**	A	*GA*	IL	65559	72559	74559	68559
360 110	**FB**	A	*GA*	IL	65560	72560	74560	68560
360 111	**FB**	A	*GA*	IL	65561	72561	74561	68561
360 112	**FB**	A	*GA*	IL	65562	72562	74562	68562
360 113	**FB**	A	*GA*	IL	65563	72563	74563	68563
360 114	**FB**	A	*GA*	IL	65564	72564	74564	68564
360 115	**FB**	A	*GA*	IL	65565	72565	74565	68565
360 116	**FB**	A	*GA*	IL	65566	72566	74566	68566
360 117	**FB**	A	*GA*	IL	65567	72567	74567	68567
360 118	**FB**	A	*GA*	IL	65568	72568	74568	68568
360 119	**FB**	A	*GA*	IL	65569	72569	74569	68569
360 120	**FB**	A	*GA*	IL	65570	72570	74570	68570
360 121	**FB**	A	*GA*	IL	65571	72571	74571	68571

CLASS 360/2 DESIRO UK SIEMENS

4-car Class 350 testbed units rebuilt for use by Heathrow Express on Paddington–Heathrow Airport stopping services ("Heathrow Connect").

Original 4-car sets 360 201–204 were made up to 5-cars during 2007 using additional TSs. A fifth unit (360 205) was delivered in late 2005 as a 5-car set. In 2018 TfL Rail took over the operation of the Heathrow stopping service, as the first stage of the new Elizabeth Line service.

Formation: DMS–PTS–TS–TS–DMS.
Construction: Welded aluminium.
Traction Motors: Four Siemens 1TB2016-0GB02 asynchronous of 250 kW.
Wheel Arrangement: Bo-Bo + 2-2 + 2-2 + 2-2 + Bo-Bo.
Braking: Disc & regenerative. **Dimensions:** 20.34 x 2.80 m.
Bogies: SGP SF5000. **Couplers:** Dellner 12.
Gangways: Within unit. **Control System:** IGBT Inverter.
Doors: Sliding plug. **Maximum Speed:** 100 mph.
Heating & ventilation: Air conditioning.
Seating Layout: 3+2 (* 2+2) facing/unidirectional.
Multiple Working: Within class.

DMS(A). Siemens Krefeld 2002–06. –/63 (* –/54). 44.8 t.
PTS. Siemens Krefeld 2002–06. –/57(+9) 1TD 2W (* –/48(+9) 2W). 44.2 t.
TS(A). Siemens Krefeld 2005–06. –/74 (* –/62). 35.3 t.
TS(B). Siemens Krefeld 2002–06. –/74 (* –/62). 34.1 t.
DMS(B). Siemens Krefeld 2002–06. –/63 (* –/54). 44.4 t.

360 201		**HC**	HE	*XR*	OH	78431	63421	72431	72421	78441
360 202		**HC**	HE	*XR*	OH	78432	63422	72432	72422	78442
360 203		**HC**	HE	*XR*	OH	78433	63423	72433	72423	78443
360 204		**HC**	HE	*XR*	OH	78434	63424	72434	72424	78444
360 205	*	**HE**	HE	*XR*	OH	78435	63425	72435	72425	78445

CLASS 365 NETWORKER EXPRESS ABB YORK

Outer suburban units.

Formation: DMC–TS–PTS–DMC.
Systems: 25 kV AC overhead but with 750 V DC third rail capability (units 365 501–516 were formerly used on DC lines in the South-East).
Construction: Welded aluminium alloy.
Traction Motors: Four GEC-Alsthom G354CX asynchronous of 157 kW.
Wheel Arrangement: Bo-Bo + 2-2 + 2-2 + Bo-Bo.
Braking: Disc & rheostatic.
Dimensions: 20.89/20.06 x 2.81 m.
Bogies: ABB P3-16/T3-16.
Couplers: Tightlock.
Gangways: Within unit.
Control System: GTO Inverter.
Doors: Sliding plug.
Maximum Speed: 100 mph.
Seating Layout: 1: 2+2 facing, 2: 2+2 facing.
Multiple Working: Within class only.

DMC(A). Lot No. 31133 1994–95. 12/56. 41.7 t.
TS. Lot No. 31134 1994–95. –/58 1TD 2W 32.9 t.
PTS. Lot No. 31135 1994–95. –/70 1T. 35.2 t.
DMC(B). Lot No. 31136 1994–95. 12/56. 41.7 t.

365 501	**TL**	TF		CY	65894	72241	72240	65935
365 502	**TL**	TF	*GN*	HE	65895	72243	72242	65936
365 503	**TL**	TF		CY	65896	72245	72244	65937
365 504	**TL**	TF	*GN*	HE	65897	72247	72246	65938
365 505	**TL**	TF		CY	65898	72249	72248	65939
365 506	**TL**	TF	*GN*	HE	65899	72251	72250	65940
365 507	**TL**	TF		CY	65900	72253	72252	65941
365 508	**TL**	TF	*GN*	HE	65901	72255	72254	65942
365 509	**TL**	TF		CY	65902	72257	72256	65943
365 510	**TL**	TF	*GN*	HE	65903	72259	72258	65944
365 511	**TL**	TF	*GN*	HE	65904	72261	72260	65945
365 512	**TL**	TF	*GN*	HE	65905	72263	72262	65946
365 513	**TL**	TF		CY	65906	72265	72264	65947
365 514	**TL**	TF	*GN*	HE	65907	72267	72266	65948
365 515	**TL**	TF		CY	65908	72269	72268	65949
365 516	**TL**	TF	*GN*	HE	65909	72271	72270	65950
365 517	**TL**	TF		CY	65910	72273	72272	65951
365 518	**TL**	TF	*GN*	HE	65911	72275	72274	65952
365 519	**TL**	TF		CY	65912	72277	72276	65953

365520	**TL**	TF	*GN*	HE	65913	72279	72278	65954
365521	**TL**	TF		CY	65914	72281	72280	65955
365522	**TL**	TF	*GN*	HE	65915	72283	72282	65956
365523	**TL**	TF		CY	65916	72285	72284	65957
365524	**TL**	TF	*GN*	HE	65917	72287	72286	65958
365525	**TL**	TF		CY	65918	72289	72288	65959
365527	**TL**	TF		CY	65920	72293	72292	65961
365528	**TL**	TF	*GN*	HE	65921	72295	72294	65962
365529	**TL**	TF		CY	65922	72297	72296	65963
365530	**TL**	TF	*GN*	HE	65923	72299	72298	65964
365531	**TL**	TF		CY	65924	72301	72300	65965
365532	**TL**	TF	*GN*	HE	65925	72303	72302	65966
365533	**TL**	TF		CY	65926	72305	72304	65967
365534	**TL**	TF	*GN*	HE	65927	72307	72306	65968
365535	**TL**	TF		CY	65928	72309	72308	65969
365536	**TL**	TF	*GN*	HE	65929	72311	72310	65970
365537	**TL**	TF		CY	65930	72313	72312	65971
365538	**TL**	TF	*GN*	HE	65931	72315	72314	65972
365539	**TL**	TF	*GN*	HE	65932	72317	72316	65973
365540	**TL**	TF	*GN*	HE	65933	72319	72318	65974
365541	**TL**	TF		CY	65934	72321	72320	65975

Name (carried on each DMC):

365537 Daniel Edwards (1974–2010) Cambridge Driver

CLASS 375 ELECTROSTAR
ADTRANZ/BOMBARDIER DERBY

Express and outer suburban units.

Formation: Various, see sub-class headings.
Systems: 25 kV AC overhead/750 V DC third rail (some third rail only with provision for retro-fitting of AC equipment).
Construction: Welded aluminium alloy underframe, sides and roof with steel ends. All sections bolted together.
Traction Motors: Two Adtranz asynchronous of 250 kW.
Wheel Arrangement: 2-Bo (+ 2-Bo) + 2-2 + Bo-2.
Braking: Disc & regenerative.
Bogies: Adtranz P3-25/T3-25.
Gangways: Throughout.
Doors: Sliding plug.
Dimensions: 20.40/19.99 x 2.80 m.
Couplers: Dellner 12.
Control System: IGBT Inverter.
Maximum Speed: 100 mph.
Heating & ventilation: Air conditioning.
Seating Layout: 1: 2+2 facing/unidirectional. 2: 2+2 facing/unidirectional (except 375/9 – 3+2 facing/unidirectional).
Multiple Working: Within class and with Classes 376, 377, 378 and 379.

Class 375/3. Express units. 750 V DC only. DMS–TS–DMC.

DMS. Bombardier Derby 2001–02. –/60. 43.8 t.
TS. Bombardier Derby 2001–02. –/56 1TD 2W. 35.5 t.
DMC. Bombardier Derby 2001–02. 12/48. 43.8 t.

375301	**SB**	E	*SE*	RM	67921	74351	67931	
375302	**SB**	E	*SE*	RM	67922	74352	67932	
375303	**SB**	E	*SE*	RM	67923	74353	67933	
375304	**SB**	E	*SE*	RM	67924	74354	67934	
375305	**SB**	E	*SE*	RM	67925	74355	67935	
375306	**SB**	E	*SE*	RM	67926	74356	67936	
375307	**SB**	E	*SE*	RM	67927	74357	67937	
375308	**SB**	E	*SE*	RM	67928	74358	67938	
375309	**SB**	E	*SE*	RM	67929	74359	67939	
375310	**SB**	E	*SE*	RM	67930	74360	67940	

Class 375/6. Express units. 25 kV AC/750 V DC. DMS–MC–PTS–DMS.

DMS(A). Adtranz Derby 1999–2001. –/60. 46.2 t.
MC. Adtranz Derby 1999–2001. 16/50 1T. 40.5 t.
PTS. Adtranz Derby 1999–2001. –/56 1TD 2W. 40.7 t.
DMS(B). Adtranz Derby 1999–2001. –/60. 46.2 t.

375601	**SB**	E	*SE*	RM	67801	74251	74201	67851
375602	**SB**	E	*SE*	RM	67802	74252	74202	67852
375603	**SB**	E	*SE*	RM	67803	74253	74203	67853
375604	**SB**	E	*SE*	RM	67804	74254	74204	67854
375605	**SB**	E	*SE*	RM	67805	74255	74205	67855
375606	**SB**	E	*SE*	RM	67806	74256	74206	67856
375607	**SB**	E	*SE*	RM	67807	74257	74207	67857
375608	**SB**	E	*SE*	RM	67808	74258	74208	67858
375609	**SB**	E	*SE*	RM	67809	74259	74209	67859
375610	**SB**	E	*SE*	RM	67810	74260	74210	67860
375611	**SB**	E	*SE*	RM	67811	74261	74211	67861
375612	**SB**	E	*SE*	RM	67812	74262	74212	67862
375613	**SB**	E	*SE*	RM	67813	74263	74213	67863
375614	**SB**	E	*SE*	RM	67814	74264	74214	67864
375615	**SB**	E	*SE*	RM	67815	74265	74215	67865
375616	**SB**	E	*SE*	RM	67816	74266	74216	67866
375617	**SB**	E	*SE*	RM	67817	74267	74217	67867
375618	**SB**	E	*SE*	RM	67818	74268	74218	67868
375619	**SB**	E	*SE*	RM	67819	74269	74219	67869
375620	**SB**	E	*SE*	RM	67820	74270	74220	67870
375621	**SB**	E	*SE*	RM	67821	74271	74221	67871
375622	**SB**	E	*SE*	RM	67822	74272	74222	67872
375623	**SB**	E	*SE*	RM	67823	74273	74223	67873
375624	**SB**	E	*SE*	RM	67824	74274	74224	67874
375625	**SB**	E	*SE*	RM	67825	74275	74225	67875
375626	**SB**	E	*SE*	RM	67826	74276	74226	67876
375627	**SB**	E	*SE*	RM	67827	74277	74227	67877
375628	**SB**	E	*SE*	RM	67828	74278	74228	67878
375629	**SB**	E	*SE*	RM	67829	74279	74229	67879
375630	**SB**	E	*SE*	RM	67830	74280	74230	67880

Names (carried on one side of each MC or TS):

375619 Driver John Neve | 375623 Hospice in the Weald

Class 375/7. Express units. 750 V DC only. DMS–MC–TS–DMS.

DMS(A). Bombardier Derby 2001–02. –/60. 43.8 t.
MC. Bombardier Derby 2001–02. 16/50 1T. 36.4 t.
TS. Bombardier Derby 2001–02. –/56 1TD 2W. 34.1 t.
DMS(B). Bombardier Derby 2001–02. –/60. 43.8 t.

375701	**SB**	E	*SE*	RM	67831	74281	74231	67881
375702	**SB**	E	*SE*	RM	67832	74282	74232	67882
375703	**SB**	E	*SE*	RM	67833	74283	74233	67883
375704	**SB**	E	*SE*	RM	67834	74284	74234	67884
375705	**SB**	E	*SE*	RM	67835	74285	74235	67885
375706	**SB**	E	*SE*	RM	67836	74286	74236	67886
375707	**SB**	E	*SE*	RM	67837	74287	74237	67887
375708	**SB**	E	*SE*	RM	67838	74288	74238	67888
375709	**SB**	E	*SE*	RM	67839	74289	74239	67889
375710	**SB**	E	*SE*	RM	67840	74290	74240	67890
375711	**SB**	E	*SE*	RM	67841	74291	74241	67891
375712	**SB**	E	*SE*	RM	67842	74292	74242	67892
375713	**SB**	E	*SE*	RM	67843	74293	74243	67893
375714	**SB**	E	*SE*	RM	67844	74294	74244	67894
375715	**SB**	E	*SE*	RM	67845	74295	74245	67895

Names (carried on one side of each MC or TS):

375701 Kent Air Ambulance Explorer
375710 Rochester Castle
375714 Rochester Cathedral

Class 375/8. Express units. 750 V DC only. DMS–MC–TS–DMS.

375 801–820 are fitted with de-icing equipment. TS weighs 36.5 t.

DMS(A). Bombardier Derby 2004. –/60. 43.3 t.
MC. Bombardier Derby 2004. 16/50 1T. 39.8 t.
TS. Bombardier Derby 2004. –/52 1TD 2W. 35.9 t.
DMS(B). Bombardier Derby 2004. –/64. 43.3 t.

375801	**SB**	E	*SE*	RM	73301	79001	78201	73701
375802	**SB**	E	*SE*	RM	73302	79002	78202	73702
375803	**SB**	E	*SE*	RM	73303	79003	78203	73703
375804	**SB**	E	*SE*	RM	73304	79004	78204	73704
375805	**SB**	E	*SE*	RM	73305	79005	78205	73705
375806	**SB**	E	*SE*	RM	73306	79006	78206	73706
375807	**SB**	E	*SE*	RM	73307	79007	78207	73707
375808	**SB**	E	*SE*	RM	73308	79008	78208	73708
375809	**SB**	E	*SE*	RM	73309	79009	78209	73709
375810	**SB**	E	*SE*	RM	73310	79010	78210	73710
375811	**SB**	E	*SE*	RM	73311	79011	78211	73711
375812	**SB**	E	*SE*	RM	73312	79012	78212	73712
375813	**SB**	E	*SE*	RM	73313	79013	78213	73713
375814	**SB**	E	*SE*	RM	73314	79014	78214	73714
375815	**SB**	E	*SE*	RM	73315	79015	78215	73715
375816	**SB**	E	*SE*	RM	73316	79016	78216	73716
375817	**SB**	E	*SE*	RM	73317	79017	78217	73717
375818	**SB**	E	*SE*	RM	73318	79018	78218	73718

375819	**SB**	E	*SE*	RM	73319	79019	78219	73719
375820	**SB**	E	*SE*	RM	73320	79020	78220	73720
375821	**SB**	E	*SE*	RM	73321	79021	78221	73721
375822	**SB**	E	*SE*	RM	73322	79022	78222	73722
375823	**SB**	E	*SE*	RM	73323	79023	78223	73723
375824	**SB**	E	*SE*	RM	73324	79024	78224	73724
375825	**SB**	E	*SE*	RM	73325	79025	78225	73725
375826	**SB**	E	*SE*	RM	73326	79026	78226	73726
375827	**SB**	E	*SE*	RM	73327	79027	78227	73727
375828	**SB**	E	*SE*	RM	73328	79028	78228	73728
375829	**SB**	E	*SE*	RM	73329	79029	78229	73729
375830	**SB**	E	*SE*	RM	73330	79030	78230	73730

Names (carried on one side of each MS or TS):

375823 Ashford Proudly Served by Rail for 175 years

Class 375/9. Outer suburban units. 750 V DC only. DMC–MS–TS–DMC.

DMC(A). Bombardier Derby 2003–04. 12/59. 43.4 t.
MS. Bombardier Derby 2003–04. –/73 1T. 39.3 t.
TS. Bombardier Derby 2003–04. –/62 1TD 2W. 35.6 t.
DMC(B). Bombardier Derby 2003–04. 12/59. 43.4 t.

375901	**SB**	E	*SE*	RM	73331	79031	79061	73731
375902	**SB**	E	*SE*	RM	73332	79032	79062	73732
375903	**SB**	E	*SE*	RM	73333	79033	79063	73733
375904	**SB**	E	*SE*	RM	73334	79034	79064	73734
375905	**SB**	E	*SE*	RM	73335	79035	79065	73735
375906	**SB**	E	*SE*	RM	73336	79036	79066	73736
375907	**SB**	E	*SE*	RM	73337	79037	79067	73737
375908	**SB**	E	*SE*	RM	73338	79038	79068	73738
375909	**SB**	E	*SE*	RM	73339	79039	79069	73739
375910	**SB**	E	*SE*	RM	73340	79040	79070	73740
375911	**SB**	E	*SE*	RM	73341	79041	79071	73741
375912	**SB**	E	*SE*	RM	73342	79042	79072	73742
375913	**SB**	E	*SE*	RM	73343	79043	79073	73743
375914	**SB**	E	*SE*	RM	73344	79044	79074	73744
375915	**SB**	E	*SE*	RM	73345	79045	79075	73745
375916	**SB**	E	*SE*	RM	73346	79046	79076	73746
375917	**SB**	E	*SE*	RM	73347	79047	79077	73747
375918	**SB**	E	*SE*	RM	73348	79048	79078	73748
375919	**SB**	E	*SE*	RM	73349	79049	79079	73749
375920	**SB**	E	*SE*	RM	73350	79050	79080	73750
375921	**SB**	E	*SE*	RM	73351	79051	79081	73751
375922	**SB**	E	*SE*	RM	73352	79052	79082	73752
375923	**SB**	E	*SE*	RM	73353	79053	79083	73753
375924	**SB**	E	*SE*	RM	73354	79054	79084	73754
375925	**SB**	E	*SE*	RM	73355	79055	79085	73755
375926	**SB**	E	*SE*	RM	73356	79056	79086	73756
375927	**SB**	E	*SE*	RM	73357	79057	79087	73757

CLASS 376 ELECTROSTAR BOMBARDIER DERBY

Inner suburban units.

Formation: DMS–MS–TS–MS–DMS.
System: 750 V DC third rail.
Construction: Welded aluminium alloy underframe, sides and roof with steel ends. All sections bolted together.
Traction Motors: Two Bombardier asynchronous of 200 kW.
Wheel Arrangement: 2-Bo + 2-Bo + 2-2 + Bo-2 + Bo-2.
Braking: Disc & regenerative.
Bogies: Bombardier P3-25/T3-25.
Gangways: Within unit.
Doors: Sliding.
Dimensions: 20.40/19.99 x 2.80 m.
Couplers: Dellner 12.
Control System: IGBT Inverter.
Maximum Speed: 75 mph.
Heating & ventilation: Pressure heating and ventilation.
Seating Layout: 2+2 low density facing.
Multiple Working: Within class and with Classes 375, 377, 378 and 379.

DMS(A). Bombardier Derby 2004–05. –/36(+6) 1W. 42.1 t.
MS. Bombardier Derby 2004–05. –/48. 36.2 t.
TS. Bombardier Derby 2004–05. –/48. 36.3 t.
DMS(B). Bombardier Derby 2004–05. –/36(+6) 1W. 42.1 t.

376001	**CN**	E	*SE*	SG	61101	63301	64301	63501	61601
376002	**CN**	E	*SE*	SG	61102	63302	64302	63502	61602
376003	**CN**	E	*SE*	SG	61103	63303	64303	63503	61603
376004	**CN**	E	*SE*	SG	61104	63304	64304	63504	61604
376005	**CN**	E	*SE*	SG	61105	63305	64305	63505	61605
376006	**CN**	E	*SE*	SG	61106	63306	64306	63506	61606
376007	**CN**	E	*SE*	SG	61107	63307	64307	63507	61607
376008	**CN**	E	*SE*	SG	61108	63308	64308	63508	61608
376009	**CN**	E	*SE*	SG	61109	63309	64309	63509	61609
376010	**CN**	E	*SE*	SG	61110	63310	64310	63510	61610
376011	**CN**	E	*SE*	SG	61111	63311	64311	63511	61611
376012	**CN**	E	*SE*	SG	61112	63312	64312	63512	61612
376013	**CN**	E	*SE*	SG	61113	63313	64313	63513	61613
376014	**CN**	E	*SE*	SG	61114	63314	64314	63514	61614
376015	**CN**	E	*SE*	SG	61115	63315	64315	63515	61615
376016	**CN**	E	*SE*	SG	61116	63316	64316	63516	61616
376017	**CN**	E	*SE*	SG	61117	63317	64317	63517	61617
376018	**CN**	E	*SE*	SG	61118	63318	64318	63518	61618
376019	**CN**	E	*SE*	SG	61119	63319	64319	63519	61619
376020	**CN**	E	*SE*	SG	61120	63320	64320	63520	61620
376021	**CN**	E	*SE*	SG	61121	63321	64321	63521	61621
376022	**CN**	E	*SE*	SG	61122	63322	64322	63522	61622
376023	**CN**	E	*SE*	SG	61123	63323	64323	63523	61623
376024	**CN**	E	*SE*	SG	61124	63324	64324	63524	61624
376025	**CN**	E	*SE*	SG	61125	63325	64325	63525	61625
376026	**CN**	E	*SE*	SG	61126	63326	64326	63526	61626
376027	**CN**	E	*SE*	SG	61127	63327	64327	63527	61627
376028	**CN**	E	*SE*	SG	61128	63328	64328	63528	61628
376029	**CN**	E	*SE*	SG	61129	63329	64329	63529	61629

376 030	**CN**	E	*SE*	SG	61130	63330	64330	63530	61630
376 031	**CN**	E	*SE*	SG	61131	63331	64331	63531	61631
376 032	**CN**	E	*SE*	SG	61132	63332	64332	63532	61632
376 033	**CN**	E	*SE*	SG	61133	63333	64333	63533	61633
376 034	**CN**	E	*SE*	SG	61134	63334	64334	63534	61634
376 035	**CN**	E	*SE*	SG	61135	63335	64335	63535	61635
376 036	**CN**	E	*SE*	SG	61136	63336	64336	63536	61636

Name (carried on TSO): 376 001 Alan Doggett

CLASS 377 ELECTROSTAR BOMBARDIER DERBY

Express and outer suburban units.

Formation: Various, see sub-class headings.
Systems: 25 kV AC overhead/750 V DC third rail or third rail only with provision for retro-fitting of AC equipment.
Construction: Welded aluminium alloy underframe, sides and roof with steel ends. All sections bolted together.
Traction Motors: Two Bombardier asynchronous of 250 kW.
Wheel Arrangement: 2-Bo + 2-2 + Bo-2 or 2-Bo + 2-Bo + 2-2 + Bo-2 or 2-Bo + 2-Bo + 2-2 + Bo-2 + Bo-2.
Braking: Disc & regenerative.
Dimensions: 20.39/20.00 x 2.80 m.
Bogies: Bombardier P3-25/T3-25.
Couplers: Dellner 12.
Gangways: Throughout.
Control System: IGBT Inverter.
Doors: Sliding plug.
Maximum Speed: 100 mph.
Heating & ventilation: Air conditioning.
Seating Layout: Various, see sub-class headings.
Multiple Working: Within class and with Classes 375, 376, 378, 379 and 387.

Class 377/1. 750 V DC only. DMC–MS–TS–DMC.
Seating layout: 1: 2+2 facing/unidirectional, 2: 2+2 facing/unidirectional (377 101–119), 3+2/2+2 facing/unidirectional (377 120–139), 3+2 (middle cars and 2+2 (end cars) facing/unidirectional (377 140–164).

DMC(A). Bombardier Derby 2002–03. 12/48 (s 12/56). 44.8 t.
MS. Bombardier Derby 2002–03. –/62 (s –/70, t –/69). 1T. 39.0 t.
TS. Bombardier Derby 2002–03. –/52 (s –/60, t –/57). 1TD 2W. 35.4 t.
DMC(B). Bombardier Derby 2002–03. 12/48 (s 12/56). 43.4 t.

377 101	**SN**	P	*SN*	SU	78501	77101	78901	78701
377 102	**SN**	P	*SN*	SU	78502	77102	78902	78702
377 103	**SN**	P	*SN*	SU	78503	77103	78903	78703
377 104	**SN**	P	*SN*	SU	78504	77104	78904	78704
377 105	**SN**	P	*SN*	SU	78505	77105	78905	78705
377 106	**SN**	P	*SN*	SU	78506	77106	78906	78706
377 107	**SN**	P	*SN*	SU	78507	77107	78907	78707
377 108	**SN**	P	*SN*	SU	78508	77108	78908	78708
377 109	**SN**	P	*SN*	SU	78509	77109	78909	78709
377 110	**SN**	P	*SN*	SU	78510	77110	78910	78710
377 111	**SN**	P	*SN*	SU	78511	77111	78911	78711
377 112	**SN**	P	*SN*	SU	78512	77112	78912	78712
377 113	**SN**	P	*SN*	SU	78513	77113	78913	78713

377 114		**SN**	P	*SN*	SU	78514	77114	78914	78714
377 115		**SN**	P	*SN*	SU	78515	77115	78915	78715
377 116		**SN**	P	*SN*	SU	78516	77116	78916	78716
377 117		**SN**	P	*SN*	SU	78517	77117	78917	78717
377 118		**SN**	P	*SN*	SU	78518	77118	78918	78718
377 119		**SN**	P	*SN*	SU	78519	77119	78919	78719
377 120	s	**SN**	P	*SN*	SU	78520	77120	78920	78720
377 121	s	**SN**	P	*SN*	SU	78521	77121	78921	78721
377 122	s	**SN**	P	*SN*	SU	78522	77122	78922	78722
377 123	s	**SN**	P	*SN*	SU	78523	77123	78923	78723
377 124	s	**SN**	P	*SN*	SU	78524	77124	78924	78724
377 125	s	**SN**	P	*SN*	SU	78525	77125	78925	78725
377 126	s	**SN**	P	*SN*	SU	78526	77126	78926	78726
377 127	s	**SN**	P	*SN*	SU	78527	77127	78927	78727
377 128	s	**SN**	P	*SN*	SU	78528	77128	78928	78728
377 129	s	**SN**	P	*SN*	SU	78529	77129	78929	78729
377 130	s	**SN**	P	*SN*	SU	78530	77130	78930	78730
377 131	s	**SN**	P	*SN*	SU	78531	77131	78931	78731
377 132	s	**SN**	P	*SN*	SU	78532	77132	78932	78732
377 133	s	**SN**	P	*SN*	SU	78533	77133	78933	78733
377 134	s	**SN**	P	*SN*	SU	78534	77134	78934	78734
377 135	s	**SN**	P	*SN*	SU	78535	77135	78935	78735
377 136	s	**SN**	P	*SN*	SU	78536	77136	78936	78736
377 137	s	**SN**	P	*SN*	SU	78537	77137	78937	78737
377 138	s	**SN**	P	*SN*	SU	78538	77138	78938	78738
377 139	s	**SN**	P	*SN*	SU	78539	77139	78939	78739
377 140	t	**SN**	P	*SN*	SU	78540	77140	78940	78740
377 141	t	**SN**	P	*SN*	SU	78541	77141	78941	78741
377 142	t	**SN**	P	*SN*	SU	78542	77142	78942	78742
377 143	t	**SN**	P	*SN*	SU	78543	77143	78943	78743
377 144	t	**SN**	P	*SN*	SU	78544	77144	78944	78744
377 145	t	**SN**	P	*SN*	SU	78545	77145	78945	78745
377 146	t	**SN**	P	*SN*	SU	78546	77146	78946	78746
377 147	t	**SN**	P	*SN*	SU	78547	77147	78947	78747
377 148	t	**SN**	P	*SN*	SU	78548	77148	78948	78748
377 149	t	**SN**	P	*SN*	SU	78549	77149	78949	78749
377 150	t	**SN**	P	*SN*	SU	78550	77150	78950	78750
377 151	t	**SN**	P	*SN*	SU	78551	77151	78951	78751
377 152	t	**SN**	P	*SN*	SU	78552	77152	78952	78752
377 153	t	**SN**	P	*SN*	SU	78553	77153	78953	78753
377 154	t	**SN**	P	*SN*	SU	78554	77154	78954	78754
377 155	t	**SN**	P	*SN*	SU	78555	77155	78955	78755
377 156	t	**SN**	P	*SN*	SU	78556	77156	78956	78756
377 157	t	**SN**	P	*SN*	SU	78557	77157	78957	78757
377 158	t	**SN**	P	*SN*	SU	78558	77158	78958	78758
377 159	t	**SN**	P	*SN*	SU	78559	77159	78959	78759
377 160	t	**SN**	P	*SN*	SU	78560	77160	78960	78760
377 161	t	**SN**	P	*SN*	SU	78561	77161	78961	78761
377 162	t	**SN**	P	*SN*	SU	78562	77162	78962	78762
377 163	t	**SN**	P	*SE*	RM	78563	77163	78963	78763
377 164	t	**SN**	P	*SE*	RM	78564	77164	78964	78764

Class 377/2. 25kV AC/750V DC. DMC–MS–PTS–DMC. Dual-voltage units.
Seating layout: 1: 2+2 facing/unidirectional, 2: 2+2 and 3+2 facing/unidirectional (3+2 seating in middle cars only).

DMC(A). Bombardier Derby 2003–04. 12/48. 44.2 t.
MS. Bombardier Derby 2003–04. –/69 1T. 39.8 t.
PTS. Bombardier Derby 2003–04. –/57 1TD 2W. 40.1 t.
DMC(B). Bombardier Derby 2003–04. 12/48. 44.2 t.

377201	**SN**	P	*SN*	SU	78571	77171	78971	78771
377202	**SN**	P	*SN*	SU	78572	77172	78972	78772
377203	**SN**	P	*SN*	SU	78573	77173	78973	78773
377204	**SN**	P	*SN*	SU	78574	77174	78974	78774
377205	**SN**	P	*SN*	SU	78575	77175	78975	78775
377206	**SN**	P	*SN*	SU	78576	77176	78976	78776
377207	**SN**	P	*SN*	SU	78577	77177	78977	78777
377208	**SN**	P	*SN*	SU	78578	77178	78978	78778
377209	**SN**	P	*SN*	SU	78579	77179	78979	78779
377210	**SN**	P	*SN*	SU	78580	77180	78980	78780
377211	**SN**	P	*SN*	SU	78581	77181	78981	78781
377212	**SN**	P	*SN*	SU	78582	77182	78982	78782
377213	**SN**	P	*SN*	SU	78583	77183	78983	78783
377214	**SN**	P	*SN*	SU	78584	77184	78984	78784
377215	**SN**	P	*SN*	SU	78585	77185	78985	78785

Class 377/3. 750 V DC only. DMC–TS–DMC.
Seating Layout: 1: 2+2 facing/unidirectional, 2: 2+2 facing/unidirectional.

Units built as Class 375, but renumbered in the Class 377/3 range when fitted with Dellner couplers.

377342 was formerly 377442. It had been reformed as a 3-car unit owing to fire damage to MS vehicle 78842 in 2016.

DMC(A). Bombardier Derby 2001–02. 12/48. 43.5 t.
TS. Bombardier Derby 2001–02. –/56 1TD 2W. 35.4 t.
DMC(B). Bombardier Derby 2001–02. 12/48. 43.5 t.

377301	(375311)	**SN**	P	*SN*	SU	68201	74801	68401
377302	(375312)	**SN**	P	*SN*	SU	68202	74802	68402
377303	(375313)	**SN**	P	*SN*	SU	68203	74803	68403
377304	(375314)	**SN**	P	*SN*	SU	68204	74804	68404
377305	(375315)	**SN**	P	*SN*	SU	68205	74805	68405
377306	(375316)	**SN**	P	*SN*	SU	68206	74806	68406
377307	(375317)	**SN**	P	*SN*	SU	68207	74807	68407
377308	(375318)	**SN**	P	*SN*	SU	68208	74808	68408
377309	(375319)	**SN**	P	*SN*	SU	68209	74809	68409
377310	(375320)	**SN**	P	*SN*	SU	68210	74810	68410
377311	(375321)	**SN**	P	*SN*	SU	68211	74811	68411
377312	(375322)	**SN**	P	*SN*	SU	68212	74812	68412
377313	(375323)	**SN**	P	*SN*	SU	68213	74813	68413
377314	(375324)	**SN**	P	*SN*	SU	68214	74814	68414
377315	(375325)	**SN**	P	*SN*	SU	68215	74815	68415
377316	(375326)	**SN**	P	*SN*	SU	68216	74816	68416

377 317	(375 327)	**SN**	P	*SN*	SU	68217	74817	68417
377 318	(375 328)	**SN**	P	*SN*	SU	68218	74818	68418
377 319	(375 329)	**SN**	P	*SN*	SU	68219	74819	68419
377 320	(375 330)	**SN**	P	*SN*	SU	68220	74820	68420
377 321	(375 331)	**SN**	P	*SN*	SU	68221	74821	68421
377 322	(375 332)	**SN**	P	*SN*	SU	68222	74822	68422
377 323	(375 333)	**SN**	P	*SN*	SU	68223	74823	68423
377 324	(375 334)	**SN**	P	*SN*	SU	68224	74824	68424
377 325	(375 335)	**SN**	P	*SN*	SU	68225	74825	68425
377 326	(375 336)	**SN**	P	*SN*	SU	68226	74826	68426
377 327	(375 337)	**SN**	P	*SN*	SU	68227	74827	68427
377 328	(375 338)	**SN**	P	*SN*	SU	68228	74828	68428
377 342	(377 442)	**SN**	P	*SN*	SU	73442	78642	73842

Class 377/4. 750 V DC only. DMC–MS–TS–DMC.
Seating Layout: 1: 2+2 facing/two seats longitudinal, 2: 2+2 and 3+2 facing/unidirectional (3+2 seating in middle cars only).

DMC(A). Bombardier Derby 2004–05. 10/48. 43.1 t.
MS. Bombardier Derby 2004–05. –/69 1T. 39.3 t.
TS. Bombardier Derby 2004–05. –/56 1TD 2W. 35.3 t.
DMC(B). Bombardier Derby 2004–05. 10/48. 43.2 t.

377 401	**SN**	P	*SN*	SU	73401	78801	78601	73801
377 402	**SN**	P	*SN*	SU	73402	78802	78602	73802
377 403	**SN**	P	*SN*	SU	73403	78803	78603	73803
377 404	**SN**	P	*SN*	SU	73404	78804	78604	73804
377 405	**SN**	P	*SN*	SU	73405	78805	78605	73805
377 406	**SN**	P	*SN*	SU	73406	78806	78606	73806
377 407	**SN**	P	*SN*	SU	73407	78807	78607	73807
377 408	**SN**	P	*SN*	SU	73408	78808	78608	73808
377 409	**SN**	P	*SN*	SU	73409	78809	78609	73809
377 410	**SN**	P	*SN*	SU	73410	78810	78610	73810
377 411	**SN**	P	*SN*	SU	73411	78811	78611	73811
377 412	**SN**	P	*SN*	SU	73412	78812	78612	73812
377 413	**SN**	P	*SN*	SU	73413	78813	78613	73813
377 414	**SN**	P	*SN*	SU	73414	78814	78614	73814
377 415	**SN**	P	*SN*	SU	73415	78815	78615	73815
377 416	**SN**	P	*SN*	SU	73416	78816	78616	73816
377 417	**SN**	P	*SN*	SU	73417	78817	78617	73817
377 418	**SN**	P	*SN*	SU	73418	78818	78618	73818
377 419	**SN**	P	*SN*	SU	73419	78819	78619	73819
377 420	**SN**	P	*SN*	SU	73420	78820	78620	73820
377 421	**SN**	P	*SN*	SU	73421	78821	78621	73821
377 422	**SN**	P	*SN*	SU	73422	78822	78622	73822
377 423	**SN**	P	*SN*	SU	73423	78823	78623	73823
377 424	**SN**	P	*SN*	SU	73424	78824	78624	73824
377 425	**SN**	P	*SN*	SU	73425	78825	78625	73825
377 426	**SN**	P	*SN*	SU	73426	78826	78626	73826
377 427	**SN**	P	*SN*	SU	73427	78827	78627	73827
377 428	**SN**	P	*SN*	SU	73428	78828	78628	73828
377 429	**SN**	P	*SN*	SU	73429	78829	78629	73829

377430	**SN**	P	*SN*	SU	73430	78830	78630	73830
377431	**SN**	P	*SN*	SU	73431	78831	78631	73831
377432	**SN**	P	*SN*	SU	73432	78832	78632	73832
377433	**SN**	P	*SN*	SU	73433	78833	78633	73833
377434	**SN**	P	*SN*	SU	73434	78834	78634	73834
377435	**SN**	P	*SN*	SU	73435	78835	78635	73835
377436	**SN**	P	*SN*	SU	73436	78836	78636	73836
377437	**SN**	P	*SN*	SU	73437	78837	78637	73837
377438	**SN**	P	*SN*	SU	73438	78838	78638	73838
377439	**SN**	P	*SN*	SU	73439	78839	78639	73839
377440	**SN**	P	*SN*	SU	73440	78840	78640	73840
377441	**SN**	P	*SN*	SU	73441	78841	78641	73841
377443	**SN**	P	*SN*	SU	73443	78843	78643	73843
377444	**SN**	P	*SN*	SU	73444	78844	78644	73844
377445	**SN**	P	*SN*	SU	73445	78845	78645	73845
377446	**SN**	P	*SN*	SU	73446	78846	78646	73846
377447	**SN**	P	*SN*	SU	73447	78847	78647	73847
377448	**SN**	P	*SN*	SU	73448	78848	78648	73848
377449	**SN**	P	*SN*	SU	73449	78849	78649	73849
377450	**SN**	P	*SN*	SU	73450	78850	78650	73850
377451	**SN**	P	*SN*	SU	73451	78851	78651	73851
377452	**SN**	P	*SN*	SU	73452	78852	78652	73852
377453	**SN**	P	*SN*	SU	73453	78853	78653	73853
377454	**SN**	P	*SN*	SU	73454	78854	78654	73854
377455	**SN**	P	*SN*	SU	73455	78855	78655	73855
377456	**SN**	P	*SN*	SU	73456	78856	78656	73856
377457	**SN**	P	*SN*	SU	73457	78857	78657	73857
377458	**SN**	P	*SN*	SU	73458	78858	78658	73858
377459	**SN**	P	*SN*	SU	73459	78859	78659	73859
377460	**SN**	P	*SN*	SU	73460	78860	78660	73860
377461	**SN**	P	*SN*	SU	73461	78861	78661	73861
377462	**SN**	P	*SN*	SU	73462	78862	78662	73862
377463	**SN**	P	*SN*	SU	73463	78863	78663	73863
377464	**SN**	P	*SN*	SU	73464	78864	78664	73864
377465	**SN**	P	*SN*	SU	73465	78865	78665	73865
377466	**SN**	P	*SN*	SU	73466	78866	78666	73866
377467	**SN**	P	*SN*	SU	73467	78867	78667	73867
377468	**SN**	P	*SN*	SU	73468	78868	78668	73868
377469	**SN**	P	*SN*	SU	73469	78869	78669	73869
377470	**SN**	P	*SN*	SU	73470	78870	78670	73870
377471	**SN**	P	*SN*	SU	73471	78871	78671	73871
377472	**SN**	P	*SN*	SU	73472	78872	78672	73872
377473	**SN**	P	*SN*	SU	73473	78873	78673	73873
377474	**SN**	P	*SN*	SU	73474	78874	78674	73874
377475	**SN**	P	*SN*	SU	73475	78875	78675	73875
Spare	**SN**	P		ZN		78842		

Class 377/5. 25 kV AC/750 V DC. DMC–MS–PTS–DMS. Dual-voltage units. Details as Class 377/2 unless stated.

DMC. Bombardier Derby 2008–09. 10/48. 43.1 t.
MS. Bombardier Derby 2008–09. –/69 1T. 40.3 t.

PTS. Bombardier Derby 2008–09. –/56 1TD 2W. 40.6 t.
DMS. Bombardier Derby 2008–09. –/58. 44.9t.

377501	**FB**	P	*SE*	RM	73501	75901	74901	73601
377502	**FB**	P	*SE*	RM	73502	75902	74902	73602
377503	**FB**	P	*SE*	RM	73503	75903	74903	73603
377504	**FB**	P	*SE*	RM	73504	75904	74904	73604
377505	**FB**	P	*SE*	RM	73505	75905	74905	73605
377506	**FB**	P	*SE*	RM	73506	75906	74906	73606
377507	**FB**	P	*SE*	RM	73507	75907	74907	73607
377508	**FB**	P	*SE*	RM	73508	75908	74908	73608
377509	**FB**	P	*SE*	RM	73509	75909	74909	73609
377510	**FB**	P	*SE*	RM	73510	75910	74910	73610
377511	**FB**	P	*SE*	RM	73511	75911	74911	73611
377512	**FB**	P	*SE*	RM	73512	75912	74912	73612
377513	**FB**	P	*SE*	RM	73513	75913	74913	73613
377514	**FB**	P	*SE*	RM	73514	75914	74914	73614
377515	**FB**	P	*SE*	RM	73515	75915	74915	73615
377516	**FB**	P	*SE*	RM	73516	75916	74916	73616
377517	**FB**	P	*SE*	RM	73517	75917	74917	73617
377518	**FB**	P	*SE*	RM	73518	75918	74918	73618
377519	**FB**	P	*SE*	RM	73519	75919	74919	73619
377520	**FB**	P	*SE*	RM	73520	75920	74920	73620
377521	**FB**	P	*SE*	RM	73521	75921	74921	73621
377522	**FB**	P	*SE*	RM	73522	75922	74922	73622
377523	**FB**	P	*SE*	RM	73523	75923	74923	73623

Class 377/6. 750V DC. DMS–MS–TS–MS–DMS. 5-car suburban units fitted with Fainsa seating. Technically the same as the 377/5s but using the slightly modified Class 379-style bodyshell.

Seating Layout: 2+2 facing/unidirectional.

DMS. Bombardier Derby 2012–13. 24/36. 44.7 t.
MS. Bombardier Derby 2012–13. –/64 1T. 38.8 t.
TS. Bombardier Derby 2012–13. –/46(+2) 1TD 2W. 37.8 t.
MS. Bombardier Derby 2012–13. –/66. 38.3 t.
DMS. Bombardier Derby 2012–13. –/62. 44.7 t.

377601	**SN**	P	*SN*	SU	70101	70201	70301	70401	70501
377602	**SN**	P	*SN*	SU	70102	70202	70302	70402	70502
377603	**SN**	P	*SN*	SU	70103	70203	70303	70403	70503
377604	**SN**	P	*SN*	SU	70104	70204	70304	70404	70504
377605	**SN**	P	*SN*	SU	70105	70205	70305	70405	70505
377606	**SN**	P	*SN*	SU	70106	70206	70306	70406	70506
377607	**SN**	P	*SN*	SU	70107	70207	70307	70407	70507
377608	**SN**	P	*SN*	SU	70108	70208	70308	70408	70508
377609	**SN**	P	*SN*	SU	70109	70209	70309	70409	70509
377610	**SN**	P	*SN*	SU	70110	70210	70310	70410	70510
377611	**SN**	P	*SN*	SU	70111	70211	70311	70411	70511
377612	**SN**	P	*SN*	SU	70112	70212	70312	70412	70512
377613	**SN**	P	*SN*	SU	70113	70213	70313	70413	70513
377614	**SN**	P	*SN*	SU	70114	70214	70314	70414	70514

377615	**SN**	P	*SN*	SU	70115	70215	70315	70415	70515
377616	**SN**	P	*SN*	SU	70116	70216	70316	70416	70516
377617	**SN**	P	*SN*	SU	70117	70217	70317	70417	70517
377618	**SN**	P	*SN*	SU	70118	70218	70318	70418	70518
377619	**SN**	P	*SN*	SU	70119	70219	70319	70419	70519
377620	**SN**	P	*SN*	SU	70120	70220	70320	70420	70520
377621	**SN**	P	*SN*	SU	70121	70221	70321	70421	70521
377622	**SN**	P	*SN*	SU	70122	70222	70322	70422	70522
377623	**SN**	P	*SN*	SU	70123	70223	70323	70423	70523
377624	**SN**	P	*SN*	SU	70124	70224	70324	70424	70524
377625	**SN**	P	*SN*	SU	70125	70225	70325	70425	70525
377626	**SN**	P	*SN*	SU	70126	70226	70326	70426	70526

Class 377/7. 25kV AC/750V DC. DMS–MS–TS–MS–DMS. Dual-voltage units, used on both the South Croydon–Milton Keynes cross-London services and on suburban services alongside the Class 377/6s.

DMS. Bombardier Derby 2013–14. 24/36. 45.6 t.
MS. Bombardier Derby 2013–14. –/64 1T. 41.0 t.
PTS. Bombardier Derby 2013–14. –/46(+2) 1TD 2W. 40.9 t.
MS. Bombardier Derby 2013–14. –/66. 39.6 t.
DMS. Bombardier Derby 2013–14. –/62. 45.2 t.

377701	**SN**	P	*SN*	SU	65201	70601	65601	70701	65401
377702	**SN**	P	*SN*	SU	65202	70602	65602	70702	65402
377703	**SN**	P	*SN*	SU	65203	70603	65603	70703	65403
377704	**SN**	P	*SN*	SU	65204	70604	65604	70704	65404
377705	**SN**	P	*SN*	SU	65205	70605	65605	70705	65405
377706	**SN**	P	*SN*	SU	65206	70606	65606	70706	65406
377707	**SN**	P	*SN*	SU	65207	70607	65607	70707	65407
377708	**SN**	P	*SN*	SU	65208	70608	65608	70708	65408

CLASS 378 CAPITALSTAR BOMBARDIER DERBY

These suburban Electrostars are designated "Capitalstars" by TfL.

Formation: DMS–MS–TS–MS–DMS or DMS–MS–PTS–MS–DMS.
System: Class 378/1 750 V DC third rail only. Class 378/2 25 kV AC overhead and 750 V DC third rail.
Construction: Welded aluminium alloy underframe, sides and roof with steel ends. All sections bolted together.
Traction Motors: Three Bombardier asynchronous of 200 kW.
Wheel Arrangement: 1A-Bo + 1A-Bo + 2-2 + Bo-1A + Bo-1A.
Braking: Disc & regenerative.
Dimensions: 20.46/20.14 x 2.80 m.
Bogies: Bombardier P3-25/T3-25.
Couplers: Dellner 12.
Gangways: Within unit + end doors.
Control System: IGBT Inverter.
Doors: Sliding.
Maximum Speed: 75 mph.
Heating & ventilation: Air conditioning.
Seating Layout: Longitudinal ("tube style") low density.
Multiple Working: Within class and with Classes 375, 376, 377 and 379.

57 extra MSs (in the 384xx number series) were delivered 2014–15 to make all units up to 5-cars.

Class 378/1. 750V DC. DMS–MS–TS–MS–DMS. Third rail only units used on the East London Line. Provision for retro-fitting as dual voltage.

378150–154 are fitted with de-icing equipment.

DMS(A). Bombardier Derby 2009–10. –/36. 43.1 t.
MS(A). Bombardier Derby 2009–10. –/40. 39.3 t.
TS. Bombardier Derby 2009–10. –/34(+6) 2W. 34.3t.
MS(B). Bombardier Derby 2014–15. –/40. 40.2 t.
DMS(B). Bombardier Derby 2009–10. –/36. 42.7 t.

378135	**LD**	QW	*LO*	NG	38035	38235	38335	38435	38135
378136	**LD**	QW	*LO*	NG	38036	38236	38336	38436	38136
378137	**LO**	QW	*LO*	NG	38037	38237	38337	38437	38137
378138	**LO**	QW	*LO*	NG	38038	38238	38338	38438	38138
378139	**LO**	QW	*LO*	NG	38039	38239	38339	38439	38139
378140	**LO**	QW	*LO*	NG	38040	38240	38340	38440	38140
378141	**LO**	QW	*LO*	NG	38041	38241	38341	38441	38141
378142	**LO**	QW	*LO*	NG	38042	38242	38342	38442	38142
378143	**LO**	QW	*LO*	NG	38043	38243	38343	38443	38143
378144	**LO**	QW	*LO*	NG	38044	38244	38344	38444	38144
378145	**LO**	QW	*LO*	NG	38045	38245	38345	38445	38145
378146	**LO**	QW	*LO*	NG	38046	38246	38346	38446	38146
378147	**LD**	QW	*LO*	NG	38047	38247	38347	38447	38147
378148	**LO**	QW	*LO*	NG	38048	38248	38348	38448	38148
378149	**LO**	QW	*LO*	NG	38049	38249	38349	38449	38149
378150	**LD**	QW	*LO*	NG	38050	38250	38350	38450	38150
378151	**LO**	QW	*LO*	NG	38051	38251	38351	38451	38151
378152	**LO**	QW	*LO*	NG	38052	38252	38352	38452	38152
378153	**LO**	QW	*LO*	NG	38053	38253	38353	38453	38153
378154	**LO**	QW	*LO*	NG	38054	38254	38354	38454	38154

Name (carried on DMS(A)): 378135 Daks Hamilton

Class 378/2. 25kV AC/750V DC. DMS–MS–PTS–MS–DMS or DMS–MS–PTS–DMS. Dual-voltage units mainly used on North London Railway services. 378201–224 were built as 3-car units 378001–024 and extended to 4-car units in 2010.

Fitted with tripcocks for operation on the tracks shared with London Underground between Queens Park and Harrow & Wealdstone.

378216–220 are fitted with de-icing equipment.

DMS(A). Bombardier Derby 2008–11. –/36. 43.4 t.
MS(A). Bombardier Derby 2008–11. –/40. 39.6 t.
PTS. Bombardier Derby 2008–11. –/34(+6) 2W. 39.2t.
MS(B). Bombardier Derby 2014–15. –/40. 40.4 t.
DMS(B). Bombardier Derby 2008–11. –/36. 43.1 t.

378201	**LO**	QW	*LO*	NG	38001	38201	38301	38401	38101
378202	**LO**	QW	*LO*	NG	38002	38202	38302	38402	38102
378203	**LO**	QW	*LO*	NG	38003	38203	38303	38403	38103
378204	**LO**	QW	*LO*	NG	38004	38204	38304	38404	38104
378205	**LO**	QW	*LO*	NG	38005	38205	38305	38405	38105

378 206	**LO**	QW	*LO*	NG	38006	38206	38306	38406	38106
378 207	**LO**	QW	*LO*	NG	38007	38207	38307	38407	38107
378 208	**LO**	QW	*LO*	NG	38008	38208	38308	38408	38108
378 209	**LO**	QW	*LO*	NG	38009	38209	38309	38409	38109
378 210	**LO**	QW	*LO*	NG	38010	38210	38310	38410	38110
378 211	**LO**	QW	*LO*	NG	38011	38211	38311	38411	38111
378 212	**LO**	QW	*LO*	NG	38012	38212	38312	38412	38112
378 213	**LO**	QW	*LO*	NG	38013	38213	38313	38413	38113
378 214	**LO**	QW	*LO*	NG	38014	38214	38314	38414	38114
378 215	**LO**	QW	*LO*	NG	38015	38215	38315	38415	38115
378 216	**LO**	QW	*LO*	NG	38016	38216	38316	38416	38116
378 217	**LO**	QW	*LO*	NG	38017	38217	38317	38417	38117
378 218	**LO**	QW	*LO*	NG	38018	38218	38318	38418	38118
378 219	**LO**	QW	*LO*	NG	38019	38219	38319	38419	38119
378 220	**LO**	QW	*LO*	NG	38020	38220	38320	38420	38120
378 221	**LO**	QW	*LO*	NG	38021	38221	38321	38421	38121
378 222	**LO**	QW	*LO*	NG	38022	38222	38322	38422	38122
378 223	**LO**	QW	*LO*	NG	38023	38223	38323	38423	38123
378 224	**LO**	QW	*LO*	NG	38024	38224	38324	38424	38124
378 225	**LO**	QW	*LO*	NG	38025	38225	38325	38425	38125
378 226	**LO**	QW	*LO*	NG	38026	38226	38326	38426	38126
378 227	**LO**	QW	*LO*	NG	38027	38227	38327	38427	38127
378 228	**LO**	QW	*LO*	NG	38028	38228	38328	38428	38128
378 229	**LO**	QW	*LO*	NG	38029	38229	38329	38429	38129
378 230	**LO**	QW	*LO*	NG	38030	38230	38330	38430	38130
378 231	**LO**	QW	*LO*	NG	38031	38231	38331	38431	38131
378 232	**LD**	QW	*LO*	NG	38032	38232	38332	38432	38132
378 233	**LO**	QW	*LO*	NG	38033	38233	38333	38433	38133
378 234	**LO**	QW	*LO*	NG	38034	38234	38334	38434	38134
378 255	**LO**	QW	*LO*	NG	38055	38255	38355	38455	38155
378 256	**LO**	QW	*LO*	NG	38056	38256	38356	38456	38156
378 257	**LO**	QW	*LO*	NG	38057	38257	38357	38457	38157

Names (carried on DMS(A)):

378 204 Professor Sir Peter Hall | 378 233 Ian Brown CBE

CLASS 379 ELECTROSTAR BOMBARDIER DERBY

Express Electrostars used on Liverpool Street–Stansted Airport and Liverpool Street–Cambridge services.

Formation: DMS–MS–PTS–DMC.
System: 25 kV AC overhead.
Construction: Welded aluminium alloy underframe, sides and roof with steel ends. All sections bolted together.
Traction Motors: Two Bombardier asynchronous of 200 kW.
Wheel Arrangement: 2-Bo + 2-Bo + 2-2 + Bo-2.
Braking: Disc & regenerative.
Bogies: Bombardier P3-25/T3-25.
Gangways: Throughout.
Dimensions: 20.00 x 2.80 m.
Couplers: Dellner 12.
Control System: IGBT Inverter.

Doors: Sliding plug. **Maximum Speed:** 100 mph.
Heating & ventilation: Air conditioning.
Seating Layout: 1: 2+1 facing. 2: 2+2 facing/unidirectional.
Multiple Working: Within class and with Classes 375, 376, 377 and 378.

DMS. Bombardier Derby 2010–11. –/60. 42.1 t.
MS. Bombardier Derby 2010–11. –/62 1T. 38.6 t.
PTS. Bombardier Derby 2010–11. –/43(+2) 1TD 2W. 40.9 t.
DMC. Bombardier Derby 2010–11. 20/24. 42.3 t.

379 001	**NC**	MQ	*GA*	IL	61201	61701	61901	62101
379 002	**NC**	MQ	*GA*	IL	61202	61702	61902	62102
379 003	**NC**	MQ	*GA*	IL	61203	61703	61903	62103
379 004	**NC**	MQ	*GA*	IL	61204	61704	61904	62104
379 005	**NC**	MQ	*GA*	IL	61205	61705	61905	62105
379 006	**NC**	MQ	*GA*	IL	61206	61706	61906	62106
379 007	**NC**	MQ	*GA*	IL	61207	61707	61907	62107
379 008	**NC**	MQ	*GA*	IL	61208	61708	61908	62108
379 009	**NC**	MQ	*GA*	IL	61209	61709	61909	62109
379 010	**NC**	MQ	*GA*	IL	61210	61710	61910	62110
379 011	**NC**	MQ	*GA*	IL	61211	61711	61911	62111
379 012	**NC**	MQ	*GA*	IL	61212	61712	61912	62112
379 013	**NC**	MQ	*GA*	IL	61213	61713	61913	62113
379 014	**NC**	MQ	*GA*	IL	61214	61714	61914	62114
379 015	**NC**	MQ	*GA*	IL	61215	61715	61915	62115
379 016	**NC**	MQ	*GA*	IL	61216	61716	61916	62116
379 017	**NC**	MQ	*GA*	IL	61217	61717	61917	62117
379 018	**NC**	MQ	*GA*	IL	61218	61718	61918	62118
379 019	**NC**	MQ	*GA*	IL	61219	61719	61919	62119
379 020	**NC**	MQ	*GA*	IL	61220	61720	61920	62120
379 021	**NC**	MQ	*GA*	IL	61221	61721	61921	62121
379 022	**NC**	MQ	*GA*	IL	61222	61722	61922	62122
379 023	**NC**	MQ	*GA*	IL	61223	61723	61923	62123
379 024	**NC**	MQ	*GA*	IL	61224	61724	61924	62124
379 025	**NC**	MQ	*GA*	IL	61225	61725	61925	62125
379 026	**NC**	MQ	*GA*	IL	61226	61726	61926	62126
379 027	**NC**	MQ	*GA*	IL	61227	61727	61927	62127
379 028	**NC**	MQ	*GA*	IL	61228	61728	61928	62128
379 029	**NC**	MQ	*GA*	IL	61229	61729	61929	62129
379 030	**NC**	MQ	*GA*	IL	61230	61730	61930	62130

Names (carried on end cars):

379 005 Stansted Express
379 011 Ely Cathedral
379 012 The West Anglian
379 015 City of Cambridge
379 025 Go Discover

CLASS 380 DESIRO UK SIEMENS

ScotRail units mainly used on Strathclyde area services.

Formation: DMS–PTS–DMS or DMS–PTS–TS–DMS.
System: 25 kV AC overhead.
Construction: Welded aluminium with steel ends.
Traction Motors: Four Siemens ITB2016-0GB02 asynchronous of 250 kW.
Wheel Arrangement: Bo-Bo + 2-2 (+2-2) + Bo-Bo
Braking: Disc & regenerative.
Bogies: SGP SF5000.
Gangways: Throughout.
Doors: Sliding plug.
Heating & ventilation: Air conditioning.
Multiple Working: Within class.
Dimensions: 23.78/23.57 x 2.80 m.
Couplers: Voith.
Control System: IGBT Inverter.
Maximum Speed: 100 mph.
Seating Layout: 2+2 facing/unidirectional.

DMS(A). Siemens Krefeld 2009–10. –/70. 45.0t.
PTS. Siemens Krefeld 2009–10. –/57(+12) 1TD 2W. 42.7t.
TS. Siemens Krefeld 2009–10. –/74 1T. 34.8t.
DMS(B). Siemens Krefeld 2009–10. –/64(+5). 44.9t.

Class 380/0. 3-car units. **Formation**: DMS–PTS–DMS.

380 001	**SR**	E	*SR*	GW	38501	38601		38701
380 002	**SR**	E	*SR*	GW	38502	38602		38702
380 003	**SR**	E	*SR*	GW	38503	38603		38703
380 004	**SR**	E	*SR*	GW	38504	38604		38704
380 005	**SR**	E	*SR*	GW	38505	38605		38705
380 006	**SR**	E	*SR*	GW	38506	38606		38706
380 007	**SR**	E	*SR*	GW	38507	38607		38707
380 008	**SR**	E	*SR*	GW	38508	38608		38708
380 009	**SR**	E	*SR*	GW	38509	38609		38709
380 010	**SR**	E	*SR*	GW	38510	38610		38710
380 011	**SR**	E	*SR*	GW	38511	38611		38711
380 012	**SR**	E	*SR*	GW	38512	38612		38712
380 013	**SR**	E	*SR*	GW	38513	38613		38713
380 014	**SR**	E	*SR*	GW	38514	38614		38714
380 015	**SR**	E	*SR*	GW	38515	38615		38715
380 016	**SR**	E	*SR*	GW	38516	38616		38716
380 017	**SR**	E	*SR*	GW	38517	38617		38717
380 018	**SR**	E	*SR*	GW	38518	38618		38718
380 019	**SR**	E	*SR*	GW	38519	38619		38719
380 020	**SR**	E	*SR*	GW	38520	38620		38720
380 021	**SR**	E	*SR*	GW	38521	38621		38721
380 022	**SR**	E	*SR*	GW	38522	38622		38722

Class 380/1. 4-car units. **Formation**: DMS–PTS–TS–DMS.

380 101	**SR**	E	*SR*	GW	38551	38651	38851	38751
380 102	**SR**	E	*SR*	GW	38552	38652	38852	38752
380 103	**SR**	E	*SR*	GW	38553	38653	38853	38753
380 104	**SR**	E	*SR*	GW	38554	38654	38854	38754
380 105	**SR**	E	*SR*	GW	38555	38655	38855	38755
380 106	**SR**	E	*SR*	GW	38556	38656	38856	38756

380 107	**SR**	E	*SR*	GW	38557	38657	38857	38757
380 108	**SR**	E	*SR*	GW	38558	38658	38858	38758
380 109	**SR**	E	*SR*	GW	38559	38659	38859	38759
380 110	**SR**	E	*SR*	GW	38560	38660	38860	38760
380 111	**SR**	E	*SR*	GW	38561	38661	38861	38761
380 112	**SR**	E	*SR*	GW	38562	38662	38862	38762
380 113	**SR**	E	*SR*	GW	38563	38663	38863	38763
380 114	**SR**	E	*SR*	GW	38564	38664	38864	38764
380 115	**SR**	E	*SR*	GW	38565	38665	38865	38765
380 116	**SR**	E	*SR*	GW	38566	38666	38866	38766

CLASS 385 AT200 HITACHI

New 3- and 4-car ScotRail units, financed by Caledonian Rail Leasing.

Formation: DMS–PTS–DMS or DMC–PTS–TS–DMS.
System: 25 kV AC overhead.
Construction: Aluminium.
Traction Motors: Four Hitachi asynchronous of 250 kW.
Wheel Arrangement: Bo-Bo + 2-2 + Bo-2 or Bo-Bo + 2-2 + 2-2 + Bo-Bo.
Braking: Disc & regenerative.
Dimensions: 23.18/22.08 x 2.74 m.
Bogies: Hitachi.
Gangways: Throughout.
Doors: Sliding plug.
Couplers: Dellner.
Control System: IGBT Inverter.
Maximum Speed: 100 mph.
Multiple Working: Within class only.
Heating & ventilation: Air conditioning.
Seating Layout: 1: 2+1 facing. 2: 2+2 facing/unidirectional.

Class 385/0. 3-car units. Standard Class only. **Formation**: DMS–PTS–DMS.

DMS(A): Hitachi Newton Aycliffe/Kasado 2016–18. –/48(+9) 1TD 2W. 44.6 t.
PTS: Hitachi Newton Aycliffe/Kasado 2016–18. –/80. 38.4 t.
DMS(B): Hitachi Newton Aycliffe/Kasado 2016–18. –62(+5) 1T. 42.0 t.

385 001	**SR**	CL	*SR*	EC	441001	442001	444001
385 002	**SR**	CL	*SR*	EC	441002	442002	444002
385 003	**SR**	CL	*SR*	EC	441003	442003	444003
385 004	**SR**	CL	*SR*	EC	441004	442004	444004
385 005	**SR**	CL	*SR*	EC	441005	442005	444005
385 006	**SR**	CL	*SR*	EC	441006	442006	444006
385 007	**SR**	CL	*SR*	EC	441007	442007	444007
385 008	**SR**	CL	*SR*	EC	441008	442008	444008
385 009	**SR**	CL	*SR*	EC	441009	442009	444009
385 010	**SR**	CL	*SR*	EC	441010	442010	444010
385 011	**SR**	CL	*SR*	EC	441011	442011	444011
385 012	**SR**	CL	*SR*	EC	441012	442012	444012
385 013	**SR**	CL	*SR*	EC	441013	442013	444013
385 014	**SR**	CL	*SR*	EC	441014	442014	444014
385 015	**SR**	CL	*SR*	EC	441015	442015	444015
385 016	**SR**	CL	*SR*	EC	441016	442016	444016
385 017	**SR**	CL	*SR*	EC	441017	442017	444017
385 018	**SR**	CL	*SR*	EC	441018	442018	444018

385 019	**SR**	CL	*SR*	EC	441019	442019	444019
385 020	**SR**	CL	*SR*	EC	441020	442020	444020
385 021	**SR**	CL	*SR*	EC	441021	442021	444021
385 022	**SR**	CL	*SR*	EC	441022	442022	444022
385 023	**SR**	CL	*SR*	EC	441023	442023	444023
385 024	**SR**	CL	*SR*	EC	441024	442024	444024
385 025	**SR**	CL	*SR*	EC	441025	442025	444025
385 026	**SR**	CL	*SR*	EC	441026	442026	444026
385 027	**SR**	CL	*SR*	EC	441027	442027	444027
385 028	**SR**	CL	*SR*	EC	441028	442028	444028
385 029	**SR**	CL	*SR*	EC	441029	442029	444029
385 030	**SR**	CL	*SR*	EC	441030	442030	444030
385 031	**SR**	CL	*SR*	EC	441031	442031	444031
385 032	**SR**	CL	*SR*	EC	441032	442032	444032
385 033	**SR**	CL	*SR*	EC	441033	442033	444033
385 034	**SR**	CL	*SR*	EC	441034	442034	444034
385 035	**SR**	CL	*SR*	EC	441035	442035	444035
385 036	**SR**	CL	*SR*	EC	441036	442036	444036
385 037	**SR**	CL	*SR*	EC	441037	442037	444037
385 038	**SR**	CL	*SR*	EC	441038	442038	444038
385 039	**SR**	CL	*SR*	EC	441039	442039	444039
385 040	**SR**	CL	*SR*	EC	441040	442040	444040
385 041	**SR**	CL	*SR*	EC	441041	442041	444041
385 042	**SR**	CL	*SR*	EC	441042	442042	444042
385 043	**SR**	CL	*SR*	EC	441043	442043	444043
385 044	**SR**	CL	*SR*	EC	441044	442044	444044
385 045	**SR**	CL	*SR*	EC	441045	442045	444045
385 046	**SR**	CL	*SR*	EC	441046	442046	444046

Class 385/1. 4-car units. Standard Class and First Class seating.
Formation: DMC–PTS–TS–DMS.

DMC: Hitachi Newton Aycliffe/Kasado 2016–18. 20/15(+9) 1TD 2W. 44.7 t.
PTS: Hitachi Newton Aycliffe/Kasado 2016–18. –/80. 38.4 t.
TS: Hitachi Newton Aycliffe/Kasado 2016–18. –/80. 31.5 t.
DMS: Hitachi Newton Aycliffe/Kasado 2016–18. –62(+5) 1T. 44.5 t.

385 101	**SR**	CL	*SR*	EC	441101	442101	443101	444101
385 102	**SR**	CL	*SR*	EC	441102	442102	443102	444102
385 103	**SR**	CL	*SR*	EC	441103	442103	443103	444103
385 104	**SR**	CL	*SR*	EC	441104	442104	443104	444104
385 105	**SR**	CL	*SR*	EC	441105	442105	443105	444105
385 106	**SR**	CL	*SR*	EC	441106	442106	443106	444106
385 107	**SR**	CL	*SR*	EC	441107	442107	443107	444107
385 108	**SR**	CL	*SR*	EC	441108	442108	443108	444108
385 109	**SR**	CL	*SR*	EC	441109	442109	443109	444109
385 110	**SR**	CL	*SR*	EC	441110	442110	443110	444110
385 111	**SR**	CL	*SR*	EC	441111	442111	443111	444111
385 112	**SR**	CL	*SR*	EC	441112	442112	443112	444112
385 113	**SR**	CL	*SR*	EC	441113	442113	443113	444113
385 114	**SR**	CL	*SR*	EC	441114	442114	443114	444114
385 115	**SR**	CL	*SR*	EC	441115	442115	443115	444115
385 116	**SR**	CL	*SR*	EC	441116	442116	443116	444116

385117	**SR**	CL	*SR*	EC	441117	442117	443117	444117
385118	**SR**	CL	*SR*	EC	441118	442118	443118	444118
385119	**SR**	CL	*SR*	EC	441119	442119	443119	444119
385120	**SR**	CL	*SR*	EC	441120	442120	443120	444120
385121	**SR**	CL	*SR*	EC	441121	442121	443121	444121
385122	**SR**	CL	*SR*	EC	441122	442122	443122	444122
385123	**SR**	CL	*SR*	EC	441123	442123	443123	444123
385124	**SR**	CL	*SR*	EC	441124	442124	443124	444124

CLASS 387 ELECTROSTAR BOMBARDIER DERBY

The first 29 110 mph Class 387/1s were delivered in 2014–15 for Thameslink. In 2016–17 these transferred to Great Northern for services from King's Cross to Cambridge/King's Lynn and Peterborough.

A further 27 Class 387/2 units were delivered to Southern for Gatwick Express services in 2016.

Great Western Railway has taken delivery of 45 Class 387/1s for services between London Paddington and Reading, Didcot Parkway and Newbury and these now reach Swindon for stabling. 387 130–141 are currently being refurbished and fitted with ETCS for use on the Heathrow Express service.

Part of a speculative order by Porterbrook Leasing, c2c has six Class 387/3s on lease for 5 years from late 2016. Porterbrook had originally placed an order for 20 speculative units but the other 14 from this order were later incorporated into the GWR fleet.

Formation: DMC–MS–PTS–DMS.
System: 25 kV AC overhead and 750 V DC third rail.
Construction: Welded aluminium alloy underframe, sides and roof with steel ends. All sections bolted together.
Traction Motors: Two Bombardier asynchronous of 250 kW.
Wheel Arrangement: 2-Bo + 2-Bo + 2-2 + Bo-2.
Braking: Disc & regenerative.
Dimensions: 20.39/20.00 x 2.80 m.
Bogies: Bombardier P3-25/T3-25.
Couplers: Dellner 12.
Gangways: Throughout.
Control System: IGBT Inverter.
Doors: Sliding plug.
Maximum Speed: 110 mph.
Heating & ventilation: Air conditioning.
Seating Layout: 2+2 facing/unidirectional.
Multiple Working: Within class and with Class 377.

Class 387/1. Units built for Thameslink, but now used by Great Northern.

DMC. Bombardier Derby 2014–15. 22/34. 46.0 t.
MS. Bombardier Derby 2014–15. –/62 1T. 41.3 t.
PTS. Bombardier Derby 2014–15. –/45(+2) 1TD 2W. 41.6 t.
DMS. Bombardier Derby 2014–15. –/60. 45.9 t.

387101	**TG**	P	*GN*	HE	421101	422101	423101	424101
387102	**TG**	P	*GN*	HE	421102	422102	423102	424102
387103	**TG**	P	*GN*	HE	421103	422103	423103	424103
387104	**TG**	P	*GN*	HE	421104	422104	423104	424104
387105	**TG**	P	*SN*	SL	421105	422105	423105	424105

387 106	**TG**	P	*GN*	HE	421106	422106	423106	424106
387 107	**TG**	P	*GN*	HE	421107	422107	423107	424107
387 108	**TG**	P	*GN*	HE	421108	422108	423108	424108
387 109	**TG**	P	*GN*	HE	421109	422109	423109	424109
387 110	**TG**	P	*GN*	HE	421110	422110	423110	424110
387 111	**TG**	P	*GN*	HE	421111	422111	423111	424111
387 112	**TG**	P	*GN*	HE	421112	422112	423112	424112
387 113	**TG**	P	*GN*	HE	421113	422113	423113	424113
387 114	**TG**	P	*GN*	HE	421114	422114	423114	424114
387 115	**TG**	P	*GN*	HE	421115	422115	423115	424115
387 116	**TG**	P	*GN*	HE	421116	422116	423116	424116
387 117	**TG**	P	*GN*	HE	421117	422117	423117	424117
387 118	**TG**	P	*GN*	HE	421118	422118	423118	424118
387 119	**TG**	P	*GN*	HE	421119	422119	423119	424119
387 120	**TG**	P	*GN*	HE	421120	422120	423120	424120
387 121	**TG**	P	*GN*	HE	421121	422121	423121	424121
387 122	**TG**	P	*GN*	HE	421122	422122	423122	424122
387 123	**TG**	P	*GN*	HE	421123	422123	423123	424123
387 124	**TG**	P	*GN*	HE	421124	422124	423124	424124
387 125	**TG**	P	*GN*	HE	421125	422125	423125	424125
387 126	**TG**	P	*GN*	HE	421126	422126	423126	424126
387 127	**TG**	P	*GN*	HE	421127	422127	423127	424127
387 128	**TG**	P	*GN*	HE	421128	422128	423128	424128
387 129	**TG**	P	*GN*	HE	421129	422129	423129	424129

Name (carried on DMC): 387 124 Paul McCann

Class 387/1. Great Western Railway units.

DMC. Bombardier Derby 2016–17. –/56. 46.0 t.
MS. Bombardier Derby 2016–17. –/62 1T. 41.3 t.
PTS. Bombardier Derby 2016–17. –/45(+2) 1TD 2W. 41.6 t.
DMS. Bombardier Derby 2016–17. –/60. 45.9 t.

387 130	**HX**	P	*GW*	RG	421130	422130	423130	424130
387 131	**HX**	P	*GW*	RG	421131	422131	423131	424131
387 132	**HX**	P	*GW*	RG	421132	422132	423132	424132
387 133	**HX**	P	*GW*	RG	421133	422133	423133	424133
387 134	**HX**	P	*GW*	RG	421134	422134	423134	424134
387 135	**HX**	P	*GW*	RG	421135	422135	423135	424135
387 136	**HX**	P	*GW*	RG	421136	422136	423136	424136
387 137	**GW**	P	*GW*	RG	421137	422137	423137	424137
387 138	**GW**	P	*GW*	RG	421138	422138	423138	424138
387 139	**HX**	P	*GW*	RG	421139	422139	423139	424139
387 140	**HX**	P	*GW*	RG	421140	422140	423140	424140
387 141	**GW**	P	*GW*	RG	421141	422141	423141	424141
387 142	**GW**	P	*GW*	RG	421142	422142	423142	424142
387 143	**GW**	P	*GW*	RG	421143	422143	423143	424143
387 144	**GW**	P	*GW*	RG	421144	422144	423144	424144
387 145	**GW**	P	*GW*	RG	421145	422145	423145	424145
387 146	**GW**	P	*GW*	RG	421146	422146	423146	424146
387 147	**GW**	P	*GW*	RG	421147	422147	423147	424147
387 148	**GW**	P	*GW*	RG	421148	422148	423148	424148

387 149	**GW**	P	*GW*	RG	421149	422149	423149	424149
387 150	**GW**	P	*GW*	RG	421150	422150	423150	424150
387 151	**GW**	P	*GW*	RG	421151	422151	423151	424151
387 152	**GW**	P	*GW*	RG	421152	422152	423152	424152
387 153	**GW**	P	*GW*	RG	421153	422153	423153	424153
387 154	**GW**	P	*GW*	RG	421154	422154	423154	424154
387 155	**GW**	P	*GW*	RG	421155	422155	423155	424155
387 156	**GW**	P	*GW*	RG	421156	422156	423156	424156
387 157	**GW**	P	*GW*	RG	421157	422157	423157	424157
387 158	**GW**	P	*GW*	RG	421158	422158	423158	424158
387 159	**GW**	P	*GW*	RG	421159	422159	423159	424159
387 160	**GW**	P	*GW*	RG	421160	422160	423160	424160
387 161	**GW**	P	*GW*	RG	421161	422161	423161	424161
387 162	**GW**	P	*GW*	RG	421162	422162	423162	424162
387 163	**GW**	P	*GW*	RG	421163	422163	423163	424163
387 164	**GW**	P	*GW*	RG	421164	422164	423164	424164
387 165	**GW**	P	*GW*	RG	421165	422165	423165	424165
387 166	**GW**	P	*GW*	RG	421166	422166	423166	424166
387 167	**GW**	P	*GW*	RG	421167	422167	423167	424167
387 168	**GW**	P	*GW*	RG	421168	422168	423168	424168
387 169	**GW**	P	*GW*	RG	421169	422169	423169	424169
387 170	**GW**	P	*GW*	RG	421170	422170	423170	424170
387 171	**GW**	P	*GW*	RG	421171	422171	423171	424171
387 172	**GW**	P	*GW*	RG	421172	422172	423172	424172
387 173	**GW**	P	*GW*	RG	421173	422173	423173	424173
387 174	**GW**	P	*GW*	RG	421174	422174	423174	424174

Class 387/2. Southern units used on Gatwick Express-branded services on the London Victoria–Gatwick Airport–Brighton route.

DMC. Bombardier Derby 2015–16. 22/34. 46.0 t.
MS. Bombardier Derby 2015–16. –/60 1T. 41.3 t.
PTS. Bombardier Derby 2015–16. –/45(+2) 1TD 2W. 41.6 t.
DMS. Bombardier Derby 2015–16. –/60. 45.9 t.

387 201	**GX**	P	*SN*	SL	421201	422201	423201	424201
387 202	**GX**	P	*SN*	SL	421202	422202	423202	424202
387 203	**GX**	P	*SN*	SL	421203	422203	423203	424203
387 204	**GX**	P	*SN*	SL	421204	422204	423204	424204
387 205	**GX**	P	*SN*	SL	421205	422205	423205	424205
387 206	**GX**	P	*SN*	SL	421206	422206	423206	424206
387 207	**GX**	P	*SN*	SL	421207	422207	423207	424207
387 208	**GX**	P	*SN*	SL	421208	422208	423208	424208
387 209	**GX**	P	*SN*	SL	421209	422209	423209	424209
387 210	**GX**	P	*SN*	SL	421210	422210	423210	424210
387 211	**GX**	P	*SN*	SL	421211	422211	423211	424211
387 212	**GX**	P	*SN*	SL	421212	422212	423212	424212
387 213	**GX**	P	*SN*	SL	421213	422213	423213	424213
387 214	**GX**	P	*SN*	SL	421214	422214	423214	424214
387 215	**GX**	P	*SN*	SL	421215	422215	423215	424215
387 216	**GX**	P	*SN*	SL	421216	422216	423216	424216
387 217	**GX**	P	*SN*	SL	421217	422217	423217	424217

387218	**GX**	P	*SN*	SL	421218	422218	423218	424218
387219	**GX**	P	*SN*	SL	421219	422219	423219	424219
387220	**GX**	P	*SN*	SL	421220	422220	423220	424220
387221	**GX**	P	*SN*	SL	421221	422221	423221	424221
387222	**GX**	P	*SN*	SL	421222	422222	423222	424222
387223	**GX**	P	*SN*	SL	421223	422223	423223	424223
387224	**GX**	P	*SN*	SL	421224	422224	423224	424224
387225	**GX**	P	*SN*	SL	421225	422225	423225	424225
387226	**GX**	P	*SN*	SL	421226	422226	423226	424226
387227	**GX**	P	*SN*	SL	421227	422227	423227	424227

Class 387/3. c2c units, originally ordered speculatively by Porterbrook Leasing.

DMS(A). Bombardier Derby 2016. –/56. 46.0 t.
MS. Bombardier Derby 2016. –/62 1T. 41.3 t.
PTS. Bombardier Derby 2016. –/45(+2) 1TD 2W. 41.6 t.
DMS(B). Bombardier Derby 2016. –/60. 45.9 t.

387301	**C2**	P	*C2*	EM	421301	422301	423301	424301
387302	**C2**	P	*C2*	EM	421302	422302	423302	424302
387303	**C2**	P	*C2*	EM	421303	422303	423303	424303
387304	**C2**	P	*C2*	EM	421304	422304	423304	424304
387305	**C2**	P	*C2*	EM	421305	422305	423305	424305
387306	**C2**	P	*C2*	EM	421306	422306	423306	424306

CLASS 390 PENDOLINO ALSTOM

Tilting units used on the West Coast Main Line.

Formation: As listed below.
Construction: Welded aluminium alloy.
Traction Motors: Two Alstom ONIX 800 of 425 kW.
Wheel Arrangement: 1A-A1 + 1A-A1 + 2-2 + 1A-A1 (+ 2-2 + 1A-A1) + 2-2 + 1A-A1 + 2-2 + 1A-A1 + 1A-A1.
Braking: Disc, rheostatic & regenerative.
Dimensions: 24.80/23.90 x 2.73 m.
Couplers: Dellner 12.
Bogies: Fiat-SIG.
Control System: IGBT Inverter.
Gangways: Within unit.
Maximum Speed: 125 mph.
Doors: Sliding plug.
Heating & ventilation: Air conditioning.
Seating Layout: 1: 2+1 facing/unidirectional, 2: 2+2 facing/unidirectional.
Multiple Working: Within class. Can also be controlled from Class 57/3 locos.

Units up to 390034 were delivered as 8-car sets, without the TS (688xx). During 2004–05 these units were increased to 9-cars.

62 extra vehicles were built 2010–12 to lengthen 31 sets to 11-cars. On renumbering units were renumbered by adding 100 to the set number. Four new complete 11-car units were also delivered. All these extra vehicles were built at Savigliano, Italy (all original Pendolino vehicles were built at Birmingham).

The 9-car units had their MF(B) converted to an MS in 2015 to give them a better balance of Standard to First Class seating.

390033 was written off in the Lambrigg accident of February 2007.

DMRBF: Alstom Birmingham/Savigliano 2001–05/2010–12. 18/–. 56.3 t.
MF(A): Alstom Birmingham/Savigliano 2001–05/2010–12. 37/–(+2) 1TD 1W. 52.3 t.
PTF: Alstom Birmingham/Savigliano 2001–05/2010–12. 44/– 1T. 51.2 t.
MF(B: 11-car): Alstom Birmingham/Savigliano 2001–05/2010–12. 46/– 1T. 52.3 t.
MS(C: 9-car): Alstom Birmingham/Savigliano 2001–05/2010–12. –/76 1T. 52.3 t.
(**TS**: Alstom Savigliano 2010–12. –/74 1T. 49.2 t.)
(**MS**: Alstom Savigliano 2010–12. –/76 1T. 52.2 t.)
TS: Alstom Birmingham/Savigliano 2001–05/2010–12. –/76 1T. 45.5 t.
MS(A): Alstom Birmingham/Savigliano 2001–05/2010–12. –/62(+4) 1TD 1W. 52.0 t.
PTSRMB: Alstom Birmingham/Savigliano 2001–05/2010–12. –/48. 53.2 t.
MS(B): Alstom Birmingham/Savigliano 2001–05/2010–12. –/62(+2) 1TD 1W. 52.5 t.
DMS: Alstom Birmingham/Savigliano 2001–05/2010–12. –/46 1T. 54.5 t.

Class 390/0. Original build 9-car units.

Formation: DMRF–MF–PTF–MS–TS–MS–PTSRMB–MS–DMS.

390 001	**VW**	A	*AW*	MA	69101	69401	69501	69601	68801
					69701	69801	69901	69201	
390 002	**VW**	A	*AW*	MA	69102	69402	69502	69602	68802
					69702	69802	69902	69202	
390 005	**VW**	A	*AW*	MA	69105	69405	69505	69605	68805
					69705	69805	69905	69205	
390 006	**VW**	A	*AW*	MA	69106	69406	69506	69606	68806
					69706	69806	69906	69206	
390 008	**VW**	A	*AW*	MA	69108	69408	69508	69608	68808
					69708	69808	69908	69208	
390 009	**VW**	A	*AW*	MA	69109	69409	69509	69609	68809
					69709	69809	69909	69209	
390 010	**VW**	A	*AW*	MA	69110	69410	69510	69610	68810
					69710	69810	69910	69210	
390 011	**VW**	A	*AW*	MA	69111	69411	69511	69611	68811
					69711	69811	69911	69211	
390 013	**VW**	A	*AW*	MA	69113	69413	69513	69613	68813
					69713	69813	69913	69213	
390 016	**VW**	A	*AW*	MA	69116	69416	69516	69616	68816
					69716	69816	69916	69216	
390 020	**VW**	A	*AW*	MA	69120	69420	69520	69620	68820
					69720	69820	69920	69220	
390 039	**VW**	A	*AW*	MA	69139	69439	69539	69639	68839
					69739	69839	69939	69239	
390 040	**VW**	A	*AW*	MA	69140	69440	69540	69640	68840
					69740	69840	69940	69240	
390 042	**VW**	A	*AW*	MA	69142	69442	69542	69642	68842
					69742	69842	69942	69242	
390 043	**VW**	A	*AW*	MA	69143	69443	69543	69643	68843
					69743	69843	69943	69243	
390 044	**VW**	A	*AW*	MA	69144	69444	69544	69644	68844
					69744	69844	69944	69244	
390 045	**VW**	A	*AW*	MA	69145	69445	69545	69645	68845
					69745	69845	69945	69245	
390 046	**VW**	A	*AW*	MA	69146	69446	69546	69646	68846
					69746	69846	69946	69246	

390 047	**VW**	A	*AW*	MA	69147 69447 69547 69647 68847 69747 69847 69947 69247
390 049	**VW**	A	*AW*	MA	69149 69449 69549 69649 68849 69749 69849 69949 69249
390 050	**VW**	A	*AW*	MA	69150 69450 69550 69650 68850 69750 69850 69950 69250

Class 390/1. Original build 9-car units later extended to 11-cars, except 390 154–157 which were built new (in Italy) as 11-cars.
Formation: DMRF–MF–PTF–MF–TS–MS–TS–MS–PTSRMB–MS–DMS.

390 103	**VW**	A	*AW*	MA	69103 69403 69503 69603 65303 68903 68803 69703 69803 69903 69203
390 104	**VW**	A	*AW*	MA	69104 69404 69504 69604 65304 68904 68804 69704 69804 69904 69204
390 107	**VW**	A	*AW*	MA	69107 69407 69507 69607 65307 68907 68807 69707 69807 69907 69207
390 112	**VW**	A	*AW*	MA	69112 69412 69512 69612 65312 68912 68812 69712 69812 69912 69212
390 114	**VW**	A	*AW*	MA	69114 69414 69514 69614 65314 68914 68814 69714 69814 69914 69214
390 115	**VW**	A	*AW*	MA	69115 69415 69515 69615 65315 68915 68815 69715 69815 69915 69215
390 117	**VW**	A	*AW*	MA	69117 69417 69517 69617 65317 68917 68817 69717 69817 69917 69217
390 118	**VW**	A	*AW*	MA	69118 69418 69518 69618 65318 68918 68818 69718 69818 69918 69218
390 119	**VW**	A	*AW*	MA	69119 69419 69519 69619 65319 68919 68819 69719 69819 69919 69219
390 121	**VW**	A	*AW*	MA	69121 69421 69521 69621 65321 68921 68821 69721 69821 69921 69221
390 122	**VW**	A	*VW*	MA	69122 69422 69522 69622 65322 68922 68822 69722 69822 69922 69222
390 123	**VW**	A	*AW*	MA	69123 69423 69523 69623 65323 68923 68823 69723 69823 69923 69223
390 124	**VW**	A	*AW*	MA	69124 69424 69524 69624 65324 68924 68824 69724 69824 69924 69224
390 125	**VW**	A	*AW*	MA	69125 69425 69525 69625 65325 68925 68825 69725 69825 69925 69225
390 126	**VW**	A	*AW*	MA	69126 69426 69526 69626 65326 68926 68826 69726 69826 69926 69226
390 127	**VW**	A	*AW*	MA	69127 69427 69527 69627 65327 68927 68827 69727 69827 69927 69227
390 128	**VW**	A	*AW*	MA	69128 69428 69528 69628 65328 68928 68828 69728 69828 69928 69228
390 129	**VW**	A	*AW*	MA	69129 69429 69529 69629 65329 68929 68829 69729 69829 69929 69229
390 130	**VW**	A	*AW*	MA	69130 69430 69530 69630 65330 68930 68830 69730 69830 69930 69230
390 131	**VW**	A	*AW*	MA	69131 69431 69531 69631 65331 68931 68831 69731 69831 69931 69231

390 132	**VW**	A	*AW* MA	69132 69432 69532 69632 65332 68932 68832 69732 69832 69932 69232
390 134	**VW**	A	*AW* MA	69134 69434 69534 69634 65334 68934 68834 69734 69834 69934 69234
390 135	**VW**	A	*AW* MA	69135 69435 69535 69635 65335 68935 68835 69735 69835 69935 69235
390 136	**VW**	A	*AW* MA	69136 69436 69536 69636 65336 68936 68836 69736 69836 69936 69236
390 137	**VW**	A	*VW* MA	69137 69437 69537 69637 65337 68937 68837 69737 69837 69937 69237
390 138	**VW**	A	*AW* MA	69138 69438 69538 69638 65338 68938 68838 69738 69838 69938 69238
390 141	**VW**	A	*AW* MA	69141 69441 69541 69641 65341 68941 68841 69741 69841 69941 69241
390 148	**VW**	A	*AW* MA	69148 69448 69548 69648 65348 68948 68848 69748 69848 69948 69248
390 151	**VW**	A	*VW* MA	69151 69451 69551 69651 65351 68951 68851 69751 69851 69951 69251
390 152	**VW**	A	*VW* MA	69152 69452 69552 69652 65352 68952 68852 69752 69852 69952 69252
390 153	**VW**	A	*AW* MA	69153 69453 69553 69653 65353 68953 68853 69753 69853 69953 69253
390 154	**VW**	A	*AW* MA	69154 69454 69554 69654 65354 68954 68854 69754 69854 69954 69254
390 155	**AT**	A	*AW* MA	69155 69455 69555 69655 65355 68955 68855 69755 69855 69955 69255
390 156	**AT**	A	*AW* MA	69156 69456 69556 69656 65356 68956 68856 69756 69856 69956 69256
390 157	**VW**	A	*AW* MA	69157 69457 69557 69657 65357 68957 68857 69757 69857 69957 69257

Names (carried on MF No. 696xx):

390 001 Bee Together
390 002 Stephen Sutton
390 005 City of Wolverhampton
390 006 Rethink Mental Illness
390 008 CHARLES RENNIE MACKINTOSH
390 009 Treaty of Union
390 010 Cumbrian Spirit
390 011 City of Lichfield
390 013 Blackpool Belle
390 039 Lady Godiva
390 047 CLIC Sargent
390 104 Alstom Pendolino
390 114 City of Manchester
390 115 Crewe – All Change
390 117 Blue Peter
390 119 Unknown Soldier
390 122 Penny the Pendolino
390 125 Virgin Stagecoach
390 128 City of Preston
390 129 City of Stoke-on-Trent
390 130 City of Edinburgh
390 131 City of Liverpool
390 132 City of Birmingham
390 134 City of Carlisle
390 135 City of Lancaster
390 136 City of Coventry
390 138 City of London
390 148 Flying Scouseman
390 154 Matthew Flinders
390 156 Pride and Prosperity
390 157 Chad Varah

CLASS 395 JAVELIN HITACHI JAPAN

6-car dual-voltage units used on Southeastern High Speed trains from London St Pancras.

Formation: PDTS–MS–MS–MS–MS–PDTS.
Systems: 25 kV AC overhead/750 V DC third rail.
Construction: Aluminium.
Traction Motors: Four Hitachi asynchronous of 210 kW.
Wheel Arrangement: 2-2 + Bo-Bo + Bo-Bo + Bo-Bo + Bo-Bo + 2-2.
Braking: Disc, rheostatic & regenerative.
Dimensions: 20.88/20.0 x 2.81 m.
Couplers: Scharfenberg.
Bogies: Hitachi.
Control System: IGBT Inverter.
Gangways: Within unit.
Maximum Speed: 140 mph.
Doors: Single-leaf sliding.
Multiple Working: Within class only.
Heating & ventilation: Air conditioning.
Seating Layout: 2+2 facing/unidirectional (mainly unidirectional).

PDTS(A): Hitachi Kasado, Japan 2006–09. –/28(+12) 1TD 2W. 46.7 t.
MS: Hitachi Kasado, Japan 2006–09. –/66. 45.0t–45.7 t.
PDTS(B): Hitachi Kasado, Japan 2006–09. –/48 1T. 46.7 t.

395 001	**SB**	E	*SE*	AD	39011	39012	39013	39014	39015	39016
395 002	**SB**	E	*SE*	AD	39021	39022	39023	39024	39025	39026
395 003	**SB**	E	*SE*	AD	39031	39032	39033	39034	39035	39036
395 004	**SB**	E	*SE*	AD	39041	39042	39043	39044	39045	39046
395 005	**SB**	E	*SE*	AD	39051	39052	39053	39054	39055	39056
395 006	**SB**	E	*SE*	AD	39061	39062	39063	39064	39065	39066
395 007	**SB**	E	*SE*	AD	39071	39072	39073	39074	39075	39076
395 008	**SB**	E	*SE*	AD	39081	39082	39083	39084	39085	39086
395 009	**SB**	E	*SE*	AD	39091	39092	39093	39094	39095	39096
395 010	**SB**	E	*SE*	AD	39101	39102	39103	39104	39105	39106
395 011	**SB**	E	*SE*	AD	39111	39112	39113	39114	39115	39116
395 012	**SB**	E	*SE*	AD	39121	39122	39123	39124	39125	39126
395 013	**SB**	E	*SE*	AD	39131	39132	39133	39134	39135	39136
395 014	**SB**	E	*SE*	AD	39141	39142	39143	39144	39145	39146
395 015	**SB**	E	*SE*	AD	39151	39152	39153	39154	39155	39156
395 016	**SB**	E	*SE*	AD	39161	39162	39163	39164	39165	39166
395 017	**SB**	E	*SE*	AD	39171	39172	39173	39174	39175	39176
395 018	**SB**	E	*SE*	AD	39181	39182	39183	39184	39185	39186
395 019	**SB**	E	*SE*	AD	39191	39192	39193	39194	39195	39196
395 020	**SB**	E	*SE*	AD	39201	39202	39203	39204	39205	39206
395 021	**SB**	E	*SE*	AD	39211	39212	39213	39214	39215	39216
395 022	**SB**	E	*SE*	AD	39221	39222	39223	39224	39225	39226
395 023	**SB**	E	*SE*	AD	39231	39232	39233	39234	39235	39236
395 024	**SB**	E	*SE*	AD	39241	39242	39243	39244	39245	39246
395 025	**SB**	E	*SE*	AD	39251	39252	39253	39254	39255	39256
395 026	**SB**	E	*SE*	AD	39261	39262	39263	39264	39265	39266
395 027	**SB**	E	*SE*	AD	39271	39272	39273	39274	39275	39276
395 028	**SB**	E	*SE*	AD	39281	39282	39283	39284	39285	39286
395 029	**SB**	E	*SE*	AD	39291	39292	39293	39294	39295	39296

Names (carried on end cars):

395 001	Dame Kelly Holmes
395 002	Sebastian Coe
395 003	Sir Steve Redgrave
395 004	Sir Chris Hoy
395 005	Dame Tanni Grey-Thompson
395 006	Daley Thompson
395 007	Steve Backley
395 008	Ben Ainslie
395 009	Rebecca Adlington
395 010	Duncan Goodhew
395 011	Katherine Grainger
395 013	HORNBY Visitor Centre Margate, Kent
395 017	PASSCHENDAELE Javelin
395 018	THE VICTORY Javelin
395 019	Jessica Ennis
395 020	Jason Kenny
395 021	Ed Clancy MBE
395 022	Alistair Brownlee
395 023	Ellie Simmonds
395 024	Jonnie Peacock
395 025	Victoria Pendleton
395 026	Marc Woods
395 027	Hannah Cockcroft
395 028	Laura Trott
395 029	David Weir

CLASS 397 CIVITY CAF

New units currently entering service with TransPennine Express on Manchester Airport–Edinburgh/Glasgow services.

Formation: DMF–PTS–MS–PTS–DMS.
Construction: Aluminium.
Traction Motors: Four TSA of 220 kW.
Wheel Arrangement:
Braking: Disc and regenerative.
Bogies: CAF.
Gangways: Within unit.
Doors: Sliding plug.
Dimensions: 24.03/23.35 x 2.71 m.
Couplers: Dellner.
Control System: IGBT Inverter.
Maximum Speed: 125 mph.
Heating & ventilation: Air conditioning.
Seating: 1: 2+1 facing/unidirectional; 2: 2+2 facing/unidirectional.
Multiple Working: Within class.

DMF. CAF Beasain 2017–19. 24/– 1TD 2W. 41.4 t.
PTS(A). CAF Beasain 2017–19. –/76. 34.5 t.
MS. CAF Beasain 2017–19. –/68 2T. 36.6 t.
PTS(B). CAF Beasain 2017–19. –/76. 34.9 t.
DMS. CAF Beasain 2017–19. –/44(+8) 1T. 39.2 t.

397 001	**TP**	E			471001	472001	473001	474001	475001
397 002	**TP**	E			471002	472002	473002	474002	475002
397 003	**TP**	E	*TP*	MA	471003	472003	473003	474003	475003
397 004	**TP**	E			471004	472004	473004	474004	475004
397 005	**TP**	E	*TP*	MA	471005	472005	473005	474005	475005
397 006	**TP**	E	*TP*	MA	471006	472006	473006	474006	475006
397 007	**TP**	E	*TP*	MA	471007	472007	473007	474007	475007
397 008	**TP**	E			471008	472008	473008	474008	475008
397 009	**TP**	E			471009	472009	473009	474009	475009
397 010	**TP**	E			471010	472010	473010	474010	475010
397 011	**TP**	E			471011	472011	473011	474011	475011
397 012	**TP**	E			471012	472012	473012	474012	475012

CLASS 399 CITYLINK VOSSLOH/STADLER

The Class 399s are tram-trains used on the pilot Sheffield–Rotherham Parkgate tram-train service, operated by Stagecoach Supertram. Dual-voltage 750 V DC/25 kV AC (although currently only planned to operate on 750 V DC). For operation on Network Rail lines EMU running numbers 399201–207 are carried (as well as vehicle numbers in the 999xxx series), as well as the Stagecoach Supertram fleet numbers 201–207.

Entered service on the Supertram network in autumn 2017 and on the national railway network as tram-trains from October 2018.

Following two accidents in autumn 2018 unit 399202 is currently operating as a hybrid set, using one end vehicle from 399204. The other three vehicles were returned to Spain for repairs and 399204 is expected to return to traffic in the formation shown.

At the time of writing units 399201/202/203/206 have tram-train wheel profiles for operating on the National Rail network to Rotherham Parkgate. 399205/207 can only operate on the tramway network, but could be modified to operate to Rotherham if required.

Formation: DMS–MS–DMS.
Systems: 750 V DC/25 kV AC overhead.
Construction: Steel.
Traction Motors: Six VEM of 145 kW (per unit).
Wheel Arrangement: Bo-2-Bo-Bo.
Braking: Disc, regenerative & emergency track.
Dimensions: 37.20 x 2.65 m (full set).
Bogies: Vossloh.
Gangways: Within unit.
Doors: Sliding plug.
Seating Layout: 2+2 facing/unidirectional.
Weight: 64 t.
Couplers: Albert (emergency use).
Control System: IGBT Inverter.
Maximum Speed: 60 mph.
Multiple Working: Within class only.

DMS(A): Vossloh, Valencia 2014–15. –/22(+4) 1W.
MS: Vossloh, Valencia 2014–15. –/44.
DMS(B): Vossloh, Valencia 2014–15. –/22(+4) 1W.

399201	**SD**	SY	*SY*	NU	999001	999101	999201
399202	**SD**	SY	*SY*	NU	999002	999102	999204
399203	**SD**	SY	*SY*	NU	999003	999103	999203
399204	**SD**	SY	*SY*	NU	999004	999104	999202
399205	**SD**	SY	*SY*	NU	999005	999105	999205
399206	**SD**	SY	*SY*	NU	999006	999106	999206
399207	**SD**	SY	*SY*	NU	999007	999107	999207

Name (carried on cars 999002 and 999204):

399202 Theo – The Children's Hospital Charity

4.2. 750 V DC THIRD RAIL EMUs

These classes use the third rail system at 750 V DC (unless stated). Outer couplers are buckeyes on units built before 1982 with bar couplers within the units. Newer units generally have Dellner outer couplers.

CLASS 442 WESSEX EXPRESS BREL DERBY

Units built for Waterloo–Bournemouth–Weymouth services. Previously operated by South West Trains and latterly by Southern until 2017. 18 units are being refurbished and returned to service with South Western Railway during 2019–20, mainly on the Portsmouth route. These will also be retractioned with AC motors.

Units 442401/405/407/412/421/424 are in long-term store and are not planned to be returned to service.

Formation: DTS(A)–TS–MBC–TS(W)–DTS(B) (* DTC–TS–MBS–TS–DTS).
Construction: Steel.
Traction Motors: Four EE546 of 300 kW recovered from Class 432s.
Wheel Arrangement: 2-2 + 2-2 + Bo-Bo + 2-2 + 2-2.
Braking: Disc.
Dimensions: 23.15/23.00 x 2.74 m.
Bogies: Two BREL P7 motor bogies (MBS). T3 bogies (trailer cars).
Couplers: Buckeye.
Control System: 1986-type.
Gangways: Throughout.
Maximum Speed: 100 mph.
Doors: Sliding plug.
Heating & Ventilation: Air conditioning.
Seating Layout (rebuilt): 1: 2+2 unidirectional/facing; 2: 2+2 unidirectional/facing.
Multiple Working: Within class and Class 33/1 & 73 locos in an emergency.

DTS(A) (* DTC). Lot No. 31030 Derby 1988–89. –/74 (* 32/44). 38.5 t.
TS. Lot No. 31032 Derby 1988–89. –/76 2T. 37.5 t.
MBC (* MBS). Lot No. 31034 Derby 1988–89. 24/28 (* –/66). 55.0 t.
TS(W). Lot No. 31033 Derby 1988–89. –/66(+4) 1TD 1T 2W (* –/64(+3) 1TD 1T 2W. 37.8 t.
DTS(B). Lot No. 31031 Derby 1988–89. –/74 (* –/80). 37.3 t.

* Refurbished South Western Railway units with new seating in First Class which is now in one driving car.

442401		**GV**	A		EP	77382	71818	62937	71842	77414
442402	*	**SW**	A		ZG	77383	71819	62938	71843	77407
442403	*	**SW**	A	*SW*	BM	77384	71820	62941	71844	77408
442404	*	**SW**	A		ZG	77385	71821	62939	71845	77409
442405		**GV**	A		ZG	77386	71822	62944	71846	77410
442406	*	**SW**	A	*SW*	BM	77389	71823	62942	71847	77411
442407		**GV**	A		EP	77388	71824	62943	71848	77412
442408	*	**SW**	A	*SW*	BM	77387	71825	62945	71849	77413
442409	*	**SW**	A		BM	77390	71826	62946	71850	77406
442410	*	**SW**	A	*SW*	BM	77391	71827	62948	71851	77415
442411	*	**SW**	A		BM	77392	71828	62940	71858	77422
442412		**GV**	A		EP	77393	71829	62947	71853	77417
442413	*	**SW**	A	*SW*	BM	77394	71830	62949	71854	77418

442414	*	**SW**	A	*SW*	BM	77395	71831	62950	71855	77419
442415	*	**SW**	A		ZG	77396	71832	62951	71856	77420
442416	*	**SW**	A		BM	77397	71833	62952	71857	77421
442417	*	**SW**	A	*SW*	BM	77398	71834	62953	71852	77416
442418	*	**SW**	A		BM	77399	71835	62954	71859	77423
442419	*	**SW**	A		BM	77400	71836	62955	71860	77424
442420	*	**SW**	A	*SW*	BM	77401	71837	62956	71861	77425
442421		**GV**	A		EP	77402	71838	62957	71862	77426
442422	*	**SW**	A		ZG	77403	71839	62958	71863	77427
442423	*	**SW**	A	*SW*	BM	77404	71840	62959	71864	77428
442424		**GV**	A		ZG	77405	71841	62960	71865	77429

CLASS 444 DESIRO UK SIEMENS

Express units.

Formation: DMS–TS–TS–TS–DMC.
Construction: Aluminium.
Traction Motors: Four Siemens 1TB2016-0GB02 asynchronous of 250 kW.
Wheel Arrangement: Bo-Bo + 2-2 + 2-2 + 2-2 + Bo-Bo.
Braking: Disc, rheostatic & regenerative.
Bogies: SGP SF5000.
Gangways: Throughout.
Doors: Single-leaf sliding plug.
Dimensions: 23.57 x 2.69 m.
Couplers: Dellner 12.
Control System: IGBT Inverter.
Maximum Speed: 100 mph.
Heating & Ventilation: Air conditioning.
Seating Layout: 1: 2+2 facing/unidirectional, 2: 2+2 facing/unidirectional.
Multiple Working: Within class and with Class 450.

DMS. Siemens Vienna/Krefeld 2003–04. –/76. 51.0t.
TS 67101–145. Siemens Vienna/Krefeld 2003–04. –/76 1T. 40.3t.
TS 67151–195. Siemens Vienna/Krefeld 2003–04. –/76 1T. 36.8t.
TS. Siemens Vienna/Krefeld 2003–04. –59 1TD 1T 2W. 42.1t.
DMC. Siemens Vienna/Krefeld 2003–04. 32/40. 51.3t.

444001	**ST**	A	*SW*	NT	63801	67101	67151	67201	63851
444002	**ST**	A	*SW*	NT	63802	67102	67152	67202	63852
444003	**ST**	A	*SW*	NT	63803	67103	67153	67203	63853
444004	**ST**	A	*SW*	NT	63804	67104	67154	67204	63854
444005	**ST**	A	*SW*	NT	63805	67105	67155	67205	63855
444006	**SW**	A	*SW*	NT	63806	67106	67156	67206	63856
444007	**ST**	A	*SW*	NT	63807	67107	67157	67207	63857
444008	**ST**	A	*SW*	NT	63808	67108	67158	67208	63858
444009	**ST**	A	*SW*	NT	63809	67109	67159	67209	63859
444010	**ST**	A	*SW*	NT	63810	67110	67160	67210	63860
444011	**ST**	A	*SW*	NT	63811	67111	67161	67211	63861
444012	**ST**	A	*SW*	NT	63812	67112	67162	67212	63862
444013	**ST**	A	*SW*	NT	63813	67113	67163	67213	63863
444014	**ST**	A	*SW*	NT	63814	67114	67164	67214	63864
444015	**SW**	A	*SW*	NT	63815	67115	67165	67215	63865
444016	**ST**	A	*SW*	NT	63816	67116	67166	67216	63866
444017	**ST**	A	*SW*	NT	63817	67117	67167	67217	63867
444018	**ST**	A	*SW*	NT	63818	67118	67168	67218	63868

444019	**ST**	A	*SW*	NT	63819	67119	67169	67219	63869
444020	**ST**	A	*SW*	NT	63820	67120	67170	67220	63870
444021	**ST**	A	*SW*	NT	63821	67121	67171	67221	63871
444022	**ST**	A	*SW*	NT	63822	67122	67172	67222	63872
444023	**ST**	A	*SW*	NT	63823	67123	67173	67223	63873
444024	**ST**	A	*SW*	NT	63824	67124	67174	67224	63874
444025	**ST**	A	*SW*	NT	63825	67125	67175	67225	63875
444026	**ST**	A	*SW*	NT	63826	67126	67176	67226	63876
444027	**ST**	A	*SW*	NT	63827	67127	67177	67227	63877
444028	**ST**	A	*SW*	NT	63828	67128	67178	67228	63878
444029	**ST**	A	*SW*	NT	63829	67129	67179	67229	63879
444030	**ST**	A	*SW*	NT	63830	67130	67180	67230	63880
444031	**ST**	A	*SW*	NT	63831	67131	67181	67231	63881
444032	**ST**	A	*SW*	NT	63832	67132	67182	67232	63882
444033	**ST**	A	*SW*	NT	63833	67133	67183	67233	63883
444034	**ST**	A	*SW*	NT	63834	67134	67184	67234	63884
444035	**ST**	A	*SW*	NT	63835	67135	67185	67235	63885
444036	**ST**	A	*SW*	NT	63836	67136	67186	67236	63886
444037	**ST**	A	*SW*	NT	63837	67137	67187	67237	63887
444038	**ST**	A	*SW*	NT	63838	67138	67188	67238	63888
444039	**ST**	A	*SW*	NT	63839	67139	67189	67239	63889
444040	**SW**	A	*SW*	NT	63840	67140	67190	67240	63890
444041	**ST**	A	*SW*	NT	63841	67141	67191	67241	63891
444042	**ST**	A	*SW*	NT	63842	67142	67192	67242	63892
444043	**ST**	A	*SW*	NT	63843	67143	67193	67243	63893
444044	**ST**	A	*SW*	NT	63844	67144	67194	67244	63894
444045	**ST**	A	*SW*	NT	63845	67145	67195	67245	63895

Names (carried on TSRMB):

444001 NAOMI HOUSE
444012 DESTINATION WEYMOUTH
444018 THE FAB 444
444038 SOUTH WESTERN RAILWAY
444040 THE D-DAY STORY PORTSMOUTH

CLASS 450 DESIRO UK SIEMENS

Outer suburban units.

Formation: DMC–TS–TS–DMC.
Construction: Aluminium.
Traction Motors: Four Siemens 1TB2016-0GB02 asynchronous of 250 kW.
Wheel Arrangement: Bo-Bo + 2-2 + 2-2 + Bo-Bo.
Braking: Disc, rheostatic & regenerative.
Bogies: SGP SF5000.
Gangways: Throughout.
Doors: Sliding plug.
Heating & Ventilation: Air conditioning.
Dimensions: 20.34 x 2.79 m.
Couplers: Dellner 12.
Control System: IGBT Inverter.
Maximum Speed: 100 mph.
Seating Layout: 1: 2+2 facing/unidirectional, 2: 3+2 facing/unidirectional.
Multiple Working: Within class and with Class 444.

Class 450/0. Standard units.

450043–070 were numbered 450543–570 between 2007/08 and 2019. Some seats were removed to create more standing room. They were renumbered back into the 450/0 series in 2019 at the same time as the whole class was refurbished.

DMC(A). Siemens Krefeld/Vienna 2002–06. 8/62. 48.0 t.
TS(A). Siemens Krefeld/Vienna 2002–06. –/69(+4) 1T. 35.8 t.
TS(B). Siemens Krefeld/Vienna 2002–06. –/61(+9) 1TD 2W. 39.8 t.
DMC(B). Siemens Krefeld/Vienna 2002–06. 8/62. 48.6 t.

450001	**SD**	A	*SW*	NT	63201	64201	68101	63601
450002	**SD**	A	*SW*	NT	63202	64202	68102	63602
450003	**SD**	A	*SW*	NT	63203	64203	68103	63603
450004	**SD**	A	*SW*	NT	63204	64204	68104	63604
450005	**SD**	A	*SW*	NT	63205	64205	68105	63605
450006	**SD**	A	*SW*	NT	63206	64206	68106	63606
450007	**SD**	A	*SW*	NT	63207	64207	68107	63607
450008	**SD**	A	*SW*	NT	63208	64208	68108	63608
450009	**SD**	A	*SW*	NT	63209	64209	68109	63609
450010	**SD**	A	*SW*	NT	63210	64210	68110	63610
450011	**SD**	A	*SW*	NT	63211	64211	68111	63611
450012	**SD**	A	*SW*	NT	63212	64212	68112	63612
450013	**SD**	A	*SW*	NT	63213	64213	68113	63613
450014	**SD**	A	*SW*	NT	63214	64214	68114	63614
450015	**SD**	A	*SW*	NT	63215	64215	68115	63615
450016	**SD**	A	*SW*	NT	63216	64216	68116	63616
450017	**SD**	A	*SW*	NT	63217	64217	68117	63617
450018	**SD**	A	*SW*	NT	63218	64218	68118	63618
450019	**SD**	A	*SW*	NT	63219	64219	68119	63619
450020	**SD**	A	*SW*	NT	63220	64220	68120	63620
450021	**SD**	A	*SW*	NT	63221	64221	68121	63621
450022	**SD**	A	*SW*	NT	63222	64222	68122	63622
450023	**SD**	A	*SW*	NT	63223	64223	68123	63623
450024	**SD**	A	*SW*	NT	63224	64224	68124	63624
450025	**SD**	A	*SW*	NT	63225	64225	68125	63625
450026	**SD**	A	*SW*	NT	63226	64226	68126	63626
450027	**SD**	A	*SW*	NT	63227	64227	68127	63627
450028	**SD**	A	*SW*	NT	63228	64228	68128	63628
450029	**SD**	A	*SW*	NT	63229	64229	68129	63629
450030	**SD**	A	*SW*	NT	63230	64230	68130	63630
450031	**SD**	A	*SW*	NT	63231	64231	68131	63631
450032	**SD**	A	*SW*	NT	63232	64232	68132	63632
450033	**SD**	A	*SW*	NT	63233	64233	68133	63633
450034	**SD**	A	*SW*	NT	63234	64234	68134	63634
450035	**SD**	A	*SW*	NT	63235	64235	68135	63635
450036	**SD**	A	*SW*	NT	63236	64236	68136	63636
450037	**SD**	A	*SW*	NT	63237	64237	68137	63637
450038	**SD**	A	*SW*	NT	63238	64238	68138	63638
450039	**SD**	A	*SW*	NT	63239	64239	68139	63639
450040	**SD**	A	*SW*	NT	63240	64240	68140	63640

450 041	**SD**	A	*SW*	NT	63241	64241	68141	63641
450 042	**SD**	A	*SW*	NT	63242	64242	68142	63642
450 043	**SD**	A	*SW*	NT	63243	64243	68143	63643
450 044	**SD**	A	*SW*	NT	63244	64244	68144	63644
450 045	**SD**	A	*SW*	NT	63245	64245	68145	63645
450 046	**SD**	A	*SW*	NT	63246	64246	68146	63646
450 047	**SD**	A	*SW*	NT	63247	64247	68147	63647
450 048	**SD**	A	*SW*	NT	63248	64248	68148	63648
450 049	**SD**	A	*SW*	NT	63249	64249	68149	63649
450 050	**SD**	A	*SW*	NT	63250	64250	68150	63650
450 051	**SD**	A	*SW*	NT	63251	64251	68151	63651
450 052	**SD**	A	*SW*	NT	63252	64252	68152	63652
450 053	**SD**	A	*SW*	NT	63253	64253	68153	63653
450 054	**SD**	A	*SW*	NT	63254	64254	68154	63654
450 055	**SD**	A	*SW*	NT	63255	64255	68155	63655
450 056	**SD**	A	*SW*	NT	63256	64256	68156	63656
450 057	**SD**	A	*SW*	NT	63257	64257	68157	63657
450 058	**SD**	A	*SW*	NT	63258	64258	68158	63658
450 059	**SD**	A	*SW*	NT	63259	64259	68159	63659
450 060	**SD**	A	*SW*	NT	63260	64260	68160	63660
450 061	**SD**	A	*SW*	NT	63261	64261	68161	63661
450 062	**SD**	A	*SW*	NT	63262	64262	68162	63662
450 063	**SD**	A	*SW*	NT	63263	64263	68163	63663
450 064	**SD**	A	*SW*	NT	63264	64264	68164	63664
450 065	**SD**	A	*SW*	NT	63265	64265	68165	63665
450 066	**SD**	A	*SW*	NT	63266	64266	68166	63666
450 067	**SD**	A	*SW*	NT	63267	64267	68167	63667
450 068	**SD**	A	*SW*	NT	63268	64268	68168	63668
450 069	**SD**	A	*SW*	NT	63269	64269	68169	63669
450 070	**SD**	A	*SW*	NT	63270	64270	68170	63670
450 071	**SD**	A	*SW*	NT	63271	64271	68171	63671
450 072	**SD**	A	*SW*	NT	63272	64272	68172	63672
450 073	**SD**	A	*SW*	NT	63273	64273	68173	63673
450 074	**SD**	A	*SW*	NT	63274	64274	68174	63674
450 075	**SD**	A	*SW*	NT	63275	64275	68175	63675
450 076	**SD**	A	*SW*	NT	63276	64276	68176	63676
450 077	**SD**	A	*SW*	NT	63277	64277	68177	63677
450 078	**SD**	A	*SW*	NT	63278	64278	68178	63678
450 079	**SD**	A	*SW*	NT	63279	64279	68179	63679
450 080	**SD**	A	*SW*	NT	63280	64280	68180	63680
450 081	**SD**	A	*SW*	NT	63281	64281	68181	63681
450 082	**SD**	A	*SW*	NT	63282	64282	68182	63682
450 083	**SD**	A	*SW*	NT	63283	64283	68183	63683
450 084	**SD**	A	*SW*	NT	63284	64284	68184	63684
450 085	**SD**	A	*SW*	NT	63285	64285	68185	63685
450 086	**SD**	A	*SW*	NT	63286	64286	68186	63686
450 087	**SD**	A	*SW*	NT	63287	64287	68187	63687
450 088	**SD**	A	*SW*	NT	63288	64288	68188	63688
450 089	**SD**	A	*SW*	NT	63289	64289	68189	63689
450 090	**SD**	A	*SW*	NT	63290	64290	68190	63690
450 091	**SD**	A	*SW*	NT	63291	64291	68191	63691

450092	**SD**	A	*SW*	NT	63292	64292	68192	63692
450093	**SD**	A	*SW*	NT	63293	64293	68193	63693
450094	**SD**	A	*SW*	NT	63294	64294	68194	63694
450095	**SD**	A	*SW*	NT	63295	64295	68195	63695
450096	**SD**	A	*SW*	NT	63296	64296	68196	63696
450097	**SD**	A	*SW*	NT	63297	64297	68197	63697
450098	**SD**	A	*SW*	NT	63298	64298	68198	63698
450099	**SD**	A	*SW*	NT	63299	64299	68199	63699
450100	**SD**	A	*SW*	NT	63300	64300	68200	63700
450101	**SD**	A	*SW*	NT	63701	66851	66801	63751
450102	**SD**	A	*SW*	NT	63702	66852	66802	63752
450103	**SD**	A	*SW*	NT	63703	66853	66803	63753
450104	**SD**	A	*SW*	NT	63704	66854	66804	63754
450105	**SD**	A	*SW*	NT	63705	66855	66805	63755
450106	**SD**	A	*SW*	NT	63706	66856	66806	63756
450107	**SD**	A	*SW*	NT	63707	66857	66807	63757
450108	**SD**	A	*SW*	NT	63708	66858	66808	63758
450109	**SD**	A	*SW*	NT	63709	66859	66809	63759
450110	**SD**	A	*SW*	NT	63710	66860	66810	63760
450111	**SW**	A	*SW*	NT	63901	66921	66901	63921
450112	**SD**	A	*SW*	NT	63902	66922	66902	63922
450113	**SD**	A	*SW*	NT	63903	66923	66903	63923
450114	**SD**	A	*SW*	NT	63904	66924	66904	63924
450115	**SD**	A	*SW*	NT	63905	66925	66905	63925
450116	**SD**	A	*SW*	NT	63906	66926	66906	63926
450117	**SD**	A	*SW*	NT	63907	66927	66907	63927
450118	**SD**	A	*SW*	NT	63908	66928	66908	63928
450119	**SD**	A	*SW*	NT	63909	66929	66909	63929
450120	**SD**	A	*SW*	NT	63910	66930	66910	63930
450121	**SD**	A	*SW*	NT	63911	66931	66911	63931
450122	**SD**	A	*SW*	NT	63912	66932	66912	63932
450123	**SD**	A	*SW*	NT	63913	66933	66913	63933
450124	**SD**	A	*SW*	NT	63914	66934	66914	63934
450125	**SD**	A	*SW*	NT	63915	66935	66915	63935
450126	**SD**	A	*SW*	NT	63916	66936	66916	63936
450127	**SD**	A	*SW*	NT	63917	66937	66917	63937

Names (carried on DMSO(B)):

450015 DESIRO
450042 TRELOAR COLLEGE
450114 FAIRBRIDGE investing in the future
450127 DAVE GUNSON

CLASS 455 BREL YORK

Inner suburban units. During 2016–17 the South Western Railway fleet was fitted with new AC traction motors by Vossloh Kiepe.

Formation: DTS–MS–TS–DTS.
Construction: Steel. Class 455/7 TS have a steel underframe and an aluminium alloy body and roof.
Traction Motors: Four GEC507-20J of 185 kW, some recovered from Class 405s (* Four TSA010163 AC motors of 240 kW).

Wheel Arrangement: 2-2 + Bo-Bo + 2-2 + 2-2.
Braking: Disc (* and regenerative). **Dimensions:** 19.92/19.83 x 2.82 m.
Bogies: P7 (motor) and T3 (455/8 & 455/9) BX1 (455/7) trailer.
Gangways: Within unit + end doors (sealed on Southern units).
Couplers: Tightlock. **Maximum Speed:** 75 mph.
Control System: 1982-type, camshaft (* IGBT Inverter).
Doors: Sliding. **Heating & Ventilation:** Various.
Seating Layout: All units refurbished. SWR units: 2+2 high-back unidirectional/facing seating. Southern units: 3+2 high back mainly facing seating.
Multiple Working: Within class and with Class 456.

Class 455/7. South Western Railway units. Second series with TSs originally in Class 508s. Pressure heating & ventilation.

DTS. Lot No. 30976 1984–85. –/50(+4) 1W. 30.8t.
MS. Lot No. 30975 1984–85. –/68. 45.7t.
TS. Lot No. 30944 1979–80. –/68. 26.1t.

5701	*	**SS**	P	*SW*	WD	77727	62783	71545	77728
5702	*	**SS**	P	*SW*	WD	77729	62784	71547	77730
5703	*	**SS**	P	*SW*	WD	77731	62785	71540	77732
5704	*	**SS**	P	*SW*	WD	77733	62786	71548	77734
5705	*	**SS**	P	*SW*	WD	77735	62787	71565	77736
5706	*	**SS**	P	*SW*	WD	77737	62788	71534	77738
5707	*	**SS**	P	*SW*	WD	77739	62789	71536	77740
5708	*	**SS**	P	*SW*	WD	77741	62790	71560	77742
5709	*	**SS**	P	*SW*	WD	77743	62791	71532	77744
5710	*	**SS**	P	*SW*	WD	77745	62792	71566	77746
5711	*	**SS**	P	*SW*	WD	77747	62793	71542	77748
5712	*	**SS**	P	*SW*	WD	77749	62794	71546	77750
5713	*	**SS**	P	*SW*	WD	77751	62795	71567	77752
5714	*	**SS**	P	*SW*	WD	77753	62796	71539	77754
5715	*	**SS**	P	*SW*	WD	77755	62797	71535	77756
5716	*	**SS**	P	*SW*	WD	77757	62798	71564	77758
5717	*	**SS**	P	*SW*	WD	77759	62799	71528	77760
5718	*	**SS**	P	*SW*	WD	77761	62800	71557	77762
5719	*	**SS**	P	*SW*	WD	77763	62801	71558	77764
5720	*	**SS**	P	*SW*	WD	77765	62802	71568	77766
5721	*	**SS**	P	*SW*	WD	77767	62803	71553	77768
5722	*	**SS**	P	*SW*	WD	77769	62804	71533	77770
5723	*	**SS**	P	*SW*	WD	77771	62805	71526	77772
5724	*	**SS**	P	*SW*	WD	77773	62806	71561	77774
5725	*	**SS**	P	*SW*	WD	77775	62807	71541	77776
5726	*	**SS**	P	*SW*	WD	77777	62808	71556	77778
5727	*	**SS**	P	*SW*	WD	77779	62809	71562	77780
5728	*	**SS**	P	*SW*	WD	77781	62810	71527	77782
5729	*	**SS**	P	*SW*	WD	77783	62811	71550	77784
5730	*	**SS**	P	*SW*	WD	77785	62812	71551	77786
5731	*	**SS**	P	*SW*	WD	77787	62813	71555	77788
5732	*	**SS**	P	*SW*	WD	77789	62814	71552	77790
5733	*	**SS**	P	*SW*	WD	77791	62815	71549	77792
5734	*	**SS**	P	*SW*	WD	77793	62816	71531	77794

5735	*	**SS**	P	*SW*	WD	77795	62817	71563	77796
5736	*	**SS**	P	*SW*	WD	77797	62818	71554	77798
5737	*	**SS**	P	*SW*	WD	77799	62819	71544	77800
5738	*	**SS**	P	*SW*	WD	77801	62820	71529	77802
5739	*	**SS**	P	*SW*	WD	77803	62821	71537	77804
5740	*	**SS**	P	*SW*	WD	77805	62822	71530	77806
5741	*	**SS**	P	*SW*	WD	77807	62823	71559	77808
5742	*	**SS**	P	*SW*	WD	77809	62824	71543	77810
5750	*	**SS**	P	*SW*	WD	77811	62825	71538	77812

Class 455/8. Southern units. First series. Pressure heating & ventilation. Fitted with in-cab air conditioning systems meaning that the end door has been sealed.

DTS. Lot No. 30972 York 1982–84. –/74. 33.6 t.
MS. Lot No. 30973 York 1982–84. –/84. 45.6 t.
TS. Lot No. 30974 York 1982–84. –/75(+3) 2W. 34.0 t.

455801	**SN**	E	*SN*	SL	77627	62709	71657	77580
455802	**SN**	E	*SN*	SL	77581	62710	71664	77582
455803	**SN**	E	*SN*	SL	77583	62711	71639	77584
455804	**SN**	E	*SN*	SL	77585	62712	71640	77586
455805	**SN**	E	*SN*	SL	77587	62713	71641	77588
455806	**SN**	E	*SN*	SL	77589	62714	71642	77590
455807	**SN**	E	*SN*	SL	77591	62715	71643	77592
455808	**SN**	E	*SN*	SL	77637	62716	71644	77594
455809	**SN**	E	*SN*	SL	77623	62717	71648	77602
455810	**SN**	E	*SN*	SL	77597	62718	71646	77598
455811	**SN**	E	*SN*	SL	77599	62719	71647	77600
455812	**SN**	E	*SN*	SL	77595	62720	71645	77626
455813	**SN**	E	*SN*	SL	77603	62721	71649	77604
455814	**SN**	E	*SN*	SL	77605	62722	71650	77606
455815	**SN**	E	*SN*	SL	77607	62723	71651	77608
455816	**SN**	E	*SN*	SL	77609	62724	71652	77633
455817	**SN**	E	*SN*	SL	77611	62725	71653	77612
455818	**SN**	E	*SN*	SL	77613	62726	71654	77632
455819	**SN**	E	*SN*	SL	77615	62727	71637	77616
455820	**SN**	E	*SN*	SL	77617	62728	71656	77618
455821	**SN**	E	*SN*	SL	77619	62729	71655	77620
455822	**SN**	E	*SN*	SL	77621	62730	71658	77622
455823	**SN**	E	*SN*	SL	77601	62731	71659	77596
455824	**SN**	E	*SN*	SL	77593	62732	71660	77624
455825	**SN**	E	*SN*	SL	77579	62733	71661	77628
455826	**SN**	E	*SN*	SL	77630	62734	71662	77629
455827	**SN**	E	*SN*	SL	77610	62735	71663	77614
455828	**SN**	E	*SN*	SL	77631	62736	71638	77634
455829	**SN**	E	*SN*	SL	77635	62737	71665	77636
455830	**SN**	E	*SN*	SL	77625	62743	71666	77638
455831	**SN**	E	*SN*	SL	77639	62739	71667	77640
455832	**SN**	E	*SN*	SL	77641	62740	71668	77642
455833	**SN**	E	*SN*	SL	77643	62741	71669	77644
455834	**SN**	E	*SN*	SL	77645	62742	71670	77646

▲ Southern operates the oldest EMUs on the mainland in the form of the 313s on the Brighton Coastway routes. On 21/07/19 313 213 leaves Seaford with the 15.29 Seaford–Brighton. **Jamie Squibbs**

▼ ScotRail Saltire-liveried 318 256 and 320 315 pass Craigenhill with the 09.28 Glasgow Central–Lanark on 23/09/18. **Robin Ralston**

▲ New Greater Anglia-liveried "Renatus" 321 317 leads 321 426 into Chelmsford with the 17.44 Braintree–London Liverpool Street on 06/08/19. **Robert Pritchard**

▼ Royal Mail-liveried 325 002+325 013+325 012 pass Crawford with 1M44 16.20 Shieldmuir–Warrington RMT postal on 10/10/18. **Robin Ralston**

▲ New Northern-liveried 331 009 passes Longport with a driver training run from Stoke-on-Trent to Macclesfield on 19/09/19. **Cliff Beeton**

▼ New Northern-liveried 333 001 leaves Cononley with the 13.47 Skipton–Leeds on 14/03/19. **Paul Biggs**

▲ ScotRail Saltire-liveried 334 027+334 023 pass Hillend Reservoir with the 09.24 Milngavie–Edinburgh on 24/09/18. **Robin Ralston**

▼ Elizabeth Line unit 345 008, running as a 7-car set, stands at Shenfield with the 09.14 to London Liverpool Street on 20/06/19. **Andy Chard**

▲ London Northwestern Railway-liveried 350 372 passes Ansty with the 16.07 London Euston–Liverpool Lime Street on 29/07/19. **Dave Gommersall**

▼ c2c-liveried 357 009 passes Shadwell with the 12.24 London Fenchurch Street–Southend Central on 13/10/18. **Alex Dasi-Sutton**

▲ Southeastern blue-liveried 375 622 brings up the rear of the 17.10 London Charing Cross–Ramsgate led by 375 630 at St Johns on 05/08/18. **Robert Pritchard**

▼ ScotRail Saltire-liveried 380 103 passes Breich with the 11.16 Glasgow Central–Edinburgh Waverley on 17/09/19. **Ian Lothian**

▲ ScotRail Saltire-liveried 385 015 has just left Lanark with the 08.53 to Glasgow Central on 22/05/19. **Robin Ralston**

▼ Great Western Railway-liveried 387 158 and 387 141 pass Acton Main Line with the 17.42 London Paddington–Reading on 31/05/19. **Robert Pritchard**

▲ New Virgin Trains-liveried 390 045, with "Pride" vinyls, passes Lamington with the 16.38 Glasgow Central–London Euston on 12/05/19. **Robin Ralston**

▼ Southeastern blue-liveried 395 017 passes Rainham on HS1 with 15.37 St Pancras–Ramsgate on 22/10/17. **Robert Pritchard**

▲ One of the new CAF-built TransPennine Express Class 397s, 397 005, is seen near Lanark Junction with the 12.05 Glasgow Central–Liverpool Lime Street crew training run on 02/10/19. **Robin Ralston**

▼ South Western Railway-liveried 442 420 and 442 410 are seen on a gauging run at London Waterloo before leaving to Bournemouth on 19/06/19. **Chris Wilson**

▲ In South West Trains blue livery, with South Western Railway branding, 450 017 leaves Weymouth with the 15.20 to London Waterloo on 26/06/19. **Stephen Ginn**

▼ South West Trains red-liveried 456 016, with Class 455s 5702 and 5704, pass Raynes Park with the 09.37 Guildford–London Waterloo on 12/07/19.
Alex Dasi-Sutton

▲ South West Trains blue-liveried 458 535 and 458 503 leave Wimbledon with the diverted 10.09 London Waterloo–Reading on 17/08/19. **Robin Ralston**

▼ Southeastern suburban-liveried 465 191+465 019 approach Slade Green with the 13.12 London Charing Cross–Dartford on 05/04/19. **Robert Pritchard**

▲ London Transport maroon-liveried 483 008 arrives at Smallbrook Junction with a Ryde Pier Head–Shanklin service on 26/08/19. **Tony Christie**

▼ Merseyrail-liveried 508 139 arrives at Birkenhead Central with a Liverpool Central–Chester service on 07/09/19. **Paul Senior**

▲ Thameslink-liveried 700 138 passes Stoats Nest Junction (Coulsdon) with the 07.59 Brighton–Bedford on 07/08/18. **Robert Pritchard**

▼ Revised London Overground-liveried 710 261 arrives at Leyton Midland Road with a Gospel Oak–Barking service on 23/09/19. **Stuart Hicks**

▲ New Great Northern unit 717 014 passes Enfield Chase with the 15.27 Gordon Hill–Hornsey depot empty stock on 14/02/19. **Robert Pritchard**

▼ Greater Anglia 745 005, one of ten new 12-car sets for the Norwich route, passes Brantham on test from Norwich to London Liverpool Street on 02/10/19. **Paul Biggs**

▲ New Greater Anglia bi-mode unit 755 413 is seen at Lowestoft with a 15.27 press special to Norwich on 04/09/19. **Robert Pritchard**

▼ LNER bi-mode Azuma 800 107 passes Eaton Lane crossing near Retford with the 18.03 London King's Cross–Skipton on 22/07/19. **Robert Pritchard**

▲ TransPennine Express-liveried 802 201 is seen near Burnmouth on the ECML with the 11.33 Edinburgh–Newcastle test run on 17/09/19. **Robin Ralston**

▼ Siemens e320 Eurostar 4022/21 passes Westenhanger with the 13.40 Paris–London St Pancras on 05/08/18. **Robert Pritchard**

455835	**SN**	E	*SN*	SL	77647	62738	71671	77648
455836	**SN**	E	*SN*	SL	77649	62744	71672	77650
455837	**SN**	E	*SN*	SL	77651	62745	71673	77652
455838	**SN**	E	*SN*	SL	77653	62746	71674	77654
455839	**SN**	E	*SN*	SL	77655	62747	71675	77656
455840	**SN**	E	*SN*	SL	77657	62748	71676	77658
455841	**SN**	E	*SN*	SL	77659	62749	71677	77660
455842	**SN**	E	*SN*	SL	77661	62750	71678	77662
455843	**SN**	E	*SN*	SL	77663	62751	71679	77664
455844	**SN**	E	*SN*	SL	77665	62752	71680	77666
455845	**SN**	E	*SN*	SL	77667	62753	71681	77668
455846	**SN**	E	*SN*	SL	77669	62754	71682	77670

Class 455/8. South Western Railway units. First series. Pressure heating & ventilation.

DTS. Lot No. 30972 York 1982–84. –50(+4) 1W. 29.5 t.
MS. Lot No. 30973 York 1982–84. –/68. 45.6 t.
TS. Lot No. 30974 York 1982–84. –/68. 27.1 t.

5847	*	**SS**	P	*SW*	WD	77671	62755	71683	77672
5848	*	**SS**	P	*SW*	WD	77673	62756	71684	77674
5849	*	**SS**	P	*SW*	WD	77675	62757	71685	77676
5850	*	**SS**	P	*SW*	WD	77677	62758	71686	77678
5851	*	**SS**	P	*SW*	WD	77679	62759	71687	77680
5852	*	**SS**	P	*SW*	WD	77681	62760	71688	77682
5853	*	**SS**	P	*SW*	WD	77683	62761	71689	77684
5854	*	**SS**	P	*SW*	WD	77685	62762	71690	77686
5855	*	**SS**	P	*SW*	WD	77687	62763	71691	77688
5856	*	**SS**	P	*SW*	WD	77689	62764	71692	77690
5857	*	**SS**	P	*SW*	WD	77691	62765	71693	77692
5858	*	**SS**	P	*SW*	WD	77693	62766	71694	77694
5859	*	**SS**	P	*SW*	WD	77695	62767	71695	77696
5860	*	**SS**	P	*SW*	WD	77697	62768	71696	77698
5861	*	**SS**	P	*SW*	WD	77699	62769	71697	77700
5862	*	**SS**	P	*SW*	WD	77701	62770	71698	77702
5863	*	**SS**	P	*SW*	WD	77703	62771	71699	77704
5864	*	**SS**	P	*SW*	WD	77705	62772	71700	77706
5865	*	**SS**	P	*SW*	WD	77707	62773	71701	77708
5866	*	**SS**	P	*SW*	WD	77709	62774	71702	77710
5867	*	**SS**	P	*SW*	WD	77711	62775	71703	77712
5868	*	**SS**	P	*SW*	WD	77713	62776	71704	77714
5869	*	**SS**	P	*SW*	WD	77715	62777	71705	77716
5870	*	**SS**	P	*SW*	WD	77717	62778	71706	77718
5871	*	**SS**	P	*SW*	WD	77719	62779	71707	77720
5872	*	**SS**	P	*SW*	WD	77721	62780	71708	77722
5873	*	**SS**	P	*SW*	WD	77723	62781	71709	77724
5874	*	**SS**	P	*SW*	WD	77725	62782	71710	77726

Class 455/9. South Western Railway units. Third series. Convection heating.
Dimensions: 19.96/20.18 x 2.82 m.

67301 and 67400 were converted from Class 210 DEMU vehicles to replace accident damaged cars.

DTS. Lot No. 30991 York 1985. –/50(+4) 1W. 30.7 t.
MS. Lot No. 30992 York 1985. –/68. 46.3 t.
MS 67301. Lot No. 30932 Derby 1981. –/68. t.
TS. Lot No. 30993 York 1985. –/68. 28.3 t.
TS 67400. Lot No. 30932 Derby 1981. –/68. 26.5 t.

5901	*	**SS**	P	*SW*	WD	77813	62826	71714	77814
5902	*	**SS**	P	*SW*	WD	77815	62827	71715	77816
5903	*	**SS**	P	*SW*	WD	77817	62828	71716	77818
5904	*	**SS**	P	*SW*	WD	77819	62829	71717	77820
5905	*	**SS**	P	*SW*	WD	77821	62830	71725	77822
5906	*	**SS**	P	*SW*	WD	77823	62831	71719	77824
5907	*	**SS**	P	*SW*	WD	77825	62832	71720	77826
5908	*	**SS**	P	*SW*	WD	77827	62833	71721	77828
5909	*	**SS**	P	*SW*	WD	77829	62834	71722	77830
5910	*	**SS**	P	*SW*	WD	77831	62835	71723	77832
5911	*	**SS**	P	*SW*	WD	77833	62836	71724	77834
5912	*	**SS**	P	*SW*	WD	77835	62837	67400	77836
5913	*	**SS**	P	*SW*	WD	77837	67301	71726	77838
5914	*	**SS**	P	*SW*	WD	77839	62839	71727	77840
5915	*	**SS**	P	*SW*	WD	77841	62840	71728	77842
5916	*	**SS**	P	*SW*	WD	77843	62841	71729	77844
5917	*	**SS**	P	*SW*	WD	77845	62842	71730	77846
5918	*	**SS**	P	*SW*	WD	77847	62843	71732	77848
5919	*	**SS**	P	*SW*	WD	77849	62844	71718	77850
5920	*	**SS**	P	*SW*	WD	77851	62845	71733	77852

CLASS 456 BREL YORK

Inner suburban units previously operated by Southern, but now operated by South Western Railway.

Formation: DMS–DTS.
Construction: Steel underframe, aluminium alloy body & roof.
Traction Motors: Two GEC507-21J of 185 kW, some recovered from Class 405s.
Wheel Arrangement: 2-Bo + 2-2.
Braking: Disc.
Bogies: P7 (motor) and T3 (trailer).
Gangways: Within unit.
Doors: Sliding.
Seating Layout: 2+2 facing/unidirectional.
Heating & Ventilation: Convection heating.
Multiple Working: Within class and with Class 455.
Dimensions: 20.61 x 2.82 m.
Couplers: Tightlock.
Control System: GTO Chopper.
Maximum Speed: 75 mph.

DMS. Lot No. 31073 1990–91. –/59. 43.3 t.
DTS. Lot No. 31074 1990–91. –/54(+5). 32.3 t.

456001	**SS**	P	*SW*	WD	64735	78250
456002	**SS**	P	*SW*	WD	64736	78251
456003	**SS**	P	*SW*	WD	64737	78252
456004	**SS**	P	*SW*	WD	64738	78253
456005	**SS**	P	*SW*	WD	64739	78254
456006	**SS**	P	*SW*	WD	64740	78255

456007	**SS**	P	*SW*	WD	64741	78256
456008	**SS**	P	*SW*	WD	64742	78257
456009	**SS**	P	*SW*	WD	64743	78258
456010	**SS**	P	*SW*	WD	64744	78259
456011	**SS**	P	*SW*	WD	64745	78260
456012	**SS**	P	*SW*	WD	64746	78261
456013	**SS**	P	*SW*	WD	64747	78262
456014	**SS**	P	*SW*	WD	64748	78263
456015	**SS**	P	*SW*	WD	64749	78264
456016	**SS**	P	*SW*	WD	64750	78265
456017	**SS**	P	*SW*	WD	64751	78266
456018	**SS**	P	*SW*	WD	64752	78267
456019	**SS**	P	*SW*	WD	64753	78268
456020	**SS**	P	*SW*	WD	64754	78269
456021	**SS**	P	*SW*	WD	64755	78270
456022	**SS**	P	*SW*	WD	64756	78271
456023	**SS**	P	*SW*	WD	64757	78272
456024	**SS**	P	*SW*	WD	64758	78273

CLASS 458 JUNIPER ALSTOM BIRMINGHAM

Outer suburban units. Between 2013 and 2016 the fleet of 30 4-car Class 458 units and the former Gatwick Express fleet of eight 8-car Class 460 units was combined to form a fleet of 36 5-car Standard Class only Class 458/5s. The work was carried out at Wabtec Doncaster and Brush Loughborough. Former Class 460 driving cars 67901/903/907/908 were not included in this programme and have been scrapped.

After lengthening each unit was renumbered into the 458 5xx series. All individual vehicles retained their original numbers.

Formation: DMC–TS*–TS–MS–DMC (* ex-Class 460 in 458 501–530).
Construction: Steel. **Dimensions:** 21.16 or 21.06 x 2.80 m.
Traction Motors: Two Alstom ONIX 800 asynchronous of 270 kW.
Wheel Arrangement: 2-Bo + 2-2 + 2-2 + Bo-2 + Bo-2.
Braking: Disc & regenerative. **Control System:** IGBT Inverter.
Bogies: ACR. **Doors:** Sliding plug.
Gangways: Throughout.
Couplers: Voith 136.
Maximum Speed: 75 mph.
Heating & Ventilation: Air conditioning. **Multiple Working:** Within class.
Seating Layout: 2+2 facing/unidirectional.

DMC(A). Alstom 1998–2000. –/60. 45.7 t.
TS. Alstom 1998–99. 458 501–530 –/56; 458 531–536 –/52 1T. 34.4 t.
TS. Alstom 1998–2000. –/42 1TD 2W. 34.1 t.
MS. Alstom 1998–2000. 458 501–530 –56 1T; 458 531–536 –/56. 40.1 t.
DMC(B). Alstom 1998–2000. –/60. 44.9 t.

458501	**SD**	P	*SW*	WD	67601	74431	74001	74101	67701
458502	**SD**	P	*SW*	WD	67602	74421	74002	74102	67702
458503	**SD**	P	*SW*	WD	67603	74441	74003	74103	67703

458 504	**SD**	P	*SW*	WD	67604	74451	74004	74104	67704
458 505	**SD**	P	*SW*	WD	67605	74425	74005	74105	67705
458 506	**SD**	P	*SW*	WD	67606	74436	74006	74106	67706
458 507	**SD**	P	*SW*	WD	67607	74428	74007	74107	67707
458 508	**SD**	P	*SW*	WD	67608	74433	74008	74108	67708
458 509	**SD**	P	*SW*	WD	67609	74452	74009	74109	67709
458 510	**SD**	P	*SW*	WD	67610	74405	74010	74110	67710
458 511	**SD**	P	*SW*	WD	67611	74435	74011	74111	67711
458 512	**SD**	P	*SW*	WD	67612	74427	74012	74112	67712
458 513	**SD**	P	*SW*	WD	67613	74437	74013	74113	67713
458 514	**SD**	P	*SW*	WD	67614	74407	74014	74114	67714
458 515	**SD**	P	*SW*	WD	67615	74404	74015	74115	67715
458 516	**SD**	P	*SW*	WD	67616	74406	74016	74116	67716
458 517	**SD**	P	*SW*	WD	67617	74426	74017	74117	67717
458 518	**SD**	P	*SW*	WD	67618	74432	74018	74118	67718
458 519	**SD**	P	*SW*	WD	67619	74403	74019	74119	67719
458 520	**SD**	P	*SW*	WD	67620	74401	74020	74120	67720
458 521	**SD**	P	*SW*	WD	67621	74438	74021	74121	67721
458 522	**SD**	P	*SW*	WD	67622	74424	74022	74122	67722
458 523	**SD**	P	*SW*	WD	67623	74434	74023	74123	67723
458 524	**SD**	P	*SW*	WD	67624	74402	74024	74124	67724
458 525	**SD**	P	*SW*	WD	67625	74422	74025	74125	67725
458 526	**SD**	P	*SW*	WD	67626	74442	74026	74126	67726
458 527	**SD**	P	*SW*	WD	67627	74412	74027	74127	67727
458 528	**SD**	P	*SW*	WD	67628	74408	74028	74128	67728
458 529	**SD**	P	*SW*	WD	67629	74423	74029	74129	67729
458 530	**SD**	P	*SW*	WD	67630	74411	74030	74130	67730

The following units were converted entirely from Class 460s.

458 531	**SD**	P	*SW*	WD	67913	74418	74446	74458	67912
458 532	**SD**	P	*SW*	WD	67904	74417	74447	74457	67905
458 533	**SD**	P	*SW*	WD	67917	74413	74443	74453	67916
458 534	**SD**	P	*SW*	WD	67914	74414	74444	74454	67918
458 535	**SD**	P	*SW*	WD	67915	74415	74445	74455	67911
458 536	**SD**	P	*SW*	WD	67906	74416	74448	74456	67902

CLASS 465 NETWORKER

Inner and outer suburban units.

Formation: DMS–TS–TS–DMS.
Construction: Welded aluminium alloy.
Traction Motors: Four Hitachi asynchronous of 280 kW (Classes 465/0 and 465/1) or Four GEC-Alsthom G352BY of 280 kW (Classes 465/2 and 465/9).
Wheel Arrangement: Bo-Bo + 2-2 + 2-2 + Bo-Bo.
Braking: Disc & rheostatic and regenerative (Classes 465/0 and 465/1 only).
Bogies: BREL P3/T3 (465/0 and 465/1), SRP BP62/BT52 (465/2 and 465/9).
Dimensions: 20.89/20.06 x 2.81 m.
Control System: IGBT Inverter (465/0 and 465/1) or 1992-type GTO Inverter.
Gangways: Within unit. **Couplers:** Tightlock.
Doors: Sliding plug. **Maximum Speed:** 75 mph.

Seating Layout: 3+2 facing/unidirectional.
Multiple Working: Within class and with Class 466.

64759–808. DMS(A). Lot No. 31100 BREL York 1991–93. –/86. 39.2t.
64809–858. DMS(B). Lot No. 31100 BREL York 1991–93. –/86. 39.2t.
65734–749. DMS(A). Lot No. 31103 Metro-Cammell 1991–93. –/86. 39.2t.
65784–799. DMS(B). Lot No. 31103 Metro-Cammell 1991–93. –/86. 39.2t.
65800–846. DMS(A). Lot No. 31130 ABB York 1993–94. –/86. 39.2t.
65847–893. DMS(B). Lot No. 31130 ABB York 1993–94. –/86. 39.2t.
72028–126 (even nos.) TS. Lot No. 31102 BREL York 1991–93. –/90. 27.2t.
72029–127 (odd nos.) TS. Lot No. 31101 BREL York 1991–93. –/65(+7) 1TD 2W. 29.6 t.
72787–817 (odd nos.) TS. Lot No. 31104 Metro-Cammell 1991–92. –/65(+7) 1TD 2W. 30.2 t.
72788–818 (even nos.) TS. Lot No. 31105 Metro-Cammell 1991–92. –/90. 29.4t.
72900–992 (even nos.) TS. Lot No. 31102 ABB York 1993–94. –/90. 27.2t.
72901–993 (odd nos.) TS. Lot No. 31101 ABB York 1993–94. –/65(+7) 1TD 2W. 29.6 t.

Class 465/0. Built by BREL/ABB.

465001	**SE**	E	*SE*	SG	64759	72028	72029	64809
465002	**SE**	E	*SE*	SG	64760	72030	72031	64810
465003	**SE**	E	*SE*	SG	64761	72032	72033	64811
465004	**SE**	E	*SE*	SG	64762	72034	72035	64812
465005	**SE**	E	*SE*	SG	64763	72036	72037	64813
465006	**SE**	E	*SE*	SG	64764	72038	72039	64814
465007	**SE**	E	*SE*	SG	64765	72040	72041	64815
465008	**SE**	E	*SE*	SG	64766	72042	72043	64816
465009	**SE**	E	*SE*	SG	64767	72044	72045	64817
465010	**SE**	E	*SE*	SG	64768	72046	72047	64818
465011	**SE**	E	*SE*	SG	64769	72048	72049	64819
465012	**SE**	E	*SE*	SG	64770	72050	72051	64820
465013	**SE**	E	*SE*	SG	64771	72052	72053	64821
465014	**SE**	E	*SE*	SG	64772	72054	72055	64822
465015	**SE**	E	*SE*	SG	64773	72056	72057	64823
465016	**SE**	E	*SE*	SG	64774	72058	72059	64824
465017	**SE**	E	*SE*	SG	64775	72060	72061	64825
465018	**SE**	E	*SE*	SG	64776	72062	72063	64826
465019	**SE**	E	*SE*	SG	64777	72064	72065	64827
465020	**SE**	E	*SE*	SG	64778	72066	72067	64828
465021	**SE**	E	*SE*	SG	64779	72068	72069	64829
465022	**SE**	E	*SE*	SG	64780	72070	72071	64830
465023	**SE**	E	*SE*	SG	64781	72072	72073	64831
465024	**SE**	E	*SE*	SG	64782	72074	72075	64832
465025	**SE**	E	*SE*	SG	64783	72076	72077	64833
465026	**SE**	E	*SE*	SG	64784	72078	72079	64834
465027	**SE**	E	*SE*	SG	64785	72080	72081	64835
465028	**SE**	E	*SE*	SG	64786	72082	72083	64836
465029	**SE**	E	*SE*	SG	64787	72084	72085	64837
465030	**SE**	E	*SE*	SG	64788	72086	72087	64838
465031	**SE**	E	*SE*	SG	64789	72088	72089	64839

465 032	**SE**	E	*SE*	SG	64790	72090	72091	64840
465 033	**SE**	E	*SE*	SG	64791	72092	72093	64841
465 034	**SE**	E	*SE*	SG	64792	72094	72095	64842
465 035	**SE**	E	*SE*	SG	64793	72096	72097	64843
465 036	**SE**	E	*SE*	SG	64794	72098	72099	64844
465 037	**SE**	E	*SE*	SG	64795	72100	72101	64845
465 038	**SE**	E	*SE*	SG	64796	72102	72103	64846
465 039	**SE**	E	*SE*	SG	64797	72104	72105	64847
465 040	**SE**	E	*SE*	SG	64798	72106	72107	64848
465 041	**SE**	E	*SE*	SG	64799	72108	72109	64849
465 042	**SE**	E	*SE*	SG	64800	72110	72111	64850
465 043	**SE**	E	*SE*	SG	64801	72112	72113	64851
465 044	**SE**	E	*SE*	SG	64802	72114	72115	64852
465 045	**SE**	E	*SE*	SG	64803	72116	72117	64853
465 046	**SE**	E	*SE*	SG	64804	72118	72119	64854
465 047	**SE**	E	*SE*	SG	64805	72120	72121	64855
465 048	**SE**	E	*SE*	SG	64806	72122	72123	64856
465 049	**SE**	E	*SE*	SG	64807	72124	72125	64857
465 050	**SE**	E	*SE*	SG	64808	72126	72127	64858

Class 465/1. Built by BREL/ABB. Similar to Class 465/0 but with detail differences.

465 151	**SE**	E	*SE*	SG	65800	72900	72901	65847
465 152	**SE**	E	*SE*	SG	65801	72902	72903	65848
465 153	**SE**	E	*SE*	SG	65802	72904	72905	65849
465 154	**SE**	E	*SE*	SG	65803	72906	72907	65850
465 155	**SE**	E	*SE*	SG	65804	72908	72909	65851
465 156	**SE**	E	*SE*	SG	65805	72910	72911	65852
465 157	**SE**	E	*SE*	SG	65806	72912	72913	65853
465 158	**SE**	E	*SE*	SG	65807	72914	72915	65854
465 159	**SE**	E	*SE*	SG	65808	72916	72917	65855
465 160	**SE**	E	*SE*	SG	65809	72918	72919	65856
465 161	**SE**	E	*SE*	SG	65810	72920	72921	65857
465 162	**SE**	E	*SE*	SG	65811	72922	72923	65858
465 163	**SE**	E	*SE*	SG	65812	72924	72925	65859
465 164	**SE**	E	*SE*	SG	65813	72926	72927	65860
465 165	**SE**	E	*SE*	SG	65814	72928	72929	65861
465 166	**SE**	E	*SE*	SG	65815	72930	72931	65862
465 167	**SE**	E	*SE*	SG	65816	72932	72933	65863
465 168	**SE**	E	*SE*	SG	65817	72934	72935	65864
465 169	**SE**	E	*SE*	SG	65818	72936	72937	65865
465 170	**SE**	E	*SE*	SG	65819	72938	72939	65866
465 171	**SE**	E	*SE*	SG	65820	72940	72941	65867
465 172	**SE**	E	*SE*	SG	65821	72942	72943	65868
465 173	**SE**	E	*SE*	SG	65822	72944	72945	65869
465 174	**SE**	E	*SE*	SG	65823	72946	72947	65870
465 175	**SE**	E	*SE*	SG	65824	72948	72949	65871
465 176	**SE**	E	*SE*	SG	65825	72950	72951	65872
465 177	**SE**	E	*SE*	SG	65826	72952	72953	65873
465 178	**SE**	E	*SE*	SG	65827	72954	72955	65874
465 179	**SE**	E	*SE*	SG	65828	72956	72957	65875

465180	**SE**	E	*SE*	SG	65829	72958	72959	65876
465181	**SE**	E	*SE*	SG	65830	72960	72961	65877
465182	**SE**	E	*SE*	SG	65831	72962	72963	65878
465183	**SE**	E	*SE*	SG	65832	72964	72965	65879
465184	**SE**	E	*SE*	SG	65833	72966	72967	65880
465185	**SE**	E	*SE*	SG	65834	72968	72969	65881
465186	**SE**	E	*SE*	SG	65835	72970	72971	65882
465187	**SE**	E	*SE*	SG	65836	72972	72973	65883
465188	**SE**	E	*SE*	SG	65837	72974	72975	65884
465189	**SE**	E	*SE*	SG	65838	72976	72977	65885
465190	**SE**	E	*SE*	SG	65839	72978	72979	65886
465191	**SE**	E	*SE*	SG	65840	72980	72981	65887
465192	**SE**	E	*SE*	SG	65841	72982	72983	65888
465193	**SE**	E	*SE*	SG	65842	72984	72985	65889
465194	**SE**	E	*SE*	SG	65843	72986	72987	65890
465195	**SE**	E	*SE*	SG	65844	72988	72989	65891
465196	**SE**	E	*SE*	SG	65845	72990	72991	65892
465197	**SE**	E	*SE*	SG	65846	72992	72993	65893

Class 465/2. Built by Metro-Cammell. **Dimensions:** 20.80/20.15 x 2.81 m.

465235	**SE**	A	*SE*	SG	65734	72787	72788	65784
465236	**SE**	A	*SE*	SG	65735	72789	72790	65785
465237	**SE**	A	*SE*	SG	65736	72791	72792	65786
465238	**SE**	A	*SE*	SG	65737	72793	72794	65787
465239	**SE**	A	*SE*	SG	65738	72795	72796	65788
465240	**SE**	A	*SE*	SG	65739	72797	72798	65789
465241	**SE**	A	*SE*	SG	65740	72799	72800	65790
465242	**SE**	A	*SE*	SG	65741	72801	72802	65791
465243	**SE**	A	*SE*	SG	65742	72803	72804	65792
465244	**SE**	A	*SE*	SG	65743	72805	72806	65793
465245	**SE**	A	*SE*	SG	65744	72807	72808	65794
465246	**SE**	A	*SE*	SG	65745	72809	72810	65795
465247	**SE**	A	*SE*	SG	65746	72811	72812	65796
465248	**SE**	A	*SE*	SG	65747	72813	72814	65797
465249	**SE**	A	*SE*	SG	65748	72815	72816	65798
465250	**SE**	A	*SE*	SG	65749	72817	72818	65799

Class 465/9. Built by Metro-Cammell. Refurbished 2005 for longer distance services, with the addition of First Class. Details as Class 465/0 unless stated.

Formation: DMC–TS–TS–DMC.
Seating Layout: 1: 2+2 facing/unidirectional, 2: 3+2 facing/unidirectional.

65700–733. DMC(A). Lot No. 31103 Metro-Cammell 1991–93. 12/68. 39.2t.
72719–785 (odd nos.) TS(A). Lot No. 31104 Metro-Cammell 1991–92. –/65(+7) 1TD 2W. 30.3t.
72720–786 (even nos.) TS(B). Lot No. 31105 Metro-Cammell 1991–92. –/90. 29.5t.
65750–783. DMC(B). Lot No. 31103 Metro-Cammell 1991–93. 12/68. 39.2t.

465901	(465201)	**SE**	A	*SE*	SG	65700	72719	72720	65750
465902	(465202)	**SE**	A	*SE*	SG	65701	72721	72722	65751
465903	(465203)	**SE**	A	*SE*	SG	65702	72723	72724	65752
465904	(465204)	**SE**	A	*SE*	SG	65703	72725	72726	65753

465 905	(465 205)	**SE**	A	*SE*	SG	65704	72727	72728	65754
465 906	(465 206)	**SE**	A	*SE*	SG	65705	72729	72730	65755
465 907	(465 207)	**SE**	A	*SE*	SG	65706	72731	72732	65756
465 908	(465 208)	**SE**	A	*SE*	SG	65707	72733	72734	65757
465 909	(465 209)	**SE**	A	*SE*	SG	65708	72735	72736	65758
465 910	(465 210)	**SE**	A	*SE*	SG	65709	72737	72738	65759
465 911	(465 211)	**SE**	A	*SE*	SG	65710	72739	72740	65760
465 912	(465 212)	**SE**	A	*SE*	SG	65711	72741	72742	65761
465 913	(465 213)	**SE**	A	*SE*	SG	65712	72743	72744	65762
465 914	(465 214)	**SE**	A	*SE*	SG	65713	72745	72746	65763
465 915	(465 215)	**SE**	A	*SE*	SG	65714	72747	72748	65764
465 916	(465 216)	**SE**	A	*SE*	SG	65715	72749	72750	65765
465 917	(465 217)	**SE**	A	*SE*	SG	65716	72751	72752	65766
465 918	(465 218)	**SE**	A	*SE*	SG	65717	72753	72754	65767
465 919	(465 219)	**SE**	A	*SE*	SG	65718	72755	72756	65768
465 920	(465 220)	**SE**	A	*SE*	SG	65719	72757	72758	65769
465 921	(465 221)	**SE**	A	*SE*	SG	65720	72759	72760	65770
465 922	(465 222)	**SE**	A	*SE*	SG	65721	72761	72762	65771
465 923	(465 223)	**SE**	A	*SE*	SG	65722	72763	72764	65772
465 924	(465 224)	**SE**	A	*SE*	SG	65723	72765	72766	65773
465 925	(465 225)	**SE**	A	*SE*	SG	65724	72767	72768	65774
465 926	(465 226)	**SE**	A	*SE*	SG	65725	72769	72770	65775
465 927	(465 227)	**SE**	A	*SE*	SG	65726	72771	72772	65776
465 928	(465 228)	**SE**	A	*SE*	SG	65727	72773	72774	65777
465 929	(465 229)	**SE**	A	*SE*	SG	65728	72775	72776	65778
465 930	(465 230)	**SE**	A	*SE*	SG	65729	72777	72778	65779
465 931	(465 231)	**SE**	A	*SE*	SG	65730	72779	72780	65780
465 932	(465 232)	**SE**	A	*SE*	SG	65731	72781	72782	65781
465 933	(465 233)	**SE**	A	*SE*	SG	65732	72783	72784	65782
465 934	(465 234)	**SE**	A	*SE*	SG	65733	72785	72786	65783

CLASS 466 NETWORKER GEC-ALSTHOM

Inner and outer suburban units.

Formation: DMS–DTS.
Construction: Welded aluminium alloy.
Traction Motors: Two GEC-Alsthom G352AY asynchronous of 280 kW.
Wheel Arrangement: Bo-Bo + 2-2. **Couplers**: Tightlock.
Braking: Disc, rheostatic & regen. **Control System**: 1992-type GTO Inverter.
Dimensions: 20.80 x 2.80 m. **Maximum Speed**: 75 mph.
Bogies: BREL P3/T3. **Doors**: Sliding plug.
Gangways: Within unit.
Seating Layout: 3+2 facing/unidirectional.
Multiple Working: Within class and with Class 465.

DMS. Lot No. 31128 Birmingham 1993–94. –/86. 40.6 t.
DTS. Lot No. 31129 Birmingham 1993–94. –/82 1T. 31.4 t.

466 001	**SE**	A	*SE*	SG	64860	78312
466 002	**SE**	A	*SE*	SG	64861	78313
466 003	**SE**	A	*SE*	SG	64862	78314

466 004	**SE**	A	*SE*	SG	64863	78315
466 005	**SE**	A	*SE*	SG	64864	78316
466 006	**SE**	A	*SE*	SG	64865	78317
466 007	**SE**	A	*SE*	SG	64866	78318
466 008	**SE**	A	*SE*	SG	64867	78319
466 009	**SE**	A	*SE*	SG	64868	78320
466 010	**SE**	A	*SE*	SG	64869	78321
466 011	**SE**	A	*SE*	SG	64870	78322
466 012	**SE**	A	*SE*	SG	64871	78323
466 013	**SE**	A	*SE*	SG	64872	78324
466 014	**SE**	A	*SE*	SG	64873	78325
466 015	**SE**	A	*SE*	SG	64874	78326
466 016	**SE**	A	*SE*	SG	64875	78327
466 017	**SE**	A	*SE*	SG	64876	78328
466 018	**SE**	A	*SE*	SG	64877	78329
466 019	**SE**	A	*SE*	SG	64878	78330
466 020	**SE**	A	*SE*	SG	64879	78331
466 021	**SE**	A	*SE*	SG	64880	78332
466 022	**SE**	A	*SE*	SG	64881	78333
466 023	**SE**	A	*SE*	SG	64882	78334
466 024	**SE**	A	*SE*	SG	64883	78335
466 025	**SE**	A	*SE*	SG	64884	78336
466 026	**SE**	A	*SE*	SG	64885	78337
466 027	**SE**	A	*SE*	SG	64886	78338
466 028	**SE**	A	*SE*	SG	64887	78339
466 029	**SE**	A	*SE*	SG	64888	78340
466 030	**SE**	A	*SE*	SG	64889	78341
466 031	**SE**	A	*SE*	SG	64890	78342
466 032	**SE**	A	*SE*	SG	64891	78343
466 033	**SE**	A	*SE*	SG	64892	78344
466 034	**SE**	A	*SE*	SG	64893	78345
466 035	**SE**	A	*SE*	SG	64894	78346
466 036	**SE**	A	*SE*	SG	64895	78347
466 037	**SE**	A	*SE*	SG	64896	78348
466 038	**SE**	A	*SE*	SG	64897	78349
466 039	**SE**	A	*SE*	SG	64898	78350
466 040	**SE**	A	*SE*	SG	64899	78351
466 041	**SE**	A	*SE*	SG	64900	78352
466 042	**SE**	A	*SE*	SG	64901	78353
466 043	**SE**	A	*SE*	SG	64902	78354

CLASS 483 METRO-CAMMELL

Built 1938 onwards for LTE. Converted 1989–90 for the Isle of Wight Line.

Formation: DMS–DMS.
System: 660 V DC third rail.
Construction: Steel.
Wheel arrangement: A1-1A + A1-1A.
Traction Motors: Two Crompton Parkinson/GEC/BTH LT100 of 125 kW.
Braking: Tread.
Dimensions: 16.15 x 2.69 m.
Bogies: LT design.
Couplers: Wedgelock.
Gangways: None. End doors.
Control System: Pneumatic Camshaft Motor (PCM).
Doors: Sliding.
Maximum Speed: 45 mph.
Seating Layout: Longitudinal or 2+2 facing/unidirectional.
Multiple Working: Within class.
The last three numbers of the unit number only are carried.

Former London Underground numbers are shown in parentheses.

DMS(A). Lot No. 31071. –/40. 27.4 t.
DMS(B). Lot No. 31072. –/42. 27.4 t.

483 002	**LT**	SW		RY (S)	122	(10221)	225	(11142)	RAPTOR
483 004	**LT**	SW	*SW*	RY	124	(10205)	224	(11205)	
483 006	**LT**	SW	*SW*	RY	126	(10297)	226	(11297)	
483 007	**LT**	SW	*SW*	RY	127	(10291)	227	(11291)	
483 008	**LT**	SW	*SW*	RY	128	(10255)	228	(11255)	
483 009	**LT**	SW		RY (S)	129	(10229)	229	(11229)	

CLASS 484 D-TRAIN METRO-CAMMELL/VIVARAIL

South Western Railway has five 2-car D-Trains on order for the Isle of Wight Line, due for delivery 2020–21. Similar to the converted Class 230 DMUs or diesel-battery units, these will be straight third-rail EMUs, rebuilt from former London Underground D78 stock. Full details awaited.

Formation: DMS–DMS.
System: 660 V DC third rail.
Construction: Aluminium.
Wheel Arrangement:
Traction motors:
Couplers:
Braking: Rheostatic & Dynamic.
Dimensions: 18.37 x 2.85 m.
Bogies: Bombardier FLEXX1000 flexible-frame.
Gangways: Within unit only.
Control System: IGBT Inverter.
Doors: Sliding.
Maximum Speed: 60 mph.
Seating Layout: Longitudinal or 2+2 facing.
Multiple Working: Within class.

DMS(A). Metro-Cammell Birmingham 1979–83.
DMS(B). Metro-Cammell Birmingham 1979–83.

484 001	LF	131	231
484 002	LF	132	232
484 003	LF	133	233
484 004	LF	134	234
484 005	LF	135	235

CLASS 507 BREL YORK

Formation: BDMS–TS–DMS.
Construction: Steel underframe, aluminium alloy body and roof.
Traction Motors: Four GEC G310AZ of 82.125 kW.
Wheel Arrangement: Bo-Bo + 2-2 + Bo-Bo.
Braking: Disc & rheostatic.
Dimensions: 20.18 x 2.82 m.
Bogies: BX1.
Couplers: Tightlock.
Gangways: Within unit + end doors.
Control System: Camshaft.
Doors: Sliding.
Maximum Speed: 75 mph.
Seating Layout: All refurbished with 2+2 high-back facing seating.
Multiple Working: Within class and with Class 508.

Fitted with tripcocks for operating on the Merseyrail Wirral Lines.

Advertising livery: 507 002 Liverpool Hope University (white).

BDMS. Lot No. 30906 1978–80. –/56(+3) 1W. 37.0 t.
TS. Lot No. 30907 1978–80. –/74. 25.5 t.
DMS. Lot No. 30908 1978–80. –/56(+3) 1W. 35.5 t.

507 001	**MY**	A	*ME*	BD	64367	71342	64405
507 002	**AL**	A	*ME*	BD	64368	71343	64406
507 003	**MY**	A	*ME*	BD	64369	71344	64407
507 004	**MY**	A	*ME*	BD	64388	71345	64408
507 005	**MY**	A	*ME*	BD	64371	71346	64409
507 006	**MY**	A	*ME*	BD	64372	71347	64410
507 007	**MY**	A	*ME*	BD	64373	71348	64411
507 008	**MY**	A	*ME*	BD	64374	71349	64412
507 009	**MY**	A	*ME*	BD	64375	71350	64413
507 010	**MY**	A	*ME*	BD	64376	71351	64414
507 011	**MY**	A	*ME*	BD	64377	71352	64415
507 012	**MY**	A	*ME*	BD	64378	71353	64416
507 013	**MY**	A	*ME*	BD	64379	71354	64417
507 014	**MY**	A	*ME*	BD	64380	71355	64418
507 015	**MY**	A	*ME*	BD	64381	71356	64419
507 016	**MY**	A	*ME*	BD	64382	71357	64420
507 017	**MY**	A	*ME*	BD	64383	71358	64421
507 018	**MY**	A	*ME*	BD	64384	71359	64422
507 019	**MY**	A	*ME*	BD	64385	71360	64423
507 020	**MY**	A	*ME*	BD	64386	71361	64424
507 021	**MY**	A	*ME*	BD	64387	71362	64425
507 023	**MY**	A	*ME*	BD	64389	71364	64427
507 024	**MY**	A	*ME*	BD	64390	71365	64428
507 025	**MY**	A	*ME*	BD	64391	71366	64429
507 026	**MY**	A	*ME*	BD	64392	71367	64430
507 027	**MY**	A	*ME*	BD	64393	71368	64431
507 028	**MY**	A	*ME*	BD	64394	71369	64432
507 029	**MY**	A	*ME*	BD	64395	71370	64433
507 030	**MY**	A	*ME*	BD	64396	71371	64434
507 031	**MY**	A	*ME*	BD	64397	71372	64435
507 032	**MY**	A	*ME*	BD	64398	71373	64436
507 033	**MY**	A	*ME*	BD	64399	71374	64437

Names:

507 004 Bob Paisley
507 008 Harold Wilson
507 009 Dixie Dean
507 016 Merseyrail – celebrating the first ten years (2003–2013)
507 020 John Peel
507 021 Red Rum
507 023 Operations Inspector Stuart Mason
507 026 Councillor George Howard
507 033 Councillor Jack Spriggs

CLASS 508 BREL YORK

Formation: DMS–TS–BDMS.
Construction: Steel underframe, aluminium alloy body and roof.
Traction Motors: Four GEC G310AZ of 82.125 kW.
Wheel Arrangement: Bo-Bo + 2-2 + Bo-Bo.
Braking: Disc & rheostatic.
Dimensions: 20.18 x 2.82 m.
Bogies: BX1.
Couplers: Tightlock.
Gangways: Within unit + end doors.
Control System: Camshaft.
Doors: Sliding.
Maximum Speed: 75 mph.
Seating Layout: All refurbished with 2+2 high-back facing seating.
Multiple Working: Within class and with Class 507.

Fitted with tripcocks for operating on the Merseyrail Wirral Lines.

Advertising livery: 508 111 Beatles Story (blue).

DMS. Lot No. 30979 1979–80. –/56(+3) 1W. 36.0 t.
TS. Lot No. 30980 1979–80. –/74. 26.5 t.
BDMS. Lot No. 30981 1979–80. –/56(+3) 1W. 36.5 t.

508 103	**MY**	A	*ME*	BD	64651	71485	64694
508 104	**MY**	A	*ME*	BD	64652	71486	64695
508 108	**MY**	A	*ME*	BD	64656	71490	64699
508 110	**MY**	A	*ME*	BD	64658	71492	64701
508 111	**AL**	A	*ME*	BD	64659	71493	64702
508 112	**MY**	A	*ME*	BD	64660	71494	64703
508 114	**MY**	A	*ME*	BD	64662	71496	64705
508 115	**MY**	A	*ME*	BD	64663	71497	64706
508 117	**MY**	A	*ME*	BD	64665	71499	64708
508 120	**MY**	A	*ME*	BD	64668	71502	64711
508 122	**MY**	A	*ME*	BD	64670	71504	64713
508 123	**MY**	A	*ME*	BD	64671	71505	64714
508 124	**MY**	A	*ME*	BD	64672	71506	64715
508 125	**MY**	A	*ME*	BD	64673	71507	64716
508 126	**MY**	A	*ME*	BD	64674	71508	64717
508 127	**MY**	A	*ME*	BD	64675	71509	64718
508 128	**MY**	A	*ME*	BD	64676	71510	64719
508 130	**MY**	A	*ME*	BD	64678	71512	64721
508 131	**MY**	A	*ME*	BD	64679	71513	64722
508 134	**MY**	A	*ME*	BD	64682	71516	64725

508 136	**MY**	A	*ME*	BD	64684	71518	64727
508 137	**MY**	A	*ME*	BD	64685	71519	64728
508 138	**MY**	A	*ME*	BD	64686	71520	64729
508 139	**MY**	A	*ME*	BD	64687	71521	64730
508 140	**MY**	A	*ME*	BD	64688	71522	64731
508 141	**MY**	A	*ME*	BD	64689	71523	64732
508 143	**MY**	A	*ME*	BD	64691	71525	64734

Names:

508 111 The Beatles
508 123 William Roscoe
508 136 Wilfred Owen MC

4.3. DUAL VOLTAGE OR 25 kV AC OVERHEAD UNITS

The Class 7xx series is being used for some new-build EMUs built from 2014 onwards as freight wagons take up many of the remaining potential Class 3xx series'.

CLASS 700 DESIRO CITY SIEMENS

The Class 700s are the large new fleet of EMUs for Govia Thameslink, entering service between 2016 and 2018. The units are financed by Cross London Trains (a consortium of Siemens Project Ventures, Innisfree Ltd and 3i Infrastructure Ltd).

Formation (8-car): DMC–PTS–MS–TS–TS–MS–PTS–DMC or
(12-car): DMC–PTS–MS–MS–TS–TS–TS–TS–MS–MS–PTS–DMC.
Systems: 25 kV AC overhead/750 V DC third rail.
Construction: Aluminium.
Traction Motors: Four Siemens asynchronous of 200 kW.
Wheel Arrangement (8-car): Bo-Bo + 2-2 + Bo-Bo + 2-2 + 2-2 + Bo-Bo + 2-2 + Bo-Bo. **(12-car)**: Bo-Bo + 2-2 + Bo-Bo + Bo-Bo + 2-2 + 2-2 + 2-2 + 2-2 + Bo-Bo + Bo-Bo + 2-2 + Bo-Bo.
Braking: Disc, tread & regenerative.
Dimensions: 20.52/20.16 m x 2.80 m.
Bogies: Siemens SF7000 inside-frame.
Couplers: Dellner 12.
Gangways: Within unit.
Control System: IGBT Inverter.
Doors: Sliding plug.
Maximum Speed: 100 mph.
Heating & ventilation: Air conditioning.
Seating Layout: 2+2 facing/unidirectional.
Multiple Working: Within class and with Classes 707 and 717.

Class 700/0. 8-car units.

DMC(A). Siemens Krefeld 2014–18. 26/16(+3). 38.5 t.
PTS. Siemens Krefeld 2014–18. –/54 1T. 33.1 t.
MS. Siemens Krefeld 2014–18. –/64. 36.2 t.
TS. Siemens Krefeld 2014–18. –/56(+3). 28.7 t.
TS(W). Siemens Krefeld 2014–18. –/40(+8) 1TD 2W. 29.1 t.
MS. Siemens Krefeld 2014–18. –/64. 36.2 t.

PTS. Siemens Krefeld 2014–18. –/54 1T. 33.2 t.
DMC(B). Siemens Krefeld 2014–18. 26/16(+3). 38.5 t.

700001	**TL**	CT	*TL*	TB	401001 402001 403001 406001 407001 410001 411001 412001
700002	**TL**	CT	*TL*	TB	401002 402002 403002 406002 407002 410002 411002 412002
700003	**TL**	CT	*TL*	TB	401003 402003 403003 406003 407003 410003 411003 412003
700004	**TL**	CT	*TL*	TB	401004 402004 403004 406004 407004 410004 411004 412004
700005	**TL**	CT	*TL*	TB	401005 402005 403005 406005 407005 410005 411005 412005
700006	**TL**	CT	*TL*	TB	401006 402006 403006 406006 407006 410006 411006 412006
700007	**TL**	CT	*TL*	TB	401007 402007 403007 406007 407007 410007 411007 412007
700008	**TL**	CT	*TL*	TB	401008 402008 403008 406008 407008 410008 411008 412008
700009	**TL**	CT	*TL*	TB	401009 402009 403009 406009 407009 410009 411009 412009
700010	**TL**	CT	*TL*	TB	401010 402010 403010 406010 407010 410010 411010 412010
700011	**TL**	CT	*TL*	TB	401011 402011 403011 406011 407011 410011 411011 412011
700012	**TL**	CT	*TL*	TB	401012 402012 403012 406012 407012 410012 411012 412012
700013	**TL**	CT	*TL*	TB	401013 402013 403013 406013 407013 410013 411013 412013
700014	**TL**	CT	*TL*	TB	401014 402014 403014 406014 407014 410014 411014 412014
700015	**TL**	CT	*TL*	TB	401015 402015 403015 406015 407015 410015 411015 412015
700016	**TL**	CT	*TL*	TB	401016 402016 403016 406016 407016 410016 411016 412016
700017	**TL**	CT	*TL*	TB	401017 402017 403017 406017 407017 410017 411017 412017
700018	**TL**	CT	*TL*	TB	401018 402018 403018 406018 407018 410018 411018 412018
700019	**TL**	CT	*TL*	TB	401019 402019 403019 406019 407019 410019 411019 412019
700020	**TL**	CT	*TL*	TB	401020 402020 403020 406020 407020 410020 411020 412020
700021	**TL**	CT	*TL*	TB	401021 402021 403021 406021 407021 410021 411021 412021
700022	**TL**	CT	*TL*	TB	401022 402022 403022 406022 407022 410022 411022 412022
700023	**TL**	CT	*TL*	TB	401023 402023 403023 406023 407023 410023 411023 412023
700024	**TL**	CT	*TL*	TB	401024 402024 403024 406024 407024 410024 411024 412024

700025	**TL**	CT	*TL*	TB	401025	402025	403025	406025
					407025	410025	411025	412025
700026	**TL**	CT	*TL*	TB	401026	402026	403026	406026
					407026	410026	411026	412026
700027	**TL**	CT	*TL*	TB	401027	402027	403027	406027
					407027	410027	411027	412027
700028	**TL**	CT	*TL*	TB	401028	402028	403028	406028
					407028	410028	411028	412028
700029	**TL**	CT	*TL*	TB	401029	402029	403029	406029
					407029	410029	411029	412029
700030	**TL**	CT	*TL*	TB	401030	402030	403030	406030
					407030	410030	411030	412030
700031	**TL**	CT	*TL*	TB	401031	402031	403031	406031
					407031	410031	411031	412031
700032	**TL**	CT	*TL*	TB	401032	402032	403032	406032
					407032	410032	411032	412032
700033	**TL**	CT	*TL*	TB	401033	402033	403033	406033
					407033	410033	411033	412033
700034	**TL**	CT	*TL*	TB	401034	402034	403034	406034
					407034	410034	411034	412034
700035	**TL**	CT	*TL*	TB	401035	402035	403035	406035
					407035	410035	411035	412035
700036	**TL**	CT	*TL*	TB	401036	402036	403036	406036
					407036	410036	411036	412036
700037	**TL**	CT	*TL*	TB	401037	402037	403037	406037
					407037	410037	411037	412037
700038	**TL**	CT	*TL*	TB	401038	402038	403038	406038
					407038	410038	411038	412038
700039	**TL**	CT	*TL*	TB	401039	402039	403039	406039
					407039	410039	411039	412039
700040	**TL**	CT	*TL*	TB	401040	402040	403040	406040
					407040	410040	411040	412040
700041	**TL**	CT	*TL*	TB	401041	402041	403041	406041
					407041	410041	411041	412041
700042	**TL**	CT	*TL*	TB	401042	402042	403042	406042
					407042	410042	411042	412042
700043	**TL**	CT	*TL*	TB	401043	402043	403043	406043
					407043	410043	411043	412043
700044	**TL**	CT	*TL*	TB	401044	402044	403044	406044
					407044	410044	411044	412044
700045	**TL**	CT	*TL*	TB	401045	402045	403045	406045
					407045	410045	411045	412045
700046	**TL**	CT	*TL*	TB	401046	402046	403046	406046
					407046	410046	411046	412046
700047	**TL**	CT	*TL*	TB	401047	402047	403047	406047
					407047	410047	411047	412047
700048	**TL**	CT	*TL*	TB	401048	402048	403048	406048
					407048	410048	411048	412048
700049	**TL**	CT	*TL*	TB	401049	402049	403049	406049
					407049	410049	411049	412049

700 050	**TL**	CT	*TL*	TB	401050	402050	403050	406050
					407050	410050	411050	412050
700 051	**TL**	CT	*TL*	TB	401051	402051	403051	406051
					407051	410051	411051	412051
700 052	**TL**	CT	*TL*	TB	401052	402052	403052	406052
					407052	410052	411052	412052
700 053	**TL**	CT	*TL*	TB	401053	402053	403053	406053
					407053	410053	411053	412053
700 054	**TL**	CT	*TL*	TB	401054	402054	403054	406054
					407054	410054	411054	412054
700 055	**TL**	CT	*TL*	TB	401055	402055	403055	406055
					407055	410055	411055	412055
700 056	**TL**	CT	*TL*	TB	401056	402056	403056	406056
					407056	410056	411056	412056
700 057	**TL**	CT	*TL*	TB	401057	402057	403057	406057
					407057	410057	411057	412057
700 058	**TL**	CT	*TL*	TB	401058	402058	403058	406058
					407058	410058	411058	412058
700 059	**TL**	CT	*TL*	TB	401059	402059	403059	406059
					407059	410059	411059	412059
700 060	**TL**	CT	*TL*	TB	401060	402060	403060	406060
					407060	410060	411060	412060

Class 700/1. 12-car units.

DMC(A). Siemens Krefeld 2013–18. 26/20. 38.2 t.
PTS. Siemens Krefeld 2013–18. –/54 1T. 34.4 t.
MS. Siemens Krefeld 2013–18. –/60(+3). 36.0 t.
MS. Siemens Krefeld 2013–18. –/56 1T. 35.8 t.
TS. Siemens Krefeld 2013–18. –/64. 26.8 t.
TS. Siemens Krefeld 2013–18. –/56(+3). 28.3 t.
TS(W). Siemens Krefeld 2013–18. –/38(+9) 1TD 2W. 28.7 t.
TS. Siemens Krefeld 2013–18. –/64. 27.9 t.
MS. Siemens Krefeld 2013–18. –/56 1T. 35.6 t.
MS. Siemens Krefeld 2013–18. –/60(+3). 35.3 t.
PTS. Siemens Krefeld 2013–18. –/54 1T. 34.4 t.
DMC(B). Siemens Krefeld 2013–18. 26/20. 38.2 t.

700 101	**TL**	CT	*TL*	TB	401101	402101	403101	404101	405101	406101
					407101	408101	409101	410101	411101	412101
700 102	**TL**	CT	*TL*	TB	401102	402102	403102	404102	405102	406102
					407102	408102	409102	410102	411102	412102
700 103	**TL**	CT	*TL*	TB	401103	402103	403103	404103	405103	406103
					407103	408103	409103	410103	411103	412103
700 104	**TL**	CT	*TL*	TB	401104	402104	403104	404104	405104	406104
					407104	408104	409104	410104	411104	412104
700 105	**TL**	CT	*TL*	TB	401105	402105	403105	404105	405105	406105
					407105	408105	409105	410105	411105	412105
700 106	**TL**	CT	*TL*	TB	401106	402106	403106	404106	405106	406106
					407106	408106	409106	410106	411106	412106
700 107	**TL**	CT	*TL*	TB	401107	402107	403107	404107	405107	406107
					407107	408107	409107	410107	411107	412107

700 108	**TL**	CT	*TL*	TB	401108 402108 403108 404108 405108 406108 407108 408108 409108 410108 411108 412108
700 109	**TL**	CT	*TL*	TB	401109 402109 403109 404109 405109 406109 407109 408109 409109 410109 411109 412109
700 110	**TL**	CT	*TL*	TB	401110 402110 403110 404110 405110 406110 407110 408110 409110 410110 411110 412110
700 111	**TL**	CT	*TL*	TB	401111 402111 403111 404111 405111 406111 407111 408111 409111 410111 411111 412111
700 112	**TL**	CT	*TL*	TB	401112 402112 403112 404112 405112 406112 407112 408112 409112 410112 411112 412112
700 113	**TL**	CT	*TL*	TB	401113 402113 403113 404113 405113 406113 407113 408113 409113 410113 411113 412113
700 114	**TL**	CT	*TL*	TB	401114 402114 403114 404114 405114 406114 407114 408114 409114 410114 411114 412114
700 115	**TL**	CT	*TL*	TB	401115 402115 403115 404115 405115 406115 407115 408115 409115 410115 411115 412115
700 116	**TL**	CT	*TL*	TB	401116 402116 403116 404116 405116 406116 407116 408116 409116 410116 411116 412116
700 117	**TL**	CT	*TL*	TB	401117 402117 403117 404117 405117 406117 407117 408117 409117 410117 411117 412117
700 118	**TL**	CT	*TL*	TB	401118 402118 403118 404118 405118 406118 407118 408118 409118 410118 411118 412118
700 119	**TL**	CT	*TL*	TB	401119 402119 403119 404119 405119 406119 407119 408119 409119 410119 411119 412119
700 120	**TL**	CT	*TL*	TB	401120 402120 403120 404120 405120 406120 407120 408120 409120 410120 411120 412120
700 121	**TL**	CT	*TL*	TB	401121 402121 403121 404121 405121 406121 407121 408121 409121 410121 411121 412121
700 122	**TL**	CT	*TL*	TB	401122 402122 403122 404122 405122 406122 407122 408122 409122 410122 411122 412122
700 123	**TL**	CT	*TL*	TB	401123 402123 403123 404123 405123 406123 407123 408123 409123 410123 411123 412123
700 124	**TL**	CT	*TL*	TB	401124 402124 403124 404124 405124 406124 407124 408124 409124 410124 411124 412124
700 125	**TL**	CT	*TL*	TB	401125 402125 403125 404125 405125 406125 407125 408125 409125 410125 411125 412125
700 126	**TL**	CT	*TL*	TB	401126 402126 403126 404126 405126 406126 407126 408126 409126 410126 411126 412126
700 127	**TL**	CT	*TL*	TB	401127 402127 403127 404127 405127 406127 407127 408127 409127 410127 411127 412127
700 128	**TL**	CT	*TL*	TB	401128 402128 403128 404128 405128 406128 407128 408128 409128 410128 411128 412128
700 129	**TL**	CT	*TL*	TB	401129 402129 403129 404129 405129 406129 407129 408129 409129 410129 411129 412129
700 130	**TL**	CT	*TL*	TB	401130 402130 403130 404130 405130 406130 407130 408130 409130 410130 411130 412130
700 131	**TL**	CT	*TL*	TB	401131 402131 403131 404131 405131 406131 407131 408131 409131 410131 411131 412131
700 132	**TL**	CT	*TL*	TB	401132 402132 403132 404132 405132 406132 407132 408132 409132 410132 411132 412132

700 133	**TL**	CT	*TL*	TB	401133 402133 403133 404133 405133 406133 407133 408133 409133 410133 411133 412133
700 134	**TL**	CT	*TL*	TB	401134 402134 403134 404134 405134 406134 407134 408134 409134 410134 411134 412134
700 135	**TL**	CT	*TL*	TB	401135 402135 403135 404135 405135 406135 407135 408135 409135 410135 411135 412135
700 136	**TL**	CT	*TL*	TB	401136 402136 403136 404136 405136 406136 407136 408136 409136 410136 411136 412136
700 137	**TL**	CT	*TL*	TB	401137 402137 403137 404137 405137 406137 407137 408137 409137 410137 411137 412137
700 138	**TL**	CT	*TL*	TB	401138 402138 403138 404138 405138 406138 407138 408138 409138 410138 411138 412138
700 139	**TL**	CT	*TL*	TB	401139 402139 403139 404139 405139 406139 407139 408139 409139 410139 411139 412139
700 140	**TL**	CT	*TL*	TB	401140 402140 403140 404140 405140 406140 407140 408140 409140 410140 411140 412140
700 141	**TL**	CT	*TL*	TB	401141 402141 403141 404141 405141 406141 407141 408141 409141 410141 411141 412141
700 142	**TL**	CT	*TL*	TB	401142 402142 403142 404142 405142 406142 407142 408142 409142 410142 411142 412142
700 143	**TL**	CT	*TL*	TB	401143 402143 403143 404143 405143 406143 407143 408143 409143 410143 411143 412143
700 144	**TL**	CT	*TL*	TB	401144 402144 403144 404144 405144 406144 407144 408144 409144 410144 411144 412144
700 145	**TL**	CT	*TL*	TB	401145 402145 403145 404145 405145 406145 407145 408145 409145 410145 411145 412145
700 146	**TL**	CT	*TL*	TB	401146 402146 403146 404146 405146 406146 407146 408146 409146 410146 411146 412146
700 147	**TL**	CT	*TL*	TB	401147 402147 403147 404147 405147 406147 407147 408147 409147 410147 411147 412147
700 148	**TL**	CT	*TL*	TB	401148 402148 403148 404148 405148 406148 407148 408148 409148 410148 411148 412148
700 149	**TL**	CT	*TL*	TB	401149 402149 403149 404149 405149 406149 407149 408149 409149 410149 411149 412149
700 150	**TL**	CT	*TL*	TB	401150 402150 403150 404150 405150 406150 407150 408150 409150 410150 411150 412150
700 151	**TL**	CT	*TL*	TB	401151 402151 403151 404151 405151 406151 407151 408151 409151 410151 411151 412151
700 152	**TL**	CT	*TL*	TB	401152 402152 403152 404152 405152 406152 407152 408152 409152 410152 411152 412152
700 153	**TL**	CT	*TL*	TB	401153 402153 403153 404153 405153 406153 407153 408153 409153 410153 411153 412153
700 154	**TL**	CT	*TL*	TB	401154 402154 403154 404154 405154 406154 407154 408154 409154 410154 411154 412154
700 155	**TL**	CT	*TL*	TB	401155 402155 403155 404155 405155 406155 407155 408155 409155 410155 411155 412155

CLASS 701 AVENTRA BOMBARDIER DERBY

South Western Railway has 60 10-car and 30 5-car Aventra EMUs on order from Bombardier, financed by Rock Rail. They are due to enter service in 2020–21. The units will be used mainly on inner and outer suburban duties, replacing Classes 455, 456, 458 and 707.

Formation (10-car): DMS–MS–TS–MS–MS–MS–MS–TS–MS–DMS or **(5-car):** DMS–MS–TS–MS–DMS.
Systems: 750 V DC third rail.
Construction: Aluminium.
Traction Motors: Two Bombardier asynchronous of 250 kW.
Wheel Arrangement (10-car): 2-Bo + Bo-2 + 2-2 + 2-Bo + Bo-2 + 2-Bo + Bo-2 + 2-2 + 2-Bo + Bo-2 or (5-car): 2-Bo + Bo-2 + 2-2 + 2-Bo + Bo-2.
Braking: Disc, rheostatic & regenerative.
Dimensions: 20.88/19.90 m x 2.78 m.
Bogies: FLEXX B5000 inside-frame.
Couplers: Dellner 12.
Gangways: Within unit.
Control System: IGBT Inverter.
Doors: Sliding plug.
Maximum Speed: 100 mph.
Heating & ventilation: Air conditioning.
Seating Layout: 2+2 unidirectional/facing.
Multiple Working: Within class.

Class 701/0. 10-car units.

701 001	RR	480001	481001	482001	483001	484001
		485001	486001	487001	488001	489001
701 002	RR	480002	481002	482002	483002	484002
		485002	486002	487002	488002	489002
701 003	RR	480003	481003	482003	483003	484003
		485003	486003	487003	488003	489003
701 004	RR	480004	481004	482004	483004	484004
		485004	486004	487004	488004	489004
701 005	RR	480005	481005	482005	483005	484005
		485005	486005	487005	488005	489005
701 006	RR	480006	481006	482006	483006	484006
		485006	486006	487006	488006	489006
701 007	RR	480007	481007	482007	483007	484007
		485007	486007	487007	488007	489007
701 008	RR	480008	481008	482008	483008	484008
		485008	486008	487008	488008	489008
701 009	RR	480009	481009	482009	483009	484009
		485009	486009	487009	488009	489009
701 010	RR	480010	481010	482010	483010	484010
		485010	486010	487010	488010	489010
701 011	RR	480011	481011	482011	483011	484011
		485011	486011	487011	488011	489011
701 012	RR	480012	481012	482012	483012	484012
		485012	486012	487012	488012	489012
701 013	RR	480013	481013	482013	483013	484013
		485013	486013	487013	488013	489013

701014	RR	480014	481014	482014	483014	484014
		485014	486014	487014	488014	489014
701015	RR	480015	481015	482015	483015	484015
		485015	486015	487015	488015	489015
701016	RR	480016	481016	482016	483016	484016
		485016	486016	487016	488016	489016
701017	RR	480017	481017	482017	483017	484017
		485017	486017	487017	488017	489017
701018	RR	480018	481018	482018	483018	484018
		485018	486018	487018	488018	489018
701019	RR	480019	481019	482019	483019	484019
		485019	486019	487019	488019	489019
701020	RR	480020	481020	482020	483020	484020
		485020	486020	487020	488020	489020
701021	RR	480021	481021	482021	483021	484021
		485021	486021	487021	488021	489021
701022	RR	480022	481022	482022	483022	484022
		485022	486022	487022	488022	489022
701023	RR	480023	481023	482023	483023	484023
		485023	486023	487023	488023	489023
701024	RR	480024	481024	482024	483024	484024
		485024	486024	487024	488024	489024
701025	RR	480025	481025	482025	483025	484025
		485025	486025	487025	488025	489025
701026	RR	480026	481026	482026	483026	484026
		485026	486026	487026	488026	489026
701027	RR	480027	481027	482027	483027	484027
		485027	486027	487027	488027	489027
701028	RR	480028	481028	482028	483028	484028
		485028	486028	487028	488028	489028
701029	RR	480029	481029	482029	483029	484029
		485029	486029	487029	488029	489029
701030	RR	480030	481030	482030	483030	484030
		485030	486030	487030	488030	489030
701031	RR	480031	481031	482031	483031	484031
		485031	486031	487031	488031	489031
701032	RR	480032	481032	482032	483032	484032
		485032	486032	487032	488032	489032
701033	RR	480033	481033	482033	483033	484033
		485033	486033	487033	488033	489033
701034	RR	480034	481034	482034	483034	484034
		485034	486034	487034	488034	489034
701035	RR	480035	481035	482035	483035	484035
		485035	486035	487035	488035	489035
701036	RR	480036	481036	482036	483036	484036
		485036	486036	487036	488036	489036
701037	RR	480037	481037	482037	483037	484037
		485037	486037	487037	488037	489037
701038	RR	480038	481038	482038	483038	484038
		485038	486038	487038	488038	489038

701 039		RR	480039	481039	482039	483039	484039
			485039	486039	487039	488039	489039
701 040		RR	480040	481040	482040	483040	484040
			485040	486040	487040	488040	489040
701 041		RR	480041	481041	482041	483041	484041
			485041	486041	487041	488041	489041
701 042		RR	480042	481042	482042	483042	484042
			485042	486042	487042	488042	489042
701 043		RR	480043	481043	482043	483043	484043
			485043	486043	487043	488043	489043
701 044		RR	480044	481044	482044	483044	484044
			485044	486044	487044	488044	489044
701 045		RR	480045	481045	482045	483045	484045
			485045	486045	487045	488045	489045
701 046		RR	480046	481046	482046	483046	484046
			485046	486046	487046	488046	489046
701 047		RR	480047	481047	482047	483047	484047
			485047	486047	487047	488047	489047
701 048		RR	480048	481048	482048	483048	484048
			485048	486048	487048	488048	489048
701 049		RR	480049	481049	482049	483049	484049
			485049	486049	487049	488049	489049
701 050		RR	480050	481050	482050	483050	484050
			485050	486050	487050	488050	489050
701 051		RR	480051	481051	482051	483051	484051
			485051	486051	487051	488051	489051
701 052		RR	480052	481052	482052	483052	484052
			485052	486052	487052	488052	489052
701 053		RR	480053	481053	482053	483053	484053
			485053	486053	487053	488053	489053
701 054		RR	480054	481054	482054	483054	484054
			485054	486054	487054	488054	489054
701 055		RR	480055	481055	482055	483055	484055
			485055	486055	487055	488055	489055
701 056		RR	480056	481056	482056	483056	484056
			485056	486056	487056	488056	489056
701 057		RR	480057	481057	482057	483057	484057
			485057	486057	487057	488057	489057
701 058		RR	480058	481058	482058	483058	484058
			485058	486058	487058	488058	489058
701 059		RR	480059	481059	482059	483059	484059
			485059	486059	487059	488059	489059
701 060		RR	480060	481060	482060	483060	484060
			485060	486060	487060	488060	489060

Class 701/5. 5-car units.

701 501	**SW**	RR	480101	481101	482101	483101	484101
701 502	**SW**	RR	480102	481102	482102	483102	484102
701 503		RR	480103	481103	482103	483103	484103
701 504		RR	480104	481104	482104	483104	484104
701 505		RR	480105	481105	482105	483105	484105

701 506	RR	480106	481106	482106	483106	484106
701 507	RR	480107	481107	482107	483107	484107
701 508	RR	480108	481108	482108	483108	484108
701 509	RR	480109	481109	482109	483109	484109
701 510	RR	480110	481110	482110	483110	484110
701 511	RR	480111	481111	482111	483111	484111
701 512	RR	480112	481112	482112	483112	484112
701 513	RR	480113	481113	482113	483113	484113
701 514	RR	480114	481114	482114	483114	484114
701 515	RR	480115	481115	482115	483115	484115
701 516	RR	480116	481116	482116	483116	484116
701 517	RR	480117	481117	482117	483117	484117
701 518	RR	480118	481118	482118	483118	484118
701 519	RR	480119	481119	482119	483119	484119
701 520	RR	480120	481120	482120	483120	484120
701 521	RR	480121	481121	482121	483121	484121
701 522	RR	480122	481122	482122	483122	484122
701 523	RR	480123	481123	482123	483123	484123
701 524	RR	480124	481124	482124	483124	484124
701 525	RR	480125	481125	482125	483125	484125
701 526	RR	480126	481126	482126	483126	484126
701 527	RR	480127	481127	482127	483127	484127
701 528	RR	480128	481128	482128	483128	484128
701 529	RR	480129	481129	482129	483129	484129
701 530	RR	480130	481130	482130	483130	484130

CLASS 707 DESIRO CITY SIEMENS

South Western Railway suburban units. Built with the capability to be easily converted to dual-voltage units.

Formation: DMS–TS–TS–TS–DMS.
Systems: 750 V DC third rail but with 25 kV AC overhead capability.
Construction: Aluminium.
Traction Motors: Four Siemens asynchronous of 200 kW.
Wheel Arrangement: Bo-Bo + 2-2 + 2-2 + 2-2 + Bo-Bo.
Braking: Disc, tread & regenerative.
Dimensions: 20.00/20.16 m x 2.80 m.
Bogies: Siemens SF7000 inside-frame.
Couplers: Dellner 12.
Gangways: Within unit.
Control System: IGBT Inverter.
Doors: Sliding plug.
Maximum Speed: 100 mph.
Heating & ventilation: Air conditioning.
Seating Layout: 2+2/2+1 facing/unidirectional.
Multiple Working: Within class and with Classes 700 and 717.

DMS(A). Siemens Krefeld 2015–17. –/46. 37.9 t.
TS. Siemens Krefeld 2015–17. –/64. 28.3 t.
TS. Siemens Krefeld 2015–17. –/53(+4) 2W. 28.5 t.
TS. Siemens Krefeld 2015–17. –/62. 27.7 t.
DMS(B). Siemens Krefeld 2015–17. –/46. 37.9 t.

707 001	**SS**	A	*SW*	WD	421001	422001	423001	424001	425001
707 002	**SS**	A	*SW*	WD	421002	422002	423002	424002	425002

707 003	**SS**	A	*SW*	WD	421003	422003	423003	424003	425003
707 004	**SS**	A	*SW*	WD	421004	422004	423004	424004	425004
707 005	**SS**	A	*SW*	WD	421005	422005	423005	424005	425005
707 006	**SS**	A	*SW*	WD	421006	422006	423006	424006	425006
707 007	**SS**	A	*SW*	WD	421007	422007	423007	424007	425007
707 008	**SS**	A	*SW*	WD	421008	422008	423008	424008	425008
707 009	**SS**	A	*SW*	WD	421009	422009	423009	424009	425009
707 010	**SS**	A	*SW*	WD	421010	422010	423010	424010	425010
707 011	**SS**	A	*SW*	WD	421011	422011	423011	424011	425011
707 012	**SS**	A	*SW*	WD	421012	422012	423012	424012	425012
707 013	**SS**	A	*SW*	WD	421013	422013	423013	424013	425013
707 014	**SS**	A	*SW*	WD	421014	422014	423014	424014	425014
707 015	**SS**	A	*SW*	WD	421015	422015	423015	424015	425015
707 016	**SS**	A	*SW*	WD	421016	422016	423016	424016	425016
707 017	**SS**	A	*SW*	WD	421017	422017	423017	424017	425017
707 018	**SS**	A	*SW*	WD	421018	422018	423018	424018	425018
707 019	**SS**	A	*SW*	WD	421019	422019	423019	424019	425019
707 020	**SS**	A	*SW*	WD	421020	422020	423020	424020	425020
707 021	**SS**	A	*SW*	WD	421021	422021	423021	424021	425021
707 022	**SS**	A	*SW*	WD	421022	422022	423022	424022	425022
707 023	**SS**	A	*SW*	WD	421023	422023	423023	424023	425023
707 024	**SS**	A	*SW*	WD	421024	422024	423024	424024	425024
707 025	**SS**	A	*SW*	WD	421025	422025	423025	424025	425025
707 026	**SS**	A	*SW*	WD	421026	422026	423026	424026	425026
707 027	**SS**	A	*SW*	WD	421027	422027	423027	424027	425027
707 028	**SS**	A	*SW*	WD	421028	422028	423028	424028	425028
707 029	**SS**	A	*SW*	WD	421029	422029	423029	424029	425029
707 030	**SS**	A	*SW*	WD	421030	422030	423030	424030	425030

CLASS 710 AVENTRA BOMBARDIER DERBY

These suburban 4-car Aventras are now being delivered to London Overground for use on Gospel Oak–Barking, London Euston–Watford Junction and Liverpool Street local services. There are a mix of AC only and dual-voltage units.

Originally 45 4-car units were ordered. In 2018 an extra three 4-cars and six 5-cars were ordered.

Formation: DMS–MS–PMS–DMS or DMS–MS–PMS–MS–DMS.
Systems: Class 710/1 25 kV AC overhead only. Class 710/2 25 kV AC overhead and 750 V DC third rail.
Construction: Aluminium.
Traction Motors: Two Bombardier asynchronous of 265 kW.
Wheel Arrangement: Bo-2 + 2-Bo + Bo-2 (+ 2-Bo) + 2-Bo.
Braking: Disc & regenerative.
Dimensions: 21.45/19.99 m x 2.78 m.
Bogies: FLEXX B5000 inside-frame.
Couplers: Dellner 12.
Gangways: Within unit.
Control System: IGBT Inverter.
Doors: Sliding plug.
Maximum Speed: 75 mph.
Heating & ventilation: Air conditioning.
Seating Layout: Longitudinal ("tube style") low density.
Multiple Working: Within class.

Class 710/1. 25 kV AC only 4-car units.

DMS(A). Bombardier Derby 2017–19. –/40(+6). t.
MS. Bombardier Derby 2017–19. –/46. t.
PMS. Bombardier Derby 2017–19. –/45(+6) 2W. t.
DMS(B). Bombardier Derby 2017–19. –/40(+6). t.

710 101	**LD**	RF			431101	431201	431301	431501
710 102	**LD**	RF			431102	431202	431302	431502
710 103	**LD**	RF	*LO*	WN	431103	431203	431303	431503
710 104	**LD**	RF			431104	431204	431304	431504
710 105	**LD**	RF	*LO*	WN	431105	431205	431305	431505
710 106	**LD**	RF			431106	431206	431306	431506
710 107	**LD**	RF			431107	431207	431307	431507
710 108	**LD**	RF			431108	431208	431308	431508
710 109	**LD**	RF			431109	431209	431309	431509
710 110	**LD**	RF			431110	431210	431310	431510
710 111	**LD**	RF			431111	431211	431311	431511
710 112	**LD**	RF			431112	431212	431312	431512
710 113	**LD**	RF			431113	431213	431313	431513
710 114	**LD**	RF		WS(S)	431114	431214	431314	431514
710 115	**LD**	RF			431115	431215	431315	431515
710 116	**LD**	RF		WS(S)	431116	431216	431316	431516
710 117	**LD**	RF			431117	431217	431317	431517
710 118	**LD**	RF			431118	431218	431318	431518
710 119	**LD**	RF			431119	431219	431319	431519
710 120	**LD**	RF			431120	431220	431320	431520
710 121	**LD**	RF			431121	431221	431321	431521
710 122	**LD**	RF			431122	431222	431322	431522
710 123	**LD**	RF			431123	431223	431323	431523
710 124	**LD**	RF		WS(S)	431124	431224	431324	431524
710 125	**LD**	RF		WS(S)	431125	431225	431325	431525
710 126	**LD**	RF			431126	431226	431326	431526
710 127	**LD**	RF			431127	431227	431327	431527
710 128	**LD**	RF			431128	431228	431328	431528
710 129	**LD**	RF			431129	431229	431329	431529
710 130	**LD**	RF		WS(S)	431130	431230	431330	431530

Class 710/2. 25 kV AC/750 V DC 4-car units.

DMS(A). Bombardier Derby 2017–19. –/40(+6). 43.5 t.
MS. Bombardier Derby 2017–19. –/46. 32.3 t.
PMS. Bombardier Derby 2017–19. –/45(+6) 2W. 38.5 t.
DMS(B). Bombardier Derby 2017–19. –/40(+6).43.5 t.

710 256	**LD**	RF			432156	432256	432356	432556
710 257	**LD**	RF	*LO*	WN	432157	432257	432357	432557
710 258	**LD**	RF	*LO*	WN	432158	432258	432358	432558
710 259	**LD**	RF	*LO*	WN	432159	432259	432359	432559
710 260	**LD**	RF	*LO*	WN	432160	432260	432360	432560
710 261	**LD**	RF	*LO*	WN	432161	432261	432361	432561
710 262	**LD**	RF	*LO*	WN	432162	432262	432362	432562
710 263	**LD**	RF	*LO*	WN	432163	432263	432363	432563

710264	**LD**	RF	*LO*	WN	432164	432264	432364	432564
710265	**LD**	RF	*LO*	WN	432165	432265	432365	432565
710266	**LD**	RF	*LO*	WN	432166	432266	432366	432566
710267	**LD**	RF	*LO*	WN	432167	432267	432367	432567
710268	**LD**	RF	*LO*	WN	432168	432268	432368	432568
710269	**LD**	RF	*LO*	WN	432169	432269	432369	432569
710270	**LD**	RF			432170	432270	432370	432570
710271	**LD**	RF	*LO*	WN	432171	432271	432371	432571
710272	**LD**	RF		WS(S)	432172	432272	432372	432572
710273	**LD**	RF			432173	432273	432373	432573

Class 710/2. 25 kV AC/750 V DC 5-car units.

DMS(A). Bombardier Derby 2019–20. –/40(+6). t.
MS. Bombardier Derby 2019–20. –/46. t.
PMS. Bombardier Derby 2019–20. –/45(+6) 2W. t.
MS. Bombardier Derby 2019–20. t.
DMS(B). Bombardier Derby 2019–20. –/40(+6). t.

710274	**LD**	RF	432174	432274	432374	432474	432574
710275	**LD**	RF	432175	432275	432375	432475	432575
710276	**LD**	RF	432176	432276	432376	432476	432576
710277	**LD**	RF	432177	432277	432377	432477	432577
710278	**LD**	RF	432178	432278	432378	432478	432578
710279	**LD**	RF	432179	432279	432379	432479	432579

CLASS 717 DESIRO CITY SIEMENS

New dual-voltage 6-car units used on Great Northern services from London Moorgate. The design is based on Classes 700/707, but has emergency end doors for tunnel operation. Fitted with tripcocks for operation between Moorgate and Drayton Park.

Formation: DMS–TS–TS–MS–PTS–DMS.
Systems: 25 kV AC overhead and 750 V DC third rail.
Construction: Aluminium.
Traction Motors: Four Siemens asynchronous of 200 kW.
Wheel Arrangement: Bo-Bo + 2-2 + 2-2 + Bo-Bo + 2-2 + Bo-Bo.
Braking: Disc, tread & regenerative. **Dimensions:** 20.00 x 2.80 m.
Bogies: Siemens SF7000 inside-frame. **Couplers:** Dellner 12.
Gangways: Within unit + end doors. **Control System:** IGBT Inverter.
Doors: Sliding plug. **Maximum Speed:** 85 mph.
Heating & ventilation: Air conditioning.
Seating Layout: 2+2 facing/unidirectional.
Multiple Working: Within class and with Classes 700 and 707.

DMS(A). Siemens Krefeld 2017–18. –/52(+4). 38.8 t.
TS. Siemens Krefeld 2017–18. –/68. 28.8 t.
TS. Siemens Krefeld 2017–18. –/61(+4) 2W. 28.7 t.
MS. Siemens Krefeld 2017–18. –/68. 35.5 t.
PTS. Siemens Krefeld 2017–18. –/61(+3). 33.9 t.
DMS(B). Siemens Krefeld 2017–18. –/52(+4). 38.8 t.

717001	**TL**	RR	*GN*	HE	451001	452001	453001	454001	455001	456001
717002	**TL**	RR	*GN*	HE	451002	452002	453002	454002	455002	456002
717003	**TL**	RR	*GN*	HE	451003	452003	453003	454003	455003	456003
717004	**TL**	RR	*GN*	HE	451004	452004	453004	454004	455004	456004
717005	**TL**	RR	*GN*	HE	451005	452005	453005	454005	455005	456005
717006	**TL**	RR	*GN*	HE	451006	452006	453006	454006	455006	456006
717007	**TL**	RR	*GN*	HE	451007	452007	453007	454007	455007	456007
717008	**TL**	RR	*GN*	HE	451008	452008	453008	454008	455008	456008
717009	**TL**	RR	*GN*	HE	451009	452009	453009	454009	455009	456009
717010	**TL**	RR	*GN*	HE	451010	452010	453010	454010	455010	456010
717011	**TL**	RR	*GN*	HE	451011	452011	453011	454011	455011	456011
717012	**TL**	RR	*GN*	HE	451012	452012	453012	454012	455012	456012
717013	**TL**	RR	*GN*	HE	451013	452013	453013	454013	455013	456013
717014	**TL**	RR	*GN*	HE	451014	452014	453014	454014	455014	456014
717015	**TL**	RR	*GN*	HE	451015	452015	453015	454015	455015	456015
717016	**TL**	RR	*GN*	HE	451016	452016	453016	454016	455016	456016
717017	**TL**	RR	*GN*	HE	451017	452017	453017	454017	455017	456017
717018	**TL**	RR	*GN*	HE	451018	452018	453018	454018	455018	456018
717019	**TL**	RR	*GN*	HE	451019	452019	453019	454019	455019	456019
717020	**TL**	RR	*GN*	HE	451020	452020	453020	454020	455020	456020
717021	**TL**	RR	*GN*	HE	451021	452021	453021	454021	455021	456021
717022	**TL**	RR	*GN*	HE	451022	452022	453022	454022	455022	456022
717023	**TL**	RR	*GN*	HE	451023	452023	453023	454023	455023	456023
717024	**TL**	RR	*GN*	HE	451024	452024	453024	454024	455024	456024
717025	**TL**	RR	*GN*	HE	451025	452025	453025	454025	455025	456025

CLASS 720 AVENTRA BOMBARDIER DERBY

This large fleet of Aventra EMUs was ordered by Greater Anglia in 2016 to replace its entire Class 317, 321, 360 and 379 fleets on outer suburban and medium-distance services. The units will be around a year late entering service owing to Bombardier Aventra software issues. They are expected to enter service from spring 2020. Full details awaited.

Formation (10-car): DMS–PMS–MS–MS–TS–MS–PMS–MS–MS–DTS or **(5-car)**: DMS–PMS–MS–MS–DTS.
Systems: 25 kV AC overhead.
Construction: Aluminium.
Traction Motors: Two Bombardier asynchronous of 265 kW.
Wheel Arrangement:
Braking: Disc & regenerative
Bogies: FLEXX B5000 inside-frame.
Gangways: Within unit.
Doors: Sliding plug.
Dimensions: 24.47/24.21 x 2.78 m.
Couplers: Dellner 12.
Control System: IGBT Inverter.
Maximum Speed: 100 mph.
Heating & ventilation: Air conditioning.
Seating Layout: 3+2 facing/unidirectional.
Multiple Working: Within class.

Class 720/1. 10-car units.

DMS. Bombardier Derby 2019–20. t.
PMS(A). Bombardier Derby 2019–20. t.
MS(A). Bombardier Derby 2019–20. t.
MS(B). Bombardier Derby 2019–20. t.
TS. Bombardier Derby 2019–20. t.
MS(C). Bombardier Derby 2019–20. t.
PMS(B). Bombardier Derby 2019–20. t.
MS(D). Bombardier Derby 2019–20. t.
MS(E). Bombardier Derby 2019–20. t.
DTS. Bombardier Derby 2019–20. t.

720 101	**GR**	A	450101	451101	452101	453101	454101
			455101	456101	457101	458101	459101
720 102	**GR**	A	450102	451102	452102	453102	454102
			455102	456102	457102	458102	459102
720 103	**GR**	A	450103	451103	452103	453103	454103
			455103	456103	457103	458103	459103
720 104	**GR**	A	450104	451104	452104	453104	454104
			455104	456104	457104	458104	459104
720 105	**GR**	A	450105	451105	452105	453105	454105
			455105	456105	457105	458105	459105
720 106	**GR**	A	450106	451106	452106	453106	454106
			455106	456106	457106	458106	459106
720 107	**GR**	A	450107	451107	452107	453107	454107
			455107	456107	457107	458107	459107
720 108	**GR**	A	450108	451108	452108	453108	454108
			455108	456108	457108	458108	459108
720 109	**GR**	A	450109	451109	452109	453109	454109
			455109	456109	457109	458109	459109
720 110	**GR**	A	450110	451110	452110	453110	454110
			455110	456110	457110	458110	459110
720 111	**GR**	A	450111	451111	452111	453111	454111
			455111	456111	457111	458111	459111
720 112	**GR**	A	450112	451112	452112	453112	454112
			455112	456112	457112	458112	459112
720 113	**GR**	A	450113	451113	452113	453113	454113
			455113	456113	457113	458113	459113
720 114	**GR**	A	450114	451114	452114	453114	454114
			455114	456114	457114	458114	459114
720 115	**GR**	A	450115	451115	452115	453115	454115
			455115	456115	457115	458115	459115
720 116	**GR**	A	450116	451116	452116	453116	454116
			455116	456116	457116	458116	459116
720 117	**GR**	A	450117	451117	452117	453117	454117
			455117	456117	457117	458117	459117
720 118	**GR**	A	450118	451118	452118	453118	454118
			455118	456118	457118	458118	459118
720 119	**GR**	A	450119	451119	452119	453119	454119
			455119	456119	457119	458119	459119

720 120	**GR**	A	450120	451120	452120	453120	454120
			455120	456120	457120	458120	459120
720 121	**GR**	A	450121	451121	452121	453121	454121
			455121	456121	457121	458121	459121
720 122	**GR**	A	450122	451122	452122	453122	454122
			455122	456122	457122	458122	459122

Class 720/5. 5-car units.

DMS. Bombardier Derby 2018–20. t.
PMS. Bombardier Derby 2018–20. t.
MS(A). Bombardier Derby 2018–20. t.
MS(B). Bombardier Derby 2018–20. t.
DTS. Bombardier Derby 2018–20. t.

720 501	**GR**	A	450501	451501	452501	453501	459501
720 502	**GR**	A	450502	451502	452502	453502	459502
720 503	**GR**	A	450503	451503	452503	453503	459503
720 504	**GR**	A	450504	451504	452504	453504	459504
720 505	**GR**	A	450505	451505	452505	453505	459505
720 506	**GR**	A	450506	451506	452506	453506	459506
720 507	**GR**	A	450507	451507	452507	453507	459507
720 508	**GR**	A	450508	451508	452508	453508	459508
720 509	**GR**	A	450509	451509	452509	453509	459509
720 510	**GR**	A	450510	451510	452510	453510	459510
720 511	**GR**	A	450511	451511	452511	453511	459511
720 512	**GR**	A	450512	451512	452512	453512	459512
720 513	**GR**	A	450513	451513	452513	453513	459513
720 514	**GR**	A	450514	451514	452514	453514	459514
720 515	**GR**	A	450515	451515	452515	453515	459515
720 516	**GR**	A	450516	451516	452516	453516	459516
720 517	**GR**	A	450517	451517	452517	453517	459517
720 518	**GR**	A	450518	451518	452518	453518	459518
720 519	**GR**	A	450519	451519	452519	453519	459519
720 520	**GR**	A	450520	451520	452520	453520	459520
720 521	**GR**	A	450521	451521	452521	453521	459521
720 522	**GR**	A	450522	451522	452522	453522	459522
720 523	**GR**	A	450523	451523	452523	453523	459523
720 524	**GR**	A	450524	451524	452524	453524	459524
720 525	**GR**	A	450525	451525	452525	453525	459525
720 526	**GR**	A	450526	451526	452526	453526	459526
720 527	**GR**	A	450527	451527	452527	453527	459527
720 528	**GR**	A	450528	451528	452528	453528	459528
720 529	**GR**	A	450529	451529	452529	453529	459529
720 530	**GR**	A	450530	451530	452530	453530	459530
720 531	**GR**	A	450531	451531	452531	453531	459531
720 532	**GR**	A	450532	451532	452532	453532	459532
720 533	**GR**	A	450533	451533	452533	453533	459533
720 534	**GR**	A	450534	451534	452534	453534	459534
720 535	**GR**	A	450535	451535	452535	453535	459535
720 536	**GR**	A	450536	451536	452536	453536	459536
720 537	**GR**	A	450537	451537	452537	453537	459537
720 538	**GR**	A	450538	451538	452538	453538	459538

720 539	GR	A	450539	451539	452539	453539	459539
720 540	GR	A	450540	451540	452540	453540	459540
720 541	GR	A	450541	451541	452541	453541	459541
720 542	GR	A	450542	451542	452542	453542	459542
720 543	GR	A	450543	451543	452543	453543	459543
720 544	GR	A	450544	451544	452544	453544	459544
720 545	GR	A	450545	451545	452545	453545	459545
720 546	GR	A	450546	451546	452546	453546	459546
720 547	GR	A	450547	451547	452547	453547	459547
720 548	GR	A	450548	451548	452548	453548	459548
720 549	GR	A	450549	451549	452549	453549	459549
720 550	GR	A	450550	451550	452550	453550	459550
720 551	GR	A	450551	451551	452551	453551	459551
720 552	GR	A	450552	451552	452552	453552	459552
720 553	GR	A	450553	451553	452553	453553	459553
720 554	GR	A	450554	451554	452554	453554	459554
720 555	GR	A	450555	451555	452555	453555	459555
720 556	GR	A	450556	451556	452556	453556	459556
720 557	GR	A	450557	451557	452557	453557	459557
720 558	GR	A	450558	451558	452558	453558	459558
720 559	GR	A	450559	451559	452559	453559	459559
720 560	GR	A	450560	451560	452560	453560	459560
720 561	GR	A	450561	451561	452561	453561	459561
720 562	GR	A	450562	451562	452562	453562	459562
720 563	GR	A	450563	451563	452563	453563	459563
720 564	GR	A	450564	451564	452564	453564	459564
720 565	GR	A	450565	451565	452565	453565	459565
720 566	GR	A	450566	451566	452566	453566	459566
720 567	GR	A	450567	451567	452567	453567	459567
720 568	GR	A	450568	451568	452568	453568	459568
720 569	GR	A	450569	451569	452569	453569	459569
720 570	GR	A	450570	451570	452570	453570	459570
720 571	GR	A	450571	451571	452571	453571	459571
720 572	GR	A	450572	451572	452572	453572	459572
720 573	GR	A	450573	451573	452573	453573	459573
720 574	GR	A	450574	451574	452574	453574	459574
720 575	GR	A	450575	451575	452575	453575	459575
720 576	GR	A	450576	451576	452576	453576	459576
720 577	GR	A	450577	451577	452577	453577	459577
720 578	GR	A	450578	451578	452578	453578	459578
720 579	GR	A	450579	451579	452579	453579	459579
720 580	GR	A	450580	451580	452580	453580	459580
720 581	GR	A	450581	451581	452581	453581	459581
720 582	GR	A	450582	451582	452582	453582	459582
720 583	GR	A	450583	451583	452583	453583	459583
720 584	GR	A	450584	451584	452584	453584	459584
720 585	GR	A	450585	451585	452585	453585	459585
720 586	GR	A	450586	451586	452586	453586	459586
720 587	GR	A	450587	451587	452587	453587	459587
720 588	GR	A	450588	451588	452588	453588	459588
720 589	GR	A	450589	451589	452589	453589	459589

CLASS 730 AVENTRA BOMBARDIER DERBY

West Midlands Trains has a mixed fleet of 3- and 5-car Aventra EMUs on order from Bombardier, for delivery 2020–21. The 3-car units will be used on suburban services around Birmingham, including on the Cross City line, while the 5-car units will be used on outer suburban and inter urban services from London Euston and in the West Midlands. Full details awaited.

Formation: DMS–PMS–DMS or DMC–MS–PMS–MS–DMS.
Systems: 25 kV AC overhead.
Construction: Aluminium.
Traction Motors: Two Bombardier asynchronous of 250 kW.
Wheel Arrangement:
Braking: Disc & regenerative.
Bogies: FLEXX B5000 inside-frame.
Gangways: End gangways.
Doors: Sliding plug.
Dimensions: 24.47/24.21 x 2.78 m.
Couplers: Dellner 12.
Control System: IGBT Inverter.
Maximum Speed:
Heating & ventilation: Air conditioning.
Seating Layout:
Multiple Working: Within class.

Class 730/0. 3-car West Midlands area units.

DMS. Bombardier Derby 2020–21. t.
PMS. Bombardier Derby 2020–21. t.
DMS. Bombardier Derby 2020–21. t.

730001	CO	490001	491001	492001
730002	CO	490002	491002	492002
730003	CO	490003	491003	492003
730004	CO	490004	491004	492004
730005	CO	490005	491005	492005
730006	CO	490006	491006	492006
730007	CO	490007	491007	492007
730008	CO	490008	491008	492008
730009	CO	490009	491009	492009
730010	CO	490010	491010	492010
730011	CO	490011	491011	492011
730012	CO	490012	491012	492012
730013	CO	490013	491013	492013
730014	CO	490014	491014	492014
730015	CO	490015	491015	492015
730016	CO	490016	491016	492016
730017	CO	490017	491017	492017
730018	CO	490018	491018	492018
730019	CO	490019	491019	492019
730020	CO	490020	491020	492020
730021	CO	490021	491021	492021
730022	CO	490022	491022	492022
730023	CO	490023	491023	492023
730024	CO	490024	491024	492024
730025	CO	490025	491025	492025
730026	CO	490026	491026	492026

730027	CO	490027	491027	492027
730028	CO	490028	491028	492028
730029	CO	490029	491029	492029
730030	CO	490030	491030	492030
730031	CO	490031	491031	492031
730032	CO	490032	491032	492032
730033	CO	490033	491033	492033
730034	CO	490034	491034	492034
730035	CO	490035	491035	492035
730036	CO	490036	491036	492036

Class 730/1. 5-car outer suburban units.

DMC. Bombardier Derby 2020–21. t.
MS. Bombardier Derby 2020–21. t.
PMS. Bombardier Derby 2020–21. t.
MS. Bombardier Derby 2020–21. t.
DMS. Bombardier Derby 2020–21. t.

730101	CO	490101	491101	492101	493101	494101
730102	CO	490102	491102	492102	493102	494102
730103	CO	490103	491103	492103	493103	494103
730104	CO	490104	491104	492104	493104	494104
730105	CO	490105	491105	492105	493105	494105
730106	CO	490106	491106	492106	493106	494106
730107	CO	490107	491107	492107	493107	494107
730108	CO	490108	491108	492108	493108	494108
730109	CO	490109	491109	492109	493109	494109
730110	CO	490110	491110	492110	493110	494110
730111	CO	490111	491111	492111	493111	494111
730112	CO	490112	491112	492112	493112	494112
730113	CO	490113	491113	492113	493113	494113
730114	CO	490114	491114	492114	493114	494114
730115	CO	490115	491115	492115	493115	494115
730116	CO	490116	491116	492116	493116	494116
730117	CO	490117	491117	492117	493117	494117
730118	CO	490118	491118	492118	493118	494118
730119	CO	490119	491119	492119	493119	494119
730120	CO	490120	491120	492120	493120	494120
730121	CO	490121	491121	492121	493121	494121
730122	CO	490122	491122	492122	493122	494122
730123	CO	490123	491123	492123	493123	494123
730124	CO	490124	491124	492124	493124	494124
730125	CO	490125	491125	492125	493125	494125
730126	CO	490126	491126	492126	493126	494126
730127	CO	490127	491127	492127	493127	494127
730128	CO	490128	491128	492128	493128	494128
730129	CO	490129	491129	492129	493129	494129

Class 730/2. 5-car long distance units.

DMC. Bombardier Derby 2020–21. t.
MS. Bombardier Derby 2020–21. t.

PMS. Bombardier Derby 2020–21. t.
MS. Bombardier Derby 2020–21. t.
DMS. Bombardier Derby 2020–21. t.

730 201	CO	490201	491201	492201	493201	494201
730 202	CO	490202	491202	492202	493202	494202
730 203	CO	490203	491203	492203	493203	494203
730 204	CO	490204	491204	492204	493204	494204
730 205	CO	490205	491205	492205	493205	494205
730 206	CO	490206	491206	492206	493206	494206
730 207	CO	490207	491207	492207	493207	494207
730 208	CO	490208	491208	492208	493208	494208
730 209	CO	490209	491209	492209	493209	494209
730 210	CO	490210	491210	492210	493210	494210
730 211	CO	490211	491211	492211	493211	494211
730 212	CO	490212	491212	492212	493212	494212
730 213	CO	490213	491213	492213	493213	494213
730 214	CO	490214	491214	492214	493214	494214
730 215	CO	490215	491215	492215	493215	494215
730 216	CO	490216	491216	492216	493216	494216

CLASS 745 FLIRT ELECTRIC STADLER

This fleet of 20 12-car articulated Stadler EMUs was ordered by Greater Anglia in 2016 to replace its locomotive-hauled sets on Liverpool Street–Norwich services and Class 379s on the Liverpool Street–Stansted Airport route. The first unit entered service in early 2020. The 12-car units are formed of two 6-car half units formed of three coupled articulated pairs. Full details awaited.

Formation (745/0): DMF–PTF–TS–TS–TS–MS–MS–TS–TS–TS–PTS–DMS or **(745/1)**: DMS–PTS–TS–TS–TS–MS–MS–TS–TS–TS–PTS–DMS.
Systems: 25 kV AC overhead.
Construction: Aluminium.
Traction Motors: Four TSA of 325 kW.
Wheel Arrangement: Bo-2-2 + 2-2-2 + 2-2-Bo + Bo-2-2 + 2-2-2 + 2-2-Bo.
Braking: Disc & regenerative
Bogies: Stadler/Jacobs.
Gangways: Within unit.
Doors: Sliding plug (one per vehicle).
Dimensions:
Couplers: Dellner 10.
Control System: IGBT Inverter.
Maximum Speed: 100 mph.
Heating & ventilation: Air conditioning.
Seating Layout: 1: 2+1 facing/unidirectional, 2: 2+2 unidirectional/facing.
Multiple Working: Within class.

Class 745/0. Fitted with First Class and café bar area for use on the London Liverpool Street–Norwich route.

DMF. Stadler Bussnang/Szolnok 2018–19. t.
PTF. Stadler Bussnang/Szolnok 2018–19. t.
TS(A). Stadler Bussnang/Szolnok 2018–19. t.
TS(B). Stadler Bussnang/Szolnok 2018–19. t.
TS(C). Stadler Bussnang/Szolnok 2018–19. t.
MS(A). Stadler Bussnang/Szolnok 2018–19. t.
MS(B). Stadler Bussnang/Szolnok 2018–19. t.

TS(D). Stadler Bussnang/Szolnok 2018–19. t.
TS(E). Stadler Bussnang/Szolnok 2018–19. t.
TS(F). Stadler Bussnang/Szolnok 2018–19. t.
PTS. Stadler Bussnang/Szolnok 2018–19. t.
DMS. Stadler Bussnang/Szolnok 2018–19. t.

745 001	**GR**	RR			413001 426001 332001 343001 341001 301001 302001 342001 344001 346001 322001 312001
745 002	**GR**	RR			413002 426002 332002 343002 341002 301002 302002 342002 344002 346002 322002 312002
745 003	**GR**	RR			413003 426003 332003 343003 341003 301003 302003 342003 344003 346003 322003 312003
745 004	**GR**	RR			413004 426004 332004 343004 341004 301004 302004 342004 344004 346004 322004 312004
745 005	**GR**	RR			413005 426005 332005 343005 341005 301005 302005 342005 344005 346005 322005 312005
745 006	**GR**	RR			413006 426006 332006 343006 341006 301006 302006 342006 344006 346006 322006 312006
745 007	**GR**	RR	*GA*	NC	413007 426007 332007 343007 341007 301007 302007 342007 344007 346007 322007 312007
745 008	**GR**	RR			413008 426008 332008 343008 341008 301008 302008 342008 344008 346008 322008 312008
745 009	**GR**	RR			413009 426009 332009 343009 341009 301009 302009 342009 344009 346009 322009 312009
745 010	**GR**	RR			413010 426010 332010 343010 341010 301010 302010 342010 344010 346010 322010 312010

Class 745/1. Standard Class only units for use between London Liverpool Street and Stansted Airport.

DMS. Stadler Bussnang/Szolnok 2018–19. t.
PTS. Stadler Bussnang/Szolnok 2018–19. t.
TS(A). Stadler Bussnang/Szolnok 2018–19. t.
TS(B). Stadler Bussnang/Szolnok 2018–19. t.
TS(C). Stadler Bussnang/Szolnok 2018–19. t.
MS(A). Stadler Bussnang/Szolnok 2018–19. t.
MS(B). Stadler Bussnang/Szolnok 2018–19. t.
TS(D). Stadler Bussnang/Szolnok 2018–19. t.
TS(E). Stadler Bussnang/Szolnok 2018–19. t.
TS(F). Stadler Bussnang/Szolnok 2018–19. t.
PTS. Stadler Bussnang/Szolnok 2018–19. t.
DMS. Stadler Bussnang/Szolnok 2018–19. t.

745 101	**GR**	RR	313101 326101 332101 343101 341101 301101 302101 342101 344101 346101 322101 312101
745 102	**GR**	RR	313102 326102 332102 343102 341102 301102 302102 342102 344102 346102 322102 312102
745 103	**GR**	RR	313103 326103 332103 343103 341103 301103 302103 342103 344103 346103 322103 312103
745 104	**GR**	RR	313104 326104 332104 343104 341104 301104 302104 342104 344104 346104 322104 312104
745 105	**GR**	RR	313105 326105 332105 343105 341105 301105 302105 342105 344105 346105 322105 312105

745 106	**GR**	RR	313106 326106 332106 343106 341106 301106 302106 342106 344106 346106 322106 312106
745 107	**GR**	RR	313107 326107 332107 343107 341107 301107 302107 342107 344107 346107 322107 312107
745 108	**GR**	RR	313108 326108 332108 343108 341108 301108 302108 342108 344108 346108 322108 312108
745 109	**GR**	RR	313109 326109 332109 343109 341109 301109 302109 342109 344109 346109 322109 312109
745 110	**GR**	RR	313110 326110 332110 343110 341110 301110 302110 342110 344110 346110 322110 312110

CLASS 755 FLIRT BI-MODE STADLER

This fleet of 3- and 4-car articulated Stadler bi-mode units was ordered by Greater Anglia in 2016 to replace all of its older DMU fleets. The first units entered service in summer 2019. The design features a "power pack" in the middle that houses two diesel engines for the 3-car units and four diesel engines for the 4-car units. This has been given its own number, effectively making the units 4- and 5-car, although there is no passenger accommodation in the power pack car.

Formation: DMS–PP–PTS–DMS or DMS–PTS–PP–PTS–DMS.
Systems: Diesel/25 kV AC overhead.
Construction: Aluminium.
Engines: (4-car): Four Deutz V8 of 480 kW (645 hp), (3-car): Two Four Deutz V8 of 480 kW (645 hp).
Traction Motors: Four TSA of 325 kW.
Wheel Arrangement: Bo-2-2-2-Bo or Bo-2-2-2-2-Bo.
Braking: Disc & regenerative
Dimensions: 20.81/15.22/6.69 (PP) m x 2.72/2.82 (PP) m.
Bogies: Stadler/Jacobs.
Couplers: Dellner 10.
Gangways: Within unit.
Control System: IGBT Inverter.
Doors: Sliding plug (one per vehicle).
Maximum Speed: 100 mph.
Heating & ventilation: Air conditioning.
Seating Layout: 2+2 unidirectional/facing.
Multiple Working: Within class.

Class 755/3. 3-car (plus power pack) units.

DMS(A). Stadler Szolnok/Siedlce/Bussnang/Valencia 2018–19. –/60(+4).
PP. Stadler Bussnang/Valencia 2018–19.
PTS. Stadler Szolnok/Siedlce/Bussnang/Valencia 2018–19. –/32(+7) 1TD 1T 2W.
DMS(B). Stadler Szolnok/Siedlce/Bussnang/Valencia 2018–19. –/52(+12).

755 325	**GR**	RR			911325	971325	981325	912325
755 326	**GR**	RR			911326	971326	981326	912326
755 327	**GR**	RR	*GA*	NC	911327	971327	981327	912327
755 328	**GR**	RR	*GA*	NC	911328	971328	981328	912328
755 329	**GR**	RR	*GA*	NC	911329	971329	981329	912329
755 330	**GR**	RR	*GA*	NC	911330	971330	981330	912330
755 331	**GR**	RR			911331	971331	981331	912331
755 332	**GR**	RR	*GA*	NC	911332	971332	981332	912332
755 333	**GR**	RR	*GA*	NC	911333	971333	981333	912333

755334	**GR**	RR			911334	971334	981334	912334
755335	**GR**	RR	*GA*	NC	911335	971335	981335	912335
755336	**GR**	RR	*GA*	NC	911336	971336	981336	912336
755337	**GR**	RR	*GA*	NC	911337	971337	981337	912337
755338	**GR**	RR			911338	971338	981338	912338

Class 755/4. 4-car (plus power pack) units.

DMS(A). Stadler Szolnok/Siedlce/Bussnang/Valencia 2018–19. –/60(+4). 41.4 t.
PTS(A). Stadler Szolnok/Siedlce/Bussnang/Valencia 2018–19. –/58(+4). 25.0 t.
PP. Stadler Bussnang/Valencia 2018–19. 28.5 t.
PTS(B). Stadler Szolnok/Siedlce/Bussnang/Valencia 2018–19. –/32(+7). 1TD 1T 2W. 26.4 t.
DMS(B). Stadler Szolnok/Siedlce/Bussnang/Valencia 2018–19. –/52(+12). 42.2 t.

755401	**GR**	RR			911401	961401	971401	981401	912401
755402	**GR**	RR	*GA*	NC	911402	961402	971402	981402	912402
755403	**GR**	RR			911403	961403	971403	981403	912403
755404	**GR**	RR	*GA*	NC	911404	961404	971404	981404	912404
755405	**GR**	RR			911405	961405	971405	981405	912405
755406	**GR**	RR			911406	961406	971406	981406	912406
755407	**GR**	RR	*GA*	NC	911407	961407	971407	981407	912407
755408	**GR**	RR			911408	961408	971408	981408	912408
755409	**GR**	RR	*GA*	NC	911409	961409	971409	981409	912409
755410	**GR**	RR	*GA*	NC	911410	961410	971410	981410	912410
755411	**GR**	RR	*GA*	NC	911411	961411	971411	981411	912411
755412	**GR**	RR	*GA*	NC	911412	961412	971412	981412	912412
755413	**GR**	RR	*GA*	NC	911413	961413	971413	981413	912413
755414	**GR**	RR	*GA*	NC	911414	961414	971414	981414	912414
755415	**GR**	RR	*GA*	NC	911415	961415	971415	981415	912415
755416	**GR**	RR	*GA*	NC	911416	961416	971416	981416	912416
755417	**GR**	RR	*GA*	NC	911417	961417	971417	981417	912417
755418	**GR**	RR	*GA*	NC	911418	961418	971418	981418	912418
755419	**GR**	RR	*GA*	NC	911419	961419	971419	981419	912419
755420	**GR**	RR	*GA*	NC	911420	961420	971420	981420	912420
755421	**GR**	RR	*GA*	NC	911421	961421	971421	981421	912421
755422	**GR**	RR	*GA*	NC	911422	961422	971422	981422	912422
755423	**GR**	RR	*GA*	NC	911423	961423	971423	981423	912423
755424	**GR**	RR	*GA*	NC	911424	961424	971424	981424	912424

CLASS 769 FLEX BREL YORK/BRUSH

In 2017 it was announced that Porterbrook would be converting eight Class 319s into bi-mode "Flex" units for Northern, with two new diesel engines being fitted (one under each of the driving trailer cars) to drive ABB alternators. Subsequently orders have been placed by Transport for Wales for nine units and Great Western Railway for 19 units. The GWR units will be "tri-mode", with both AC overhead and DC third rail capability.

Work on the conversions is taking place at Brush Loughborough but the project has been beset by delays, with the first Northern units not due to enter traffic until spring 2020. Identities of four of the TfW units is not yet known. All conversions are from Class 319/0 or 319/4 Phase 1 units. Full details awaited.

Formation: DMC–MS–TS–DMS.
Systems: Diesel/25 kV AC overhead/750 V DC third rail (GWR units only).
Construction: Steel.
Engines: Two MAN D2876 of 390 kW (523 hp).
Traction Motors: Four GEC G315BZ of 268 kW.
Wheel Arrangement: 2-2 + Bo-Bo + 2-2 + 2-2.
Braking: Disc. **Dimensions**: 20.17/20.16 x 2.82 m.
Bogies: P7-4 (MS), T3-7 (others). **Couplers**: Tightlock.
Gangways: Within unit + end doors. **Control System**: GTO chopper.
Doors: Sliding.
Maximum Speed: 100 mph (electric); 85 mph (diesel).
Seating Layout: 1: 2+1 facing (declassified); 2: 2+2/3+2 facing.
Multiple Working: Within class and with Class 319.

77291–381. DMC. Lot No. 31022 (odd nos.) 1987–88.
77431–457. DMC. Lot No. 31038 (odd nos.) 1988.
62891–936. MS. Lot No. 31023 1987–88.
62961–974. MS. Lot No. 31039 1988.
71772–817. TS. Lot No. 31024 1987–88.
71866–879. TS. Lot No. 31040 1988.
77330–380. DMS. Lot No. 31025 (even nos.) 1987–88.
77430–456. DMS. Lot No. 31041 (even nos.) 1988.

Class 769/0. Transport for Wales units.

769002	(319002)	**TL**	P	CF	77293	62892	71773	77292
769003	(319003)		P		77295	62893	71774	77294
769006	(319006)	**TL**	P	CF	77301	62896	71777	77300
769007	(319007)		P		77303	62897	71778	77302
769008	(319008)	**TW**	P	CF	77305	62898	71779	77304

Class 769/4. Northern units.

769424	(319424)	**NR**	P	AN	77337	62914	71795	77336
769431	(319431)	**NR**	P	AN	77351	62921	71802	77350
769434	(319434)	**NR**	P	AN	77357	62924	71805	77356
769442	(319442)	**NR**	P	AN	77373	62932	71813	77372
769448	(319448)	**NR**	P	AN	77433	62962	71867	77432
769450	(319450)	**NR**	P	AN	77437	62964	71869	77436
769456	(319456)	**NR**	P	AN	77449	62970	71875	77448
769458	(319458)	**NR**	P	AN	77453	62972	71877	77452

Class 769/9. Great Western Railway units.

769922	(319422)	P	77333	62912	71793	77332
769923	(319423)	P	77335	62913	71794	77334
769925	(319425)	P	77339	62915	71796	77338
769927	(319427)	P	77343	62917	71798	77342
769928	(319428)	P	77345	62918	71799	77344
769930	(319430)	P	77349	62920	71801	77348
769932	(319432)	P	77353	62922	71803	77352
769935	(319435)	P	77359	62925	71806	77358
769936	(319436)	P	77361	62926	71807	77360
769937	(319437)	P	77363	62927	71808	77362

769938	(319438)	P	77365	62928	71809	77364
769939	(319439)	P	77367	62929	71810	77366
769940	(319440)	P	77369	62930	71811	77368
769943	(319443)	P	77375	62933	71814	77374
769945	(319445)	P	77379	62935	71816	77378
769947	(319447)	P	77431	62961	71866	77430
769949	(319449)	P	77435	62963	71868	77434
769952	(319452)	P	77441	62966	71871	77440
769959	(319459)	P	77455	62973	71878	77454

CLASS 777 STADLER

This fleet of articulated 4-car units was ordered from Stadler in 2017 by Merseytravel for the DC third rail Merseyrail suburban network, to replace Classes 507–508 in 2020–21. The fleet will be owned by Merseytravel. An option exists for up to a further 60 units. Full details awaited.

Formation: DMS–MS–MS–DMS.
System: 750 V DC third rail.
Construction: Aluminium.
Traction Motors: Six TSA of 350 kW (470 hp) per unit.
Wheel Arrangement: 2-Bo-Bo-Bo-2.
Braking: Tread & regenerative.
Bogies: Jakobs.
Gangways: Within unit.
Doors: Sliding plug.
Dimensions: 19.00/13.50 x 2.82 m.
Couplers: Dellner 12.
Control System: IGBT Inverter.
Maximum Speed: 75 mph.
Heating & ventilation: Air conditioning.
Seating Layout: 2+2 facing/unidirectional.
Multiple Working: Within class.

DMS(A). Stadler Szolnok/Siedlce/Altenrhein 2018–20. –/53. t.
MS(A). Stadler Szolnok/Siedlce/Altenrhein 2018–20. –/39 1W. t.
MS(B). Stadler Szolnok/Siedlce/Altenrhein 2018–20. –/39 1W. t.
DMS(B). Stadler Szolnok/Siedlce/Altenrhein 2018–20. –/53. t.

777001	427001	428001	429001	430001
777002	427002	428002	429002	430002
777003	427003	428003	429003	430003
777004	427004	428004	429004	430004
777005	427005	428005	429005	430005
777006	427006	428006	429006	430006
777007	427007	428007	429007	430007
777008	427008	428008	429008	430008
777009	427009	428009	429009	430009
777010	427010	428010	429010	430010
777011	427011	428011	429011	430011
777012	427012	428012	429012	430012
777013	427013	428013	429013	430013
777014	427014	428014	429014	430014
777015	427015	428015	429015	430015
777016	427016	428016	429016	430016
777017	427017	428017	429017	430017

777 018	427018	428018	429018	430018
777 019	427019	428019	429019	430019
777 020	427020	428020	429020	430020
777 021	427021	428021	429021	430021
777 022	427022	428022	429022	430022
777 023	427023	428023	429023	430023
777 024	427024	428024	429024	430024
777 025	427025	428025	429025	430025
777 026	427026	428026	429026	430026
777 027	427027	428027	429027	430027
777 028	427028	428028	429028	430028
777 029	427029	428029	429029	430029
777 030	427030	428030	429030	430030
777 031	427031	428031	429031	430031
777 032	427032	428032	429032	430032
777 033	427033	428033	429033	430033
777 034	427034	428034	429034	430034
777 035	427035	428035	429035	430035
777 036	427036	428036	429036	430036
777 037	427037	428037	429037	430037
777 038	427038	428038	429038	430038
777 039	427039	428039	429039	430039
777 040	427040	428040	429040	430040
777 041	427041	428041	429041	430041
777 042	427042	428042	429042	430042
777 043	427043	428043	429043	430043
777 044	427044	428044	429044	430044
777 045	427045	428045	429045	430045
777 046	427046	428046	429046	430046
777 047	427047	428047	429047	430047
777 048	427048	428048	429048	430048
777 049	427049	428049	429049	430049
777 050	427050	428050	429050	430050
777 051	427051	428051	429051	430051
777 052	427052	428052	429052	430052

CLASS 799 HYDROFLEX BREL YORK/BRUSH

This hydrogen demonstrator unit was converted in 2019 from a Class 319 as part of a partnership between Porterbrook and the University of Birmingham. It is due to commence main line testing during 2020.

The Class 799 MS has been heavily modified and is now fitted with batteries, a hydrogen fuel cell and four hydrogen tanks. Hydrogen is stored in tanks at high pressure, from where it is piped into fuel cells where it is mixed with oxygen to create electricity to power the motors. The energy can also be stored in the batteries, these being used at times of high demand.

Formation: DMC–MS–TS–DMS.
Systems: Hydrogen/25 kV AC overhead/750 V DC third rail.
Construction: Steel.

Traction Motors: Four GEC G315BZ of 268 kW.
Wheel Arrangement: 2-2 + Bo-Bo + 2-2 + 2-2.
Braking: Disc. **Dimensions:** 20.17/20.16 x 2.82 m.
Bogies: P7-4 (MS), T3-7 (others). **Couplers:** Tightlock.
Gangways: Within unit + end doors. **Doors:** Sliding.
Maximum Speed: 75 mph.
Seating Layout: 1: 2+1 facing (declassified); 2: 2+2/3+2 facing.

Non-standard livery: HydroFlex (green, grey and white).

77291. DMC. Lot No. 31022. 1987–88.
62891. MS. Lot No. 31023 1987–88.
71772. TS. Lot No. 31024 1987–88.
77290. DMS. Lot No. 31025 1987–88.

769001	(319001)	**0**	P	LM	77291	62891	71772	77290

4.4. HITACHI IEP UNITS

CLASS 800 INTERCITY EXPRESS PROGRAMME BI-MODE HITACHI

In 2012 Agility Trains, a consortium of Hitachi and John Laing, signed a deal with the DfT to design, build, finance and maintain the next generation of InterCity rolling stock for the Great Western and East Coast Main Lines, principally to replace ageing High Speed Trains on these routes. A follow-on order in 2013 was placed for 30 9-car trains to replace the Class 91 and Mark 4 carriages on the ECML. This brought the total number of vehicles ordered to 866. Both GWR and LNER were originally planned to have a mix of 5-car and 9-car units which will be bi-mode and straight electric trains (although the EMUs also have one diesel engine fitted to each set). However, owing to delays with electrification works on the GWML, in 2016 it was announced that the 21 9-car electric Class 801 units for GWR would be built as 21 9-car bi-mode units, numbered instead in the Class 800/3 series.

The units are broadly based on the Southeastern Class 395s, but have 25–25.35 m length bodyshells. They are numbered in the Class 800 (bi-mode) and Class 801 (EMU) number series'. 12 trains (76 vehicles) were fully manufactured at Kasado in Japan before the new Hitachi factory at Newton Aycliffe, County Durham was up and running. The remaining trains are being assembled at either Newton Aycliffe or Kasado. New maintenance depots for the trains have been built at Stoke Gifford (Bristol), Swansea and North Pole (London, the former Eurostar depot) for the GWR sets and at Doncaster for the LNER units.

The first trains arrived for testing in 2015. 5-car units entered service on the Great Western Main Line in autumn 2017 and Class 800s entered service on the East Coast Main Line from spring 2019.

In 2015 GWR ordered a further 22 5-car and seven 9-car IEPs, designated Class 802/0 (5-car) and Class 802/1 (9-car). These are mainly used on Paddington–West of England services.

In 2016 GWR ordered a further seven 9-car Class 802s, TransPennine Express ordered 19 5-car Class 802s and Hull Trains ordered five 5-car Class 802s, for delivery 2019–20. The majority of the Class 802s were constructed at Pistoia in Italy, with some at Kasado.

Formation: Various, see class headings for details.
Systems: Diesel/25 kV AC overhead electric.
Construction: Aluminium.
Diesel engines: In the 5-car sets diesel engines are located in cars 2, 3 and 4. In the 9-car sets diesel engines are located in cars 2, 3, 5, 7 and 8.
Engines: MTU 12V 1600 R80L of 700 kW (940 hp).
Traction Motors: Four Hitachi asynchronous of 226 kW.
Wheel Arrangement: 2-2 + Bo-Bo + Bo-Bo + Bo-Bo + 2-2 or 2-2 + Bo-Bo + Bo-Bo + 2-2 + Bo-Bo + 2-2 + Bo-Bo + Bo-Bo + 2-2.
Braking: Disc & regenerative.
Bogies: Hitachi.
Gangways: Within unit.
Doors: Single-leaf sliding.
Dimensions: 25.35/25.00 m x 2.74 m.
Couplers: Dellner 10.
Control System: IGBT Inverter.
Maximum Speed: 125 mph.
Heating & ventilation: Air conditioning.
Seating Layout: 1: 2+1 facing/unidirectional; 2+2 facing/unidirectional.
Multiple Working: Within class and with Classes 801 and 802.

Class 800/0. 5-car Great Western Railway units.
Formation: PDTS–MS–MS–MC–PDTRBF.

PDTS. Hitachi Newton Aycliffe/Kasado 2013–17. –/56 1TD. 47.8 t.
MS. Hitachi Newton Aycliffe/Kasado 2013–17. –/88. 50.1 t.
MS. Hitachi Newton Aycliffe/Kasado 2013–17. –/88 2T. 50.3 t.
MC. Hitachi Newton Aycliffe/Kasado 2013–17. 18/58 1T. 50.6 t.
PDTRBF. Hitachi Newton Aycliffe/Kasado 2013–17. 18/– 1TD 2W. 51.7 t.

800001	**GW**	AT	*GW*	NP	811001	812001	813001	814001	815001
800002	**GW**	AT	*GW*	NP	811002	812002	813002	814002	815002
800003	**GW**	AT	*GW*	NP	811003	812003	813003	814003	815003
800004	**GW**	AT	*GW*	NP	811004	812004	813004	814004	815004
800005	**GW**	AT	*GW*	NP	811005	812005	813005	814005	815005
800006	**GW**	AT	*GW*	NP	811006	812006	813006	814006	815006
800007	**GW**	AT	*GW*	NP	811007	812007	813007	814007	815007
800008	**GW**	AT	*GW*	NP	811008	812008	813008	814008	815008
800009	**GW**	AT	*GW*	NP	811009	812009	813009	814009	815009
800010	**GW**	AT	*GW*	NP	811010	812010	813010	814010	815010
800011	**GW**	AT	*GW*	NP	811011	812011	813011	814011	815011
800012	**GW**	AT	*GW*	NP	811012	812012	813012	814012	815012
800013	**GW**	AT	*GW*	NP	811013	812013	813013	814013	815013
800014	**GW**	AT	*GW*	NP	811014	812014	813014	814014	815014
800015	**GW**	AT	*GW*	NP	811015	812015	813015	814015	815015
800016	**GW**	AT	*GW*	NP	811016	812016	813016	814016	815016
800017	**GW**	AT	*GW*	NP	811017	812017	813017	814017	815017
800018	**GW**	AT	*GW*	NP	811018	812018	813018	814018	815018
800019	**GW**	AT	*GW*	NP	811019	812019	813019	814019	815019
800020	**GW**	AT	*GW*	NP	811020	812020	813020	814020	815020
800021	**GW**	AT	*GW*	NP	811021	812021	813021	814021	815021
800022	**GW**	AT	*GW*	NP	811022	812022	813022	814022	815022

800 023	**GW**	AT	*GW*	NP	811023	812023	813023	814023	815023
800 024	**GW**	AT	*GW*	NP	811024	812024	813024	814024	815024
800 025	**GW**	AT	*GW*	NP	811025	812025	813025	814025	815025
800 026	**GW**	AT	*GW*	NP	811026	812026	813026	814026	815026
800 027	**GW**	AT	*GW*	NP	811027	812027	813027	814027	815027
800 028	**GW**	AT	*GW*	NP	811028	812028	813028	814028	815028
800 029	**GW**	AT	*GW*	NP	811029	812029	813029	814029	815029
800 030	**GW**	AT	*GW*	NP	811030	812030	813030	814030	815030
800 031	**GW**	AT	*GW*	NP	811031	812031	813031	814031	815031
800 032	**GW**	AT	*GW*	NP	811032	812032	813032	814032	815032
800 033	**GW**	AT	*GW*	NP	811033	812033	813033	814033	815033
800 034	**GW**	AT	*GW*	NP	811034	812034	813034	814034	815034
800 035	**GW**	AT	*GW*	NP	811035	812035	813035	814035	815035
800 036	**GW**	AT	*GW*	NP	811036	812036	813036	814036	815036

Names (one on each driving car):

800 009 Sir Gareth Edwards/John Charles
800 010 Michael Bond/Paddington Bear
800 014 Megan Lloyd George CH/Edith New
800 019 Joy Lofthouse/Johnny Johnson MBE DFM
800 020 Bob Woodward/Elizabeth Ralph
800 023 Firefighter Fleur Lombard QGM/Kathryn Osmond
800 026 Don Cameron

Class 800/1. 9-car LNER units.
Formation: PDTS–MS–MS–TSRB–MS–TS–MC–MF–PDTRBF.

PDTS. Hitachi Kasado/Newton Aycliffe 2013–18. –/48 1TD 2W. 47.7 t.
MS. Hitachi Kasado/Newton Aycliffe 2013–18. –/88 1T. 50.5 t.
MS. Hitachi Kasado/Newton Aycliffe 2013–18. –/88 2T. 50.3 t.
TSRB. Hitachi Kasado/Newton Aycliffe 2013–18. –/72. 41.0 t.
MS. Hitachi Kasado/Newton Aycliffe 2013–18. –/88 2T. 50.3 t.
TS. Hitachi Kasado/Newton Aycliffe 2013–18. –/88 2T. 38.3 t.
MC. Hitachi Kasado/Newton Aycliffe 2013–18. 30/38. 49.1 t.
MF. Hitachi Kasado/Newton Aycliffe 2013–18. 56/– 1T. 50.6 t.
PDTRBF. Hitachi Kasado/Newton Aycliffe 2013–18. 15/– 1TD 2W. 51.7 t.

800 101	**LZ**	AT	*LN*	DN	811101	812101	813101	814101	815101
					816101	817101	818101	819101	
800 102	**LZ**	AT	*LN*	DN	811102	812102	813102	814102	815102
					816102	817102	818102	819102	
800 103	**LZ**	AT	*LN*	DN	811103	812103	813103	814103	815103
					816103	817103	818103	819103	
800 104	**LZ**	AT	*LN*	DN	811104	812104	813104	814104	815104
					816104	817104	818104	819104	
800 105	**LZ**	AT	*LN*	DN	811105	812105	813105	814105	815105
					816105	817105	818105	819105	
800 106	**LZ**	AT	*LN*	DN	811106	812106	813106	814106	815106
					816106	817106	818106	819106	
800 107	**LZ**	AT	*LN*	DN	811107	812107	813107	814107	815107
					816107	817107	818107	819107	
800 108	**LZ**	AT	*LN*	DN	811108	812108	813108	814108	815108
					816108	817108	818108	819108	

800109	**LZ**	AT	*LN*	DN	811109	812109	813109	814109	815109
					816109	817109	818109	819109	
800110	**LZ**	AT	*LN*	DN	811110	812110	813110	814110	815110
					816110	817110	818110	819110	
800111	**LZ**	AT	*LN*	DN	811111	812111	813111	814111	815111
					816111	817111	818111	819111	
800112	**LZ**	AT	*LN*	DN	811112	812112	813112	814112	815112
					816112	817112	818112	819112	
800113	**LZ**	AT	*LN*	DN	811113	812113	813113	814113	815113
					816113	817113	818113	819113	

Class 800/2. 5-car LNER units.
Formation: PDTS–MSRB–MS–MC–PDTRBF.

PDTS. Hitachi Newton Aycliffe/Kasado 2018–19. –/56 1TD. 47.8 t.
MSRB. Hitachi Newton Aycliffe/Kasado 2018–19. –/72. 50.1 t.
MS. Hitachi Newton Aycliffe/Kasado 2018–19. –/88 2T. 50.3 t.
MC. Hitachi Newton Aycliffe/Kasado 2018–19. 30/38 1T. 50.6 t.
PDTRBF. Hitachi Newton Aycliffe/Kasado 2018–19. 18/– 1TD 2W. 51.7 t.

800201	**LZ**	AT	*LN*	DN	811201	812201	813201	814201	815201
800202	**LZ**	AT	*LN*	DN	811202	812202	813202	814202	815202
800203	**LZ**	AT	*LN*	DN	811203	812203	813203	814203	815203
800204	**LZ**	AT	*LN*	DN	811204	812204	813204	814204	815204
800205	**LZ**	AT	*LN*	DN	811205	812205	813205	814205	815205
800206	**LZ**	AT	*LN*	DN	811206	812206	813206	814206	815206
800207	**LZ**	AT	*LN*	DN	811207	812207	813207	814207	815207
800208	**LZ**	AT	*LN*	DN	811208	812208	813208	814208	815208
800209	**LZ**	AT	*LN*	DN	811209	812209	813209	814209	815209
800210	**LZ**	AT	*LN*	DN	811210	812210	813210	814210	815210

Class 800/3. 9-car Great Western Railway units. Originally to be built as electric trains and numbered in the Class 801/0 series.
Formation: PDTS–MS–MS–TS–MS–TS–MS–MF–PDTRBF.

PDTS. Hitachi Newton Aycliffe/Kasado 2017–18. –/48 1TD 2W. 47.8 t.
MS. Hitachi Newton Aycliffe/Kasado 2017–18. –/88 1T. 50.1 t.
MS. Hitachi Newton Aycliffe/Kasado 2017–18. –/88 2T. 50.3 t.
TS. Hitachi Newton Aycliffe/Kasado 2017–18. –/88. 41.0 t.
MS. Hitachi Newton Aycliffe/Kasado 2017–18. –/88 2T. 50.3 t.
TS. Hitachi Newton Aycliffe/Kasado 2017–18. –/88 2T. 38.3 t.
MS. Hitachi Newton Aycliffe/Kasado 2017–18. –/88. 49.1 t.
MF. Hitachi Newton Aycliffe/Kasado 2017–18. 56/– 1T. 50.6 t.
PDTRBF. Hitachi Newton Aycliffe/Kasado 2017–18. 15/– 1TD 2W. 51.7 t.

800301	**GW**	AT	*GW*	NP	821001	822001	823001	824001	825001
					826001	827001	828001	829001	
800302	**GW**	AT	*GW*	NP	821002	822002	823002	824002	825002
					826002	827002	828002	829002	
800303	**GW**	AT	*GW*	NP	821003	822003	823003	824003	825003
					826003	827003	828003	829003	
800304	**GW**	AT	*GW*	NP	821004	822004	823004	824004	825004
					826004	827004	828004	829004	
800305	**GW**	AT	*GW*	NP	821005	822005	823005	824005	825005
					826005	827005	828005	829005	

800306	**GW**	AT *GW* NP	821006	822006	823006	824006	825006		
			826006	827006	828006	829006			
800307	**GW**	AT *GW* NP	821007	822007	823007	824007	825007		
			826007	827007	828007	829007			
800308	**GW**	AT *GW* NP	821008	822008	823008	824008	825008		
			826008	827008	828008	829008			
800309	**GW**	AT *GW* NP	821009	822009	823009	824009	825009		
			826009	827009	828009	829009			
800310	**GW**	AT *GW* NP	821010	822010	823010	824010	825010		
			826010	827010	828010	829010			
800311	**GW**	AT *GW* NP	821011	822011	823011	824011	825011		
			826011	827011	828011	829011			
800312	**GW**	AT *GW* NP	821012	822012	823012	824012	825012		
			826012	827012	828012	829012			
800313	**GW**	AT *GW* NP	821013	822013	823013	824013	825013		
			826013	827013	828013	829013			
800314	**GW**	AT *GW* NP	821014	822014	823014	824014	825014		
			826014	827014	828014	829014			
800315	**GW**	AT *GW* NP	821015	822015	823015	824015	825015		
			826015	827015	828015	829015			
800316	**GW**	AT *GW* NP	821016	822016	823016	824016	825016		
			826016	827016	828016	829016			
800317	**GW**	AT *GW* NP	821017	822017	823017	824017	825017		
			826017	827017	828017	829017			
800318	**GW**	AT *GW* NP	821018	822018	823018	824018	825018		
			826018	827018	828018	829018			
800319	**GW**	AT *GW* NP	821019	822019	823019	824019	825019		
			826019	827019	828019	829019			
800320	**GW**	AT *GW* NP	821020	822020	823020	824020	825020		
			826020	827020	828020	829020			
800321	**GW**	AT *GW* NP	821021	822021	823021	824021	825021		
			826021	827021	828021	829021			

Name (carried on alternative driving cars):

800306 Allan Leonard Lewis VC/Harold Day DSC

CLASS 801 INTERCITY EXPRESS PROGRAMME ELECTRIC HITACHI

The Class 801s are electric units, but still have one diesel engine fitted per unit for emergency use.

Formation: Various, see class headings for details.
Systems: 25 kV AC overhead electric, plus one diesel engine per set.
Construction: Aluminium.
Diesel engines: In the 5-car sets the single diesel engine is located in car 2 and in the 9-car sets the diesel engine is located in car 8.
Engines: MTU 12V 1600 R80L of 700 kW (940 hp).
Traction Motors: Four Hitachi asynchronous of 226 kW.
Wheel Arrangement: 2-2 + Bo-Bo + Bo-Bo + Bo-Bo + 2-2 or
2-2 + Bo-Bo + Bo-Bo + 2-2 + Bo-Bo + 2-2 + Bo-Bo + Bo-Bo + 2-2.

Braking: Disc & regenerative.
Bogies: Hitachi.
Gangways: Within unit.
Doors: Single-leaf sliding.
Dimensions: 25.35/25.00 m x 2.74 m.
Couplers: Dellner 10.
Control System: IGBT Inverter.
Maximum Speed: 125 mph.
Heating & ventilation: Air conditioning.
Seating Layout: 1: 2+1 facing/unidirectional; 2+2 facing/unidirectional.
Multiple Working: Within class and with Classes 800 and 802.

Class 801/1. 5-car LNER units.
Formation: PDTS–MSRB–MS–MC–PDTRBF.

PDTS. Hitachi Newton Aycliffe/Kasado 2016–19. –/56 1TD. 47.8 t.
MSRB. Hitachi Newton Aycliffe/Kasado 2016–19. –/72. 52.1 t.
MS. Hitachi Newton Aycliffe/Kasado 2016–19. –/88 2T. 43.5 t.
MC. Hitachi Newton Aycliffe/Kasado 2016–19. 30/38 1T. 44.1 t.
PDTRBF. Hitachi Newton Aycliffe/Kasado 2016–19. 18/– 1TD 2W. 51.2 t.

801 101	**LZ**	AT	*LN*	DN	821101	822101	823101	824101	825101
801 102	**LZ**	AT	*LN*	DN	821102	822102	823102	824102	825102
801 103	**LZ**	AT	*LN*	DN	821103	822103	823103	824103	825103
801 104	**LZ**	AT	*LN*	DN	821104	822104	823104	824104	825104
801 105	**LZ**	AT	*LN*	DN	821105	822105	823105	824105	825105
801 106	**LZ**	AT	*LN*	DN	821106	822106	823106	824106	825106
801 107	**LZ**	AT	*LN*	DN	821107	822107	823107	824107	825107
801 108	**LZ**	AT	*LN*	DN	821108	822108	823108	824108	825108
801 109	**LZ**	AT	*LN*	DN	821109	822109	823109	824109	825109
801 110	**LZ**	AT	*LN*	DN	821110	822110	823110	824110	825110
801 111	**LZ**	AT	*LN*	DN	821111	822111	823111	824111	825111
801 112	**LZ**	AT	*LN*	DN	821112	822112	823112	824112	825112

Class 801/2. 9-car LNER units.
Formation: PDTS–MS–MS–TSRB–MS–TS–MC–MF–PDTRBF.

PDTS. Hitachi Newton Aycliffe/Kasado 2018–20. –/48 1TD 2W. 47.7 t.
MS. Hitachi Newton Aycliffe/Kasado 2018–20. –/88 1T. 50.5 t.
MS. Hitachi Newton Aycliffe/Kasado 2018–20. –/88 2T. 43.5 t.
TSRB. Hitachi Newton Aycliffe/Kasado 2018–20. –/72. 43.0 t.
MS. Hitachi Newton Aycliffe/Kasado 2018–20. –/88 2T. 43.5 t.
TS. Hitachi Newton Aycliffe/Kasado 2018–20. –/88 2T. 38.3 t.
MC. Hitachi Newton Aycliffe/Kasado 2018–20. 30/38. 42.6 t.
MF. Hitachi Newton Aycliffe/Kasado 2018–20. 56/– 1T. 43.8 t.
PDTRBF. Hitachi Newton Aycliffe/Kasado 2018–20. 15/– 1TD 2W. 51.7 t.

801 201		AT			821201	822201	823201	824201	825201
					826201	827201	828201	829201	
801 202		AT			821202	822202	823202	824202	825202
					826202	827202	828202	829202	
801 203	**LZ**	AT	*LN*	BN	821203	822203	823203	824203	825203
					826203	827203	828203	829203	
801 204		AT			821204	822204	823204	824204	825204
					826204	827204	828204	829204	
801 205	**LZ**	AT	*LN*	BN	821205	822205	823205	824205	825205
					826205	827205	828205	829205	

801206		AT			821206	822206	823206	824206	825206
					826206	827206	828206	829206	
801207	**LZ**	AT	*LN*	BN	821207	822207	823207	824207	825207
					826207	827207	828207	829207	
801208		AT			821208	822208	823208	824208	825208
					826208	827208	828208	829208	
801209	**LZ**	AT	*LN*	BN	821209	822209	823209	824209	825209
					826209	827209	828209	829209	
801210		AT			821210	822210	823210	824210	825210
					826210	827210	828210	829210	
801211	**LZ**	AT	*LN*	BN	821211	822211	823211	824211	825211
					826211	827211	828211	829211	
801212		AT			821212	822212	823212	824212	825212
					826212	827212	828212	829212	
801213	**LZ**	AT	*LN*	BN	821213	822213	823213	824213	825213
					826213	827213	828213	829213	
801214		AT			821214	822214	823214	824214	825214
					826214	827214	828214	829214	
801215	**LZ**	AT	*LN*	BN	821215	822215	823215	824215	825215
					826215	827215	828215	829215	
801216		AT			821216	822216	823216	824216	825216
					826216	827216	828216	829216	
801217	**LZ**	AT	*LN*	BN	821217	822217	823217	824217	825217
					826217	827217	828217	829217	
801218		AT			821218	822218	823218	824218	825218
					826218	827218	828218	829218	
801219	**LZ**	AT			821219	822219	823219	824219	825219
					826219	827219	828219	829219	
801220	**LZ**	AT			821220	822220	823220	824220	825220
					826220	827220	828220	829220	
801221	**LZ**	AT			821221	822221	823221	824221	825221
					826221	827221	828221	829221	
801222	**LZ**	AT			821222	822222	823222	824222	825222
					826222	827222	828222	829222	
801223		AT			821223	822223	823223	824223	825223
					826223	827223	828223	829223	
801224		AT			821224	822224	823224	824224	825224
					826224	827224	828224	829224	
801225		AT			821225	822225	823225	824225	825225
					826225	827225	828225	829225	
801226		AT			821226	822226	823226	824226	825226
					826226	827226	828226	829226	
801227		AT			821227	822227	823227	824227	825227
					826227	827227	828227	829227	
801228		AT			821228	822228	823228	824228	825228
					826228	827228	828228	829228	
801229		AT			821229	822229	823229	824229	825229
					826229	827229	828229	829229	
801230		AT			821230	822230	823230	824230	825230
					826230	827230	828230	829230	

CLASS 802 AT300 HITACHI

These units are technically very similar to the Class 800s. The GWR units have modifications to the roof-mounted brake resistors for operation along the Dawlish seawall.

Formation: Various, full details awaited.
Systems: Diesel/25 kV AC overhead electric.
Construction: Aluminium.
Diesel engines: In the 5-car sets diesel engines are located in cars 2, 3 and 4. In the 9-car sets diesel engines are located in cars 2, 3, 5, 7 and 8.
Engines: MTU 12V 1600 R80L of 700 kW (940 hp).
Traction Motors: Four Hitachi asynchronous of 226 kW.
Wheel Arrangement: 2-2 + Bo-Bo + Bo-Bo + Bo-Bo + 2-2 or 2-2 + Bo-Bo + Bo-Bo + 2-2 + Bo-Bo + 2-2 + Bo-Bo + Bo-Bo + 2-2.
Braking: Disc & regenerative.
Dimensions: 25.35/25.00 m x 2.74 m.
Bogies: Hitachi.
Couplers: Dellner 10.
Gangways: Within unit.
Control System: IGBT Inverter.
Doors: Single-leaf sliding.
Maximum Speed: 125 mph.
Heating & ventilation: Air conditioning.
Seating Layout: 1: 2+1 facing/unidirectional; 2+2 facing/unidirectional.
Multiple Working: Within class and with Classes 800 and 801.

Class 802/0. 5-car Great Western Railway units. Pre-series units 802 001/002 were built at Kasado and the remainder at Pistoia.
Formation: PDTS–MS–MS–MC–PDTRBF.

PDTS. Hitachi Pistoia/Kasado 2017–18. –/56 1TD. 48.0 t.
MS. Hitachi Pistoia/Kasado 2017–18. –/88. 50.9 t.
MS. Hitachi Pistoia/Kasado 2017–18. –/88 2T 51.1 t.
MC. Hitachi Pistoia/Kasado 2017–18. 18/58 1T. 51.5 t.
PDTRBF. Hitachi Pistoia/Kasado 2017–18. 18/– 1TD 2W. 51.3 t.

802001	**GW**	E	*GW*	NP	831001	832001	833001	834001	835001
802002	**GW**	E	*GW*	NP	831002	832002	833002	834002	835002
802003	**GW**	E	*GW*	NP	831003	832003	833003	834003	835003
802004	**GW**	E	*GW*	NP	831004	832004	833004	834004	835004
802005	**GW**	E	*GW*	NP	831005	832005	833005	834005	835005
802006	**GW**	E	*GW*	NP	831006	832006	833006	834006	835006
802007	**GW**	E	*GW*	NP	831007	832007	833007	834007	835007
802008	**GW**	E	*GW*	NP	831008	832008	833008	834008	835008
802009	**GW**	E	*GW*	NP	831009	832009	833009	834009	835009
802010	**GW**	E	*GW*	NP	831010	832010	833010	834010	835010
802011	**GW**	E	*GW*	NP	831011	832011	833011	834011	835011
802012	**GW**	E	*GW*	NP	831012	832012	833012	834012	835012
802013	**GW**	E	*GW*	NP	831013	832013	833013	834013	835013
802014	**GW**	E	*GW*	NP	831014	832014	833014	834014	835014
802015	**GW**	E	*GW*	NP	831015	832015	833015	834015	835015
802016	**GW**	E	*GW*	NP	831016	832016	833016	834016	835016
802017	**GW**	E	*GW*	NP	831017	832017	833017	834017	835017
802018	**GW**	E	*GW*	NP	831018	832018	833018	834018	835018
802019	**GW**	E	*GW*	NP	831019	832019	833019	834019	835019

802020	**GW**	E	*GW*	NP	831020	832020	833020	834020	835020
802021	**GW**	E	*GW*	NP	831021	832021	833021	834021	835021
802022	**GW**	E	*GW*	NP	831022	832022	833022	834022	835022

Names (one on each driving car):

802008 Rick Rescorla/RNLB Solomon Browne
802011 Sir Joshua Reynolds PRA/Capt. Robert Falcon Scott RN CVO
802013 Michael Eavis CBE

Class 802/1. 9-car Great Western Railway units. Pre-series unit 802 101 was built at Kasado and the remainder at Pistoia.
Formation: PDTS–MS–MS–TS–MS–TS–MC–MF–PDTRBF.

PDTS. Hitachi Pistoia/Kasado 2017–18. –/48 1TD 2W. 47.7 t.
MS. Hitachi Pistoia/Kasado 2017–18. –/88 1T. 50.1 t.
MS. Hitachi Pistoia/Kasado 2017–18. –/88 2T. 50.3 t.
TS. Hitachi Pistoia/Kasado 2017–18. –/88. 41.0 t.
MS. Hitachi Pistoia/Kasado 2017–18. –/88 2T. 50.3 t.
TS. Hitachi Pistoia/Kasado 2017–18. –/88 2T. 38.3 t.
MS. Hitachi Pistoia/Kasado 2017–18. –/88. 50.3 t.
MF. Hitachi Pistoia/Kasado 2017–18. 56/– 1T. 50.6 t.
PDTRBF. Hitachi Pistoia/Kasado 2017–18. 15/– 1TD 2W. 51.7 t.

802101	**GW**	E	*GW*	NP	831101	832101	833101	834101	835101
					836101	837101	838101	839101	
802102	**GW**	E	*GW*	NP	831102	832102	833102	834102	835102
					836102	837102	838102	839102	
802103	**GW**	E	*GW*	NP	831103	832103	833103	834103	835103
					836103	837103	838103	839103	
802104	**GW**	E	*GW*	NP	831104	832104	833104	834104	835104
					836104	837104	838104	839104	
802105	**GW**	E	*GW*	NP	831105	832105	833105	834105	835105
					836105	837105	838105	839105	
802106	**GW**	E	*GW*	NP	831106	832106	833106	834106	835106
					836106	837106	838106	839106	
802107	**GW**	E	*GW*	NP	831107	832107	833107	834107	835107
					836107	837107	838107	839107	
802108	**GW**	E	*GW*	NP	831108	832108	833108	834108	835108
					836108	837108	838108	839108	
802109	**GW**	E	*GW*	NP	831109	832109	833109	834109	835109
					836109	837109	838109	839109	
802110	**GW**	E	*GW*	NP	831110	832110	833110	834110	835110
					836110	837110	838110	839110	
802111	**GW**	E	*GW*	NP	831111	832111	833111	834111	835111
					836111	837111	838111	839111	
802112	**GW**	E	*GW*	NP	831112	832112	833112	834112	835112
					836112	837112	838112	839112	
802113	**GW**	E	*GW*	NP	831113	832113	833113	834113	835113
					836113	837113	838113	839113	
802114	**GW**	E	*GW*	NP	831114	832114	833114	834114	835114
					836114	837114	838114	839114	

Name: 802101 Nancy Astor CH

Class 802/2. TransPennine Express units. Units accepted into service 2019–20.

PDTS. Hitachi Pistoia/Kasado 2018–19. –/56 1TD. 48.0 t.
MS. Hitachi Pistoia/Kasado 2018–19. –/86. 50.9 t.
MS. Hitachi Pistoia/Kasado 2018–19. –/88 2T 51.1 t.
MS. Hitachi Pistoia/Kasado 2018–19. –/88 1T 51.3 t.
PDTF. Hitachi Pistoia/Kasado 2018–19. 24/– 1TD 2W. 50.2 t.

802 201	**TP**	A	*TP*	DN	831201	832201	833201	834201	835201
802 202	**TP**	A	*TP*	DN	831202	832202	833202	834202	835202
802 203	**TP**	A	*TP*	DN	831203	832203	833203	834203	835203
802 204	**U**	A	*TP*	DN	831204	832204	833204	834204	835204
802 205	**U**	A			831205	832205	833205	834205	835205
802 206	**TP**	A	*TP*	DN	831206	832206	833206	834206	835206
802 207	**TP**	A	*TP*	DN	831207	832207	833207	834207	835207
802 208	**TP**	A	*TP*	DN	831208	832208	833208	834208	835208
802 209	**TP**	A	*TP*	DN	831209	832209	833209	834209	835209
802 210	**TP**	A	*TP*	DN	831210	832210	833210	834210	835210
802 211	**TP**	A	*TP*	DN	831211	832211	833211	834211	835211
802 212	**TP**	A	*TP*	DN	831212	832212	833212	834212	835212
802 213	**TP**	A	*TP*	DN	831213	832213	833213	834213	835213
802 214	**TP**	A	*TP*	DN	831214	832214	833214	834214	835214
802 215	**TP**	A	*TP*	DN	831215	832215	833215	834215	835215
802 216	**TP**	A	*TP*	DN	831216	832216	833216	834216	835216
802 217	**TP**	A	*TP*	DN	831217	832217	833217	834217	835217
802 218	**U**	A	*TP*	DN	831218	832218	833218	834218	835218
802 219	**U**	A	*TP*	DN	831219	832219	833219	834219	835219

Class 802/3. Hull Trains units. Units accepted into service 2019–20.

PDTS. Hitachi Pistoia 2018–19. –/50 1TD 1W. 48.0 t.
MS. Hitachi Pistoia 2018–19. –/88. 49.6 t.
MS. Hitachi Pistoia 2018–19. –/88 2T 50.4 t.
MC. Hitachi Pistoia 2018–19. 18/58 1T 50.4 t.
PDTF. Hitachi Pistoia 2018–19. 25/– 1TD 2W. 49.6 t.

802 301	**HT**	A	*HT*	BN	831301	832301	833301	834301	835301
802 302	**HT**	A	*HT*	BN	831302	832302	833302	834302	835302
802 303	**HT**	A	*HT*	BN	831303	832303	833303	834303	835303
802 304	**HT**	A			831304	832304	833304	834304	835304
802 305	**HT**	A			831305	832305	833305	834305	835305

4.5. EUROSTAR UNITS

The original Eurostar Class 373 units were built for and are normally used on services between Britain and continental Europe via the Channel Tunnel. SNCF-owned units 3225/26 and 3227/28 have been removed from the Eurostar pool and withdrawn. As they are not now permitted through the Channel Tunnel they are not listed here.

The trailers from SNCF set 3203/04 were refurbished and renumbered to run with power cars 3211/12 (original power cars 3203/04 have been scrapped, as have the trailers from 3211/12).

Each Class 373 train consists of two 10-car units coupled, with a motor car at each driving end. All units are articulated with an extra motor bogie on the coach adjacent to the motor car.

All Class 373 sets can be used between London St Pancras and Paris, Brussels and Disneyland Paris. Certain sets (shown *) are equipped for 1500 V DC operation and are used for the winter service to Bourg Saint Maurice and the summer service to Avignon. All eight refurbished units are fitted for operation on 1500 V DC.

Seven 8-car Class 373 sets were built for Regional Eurostar services, but apart from power cars 3304 and 3308 which have been preserved, the rest have been scrapped.

The second generation Eurostar trains, the Siemens Class 374s, have now been introduced and have replaced most of the Class 373s. Eight sets have been fully refurbished and will be retained as part of Eurostar's long-term fleet – 3007/08, 3015/16, 3205/06, 3209/10, 3211/12, 3219/20, 3221/22 and 3229/30.

CLASS 373 "THREE CAPITALS" EUROSTARS

10-car half-sets. Built for services starting from or terminating in London Waterloo (now St Pancras). Individual vehicles in each set are allocated numbers 373xxx0 + 373xxx1 + 373xxx2 + 373xxx3 + 373xxx4 + 373xxx5 + 373xxx6 + 373xxx7 + 373xxx8 + 373xxx9, where 3xxx denotes the set number.

Formation: DM–MS–4TS–RB–2TF–TBF. Gangwayed within pair of units. Air conditioned.
Construction: Steel.
Supply Systems: 25 kV AC 50 Hz overhead or 3000 V DC overhead (* also equipped for 1500 V DC overhead operation).
Control System: GTO–GTO Inverter on UK 750V DC and 25kVAC, GTO Chopper on SNCB 3000VDC.
Continuous rating: 12 x 240 kW (25 kV AC); 5700 kW (1500 and 3000 V DC).
Wheel Arrangement: Bo-Bo + Bo–2–2–2–2–2–2–2–2–2.
Lengths: 22.15 m (DM), 21.85 m (MS & TBF), 18.70 m (other cars).
Couplers: Schaku 10S at outer ends, Schaku 10L at inner end of each DM and outer ends of each sub set.
Maximum Speed: 186mph (300km/h).

Built: 1992–93 by GEC-Alsthom/Brush/ANF/De Dietrich/BN Construction/ACEC.

DM vehicles carry the set numbers indicated below.

Non-standard livery: 3213 and 3224 – Izy (green, white & purple).

† Refurbished.

At the time of writing the following sets were misformed: 3213 with 3224 and 3214 with 3223.
3213/24 is currently on hire to Thalys for the Paris–Brussels "Izy" service.

373xxx0 series. DM. Lot No. 31118 1992–95. 68.5 t.
373xxx1 series. MS. Lot No. 31119 1992–95. –/48 2T. 44.6 t.
373xxx2 series. TS. Lot No. 31120 1992–95. –/56 1T. 28.1 t.
373xxx3 series. TS. Lot No. 31121 1992–95. –/56 2T. 29.7 t.
373xxx4 series. TS. Lot No. 31122 1992–95. –/56 1T. 28.3 t.
373xxx5 series. TS. Lot No. 31123 1992–95. –/56 2T. 29.2 t.
373xxx6 series. RB. Lot No. 31124 1992–95. 31.1 t.
373xxx7 series. TF. Lot No. 31125 1992–95. 39/– 1T. 29.6 t.
373xxx8 series. TF. Lot No. 31126 1992–95. 39/– 1T. 32.2 t.
373xxx9 series. TBF. Lot No. 31127 1992–95. 25/– 1TD. 39.4 t.

3007	†*	**ES**	EU	*EU*	TI
3008	†*	**ES**	EU	*EU*	TI
3015	†*	**ES**	EU	*EU*	TI
3016	†*	**ES**	EU	*EU*	TI
3205	†*	**ES**	SF	*EU*	LY
3206	†*	**ES**	SF	*EU*	LY
3209	†*	**ES**	SF	*EU*	LY
3210	†*	**ES**	SF	*EU*	LY
3211	†*	**ES**	SF	*EU*	LY
3212	†*	**ES**	SF	*EU*	LY
3213	*	**0**	SF	*EU*	LY
3214	*	**EU**	SF	*EU*	LY
3215	*	**EU**	SF	*EU*	LY
3216	*	**EU**	SF	*EU*	LY
3217		**EU**	SF	*EU*	LY
3218		**EU**	SF	*EU*	LY
3219	†*	**ES**	SF	*EU*	LY
3220	†*	**ES**	SF	*EU*	LY
3221	†*	**ES**	SF	*EU*	LY
3222	†*	**ES**	SF	*EU*	LY
3223	*	**EU**	SF	*EU*	LY
3224	*	**0**	SF	*EU*	LY
3229	†*	**ES**	SF	*EU*	LY
3230	†*	**ES**	SF	*EU*	LY

Spare DM:

3999		**ES**	EU	*EU*	TI

CLASS 374 SIEMENS VELARO e320

8-car half-sets. These units are similar to the DB Class 407 ICE sets, with distributed power rather than a power car at either end like the Class 373s. The first sets entered service in November 2015, operating initially on the St Pancras–Paris route. They have also been used on the new St Pancras–Amsterdam service from 2018.

The initial order was for ten units (4001–20) and this was then increased by another seven (4021–34) in 2014. An option exists for a further six units.

Formation: DMF–TBF–MS–TS–TS–MS–TS–MSRB.
Gangwayed within pair of units. Air conditioned.
Construction: Aluminium. **Control System**: IGBT Inverter.
Supply Systems: 25 kV AC 50 Hz overhead, 1500 V DC overhead and 3000 V DC overhead.
Continuous rating: 8000 kW (25 kV AC), 4200 kW (1500 and 3000 V DC).
Wheel Arrangement: Bo-Bo + 2-2 + Bo-Bo + 2-2 + 2-2 + Bo-Bo + 2-2 + Bo-Bo.
Lengths: 26.035 m (DMF), 24.775 m (other cars).
Couplers: Dellner 12. **Maximum Speed**: 200 mph (320 km/h).
Built: 2012–17 by Siemens, Krefeld, Germany.

DM vehicles carry the full 12-digit EVNs as indicated below. For example set 4001/02 carries the numbers 93703740011-9 + 93703740012-7 + 93703740013-5 + 93703740014-3 + 93703740015-0 + 93703740016-8 + 93703740017-6 + 93703740018-4 + 93703740028-3 + 93703740027-5 + 93703740026-7 + 93703740025-9 + 93703740024-2 + 93703740023-4 + 93703740022-6 + 93703740021-8.

93703740xx1-c series. DMF. Siemens Krefeld 2012–17. 40/–. 58.0 t.
93703740xx2-c series. TBF. Siemens Krefeld 2012–17. 36/– 2T. 59.0 t.
93703740xx3-c series. MF. Siemens Krefeld 2012–17. 34/–(+2) 1TD 2W. 59.0 t.
93703740xx4-c series. TS. Siemens Krefeld 2012–17. –/76 2T. 53.0 t.
93703740xx5-c series. TS. Siemens Krefeld 2012–17. –/76 2T. 53.0 t.
93703740xx6-c series. MS. Siemens Krefeld 2012–17. –/76 2T. 58.0 t.
93703740xx7-c series. TS. Siemens Krefeld 2012–17. –/76 2T. 57.0 t.
93703740xx8-c series. MSRB. Siemens Krefeld 2012–17. –/32 2T. 58.0 t.

4001	**ES**	EU	*EU*	TI
4002	**ES**	EU	*EU*	TI
4003	**ES**	EU	*EU*	TI
4004	**ES**	EU	*EU*	TI
4005	**ES**	EU	*EU*	TI
4006	**ES**	EU	*EU*	TI
4007	**ES**	EU	*EU*	TI
4008	**ES**	EU	*EU*	TI
4009	**ES**	EU	*EU*	TI
4010	**ES**	EU	*EU*	TI
4011	**ES**	EU	*EU*	TI
4012	**ES**	EU	*EU*	TI
4013	**ES**	EU	*EU*	TI
4014	**ES**	EU	*EU*	TI
4015	**ES**	EU	*EU*	TI
4016	**ES**	EU	*EU*	TI
4017	**ES**	EU	*EU*	TI
4018	**ES**	EU	*EU*	TI
4019	**ES**	EU	*EU*	TI
4020	**ES**	EU	*EU*	TI
4021	**ES**	EU	*EU*	TI
4022	**ES**	EU	*EU*	TI
4023	**ES**	EU	*EU*	TI
4024	**ES**	EU	*EU*	TI
4025	**ES**	EU	*EU*	TI
4026	**ES**	EU	*EU*	TI
4027	**ES**	EU	*EU*	TI
4028	**ES**	EU	*EU*	TI
4029	**ES**	EU	*EU*	TI
4030	**ES**	EU	*EU*	TI
4031	**ES**	EU	*EU*	TI
4032	**ES**	EU	*EU*	TI
4033	**ES**	EU	*EU*	TI
4034	**ES**	EU	*EU*	TI

4.6. SERVICE EMUS

The following unit was used by Network Rail for ERTMS testing on the Hertford Loop. It has been heavily modified from its original condition, and now includes a toilet.

313 121	**Y**	BN	ZG	62549	71233	62613

4.7. EMU VEHICLES IN INDUSTRIAL SERVICE

This list comprises EMU vehicles that have been withdrawn from active service but continue to be used in industrial service or for emergency training.

Cl. 390	69133	69833		Avanti West Coast Training Centre, Westmere Drive, Crewe, Cheshire (ex-unit 390 033)
Cl. 390	69633	69733		The Fire Service College, Moreton-in-Marsh, Gloucestershire (ex-unit 390 033)
Cl. 390	69933			Safety & Accident Investigation Centre, Cranfield University, Cranfield, Bedfordshire (ex-unit 390 033)
Cl. 508	64649	64712		Emergency Services Training Centre, Seacombe, Merseyside (ex-units 508 201/209)
Cl. 508	64681	71511	64724	The Fire Service College, Moreton-in-Marsh, Gloucestershire (unit 508 212)

4.8. EMUS AWAITING DISPOSAL

This list comprises former main line EMU vehicles which are awaiting disposal.

25 kV AC 50 Hz OVERHEAD UNITS:

Cl. 309	**RR**	WC	CS	71758
Cl. 314	**SR**	X	LM	71452
Cl. 365	**N**	X	ZN	65919

PLATFORM 5 MAIL ORDER

UK METRO & LIGHT RAIL SYSTEMS

INCLUDING LONDON UNDERGROUND

The latest edition of the Platform 5 guide to the rolling stock of London Underground and all public-carrier light rail and metro systems in the UK.

For every LU line and light rail/metro undertaking, a general introduction provides a brief history of each line and details of day-to-day operations including service frequencies, operating times and depot/ maintenance information. This introduction is followed by detailed fleet lists with tabulated technical data and unit formations. Technical specifications are explained using notes and appendices.

Includes specially comissioned and updated maps for this publication and the book is well illustrated throughout using colour photography. A5 size. 160 pages. **£19.95**

Please add postage: 10% UK, 20% Europe, 30% Rest of World.

Telephone, fax or send your order to the Platform 5 Mail Order Department. **See page 432 of this book for details.**

5. ON-TRACK MACHINES

These machines are used for maintaining, renewing and enhancing the infrastructure of the national railway network. With the exception of snowploughs all can be self-propelled, controlled either from a cab mounted on the machine or remotely. They are permitted to operate either under their own power or in train formations throughout the network both within and outside engineering possessions. Machines only permitted to be used within engineering possessions, referred to as On-Track Plant, are not included. Also not included are wagons included in OTM consists and overseas based machines that might make occasional short visits.

For each machine its GB operational number, owner or responsible custodian and type is given, plus its name if carried. In addition, for snow clearance equipment the berthing location is given. Actual operation of each machine is undertaken by either the owner/responsible custodian or a contracted responsible custodian.

Machines were numbered by British Rail with either six-digit wagon series numbers or in the CEPS (Civil Engineers Plant System) series with five prefixed digits. Machines delivered from 2013 onwards carry 12-digit EVN series numbers, most additionally carrying a shorter GB operational number. In most cases the later resemble CEPS numbers. Machines are listed here by GB operational number, which in some cases is also the EVN number. Anomalies in such numbering mean this is not strictly numeric, but the order they would have been if allocated CEPS numbers correctly. Machines that carry additional identifying numbers have these shown "xxxx".

(S) after the registered number designates a machine that is currently stored (the storage location of each is given at the end of this section).

DYNAMIC TRACK STABILISERS

DR 72211	BB	Plasser & Theurer DGS 62-N
DR 72213	BB	Plasser & Theurer DGS 62-N

TAMPERS

Plasser & Theurer 09 Series

DR 73109	SK	Plasser & Theurer 09-3X-RT	
DR 73110	SK	Plasser & Theurer 09-3X-RT	PETER WHITE
DR 73111	NR	Plasser & Theurer 09-3X-Dynamic	
DR 73113	NR	Plasser & Theurer 09-3X-Dynamic	
DR 73114	NR	Plasser & Theurer 09-3X-Dynamic	Ron Henderson
DR 73115	NR	Plasser & Theurer 09-3X-Dynamic	
DR 73116	NR	Plasser & Theurer 09-3X Dynamic	
DR 73117	NR	Plasser & Theurer 09-3X Dynamic	
DR 73118	NR	Plasser & Theurer 09-3X Dynamic	
DR 73120	NR	Plasser & Theurer 09-3X Dynamic	"99 70 9123 120-6"

DR 73121	NR	Plasser & Theurer 09-2X Dynamic	"99 70 9123 121-4"
DR 73122	NR	Plasser & Theurer 09-2X Dynamic	"99 70 9123 122-2"
928001	SK	Plasser & Theurer Unimat 09-4x4/4S Dynamic	"99 70 9128 001-3"
DR 74002	SK	Plasser & Theurer Unimat 09-4x4/4S Dynamic	"99 70 9128 002-1"
DR 75008	CS	Plasser & Theurer 09-4x4/4S Dynamic	"99 70 9123 008-3"
DR 75009	CS	Plasser & Theurer 09-4x4/4S Dynamic	"99 70 9123 009-1"
DR 75010	CS	Plasser & Theurer 09-4x4/4S Dynamic	"99 70 9123 010-9"
DR 75011	CS	Plasser & Theurer 09-4x4/4S Dynamic	"99 70 9123 011-7"
DR 75012	SK	Plasser & Theurer 09-4x4/4S Dynamic	"99 70 9123 012-5"
DR 75013	SK	Plasser & Theurer 09-4x4/4S Dynamic	"99 70 9123 013-3"

Plasser & Theurer 08 Series and 08 Series (compact)

DR 73803	SK	Plasser & Theurer 08-32U-RT	Alexander Graham Bell
DR 73804	SK	Plasser & Theurer 08-32U-RT	James Watt
DR 73805 (S)	CS	Plasser & Theurer 08-16/32U-RT	
DR 73806	CS	Plasser & Theurer 08-16/32U-RT	Karine
DR 73904	SK	Plasser & Theurer 08-4x4/4S-RT	Thomas Telford
DR 73905	CS	Plasser & Theurer 08-4x4/4S-RT	
DR 73906	CS	Plasser & Theurer 08-4x4/4S-RT	Panther
DR 73907	CS	Plasser & Theurer 08-4x4/4S-RT	
DR 73908	CS	Plasser & Theurer 08-4x4/4S-RT	
DR 73909	CS	Plasser & Theurer 08-4x4/4S-RT	Saturn
DR 73910	CS	Plasser & Theurer 08-4x4/4S-RT	Jupiter
DR 73911	CS	Plasser & Theurer 08-16/4x4C-RT	Puma
DR 73912	CS	Plasser & Theurer 08-16/4x4C-RT	Lynx
DR 73913	CS	Plasser & Theurer 08-12/4x4C-RT	
DR 73914	SK	Plasser & Theurer 08-4x4/4S-RT	Robert McAlpine
DR 73915	SK	Plasser & Theurer 08-16/4x4C-RT	William Arrol
DR 73916	SK	Plasser & Theurer 08-16/4x4C-RT	First Engineering
DR 73917	BB	Plasser & Theurer 08-4x4/4S-RT	
DR 73918	BB	Plasser & Theurer 08-4x4/4S-RT	
DR 73919	CS	Plasser & Theurer 08-16/4x4C100-RT (with trailer)	
DR 73920	CS	Plasser & Theurer 08-16/4x4C80-RT	
DR 73921	CS	Plasser & Theurer 08-16/4x4C80-RT	
DR 73922	CS	Plasser & Theurer 08-16/4x4C80-RT	John Snowdon
DR 73923	CS	Plasser & Theurer 08-4x4/4S-RT	Mercury
DR 73924	CS	Plasser & Theurer 08-16/4x4C100-RT	
DR 73925	CS	Plasser & Theurer 08-16/4x4C100-RT	Europa
DR 73926	BB	Plasser & Theurer 08-16/4x4C100-RT	Stephen Keith Blanchard
DR 73927 (S)	BB	Plasser & Theurer 08-16/4x4C100-RT	
DR 73929	CS	Plasser & Theurer 08-4x4/4S-RT	
DR 73930	CS	Plasser & Theurer 08-4x4/4S-RT	
DR 73931	CS	Plasser & Theurer 08-16/4x4C100-RT	
DR 73932	SK	Plasser & Theurer 08-4x4/4S-RT	
DR 73933	SK	Plasser & Theurer 08-16/4x4/C100-RT (with trailer)	
DR 73934	SK	Plasser & Theurer 08-16/4x4/C100-RT (with trailer)	
DR 73935	CS	Plasser & Theurer 08-4x4/4S-RT	
DR 73936	CS	Plasser & Theurer 08-4x4/4S-RT	
DR 73937	BB	Plasser & Theurer 08-16/4x4C100-RT	
DR 73938	BB	Plasser & Theurer 08-16/4x4C100-RT	

DR 73939	BB	Plasser & Theurer 08-16/4x4C100-RT	Pat Best
DR 73940	SK	Plasser & Theurer 08-4x4/4S-RT	
DR 73941	SK	Plasser & Theurer 08-4x4/4S-RT	
DR 73942	CS	Plasser & Theurer 08-4x4/4S-RT	
DR 73943	BB	Plasser & Theurer 08-16/4x4C100-RT	
DR 73944	BB	Plasser & Theurer 08-16/4x4C100-RT	
DR 73945	BB	Plasser & Theurer 08-16/4x4C100-RT	
DR 73946	VO	Plasser & Theurer Euromat 08-4x4/4S	
DR 73947	CS	Plasser & Theurer 08-4x4/4S-RT	
DR 73948	CS	Plasser & Theurer 08-4x4/4S-RT	

Matisa

DR 75301	VO	Matisa B 45 UE	
DR 75302	VO	Matisa B 45 UE	Gary Wright
DR 75303	VO	Matisa B 45 UE	
DR 75401	VO	Matisa B 41 UE	
DR 75402	VO	Matisa B 41 UE	
DR 75404	VO	Matisa B 41 UE	
DR 75405	VO	Matisa B 41 UE	
DR 75406	CS	Matisa B 41 UE	Eric Machell
DR 75407	CS	Matisa B 41 UE	Gerry Taylor
DR 75408	BB	Matisa B 41 UE	
DR 75409	BB	Matisa B 41 UE	
DR 75410	BB	Matisa B 41 UE	
DR 75411	BB	Matisa B 41 UE	
DR 75501	BB	Matisa B 66 UC	
DR 75502	BB	Matisa B 66 UC	
DR 75503	VO	Matisa B 66 UC	"99 70 9124 001-7"
DR 75504	VO	Matisa B 66 UC	"99 70 9124 002-5"

BALLAST CLEANERS

DR 76501	NR	Plasser & Theurer RM-900-RT	
DR 76502	NR	Plasser & Theurer RM-900-RT	
DR 76503	NR	Plasser & Theurer RM-900-RT	
DR 76504	NR	Plasser & Theurer RM-900	"99 70 9314 504-0"

VACUUM PREPARATION MACHINES

DR 76701 (S)	NR	Plasser & Theurer VM80-NR
DR 76703 (S)	NR	Plasser & Theurer VM80-NR

RAIL VACUUM MACHINES

99 70 9515 002-2	RC	Railcare 16000-480-UK RailVac OTM
99 70 9515 003-0	RC	Railcare 16000-480-UK RailVac OTM
99 70 9515 004-8	RC	Railcare 16000-480-UK RailVac OTM
99 70 9515 005-5	RC	Railcare 16000-480-UK RailVac OTM

BALLAST FEEDER MACHINE

99 70 9552 020-8 RC Railcare Ballast Feeder UK

BALLAST TRANSFER MACHINES

DR 76750 NR Matisa D75 *(works with DR 78802/DR 78812/ DR 78822/DR 78832)*

DR 76751 NR Matisa D75 *(works with DR 78801/DR 78811/ DR 78821/DR 78831)*

CONSOLIDATION MACHINES

DR 76801 NR Plasser & Theurer 09-CM-NR
DR 76802 NR Plasser & Theurer 09-2X-CM "99 70 9320 802-0"

FINISHING MACHINES & BALLAST REGULATORS

DR 77001 SK Plasser & Theurer AFM 2000-RT Finishing Machine Anthony Lou Phillips

DR 77002 SK Plasser & Theurer AFM 2000-RT Finishing Machine

DR 77010 NR Plasser & Theurer USP 6000 Regulator "99 70 9125 010-7"
DR 77315 (S) BB Plasser & Theurer USP 5000C Regulator
DR 77316 (S) BB Plasser & Theurer USP 5000C Regulator
DR 77322 (S) BB Plasser & Theurer USP 5000C Regulator
DR 77327 CS Plasser & Theurer USP 5000C Regulator
DR 77336 (S) BB Plasser & Theurer USP 5000C Regulator
DR 77801 VO Matisa R 24 S Regulator
DR 77802 VO Matisa R 24 S Regulator
DR 77901 CS Plasser & Theurer USP 5000-RT Regulator
DR 77903 NR Plasser & Theurer USP 5000-RT Regulator
DR 77904 NR Plasser & Theurer USP 5000-RT Regulator
DR 77905 NR Plasser & Theurer USP 5000-RT Regulator
DR 77906 NR Plasser & Theurer USP 5000-RT Regulator
DR 77907 NR Plasser & Theurer USP 5000-RT Regulator
DR 77908 SK Plasser & Theurer USP 5000-RT Regulator
DR 77909 NR Plasser & Theurer USP 5000 Regulator "99 70 9125 909-0"

TWIN JIB TRACK RELAYERS

DRP 78213 VO Plasser & Theurer Self-Propelled Heavy Duty
DRP 78215 BA Plasser & Theurer Self-Propelled Heavy Duty
DRP 78216 (S) BB Plasser & Theurer Self-Propelled Heavy Duty
DRP 78217 (S) BA Plasser & Theurer Self-Propelled Heavy Duty
DRP 78218 (S) BB Plasser & Theurer Self-Propelled Heavy Duty
DRP 78219 BA Plasser & Theurer Self-Propelled Heavy Duty
DRP 78221 (S) BB Plasser & Theurer Self-Propelled Heavy Duty
DRP 78222 (S) BB Plasser & Theurer Self-Propelled Heavy Duty

DRP 78223 (S) BB Plasser & Theurer Self-Propelled Heavy Duty
DRP 78224 (S) BB Plasser & Theurer Self-Propelled Heavy Duty
DRC 78226 CS Cowans Sheldon Self-Propelled Heavy Duty
DRC 78229 (S) NR Cowans Sheldon Self-Propelled Heavy Duty
DRC 78231 (S) NR Cowans Sheldon Self-Propelled Heavy Duty
DRC 78234 (S) NR Cowans Sheldon Self-Propelled Heavy Duty
DRC 78235 CS Cowans Sheldon Self-Propelled Heavy Duty
DRC 78237 (S) CS Cowans Sheldon Self-Propelled Heavy Duty

NEW TRACK CONSTRUCTION TRAIN PROPULSION MACHINES

DR 78701 BB Harsco Track Technologies NTC-PW
DR 78702 BB Harsco Track Technologies NTC-PW

TRACK RENEWAL MACHINES

Matisa P95 Track Renewals Trains
DR 78801+DR 78811+DR 78821+DR 78831 NR *(works with DR 76751)*
DR 78802+DR 78812+DR 78822+DR 78832 NR *(works with DR 76750)*

RAIL GRINDING TRAINS

Loram C21
DR 79231 + DR 79232 + DR 79233 + DR 79236 + DR 79237 LO
DR 79241 + DR 79242 + DR 79243 + DR 79244 + DR 79245 + DR 79246 + DR 79247 NR
DR 79251 + DR 79252 + DR 79253 + DR 79254 + DR 79255 + DR 79256 + DR 79257 NR

Names: DR 79241/247 Roger South *(one plate on opposite sides of each)*
DR 79251/257 Martin Elwood *(one plate on opposite sides of each)*

Harsco Track Technologies RGH20C
DR 79261 + DR 79271 NR
DR 79262 + DR 79272 NR
DR 79263 + DR 79273 NR
DR 79265 + DR 79264 +DR 79274 NR
DR 79267 + DR 79277 NR

Loram C44
DR 79301+DR 79302+ NR 99 70 9427 038-3 + 99 70 9427 039-1+
DR 79303+DR 79304 99 70 9427 040-9 + 99 70 9427 041-7
DR 79401+DR 79402+ NR 99 70 9427 042-5 + 99 70 9427 043-3+
DR 79403+DR 79404 99 70 9427 044-1 + 99 70 9427 045-8
DR 79501+DR 79502+ NR 99 70 9427 046-6 + 99 70 9427 047-4 +
DR 79503+DR 79504+ 99 70 9427 048-2 + 99 70 9427 049-0+
DR 79505+DR 79506+ 99 70 9427 050-8 + 99 70 9427 051-6 +
DR 79507 99 70 9427 052-4

RAIL MILLING MACHINES

DR 79101	XR	Linsinger MG31-UK Milling Machine	"99 70 9127 006-3"
DR 79601	SC	Schweerbau High Speed Milling Machine	"99 70 9427 063-1"

STONEBLOWERS

DR 80200 (S)	HR	Pandrol Jackson Plain Line	
DR 80201	NR	Pandrol Jackson Plain Line	
DR 80202 (S)	HR	Pandrol Jackson Plain Line	
DR 80203 (S)	HR	Pandrol Jackson Plain Line	
DR 80204 (S)	HR	Pandrol Jackson Plain Line	
DR 80205	NR	Pandrol Jackson Plain Line	
DR 80206	NR	Pandrol Jackson Plain Line	
DR 80208	NR	Pandrol Jackson Plain Line	
DR 80209	NR	Pandrol Jackson Plain Line	
DR 80210	NR	Pandrol Jackson Plain Line	
DR 80211	NR	Pandrol Jackson Plain Line	
DR 80213	NR	Harsco Track Technologies Plain Line	
DR 80214	NR	Harsco Track Technologies Plain Line	
DR 80215	NR	Harsco Track Technologies Plain Line	
DR 80216	NR	Harsco Track Technologies Plain Line	
DR 80217	NR	Harsco Track Technologies Plain Line	
DR 80301	NR	Harsco Track Technologies Multi-purpose	Stephen Cornish
DR 80302	NR	Harsco Track Technologies Multi-purpose	
DR 80303	NR	Harsco Track Technologies Multi-purpose	

CRANES

DRP 81505	BB	Plasser & Theurer 12 tonne Heavy Duty Diesel Hydraulic
DRP 81507 (S)	BB	Plasser & Theurer 12 tonne Heavy Duty Diesel Hydraulic
DRP 81508	BB	Plasser & Theurer 12 tonne Heavy Duty Diesel Hydraulic
DRP 81511 (S)	BB	Plasser & Theurer 12 tonne Heavy Duty Diesel Hydraulic
DRP 81513	BB	Plasser & Theurer 12 tonne Heavy Duty Diesel Hydraulic
DRP 81517	BB	Plasser & Theurer 12 tonne Heavy Duty Diesel Hydraulic
DRP 81519 (S)	BB	Plasser & Theurer 12 tonne Heavy Duty Diesel Hydraulic
DRP 81522 (S)	BB	Plasser & Theurer 12 tonne Heavy Duty Diesel Hydraulic
DRP 81525	BB	Plasser & Theurer 12 tonne Heavy Duty Diesel Hydraulic
DRP 81532	BB	Plasser & Theurer 12 tonne Heavy Duty Diesel Hydraulic
DRK 81601	VO	Kirow KRC 810UK 100 tonne Heavy Duty Diesel Hydraulic
DRK 81602	BB	Kirow KRC 810UK 100 tonne Heavy Duty Diesel Hydraulic
DRK 81611	BB	Kirow KRC 1200UK 125 tonne Heavy Duty Diesel Hydraulic
DRK 81612	CS	Kirow KRC 1200UK 125 tonne Heavy Duty Diesel Hydraulic
DRK 81613	VO	Kirow KRC 1200UK 125 tonne Heavy Duty Diesel Hydraulic
DRK 81621	VO	Kirow KRC 250UK 25 tonne Diesel Hydraulic
DRK 81622	VO	Kirow KRC 250UK 25 tonne Diesel Hydraulic
DRK 81623	SK	Kirow KRC 250UK 25 tonne Diesel Hydraulic
DRK 81624	SK	Kirow KRC 250UK 25 tonne Diesel Hydraulic
DRK 81625	SK	Kirow KRC 250UK 25 tonne Diesel Hydraulic

DRK 81626 SK Kirow KRC 250S 25 tonne Diesel Hydraulic "99 70 9319 012-9"

99 70 9319 013-7 NR Kirow KRC 1200UK 125 tonne Heavy Duty Diesel Hydraulic

Names:

DRK 81601	Nigel Chester	DRK 81611	Malcolm L. Pearce

LONG WELDED RAIL TRAIN PROPULSION MACHINES

DR 89005	NR	Cowans Boyd PW
DR 89007	NR	Cowans Boyd PW
DR 89008	NR	Cowans Boyd PW

BALLAST SYSTEM PROPULSION MACHINES

DR 92285	NR	Plasser & Theurer PW-RT	
DR 92286	NR	Plasser & Theurer NPW-RT	
DR 92331	NR	Plasser & Theurer PW-RT	
DR 92332	NR	Plasser & Theurer NPW-RT	
DR 92431	NR	Plasser & Theurer PW-RT	
DR 92432	NR	Plasser & Theurer NPW-RT	
DR 92477	NR	Plasser & Theurer PW	"99 70 9310 477-3"
DR 92478	NR	Plasser & Theurer NPW	"99 70 9310 478-1"

BREAKDOWN CRANES

ADRC 96710 (S)	NR	Cowans Sheldon 75 tonne Diesel Hydraulic
ADRC 96713	NR	Cowans Sheldon 75 tonne Diesel Hydraulic
ADRC 96714 (S)	NR	Cowans Sheldon 75 tonne Diesel Hydraulic
ADRC 96715	NR	Cowans Sheldon 75 tonne Diesel Hydraulic

HIGH SPEED 1 MAINTENANCE TRAIN VEHICLES

DR 97001	H1	Eiv de Brieve DU94BA TRAMM with Crane	"DU 94 B 001 URS"
DR 97011	H1	Windhoff MPV (Modular)	
DR 97012	H1	Windhoff MPV (Modular)	Geoff Bell
DR 97013	H1	Windhoff MPV (Modular)	
DR 97014	H1	Windhoff MPV (Modular)	

MOBILE MAINTENANCE TRAINS

Robel Type 69.70 Mobile Maintenance System

DR 97501/601/801	NR	"99 70 9481 001-4 + 99 70 9559 001-1 + 99 70 9580 001-4"
DR 97502/602/802	NR	"99 70 9481 002-2 + 99 70 9559 002-9 + 99 70 9580 002-2"
DR 97503/603/803	NR	"99 70 9481 003-0 + 99 70 9559 003-7 + 99 70 9580 003-0"
DR 97504/604/804	NR	"99 70 9481 004-8 + 99 70 9559 004-5 + 99 70 9580 004-8"
DR 97505/605/805	NR	"99 70 9481 005-5 + 99 70 9559 005-2 + 99 70 9580 005-5"
DR 97506/606/806	NR	"99 70 9481 006-3 + 99 70 9559 006-0 + 99 70 9580 006-3"
DR 97507/607/807	NR	"99 70 9481 007-1 + 99 70 9559 007-8 + 99 70 9580 007-1"
DR 97508/608/808	NR	"99 70 9481 008-9 + 99 70 9559 008-6 + 99 70 9580 008-9"

ELIZABETH LINE MAINTENANCE TRAIN VEHICLES

DR 97509	XR	Robel Power Car A	"99 70 9481 009-7"
DR 97510	XR	Robel Power Car B	"99 70 9481 010-5"
DR 97511	XR	Robel Power Car B	"99 70 9481 011-3"
DR 97512	XR	Robel Power Car E	"99 70 9481 012-1"

ELECTRIFICATION VEHICLES

DR 76901	NR	Windhoff MPV with Piling Equipment	"99 70 9131 001-8"
DR 76903	NR	Windhoff MPV with Piling Equipment	"99 70 9131 003-4"
DR 76905	NR	Windhoff MPV with Piling Equipment	"99 70 9131 005-9"
DR 76906	NR	Windhoff MPV with Concrete Equipment	"99 70 9131 006-7"
DR 76910	NR	Windhoff MPV with Concrete Equipment	"99 70 9131 010-9"
DR 76911	NR	Windhoff MPV with Structure Equipment	"99 70 9131 011-7"
DR 76913	NR	Windhoff MPV with Structure Equipment	"99 70 9131 013-3"
DR 76914	NR	Windhoff MPV with Overhead Line Equipment	"99 70 9131 014-1"
DR 76915	NR	Windhoff MPV with Overhead Line Equipment	"99 70 9131 015-8"
DR 76918	NR	Windhoff MPV with Overhead Line Equipment	"99 70 9131 018-2"
DR 76920	NR	Windhoff MPV with Overhead Line Equipment	"99 70 9131 020-8"
DR 76921	NR	Windhoff MPV with Overhead Line Equipment	"99 70 9131 021-6"
DR 76922	NR	Windhoff MPV with Final Works Equipment	"99 70 9131 022-4"
DR 76923	NR	Windhoff MPV with Final Works Equipment	"99 70 9131 023-2"

DR 98001	NR	Windhoff MPV with Piling Equipment
DR 98002	NR	Windhoff MPV with Overhead Line Renewal Equipment
DR 98003	NR	Windhoff MPV with Overhead Line Renewal Equipment
DR 98004	NR	Windhoff MPV with Overhead Line Renewal Equipment
DR 98005	NR	Windhoff MPV with Overhead Line Renewal Equipment
DR 98006	NR	Windhoff MPV with Overhead Line Renewal Equipment
DR 98007	NR	Windhoff MPV with Piling Equipment
DR 98009	NR	Windhoff MPV with Overhead Line Renewal Equipment
DR 98010	NR	Windhoff MPV with Overhead Line Renewal Equipment
DR 98011	NR	Windhoff MPV with Overhead Line Renewal Equipment
DR 98012	NR	Windhoff MPV with Overhead Line Renewal Equipment
DR 98013	NR	Windhoff MPV with Overhead Line Renewal Equipment
DR 98014	NR	Windhoff MPV with Overhead Line Renewal Equipment

99 70 9231 001-7	AM	SVI RT250 with crane & access platform
99 70 9231 004-1	AM	SVI PT500 with wire manipulator & access platform
99 70 9231 005-8	AM	SVI RSM9 with access platform
99 70 9231 006-6	AM	SVI RSM9 with access platform
99 70 9231 007-4	AM	APV250 with access platform

Names:

DR 76901	BRUNEL
DR 76923	GAVIN ROBERTS
DR 98003	ANTHONY WRIGHTON 1944–2011
DR 98004	PHILIP CATTRELL 1961–2011
DR 98006	JASON MCDONNELL 1970–2016
DR 98009	MELVYN SMITH 1953–2011

DR 98010	BENJAMIN GAUTREY 1992–2011
DR 98012	TERENCE HAND 1962–2016
DR 98013	DAVID WOOD 1951–2015
DR 98014	WAYNE IMLACH 1955–2015

GENERAL PURPOSE VEHICLES

DR 98215A + DR 98215B	BB	Plasser & Theurer GP-TRAMM with Trailer
DR 98216A + DR 98216B	BB	Plasser & Theurer GP-TRAMM with Trailer
DR 98217A + DR 98217B	BB	Plasser & Theurer GP-TRAMM with Trailer
DR 98218A + DR 98218B	BB	Plasser & Theurer GP-TRAMM with Trailer
DR 98219A + DR 98219B	BB	Plasser & Theurer GP-TRAMM with Trailer
DR 98220A + DR 98220B	BB	Plasser & Theurer GP-TRAMM with Trailer

DR 98307A (S)	CS	Geismar GP-TRAMM VMT 860 PL/UM
DR 98307B*	CS	Geismar GP-TRAMM Trailer
DR 98308A + DR 98308B (S)	CS	Geismar GP-TRAMM VMT 860 PL/UM with Trailer

* In use as a propelling control vehicle at Baglan Bay Yard.

DR 98901 + DR 98951	NR	Windhoff MPV Master & Slave
DR 98902 + DR 98952	NR	Windhoff MPV Master & Slave
DR 98903 + DR 98953	NR	Windhoff MPV Master & Slave
DR 98904 + DR 98954	NR	Windhoff MPV Master & Slave
DR 98905 + DR 98955	NR	Windhoff MPV Master & Slave
DR 98906 + DR 98956	NR	Windhoff MPV Master & Slave
DR 98907 + DR 98957	NR	Windhoff MPV Master & Slave
DR 98908 + DR 98958	NR	Windhoff MPV Master & Slave
DR 98909 + DR 98959	NR	Windhoff MPV Master & Slave
DR 98910 + DR 98960	NR	Windhoff MPV Master & Slave
DR 98911 + DR 98961	NR	Windhoff MPV Master & Slave
DR 98912 + DR 98962	NR	Windhoff MPV Master & Slave
DR 98913 + DR 98963	NR	Windhoff MPV Master & Slave
DR 98914 + DR 98964	NR	Windhoff MPV Master & Slave
DR 98915 + DR 98965	NR	Windhoff MPV Master & Slave
DR 98916 + DR 98966	NR	Windhoff MPV Master & Slave
DR 98917 + DR 98967	NR	Windhoff MPV Master & Slave
DR 98918 + DR 98968	NR	Windhoff MPV Master & Slave
DR 98919 + DR 98969	NR	Windhoff MPV Master & Slave
DR 98920 + DR 98970	NR	Windhoff MPV Master & Slave
DR 98921 + DR 98971	NR	Windhoff MPV Master & Slave
DR 98922 + DR 98972	NR	Windhoff MPV Master & Slave
DR 98923 + DR 98973	NR	Windhoff MPV Master & Slave
DR 98924 + DR 98974	NR	Windhoff MPV Master & Slave
DR 98925 + DR 98975	NR	Windhoff MPV Master & Slave
DR 98926 + DR 98976	NR	Windhoff MPV Master & Powered Slave
DR 98927 + DR 98977	NR	Windhoff MPV Master & Powered Slave
DR 98928 + DR 98978	NR	Windhoff MPV Master & Powered Slave
DR 98929 + DR 98979	NR	Windhoff MPV Master & Powered Slave
DR 98930 + DR 98980	NR	Windhoff MPV Master & Powered Slave
DR 98931 + DR 98981	NR	Windhoff MPV Master & Powered Slave
DR 98932 + DR 98982	NR	Windhoff MPV Master & Powered Slave

Names:

DR 98914+DR 98964	Dick Preston
DR 98915+DR 98965	Nigel Cummins
DR 98923+DR 98973	Chris Lemon
DR 98926+DR 98976	John Denyer

INFRASTRUCTURE MONITORING VEHICLES

Note: "950 001" is a purpose-built Track Assessment Unit based on the BREL Class 150/1 design.

DR 98008	NR	Windhoff MPV Twin-cab with surveying equipment
999600+999601	NR	BREL York Track Assessment Unit "950 001"

SNOWPLOUGHS

ADB 965203	NR	Independent Drift Plough	Carlisle Kingmoor Depot
ADB 965206	NR	Independent Drift Plough	Leeman Road Sidings, York
ADB 965208	NR	Independent Drift Plough	Norwich Thorpe Yard
ADB 965209	NR	Independent Drift Plough	Motherwell Depot
ADB 965210	NR	Independent Drift Plough	West Yard, Tonbridge
ADB 965211	NR	Independent Drift Plough	Tonbridge West Yard
ADB 965217	NR	Independent Drift Plough	Leeman Road Sidings, York
ADB 965219	NR	Independent Drift Plough	Norwich Thorpe Yard
ADB 965223	NR	Independent Drift Plough	Fairwater Yard, Taunton
ADB 965224	NR	Independent Drift Plough	Millburn Yard, Inverness
ADB 965230	NR	Independent Drift Plough	Millburn Yard, Inverness
ADB 965231	NR	Independent Drift Plough	Motherwell Depot
ADB 965234	NR	Independent Drift Plough	Millburn Yard, Inverness
ADB 965235	NR	Independent Drift Plough	Fairwater Yard, Taunton
ADB 965236	NR	Independent Drift Plough	West Yard, Tonbridge
ADB 965237	NR	Independent Drift Plough	Tonbridge West Yard
ADB 965240	NR	Independent Drift Plough	York North Yard Sidings
ADB 965241	NR	Independent Drift Plough	York Yard North Sidings
ADB 965242	NR	Independent Drift Plough	Carlisle Kingmoor Depot
ADB 965243	NR	Independent Drift Plough	Millburn Yard, Inverness
ADB 965576	NR	Beilhack Type PB600 Plough	West Yard, Doncaster
ADB 965577	NR	Beilhack Type PB600 Plough	West Yard, Doncaster
ADB 965578	NR	Beilhack Type PB600 Plough	Kingmoor Yard, Carlisle
ADB 965579	NR	Beilhack Type PB600 Plough	Kingmoor Yard, Carlisle
ADB 965580	NR	Beilhack Type PB600 Plough	Crewe Gresty Bridge Depot
ADB 965581	NR	Beilhack Type PB600 Plough	Crewe Gresty Bridge Depot
ADB 966098	NR	Beilhack Type PB600 Plough	West Yard, Doncaster
ADB 966099	NR	Beilhack Type PB600 Plough	West Yard, Doncaster

SNOWBLOWERS

ADB 968500	NR	Beilhack Self-Propelled Rotary	Edinburgh Slateford Depot
ADB 968501	NR	Beilhack Self-Propelled Rotary	Edinburgh Slateford Depot

ON-TRACK MACHINES AWAITING DISPOSAL

Tampers

DR 73105	Plasser & Theurer 09-32 CSM	Cardiff Canton Depot
DR 75201	Plasser & Theurer 08-275 S&C	Hither Green Depot
DR 75202	Plasser & Theurer 08-275 S&C	Hither Green Depot
DR 75403	Matisa B 41 UE	France/Eastleigh Works

Twin Jib track relayer

DRB 78123	British Hoist & Crane Non-Self-Propelled	Polmadie DHS

Infrastructure Monitoring Vehicles

999800	Plasser & Theurer EM-SAT 100/RT Track Survey Car	Thuxton
999801	Plasser & Theurer EM-SAT 100/RT Track Survey Car	Eastleigh Works

LOCATIONS OF STORED ON-TRACK MACHINES

The locations of machines shown above as stored (S) are shown here.

DR 73805	Rugby Depot
DR 73927	Ashford OTM Depot
DR 76701	Fairwater Yard, Taunton
DR 76703	Fairwater Yard, Taunton
DR 77315	Ashford OTM Depot
DR 77316	Ashford OTM Depot
DR 77322	Colchester OTM Depot
DR 77336	Hither Green Depot
DRP 78216	Hither Green Depot
DRP 78217	Glasgow Rutherglen Depot
DRP 78218	Ashford OTM Depot
DRP 78221	Ashford OTM Depot
DRP 78222	Ashford OTM Depot
DRP 78223	Ashford OTM Depot
DRP 78224	Hither Green Depot
DRC 78229	Beeston Sidings
DRC 78231	Beeston Sidings
DRC 78234	Beeston Sidings
DRC 78237	Rugby Depot
DR 79234+	
DR 79235	RTC Business Park, Derby
DR 80200	Thuxton
DR 80202	Leeds Holbeck Depot
DR 80203	Leeds Holbeck Depot
DR 80204	Thuxton
DRP 81507	Ashford OTM Depot
DRP 81511	Ashford OTM Depot
DRP 81519	Woking OTM Depot
DRP 81522	Ashford OTM Depot
ARDC 96710	Wigan Springs Branch Depot
ARDC 96714	Wigan Springs Branch Depot
DR 98307A	Darley Dale
DR 98308A+	
DR 98308B	Barry Rail Centre

6. CODES

6.1. LIVERY CODES

Livery codes are used to denote the various liveries carried. It is impossible to list every livery variation which currently exists. In particular items ignored for this publication include:

- Minor colour variations.
- Omission of logos.
- All numbering, lettering and brandings.

Descriptions quoted are thus a general guide only. Logos as appropriate for each livery are normally deemed to be carried. The colour of the lower half of the bodyside is generally stated first.

Code	*Description*
AB	Arriva Trains Wales/Welsh Government sponsored all over dark blue.
AG	Arlington Fleet Services (green).
AI	Aggregate Industries (green, light grey & blue).
AL	Advertising/promotional livery (see class heading for details).
AR	Anglia Railways (turquoise blue with a white stripe).
AT	Avanti West Coast (dark green, dark grey, white, cream & orange).
AV	Arriva Trains (turquoise blue with white doors & a cream "swish").
AW	Arriva Trains Wales/Welsh Government sponsored dark & light blue.
AZ	Advenza Freight (deep blue with green Advenza brandings).
B	BR blue.
BG	BR blue & grey lined out in white.
BL	BR Revised blue with yellow cabs, grey roof, large numbers & logo.
C2	c2c (white with dark blue doors).
CA	Caledonian Sleeper (dark blue).
CC	BR Carmine & Cream.
CD	Cotswold Rail (silver with blue & red logo).
CE	BR Civil Engineers (yellow & grey with black cab doors & window surrounds).
CH	BR Western Region/GWR (chocolate & cream lined out in gold).
CL	Chiltern Railways Mainline Class 168 (white & silver).
CM	Chiltern Railways Mainline loco-hauled (two-tone grey/white & silver with blue stripes).
CN	Connex/Southeastern (white with black window surrounds & grey lower band).
CR	Chiltern Railways (blue & white with a red stripe).
CS	Colas Rail (yellow, orange & black).
CU	Corus (silver with red logos).
DB	DB Cargo (Deutsche Bahn red with grey roof & solebar).
DC	Devon & Cornwall Railways (metallic silver).
DG	BR Departmental (dark grey with black cab doors & window surrounds).
DI	New DRS {Class 68 style} (deep blue & aquamarine with large compass logo).
DR	Direct Rail Services (dark blue with light blue or dark grey roof).
DS	Revised Direct Rail Services (dark blue, light blue & green. "Compass" logo).

E English Welsh & Scottish Railway (maroon bodyside & roof with a broad gold bodyside band).
EA East Midlands Trains revised HST (dark blue, orange & red).
EB Eurotunnel (two-tone grey with a broad blue stripe).
EG "EWS grey" (as **F** but with large yellow & red EWS logo).
EI East Midlands Railway {interim} (white with deep purple swish at unit ends).
EP European Passenger Services (two-tone grey with dark blue roof).
EM East Midlands Trains {Connect} (blue with red & orange swish at unit ends).
ER East Midlands Railway (two-tone purple with white lower bodyside lining and doors).
ES Revised Eurostar (deep blue & two-tone grey).
EU Eurostar (white with dark blue & yellow stripes).
EX Europhoenix (silver, blue & red).
F BR Trainload Freight (two-tone grey with black cab doors & window surrounds. Various logos).
FA Fastline Freight (grey & black with white & orange stripes).
FB First Group dark blue.
FD First Great Western & Hull Trains "Dynamic Lines" (dark blue with thin multi-coloured lines on the lower bodyside).
FE Railfreight Distribution International (two tone-grey with black cab doors & dark blue roof).
FER Fertis (light grey with a dark grey roof & solebar).
FF Freightliner grey (two-tone grey with black cab doors & window surrounds. Freightliner logo).
FG New Freightliner Genesee & Wyoming style (orange with black & yellow lower bodyside stripes).
FH Revised Freightliner {PowerHaul} (dark green with yellow cab ends & grey stripe/buffer beam).
FI First Great Western "Local Lines" DMU (varying blue with local visitor attractions applied to the lower bodyside).
FL Freightliner (dark green with yellow cabs).
FP Old First Great Western (green & ivory with thin green & gold stripes).
FO BR Railfreight (grey bodysides, yellow cabs & red lower bodyside stripe, large BR logo).
FR Fragonset Railways (black with silver roof & a red bodyside band lined out in white).
FS First Group (indigo blue with pink & white stripes).
FU First Group "Urban Lights" (varying blue or uniform indigo blue with pink, white & blue markings on the lower bodyside).
G[1] BR Green (plain green, with white stripe on main line locomotives).
G[2] BR Southern Region/SR or BR DMU green.
GA Greater Anglia (white with red doors & black window surrounds).
GB GB Railfreight (blue with orange cantrail & solebar stripes, orange cabs).
GC Grand Central (all over black with an orange stripe).
GG BR two-tone green.
GL First Great Western locomotives (green with a gold stripe).
GR New Greater Anglia (white/grey with black window surrounds & red & dark grey on the lower bodyside).
GV Gatwick Express Class 442 (red, white & indigo blue with mauve & blue doors).

GW Great Western Railway (TOC) dark green.
GY Eurotunnel (grey & yellow).
GX Gatwick Express Class 387 (red with white lining and grey doors).
HA Hanson Quarry Products (dark blue/silver with oxide red roof).
HB HSBC Rail (Oxford blue & white).
HC Heathrow Connect (grey with a broad deep blue bodyside band & orange doors).
HE Heathrow Express (silver with purple doors and black window surrounds.
HN Harry Needle Railroad Company (orange with a black roof and solebar).
HT New Hull Trains (First Group dark blue with a multi-coloured band on lower bodyside depicting images from the route).
HU Hunslet Engine Company (dark blue & orange).
HX New Heathrow Express (silver, grey & purple).
IC BR InterCity (dark grey/white/red/white).
K Black.
KB Knorr-Bremse Rail UK (blue, white & light green).
LD New London Overground (black upper bodyside with white, orange & blue lower bodyside stripes & orange doors).
LH BR Loadhaul (black with orange cabsides).
LI London Northwestern Railway {interim} (dark green at unit ends and doors applied on **LM** light grey/black livery).
LM London Midland (light grey & green with black stripe around the windows).
LN London Northwestern Railway (light grey, dark green & light green).
LO London Overground (all over white with a blue solebar & black window surrounds and orange doors).
LT London Transport maroon & cream.
LZ LNER Azuma (white with red window surrounds).
M BR maroon (maroon lined out in straw & black).
ML BR Mainline Freight (aircraft blue with a silver stripe).
MT Maritime (blue with white lettering).
MY Merseyrail (all over yellow or all over grey (alternate sides)).
N BR Network SouthEast (white & blue with red lower bodyside stripe, grey solebar & cab ends).
NB Northern all over dark blue.
NC National Express white (white with blue doors).
NO Northern (deep blue, purple & white). Some units have area-specific promotional vinyls (see class heading for details).
NR New Northern (white & purple).
NX National Express (white with grey ends).
0 Non-standard (see class heading for details).
PB Porterbrook Leasing Company (blue).
PC Pullman Car Company (umber & cream with gold lettering lined out in gold).
RB Riviera Trains Oxford blue.
RL RMS Locotec (dark blue with light grey cabsides).
RM Royal Mail revised (all over red).
RO Rail Operations Group (dark blue).
RP Royal Train (claret, lined out in red & black).
RR Regional Railways (dark blue & grey with light blue & white stripes, three narrow dark blue stripes at vehicle ends).
RS Railway Support Services (grey with a red solebar).
RV Riviera Trains Great Briton (Oxford blue & cream lined out in gold).

RX Rail Express Systems (dark grey & red with or without blue markings).
RZ Royal Train revised (plain claret, no lining).
SB Southeastern blue (all over blue with black window surrounds).
SC Strathclyde PTE (carmine & cream lined out in black & gold).
SD Stagecoach/South West Trains outer suburban {Class 450 style} (deep blue with red doors & orange & red cab sides).
SE Southeastern suburban (all over white with black window surrounds, light blue doors and (on some units) dark blue lower bodyside stripe).
SI ScotRail InterCity HST (light grey & dark blue with INTER7CITY branding).
SL Silverlink (indigo blue with white stripe, green lower body & yellow doors).
SN Southern (white & dark green with light green semi-circles at one end of each vehicle. Light grey band at solebar level).
SR ScotRail – Scotland's Railways (dark blue with Scottish Saltire flag & white/light blue flashes).
SS South West Trains inner suburban {Class 455 style} (red with blue & orange flashes at unit ends).
ST Stagecoach {long-distance stock} (white & dark blue with dark blue window surrounds and red & orange swishes at unit ends).
SW South Western Railway (two-tone grey with a yellow lower bodyside stripe).
TF TfL Rail (white with blue doors and lower bodyside stripe).
TG Govia Thameslink interim {Class 387} (white with dark green doors).
TL Govia Thameslink Railway (light grey & white with blue doors).
TP TransPennine Express (silver, grey, blue & purple).
TT Transmart Trains (all over green).
TW Transport for Wales (white with a broad red stripe at cantrail level & red doors).
U Plain white or grey undercoat.
V Virgin Trains (red with black doors extending into bodysides, three white lower bodysides stripes).
VE Virgin Trains East Coast (red & white with black window surrounds).
VP Virgin Trains shunters (black with a large black & white chequered flag on the bodyside).
VN Northern Belle (crimson lake & cream lined out in gold).
VT Virgin Trains silver (silver, with black window surrounds, white cantrail stripe & red roof. Red swept down at unit ends).
VI Vivarail (white & green).
VW New Virgin Trains {unbranded} (all over white).
WA Wabtec Rail (black).
WC West Coast Railway Company maroon.
WI West Midlands Railway {interim} (gold at unit ends & gold doors applied on **LM** light grey/black livery).
WM West Midlands Railway (gold & metallic purple).
XC CrossCountry (two-tone silver with deep crimson ends & pink doors).
XR Crossrail (white with black window surrounds and a purple lower bodyside).
Y Network Rail yellow.
YR West Yorkshire PTE/Northern EMUs (red, lilac & grey).

6.2. OWNER CODES

The following codes are used to define the ownership details of the locomotives or rolling stock listed in this book. Codes shown indicate either the legal owner or "responsible custodian" of each vehicle.

20	Class 20189
37	Scottish Thirty-Seven Group
40	Class 40 Preservation Society
47	Stratford 47 Group
50	Class 50 Alliance
56	Class 56 Locomotives
70	7029 Clun Castle
71	71A Locomotives
2L	Class 20 Locomotives
A	Angel Trains
AD	AV Dawson
AF	Arlington Fleet Services
AM	Alstom
AT	Agility Trains
AV	Arriva UK Trains
BA	Babcock Rail
BB	Balfour Beatty Rail Infrastructure Services
BD	Bardon Aggregates
BE	Belmond (UK)
BN	Beacon Rail
BR	Brodie Leasing
BT	Bombardier Transportation
CL	Caledonian Rail Leasing
CO	Corelink Rail Infrastructure
CT	Cross London Trains
CS	Colas Rail
D0	D05 Preservation Group
DA	Data Acquisition & Testing Services
DB	DB Cargo (UK)
DC	DC Rail
DP	Deltic Preservation Society
DR	Direct Rail Services
DT	The Diesel Traction Group
E	Eversholt Rail (UK)
EE	English Electric Preservation
EL	Electric Traction Limited
EM	East Midlands Railway
EO	ElectroMotive Diesel Services
EP	Europhoenix
ER	Eastern Rail Services
ET	Eurotunnel
EU	Eurostar international
EY	European Metal Recycling
FG	First Group
FL	Freightliner

GB GB Railfreight
GE Gemini Rail Group
GW Great Western Railway (assets of the Greater Western franchise)
H1 Network Rail (High Speed)
HD Hastings Diesels
HE Heathrow Airport Holdings
HN Harry Needle Railroad Company
HR Harsco Track Technologies
HT Hanson Traction
HU Hunslet Engine Company
LD Locomotive Diesels
LF Lombard North Central
LN London Overground
LO LORAM (UK)
LS Locomotive Services
LU London Underground
MG Mid Glamorgan County Council
MQ Macquarie Group
MR Mendip Rail
NB Boden Rail Engineering
NM National Museum of Science & Industry
NN North Norfolk Railway
NR Network Rail
NS Nemesis Rail
NY North Yorkshire Moors Railway Enterprises
P Porterbrook Leasing Company
PO Other private owner
PP Peter Pan Locomotive Company
PR The Princess Royal Class Locomotive Trust
QW QW Rail Leasing
RC RailCare UK
RF Rail for London (Transport for London)
RL Rail Management Services (trading as RMS Locotec)
RM Royal Mail
RO Rail Operations Group
RP Rampart Engineering
RR Rock Rail
RS Railway Support Services
RU Russell Logistics
RV Riviera Trains
SB Steve Beniston
SC Schweerbau (UK)
SF SNCF (Société Nationale des Chemins de fer Français)
SG South Glamorgan County Council
SI Speno International
SK Swietelsky Babcock Rail
SP The Scottish Railway Preservation Society
SR ScotRail
ST Shaun Wright
SU SembCorp Utilities UK
SW South Western Railway

SY South Yorkshire Passenger Transport Executive
TF Train Fleet (Department for Transport)
TT Transmart Trains
UR UK Rail Leasing
VG Victoria Group
VI Vivarail
VO VolkerRail
VT Vintage Trains
WA Wabtec Rail Group
WC West Coast Railway Company
WM West Midlands Trains
X Sold for scrap/further use and awaiting collection
XR Crossrail

6.3. LOCOMOTIVE POOL CODES

Locomotives are split into operational groups ("pools") for diagramming and maintenance purposes. The codes used to denote these pools are shown in this publication.

AWCA West Coast Railway Company operational locomotives.
AWCX West Coast Railway Company stored locomotives.
CFOL Class 50 Operations locomotives.
CFSL Class 40 Preservation Society Locomotives.
COFS Colas Rail Class 56.
COLO Colas Rail Classes 66 & 70.
COLS Colas Rail stored locomotives.
COTS Colas Rail Classes 37 & 67.
DFGI Freightliner Class 70.
DFHH Freightliner Class 66/6.
DFIM Freightliner Class 66/5.
DFIN Freightliner low emission Class 66.
DFLC Freightliner Class 90.
DFNC Freightliner Class 86/6.
DHLT Freightliner locomotives awaiting maintenance/repair/disposal.
EFOO Great Western Railway Class 57.
EFPC Great Western Railway 43.
EHPC CrossCountry Class 43.
EMPC East Midlands Railway Class 43.
EPEX Europhoenix locomotives for export.
EPUK Europhoenix UK locomotives.
GBBR GB Railfreight Class 73 for possible rebuilding.
GBBT GB Railfreight Class 66. Large fuel tanks.
GBCH GB Railfreight Class 86 & 87.
GBCS GB Railfreight Class 73/9. Caledonian Sleeper.
GBDF GB Railfreight Class 47.
GBEB GB Railfreight Class 66. Ex-European, large fuel tanks.
GBED GB Railfreight Class 73.
GBEE GB Railfreight Class 20. On hire from HNRC.
GBEL GB Railfreight Class 66. New build, small fuel tanks.
GBFM GB Railfreight Class 66. RETB fitted.

GBGD	GB Railfreight Class 56. Operational locomotives.
GBGS	GB Railfreight Class 56. Stored locomotives.
GBLT	GB Railfreight Class 66. Small fuel tanks.
GBNB	GB Railfreight Class 66. New build.
GBNR	GB Railfreight Class 73/9. Network Rail contracts.
GBOB	GB Railfreight Class 66. Former DB Cargo locomotives; large fuel tanks and buckeye couplers.
GBSD	GB Railfreight. Stored locomotives.
GBSL	GB Railfreight Class 92. Caledonian Sleeper.
GBST	GB Railfreight Class 92. Caledonian Sleeper & Channel Tunnel.
GBTG	GB Railfreight Class 60.
GBYH	GB Railfreight Class 59.
GROG	Rail Operations Group operational locomotives.
HAPC	ScotRail Class 43.
HNRL	Harry Needle Railroad Company hire locomotives.
HNRS	Harry Needle Railroad Company stored locomotives.
HTLX	DC Rail or Hanson Traction locomotives.
HYWD	South Western Railway Class 73.
IANA	Greater Anglia Class 90.
IECA	London North Eastern Railway Class 91.
IECP	London North Eastern Railway Class 43.
LSLO	Locomotive Services operational locomotives.
LSLS	Locomotive Services stored locomotives.
MBDL	Non TOC-owned diesel locomotives.
MBED	Non TOC-owned electro-diesel locomotives.
MBEL	Non TOC-owned electric locomotives.
MOLO	Class 20189 Ltd Class 20.
NRLO	Nemesis Rail locomotives.
QADD	Network Rail locomotives.
QCAR	Network Rail New Measurement Train Class 43.
QETS	Network Rail Class 37.
SAXL	Eversholt Rail off-lease locomotives.
SBXL	Porterbrook Leasing Company stored locomotives.
SCEL	Angel Trains stored locomotives.
SROG	Rail Operations Group locomotives under overhaul.
TPEX	TransPennine Express Class 68 locomotives.
UKRL	UK Rail Leasing. Operational locomotives.
UKRM	UK Rail Leasing. Locomotives for overhaul.
UKRS	UK Rail Leasing. Stored locomotives.
WAAC	DB Cargo Class 67.
WABC	DB Cargo Class 67. RETB fitted.
WACC	DB Cargo Class 67.
WAWC	DB Cargo Class 67 for hire to Transport for Wales.
WBAE	DB Cargo Class 66. Locomotives fitted with "stop-start" technology.
WBAR	DB Cargo Class 66. Fitted with remote monitoring equipment.
WBAT	DB Cargo Class 66.
WBBE	DB Cargo Class 66. RETB fitted and fitted with "stop-start" technology.
WBBT	DB Cargo Class 66. RETB fitted.
WBLE	DB Cargo Class 66. Dedicated locomotives for Lickey Incline banking duties. Fitted with "stop-start" technology.
WCAT	DB Cargo Class 60.

WCBT DB Cargo Class 60. Extended-range fuel tanks.
WEAC DB Cargo Class 90.
WEDC DB Cargo Class 90. Modified for operation with Mark 4s.
WFBC DB Cargo Class 92 with TVM430 cab signalling equipment for use on High Speed 1.
WQAA DB Cargo stored locomotives Group 1A (short-term maintenance).
WQAB DB Cargo stored locomotives Group 1B.
WQBA DB Cargo stored locomotives Group 2 (unserviceable).
WQCA DB Cargo stored locomotives Group 3 (unserviceable).
WQDA DB Cargo stored locomotives Group 4 (awaiting disposal).
XHAC Direct Rail Services Classes 37/4 & 57/3.
XHCE Direct Rail Services Class 68 for hire to Chiltern Railways.
XHCK Direct Rail Services Classes 20 & 57/0.
XHIM Direct Rail Services locomotives – Intermodal traffic.
XHNC Direct Rail Services locomotives – nuclear traffic/general.
XHSS Direct Rail Services stored locomotives.
XHTP Direct Rail Services Class 68 for hire to TransPennine Express.
XHVE Direct Rail Services Classes 68 & 88.
XHVT Direct Rail Services Class 57/3 for hire to Virgin Trains.

6.4. OPERATOR CODES

Operator codes are used to denote the organisation that facilitates the use of that vehicle, and may not be the actual Train Operating Company which runs the train. Where no operator code is shown, vehicles are currently not in use.

AW Avanti West Coast
BP Belmond British Pullman
C2 c2c
CA Caledonian Sleeper
CR Chiltern Railways
CS Colas Rail
DB DB Cargo (UK)
DR Direct Rail Services
EM East Midlands Railway
EU Eurostar (UK)
GA Greater Anglia
GB GB Railfreight
GC Grand Central
GN Great Northern (part of Govia Thameslink Railway)
GW Great Western Railway
HD Hastings Diesels
HE Heathrow Express
HT Hull Trains
LN London North Eastern Railway
LO London Overground
LS Locomotive Services
ME Merseyrail
NO Northern
NY North Yorkshire Moors Railway

PR	The Princess Royal Class Locomotive Trust
RO	Rail Operations Group
RS	The Royal Scotsman (Belmond)
RT	Royal Train
RV	Riviera Trains
SE	Southeastern
SN	Southern (part of Govia Thameslink Railway)
SP	The Scottish Railway Preservation Society
SR	ScotRail
SW	South Western Railway
SY	Stagecoach Supertram
TL	Thameslink (part of Govia Thameslink Railway)
TP	TransPennine Express
TW	Transport for Wales
VT	Vintage Trains
WC	West Coast Railway Company
WM	West Midlands Trains
XC	CrossCountry
XR	TfL Rail

6.5. ALLOCATION & LOCATION CODES

Allocation codes are used in this publication to denote the normal maintenance base ("depots") of each operational locomotive, multiple unit or coach. However, maintenance may be carried out at other locations and may also be carried out by mobile maintenance teams. Location codes are used to denote common storage locations whilst the full place name is used for other locations. The designation (S) denotes stored.

Code	*Depot*	*Depot Operator*
AD	Ashford (Kent)	Hitachi
AK	Ardwick (Manchester)	Siemens
AL	Aylesbury	Chiltern Railways
AN	Allerton (Liverpool)	Northern
BD	Birkenhead North	Stadler Rail Service UK
BH	Barrow Hill (Chesterfield)	Barrow Hill Engine Shed Society
BI	Brighton Lovers Walk	Govia Thameslink Railway
BL	Shackerstone, Battlefield Line	*Storage location only*
BM	Bournemouth	South Western Railway
BN	Bounds Green (London)	Hitachi
BO	Bo'ness (West Lothian)	The Bo'ness & Kinneil Railway
BQ	Bury (Greater Manchester)	East Lancashire Railway Trust
BU	Burton-upon-Trent	Nemesis Rail
BY	Bletchley	West Midlands Trains
CB	Crewe Basford Hall	Freightliner Engineering
CE	Crewe International	DB Cargo (UK)
CF	Cardiff Canton	Transport for Wales/Colas Rail
CH	Chester	Alstom
CK	Corkerhill (Glasgow)	ScotRail
CL	Crewe LNWR Heritage	LNWR Heritage Company

CM	East Cranmore	East Somerset Railway
CN	Castle Donington RFT	*Storage location only*
CO	Coquelles (France)	Eurotunnel
CP	Crewe Carriage Shed	Arriva TrainCare
CR	Crewe Gresty Bridge	Direct Rail Services
CS	Carnforth	West Coast Railway Company
CT	Cheriton (Folkestone)	Eurotunnel
CY	Crewe South Yard	*Storage location only*
CZ	Central Rivers (Barton-under-Needwood)	Bombardier Transportation
DE	East Dereham (Norfolk)	Mid Norfolk Railway
DN	Doncaster Carr	Hitachi
DR	Doncaster Belmont Yard	*Storage location only*
DY	Derby Etches Park	East Midlands Railway
EC	Edinburgh Craigentinny	Hitachi
EH	Eastleigh	Arriva TrainCare
EM	East Ham (London)	c2c
EP	Ely Papworth Sidings	*Storage location only*
EX	Exeter	Great Western Railway
FA	Fawley (Hampshire)	*Storage location only*
GA	Gascoigne Wood Sidings (South Milford)	*Storage location only*
GW	Glasgow Shields Road	ScotRail
HA	Haymarket (Edinburgh)	ScotRail
HE	Hornsey (London)	Govia Thameslink Railway
HJ	Hoo Junction (Kent)	Colas Rail
HM	Healey Mills (Wakefield)	*Storage location only*
HN	Hamilton (Glasgow)	Assenta Rail
HO	Hope Cement Works	Breedon Hope Cement
HT	Heaton (Newcastle-upon-Tyne)	Northern/LNER
IL	Ilford (London)	Greater Anglia/TfL Rail
IS	Inverness	ScotRail
KK	Kirkdale (Liverpool)	Stadler Rail Service UK
KM	Carlisle Kingmoor	Direct Rail Services
KP	Kimberley Park, Mid Norfolk Railway	*Storage location only*
KR	Kidderminster	Severn Valley Railway
LA	Laira (Plymouth)	Great Western Railway
LB	Loughborough Works	Brush Traction
LD	Leeds Midland Road	Freightliner Engineering
LE	Landore (Swansea)	Chrysalis Rail
LM	Quinton Rail Technology Centre (Long Marston, Warwickshire)	Motorail Logistics
LR	Leicester	UK Rail Leasing
LT	Longport (Stoke-on-Trent)	ElectroMotive Diesel Services
LW	MoD Longtown (Cumbria)	*Storage location only*
LY	Le Landy (Paris)	SNCF
MA	Longsight (Manchester)	Alstom
MD	Merehead	Mendip Rail
ME	Mossend Yard	*Storage location only*
ML	Motherwell	Direct Rail Services
MN	Machynlleth	Transport for Wales
NC	Norwich Crown Point	Greater Anglia
NG	New Cross Gate (London)	London Overground

NH	Newton Heath (Manchester)	Northern
NL	Neville Hill (Leeds)	East Midlands Railway/Northern
NM	Nottingham Eastcroft	East Midlands Railway/Boden Rail
NN	Northampton King's Heath	Siemens
NO	Weybourne (Norfolk)	North Norfolk Railway
NP	North Pole (London)	Hitachi
NT	Northam (Southampton)	Siemens
NU	Sheffield Nunnery	Stagecoach Supertram
NY	Grosmont (North Yorkshire)	North Yorkshire Moors Railway Enterprises
OC	Old Oak Common Crossrail (London)	TfL Rail
OH	Old Oak Common Heathrow	Heathrow Express
PM	St Philip's Marsh (Bristol)	Great Western Railway
PO	Polmadie (Glasgow)	Alstom
PZ	Penzance Long Rock	Great Western Railway
RG	Reading	Great Western Railway
RM	Ramsgate	Southeastern
RO	Rowsley (Derbyshire)	Peak Rail
RR	Doncaster Roberts Road	ElectroMotive Diesel Services
RS	Ruislip (London)	London Underground
RU	Rugby	Colas Rail
RY	Ryde (Isle of Wight)	South Western Railway
SA	Salisbury	South Western Railway
SC	Scunthorpe Steelworks	British Steel
SE	St Leonards (Hastings)	St Leonards Railway Engineering
SG	Slade Green (London)	Southeastern
SH	Southall (London)	West Coast Rly Co/Locomotive Services
SJ	Stourbridge Junction	Parry People Movers
SK	Swanwick West (Derbyshire)	The Princess Royal Locomotive Trust
SL	Stewarts Lane (London)	Govia Thameslink Railway/Belmond
SO	Soho (Birmingham)	West Midlands Trains
SP	Springs Branch (Wigan)	DB Cargo (UK)
SU	Selhurst (Croydon)	Govia Thameslink Railway
SW	Swanage	Swanage Railway
TB	Three Bridges (Crawley)	Siemens
TI	Temple Mills (London)	Eurostar International
TJ	Tavistock Junction Yard (Plymouth)	*Storage location only*
TM	Tyseley Locomotive Works	Vintage Trains
TN	Thornton (Fife)	John Cameron
TO	Toton (Nottinghamshire)	DB Cargo (UK)
TS	Tyseley (Birmingham)	West Midlands Trains
TY	Tyne Yard (Newcastle)	*Storage location only*
WB	Wembley (London)	Alstom
WD	Wimbledon (London)	South Western Railway
WE	Willesden Brent sidings	*Storage location only*
WN	Willesden (London)	Bombardier Transportation
WO	Wolsingham, Weardale Railway	RMS Locotec
WS	Worksop (Nottinghamshire)	Harry Needle Railroad Company
YK	National Railway Museum (York)	National Museum of Science & Industry
YO	Yoker (Glasgow)	ScotRail
XW	Crofton (Wakefield)	Bombardier Transportation

ZA	RTC Business Park (Derby)	LORAM (UK)
ZB	Doncaster Works	Wabtec Rail
ZC	Crewe Works	Bombardier Transportation UK
ZD	Derby Works	Bombardier Transportation UK
ZG	Eastleigh Works	Arlington Fleet Services
ZH	Springburn Depot (Glasgow)	*Closed*
ZI	Ilford Works	Bombardier Transportation UK
ZJ	Stoke-on-Trent Works	Axiom Rail (Stoke)
ZK	Kilmarnock Caledonia Works	Wabtec Rail Scotland
ZM	Kilmarnock Bonnyton Works	Brodie Engineering
ZN	Wolverton Works	Gemini Rail Group
ZR	Holgate Works (York)	Network Rail

6.6. ABBREVIATIONS

The following general abbreviations are used in this book:

AC	Alternating Current (ie Overhead supply)
AFD	Air Force Department
BAA	British Airports Authority
BR	British Railways
BSI	Bergische Stahl Industrie
CRDC	Component Recovery & Disposal Centre
C&W	Carriage & Wagon
DC	Direct Current (ie Third Rail)
DEMU	Diesel Electric Multiple Unit
DERA	Defence Evaluation & Research Agency
DfT	Department for Transport
Dia	Diagram number
DMU	Diesel Multiple Unit (general term)
DSDC	Defence Storage & Distribution Centre
DRS	Direct Rail Services
ETS	Electric Train Supply
EMU	Electric Multiple Unit (general term)
GWR	Great Western Railway
FLT	Freightliner Terminal
HB	Hunslet-Barclay
hp	Horse power
HNRC	Harry Needle Railroad Company
Hz	Hertz
kN	Kilonewtons
km/h	Kilometres per hour
kW	Kilowatts
lbf	Pounds force
LT	London Transport
LUL	London Underground Limited
m	Metres

mm	Millimetres
mph	Miles per hour
NPCCS	Non Passenger Carrying Coaching Stock
PTE	Passenger Transport Executive
RCH	Railway Clearing House
rpm	Revolutions per minute
RR	Rolls Royce
RSL	Rolling Stock Library
SR	BR Southern Region and Southern Railway
t	Tonnes
T	Toilet
TD	Toilet suitable for use by disabled passengers
TDM	Time Division Multiplex
TOPS	Total Operations Processing System
V	Volts
W	Wheelchair space

6.7 BUILDERS

Builders are shown in the class headings. The workshops of British Railways and the pre-nationalisation and pre-grouping companies were first transferred to a wholly-owned subsidiary called British Rail Engineering Ltd (BREL). These workshops were later privatised, BREL then becoming BREL Ltd. Some of the works were then taken over by ABB, which was later merged with Daimler-Benz Transportation to become Adtranz. This was later taken over by Bombardier Transportation, which now operates the important works at Derby Litchurch Lane. Bombardier also built vehicles for the British market in Brugge, Belgium.

Other workshops were the subject of separate sales, Springburn, Glasgow and Wolverton becoming "Railcare" and Eastleigh becoming "Wessex Traincare". All three were sold to GEC-Alsthom (now Alstom) but Eastleigh closed in 2006, although the site is now used as a storage and refurbishment location, now operated by Arlington Fleet Services.

Part of Doncaster Works was sold to RFS Engineering, which became insolvent and was bought out and renamed RFS Industries. Doncaster Works now forms part of Wabtec Rail Group.

A number of companies still manufacture or assemble trains in Great Britain, with others planning to open new plants. Bombardier builds trains at its Derby Works and Hitachi at Newton Aycliffe, County Durham. In 2018 CAF opened a new manufacturing and assembly plant at Llanwern, near Newport and Siemens is building a new plant at Goole, which will initially manufacture trains for London Underground.

The builder details in the class headings show the owner at the time of vehicle construction followed by details of the works as follows:

Ashford	Ashford Works (now Ashford Rail Plant depot, not the same location as the now closed Ashford Chart Leacon Works).
Birmingham	The former Metro-Cammell works at Saltley, Birmingham, later operated by Alstom.
Cowlairs	Cowlairs Works, Glasgow.
Derby	Derby Carriage Works (also known as Litchurch Lane).
Doncaster	Doncaster Works.
Eastleigh	Eastleigh Works
Swindon	Swindon Works.
Wolverton	Wolverton Works.
York	York Carriage Works.

Other builders are:

Alexander	Walter Alexander, Falkirk.
Alstom	Valencia, Spain (later sold to Vossloh and then Stadler) and Savigliano (Italy).
Barclay	Andrew Barclay, Caledonia Works, Kilmarnock (now Wabtec).
BRCW	Birmingham Railway Carriage & Wagon, Smethwick.
CAF	Construcciones y Auxiliar de Ferrocarriles (works in Newport, UK and Zaragoza, Beasain, Castejon and Irun in Spain).
Cravens	Cravens, Sheffield.
Gloucester	Gloucester Railway Carriage & Wagon, Gloucester.
Hitachi	Hitachi Rail Europe (Newton Aycliffe, UK, Kasado, Japan and Pistoia, Italy).
Hunslet-Barclay	Hunslet-Barclay, Caledonia Works, Kilmarnock (now Wabtec).
Hunslet TPL	Hunslet Transportation Projects, Leeds.
Lancing	SR, Lancing Works.
Leyland Bus	Leyland Bus, Workington.
Metro-Cammell	Metropolitan-Cammell, Saltley, Birmingham
Pressed Steel	Pressed Steel, Linwood.
Charles Roberts	Charles Roberts, Horbury Junction, Wakefield.
SGP	Simmering-Graz-Pauker, Austria (now owned by Siemens).
Siemens	Siemens Transportation Systems (principal works is in Krefeld (Germany) with others in Vienna (Austria) and Prague (Czech Republic, now closed). A new plant is under construction at Goole, UK.
SRP	Specialist Rail Products Ltd (A subsidiary of RFS).
Stadler	Stadler Rail Group. Principal works building rolling stock for the UK market at Altenrhein and Bussnang (Switzerland), Siedlce (Poland), Szolnok (Hungary) and Valencia, Spain (the former Alstom plant).
Vossloh	Vossloh Rail Vehicles, Valencia, Spain (sold to Stadler in 2015).